BUSINESS ETHICS
Readings and Cases in Corporate Morality

BUSINESS ETHICS
Readings and Cases in Corporate Morality

W. Michael Hoffman
Jennifer Mills Moore

Bentley College

McGraw-Hill Book Company
New York St. Louis San Francisco Auckland Bogotá Hamburg
Johannesburg London Madrid Mexico Montreal New Delhi
Panama Paris São Paulo Singapore Sydney Tokyo Toronto

Library of Congress Cataloging in Publication Data
Main entry under title:

Business ethics.

    Includes bibliographies.
      1. Business ethics—Addresses, essays, lectures.
2. Business ethics—Case studies.   I. Hoffman,
W. Michael.   II. Moore, Jennifer Mills.
HF5387.B873   1984   174'.4   83-11345
ISBN 0-07-029313-9

[Handwritten notes:]

1 INTRODUCTION - Utilitarianism & Deontology
2 Chapter 1 - Lawits & Nozicen
3 Chapter 2 - Capitalism & Socialism
4 Chapter 3 CBA   exam !
5 Chapter 4 Corporate Responsum
6 Chapter 5,6 Corporate Soerty, agency
7 Chapter 7, 8 Employee Rights, paternism
8 Chapter 9 Preferential hiring, Reverse Descn Exam II
9 Chapter 10 no Consumer, Advertising
10 Chapter 11,12 Regulation, Lobbying 2
11 Chapter 12 no Environment
12 Chapter 13 Multinational Corporation Exam III
13 Chapter 14 Corporate Deception
14 Chapter 15 Bribery
15 Chapter 17 no Corporate Philosophy Exam IV

BUSINESS ETHICS: Readings and Cases in Corporate Morality

34567890 DODO 876

ISBN 0-07-029313-9

This book was set in Electra by J. M. Post Graphics, Corp.
The editors were Kaye Pace, Anne Murphy, and David Dunham;
the designer was Charles A. Carson;
the production supervisor was Leroy A. Young.
The drawings were done by Fine Line Illustrations, Inc.

CONTENTS

PREFACE

As Cicero said in his *De Officiis* in 44 B.C., "To everyone who proposes to have a good career, moral philosophy is indispensable." *Business Ethics: Readings and Cases in Corporate Morality* is put forward with a commitment to this belief. We also believe that the study of ethics, especially in its application to the world of practical affairs, is perhaps more urgent today than it has ever been in the history of our civilization. Alarms have sounded from numerous ideological camps warning us of the ethical insensitivity which is dehumanizing our existence. We must not allow this to happen; we must dedicate ourselves to searching for a moral point of view on which to base our present and future decision making.

This text takes up such a challenge by focusing on the area of business activity. As does the entire field of business ethics, we reject the often-quoted cliché that the "business of business is business," that business is an amoral enterprise. Many, if not most, business decisions involve moral choices. Furthermore, the lack of an appropriate ethical climate will inevitably imperil business transactions themselves. In *Religion and the Rise of Capitalism* R. H. Tawney said that "economic organization must allow for the fact that, unless industry is to be paralyzed by recurrent revolts on the part of outraged human nature, it must satisfy criteria which are not purely economic."

The importance of studying business ethics is also heightened by the fact that the contract between business and society is radically and swiftly changing—a belief shared by leaders as different as Ralph Nader and Henry Ford II. This transformation is affecting how society perceives the corporation as well as how the corporation perceives itself. It is our hope that a study of the ethical issues discussed in this book will assist in this crucial transition and lead to an environment in which the activities of business and the needs of a humane society can be harmonized.

In this text we have tried, first, to be *comprehensive* in our coverage of important issues. In addition to presenting theories of ethics and economic justice, we deal with what we consider to be the most important currently debated moral concerns in the field of business ethics, utilizing both critical issues and case studies. Second, we have tried to be *impartial* in our inclusion of rational perspectives on these issues. The format of the text is point–counterpoint, with viewpoints expressed by thinkers from a wide range of constituencies, including business, government, labor, public interest groups, and varied professions.

Third, we have tried to be *systematic* in our organization of general topics. Although it is possible to use the text in different ways, for the most part we have proceeded from theoretical and abstract issues, or more widely focused issues, to more specific, practical issues, because we feel that the latter are given a framework for discussion and understanding by the former.

Therefore, we first provide an introduction into ethical theory which helps in understanding theories of economic justice—theories which in turn are crucial to judging the ethical appropriateness of specific economic systems within which business decision making is made. We then deal with the general nature of the corporation and set the stage for the more concrete issues regarding work inside the corporation, the relationship of the corporation to its external environment, and questionable business practices. We conclude by speculating on the development of the moral corporation of the future—a development toward which the publication of this book is dedicated.

An acknowledgment of our appreciation is extended to Bentley College for its support of this and other projects in business ethics. A special thanks also goes to Kathy Norton and Sue Zimmerman, staff assistants to the Center for Business Ethics, for help in the preparation of various stages of the manuscripts. Finally, we are obliged to our editors Kaye Pace and Anne Murphy of McGraw-Hill for their invaluable assistance and to the following scholars for their insightful critical analyses of earlier drafts of this book: John R. Danley, Southern Illinois University at Edwardsville; Joseph R. Des Jardins, Villanova University; John W. Hennessey, Amos Tuck School of Business at Dartmouth College; Mark Pastin, Center for Private and Public Sector Ethics at Arizona State University; and Clarence Walton, The American College in Bryn Mawr, Pennsylvania.

W. Michael Hoffman
Jennifer Mills Moore

BUSINESS ETHICS
Readings and Cases in Corporate Morality

GENERAL INTRODUCTION: ETHICAL FRAMEWORKS FOR APPLICATION IN BUSINESS

Business is a complex fabric of human relationships—relationships between manufacturers and consumers, employers and employees, managers and stockholders, members of corporations and members of the communities in which those corporations operate. These are economic relationships, created by the exchange of goods and services; but they are also *moral* relationships. Questions concerning profit, growth, and technological advance have ethical dimensions: Some of these include the effects of the pollution and depletion of natural resources on society at large, the quality and character of the work environment, and the safety of consumers. As an anthology in business ethics, this text proposes to explore the moral dimension of business.

Ethics may be defined as the study of what is *good* or *right* for human beings. It asks what goals people ought to pursue and what actions they ought to perform. Business ethics is a branch of applied ethics; it studies the relationship of what is good and right to business.

It is often said that business and ethics don't mix. In business, some argue, profit takes first place. Business has its own rules and objectives, and ethical concepts, standards, and judgments are inappropriate to the business context. But this view is fundamentally mistaken. Business is an economic institution, but like our economy as a whole it has a moral foundation. The free market system is a product of our convictions about the nature of the good life and the good society, about the fair distribution of goods and services, and about what kinds of goods and services to distribute. It is true that the goal of business has been profit, but profit making is not a morally neutral activity. Traditionally, we have encouraged business to pursue profits because we believed—rightly or wrongly—that profit seeking violated no rights and would be best for society as a whole. This conviction has been the source of business' legitimacy, our belief in its right to exist. In the past two decades, the traditional belief in business' contribution to the general welfare has been challenged; for many, business' connection with the moral foundation which justified it no longer seems clear. Distrust of business has increased; a 1977 Gallup poll, for example, indicated that Americans believed that the ethical standards of business were lower than those of society as a whole, and that they were declining. Many thinkers contend that business faces a true crisis of legitimacy. In such a climate an investigation of business values, of the moral dimension of business, and of the role of business in society becomes urgent. To undertake such an investigation is the task of business ethics. We view this task as taking place on four levels:

1. An ethical investigation of the context in which American business is conducted—that is, capitalism or the free market system. Does the system truly contribute to a good society and reflect our most important social values? In particular, is it a just system? What is economic justice? The selections included in Part I of this text explore the meaning of economic justice and the question of whether capitalism or socialism best embodies that ideal. It also suggests some specific ways in which ethical values have operated or should operate in business decision making.

2. An inquiry, within this broad economic context, into the nature and role of business organizations. Is the function of business activity simply to make a profit? Does business have other sorts of obligations because of its vast power or relationship to other elements of society? How might corporate structure best reflect the nature and responsibilities of corporations? Such questions are taken up in Part II of this text.

3. An examination of particular ethical issues which arise in the course of business activity, such as employee rights and duties, quality of working life, hiring practices, product safety, obligations to the environment, bluffing, and anticompetitive behavior. A range of such issues is covered in Parts III, IV, and V.

4. An examination and ethical assessment of the values which reside implicitly in business organizations and business activity in general, such as freedom of opportunity, economic growth, and material well-being. We pursue this endeavor throughout the text, and in Part VI we examine some new business values and the development of a new corporate ethos.

Engaging in ethical reflection on business at each of these levels requires the use of ethical concepts, theories, and standards of judgment. The remainder of this introduction presents some of the most important principles of ethical theory, which could serve as possible frameworks for application in business contexts.

THE AMALGAMATED MACHINERY DILEMMA

Ted Brown is worried. A salesman for Amalgamated Machinery, he has been placed in charge of negotiating an important sale of construction equipment to the government of a small but rapidly developing nation. Deeply in debt, Amalgamated has staked its future on penetrating foreign markets. Ted's potential contract not only is a very large one; it could open the door to even bigger sales in the future. If he lands the contract, Ted's promotion in the firm is practically certain—and he has been convinced he would succeed until he speaks with a powerful government official who is involved in the negotiations. Ted's bid is looked upon very favorably, the official explains, and it is in fact the lowest. A $100,000 "commission fee" payable in cash to the official would clinch the deal. If Ted does not pay the fee, the official regrets that the contract will go to a competitor.

Ted knows that the sale is crucial to the well-being of his company. He believes that his customers would get the best possible deal by buying Amalgamated's equipment. And he knows that $100,000 is a trivial sum beside the potential profits represented by the contract. Yet, although he is aware that such payments are common practice in many countries, he has always felt that they were wrong, and has never before used them to secure a deal.

Ted Brown's dilemma is a fictitious one, but it is not farfetched. Business people frequently feel torn between their desire to act in the interests of their company and their convictions about what is right. In a study reported by *Business Week* in 1977, 59 percent of the managers at Pitney Bowes and 70 percent of the managers at Uniroyal revealed that they felt pressured to compromise their personal ethical principles to achieve corporate goals.

What is the right decision for Ted to make? What are the most important factors for him to consider in making his decision? How does one determine which are most important? Such questions lead us into the area of ethical theory.

Ted might begin the decision process by considering the potential consequences of his choices. If he refuses to pay the bribe, his company will suffer a severe financial blow; stockholders will take a loss on their investment and some employees may lose their jobs. If he pays the official, his firm will be awarded the contract, he will get his promotion, the government will receive a good price on quality construction equipment, and the official will be $100,000 richer. If we assume that this payment is one of those declared illegal by the 1977 Foreign Corrupt Practices Act, then the scandal which would erupt if the bribe were discovered could hurt the company financially and ruin Ted's career. Provided the payment remains secret, however, it looks as if no harm could result from it.

Yet Ted still feels that bribery is wrong. He reflects that the practice violates the rules of the business game, which decree that one should obtain business only through the fair, free operation of the market system. The payment is also illegal, and although Ted has made no explicit promise, he feels that the rights of a citizen carry with them an obligation to obey the law. On the other hand, he has made a similar implicit promise to act in the best interests of his company.

ETHICAL RELATIVISM

Although we have identified a number of factors relevant to Ted's decision, these seem to have confused rather than simplified his dilemma. Does this mean that there is no rational way of deciding what is right in Ted's situation, that there is no universal standard to which we can appeal, that neither of the choices is better or worse than the other? Ted's colleagues might well challenge his belief that bribery is wrong, pointing out that it is standard practice in the developing nation.

The position that there is no one universal standard or set of standards by which to judge an action's morality is called *ethical relativism*. Ethical relativists may hold that the same act may be morally right for one society and morally wrong for another; or they may hold the more radical position that the same act can be right for one individual and wrong for another. At first glance ethical relativism appears persuasive. But many philosophers contend that it does not stand up well to closer scrutiny. In particular, they hold, it contradicts our everyday ethical experience and the way in which we act and speak about ethical problems and ethical judgments.

One way of stating the position of ethical relativism is to say that it holds that what a person or society *believes* is right *is* right for that person or society. But if this claim is true, it means that what a society believes is right and what is in fact right for that society are one and the same thing. In ordinary life, however, we are continually making distinctions between these two. Several cultures throughout history have believed in slavery, for example. Yet most of us would argue that slavery is not only wrong now, but was wrong then, in spite of cultural mores. Although we know that people's opinions about ethics differ widely, we do not believe that they are all correct. On the contrary, we often praise or blame other people for their ethical standards. We would not do this, it is argued, if we believed that ethical relativism is correct.

We might also ask what constitutes a "society" for the purposes of ethical relativism. If a minority group within a larger culture holds different ethical views from those of the majority, are their views wrong simply because they are in the minority? Or should that group be viewed as a society in its own right with an equally valid set of beliefs? If the minority is to be regarded as a separate society, ought not a dissenting group within the minority be seen in the same way? And should not each individual, as well, be looked upon as a society of sorts with a set of ethical beliefs which are right for himself or herself?

If this version of ethical relativism is true, however, no person can disagree with another person about ethics, because each person's opinion is equally right. In fact, if ethical relativism is true, there *is* no right or wrong in ethics apart from people's beliefs. We have no way of deciding whether one set of beliefs is any better than any other. No one can be mistaken about an ethical problem if ethical relativism is correct, for what a person believes is right *is* right for him or her. Again, these consequences seem to contradict the way we behave in real life since we habitually accuse ourselves and others of making mistakes on ethical issues.

In short, it is argued that if ethical relativism is correct, no comparative moral judgments are possible. We cannot say that any act or belief is better or worse from a moral perspective than any other. Such comparative judgments seem to require the very thing that ethical relativism denies: a universal ethical principle, standard, or framework. But much of our ethical reasoning is the making of comparative judgments. It is the weighing of alternatives, the choice of which values to embrace, and the selection of the course of action which best expresses and upholds these values. For this reason some argue that if ethical relativism is true, morality itself is impossible.

Our experience, however, indicates that we do disagree about moral issues, we do make mistakes in ethical choices, and we do make comparative ethical judgments. Moreover, we feel that this ethical dimension is a crucial dimension of human life. Of course, we may be operating under a gigantic illusion. But the fact that our moral experience not only does not support but seems to contradict ethical relativism gives us strong reasons for rejecting the theory.

This does not mean that it is always easy to decide what is right or that there are clear and undisputed criteria for doing so. But it does mean that ethical principles are either right or wrong, and can be attacked or defended with rational arguments. Let us investigate some of these principles and assess their strength as guides to ethical decision making.

As we examine the considerations raised during Ted's reflection on his dilemma, it can be seen that they fall into two distinct groups. One group is concerned with the consequences of Ted's choices—to his company, to the developing nation, to himself, and so on; the other raises issues regarding duties, promises, obligations. Some ethical theorists, called *consequentialists*, hold that the consequences of an action are the sole factors to be taken into account in determining whether that action is right or wrong. For consequentialists, good consequences make right actions. Those who conclude that Ted ought to pay the official because more benefit than harm would result from his action are making a judgment based on consequentialist standards. Others, called *deontologists* (a term derived from the Greek word meaning duty), deny the consequentialist claim. Not all actions which produce good results are right actions, deontologists argue, and some right actions may even produce unpleasant results for ourselves and others. A right action is right not solely because of its consequences, but because it satisfies the demands of justice, because it respects the rights of others, or because we have promised to perform it. Ted is expressing deontological reservations when he feels that in spite of the good consequences it might produce, succumbing to the demands of the government official is wrong.

Consequentialist and deontological theories represent two different processes for making ethical judgments. All of us operate under some such theory, although we rarely make the theory explicit to ourselves and often fail to apply it systematically. Spelled out and applied consistently, ethical theories can serve as guidelines for disciplined and informed ethical decision making. Below we examine two consequentialist theories—egoism and utilitarianism—and the deontological theory of Immanuel Kant.

ETHICAL EGOISM

Ethical egoism states that every person ought always to act so as to promote the greatest possible balance of good over evil for himself or herself. From an egoistic perspective, an act contrary to one's self-interest is an immoral act. That this is true does not mean that an egoist never takes the interests of others into account. On the contrary; most egoists argue that others' interests should be respected, because treating others well promotes our self-interest in the long run.

An egoist, then, would advise Ted to act in his own best interest—or, in his capacity as an agent of Amalgamated Machinery, in the best interest of the company. If Ted takes this advice, it need not mean that he will bribe the government official. Egoists strive to maximize long-term, not merely short-term, benefits; Ted may decide that the risks to his reputation and that of his company override the potential benefits of the payment. Or he may decide that the guilt he would suffer for having compromised his personal beliefs would outweigh the pleasure he would receive from his promotion, although it is difficult to see why he would feel guilty for doing the right (that is, the egoistic) thing.

Does egoism have a special place in business decision making? If the good mentioned in the egoist maxim is interpreted to mean profit or efficiency, ethical egoism might be seen as the standard by which business and businesspeople have traditionally judged their behavior in a free market system. Some have interpreted economist Milton Friedman's claim that the only obligation of business is to increase its profits as an expression of this traditional view. Following this interpretation, Friedman is arguing not that "good ethics is good business," but that "good business is good ethics." He sees altruistic acts on the part of business as a violation of business' function and obligations. This does not mean that business should be prohibited from performing acts which benefit others. If a business makes costly improvements in the working conditions of its employees, for example, in order to increase productivity, decrease turnover, and improve long-run efficiency, it would win the ethical egoist's approval.

Ethical egoism is often found in conjunction with a theory termed *psychological egoism*. While ethical egoism is a normative theory stating how people *ought* to behave, psychological egoism is a descriptive theory which claims that people *do in fact* act solely to promote their own interest. It is important to distinguish between the two theories, but it is also easy to see their connection: If psychological egoism is true, it is difficult to see how people could behave other than egoistically. To tell them that they ought to do so is futile. It looks as if ethical egoism is the only viable ethical theory if psychological egoism is correct.

Is psychological egoism correct, however? Most of us believe that we have observed people performing acts in order to benefit others; we probably feel that we have performed such acts ourselves. Psychological egoism counters this belief with the assertion that even people who perform acts which benefit others do so for their own satisfaction. One might argue that psychological egoism has mistaken the satisfaction which accompanies an act which benefits others for the motive of that act. Although we may receive happiness or pleasure from doing things for others, it does not follow that the pleasure is the motive or object of our action, that we want to do things for others because of the pleasure we will receive. Perhaps the benevolent act itself is our goal, and we receive pleasure from it because we wanted to do it.

Psychological egoism has often been advanced in support of ethical egoism. But some argue that what it does is make ethical egoism—and, ultimately, all ethics—superfluous. If people always act in their own self-interest, it is not necessary to tell them that they ought to do so. We do not advise stones to fall to the earth when dropped or rivers to flow downstream. Nor does it make much sense to tell people that they ought to do what they are incapable of doing. Traditionally, ethics has assumed that clashes between different interests are bound to occur. If this is true, there will be times when the right thing to do is to sacrifice one's own interest for the interests of others. But psychological egoism asserts that people are not capable of such actions. If psychological egoism is correct, ethical reflection and ethical rules seem futile.

Whether psychological egoism is true or not, the suggestion that interests may clash points to some problems with ethical egoism itself as a moral theory. Some egoists attempt to circumvent these problems with the claim that, ultimately, interests do not conflict, and that apparent oppositions can be resolved by free exchange among interested parties. But even one committed to this view could not deny that *perceived* conflicts of interest occur frequently. Some critics claim that ethical egoism provides no way of settling competing claims when they do arise, no way of determining whether one interest is more important than another. In part this is because in an egoistic society, no one occupies a *disinterested* position, which is the same reason an egoist is not equipped to give advice or to pass moral judgments on other people's actions. One could even say that an egoist cannot consistently advise others to be egoists and to pursue their own self-interest. If one is truly committed to egoism one should tell others that they ought to maximize the egoist's well-being, and not their own. Ethical egoism, then, appears self-contradictory.

It is often argued that people ought to behave egoistically because if they do, it will promote the general welfare. It is important, however, to note that this defense of ethical egoism is not itself an egoistic one. It implies that there is a different, nonegoistic basis for the rightness or wrongness of actions—their consequences for society as a whole. We have moved from egoism to utilitarianism.

UTILITARIANISM

This section examines primarily the utilitarianism of Jeremy Bentham (1748–1832), generally acknowledged as the founder of utilitarianism. Bentham argued that when evaluating an action or making a choice one ought to take into account not only the consequences of that action to oneself, but its consequences for all those affected by the act as well. Utilitarianism as Bentham conceived it, then, states that people ought to act so as to promote the greatest *total* balance of good over evil, or the greatest good for the greatest number.

Utilitarians come in two varieties. *Act utilitarians* hold that in every situation one ought to act so as to maximize total good, even if doing so means violating a rule which, when followed, generally promotes social welfare. Such rules, act utilitarians argue, are simply guidelines: They can—in fact, they must—be broken if to do so leads to the public good. *Rule utilitarians*, on the other hand, use the utilitarian principle to develop rules which they believe are in the public interest. They claim that one should obey these rules even when doing so does not lead to the best consequences, for the presence of the rule itself and consistent adherence to it does promote the general welfare.

A rule utilitarian might argue, for example, that laws against bribery are in the best interest of society. For this reason, Ted ought not to bribe the government official, even though in his particular case to agree to the bribe would produce more good than harm. An act utilitarian would counter that although it is often in the best interests of society to obey the rule against bribery, Ted's case is an exception. To insist that he obey the law violates the fundamental demand of utilitarianism that we maximize total good. An act utilitarian would probably advise Ted to pay the official.

We can see the utilitarian principle at work in the technique of cost-benefit analysis, a decision-making process familiar to businesspeople and often used as a guide to fair public policy decisions. Utilitarianism for Bentham is, in fact, a species of cost-benefit analysis, in which the painful consequences of an act are subtracted from the pleasurable ones, and the total reveals the act's moral quality.

Not all utilitarians agree as to what constitutes the "good" they believe should be maximized. Some claim that there are a number of different goods; truth, beauty, health, peace, and freedom might count as some of them. As a *hedonistic utilitarian,*

Bentham believes that ultimately there is only one good—pleasure or happiness—and that right actions are those which maximize total pleasure or happiness.

If hedonistic utilitarianism is to work, we must find an accurate way of measuring people's pleasure or happiness so as to arrive at a sum total. But this task is more difficult than it might seem, and an examination of these measurement problems reveals some weaknesses in utilitarianism as a moral theory. How exactly does one go about measuring the costs and benefits of an action? What is to be the unit of measurement? Some thinkers have suggested that, ultimately, all costs and benefits can be expressed in terms of dollars. But what about things that are not bought and sold, and therefore have no price on the market? How do we quantify such benefits as job satisfaction, equality, or the cost of a human life?

Bentham himself proposed a less rigorous measurement device which he termed the hedonic calculus. By taking into account the intensity, duration, certainty or uncertainty, nearness or remoteness, fecundity, purity, and extent of the happiness produced by an act, he claimed, one could determine individual units of happiness and subtract from them units of unhappiness to arrive at a quantitative total.

But is Bentham's calculus really adequate? Can the attempt to quantify the process of ethical judgment ever be satisfactory? Suppose for a moment that Ted does not really have to pay the government official in order to obtain the contract he wants, but that he could secure it by honest means. Suppose also that the hedonic calculus has revealed no difference in the sum total of happiness produced by either act. If Ted decides not to pay the official, the pleasure received by his company because of the savings is balanced by the official's unhappiness at his loss and vice versa. Bentham's version of utilitarianism would, in this case, see no difference between the two acts. Although by making one choice Ted is obtaining the sale honestly and by making the other he is not, the hedonic calculus has no means of taking this fact into account. Hedonistic utilitarianism would judge the two acts morally identical, because they produce the same sum total of good.

John Stuart Mill (1806–1873) objected to this failure of Bentham's utilitarianism to take account of the difference between an honest and a dishonest act which produce the same results. The problem with the hedonic calculus, he believed, was that it did not recognize the fact that pleasure or happiness differs in quality as well as in quantity. Some forms of happiness are more noble than others, he argued; some are achieved by ethical, some by unethical means. Mill thought the failing could be remedied by introducing the element of quality into the hedonic calculus. But his doing so raised as many problems as it solved. The purpose of the hedonic calculus as designed by Bentham was to express the ethical quality of an act in terms of the quantity of happiness it produces. The attempt to reduce quality to quantity is at the core of hedonistic utilitarianism. Mill's introduction of quality into the hedonic calculus suggests that an act can be good or bad independently of the amount of pleasure it produces, and thus contradicts the fundamental principle of utilitarianism. In order to define quality, Mill would have to go outside the bounds of utilitarian theory. As an attempt to revise hedonistic utilitarianism, therefore, Mill's effort seems to fail.

Because introducing the criterion of quality into a utilitarian framework poses so many difficulties, it has been argued that utilitarianism justifies—and perhaps even demands—acts which seem to us to be unjust or immoral. Imagine, for example, a group of thugs who receive their enjoyment from molesting small children. If the hedonic calculus revealed that the thugs receive more personal pleasure from their actions than their victims receive pain, would the thugs win utilitarian approval? Another way of expressing this objection to utilitarianism is to make the claim that people have *rights* which ought not to be violated even when doing so results in a greater sum total of good. It is argued that utilitarianism is incapable of respecting such rights, because they can always be overridden in favor of an act or rule which maximizes total good.

A final objection to utilitarianism is that while it insists that total good be maximized, it tells us nothing about the distribution of this good. There seems to be no reason for utilitarians to disapprove of a slave-owning society, for example, if it could be shown that such a society provided a larger sum of goodness than one in which all people are treated as equals. A familiar criticism of capitalism is that the rich become richer at the expense of the poor; although the sum total of well-being may be maximized, the system is *unjust*. As was the case with rights, utilitarianism seems to have no place in its framework for justice. Claims of justice are always subordinate to the imperative to maximize the balance of good over evil.

It seems to be true that the consequences of an action play an important part in determining whether that action is right or wrong. But egoism's failure to acknowledge that it is sometimes our duty to perform acts which are not in our own interest and utilitarianism's inability to take into account rights and justice suggest that the rightness of an action does not depend solely upon its consequences—for ourselves or for others. Other nonconsequentialist factors may also have a bearing on the moral quality of actions. For an approach which does take such factors into account we turn to the deontological theory of Immanuel Kant.

KANT'S CATEGORICAL IMPERATIVE

In contrast to the consequentialists, Immanuel Kant (1724–1804) holds that one ought to perform right actions not because they will produce good results, but because it is our *duty* to do so. For Kant, moral commands are *categorical imperatives*; that is, they are absolute and unconditional, binding for us regardless of the consequences obedience to them brings about. Ultimately, Kant argues, there is only one categorical imperative. Below we discuss two of his major formulations of this ethical principle.

In our discussion of relativism above, we noted the need for a universal moral principle or set of principles for use in making ethical judgments. For Kant this idea of universality is at the heart of morality, and it serves as the litmus test for immoral action in his first expression of the categorical imperative. In making an ethical decision about action, Kant holds, we should ask ourselves whether we would be willing to have everyone take that action. If we are not willing to permit the universal practice of the action, it is immoral. Kant claims that an act is not moral unless it can be made into a universal law.

If I am contemplating a deceptive advertisement in order to sell a product, for example, I must be willing to endorse a world in which all people lie when it seems to their advantage to do so. Not only would we not wish to see unethical behavior practiced universally; according to Kant, many principles cannot even be *conceived* of as universal. If everyone were entitled to lie, one would never be able to tell if a person is lying or telling the truth. Under such circumstances, the very practice of truth telling is undermined and lying ceases to be advantageous.

Kant would advise Ted not to pay the government official in order to obtain his contract, not because to do so would produce bad consequences, but because the universal practice of bribery would undermine the very basis of business itself. Other rules governing business practices might be justified on similar grounds. Cheating, stealing, breaking contracts, price-fixing, and so on erode the moral backdrop of business and make business activity impossible. If everyone engages in such activities, there is no longer any advantage in doing so. Kant's analysis reveals that the unethical person exempts himself or herself from moral laws without being willing to grant similar privileges to others. He or she is in effect a parasite on the very ethical system he or she violates. Unethical behavior is possible and advantageous only in an *ethical* society. When universalized, it contradicts itself. We should act only on those principles, Kant maintains, which we would be willing to see become universal law.

In a second formulation of the categorical imperative, Kant turns his attention to the rights of human beings. One ought always to act, he claims, so as to treat all human beings as ends in themselves, and never only as means to an end. Both egoism and utilitarianism seem to violate this principle. For the egoist, others have value only insofar as they promote the egoist's self-interest; for the utilitarian, every person appears to be a means for the maximization of good. Kant recognizes that we must often use others as means to an end, as we do, for example, when we hire them to do a job for us. But he emphasizes that they also have a value in and of themselves which we have a duty to respect.

Kant's respect for persons derives from the fact that they are capable of recognizing and choosing to obey moral laws, and he insists upon a close connection between freedom and morality. In a denial of psychological egoism, Kant claims that human beings are the only creatures capable of performing an act not because it is to their advantage, but because duty requires it. It is in making choices based on duty that we take full possession of our freedom, argues Kant. Kant turns his attention away, then, from the *products* of our choice—their results for oneself or for others—and toward the *process* of choice itself. To act out of duty in obedience to the categorical imperative is for Kant what it means to be moral.

Although it offers some significant advantages over consequentialism, Kant's theory is not without its difficulties. An attempt to apply the first formulation of the categorical imperative to actual problems reveals its imprecisions. We have stated above that Kant would prohibit Ted from bribing the official to obtain his contract, because bribery cannot be adopted as a universal practice without contradiction. But suppose that the act Ted chooses to put to Kant's test is not bribery in general, but bribery with qualifications, such as bribery to save one's company from bankruptcy or bribery which secures the best deal for a client. It is less clear whether Ted would be willing to permit these acts on the part of other companies or whether they contradict themselves when universalized. To express the principle of one's action accurately and to test it is not an easy task. It might be possible to describe immoral actions in so specific a way that they would pass Kant's tests, even if, when couched in general terms, they violate the categorical imperative.

A second criticism often directed at Kant is that although he provides us with a rational basis for rights and duties, he does not take into account that duties can conflict, and he does not offer a framework for resolving such conflicts. Businesspeople often feel torn between their duty to their company and their duty to society at large, for example. Although Kant would undoubtedly acknowledge that every person has a right to nondiscriminatory treatment in hiring, he might also assert that those who have been unfairly treated in the past have a right to be compensated for the injustice. What do we do, however, if the only way of compensating minorities and the disadvantaged turns out to involve discrimination against white males? Both compensating the victims of past injustice and refraining from injustice in the present seem commanded by the categorical imperative. What should we do when faced with such conflicts? Consequentialists would argue that deontologists provide no satisfactory answer to this question.

CONCLUSION

Each of the ethical theories we have considered appears to have some weaknesses. Because they identify the rightness of an act with the good results it produces, consequentialist theories can overlook claims of rights and justice and the intrinsic worth of all human beings. Kant's theory seems ambiguous in places and it fails to tell us how to deal with the problem of conflicting rights, conflicting duties. Whether these theories are totally incompatible is an ongoing debate and probably stated in their most extreme form they are. There may be ways, however, of drawing fruitfully on each theory in constructing a moral framework from which to make judgments in business. We are not suggesting that one adopt a naive eclecticism, extracting inconsistent parts from each, but one might find meaningful aspects to each position in formulating a comprehensive moral point of view. Utilitarianism, for example, could act as a check on each individual's pursuit of his or her own self-interest; Kantianism suggests some limits beyond which we ought not to go, even to maximize the sum total of good; conflicts between duties and rights which cannot be resolved within a Kantian framework might be illuminated by consequentialist reflection. We offer no comprehensive moral theory which could tell us with certainty in particular instances whether the consequentialist emphasis on good results or the deontological stress on rights and duties is more important.

A sense of the relationship among the three theories will become clearer as we begin to explore the issues which follow. Business can serve as a field for testing the strength of ethical theories and their ability to shed light on concrete problems. The further development of such a dialogue between theory and practice is one of the purposes served by a study of business ethics.

PART ONE
ETHICS AND BUSINESS:
FROM THEORY TO PRACTICE

In exploring the ethical dimensions of business activity it is not always enough to focus attention on specific ethical problems. Such issues as the rights and duties of employees, product liability, and the responsibility of business to the environment arise in the context of a comprehensive economic system which deeply influences our values and structures the range of choices available to us. Often we will find that the most important ethical question is not "What is right or wrong in this particular situation?" but rather "What is the ethical status of a situation which forces such a choice on the agent?" or "How can it be restructured to provide a more satisfactory climate for ethical decision making?" Some ethical problems are not isolated, but systemic; for this reason Chapter Two of this part examines the free market system itself from an ethical perspective.

What we seek when we evaluate economic systems ethically, at least in part, is a framework for business transactions and decisions, a set of procedures which, if followed, will generally bring about just results. Justice of this kind—called procedural justice—can be illustrated by the familiar method of dividing a piece of cake between two children: Assuming that the two should receive equal slices, if one child cuts the cake and the other chooses the first slice, justice should be served. Not all just procedures produce as completely just results as this one does. But in choosing an economic system we look for one which provides as much justice as possible. Traditionally, it has been held in America that capitalism is such a system; critics challenge this claim. An examination of this controversy requires a clear conception of what justice is, and Chapter One provides the groundwork for such a conception by presenting three important theories of economic justice.

Even if the free market system is a just one it may not mean that every event which occurs according to the rules of the system is just. Just procedures are not always sufficient to ensure just results. Suppose, for example, that a person owns one of the five waterholes on an island and that the other four unexpectedly dry up, leaving the owner with a monopoly over the water supply and the opportunity to charge exorbitantly high prices for water. It might be argued that even if the owner of the waterhole acquired it legally, did not conspire to monopolize, and allowed his prices to be determined by the fluctuations of the market, this situation is unjust. Although procedural justice may be necessary to bring about ethical outcomes, it may not be sufficient *by itself* to do so. Although a just economic system is essential for an ethical business climate, we may also find it necessary to examine the relationships and transactions which take place within the system and to make ethical reasoning a part of business decision making at a more specific, less general level. Chapter Three suggests some ways in which this might be done.

DISTRIBUTIVE JUSTICE

Questions of economic justice arise when people find themselves in competition for scarce resources—wealth, income, jobs, food, housing. If there are not enough of society's benefits—and too many of society's burdens—to satisfy everyone, we must ask how to distribute these benefits and burdens fairly. One of the most important problems of economic justice, then, is that of the fair distribution of limited commodities.

What does it mean to distribute things justly or fairly? To do justice is to give each person what he or she deserves or is owed. If those who have the most in a society deserve the most and those who have the least deserve the least, that society is a just one. If not, it is unjust. But what makes one person more, another less, deserving?

Philosophers have offered a wide range of criteria for determining who deserves what. One suggestion is that everyone deserves an equal share. Others hold that benefits and burdens should be distributed on the basis of need, merit, effort or hard work, or contribution to society. John Rawls, Robert Nozick, and J. J. C. Smart each emphasize one or more of these criteria in constructing a theory of economic justice.

The theory of economic justice underlying American capitalism has tended to emphasize contribution to society, along with merit and hard work, as the basis of distribution. We do not expect everyone to end up with an equal share of benefits and burdens under a capitalist system. But supporters of capitalism hold that those who receive more do so because of their greater contribution, and that for this reason the inequalities are just. Recalling the Kantian ethical principles examined in the introduction to the text, however, it might be argued that rewarding people on the basis of what they contribute to the general welfare implies treating them as means to an end rather than as ends in themselves and overlooks the intrinsic value of persons. Each person's contribution, furthermore, depends largely on inborn skills and qualities and circumstances which permit the development of these traits. Ought people to be rewarded in proportion to accidents of birth over which they have no control? Some philosophers, like John Rawls, think not.

As an egalitarian, Rawls believes that there are no characteristics which make one person more deserving than another; there are no differences between people which justify inequalities in the distribution of social benefits and burdens. Everyone deserves an equal share. That this is true does not mean that Rawls finds all inequalities unjust; but his theory permits only inequalities which benefit everyone and to which everyone has an equal opportunity.

Rawls' principles of distribution are just, he claims, because they are the principles which would be chosen by a group of rational persons designing a society—providing they are ignorant of their own abilities, preferences, and eventual social position. We ought to choose our principles of justice, Rawls argues, from behind a "veil of ignorance"—a position strikingly similar to that of the child who cuts the cake evenly, unsure of which piece he or she will eventually have. Although all those in Rawls' hypothetical situation seek to protect their own interest, they are prevented from choosing a principle of distribution which will benefit themselves at the expense of others. Thus they are likely to reject a utilitarian principle of justice under which the happiness of a few might be sacrificed to maximize total well-being or a notion of justice in which distribution depends in part upon luck, skill, natural endowments, or social position. Rawls believes that they would select egalitarian principles.

Some critics have challenged Rawls' claim that rational persons acting from behind a veil of ignorance would choose egalitarian principles of justice. Rawls assumes that all people are egoists, and he fails to take account of the gamblers among us. Others ask whether the choice of egalitarian principles by uninformed egoists is really enough to justify them ethically. A possible defense of Rawls' argument involves an appeal to the Kantian ethical principle examined in the introduction to the text. Kant held that one test of the ethical acceptability of a principle is whether it can be made into a universal law without contradiction. By placing us behind a hypothetical veil of ignorance, Rawls asks us to choose principles of justice which apply to ourselves and all others equally. As a universal law, Rawls seems to be saying, only the egalitarian theory of justice is fully consistent.

Because he gives everyone a voice in what the principle of justice is to be, and because equal treatment seems to recognize every person's intrinsic worth, Rawls' theory of justice also seems to satisfy the second Kantian test, the treatment of all people as ends in themselves. It is not clear, however, that the egalitarian way is the only way to treat people as ends in themselves. Robert Nozick's libertarianism, which emphasizes individual rights instead of equal distribution, might also be susceptible to a Kantian defense.

Unlike Rawls, Nozick focuses his attention not on what each person ends up with, but on how each person acquired what he or she has. Justice for Nozick is historical; it resides in the *process* of acquisition. A theory of justice thus consists of setting forth rules for just acquisition, and something which has been justly acquired justly belongs to its owner even if this means that some people will receive a far greater share of benefits or burdens than others.

Nozick objects to the attempt to bring about justice by imposing a preconceived pattern of distribution such as the egalitarian one because he believes that no such pattern can be realized without violating people's rights. As the word *libertarian* suggests, the right most heavily emphasized by Nozick is that of freedom, or noninterference. Interference, he holds, is permitted only when the rights of others are being violated. Second is the right to property which has been justly acquired. Under a libertarian theory of justice, taxation to redistribute and equalize wealth is a violation of human rights, an appropriation of the fruit of other people's freedom akin to forced labor. One might also look upon it as the treatment of others as means. The only way to treat people as ends in themselves, a libertarian might argue, is to grant them freedom from coercion. The only just pattern of distribution, libertarians claim, is not a pattern at all, but the product of a multitude of free, individual choices.

Critics of the libertarian theory generally attack what they view as its truncated conception of human rights. It may be true, they say, that persons have rights of noninterference. But surely there are other human rights more positive in nature. If persons have a right to life, for example, it could be argued that they also have a right to certain things they need in order to live: food, clothing, shelter, and so on. If this is true, their right to these things might sometimes override someone else's right to noninterference. For example, Nozick himself admits that it is unjust for one person to appropriate the entire supply of something necessary for life, as in the example of the waterhole mentioned above. If it is correct that there are positive rights which supersede the right to noninterference, libertarianism needs reexamining.

J. J. C. Smart's utilitarian theory of justice differs from both Nozick's and Rawls' in that it neither attempts to make distribution conform to a specific pattern nor focuses on the process by which distribution takes place. As a utilitarian, Smart is concerned with the maximization of happiness or pleasure, and approves of any distribution of goods which accomplishes this goal. Thus utilitarian justice could be compatible with either an equal or an unequal distribution of goods, depending on which of the two is shown to provide the greatest total happiness. Although in general Smart believes that an egalitarian distribution of benefits and burdens is the most likely to maximize happiness, he is in no way committed to equality as a principle of distribution; on the contrary, if he were to find that extreme inequalities were what maximized happiness or that the sum total of happiness would be increased if a few were sacrificed for the good of the greatest number, he would be committed to these strategies. Utilitarianism, in short, is interested in the *maximization* of happiness and not in its distribution.

Some thinkers find utilitarianism's stress on the sum total of happiness to be incompatible with the very idea of justice, and Smart admits that justice is only a subordinate interest for utilitarians. Under utilitarianism, people may be denied what they deserve because that denial increases total happiness.

JUSTICE AND ECONOMIC SYSTEMS

Rawls, Nozick, and Smart offer three different theories of economic justice. They have made no claims, however, about how their principles of justice might best be embodied in an economic system. Rawls, for example, might assert that his theory is compatible with both capitalism and socialism. In Chapter Two we examine the soundness of the concepts of justice underlying two quite different economic systems. Irving Kristol presents a defense of what he views as the capitalist conception of justice; Michael Harrington offers a critique of capitalism, claiming that only a socialist system can truly serve the interests of justice.

Perhaps the two most important characteristics of capitalism are (1) the private ownership of the means of production (as opposed to common or government ownership), such that most of us must work for others and earn wages to make a living, and (2) a free market system, in which prices and wages are not controlled by the government or by a small, powerful group, but are allowed to fluctuate. The key word here is freedom. Essential to the system is free competition: Workers must be able to move freely from job to job as they choose, and everyone must be free to enter the market to buy and sell. It is on this second characteristic which Kristol focuses in his discussion of capitalism.

Clearly, a free market system will not provide everyone with an equal share of social benefits and burdens; and indeed the conception of justice which Kristol claims lies at the heart of capitalism is a fundamentally libertarian one. Equality of rights and equality of opportunity are crucial to the system, Kristol explains; within these constraints, however, people are rewarded in proportion to their contribution to the economic system. It is important to note that Kristol does not believe that equality of opportunity requires us to give special compensation to the disadvantaged, as Rawls does. For Kristol equality of opportunity means only that there are no *official* barriers to opportunity. He recognizes that luck may play a significant role in success under a capitalist system.

Kristol defends the capitalist conception of justice because, like Nozick, he believes that it best respects people's rights and maximizes freedom. In addition, he argues that although inequalities do exist under capitalism, everyone is better off than he or she would be under another kind of economic system. A capitalist economy maximizes efficiency, for example, and provides a far greater range of goods and services than a more planned economy would. If capitalism truly benefits everybody, as Kristol claims, it might win approval not only from Nozick, but from Rawls and Smart as well.

Does everyone really benefit under a capitalist system, however? Some critics argue that the truth of this claim depends upon the freedom of the market—a freedom which, they hold, is largely illusory. Because of limitations due to lack of education, age, poverty, or social position, it is claimed, workers are not free to move from job to job and can thus become trapped in work that is hazardous or low-paying. The influence of powerful, giant corporations skews the market: Individuals are not able to compete on the same terms as large conglomerates and thus competition is not truly free. Kristol's picture of capitalism, critics might say, fails to take account of the very real constraints felt by people even in a free market system. For this reason it is not clear that every person is better off in a capitalist economy.

The objections voiced above do not challenge the concept of justice presented by Kristol; they suggest only that capitalist systems fail to achieve the justice they claim. But criticisms have also been leveled at the idea of justice which underlies capitalism. Capitalist justice as Kristol describes it ignores claims of need, for example. People are free to give to others in a capitalist economy, but the needy have no real right to demand that their needs be satisfied. Thus, critics have concluded, capitalism sanctions poverty and extreme inequalities, and pits human beings against each other in a fierce competitive struggle. Even if everyone does benefit from a capitalist economy, it might be argued, it is not clear that everyone receives what he or she *deserves*—the criterion we referred to earlier as the earmark of justice.

Capitalism rewards people in proportion to their contribution to the economy. This does not mean that they benefit in proportion to their merit, virtue, effort, or contribution to society. For Kristol, that this is true is one of the strengths of an admittedly imperfect system, for to achieve distributions of the latter kind would require restrictions on individual liberty and centralized planning on a scope and scale he would not tolerate. Others, such as Harrington, believe that extensive planning should be undertaken in the interest of social justice. In part, it is because capitalism is hostile to such planning that Harrington turns to the socialist alternative.

Although Harrington believes that a capitalist economy benefits everyone to some extent, he argues that it does so at the expense of the poor and disadvantaged. He charges capitalism with the creation of a class system in which the rich get richer and the poor poorer, and he favors a more equal distribution of goods.

One might ask if it is really necessary to discard capitalism entirely in order to bring about the kind of justice Harrington desires. The present American economic system, for example, is not the pure capitalism that Kristol describes. It incorporates a number of modifications, many of which seem to take seriously some of the criticisms of capitalism mentioned above. We do not permit distribution through the market system alone, but attend to claims of need by redistributing wealth through taxation and welfare programs. We have placed such restrictions on the free market system as minimum wage requirements, price freezes, rent control, and regulations concerning product safety, worker health and safety, and environmental protection.

Harrington, however, believes that such measures are not extensive, long range, or comprehensive enough; they are mere patches on a fundamentally unsound fabric. Even if a capitalist economy could sustain the kind of planning he believes is necessary, Harrington claims, it would have to be abandoned, for capitalism is unable to deal with its own prosperity, and defeats itself.

Although he concedes that capitalism produces great affluence, and may even benefit everyone to some extent, Harrington challenges the idea that economic well-being is identical with or leads automatically to social well-being. On the contrary, he claims, the same system which produces wealth in such abundance also encourages antisocial spending for private profit rather than for the public good. Private acts of acquisition, investment, and consumption produce tremendous social costs in the form of problems such as pollution and the deterioration of urban areas. A reversal of this trend, then, requires measures of reform which go beyond the boundaries of a capitalist economy. As a socialist, Harrington advocates social, rather than private, ownership of the means of production; comprehensive social and economic planning; the socialization of investment decisions so that large investments will be made for the public good rather than for private gain; and extensive tax reform.

Richard Titmuss provides us with the unusual opportunity to compare the advantages of market and nonmarket systems of distribution with respect to one essential commodity—human blood. The results of his comparative study of blood distribution in the United States, which has a predominantly market system of blood distribution, and in Great Britain, where a voluntary donor system prevails, seem to echo some of Harrington's claims. Although we would expect a pure market system to maximize efficiency and to provide a good quality product at a good price, Titmuss states, the commercialized blood market fails on both counts. It is far more likely to distribute contaminated blood than a voluntary donor system, it produces far greater waste, and the effort to control these problems inflates the price of blood in the United States to from five to fifteen times its price in Britain. Higher prices mean that in some cases, the poor cannot afford the blood they need. In addition, argues Titmuss, a commercialized blood system encourages lack of trust, discord, and action from self-interest, and allows us to feel that we have no obligation to give to others; it discourages the expression of altruism and erodes a sense of community.

Titmuss' findings raise a range of questions concerning distributive justice and systems of distribution, some of which have already been touched upon by Rawls, Nozick, Smart, Kristol, and Harrington. Is a free market system a just means of distributing scarce commodities? Is blood, an essential for human life, something to which everyone has a right regardless of the workings of the market? Do Titmuss' results reveal some fundamental weaknesses in market systems of distribution or is blood too unique a commodity for them to be conclusive?

FROM THEORY TO PRACTICE

In Chapter Three we turn from an examination of the justice of economic systems to an investigation of ethical business decision making within the system, at a concrete, specific level. Kermit Vandivier's discussion of his own part in the B.F. Goodrich aircraft brake scandal highlights the importance of such an investigation. Striking in Goodrich's decision to market a defective brake are the lack of clarity concerning corporate values, the evasion of responsibility, and the refusal or inability to engage in ethical reflection exhibited by those involved. Although Vandivier and his associates recognized that they were trapped in an ethical dilemma, they lacked the tools to state this dilemma clearly and to make their concerns impact upon corporate policy in an effective way.

Verne Henderson and Steven Kelman discuss some ways in which ethical concerns can be and have been significantly operative in business decisions. Henderson offers a conceptual framework for use in clarifying the ethical dimensions of a situation. He believes that the incorporation of ethical concerns into a hierarchy of multiple goals, the selection of appropriate methods for achieving these goals, the development of an awareness of motives, and the review of the potential consequences of an act comprise a decision-making process which could enable business managers to remain sensitive to the interests of all their constituencies. Again, had they been an acknowledged aspect of B.F. Goodrich's corporate policy, Henderson's guidelines might have clarified Vandivier's dilemma considerably.

Kelman sees in an already widely used technique for business decision making—cost-benefit analysis—a close resemblance to the utilitarian principle examined in the introduction to the text. He uses theoretical ethics to illuminate cost-benefit analysis and to argue for his claim that it should not be used as the sole tool in making ethical decisions. Commitment to cost-benefit analysis as Kelman describes it implies the belief that costs and benefits should be totaled and weighed against each other in making a decision, that an act should not be undertaken unless its benefits exceed its costs, and that benefits and costs must be assigned dollar values so that they can be compared on a common scale.

We have already encountered the primary objections to utilitarianism in the introduction to the text; Kelman reiterates some of these. Utilitarianism identifies what is right with what maximizes benefits and minimizes costs, Kelman explains. But he argues that there are instances—those which involve the breaking of a promise, for example, or the violation of a human right—in which an act may be wrong even if its benefits outweigh its costs. Kelman cites examples to illustrate his claim that the utilitarian principle permits or even requires some actions which we are inclined to feel are morally repugnant.

Kelman also challenges the possibility of placing dollar values on nonmarket items such as clean air, health and safety, and human life. And even if it were possible to determine prices for these goods which truly reflect their value to society, he holds, it would not be advisable to do so. Certain items like life and health are "priceless," he argues, and the very act of placing a price on them may lower their perceived value in society. Kelman fears that placing a price on things declares that they are for sale; thus a worker's health may be traded because its dollar value is less than that of the equipment required to protect it. Cost-benefit analysis is particularly inappropriate, Kelman argues, when such "specially valued things" are at stake.

But what happens when a decision must be made which balances the claims of more than one specially valued thing? A decision about environmental quality, for example, may be more than a trade-off between clean air and profits; it may also impact on the jobs of a number of workers. Moreover, people specially value a variety of different goods. How are we to decide whose claims receive preference? Critics James DeLong and Robert Nisbet point out that Kelman has failed to provide guidelines for decision making in such areas. Only some form of cost-benefit analysis, they argue, can settle competing claims regarding specially valued things.

chapter one
THEORIES OF ECONOMIC JUSTICE

JUSTICE AS FAIRNESS

JOHN RAWLS*

THE MAIN IDEA OF THE THEORY OF JUSTICE

My aim is to present a conception of justice which generalizes and carries to a higher level of abstraction the familiar theory of the social contract as found, say, in Locke, Rousseau, and Kant. In order to do this we are not to think of the original contract as one to enter a particular society or to set up a particular form of government. Rather, the guiding idea is that the principles of justice for the basic structure of society are the object of the original agreement. They are the principles that free and rational persons concerned to further their own interests would accept in an initial position of equality as defining the fundamental terms of their association. These principles are to regulate all further agreements: they specify the kinds of social cooperation that can be entered into and the forms of government that can be established. This way of regarding the principles of justice I shall call justice as fairness.

Thus we are to imagine that those who engage in social cooperation choose together, in one joint act, the principles which are to assign basic rights and duties and to determine the division of social benefits. Men are to decide in advance how they are to regulate their claims against one another and what is to be the foundation charter of their society. Just as each person must decide by rational reflection what constitutes his good, that is, the system of ends which it is rational for him to pursue, so a group of persons must decide once and for all what is to count among them as just and unjust. The choice which rational men would make in this hypothetical situation of equal liberty, assuming for the present that this choice problem has a solution, determines the principles of justice.

In justice as fairness the original position of equality corresponds to the state of nature in the traditional theory of the social contract. This original position is not, of course, thought of as an actual historical state of affairs, much less as a primitive condition of culture. It is understood as a purely hypothetical situation characterized so as to lead to a certain conception of justice. Among the essential features of this situation is that no one knows his place in society, his class position or social status, nor does any one know his fortune in the distribution of natural assets and abilities,

*Department of Philosophy, Harvard University.

his intelligence, strength, and the like. I shall even assume that the parties do not know their conceptions of the good or their special psychological propensities. The principles of justice are chosen behind a veil of ignorance. This ensures that no one is advantaged or disadvantaged in the choice of principles by the outcome of natural chance or the contingency of social circumstances. Since all are similarly situated and no one is able to design principles to favor his particular condition, the principles of justice are the result of a fair agreement or bargain. For given the circumstances of the original position, the symmetry of everyone's relations to each other, this initial situation is fair between individuals as moral persons, that is, as rational beings with their own ends and capable, I shall assume, of a sense of justice. The original position is, one might say, the appropriate initial status quo, and thus the fundamental agreements reached in it are fair. This explains the propriety of the name "justice as fairness": it conveys the idea that the principles of justice are agreed to in an initial situation that is fair. The name does not mean that the concepts of justice and fairness are the same, any more than the phrase "poetry as metaphor" means that the concepts of poetry and metaphor are the same.

Justice as fairness begins, as I have said, with one of the most general of all choices which persons might make together, namely, with the choice of the first principles of a conception of justice which is to regulate all subsequent criticism and reform of institutions. Then, having chosen a conception of justice, we can suppose that they are to choose a constitution and a legislature to enact laws, and so on, all in accordance with the principles of justice initially agreed upon. Our social situation is just if it is such that by this sequence of hypothetical agreements we would have contracted into the general system of rules which defines it.

It may be observed that once the principles of justice are thought of as arising from an original agreement in a situation of equality, it is an open question whether the principle of utility would be acknowledged. Offhand it hardly seems likely that persons who view themselves as equals, entitled to press their claims upon one another, would agree to a principle which may require lesser life prospects for some simply for the sake of a greater sum of advantages enjoyed by others. Since each desires to protect his interests, his capacity to advance his conception of the good, no one has a reason to acquiesce in an enduring loss for himself in order to bring about a greater net balance of satisfaction. In the absence of strong and lasting benevolent impulses, a rational man would not accept a basic structure merely because it maximized the algebraic sum of advantages irrespective of its permanent effects on his own basic rights and interests. Thus it seems that the principle of utility is incompatible with the conception of social cooperation among equals for mutual advantage. It appears to be inconsistent with the idea of reciprocity implicit in the notion of a well-ordered society. Or, at any rate, so I shall argue.

I shall maintain instead that the persons in the initial situation would choose two rather different principles: the first requires equality in the assignment of basic rights and duties, while the second holds that social and economic inequalities, for example inequalities of wealth and authority, are just only if they result in compensating benefits for everyone, and in particular for the least advantaged members of society. These principles rule out justifying institutions on the grounds that the hardships of some are offset by a greater good in the aggregate. It may be expedient but it is not just that some should have less in order that others may prosper. But there is no injustice in the greater benefits earned by a few provided that the situation of persons not so fortunate is thereby improved. The intuitive idea is that since everyone's well-being depends upon a scheme of cooperation without which no one could have a satisfactory life, the division of advantages should be such as to draw forth the willing cooperation of everyone taking part in it, including those less well situated. Yet this can be expected only if reasonable terms are proposed. The two principles mentioned seem to be a fair agreement on the basis of which those better endowed, or more fortunate in their social position, neither of which we can be said to deserve, could expect the willing cooperation of others when some workable scheme is a necessary condition of the welfare of all.[1] Once we decide to look for a conception of justice that nullifies the accidents of natural endowment and the contingencies of social circumstance as counters in quest for political and economic advantage, we are led to these principles. They express the result of leaving aside those aspects of the social world that seem arbitrary from a moral point of view.

The idea of the original position is to set up a fair procedure so that any principles agreed to will be just. Somehow we must nullify the effects of specific contingencies which put men at odds and tempt them to exploit social and natural circumstances to their own advantage. Now in order to do this I assume that the parties are situated behind a veil of ignorance. They do not know how the various alternatives will affect their own particular case and they are obliged to evaluate principles solely on the basis of general considerations.[2] The veil of ignorance enables us to make vivid to ourselves the restrictions that it seems reasonable to impose on arguments for principles of justice, and therefore on these principles themselves. Thus it seems reasonable and generally acceptable that no one should be advantaged or disadvantaged by natural fortune or social circumstances in the choice of principles. It also seems widely agreed that it should be impossible to tailor principles to the circumstances of one's own case. We should insure further that particular inclinations and aspirations, and persons' conceptions of their good do not affect the principles adopted. The aim is to rule out those principles that it would be rational to propose for acceptance, however little the chance of success, only if one knew certain things that are irrelevant from the standpoint of justice. For example, if a man knew that he was wealthy, he might find it rational to advance the principle that various taxes for welfare measures be counted unjust; if he knew that he was poor, he would most likely propose the contrary principle. To represent the desired restrictions one imagines a situation in which everyone is deprived of this sort of information. One excludes the knowledge of those contingencies which sets men at odds and allows them to be guided by their prejudices.

It is assumed, then, that the parties do not know certain kinds of particular facts. First of all, no one knows his place in society, his class position or social status; nor does he know his fortune in the distribution of natural assets and abilities, his intelligence and strength, and the like. Nor, again, does anyone know his conception of the good, the particulars of his rational plan of life, or even the special features of his psychology such as his aversion to risk or liability to optimism or pessimism. More than this, I assume that the parties do not know the particular circumstances of their own society. That is, they do not know its economic or political situation, or the level of civilization and culture it has been able to achieve. The persons in the original position have no information as to which generation they belong. These broader restrictions on knowledge are appropriate in part because questions of social justice arise between generations as well as within them, for example, the question of the appropriate rate of capital saving and of the conservation of natural resources and the environment of nature. There is also, theoretically anyway, the question of a reasonable genetic policy. In these cases too, in order to carry through the idea of the original position, the parties must not know the contingencies that set them in opposition. They must choose principles the consequences of which they are prepared to live with whatever generation they turn out to belong to. As far as possible, then, the only particular facts which the parties know is that their society is subject to the circumstances of justice and whatever this implies.

The restrictions on particular information in the original position are of fundamental importance. The veil of ignorance makes possible a unanimous choice of a particular conception of justice. Without these limitations on knowledge the bargaining problem of the original position would be hopelessly complicated. Even if theoretically a solution were to exist, we would not, at present anyway, be able to determine it.

THE RATIONALITY OF THE PARTIES

I have assumed throughout that the persons in the original position are rational. In choosing between principles each tries as best he can to advance his interests. But I have also assumed that the parties do not know their conception of the good. This means that while they know that they have some rational plan of life, they do not know the details of this plan, the particular ends and interests which it is calculated to promote. How, then, can they decide which conceptions of justice are most to their advantage? Or must we suppose that they are reduced to mere guessing? To meet this difficulty, I postulate that they would prefer more primary social goods rather than less (i.e., rights and liberties, powers and opportunities, income and wealth and self-respect). Of course, it may turn out, once the veil of ignorance is removed, that some of them for religious or other reasons may not, in fact, want more of these goods. But from the standpoint of the original position, it is rational for the parties to suppose that they do want a larger share, since in any case they are not compelled to accept more if they do not wish to nor does a person suffer from a greater liberty. Thus even though the parties are deprived of information about their particular ends, they have enough knowledge to rank the alternatives. They know that in general they must try to protect their liberties, widen their opportunities, and enlarge their means for promoting their aims whatever these are. Guided by the theory of the good and the general facts of moral psychology, their deliberations are no longer guesswork. They can make a rational decision in the ordinary sense.

The assumption of mutually disinterested rationality, then, comes to this: the persons in the original position try to acknowledge principles which advance their system of ends as far as possible. They do this by attempting to win for themselves the highest index of primary social goods, since this enables them to promote their conception of the good most effectively whatever it turns out to be. The parties do not seek to confer benefits or to impose injuries on one another; they are not moved by affection or rancor. Nor do they try to gain relative to each other; they are not envious or vain. Put in terms of a game, we might say: they strive for as high an absolute score as possible. They do not wish a high or a low score for their opponents, nor do they seek to maximize or minimize the difference between their successes and those of others. The idea of a game does not really apply, since the parties are not concerned to win but to get as many points as possible judged by their own system of ends.

I shall now state in a provisional form the two principles of justice that I believe would be chosen in the original position. The first statement of the two principles reads as follows.

- First: each person is to have an equal right to the most extensive basic liberty compatible with a similar liberty for others.

- Second: social and economic inequalities are to be arranged so that they are both (a) reasonably expected to be to everyone's advantage, and (b) attached to positions and offices open to all.

By way of general comment, these principles primarily apply, as I have said, to the basic structure of society. They are to govern the assignment of rights and duties and to regulate the distribution of social and economic advantages. As their formulation suggests, these principles presuppose that the social structure can be divided into two more or less distinct parts, the first principle applying to the one, the second to the other. They distinguish between those aspects of the social system that define and secure the equal liberties of citizenship and those that specify and establish social and economic inequalities. The basic liberties of citizens are, roughly speaking, political liberty (the right to vote and to be eligible for public office) together with freedom of speech and assembly; liberty of conscience and freedom of thought; freedom of the person along with the right to hold (personal) property; and freedom from arbitrary arrest and seizure as defined by the concept of the rule of law. These liberties are all required to be equal by the first principle, since citizens of a just society are to have the same basic rights.

The second principle applies, in the first approximation, to the distribution of income and wealth and to the design of organizations that make use of differences in authority and responsibility, or chains of command. While the distribution of wealth and income need not be equal, it must be to everyone's advantage, and at the same time, positions of authority and offices of command must be accessible to all. One applies the second principle by holding positions open, and then, subject to this constraint, arranges social and economic inequalities so that everyone benefits.

These principles are to be arranged in a serial order with the first principle prior to the second. This ordering means that a departure from the institutions of equal liberty required by the first principle cannot be justified by, or compensated for, by greater social and economic advantages. The distribution of wealth and income, and the hierarchies of authority, must be consistent with both the liberties of equal citizenship and equality of opportunity.

It is clear that these principles are rather specific in their content, and their acceptance rests on certain assumptions that I must eventually try to explain and justify. For the present, it should be observed that the two principles (and this holds for all formulations) are a special case of a more general conception of justice that can be expressed as follows.

> All social values—liberty and opportunity, income and wealth, and the bases of self-respect—are to be distributed equally unless an unequal distribution of any, or all, of these values is to everyone's advantage.

Injustice, then, is simply inequalities that are not to the benefit of all. Of course, this conception is extremely vague and requires interpretation.

As a first step, suppose that the basic structure of society distributes certain primary goods, that is, things that every rational man is presumed to want. These goods normally have a use whatever a person's rational plan of life. For simplicity, assume that the chief primary goods at the disposition of society are rights and liberties, powers and opportunities, income and wealth. These are the social primary goods. Other primary goods such as health and vigor, intelligence and imagination, are natural goods; although their possession is influenced by the basic structure, they are not so directly under its control. Imagine, then, a hypothetical initial arrangement in which all the social primary goods are equally distributed: everyone has similar rights and duties, and income and wealth are evenly shared. This state of affairs provides a benchmark for judging improvements. If certain inequalities of wealth and organizational powers would make everyone better off than in this hypothetical starting situation, then they accord with the general conception.

Now it is possible, at least theoretically, that by giving up some of their fundamental liberties men are sufficiently compensated by the resulting social and economic gains. The general conception of justice imposes no restrictions on what sort of inequalities are permissible; it only requires that everyone's position be improved.

The second principle insists that each person benefit from permissible inequalities in the basic structure. This means that it must be reasonable for each relevant representative man defined by this structure, when he views it as a going concern, to prefer his prospects with the inequality to his prospects without it. One is not allowed to justify differences in income or organizational powers on the ground that the disadvantages of those in one position are outweighed by the greater advantages of those in another. Much less can infringements of liberty be counterbalanced in this way. Applied to the basic structure, the principle of utility would have us maximize the sum of expectations of representative men (weighted by the number of persons they represent, on the classical view); and this would permit us to compensate for the losses of some by the gains of others. Instead, the two principles require that everyone benefit from economic and social inequalities.

THE TENDENCY TO EQUALITY

I wish to conclude this discussion of the two principles by explaining the sense in which they express an egalitarian conception of justice. Also I should like to forestall the objection to the principle of fair opportunity that it leads to a callous meritocratic society. In order to prepare the way for doing this, I note several aspects of the conception of justice that I have set out.

First we may observe that the difference principle gives some weight to the considerations singled out by the principle of redress. This is the principle that undeserved inequalities call for redress; and since inequalities of birth and natural endowment are undeserved, these inequalities are to be somehow compensated for.[3] Thus the principle holds that in order to treat all persons equally, to provide genuine equality of opportunity, society must give more attention to those with fewer native assets and to those born into the less favorable social positions. The idea is to redress the bias of contingencies in the direction of equality. In pursuit of this principle greater resources might be spent on the education of the less rather than the more intelligent, at least over a certain time of life, say the earlier years of school.

Now the principle of redress has not to my knowledge been proposed as the sole criterion of justice, as the single aim of the social order. It is plausible as most such principles are only as a prima facie principle, one that is to be weighed in the balance with others. For example, we are to weigh it against the principle to improve the average standard of life, or to advance the common good. But whatever other principles we hold, the claims of redress are to be taken into account. It is thought to represent one of the elements in our conception of justice. Now the difference principle is not of course the principle of redress. It does not require society to try to even out handicaps as if all were expected to compete on a fair basis in the same race. But the difference principle would allocate resources in education, say, so as to improve the long-term expectation of the least favored. If this end is attained by giving more attention to the better endowed, it is permissible; otherwise not. And in making this decision, the value of education should not be assessed only in terms of economic efficiency and social welfare. Equally if not more important is the role of education in enabling a person to enjoy the culture of his society and to take part in its affairs, and in this way to provide for each individual a secure sense of his own worth.

Thus although the difference principle is not the same as that of redress, it does achieve some of the intent of the latter principle. It transforms the aims of the basic structure so that the total scheme of institutions no longer emphasizes social efficiency and technocratic values. We see then that the difference principle represents, in effect, an agreement to regard the distribution of natural talents as a common asset and to share in the benefits of this distribution whatever it turns out to be. Those who have been favored by nature, whoever they are, may gain from their good fortune only on terms that improve the situation of those who have lost out. The naturally advantaged are not to gain merely because they are more gifted, but only to cover the costs of training and education and for using their endowments in ways that help the less fortunate as well. No one deserves his greater natural capacity nor merits a more favorable starting place in society. But it does not follow that one should eliminate these distinctions. There is another way to deal with them. The basic structure can be arranged so that these contingencies work for the good of the least fortunate. Thus we are led to the difference principle if we wish to set up the social system so that no one gains or loses from his arbitrary place in the distribution of natural assets or his initial position in society without giving or receiving compensating advantages in return.

The natural distribution of talents is neither just nor unjust; nor is it unjust that men are born into society at some particular position. These are simply natural facts.

What is just and unjust is the way that institutions deal with these facts. Aristocratic and caste societies are unjust because they make these contingencies the ascriptive basis for belonging to more or less enclosed and privileged social classes. The basic structure of these societies incorporates the arbitrariness found in nature. But there is no necessity for men to resign themselves to these contingencies. The social system is not an unchangeable order beyond human control but a pattern of human action. In justice as fairness men agree to share one another's fate. In designing institutions they undertake to avail themselves of the accidents of nature and social circumstance only when doing so is for the common benefit. The two principles are a fair way of meeting the arbitrariness of fortune; and while no doubt imperfect in other ways, the institutions which satisfy these principles are just.

There is a natural inclination to object that those better situated deserve their greater advantages whether or not they are to the benefit of others. At this point it is necessary to be clear about the notion of desert. It is perfectly true that given a just system of cooperation as a scheme of public rules and the expectations set up by it, those who, with the prospect of improving their condition, have done what the system announces that it will reward are entitled to their advantages. In this sense the more fortunate have a claim to their better situation; their claims are legitimate expectations established by social institutions, and the community is obligated to meet them. But this sense of desert presupposes the existence of the cooperative scheme; it is irrelevant to the question whether in the first place the scheme is to be designed in accordance with the difference principle or some other criterion.

Perhaps some will think that the person with greater natural endowments deserves those assets and the superior character that made their development possible. Because he is more worthy in this sense, he deserves the greater advantages that he could achieve with them. This view, however, is surely incorrect. It seems to be one of the fixed points of our considered judgments that no one deserves his place in the distribution of native endowments, any more than one deserves one's initial starting place in society. The assertion that a man deserves the superior character that enables him to make the effort to cultivate his abilities is equally problematic; for his character depends in large part upon fortunate family and social circumstances for which he can claim no credit. The notion of desert seems not to apply to these cases. Thus the more advantaged representative man cannot say that he deserves and therefore has a right to a scheme of cooperation in which he is permitted to acquire benefits in ways that do not contribute to the welfare of others. There is no basis for his making this claim. From the standpoint of common sense, then, the difference principle appears to be acceptable both to the more advantaged and to the less advantaged individual.

NOTES

1. For the formulation of this intuitive idea I am indebted to Allan Gibbard.

2. The veil of ignorance is so natural a condition that something like it must have occurred to many. The closest express statement of it known to me is found in J. C. Harsanyi,

"Cardinal Utility in Welfare Economics and in the Theory of Risk-Taking." *Journal of Political Economy*, vol. 61 (1953). Harsanyi uses it to develop a utilitarian theory.

3. See Herbert Spiegelberg, "A Defense of Human Equality," *Philosophical Review*, vol. 53 (1944), pp. 101, 113–123; and D. D. Raphael, "Justice and Liberty," *Proceedings of the Aristotelian Society*, vol. 51 (1950–1951), pp. 187f.

DISTRIBUTIVE JUSTICE

ROBERT NOZICK*

The minimal state is the most extensive state that can be justified. Any state more extensive violates people's rights. Yet many persons have put forth reasons purporting to justify a more extensive state. It is impossible within the compass of this book to examine all the reasons that have been put forth. Therefore, I shall focus upon those generally acknowledged to be most weighty and influential, to see precisely wherein they fail. In this paper we consider the claim that a more extensive state is justified, because necessary (or the best instrument) to achieve distributive justice.

The term "distributive justice" is not a neutral one. Hearing the term "distribution," most people presume that some thing or mechanism uses some principle or criterion to give out a supply of things. Into this process of distributing shares some error may have crept. So it is an open question, at least, whether *re*distribution should take place; whether we should do again what has already been done once, though poorly. However, we are not in the position of children who have been given portions of pie by someone who now makes last minute adjustments to rectify careless cutting. There is no *central* distribution, no person or group entitled to control all the resources, jointly deciding how they are to be doled out. What each person gets, he gets from others who give to him in exchange for something, or as a gift. In a free society, diverse persons control different resources, and new holdings arise out of the voluntary exchanges and actions of persons. There is no more a distributing or distribution of shares than there is a distributing of mates in a society in which persons choose whom they shall marry. The total result is the product of many individual decisions which the different individuals involved are entitled to make.

THE ENTITLEMENT THEORY

The subject of justice in holdings consists of three major topics. The first is the *original acquisition of holdings*, the appropriation of unheld things. This includes the issues of how unheld things may come to be held, the process, or processes, by which unheld things may come to be held, the things that may come to be held by these processes, the extent of what comes to be held by a particular process, and so on. We shall refer to the complicated truth about this topic, which we shall not formulate here, as the principle of justice in acquisition. The second topic concerns the *transfer of holdings* from one person to another. By what processes may a person transfer holdings to another? How may a person acquire a holding from another who holds it? Under this topic come general descriptions of voluntary exchange, and gift and (on the other hand) fraud, as well as reference to particular conventional details fixed upon in a given society. The complicated truth about this subject (with placeholders for con-

Excerpted from *Anarchy, State and Utopia*, by Robert Nozick, New York: Basic Books. © 1974 by Basic Books, Inc. Reprinted by permission of the publisher and Basil Blackwell.
*Department of Philosophy, Harvard University.

ventional details) we shall call the principle of justice in transfer. (And we shall suppose it also includes principles governing how a person may divest himself of a holding, passing it into an unheld state.)

If the world were wholly just, the following inductive definition would exhaustively cover the subject of justice in holdings.

1. A person who acquires a holding in accordance with the principle of justice in acquisition is entitled to that holding.

2. A person who acquires a holding in accordance with the principle of justice in transfer, from someone else entitled to the holding, is entitled to the holding.

3. No one is entitled to a holding except by (repeated) applications of 1 and 2.

The complete principle of distributive justice would say simply that a distribution is just if everyone is entitled to the holdings they possess under the distribution.

A distribution is just if it arises from another just distribution by legitimate means. The legitimate means of moving from one distribution to another are specified by the principle of justice in transfer. The legitimate first "moves" are specified by the principle of justice in acquisition. Whatever arises from a just situation by just steps is itself just. The means of change specified by the principle of justice in transfer preserve justice. As correct rules of inference are truth-preserving, and any conclusion deduced via repeated application of such rules from only true premises is itself true, so the means of transition from one situation to another specified by the principle of justice in transfer are justice-preserving, and any situation actually arising from repeated transitions in accordance with the principle from a just situation is itself just. The parallel between justice-preserving transformations and truth-preserving transformations illuminates where it fails as well as where it holds. That a conclusion could have been deduced by truth-preserving means from premises that are true suffices to show its truth. That from a just situation a situation *could* have arisen via justice-preserving means does *not* suffice to show its justice. The fact that a thief's victims voluntarily *could* have presented him with gifts does not entitle the thief to his ill-gotten gains. Justice in holdings is historical; it depends upon what actually has happened. We shall return to this point later.

Not all actual situations are generated in accordance with the two principles of justice in holdings: the principle of justice in acquisition and the principle of justice in transfer. Some people steal from others, or defraud them, or enslave them, seizing their product and preventing them from living as they choose, or forcibly exclude others from competing in exchanges. None of these are permissible modes of transition from one situation to another. And some persons acquire holdings by means not sanctioned by the principle of justice in acquisition. The existence of past injustice (previous violations of the first two principles of justice in holdings) raises the third major topic under justice in holdings: the rectification of injustice in holdings. If past injustice has shaped present holdings in various ways, some identifiable and some not, what now, if anything, ought to be done to rectify these injustices? What obligations do the performers of injustice have toward those whose position is worse than it would have been had the injustice not been done? Or, than it would have been had compensation been paid promptly? How, if at all, do things change if the beneficiaries and those made worse off are not the direct parties in the act of injustice, but, for example, their descendants? Is an injustice done to someone whose holding was itself based upon an unrectified injustice? How far back must one go in wiping clean the historical slate of injustices? What may victims of injustice permissibly do in order to rectify the injustices being done to them, including the many injustices done by persons acting through their government? I do not know of a thorough or theoretically sophisticated treatment of such issues. Idealizing greatly, let us suppose theoretical investigation will produce a principle of rectification. This principle uses historical information about previous situations and injustices done in them (as defined by the first two principles of justice and rights against interference), and information about the actual course of events that flowed from these injustices, until the present, and it yields a description (or descriptions) of holdings in the society. The principle of rectification presumably will make use of its best estimate of subjunctive information about what would have occurred (or a probability distribution over what might have occurred, using the expected value) if the injustice had not taken place. If the actual description of holdings turns out not to be one of the descriptions yielded by the principle, then one of the descriptions yielded must be realized.

The general outlines of the theory of justice in holdings are that the holdings of a person are just if he is entitled to them by the principles of justice in acquisition and transfer, or by the principle of rectification of injustice (as specified by the first two principles). If each person's holdings are just, then the total set (distribution) of holdings is just. To turn these general outlines into a specific theory we would have to specify the details of each of the three principles of justice in holdings: the principle of acquisition of holdings, the principle of transfer of holdings, and the principle of rectification of violations of the first two principles. I shall not attempt that task here. (Locke's principle of justice in acquisition is discussed below.)

HISTORICAL PRINCIPLES AND END-RESULT PRINCIPLES

The general outlines of the entitlement theory illuminate the nature and defects of other conceptions of distributive justice. The entitlement theory of justice in distribution is *historical*; whether a distribution is just depends upon how it came about. In contrast, *current time-slice principles* of justice hold that the justice of a distribution is determined by how things are distributed (who has what) as judged by some *structural* principle(s) of just distribution. A utilitarian who judges between any two distributions by seeing which has the greater sum of utility and, if the sums tie, applies some fixed equality criterion to choose the more equal distribution, would hold a current time-slice principle of justice. As would someone who had a fixed schedule of trade-offs between the sum of happiness and equality. According to a current time-slice principle, all that needs to be looked at, in judging the justice of a distribution, is who ends up with what; in comparing any two distributions one need look only at the matrix presenting the distributions. No further information need be fed into a principle of justice. It is a consequence of such principles of justice that any two structurally identical distributions are equally just. (Two distributions are structurally identical if they present the same profile, but perhaps have different persons occupying the particular slots. My having ten and your having five, and my having five and your having ten are structurally identical distributions.) Welfare economics is the theory of current time-slice principles of justice. The subject is conceived as operating on matrices representing only current information about distribution. This, as well as some of the usual conditions (for example, the choice of distribution is invariant under relabeling of columns), guarantees that welfare economics will be a current time-slice theory, with all of its inadequacies.

Most persons do not accept current time-slice principles as constituting the whole story about distributive shares. They think it relevant in assessing the justice of a situation to consider not only the distribution it embodies, but also how that distribution came about. If some persons are in prison for murder or war crimes, we do not say that to assess the justice of the distribution in the society we must look only at what this person has, and that person has, and that person has, . . . at the current time. We think it relevant to ask whether someone did something so that he *deserved* to be punished, deserved to have a lower share.

PATTERNING

The entitlement principles of justice in holdings that we have sketched are historical principles of justice. To better understand their precise character, we shall distinguish them from another subclass of the historical principles. Consider, as an example, the principle of distribution according to moral merit. This principle requires that total distributive shares vary directly with moral merit; no person should have a greater share than anyone whose moral merit is greater. Or consider the principle that results by substituting "usefulness to society" for "moral merit" in the previous principle. Or instead of "distribute according to moral merit," or "distribute according to usefulness to society," we might consider "distribute according to the weighted sum of moral merit, usefulness to society, and need," with the weights of the different dimensions equal. Let us call a principle of distribution *patterned* if it specifies that a distribution is to vary along with some natural dimension, weighted sum of natural dimensions, or lexicographic ordering of natural dimensions. And let us say a distribution is patterned if it accords with some patterned principle. The principle of distribution in accordance with moral merit is a patterned historical principle, which specifies a patterned distribution. "Distribute according to I.Q." is a patterned principle that looks to information not contained in distributional matrices. It is not historical, however, in that it does not look to any past actions creating differential entitlements to evaluate a distribution; it requires only distributional matrices whose columns are labeled by I.Q. scores. The distribution in a society, however, may be composed of such simple patterned distributions, without itself being simply patterned. Different sectors may operate different patterns, or some combination of patterns may operate in different proportions across a society. A distribution composed in this manner, from a small number of patterned distributions, we also shall term "patterned." And we extend the use of "pattern" to include the overall designs put forth by combinations of end-state principles.

Almost every suggested principle of distributive justice is patterned: to each according to his moral merit, or needs, or marginal product, or how hard he tries, or the weighted sum of the foregoing, and so on. The principle of entitlement we have sketched is *not* patterned. There is no one natural dimension or weighted sum or combination of a small number of natural dimensions that yields the distributions generated in accordance with the principle of entitlement. The set of holdings that results when some persons receive their marginal products, others win at gambling, others receive a share of their mate's income, others receive gifts from foundations, others receive interest on loans, others receive gifts from admirers, others receive returns on investment, others make for themselves much of what they have, others find things, and so on, will not be patterned.

To think that the task of a theory of distributive justice is to fill in the blank in "to each according to his ———" is to be predisposed to search for a pattern; and the separate treatment of "from each according to his ———" treats production and distribution as two separate and independent issues. On an entitlement view these are *not* two separate questions. Whoever makes something, having bought or contracted for all other held resources used in the process (transferring some of his holdings for these cooperating factors), is entitled to it. The situation is *not* one of something's getting made, and there being an open question of who is to get it. Things come into the world already attached to people having entitlements over them. From the point of view of the historical entitlement conception of justice in holdings, those who start afresh to complete "to each according to his ———" treat objects as if they appeared from nowhere, out of nothing. A complete theory of justice might cover this limited case as well; perhaps here is a use for the usual conceptions of distributive justice.

So entrenched are maxims of the usual form that perhaps we should present the entitlement conception as a competitor. Ignoring acquisition and rectification, we might say:

> From each according to what he chooses to do, to each according to what he makes for himself (perhaps with the contracted aid of others) and what others choose to do for him and choose to give him of what they've been given previously (under this maxim) and haven't yet expended or transferred.

This, the discerning reader will have noticed, has its defects as a slogan. So as a summary and great simplification (and not as a maxim with any independent meaning) we have:

> From each as they choose, to each as they are chosen.

HOW LIBERTY UPSETS PATTERNS

It is not clear how those holding alternative conceptions of distributive justice can reject the entitlement conception of justice in holdings. For suppose a distribution favored by one of these non-entitlement conceptions is realized. Let us suppose it is your favorite one and let us call this distribution D_1; perhaps everyone has an equal share, perhaps shares vary in accordance with some dimension you treasure. Now suppose that Wilt Chamberlain is greatly in demand by basketball teams, being a great gate attraction. (Also suppose contracts run only for a year, with players being free agents.) He signs the following sort of contract with a team: In each home game, twenty-five cents from the price of each ticket of admission goes to him. (We ignore the question of whether he is "gouging" the owners, letting them look out for themselves.) The season starts, and people cheerfully attend his team's games; they buy their tickets, each time dropping a separate twenty-five cents of their admission price into a special box with Chamberlain's name on it. They are excited about seeing him play; it is worth the total admission price to them. Let us suppose that in one season one million persons attend his home games, and Wilt Chamberlain winds up with $250,000, a much larger sum than the average income and larger even than anyone else has. Is he entitled to this income? Is this new distribution D_2 unjust? If so, why? There is *no* question about whether each of the people was entitled to the control over the resources they held in D_1; because that was the distribution (your favorite) that (for the purposes of argument) we assumed was acceptable. Each of these persons *chose* to give twenty-five cents of their money to Chamberlain. They could have spent it on going to the movies, or on candy bars, or on copies of *Dissent* magazine, or of *Monthly Review*. But they all, at least one million of them, converged on giving it to Wilt Chamberlain in exchange for watching him play basketball. If D_1 was a just distribution, and people voluntarily moved from it to D_2, transferring parts of their shares they were given under D_1 (what was it for if not to do something with?), isn't D_2 also just? If the people were entitled to dispose of the resources to which they were entitled (under D_1), didn't this include their being entitled to give it to, or exchange it with, Wilt Chamberlain? Can anyone else complain on grounds of justice? Each other person already has his legitimate share under D_1. Under D_1, there is nothing that anyone has that anyone else has a claim of justice against. After someone transfers something to Wilt Chamberlain, third parties *still* have their legitimate shares; *their* shares are not changed. By what process could such a transfer among two persons give rise to a legitimate claim of distributive justice on a portion of what was transferred, by a third party who had no claim of justice on any holding of the others *before* the transfer? To cut off objections irrelevant here, we might imagine the exchanges occurring in a socialist society, after hours. After playing whatever basketball he does in his daily work, or doing whatever other daily work he does, Wilt Chamberlain decides to put in *overtime* to earn additional money. (First his work quota is set; he works time over that.) Or imagine it is a skilled juggler people like to see, who puts on shows after hours.

The general point illustrated by the Wilt Chamberlain example and the example of the entrepreneur in a socialist society is that no end-state principle or distributional patterned principle of justice can be continuously realized without continuous interference with people's lives. Any favored pattern would be transformed into one unfavored by the principle, by people choosing to act in various ways; for example, by people exchanging goods and services with other people, or giving things to other people, things the transferrers are entitled to under the favored distributional pattern. To maintain a pattern one must either continually interfere to stop people from transferring resources as they wish to, or continually (or periodically) interfere to take from some persons resources that others for some reason chose to transfer to them.

Patterned principles of distributive justice necessitate *redistributive* activities. The likelihood is small that any actual freely-arrived-at set of holdings fits a given pattern; and the likelihood is nil that it will continue to fit the pattern as people exchange and give. From the point of view of an entitlement theory, redistribution is a serious matter indeed, involving, as it does, the violation of people's rights. (An exception is those takings that fall under the principle of the rectification of injustices.) From other points of view, also, it is serious.

Taxation of earnings from labor is on a par with forced labor. Some persons find this claim obviously true: taking the earnings of n hours labor is like taking n hours from the person; it is like forcing the person to work n hours for another's purpose. Others find the claim absurd. But even these, *if* they object to forced labor, would oppose forcing unemployed hippies to work for the benefit of the needy. And they would also object to forcing each person to work five extra hours each week for the benefit of the needy. But a system that takes five hours' wages in taxes does not seem to them like one that forces someone to work five hours, since it offers the person forced a wider range of choice in activities than does taxation in kind with the particular labor specified.

Whether it is done through taxation on wages or on wages over a certain amount, or through seizure of profits, or through there being a big *social pot* so that it's not clear what's coming from where and what's going where, patterned principles of distributive justice involve appropriating the actions of other persons. Seizing the results of someone's labor is equivalent to seizing hours from him and directing him to carry on various activities. If people force you to do certain work, or unrewarded work, for a certain period of time, they decide what you are to do and what purposes your work is to serve apart from your decisions. This process whereby they take this decision from you makes them a *part-owner* of you; it gives them a property right in you. Just as having such partial control and power of decision, by right, over an animal or inanimate object would be to have a property right in it.

LOCKE'S THEORY OF ACQUISITION

We must introduce an additional bit of complexity into the structure of the entitlement theory. This is best approached by considering Locke's attempt to specify a principle of justice in acquisition. Locke views property rights in an unowned object as originating through someone's mixing his labor with it. This gives rise to many questions. What are the boundaries of what labor is mixed with? If a private astronaut clears a place on Mars, has he mixed his labor with (so that he comes to own) the whole planet, the whole uninhabited universe, or just a particular plot? Which plot does an act bring under ownership?

Locke's proviso that there be "enough and as good left in common for others" is meant to ensure that the situation of others is not worsened. I assume that any adequate theory of justice in acquisition will contain a proviso similar to Locke's. A process normally giving rise to a permanent bequeathable property right in a previously unowned thing will not do so if the position of others no longer at liberty to use the thing is thereby worsened. It is important to specify *this* particular mode of worsening the situation of others, for the proviso does not encompass other modes. It does not include the worsening due to more limited opportunities to appropriate, and it does not include how I "worsen" a seller's position if I appropriate materials to make some of what he is selling, and then enter into competition with him. Someone whose appropriation otherwise would violate the proviso still may appropriate provided he compensates the others so that their situation is not thereby worsened; unless he does compensate these others, his appropriation will violate the proviso of the principle of justice in acquisition and will be an illegitimate one. A theory of appropriation incorporating this Lockean proviso will handle correctly the cases (objections to the theory lacking the proviso) where someone appropriates the total supply of something necessary for life.

A theory which includes this proviso in its principle of justice in acquisition must also contain a more complex principle of justice in transfer. Some reflection of the proviso about appropriation constrains later actions. If my appropriating all of a certain substance violates the Lockean proviso, then so does my appropriating some and purchasing all the rest from others who obtained it without otherwise violating the Lockean proviso. If the proviso excludes someone's appropriating all the drinkable water in the world, it also excludes his purchasing it all. (More weakly, and messily, it may exclude his charging certain prices for some of his supply.) This proviso (almost?) never will come into effect; the more someone acquires of a scarce substance which others want, the higher the price of the rest will go, and the more difficult it will become for him to acquire it all. But still, we can imagine, at least, that something like this occurs: someone makes simultaneous secret bids to the separate owners of a substance, each of whom sells assuming he can easily purchase more from the other owners; or some natural catastrophe destroys all of the supply of something except that in one person's possession. The total supply could not be permissibly appropriated by one person at the beginning. His later acquisition of it all does not show that the original appropriation violated the proviso. Rather, it is the combination of the original appropriation *plus* all the later transfers and actions that violates the Lockean proviso.

Each owner's title to his holding includes the historical shadow of the Lockean proviso on appropriation. This excludes his transferring it into an agglomeration that does violate the Lockean proviso and excludes his using it in a way, in coordination with others or independently of them, so as to violate the proviso by making the situation of others worse than their baseline situation. Once it is known that someone's ownership runs afoul of the Lockean proviso, there are stringent limits on what he may do with (what it is difficult any longer unreservedly to call) "his property." Thus a person may not appropriate the only water hole in a desert and charge what he will. Nor may he charge what he will if he possesses one, and unfortunately it happens that all the water holes in the desert dry up, except for his. This unfortunate circumstance, admittedly no fault of his, brings into operation the Lockean proviso and limits his property rights. Similarly, an owner's property right in the only island in an area does not allow him to order a castaway from a shipwreck off his island as a trespasser, for this would violate the Lockean proviso.

Notice that the theory does not say that owners do not have these rights, but that the rights are overridden to avoid some catastrophe. (Overridden rights do not disappear; they leave a trace of a sort absent in the cases under discussion.) There is no such external (and *ad hoc*?) overriding. Considerations internal to the theory of property itself, to its theory of acquisition and appropriation, provide the means for handling such cases.

I believe that the free operation of a market system will not actually run afoul of the Lockean proviso. If this is correct, the proviso will not provide a significant opportunity for future state action.

DISTRIBUTIVE JUSTICE AND UTILITARIANISM

J. J. C. SMART*

INTRODUCTION

In this paper I shall not be concerned with the defense of utilitarianism against other types of ethical theory. Indeed I hold that questions of ultimate ethical principle are not susceptible of proof, though something can be done to render them more acceptable by presenting them in a clear light and by clearing up certain confusions which (for some people) may get in the way of their acceptance. Ultimately the utilitarian appeals to the sentiment of generalized benevolence, and speaks to others who feel this sentiment too and for whom it is an over-riding feeling.[1] (This does not mean that he will always act from this over-riding feeling. There can be backsliding and action may result from more particular feelings, just as an egoist may go against his own interests, and may regret this.) I shall be concerned here merely to investigate certain consequences of utilitarianism, as they relate to questions of distributive justice. The type of utilitarianism with which I am concerned is act utilitarianism.

THE PLACE OF JUSTICE IN UTILITARIAN THEORY

The concept of justice as a *fundamental* ethical concept is really quite foreign to utilitarianism. A utilitarian would compromise his utilitarianism if he allowed principles of justice which might conflict with the maximization of happiness (or more generally of goodness, should he be an "ideal" utilitarian). He is concerned with the maximization of happiness[2] and not with the distribution of it. Nevertheless he may well deduce from his ethical principle that certain ways of distributing the means to happiness (e.g., money, food, housing) are more conducive to the general good than are others. He will be interested in justice in so far as it is a political or legal or quasi-legal concept. He will consider whether the legal institutions and customary sanctions which operate in particular societies are more or less conducive to the utilitarian end than are other possible institutions and customs. Even if the society consisted entirely of utilitarians (and of course no actual societies have thus consisted) it might still be important to have legal and customary sanctions relating to distribution of goods, because utilitarians might be tempted to backslide and favour non-optimific distributions, perhaps because of bias in their own favour. They might be helped to act in a more nearly utilitarian way because of the presence of these sanctions.

    As a utilitarian, therefore, I do not allow the concept of justice as a fundamental moral concept, but I am nevertheless interested in justice in a subordinate way, as a *means* to the utilitarian end. Thus even though I hold that it does not matter in what

Excerpted from "Distributive Justice and Utilitarianism," published in *Justice and Economic Distribution*, edited by John Arthur and William H. Shaw, Englewood Cliffs, N.J.: Prentice-Hall, 1978. Reprinted by permission of the author.

*Research School of Social Sciences, The Australian National University.

way happiness is distributed among different persons, provided that the total amount of happiness is maximized, I do of course hold that it can be of vital importance that the *means* to happiness should be distributed in some ways and not in others. Suppose that I have the choice of two alternative actions as follows: I can either give $500 to each of two needy men, Smith and Campbell, or else give $1000 to Smith and nothing to Campbell. It is of course likely to produce the greatest happiness if I divide the money equally. For this reason utilitarianism can often emerge as a theory with egalitarian consequences. If it does so this is because of the empirical situation, and not because of any moral commitment to egalitarianism as such. Consider, for example, another empirical situation in which the $500 was replaced by a half-dose of a life saving drug, in which case the utilitarian would advocate giving two half-doses to Smith or Campbell and none to the other. Indeed if Smith and Campbell each possessed a half-dose it would be right to take one of the half-doses and give it to the other. (I am assuming that a whole dose would preserve life and that a half-dose would not. I am also assuming a simplified situation: in some possible situations, especially in a society of nonutilitarians, the wide social ramifications of taking a half-dose from Smith and giving it to Campbell might conceivably outweigh the good results of saving Campbell's life.) However, it is probable that in most situations the equal distribution of the means to happiness will be the right utilitarian action, even though the utilitarian has no ultimate moral commitment to egalitarianism. If a utilitarian is given the choice of two actions, one of which will give 2 units of happiness to Smith and 2 to Campbell, and the other of which will give 1 unit of happiness to Smith and 9 to Campbell, he will choose the latter course.[3] It may also be that I have the choice between two alternative actions, one of which gives -1 unit of happiness to Smith and $+9$ units to Campbell, and the other of which gives $+2$ to Smith and $+2$ to Campbell. As a utilitarian I will choose the former course, and here I will be in conflict with John Rawls' theory, whose maximin principle would rule out making Smith worse off.

UTILITARIANISM AND RAWLS' THEORY

Rawls deduces his ethical principles from the contract which would be made by a group of rational egoists in an 'original position' in which they thought behind a 'veil of ignorance,' so that they would not know who they were or even what generation they belonged to.[4] Reasoning behind this veil of ignorance, they would apply the maximin principle. John Harsanyi earlier used the notion of a contract in such a position of ignorance, but used not the maximin principle but the principle of maximizing expected utility.[5] Harsanyi's method leads to a form of rule utilitarianism. I see no great merit in this roundabout approach to ethics *via* a contrary to fact supposition, which involves the tricky notion of a social contract and which thus appears already to presuppose a moral position. The approach seems also too Hobbesian: it is anthropologically incorrect to suppose that we are all originally little egoists. I prefer to base ethics on a principle of generalized benevolence, to which some of those with whom I discuss ethics may immediately respond. Possibly it might show something interesting about our common moral notions if it could be proved that they follow from what would be contracted by rational egoists in an 'original position,' but as a utilitarian I am more concerned to advocate a normative theory which might replace our common moral notions than I am to explain these notions. Though some form of utilitarianism might be deducible (as by Harsanyi) from a contract or original position theory, I do not think that it either ought to be or need be defended in this sort of way.

Be that as it may, it is clear that utilitarian views about distribution of happiness do differ from Rawls' view. I have made a distinction between justice as a moral concept and justice as a legal or quasi-legal concept. The utilitarian has no room for the former, but he can have strong views about the latter, though *what* these views are will depend on empirical considerations. Thus whether he will prefer a political theory which advocates a completely socialist state, or whether he will prefer one which advocates a minimal state (as Robert Nozick's book does[6]), or whether again he will advocate something between the two, is something which depends on the facts of economics, sociology, and so on. As someone not expert in these fields I have no desire to dogmatize on these empirical matters. (My own private non-expert opinion is that probably neither extreme leads to maximization of happiness, though I have a liking for rather more socialism than exists in Australia or U.S.A. at present.) As a utilitarian my approach to political theory has to be tentative and empirical. Not believing in moral rights as such I can not deduce theories about the best political arrangements by making deductions (as Nozick does) from propositions which purport to be about such basic rights.

Rawls deduces two principles of justice.[7] The first of these is that 'each person is to have an equal right to the most extensive basic liberty compatible with a similar liberty for others,' and the second one is that 'social and economic inequalities are to be arranged so that they are both (a) reasonably expected to be to everyone's advantage, and (b) attached to positions and offices open to all.' Though a utilitarian could (on empirical grounds) be very much in sympathy with both of these principles, he could not accept them as universal rules. Suppose that a society which had no danger of nuclear war could be achieved only by reducing the liberty of one per cent of the world's population. Might it not be right to bring about such a state of affairs if it were in one's power? Indeed might it not be right greatly to reduce the liberty of 100% of the world's population if such a desirable outcome could be achieved? Perhaps the present generation would be pretty miserable and would hanker for their lost liberties. However we must also think about the countless future generations which might exist and be happy provided that mankind can avoid exterminating itself, and we must also think of all the pain, misery and genetic damage which would be brought about by nuclear war even if this did not lead to the total extermination of mankind.

Suppose that this loss of freedom prevented a war so devastating that the whole process of evolution on this planet would come to an end. At the cost of the loss of freedom, instead of the war and the end of evolution there might occur an evolutionary process which was not only long lived but also beneficial: in millions of years there might be creatures descended from *homo sapiens* which had vastly increased talents and capacity for happiness. At least such considerations show that Rawls' first principle is far from obvious to the utilitarian, though in certain mundane contexts he might accede to it as a useful approximation. Indeed I do not believe that restriction of liberty, in our present society, could have beneficial results in helping to prevent nuclear war, though a case could be made for certain restrictions on the liberty of all present members of society so as to enable the government to prevent nuclear blackmail by gangs of terrorists.

Perhaps in the past considerable restrictions on the personal liberties of a large proportion of citizens may have been justifiable on utilitarian grounds. In view of the glories of Athens and its contributions to civilization it is possible that the Athenian slave society was justifiable. In one part of his paper, 'Nature and Soundness of the Contract and Coherence Arguments,'[8] David Lyons has judiciously discussed the question of whether in certain circumstances a utilitarian would condone slavery. He says that it would be unlikely that a utilitarian could condone slavery as it has existed in modern times. However he considers the possibility that less objectionable forms of slavery or near slavery have existed. The less objectionable these may have been, the more likely it is that utilitarianism would have condoned them. Lyons remarks that our judgments about the relative advantages of different societies must be very tentative because we do not know enough about human history to say what were the social alternatives at any juncture.[9]

Similar reflections naturally occur in connection with Rawls' second principle. Oligarchic societies, such as that of eighteenth century Britain, may well have been in fact better governed than they would have been if posts of responsibility had been available to all. Certainly to resolve this question we should have to go deeply into empirical investigations of the historical facts. (To prevent misunderstanding, I do think that in our present society utilitarianism would imply adherence to Rawls' second principle as a general rule.)

A utilitarian is concerned with maximizing total happiness (or goodness, if he is an ideal utilitarian). Rawls largely concerns himself with certain 'primary goods,' as he calls them. These include 'rights and liberties, powers and opportunities, income and wealth.'[10] A utilitarian would regard these as mere means to the ultimate good. Nevertheless if he is proposing new laws or changes to social institutions the utilitarian will have to concern himself in practice with the distribution of these 'primary goods' (as Bentham did).[11] But if as an approximation we neglect this distinction, which may be justifiable to the extent that there is a correlation between happiness and the level of these 'primary goods,' we may say that according to Rawls an action is right only if it is to the benefit of the least advantaged person. A utilitarian will hold that a redistribution of the means to happiness is right if it maximizes the general happiness, even though some persons, even the least advantaged ones, are made worse off. A position which is intermediate between the utilitarian position and Rawls' position would be one which held that one ought to maximize some sort of trade-off between total happiness and distribution of happiness. Such a position would imply that sometimes we should redistribute in such a way as to make some persons, even the least advantaged ones, worse off, but this would happen less often than it would according to the classical utilitarian theory.

UTILITARIANISM AND NOZICK'S THEORY

General adherence to Robert Nozick's theory (in his *Anarchy, State and Utopia*)[12] would be compatible with the existence of very great inequality indeed. This is because the whole theory is based quite explicitly on the notion of *rights:* in the very first sentence of the preface of his book we read 'Individuals have rights. . . .' The utilitarian would demur here. A utilitarian legislator might tax the rich in order to give aid to the poor, but a Nozickian legislator would not do so. A utilitarian legislator might impose a heavy tax on inherited wealth, whereas Nozick would allow the relatively fortunate to become even more fortunate, provided that they did not infringe the *rights* of the less fortunate. The utilitarian legislator would hope to increase the total happiness by equalizing things a bit. How far he should go in this direction would depend on empirical considerations. He would not want to equalize things too much if this led to too much weakening of the incentive to work, for example. Of course according to Nozick's system there would be no reason why members of society should not set up a utilitarian utopia, and voluntarily equalize their wealth, and also give wealth to poorer communities outside. However it is questionable whether such isolated utopias could survive in a modern environment, but if they did survive, the conformity of the behaviour of their members to utilitarian theory, rather than the conformity to Nozick's theory, would be what would commend their societies to me.

SUMMARY

In this article I have explained that the notion of justice is not a fundamental notion in utilitarianism, but that utilitarians will characteristically have certain views about such things as the distribution of wealth, savings for the benefit of future generations and for the third world countries and other practical matters. Utilitarianism differs from John Rawls' theory in that it is ready to contemplate some sacrifice to certain individuals (or classes of individuals) for the sake of the greater good of all, and in particular may allow certain limitations of personal freedom which would be ruled out by Rawls' theory. *In practice,* however, the general tendency of utilitarianism may well be towards an egalitarian form of society.

NOTES

1. In hoping that utilitarianism can be rendered acceptable to some people by presenting it in a clear light, I do not deny the possibility of the reverse happening. Thus I confess to a bit of a pull the other way when I consider Nozick's example of an 'experience machine'. See Robert Nozick, *Anarchy, State and Utopia* (Oxford: Blackwell, 1975), pp. 42–45, though I am at least partially reassured by Peter Singer's remarks towards the end of his review of Nozick, *New York Review of Books*, March 6, 1975. Nozick's example of an experience machine is more worrying than the more familiar one of a pleasure inducing machine, because it seems to apply to ideal as well as to hedonistic utilitarianism.

2. In this paper I shall assume a hedonistic utilitarianism, though most of what I have to say will be applicable to ideal utilitarianism too.

3. There are of course difficult problems about the assignment of cardinal utilities to states of mind, but for the purposes of this paper I am assuming that we can intelligibly talk, as utilitarians do, about units of happiness.

4. John Rawls, *A Theory of Justice* (Cambridge, Mass.: Harvard University Press, 1971).

5. John C. Harsanyi, 'Cardinal Utility in Welfare Economics and the Theory of Risk-Taking', *Journal of Political Economy*, 61 (1953), 434–435, and 'Cardinal Welfare, Individualistic

Ethics, and Interpersonal Comparisons of Utility', *ibid.*, **63** (1955), 309–321. Harsanyi has discussed Rawls' use of the maximin principle and has defended the principle of maximizing expected utility instead, in a paper 'Can the Maximin Principle Serve as a Basis for Morality? A Critique of John Rawls' Theory', *The American Political Science Review*, **69** (1975), 594–606. These articles have been reprinted in John C. Harsanyi, *Essays on Ethics, Social Behavior, and Scientific Explanation* (Dordrecht, Holland: D. Reidel, 1976).

6. Robert Nozick, *Anarchy, State and Utopia*. (See note 1 above.)

7. Rawls, A *Theory of Justice*, p. 60.

8. In Norman Daniels (ed.), *Reading Rawls* (Oxford: Blackwell, 1975), pp. 141–167. See pp. 148–149.

9. Lyons, *op. cit.*, p. 149, near top.

10. Rawls, *op. cit.*, p. 62.

11. On this point see Brian Barry, *The Liberal Theory of Justice* (London: Oxford University Press, 1973), p. 55.

12. See note 1.

chapter two
CAPITALISM AND SOCIALISM: A TALE OF TWO SYSTEMS

A CAPITALIST CONCEPTION OF JUSTICE

IRVING KRISTOL*

It is fashionable these days for social commentators to ask, "Is capitalism compatible with social justice?" I submit that the only appropriate answer is "No." Indeed, this is the only possible answer. The term "social justice" was invented in order *not* to be compatible with capitalism.

What is the difference between "social justice" and plain, unqualified "justice?" Why can't we ask, "Is capitalism compatible with justice?" We can, and were we to do so, we would then have to explore the idea of justice that is peculiar to the capitalist system, because capitalism certainly does have an idea of justice.

"Social justice," however, was invented and propagated by people who were not much interested in understanding capitalism. These were nineteenth-century critics of capitalism—liberals, radicals, socialists—who invented the term in order to insinuate into the argument a quite different conception of the good society from the one proposed by liberal capitalism. As it is used today, the term has an irredeemably egalitarian and authoritarian thrust. Since capitalism as a socioeconomic or political system is neither egalitarian nor authoritarian, it is in truth incompatible with "social justice."

Let us first address the issue of egalitarianism. In a liberal or democratic capitalist society there is, indeed, a connection between justice and equality. Equality before the law and equality of political rights are fundamental to a liberal capitalist system and, in historical fact, the ideological Founding Fathers of liberal capitalism all did believe in equality before the law and in some form of equality of political rights. The introduction of the term "social justice" represents an effort to stretch the idea of justice that is compatible with capitalism to cover *economic* equality as well. Proponents of something called "social justice" would persuade us that economic equality is as much a right as are equality before the law and equality of political rights. As a matter of fact, these proponents move in an egalitarian direction so formidably that inevitably *all* differences are seen sooner or later to be unjust. Differences between men and

*Graduate School of Business, New York University.

women, differences between parents and children, differences between human beings and animals—all of these, as we have seen in the last ten or fifteen years, become questionable and controversial.

A person who believes in "social justice" is an egalitarian. I do not say that he or she necessarily believes in perfect equality; I do not think anyone believes in perfect equality. But "social justice" advocates are terribly interested in far more equality than a capitalist system is likely to deliver. Capitalism delivers many good things but, on the whole, economic equality is not one of them. It has never pretended to deliver economic equality. Rather, capitalism has always stood for equality of economic opportunity, reasonably understood to mean the absence of official barriers to economic opportunity.

We are now in an egalitarian age when Harvard professors write books wondering whether there is a problem of "social justice" if some people are born of handsome parents and are therefore more attractive than others. This is seriously discussed in Cambridge and in other learned circles. Capitalism is not interested in that. Capitalism says there ought to be no *official* barriers to economic opportunity. If one is born of handsome or talented parents, if one inherits a musical skill, or mathematical skill, or whatever, that is simply good luck. No one can question the person's right to the fruits of such skills. Capitalism believes that, through equal opportunity, each individual will pursue his happiness as he defines it, and as far as his natural assets (plus luck, good or bad) will permit. In pursuit of that happiness everyone will, to use that familiar phrase of Adam Smith, "better his condition."

Thus, capitalism says that equal opportunity will result in everyone's bettering his or her condition. And it does. The history of the world over the past 200 years shows that capitalism did indeed permit and encourage ordinary men and women in the pursuit of their happiness to improve their condition. Even Marx did not deny this. We are not as poor as our grandparents. We are all better off because individuals in pursuit of happiness, and without barriers being put in their way, are very creative, innovative, and adept at finding ways for societies to be more productive, thereby creating more wealth in which everyone shares.

Now, although individuals do better their condition under capitalism, they do not better their conditions equally. In the pursuit of happiness, some will be more successful than others. Some will end up with more than others. Everyone will end up with *somewhat* more than he had—everyone. But some people will end up with a lot more than they had and some with a little more than they had. Capitalism does not perceive this as a problem. It is assumed that since everyone gets more, everyone ought to be content. If some people get more than others, the reason is to be found in their differential contributions to the economy. In a capitalist system, where the market predominates in economic decision making, people who—in whatever way—make different productive inputs into the economy receive different rewards. If one's input into the economy is great, one receives a large reward; if one's input is small, one receives a modest reward. The determination of these rewards is by public preferences and public tastes as expressed in the market. If the public wants basketball players to make $400,000 a year, then those who are good at basketball can become very, very rich. If the public wants to purchase certain paintings for $1 million or $2 million, then certain artists can become very, very rich. On the other hand, croquet players, even brilliant croquet players, won't better their condition to the same degree. And those who have no particular skill had better be lucky.

This is the way the system works. It rewards people in terms of their contribution to the economy as measured and defined by the marketplace—namely, in terms of the free preferences of individual men and women who have money in their pockets and are free to spend it or not on this, that, or the other as they please. Economic justice under capitalism means the differential reward to individuals is based on their productive input *to the economy*. I emphasize "to the economy" because input is measured by the marketplace.

Is it "just" that Mr. Ray Kroc, chairman of the board of McDonald's, should have made so much money by merely figuring out a new way of selling hamburgers? They are the same old hamburgers, just better made, better marketed. Is it fair? Capitalism says it is fair. He is selling a good product; people want it; it is fair. It is "just" that he has made so much money.

However, capitalism doesn't say only that. It also understands that it is an exaggeration to say that literally *everyone* betters his condition when rewards are based on productive input. There are some people who are really not capable of taking part in the race at all because of mental illness, physical illness, bad luck, and so on. Such persons are simply not able to take advantage of the opportunity that does exist.

Capitalism as originally conceived by Adam Smith was not nearly so heartless a system as it presented itself during the nineteenth century. Adam Smith didn't say that people who could make no productive input into the economy through no fault of their own should be permitted to starve to death. Though not a believer, he was enough of a Christian to know that such a conclusion was not consistent with the virtue of charity. He understood that such people had to be provided for. There has never been any question of that. Adam Smith wrote two books. The book that first made him famous was not *The Wealth of Nations* but *The Theory of Moral Sentiments*, in which he said that the highest human sentiment is sympathy—the sympathy that men and women have for one another as human beings. Although *The Wealth of Nations* is an analysis of an economic system based on self-interest, Adam Smith never believed for a moment that human beings were strictly economic men or women. It took some later generations of economists to come up with that idea. Adam Smith understood that people live in a society, not just in an economy, and that they feel a sense of social obligation to one another, as well as a sense of engaging in mutually satisfactory economic transactions.

In both these books, but especially in *The Theory of Moral Sentiments*, Adam Smith addressed himself to the question, "What do the rich do with their money once they get it?" His answer was that they reinvest some of it so that society as a whole will become wealthier and everyone will continue to be able to improve his or her condition to some degree. Also, however, the rich will engage in one of the great pleasures that wealth affords: the expression of sympathy for one's fellow human beings. Smith said that the people who have money can only consume so much. What are they going to do with the money aside from what they consume and reinvest? They will use it in such a way as to gain a good reputation among their fellow citizens. He said this will be the natural way for wealthy people to behave under capitalism. Perhaps he was thinking primarily of Scotsmen. Still, his perceptiveness is interesting. Although capitalism has long been accused of being an inhumane system, we forget that capitalism and humanitarianism entered the modern world together. Name a modern, humane movement—criminal reform, decent treatment of women, kindness to animals, etc. Where does it originate? They all came from the rising bourgeoisie at the end of the eighteenth century. They were all middle-class movements. The movements didn't begin with peasants or aristocrats. Peasants were always cruel to animals and aristocrats could not care less about animals, or about wives, for that matter. It was the bourgeoisie, the capitalist middle class, that said animals should be treated with consideration, that criminals should not be tortured, that prisons should be places of punishment, yes, but humane places of punishment. It was the generation that helped establish the capitalist idea and the capitalist way of thinking in the world that brought these movements to life. Incidentally, the anti-slavery movement was also founded by middle-class men and women who had a sense of social responsibility toward their fellow citizens.

So it is simply and wholly untrue that capitalism is a harsh, vindictive, soulless system. A man like Adam Smith would never have dreamed of recommending such a system. No, he recommended the economic relations which constitute the market system, the capitalist system, on the assumption that human beings would continue to recognize their social obligations to one another and act upon this recognition with some degree of consistency. Incidentally, he even seems to have believed in a progressive income tax.

However, something very peculiar happened after Adam Smith. Something very odd and very bad happened to the idea of capitalism and its reputation after the first generation of capitalism's intellectual Founding Fathers. The economics of capitalism became a "dismal science." One cannot read *The Wealth of Nations* and have any sense that economics is a dismal science. It is an inquiry into the causes of the wealth of nations that tells people how to get rich. It says, "If you organize your economic activities this way, everyone will get richer." There is nothing pessimistic about that, nothing dismal about that. It was an exhilarating message to the world.

Unfortunately, what gave capitalism a bad name in the early part of the nineteenth century was not the socialist's criticism of capitalism but, I fear, the work of the later capitalist economists. We do not even have a really good intellectual history of this episode because people who write histories of economic thought tend not to be interested in intellectual history, but in economics. For some reason, Malthus and then Ricardo decided that capitalist economics should not deal with the production of wealth but rather with its distribution. Adam Smith had said everyone could improve his condition. Malthus said the situation was hopeless, at least for the lower classes. If the lower classes improved their condition, he argued, they would start breeding like rabbits and shortly they would be right back where they started. Ricardo came along and said that the expanding population could not all be fed because there is a shortage of fertile land in the world. In his view, the condition of the working class over the long term was unimprovable.

This was the condition of capitalist economics for most of the nineteenth century. It is a most extraordinary and paradoxical episode in modern intellectual history. Throughout the nineteenth century, ordinary men and women, the masses, the working class, were clearly improving their condition. There is just no question that the working classes in England were better off in 1860 than they had been in 1810. In the United States there was never any such question and in France, too, it was quite clear that the system was working as Adam Smith had said it would. Yet all the economists of the School of Malthus and Ricardo kept saying, "It cannot happen. Sorry, people, but you're doomed to live in misery. There is nothing we can do about it. Just have fewer children and exercise continence." To which the people said, "Thank you very much. We do not much like this system you are recommending to us," as well they might not.

When the possibility of helping the average man and woman through economic growth is rejected loudly and dogmatically by the leading economists of the day, many will believe it. When they conclude that their condition cannot be improved by economic growth, they will seek to improve it by redistribution, by taking it away from others who have more. It is nineteenth-century capitalist economic thought, with its incredible emphasis on the impossibility of improving the condition of the working class—even as the improvement was obviously taking place—that gave great popularity and plausibility to the socialist critique of capitalism and to the redistributionist impulse that began to emerge. This impulse, which is still so appealing, makes no sense. A nation can redistribute to its heart's content and it will not affect the average person one bit. There just isn't ever enough to redistribute. Nevertheless, once it became "clear" in the nineteenth century that there was no other way, redistribution became a very popular subject.

Because capitalism after Adam Smith seemed to be associated with a hopeless view of the world, it provoked egalitarian impulses. Is it not a natural human sentiment to argue that, if we're all in a hopeless condition, we should be hopeless equally? Let us go down together. If that indeed is our condition, equality becomes a genuine virtue. Egalitarianism became such a plausible view of the world because capitalist apologists, for reasons which I do not understand, kept insisting that this is the nature of capitalism. Those who talk about "social justice" these days do not say that the income tax should be revised so that the rich people will get more, although there may be an economic case for it. (I am not saying there is, even though there might be.) "Social justice," the term, the idea, is intimately wedded to the notion of egalitarianism as a proper aim of social and economic policy, and capitalism is criticized as lacking in "social justice" because it does not achieve this equality. In fact, it does not, cannot, and never promised to achieve this result.

However, I think the more important thrust of the term "social justice" has to do with its authoritarian meaning rather than its egalitarian meaning. The term "social" prefixed before the word "justice" has a purpose and an effect which is to abolish the distinction between the public and the private sectors, a distinction which is absolutely crucial for a liberal society. It is the very definition of a liberal society that there be a public sector and a large, private sector where people can do what they want without government bothering them. What is a "social problem?" Is a social problem something that government can ignore? Would anyone say we have a social problem but it is not the business of government? Of course not.

The term "social justice" exists in order to identify those issues about which government should get active. A social problem is a problem that gives rise to a governmental policy, which is why people who believe in the expansion of the public sector are always inventing, discovering, or defining more and more social problems in our world. The world has not become any more problematic than it ever was. The proliferation of things called "social problems" arises out of an effort to get government more and more deeply involved in the lives of private citizens in an attempt to "cope with" or "solve" these "problems." Sometimes real problems are posed. Rarely are they followed by real solutions.

The idea of "social justice," however, assumes not only that government will intervene but that government will have, should have, and can have an authoritative knowledge as to what everyone merits or deserves in terms of the distribution of income and wealth. After all, if we do not like the inequality that results from the operation of the market, then who is going to make the decision as to the distribution of services and wealth? Some authority must be found to say so-and-so deserves more than so-and-so. Of course, the only possible such authority in the modern world is not the Church but the State. To the degree that one defines "social justice" as a kind of protest against the capitalist distribution of income, one proposes some other mechanism for the distribution of income. Government is the only other mechanism that can make the decisions as to who gets what, as to what he or she "deserves," for whatever reason.

The assumption that the government is able to make such decisions wisely, and therefore that government should make such decisions, violates the very premises of a liberal community. A liberal community exists on the premise that there is no such authority. If there were an authority which knew what everyone merited and could allocate it fairly, why would we need freedom? There would be no point in freedom. Let the authority do its work. Now, we have seen the experience of non-liberal societies, and not all of it is bad. I would not pretend that a liberal society is the only possible good society. If one likes the values of a particular non-liberal society, it may not be bad at all. There are many non-liberal societies I admire: monasteries are non-liberal societies, and I do not say they are bad societies. They are pretty good societies—but they are not liberal societies. The monk has no need for liberty if he believes there is someone else, his superior, who knows what is good for him and what reward he merits.

Once we assume that there is a superior authority who has authoritative knowledge of the common good and of the merits and demerits of every individual, the ground of a liberal society is swept away, because the very freedoms that subsist and thrive in a liberal society all assume that there is no such authoritative knowledge. Now, this assumption is not *necessarily* true. Maybe there is someone who really does have an authoritative knowledge of what is good for all of us and how much we all merit. We who choose a liberal society are skeptical as to the possibility. In any case, we think it is more likely that there will be ten people all claiming to have different versions of what is good for all of us and what we should all get, and therefore we choose to let the market settle it. It is an amicable way of not getting involved in endless philosophical or religious arguments about the nature of the true, the good, and the beautiful.

The notion of a "just society" existing on earth is a fantasy, a utopian fantasy. That is not what life on earth is like. The reason is that the world is full of other people who are different from you and me, alas, and we have to live with them. If they were all like us, we would live fine; but they are not all like us, and the point of a liberal society and of a market economy is to accept this difference and say, "Okay, you be you and I'll be I. We'll disagree, but we'll do business together. We'll mutually profit from doing business together, and we'll live not necessarily in friendship but at least in civility with one another."

I am not saying that capitalism is a just society. I am saying that there is a capitalist conception of justice which is a workable conception of justice. Anyone who promises you a just society on this earth is a fraud and a charlatan. I believe that this is not the nature of human destiny. It would mean that we all would be happy. Life is not like that. Life is doomed not to be like that. But if you do not accept this view, and if you really think that life can indeed be radically different from what it is, if you really believe that justice can prevail on earth, then you are likely to start taking phrases like "social justice" very seriously and to think that the function of politics is to rid the world of its evils: to abolish war, to abolish poverty, to abolish discrimination, to abolish envy, to abolish, abolish, abolish. We are not going to abolish any of those things. If we push them out one window, they will come in through another window in some unforeseen form. The reforms of today give rise to the evils of tomorrow. That is the history of the human race.

If one can be somewhat stoical about this circumstance, the basic precondition of social life, capitalism becomes much more tolerable. However, if one is not stoical about it, if one demands more of life than life can give, then capitalism is certainly the wrong system because capitalism does not promise that much and does not give you that much. All it gives is a greater abundance of material goods and a great deal of freedom to cope with the problems of the human condition on your own.

SOCIALISM

MICHAEL HARRINGTON*

The basic socialist indictment of capitalism is more true today than it was in the nineteenth century. The corporations have progressively "socialized" the economy, basing production on science and the most intricate web of human cooperation. Yet, for all the changes in capitalist attitudes, decision-making and appropriation have remained private even when they are exercised by corporate managers rather than owners. And so, as Marx and the early socialists predicted, the contradiction between unprecedented social productivity and the private institutions that direct it has become more and more intolerable, and made us progressively fearful of our own ingenuity. We purchase progress at the expense of the poor, the minorities, the old; we are even more threatened by our affluence than by our poverty.

The socialist solution remains utterly relevant: the social means of production must be socialized and made subject to democratic control.

I

There are three basic reasons why the reform of the welfare state will not solve our most urgent problems: the class structure of capitalist society vitiates, or subverts, almost every such effort toward social justice; private corporate power cannot tolerate the comprehensive and democratic planning we desperately need; and even if these first two obstacles to providing every citizen with a decent house, income and job were overcome, the system still has an inherent tendency to make affluence self-destructive.

First of all, the welfare state, for all the value of its institutions, tends to provide benefits in inverse relationship to human needs. And not—the point is crucial—because of a conspiracy by the affluent, but as a "natural" consequence of a society divided into unequal social classes.

It is possible to offset this inherent tendency within capitalist society to distribute public benefits according to the inequalities of private wealth, but only if there are vigorous radical reforms. What is more, any movement that attempts to carry out such reforms will be going against the grain of the system itself. This has not kept socialists from participating in every one of these struggles, nor will it in the future. But if the gains are to be permanent, if they are not to be reversed when a period of innovation is followed by a swing back to capitalist normality, then there must be basic, structural changes. Instead of episodic victories within an anti-social environment, there must be a concerted effort to create a new environment.

The class divisions of welfare capitalism are not, it must be stressed at the outset, simply unfair in some abstract sense. Were that the case, a sophisticated conservative argument might be persuasive: since to some extent the growth of the economy benefits

Adapted by permission of the publisher from *Socialism* by Michael Harrington. Copyright © 1972 by Michael Harrington. (A Saturday Review Press Book.)

*Department of Political Science, Queens College.

everyone, even those who are worst off, there is no point in endangering these gains on behalf of some ultimate egalitarianism. What really concerns the poor, this theory continues, is not the rise or fall of their *relative* share of affluence but the steady increase in their absolute standard of living. Actually, inequality does not merely mean that there are sharply unequal proportions of goods distributed among the various social sectors of the population. It signifies a socio-economic process, at once dynamic and destructive, which determines that public and private resources shall be spent in an increasingly anti-social way and thereby threatens the well-being of the entire society.

Housing is an excellent case in point. The Government, even under liberal administrations, has been much more solicitous about the comfort of the rich than the shelter of the poor. This policy is not only morally outrageous, it has had disastrous social consequences as well. Yet it must be emphasized that in thereby investing billions in the creation of public problems, Washington did not act maliciously but only followed—unconsciously, automatically, "naturally"—the priorities that are structured into America's class divisions. Thus:

- in 1962 the value of a single tax deduction to the 20 percent of Americans with the highest incomes was worth twice as much as all the monies spent on public housing for the one fifth who were poorest; and this figure does not even take into account Government support of below-market rates of interest to build suburbia;

- in 1969, the *Wall Street Journal* reported, the $2.5 billion for urban freeways was a far greater subsidy to car owners who daily fled the central city than was the $175 million provided for mass transit to city dwellers; and Richard Nixon's 1970 budget continued this perverse allocation of resources by providing public transportation with only 6 percent of the funds assigned to highways;

- and, as the National Commission on Civil Disorders (the "Riot Commission" of 1968) computed the figures, during roughly the same thirty-year period, the Government helped to construct over ten million housing units for home builders, i.e., for the middle class and the rich, but provided only 650,000 units of low-cost housing for the poor.

But it would be a mistake to think that Washington discriminates only against the poor. For, as a White House Conference told President Johnson in 1966, *the entire lower half of the American population is excluded from the market for new housing,* a market that could not exist without massive Federal support. This point needs special emphasis, if only because many people, with the best of intentions, concluded from the rediscovery of poverty in America in the sixties that the bulk of the nation was affluent while only a minority were poor. But the statistics, far from describing a simple division between the rich and the poverty-stricken, show that we have in this country a *majority*, composed of the poor, the near-poor, more than half the workers and the lower middle class, which does not even have a "moderate standard of living" as defined by the Government itself.

So when Washington used its powers to improve conditions for a wealthy elite, the poor suffered most because they had the most urgent claim on the funds thus squandered on the upper class, but a majority of the people, including tens of millions who were not poor, were also deprived of benefits that should have rightfully been theirs. Worse, in carrying out these discriminatory policies, the Federal programs did positive harm to those most in need. As an American Presidential Commission recently reported, " . . . over the last decades, Government action, through urban renewal, highway programs, demolitions on public housing sites, code enforcement, and other programs, has destroyed more housing for the poor than government at all levels has built for them.

In a society based on class inequality and suffused with commercial values, it just doesn't "make sense" to waste resources on social uses or beauty or anything that cannot be quantified in dollars and cents. Our legislators, drawn almost exclusively from the middle and upper classes, cannot bring themselves to forget those principles, which are sacred to the private economy. To them it seems logical to invest the Federal dollar in those undertakings that run the lowest risk and will show the highest and most immediate return.

To turn now to the second major reason why American society on its current basis cannot deal with its crises, there must also be national economic and social planning on a scale that our present institutional arrangements will not tolerate.

There is no question but that the seventies will see planning in the United States. The really crucial questions are: What kind of planning? Planning for whom? The problems of welfare capitalist society are becoming so obvious and overwhelming that conservatives and even reactionaries have understood the need for state intervention— if only to maintain as much of the old order as possible.

The first distinction between capitalist and socialist planning has to do with money. In 1967 Senator Abraham Ribicoff noted that the various existing programs don't even reach people with incomes of $8,000 a year. In December, 1969, three years of inflation later, *Fortune* reported that "the shortage of acceptable shelter that has been afflicting the poor and the black is reaching to the white middle class and even to quite affluent families." And in mid-1970, George Romney, the Secretary of Housing and Urban Development, estimated that 80 percent of U.S. families could not afford the average cost of a new house. To deal with a crisis of this magnitude will clearly require a shift of massive resources from the private to the public sector, since the market is not even reaching a majority of the people.

A second basic distinction between capitalist and socialist planning has to do with comprehensiveness.

When President Eisenhower proposed in May, 1958, that there be new, integrated communities with jobs, schools and parks and high-speed transportation links to the old cities, he was unwittingly committing himself to radical innovation. Assembling an integrated population and providing its members with decent work, education and transportation is not something to be accomplished by Adam Smith's "invisible hand." It requires long-range projections and a conscious coordination of Government policies. It could not be done, to take but one crucial example, if land were left to private speculation. For in order to assemble the huge areas needed for such extensive projects at a remotely reasonable cost, the public authority would have to use its power of eminent domain and establish land banks. So conservatives may be forced to recognize the magnitude of the urban crisis but they cannot solve it within their own economic calculus. What Eisenhower, Nixon and Stans really were talking about in their advocacy of new cities is a version of the old schemes to provide Federal subsidies to private interests, which are then supposed to fulfill a social purpose. But even supposing that such a tactic could provide the necessary billions in money (it cannot), the housing industry hardly has the resources, the overview or the legal right to engage in national, regional and metropolitan planning.

And yet, if it is easy enough to demonstrate that planning within a capitalist context is, at best, utterly and necessarily inadequate, this does not mean that socialist planning is without problems. These problems have to be faced candidly.

The principle of socialist planning is clear: the people rather than the corporations with Government subsidies should decide priorities. In practice, it is not that simple. Is it true, as John Kenneth Galbraith optimistically assumed in *The Affluent Society*, that the masses have basically decent values which are perverted by the manipulators who dominate the communications system? Galbraith contends that the fundamental reason why so many people regard the public sector as a place of compulsion and the private market as an area of free choice is that they have been programmed to do so by the media. If that is so, then the radical reform of the advertising industry would allow the electorate to get the truth and to vote for that social spending which is in its objective and long-term interest.

Socialist planning, in short, is not a total panacea; neither, for that matter, is democracy. The people are quite capable of making the wrong decision after having been given all the facts. But the only possibility of making a humane choice is if the institutions of democratic planning relentlessly encroach on the private sector in such areas of decisive importance as housing, transportation and education. Neo-capitalist planning with its commercial priorities is inherently limited and unable to solve the crises it recognizes. With socialist planning that is massive, comprehensive and democratic, there is at least the possibility that man will be able to master the environment he himself has created.

The third major reason why capitalist society must be basically transformed is this: Let us assume that the system proves to be much more ingenious than the preceding analysis suggests. Suppose it constructs a welfare state that really does respond to the needs of the poor and that, without fundamental changes in structure, it manages to accommodate itself to democratic planning. Even then—and I admit this possibility for the purpose of argument only—even then, it would be necessary to go beyond capitalism to socialism. For if this society somehow found a way to deal with poverty, racism, inequality and unmet social needs, it would still be incapable of dealing with its own prosperity.

This problem is not a consequence of wrong-headed choices on the part of muddled executives; it is a trend within the system and cannot be corrected without sweeping changes. The economic theory of "external economies" and "external diseconomies" helps to explain why.

An external economy occurs when an act of consumption creates a collective good, e.g., when the decision of a high school student to remain in school raises his skill level and makes him a more productive worker rather than a candidate for welfare. External economies usually derive from public investments in schools, hospitals and the like. External diseconomies are a result of an opposite phenomenon: acts of consumption that create a collective evil, e.g., the air pollution visited upon society by a private automobile. These are particularly associated with giant industries and, as one moderate economist put it, "seem to be far more prevalent than external economies."

So the fundamental tendencies of late capitalist economies toward bigness and concentration will produce goods whose social costs often exceed their social benefits. This, it must be emphasized, is an inherent pattern in a society where huge investments are privately made. To offset this trend, such decisions would have to be made with major consideration of the social costs—a kind of calculus (as will be seen shortly) that is at odds with the very character of the capitalist economy. There follows an extraordinary paradox: the richer capitalism becomes, the more self-destructive it is. (This is a sort of economic analogue to Freud's psychological insight that the more sophisticated society becomes, the more repressive it is, since instinctual energy must be disciplined in order to make large-scale organization possible.)

In traditional Marxist theory economic crisis was the result of overproduction within a society of systematically limited consumption. Many contemporary economists now argue that the cyclical breakdown of capitalism, which turned relative abundance into immediate want, has been mastered. That is much too optimistic an analysis, since the contradictions of capitalism bedevil Keynesians as well as anti-Keynesian conservatives. But even if we do assume for a moment that the cyclical crisis of capitalism is under control, it has been succeeded by an even more bizarre problem: that affluence itself is becoming increasingly counterproductive.

So contemporary capitalism is not only heir to many of the traditional evils of the system, even if sometimes in ameliorated ways, it also cannot deal adequately, no matter how sophisticated it has become, with either poverty or affluence. Left to itself, the system creates a welfare state that provides some benefits for all, yet favors the rich and discriminates against the desperate; it generates problems, like those of the urban environment, that demand comprehensive planning; and even when it functions to produce the highest standard of living the world has known, the social consequences of that achievement are so appalling as to vitiate much of it.

We socialists support every struggle for the partial and liberal reform of this inadequate structure. Yet we insist—and I believe that the previous analysis has documented the point—that the fundamental solution of these problems requires measures that go beyond the limits of the capitalist economy.

II

Neo-capitalism, for all its sophistication, cannot make desperately needed social investments, plan comprehensively and massively or cope with either poverty or affluence. Socialism can.

First of all—and this is urgent practical politics within the present confines of capitalism as well as a step toward socialism—investment must be socialized.

There are, as has just been seen, huge decisive areas of economic life in which private capital will not invest because there is no prospect of sufficient profitability (or, what amounts to the same thing, where anti-social allocations are more profitable than social allocations would be). This is true of the fundamental determinants of the urban environment, like housing and transportation. Therefore the society must shift resources from the privately profitable sector of the economy to the socially necessary. This is a decision that only the Government has the power to make and which must be taken as a result of a democratic process. And it can only be accomplished on a national scale and within the framework of planning.

There should be an Office of the Future in the White House. Each year the President should make a Report on the Future—with projections ranging five, ten or even twenty years ahead—which would be submitted to a Joint Congressional Committee where it would be debated, amended and then presented to the entire Congress for decision. This process should establish the broad priorities of the society and annually monitor the result of past efforts. It would be, for instance, the proper forum for establishing the broad concept of regional planning; but it would not engage in the actual planning of individual projects.

At this point, a candid admission is in order. The changes outlined in the previous paragraph could be welcomed by social engineers and technocrats determined to impose their values on the people. They could be used by sophisticated corporate leaders to make the status quo more rational and stable. And they might create an entrenched bureaucracy with a self-interest of its own. The critics of socialism who cite such dangers ignore, or conceal, the fact that they are the consequence of the complexity of *all forms* of modern technological society and that socialism is the only movement that seeks to make a structural and democratic challenge to the trend. But even more important, it must be understood that there is no institutional reform that, in and of itself, can guarantee genuine popular participation in this process. Only a vibrant movement of the people can do that. That is why socialists do not foresee an ultimate stage of human existence in which all questions are answered and all conflicts resolved. Even in the very best of societies the democratic majority must be on the alert.

But even if society would thus socialize more and more investment, consciously planning the allocation of resources for cities, transportation and human care, that in itself would not change the prevailing order. For the control of the means of production and of wealth is not simply economic power; it is political power as well. So if private ownership of huge corporations were to coexist over a long period of time with planned social investments, the corporate rich, be they managers or owners, would come to dominate the new, supposedly democratic institutions. That is one of the main reasons why socialists cannot abandon their insistence upon social ownership.

Paradoxically, I will base my case for social ownership on the same economic trend—the separation of ownership and control under contemporary capitalism—that was cited by many socialists in the sixties as a reason for giving up the traditional position on the nationalization of industry. Moreover, I think there is a strategy for achieving social ownership that does not involve a sudden, apocalyptic leap from private to public property (which is, in any case, impossible under democratic conditions), but rather employs structural reforms.

First, there is the trend toward the separation of ownership and control and its bearing on social ownership. I would argue that this trend increasingly demonstrates the functionless character of the legal title to property and suggests a very practical, unapocalyptic method of doing away with it.

Robin Marris, in his critique of the contemporary corporation, has pointed out that "once the classic idealization of capitalism is thus destroyed [when, that is, it is seen that the managers are not working 'for' the stockholders], there is no *economic* case for its superiority over socialism." It was a distinguished conservative, however, who most clearly drew the socialist conclusions. Frederick A. Hayek wrote, "So long as the management is supposed to serve the interests of the stockholders it is reasonable to leave the control of its actions to the stockholders. But if the management is supposed to serve wider public interest, it becomes a logical consequence of this conception that the appointed representatives of the public interests should control the management."

Private investment decisions must be socialized. The right to locate, or relocate, a plant in a given area can no longer be conceded to be a private matter. For in order to engage in regional planning and to aid in the construction of new cities and towns, the geography of employment has to be publicly determined. A strict system of licensing the permission to build a factory could work toward this end. The Attlee Government initiated some measures of this type, and various Italian governments have tried to use such techniques to promote the development of the south. There were even reports in 1970 that the Nixon Administration would have a similar policy for the location of power plants.

Technology has to be monitored too. The decision to build a supersonic transport has so many consequences (noise, air traffic congestion, airport construction) that even if it were not a Government-subsidized project, the public interest should be asserted. There is a need, as a National Academy of Science panel pointed out, for "technological forecasting." One cannot trust these matters, as the *Wall Street Journal* put it in a telling anti-capitalist phrase, to the "mindless market."

The National Academy panel made another important point about technological forecasting: that it must be carried out by an independent agency and not by an interested bureaucracy. For "the Bureau of Public Roads has hardly been noted for its devotion to the natural beauty of the countryside." More generally, as has been seen, it is quite possible for a publicly-owned enterprise to behave in the same aggressive, self-interested way as a private corporation. Here again, the crucial issue is not so much the legal form of ownership as the kind of economic calculus it follows.

Profit is still another function of property that must be subjected to social control. In 1967 the Council of Economic Advisors—hardly an anti-capitalist agency—noted that Government direction of the economy had smoothed out the cycle of boom and bust and therefore removed a great deal of the risk in the marketplace. Under such conditions, it argued, business should be prepared to take a lower rate of return. But in point of fact, American corporations chafed under the voluntary controls of the Kennedy and Johnson administrations, even though their profits rose by 78.7 percent between 1960 and 1970 and their cash flow (profits plus depreciation) was up by 85 percent in the same period. When Richard Nixon came into office, he abandoned all efforts to persuade industry and labor to obey guidelines in price and wage policy. Whereupon, the London *Economist* reported, the steel industry increased its prices in twelve months by 7 percent—as contrasted to a 6 percent rise in the previous ten years. And in 1971 a major price increase by Bethlehem Steel finally forced even the conservative Mr. Nixon to proclaim a contrary public interest.

So government cannot leave profit policy up to the good conscience of the corporation, but it can use an array of techniques to socialize this important area of economic life: selective price and wage controls in an inflationary period; a requirement that big companies open up their books and justify any increase in prices before an independent board; the use of vigorous tax policy (more on this shortly). But however it is done, the fundamental purpose of this reform is clear enough. The society cannot afford to leave to private decision how the prices of basic goods are to be set—or how the huge annual increments in wealth are to be distributed.

There is still another avenue of social action. The vigorous use of tax policy as a means of achieving a more egalitarian society is relevant to the immediate neo-capitalist present.

To a considerable extent, the Left has ignored the enormous potential of tax reform in forwarding the transition to a decent society. If there is a tendency under capitalism for reforms, and even structural changes like nationalization, to benefit the wealthy rather than the poor, then taxes provide a most important corrective. It is not simply a question of seeing to it that the wealth generated by the intervention of the state serves the society on a democratic basis, but also of the possibility of transforming the very organization of inequality itself.

In most cases the discussion of maldistribution focuses upon income, for that is an area of abundant government statistics. But if one begins instead by examining the shares of *wealth*—"the sum total of equity in a home or business, liquid assets, investment assets, the value of automobiles owned, and miscellaneous assets, such as assets held in trust, loans to individuals, oil royalties, etc."—the disproportions are even more shocking. One quarter of the consumer units in the United States have no wealth at all (or "negative" wealth, i.e., more debt than assets); 61 percent of the consumer units own 7 percent of the wealth while a little over 2 percent of the total have 43 percent. Indeed a majority of the wealth in the United States—57 percent, to be exact—is held by just a bit over 6 percent of the consumer units. It is this permanent structure of inequality which underlies, and is reinforced by, the annual inequities in income.

Thus, there has been no significant change in the distribution of income since 1944. Moreover, the effective rate of taxation on the rich and the upper middle class (the top 15 percent of the society as measured by incomes) declined in the years between 1952 and 1967. Many of the taxes in this country—for Social Security and Unemployment Insurance, to take Federal examples, and on consumption in the case of state levies—are regressive. All of these tax rates are based on reported rather than actual income and do not take into account the command over resources in expense accounts, pensions and other perquisites which are rampant in the upper reaches of the economy.

So the American and other advanced capitalist tax systems are a labyrinth designed to favor the wealthy who can afford lawyers and accountants. "Income," as defined by the Internal Revenue Service in the United States, is not income at all: it excludes a good portion of capital gains, worth $7 billion a year; it does not tax the rent a middle-class family saves by owning a house, an item worth $8 billion a year; it exempts various state and local bonds; and so on. In this setting, the simple equitable act of making income equal income for purposes of tax computation would be a major contribution to social justice.

But even such a modest reform is intolerable on the basis of the capitalist ideology. In the summer of 1969 when the Congress considered—and promptly forgot—the idea of limiting some of the privileges of stock speculators by changing the favored status of capital gains somewhat, the *Wall Street Journal* responded in an angry editorial. By requiring these people to pay a little more in the direction of a fair share, the Government would "punish the nation's most productive citizens." And this disincentive to the stockholder could actually lead to a decrease in economic activity and Federal revenues: "Obviously enough the tax reformer's chief aim is not more money for Uncle Sam but more 'justice' as among individual taxpayers."

Among the many problems with this analysis is the fact that it is based on an obsolete model of capitalist society. If the stock market had as its prime function bringing together risk capitalists and industrial innovators, it is indeed possible that an increase in justice would lower the rate of return on such money and slow down economic change. But in reality, American corporations more and more accumulate their own investment funds internally or else turn to institutional investors. In 1964, for instance, after paying taxes and dividends the corporations retained $59 billion to finance their future plans. And a good many of the people in the Market, far from being the "nation's most productive citizens," are functionless parasites. As Joan Robinson put it, "The shareholders and rentiers, indeed, make a great negative contribution to industry, for much of the best talent of every generation is engaged, one way or another, in the lucrative business of swapping securities around amongst them and so is kept from constructive activities. The notion that the Stock Exchange, with all its ancillary apparatus, is the most efficacious means of supplying finance to industry, compared with other available methods, is a fig leaf which it wears to preserve its self respect."

Effective inheritance taxes would be another important source of social funds and an opportunity for working toward greater equality. In the United States they are quite low—or quite avoidable, which amounts to the same thing. In classic capitalist theory a man must be able to leave his fortune to his children if he is to have an incentive to work hard all his life. That motive could be easily protected by providing for relatively low death duties on the first transfer from father to son, which would encourage the father, and very high rates on the second transfer, from son to grandson, which would give the son a reason to strive as hard as his father. This is something like that ingenious Saint-Simonian notion of abolishing inheritance over three generations and counting on the greed of the first generation to make it indifferent to what happens to its grandchildren.

In all these reforms, in short, the point would not be to penalize hard work or actual risk-taking but to severely limit, and eventually eliminate, the tribute society pays to passive wealth or to stock gamblers. For as the process of accumulation becomes much more social with industry generating its own investment funds or getting them from institutions, it becomes absurd to pay generations of functionless coupon-clippers on the grounds that their distant ancestors made a signal contribution to the society. So it is property income that would be the target, and it is easy enough to distinguish between it and the reward for present accomplishment. One would also seek to get the enormous increase in land values which take place without any effort on the part of the owner. This was $25 billion a year in the United States between 1956 and 1966.

Moreover, of all the reforms proposed here, the use of taxes as a means of increasing justice and equality should be the most politically promising, for it attacks the wealth of a functionless minority and would provide benefits for a huge majority. If all the artful outlived rationales for favoring the rich can be shown to be what they are, masses would support their abolition.

So there are three main areas of transitional programs moving in the direction of a socialist democratization of economic power: the socialization of investment; the progressive socialization of the functions of corporate property, and then that of property itself; the employment of tax policy as an instrument for social justice. Each one of these structural reforms corresponds to a need in the society which can be documented in the official reports, and more to the political point, several of them could become quite popular with the majority of the people. There is, then, still very much meaning to the idea of socialism.

chapter three
ETHICS AND BUSINESS DECISION MAKING

THE ETHICAL SIDE OF ENTERPRISE

VERNE E. HENDERSON*

"What! Another article on business ethics? What are they trying to ram down my throat this time?" This is a common reaction by businesspeople to what is becoming the latest fad. Peter Drucker recently called it that and stated flatly that there is no such thing as "business ethics."[1] However, there is an ethical side to enterprise, and Drucker's article convinces me that it is not well understood. In *Death in the Afternoon*, Ernest Hemingway wrote that "What is moral is what you feel good after and what is immoral is what you feel bad after." Ethics is different; it is what you do hoping that others will feel good after.

My experience indicates that business management is particularly wary and sometimes even incensed when ethical issues are raised by spokespeople from the religious community. R.H. Tawney noted the prevalence of that attitude more than half a century ago: "Trade is one thing, religion is another."[2] Yet my conversations with businesspeople reveal their frustrations and concerns: "How can we talk about ethics without raising fanatical religious or denominational flags?" "Can't we find a fresh approach, some new words, or something so that we can talk about a subject we all secretly know is very important?"

As a spokesman from the religious community, I affirm the need to remove religious brand names and denominational labels. Moreover, I believe that this new age of ever-advancing technology will require significant ethical innovation. The word "ethics" should generate a new set of feelings and perceptions.

Ethics in the broadest sense provides the basic conditions of acceptance for any activity. The ethics of a game or sport both implies its purpose and specifies rules of fair play. Business schools, for example, have traditionally focused on what we might call the business side of enterprise (finance, accounting, economics, marketing, forecasting), explaining the rules and imparting winning tactics. The human and the legal sides of enterprise have assumed increasing importance as the rules and tactics have

Reprinted from "The Ethical Side of Enterprise," by Verne E. Henderson, *Sloan Management Review*, vol. 23, no. 3, pp. 37–47, by permission of the publisher. Copyright © 1982 by the Sloan Management Review Association. All rights reserved.

*Professor of ethics and social issues and consultant to the dean of faculty, Arthur D. Little Management Education Institute.

become complex and the unresolved disputes numerous. Out of weariness and frustration, we ask a basic question: Should we play this game at all? Of course, we have to play. Business, after all, is a survival activity, isn't it . . . putting food on the table? So instead we ask: Can't we play the business game differently? The ethical side of enterprise emerges as this questioning of corporate activity grows in breadth and depth. At the macro level, one may question the legitimacy of both the corporation and capitalism as a viable economic system.[3] This article focuses on the micro level, addressing the specific decisions of enterprise on a variety of issues.

THE NEED TO DEFINE ETHICS

As a senior corporate executive recently described the major problems his firm faces in contemplating joint ventures abroad, it became clear to me that his primary concerns were ethical ones. For instance, how do you establish trust and share risk? How do you deal with two governments that have significant cultural differences? What motivates top management to undertake such complex efforts? These joint ventures are new cultural configurations in the marketplace and, as such, they will cause us to question old values and to establish new ones. The role of the ethicist is to aid the manager in negotiating the uncharted depths of this new environment. But first, the term "ethics" must be defined.

A Static Definition

Ethics is commonly defined as a set of principles prescribing a behavior code that explains what is good and right or bad and wrong; it may even outline moral duty and obligations generally. However, given the dynamic environment in which business must operate today, this conventional definition is far too static to be useful. It presumes a consensus about ethical principles that does not exist in this pluralistic age. The absence of such a consensus can be attributed to numerous changes that have occurred over time in the business environment, including the growth of conflicting interest groups, shifts in basic cultural values, the death of the Puritan ethic, and the increasing use of legal criteria in ethical decision making.

Multiple Clients. Edgar Schein cites the increasing number of clients and interests the manager must satisfy: the stockholders, the customer, the community and/ or government, the enterprise itself, subordinate employees, peers and colleagues, a superior, and perhaps the standards of a profession.[4] Since these clients may possess different and sometimes conflicting expectations, their ethical assessments of a management decision are also likely to differ. With so many clients and ethical expectations, it is never easy to know what is right or which client to heed. The multiple clients (or constituencies) factor requires a careful balancing of priorities and a situational approach to ethical issues.

Shifting Values. George Lodge argues that a new American ideology has emerged as a result of five major shifts in basic values within the American culture:[5]

1. From rugged individualism to "communitarianism";

2. From property rights to membership rights;

3. From competitive markets as the means to determine consumer needs to broader societal determination of community needs;

4. From limited government planning to expanded and extensive government planning;

5. From scientific specialization to a holistic utilization of knowledge.

These shifts in values can give rise to two types of ethical dilemmas. First, an industry can be divided in its loyalties to both old and new ideologies (i.e., to a free market versus a controlled market). Second, society at large may be divided in its loyalties to the needs of an industry versus the needs of the environment. These are tough choices: open markets or managed markets; industry or the environment. Such shifting values increase individuals' and firms' uncertainty regarding ethical issues. Moreover, this uncertainty is not likely to be resolved by simply choosing one ideology over another or one constituency over another.

Death of the Puritan Ethic. According to Daniel Bell, the "Puritan temper" or "Protestant ethic," which allegedly inspired the spirit of capitalism, is dying.[6] In the past this ethic promoted hard work, thrift, saving, moderation, and equality of opportunity or means. However, commercial success has spawned contradictory values that emphasize leisure, spending, debt accumulation, hedonism, and equality of condition or ends. The major consequence of this change is the erosion of a unifying social ethic. The fact that these two ethical systems exist simultaneously motivates and justifies a schizophrenic life-style where one is encouraged to be "straight" at work but a "swinger" on weekends. It is hardly surprising that managers often concede that their most vexing ethical dilemmas involve personnel.

Identical developments are evident at the corporate level. John K. Galbraith perceives a dichotomy within the production system; he labels one part a planning system and the other a marketing system.[7] The inordinate power of the planning system of large corporations gives them a monopoly over consumer needs; they even determine which needs will be served. If this is true, it means that large corporations have also deserted the Puritan ethic, that their only ethic is survival and self-perpetuation, and that their primary constituency consists of themselves.

The death of the Puritan ethic as the dominant ethical force in society has left us visionless. The individual and the corporation, confronting contradictions which foster uncertainty, turn inward and respond to the one constituency over which they have some sense of certainty and control—themselves. Achievement horizons are shortened: individuals expect rapid promotion, and corporations focus exclusively on quarterly progress.

Lawyers as Priests. We used to be able to look to religion for ethical guidance; the priest would bless and legitimize our enterprise. That is no longer the case. In fact, the entry of brand-name religion into the marketplace seems to divide loyalties further and inhibit ethical discussion. This vacuum has been filled by the legal profession.

Lawyers maintain that they only interpret the law and that they do not make it (at least not until they are elected to legislative office). But, as both practitioners and legislators, lawyers increasingly serve our culture as the priest once did. The law determines what is right and implicitly blesses it. In effect, the equation seems to be: if it's legal, it's ethical.

Yet this equation has its limitations. Christopher Stone argues that neither the "invisible" hand of the market nor a court of law is capable of delineating and enforcing the principles and behavior needed to solve society's problems, although both can play a positive role.[8] In his description of the history of corporations and the law, Stone documents numerous cases in which regulation of business by law has been ineffective. In addition, such regulation is rarely cost-effective, and it usually produces unanticipated and/or unacceptable consequences. Thus, while our growing dependence on the law as a substitute for ethics may be understandable, it is not necessarily desirable.

A Dynamic Definition

In these rapidly changing times, both the underlying purpose and the rules of the business game have become increasingly unclear. One consequence of these changes is that ethics can no longer be viewed as a static code or a set of principles that is understood and agreed upon by all. Charles Powers and David Vogel address this problem by providing a simple but dynamic working definition: "In essence ethics is concerned with clarifying what constitutes human welfare and the kind of conduct necessary to promote it."[9]

The first part of this definition implies both a constellation of values and a process of discussion or debate. While some values will be widely shared, individuals and groups will sometimes differ on "what constitutes human welfare." The Powers and Vogel definition is particularly suitable to the U.S., where no "ultimate authority" issues quick, precise answers. Rather, the process of clarification is an ongoing response to changing values, emerging technological or economic developments, and shifting political forces. For example, government's increasing role as an income transfer agent in recent years signifies a change in the definition of human welfare. The fact that some portion of the national income is distributed on the basis of need rather than merit affirms a particular perception of economic justice. Lester Thurow notes a correlation between environmentalism and income distribution, suggesting that environmentalism is one of the newest consumer wants for those whose basic needs already have been satisfied.[10] This represents a further refinement of the definition of human welfare.

The second part of the Powers and Vogel definition focuses on behavior. Once we have conceptualized or reached some consensus about what constitutes human welfare, the debate then focuses on the kind of conduct necessary to promote that concept of human welfare. For instance, having determined that some national income should be distributed on the basis of need rather than merit, we can use income tax legislation to establish a new code of conduct: taking from some and giving to others. In this way a new ethic is established. Most of the regulation of business that began in the last century can be viewed from this same perspective—a higher state of human welfare was clarified and complementary conduct was subsequently mandated.

New political and economic forces are continually reshaping our perception of the highest state of human welfare and altering our conduct accordingly. At the corporate level, deciding what is good and right or bad and wrong in such a dynamic environment is necessarily "situational." Therefore, instead of relying on a set of fixed ethical principles, we must now develop an ethical process. In order to do this, this article will next outline a conceptual ethical framework and then present an algorithm designed to deal with ethical questions on a situational basis.

A CONCEPTUAL FRAMEWORK

Business executives regularly wrestle with the new factors of the business environment: multiple clients and goals, shifting values and cultural contradictions, and increasing dependence on legal staffs. Although the profit-oriented corporation will naturally focus *primarily* on economic goals, decisions that focus *exclusively* on profit maximization are being challenged. Typically, all of these decisions are fashioned with care in the guarded privacy of corporate offices and boardrooms. This is due in part to the nature of the competitive business game; undoubtedly, some secrecy is also occasioned by less noble motives. Once a product or service reaches the market, these decisions face exposure to public scrutiny.

The process has become even more complex in our turbulent environment. Focusing on legal considerations, let us assume that the vast majority of businesspeople intend to function within the boundaries of the law. Unfortunately, the legal status of an increasing number of manufacturing or marketing decisions is unclear when they are initially conceived and put into operation. Public scrutiny of these decisions (by Congress, a federal or state agency, or perhaps some other client) often raises questions of legality. In cases where some law or legal precedent exists, a clear determination of status can be achieved (although this may take years).

Over time many products and services have fallen from presumed legality into illegality, including cyclamates, DDT, firecrackers, recombinant DNA, and payments to foreign officials and governments. Thus, not only must products and services face final acceptance or rejection by the consumer, but their legal status may change as new information becomes available.

According to our dynamic definition of ethics, ethical issues emerge when our perception of what constitutes human welfare receives or requires clarification. More specifically, ethical issues arise when laws or legal precedents are either unclear or at variance with shifting cultural values. The proliferation of multinational and transnational corporations has provided numerous examples of this process. Positioned between two or more legal/ethical systems, these firms face scrutiny by publics that may differ radically on significant issues: the use and distribution of material resources, the source and exercise of authority, perceptions of time, measurement of productivity, and the use of competition as a motivating force. These differences alter ethical objectives and their complementary customs and legal sanctions.

Many multinationals have been affected by the existence of the Foreign Corrupt Practices Act of 1977. Under this law, of course, it is illegal for U.S. firms to make payments to foreign officials or governments. Yet, some would argue that the Act itself is unethical insofar as it restricts international trade and thereby diminishes both human welfare and our national interest. When the Act was proposed, the Securities and Exchange Commission took the position that secret payments deprived current and prospective stockholders of potentially relevant information about company operations.

The Internal Revenue Service questioned the deduction of such payments as business expenses. In effect, the Act was passed to satisfy a constituency that includes an unknown percentage of domestic and foreign consumers, unidentified current and prospective stockholders, and an agency of the federal government (which presumably acts on behalf of taxpayers). But are there consumers, stockholders, and taxpayers who would take a different ethical stance? Probably. None of the available choices satisfies the total constituency; this is characteristic of ethical dilemmas.

The issue of foreign payments illustrates how ethical questions develop from corporate decisions that are privately conceived and executed in advance of public scrutiny and without clear legal or ethical precedent. Aside from blatant corruption and dishonesty, the above process describing the emergence of ethical issues accounts for much of the consternation and confusion about business ethics today. It is the failure to understand and anticipate this process that creates the vast majority of ethical dilemmas.

The conceptual framework described above is summarized in Figure 1. The inner circle of this figure represents corporate decisions before they are revealed to the public. Once these decisions are manifested (middle circle), they may become the subject of considerable public debate. The result of this debate is the codification process (outer circle), in which society determines the legal and ethical status of each decision.

One question continually confronts business executives as they privately ponder alternatives: What happens when our decisions become public? This question can be particularly difficult to answer, since the legal and ethical status of a decision may

FIGURE 1 A conceptual framework.

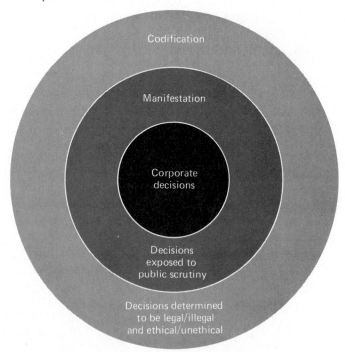

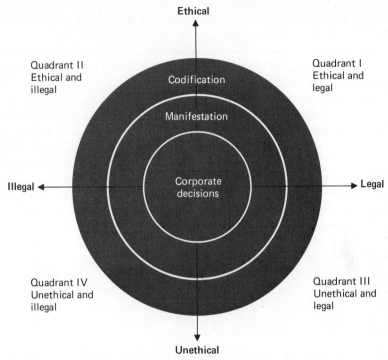

FIGURE 2 Classifying decisions using the conceptual framework.

change over time. Decision makers need to answer the question: Into which quadrant of Figure 2 will an issue with ethical implications fall?

Consider the business executive who aspires to function in Quadrant I. When his or her decisions become manifest and codified, they will prove to be both ethical and legal. In the past this was a reasonable expectation for most decision makers. While it is dangerous to make assumptions about the intentions of businesspeople today, it seems that more of their decisions now fall into Quadrants II, III, and IV.

In Quadrant II (ethical and illegal), we find a host of controversial issues that divide the country because their ethical and legal statuses conflict: selling marijuana, "whistle blowing," windfall profits, and payments to foreign officials. While many individuals will attempt to resolve such conflicts by focusing on an issue's legal status, the ethical questions surrounding an issue also should be examined. According to our conceptual framework, the ethical perceptions concerning an issue must be addressed before its legal status can be changed. This is a time-consuming task that business has been unwilling or unable to assume on a large scale.

Quadrant III contains another series of controversial subjects—those which are legal but unethical. For example, while the marketing of infant feeding formulas to developing countries is legal, a recent vote at the United Nations called it unethical. (The U.S. abstained from voting.) The following examples are legal as well, but some have questioned their ethical underpinnings: the manufacture of pesticides, the use of laetrile in cancer treatment, plant relocation based on labor cost differentials, and interlocking directorships. As in Quadrant II, it is tempting to focus corporate attention on the legal status of these issues, rather than on their ethical foundation.

In Quadrant IV (unethical and illegal), we find a wide variety of actions that have been censured, including discrimination against minorities and women, occupational hazards, disposal of chemical waste, and political slush funds. In these areas, the laws are clear and ethical support is sufficiently strong to silence open dissent.

While some issues clearly belong in one quadrant or another, there are many others whose status is unclear. How then do we decide which quadrant an issue belongs in? This is determined not only by *which* action is being examined, but also by *how* that action is undertaken. One interesting example is "whistle blowing." To the extent that some forms of whistle blowing are ethical but in clear violation of company rules or expectations, they may be placed in Quadrant II. However, where such behavior jeopardizes trade secrets or national security, we might want to place it in Quadrants III or IV. The fact that whistle blowing may be placed in any of these quadrants underscores the turbulence in our legal and ethical environments.

The conceptual framework presented here depicts a dynamic environment filled with legal and ethical uncertainty. Since decision making in such an environment must frequently be based on situational factors, an algorithm is needed that will allow us to judge each ethical issue on its own merits.

A SITUATIONAL ETHIC ALGORITHM

According to Joseph Fletcher, the basic tenet underlying situation ethics is that circumstances alter cases.[11] This theory maintains that honesty is not always the best policy—it depends on the situation. In Fletcher's judgment, complex, significant ethical decisions are made based on the situation at a given moment in time, and, therefore, no two judgments will ever be the same. As the consequences of business decisions become more complex and unpredictable, the situation ethic becomes a necessity. There is a danger, however, that disastrous outcomes will be rationalized too easily as "we did the best we could." Since a situation ethic is without ready-made answers, it is important to develop a rigorous, rational process for examining ethical issues. Such homework should precede the implementation of a decision and serve as the ethical equivalent of a cost-benefit analysis.

Fletcher identifies four factors that can serve as check points in sorting out the ethical dimensions of a given situation.[12] These factors, translated into the business context, are goals, methods, motives, and consequences. Analyzing situations from these four perspectives constitutes an ethical algorithm which can increase our sense of certainty about decisions and ultimately provide a defendable decision-making *process*. Users of the algorithm plug in their own values as they examine goals, methods, motives, and consequences. Careful consideration of these four factors before selecting a course of action is likely to yield a variety of significant insights.

Goals

The goal structure of an organization should be examined from the perspectives of goal multiplicity, constituency priority, and goal compatibility.

Goal Multiplicity. While profit maximization (subject to certain constraints) is an implicit goal of most business corporations, many firms simultaneously pursue other goals as well. Moreover, an organization's goal structure is often complicated by the imposition of constraints from outside sources. For example, a firm that relocates to another part of the country in order to maximize profits must consider the reactions of public officials and employees. A company that does business in South Africa must weigh the effect of its actions on the "ethical investor" who is opposed to apartheid. In some cases constraints such as these can eventually function as goals themselves. To the extent that these new goals can be measured, they will figure prominently in the minds of stockholders, employees, the government, and various segments of the population at large. Decision makers must be clear about this multiplicity of goals from the outset, particularly if constraints are incorporated into the goal structure.

Sometimes, however, constraints are not included in the goal structure. Some corporations, for example, treat affirmative action strictly as a constraint. It never becomes part of the goal structure, at least not in a formal sense. Minimum compliance with affirmative action guidelines may be perceived as an acceptable policy, but not as a corporate objective. Such a policy may be difficult to defend publicly, but it illustrates the importance of goal clarity and the handling of constraints.

Constituency Priority. Multiple goals can be identified as serving only corporate purposes, a specific national interest, or a minority constituency. Ranking these constituencies in terms of priorities enriches the definition of the goal structure. In most corporations, top priority is usually assigned to the enterprise itself and/or the stockholders to varying degrees. Secondary and lower priorities are given, for example, to a national interest (affirmative action) and a minority constituency (employee satisfaction), respectively. The ranking exercise itself can be illuminating, spotlighting inconsistencies and potential conflicts within the goal structure. In particular, inconsistencies are likely to appear in matching up constituent priority with goal priority. Clarity and management consensus are the operational objectives in this exercise.

Business is not always happy with morality that is legislated by others. Adopting a hierarchy of multiple goals (including those previously perceived as constraints) builds a stronger, broader ethical foundation for enterprise.

Goal Compatibility. After a firm has identified and ranked its multiple goals, the goals should be checked for compatibility. Because the ethical side of enterprise is intangible and unpredictable, an organization will frequently find that its goals conflict with one another. For example, one company that was doing business in South Africa publicly adopted the dual goals of modest profit and effective opposition to apartheid.[13] While profit was easy to measure, "effective opposition to apartheid" proved to be a much more nebulous goal. Different groups applying different standards argued that the firm should use significantly different methods to achieve these goals. One suggestion was for the firm to withdraw from South Africa, thereby sacrificing the profit goal entirely. When it finally became clear that the two goals were incompatible, the company was forced to choose between them.

Methods

Before selecting appropriate methods to achieve its goals, a firm must carefully consider the acceptability of various methods to constituents. In addition, the organization should decide whether these methods are intended to maximize goals or merely to satisfy them; whether the methods are essential, incidental, or extraneous to the goals themselves.

Constituent Acceptability. Where ethical issues emerge, the firm must consider the acceptability of various methods to its constituents. Today a corporation has more constituencies than ever before. Over time these groups have voiced a greater number of expectations and concerns, which have resulted in much new legislation. Consequently, manufacturing methods must meet new standards of product and employee safety and environmental protection. Increased SEC and IRS regulation governs investment and marketing activities in foreign countries. The passage of ERISA has regulated the vesting of employee pension benefits. As such changes in regulation and legislation continue, business can help shape them by carefully evaluating the acceptability of its methods to multiple constituencies.

Methods That Satisfy or Maximize Goals. Should the decision maker select methods that satisfy a goal or methods that maximize achievement? How safe is safe? Should a firm simply satisfy affirmative action requirements, or should it make a maximum effort to increase the employment of minorities and women? The fact that corporations have not really confronted and answered these questions has created ethical confusion. For example, such confusion has arisen in the debate over what constitutes excess or windfall profits. What is a fair or ethically acceptable return on investment? Over what period of time? The situation ethic algorithm suggests that businesspeople must confront such questions as part of the decision-making process.

Essential, Incidental, or Extraneous. It has been suggested that the decentralization of management at General Electric under Ralph Cordiner in the 1950s was a major contributor to the pricing conspiracy which ensued.[14] However, the real goals behind GE's decision to decentralize remain shrouded in controversy. Was decentralization absolutely *essential* to goal achievement? Was it *incidental*? Did management believe that it would probably have a positive impact and was worth trying at little risk? Or was it really *extraneous* to the goal itself and more a whim or personal predilection of top management? Such questions are always relevant as a firm attempts to select the most effective methods for achieving its goals.

Formal contractual arrangements and informal commitments to employees may be areas offering a number of significant choices for the future. These include such issues as the vesting of pensions, flextime, educational opportunities and on-the-job training, salary bonuses for production workers, and lifetime work contracts. In each case, business can evaluate whether such changes are essential, incidental, or extraneous to success.

Motives

It is often difficult to distinguish between motives and methods. Simply stated, corporations do not have motives. Rather, individuals have motives which find their way into corporate life through goal and method selection. In some instances, it is readily apparent that the motives of a strong or influential executive are the driving force behind a corporation's goals and methods. What drives a manager or executive to take certain actions? An instinct for survival, an innate competitive urge, a desire for power? Although employees' motives are often difficult to discern, they are the lifeblood of any institution, determining its character, climate, and degree of success. The more influential an employee, the more his or her motives will affect the firm's goals and methods. While we can only infer from an individual's behavior what his or her motives are, there are nevertheless some useful check points in this third step of the ethical algorithm.

Hidden or Known. Do others know what your motives are? As decisions with ethical implications are revealed to the public, the underlying motives of business executives tend to emerge as well. The revelation of these motives often determines the ethical or legal labeling that follows.

Motives of corporate decision makers are often suspect simply because they are somewhat hidden. The invisibility of corporate leaders makes it easy for them to be labeled "greedy" or "power hungry." If there is any substance to such accusations or if decision makers remain silent regarding their motives, the worthy goals or methods of corporate enterprise can be drowned in a sea of outraged voices. The situation ethic does not stipulate that all motives should be revealed at all times. Rather, it argues that executives should know what their motives are and when it is essential to make them public.

Shared or Selfish. In *The Gamesman*, Michael Maccoby identifies four distinct executive types, each distinguished in large measure by his motives: the Craftsman, the Companyman, the Jungle Fighter, and the Gamesman.[15] The Craftsman is absorbed in his creative process; the Companyman bases his identity on that of the firm. The Jungle Fighter is a power seeker; the Gamesman thrives on competitive activities that allow him to mark himself as a winner. In addition to underscoring the critical role that motives play, Maccoby implies that leaders driven by narrow personal or selfish motives are less likely to achieve corporate success, especially over the long term. Executives who question whether their motives are purely selfish or widely shared are moving in the direction of consensus management. Again the situation ethic does not argue that consensus is always desirable or possible, only that it is an important check point in the ethical algorithm.

Value Orientation. Commitments to certain basic values and/or religious beliefs tend to enter corporate life through the motives of key business leaders. It is becoming increasingly important for executives to be able to articulate these values and beliefs in the context of their work life. The value shifts noted by Lodge appear to have received only indirect, inconsistent attention from the business community.[16] It is not clear why business has been silent in this arena. However, it is clear that this silence has had negative effects on the ethical soundness of enterprise. In the future the success of capitalistic enterprise will be largely determined by what business leaders' motives are and by how effectively they can articulate them.

Consequences

In the final step of the ethical algorithm, the firm reviews its goals, methods, and motives and considers the potential consequences of its actions. Each of the multiple goals and methods is matched with one or more consequences. Decision makers must ask: What are the consequences of using a particular method or reaching a specific goal? These potential outcomes can be grouped into several categories.

Time Frames. Most firms will find it instructive to project the consequences of their policies over several different time periods. Of course, the appropriate time frames will vary with each firm's products and goals.

Constituency Impact. Possible consequences must be considered from the perspective of each of the firm's constituencies. This is especially important if ethical and legal precedents are unclear or if new technology is to be introduced.

Exogenous Effects. Firms must also anticipate the probable consequences of the efforts of others. In some companies such a notion is standard marketing practice. These exogenous effects are likely to grow in importance with advancing technology, increasing interdependence, global markets, and shifting values and political climates.

CONCLUSION

Sensitivity to the ethical side of enterprise means searching arduously for decisions and actions that warrant and receive the affirmation of an expanding multifarious constituency. The conceptual framework presented here is one attempt to perceive this constituency in all of its complexity. The ethical algorithm is one means of working with this constituency, rather than against it. The singular importance of enterprise to our daily lives and our collective future demands our careful attention and finest efforts.

NOTES

1. See P. E. Drucker, "Ethical Chic," *Forbes*, 14 September 1981, pp. 160–173.

2. See R. H. Tawney, *Religion and the Rise of Capitalism* (New York: Harcourt & Brace, 1926).

3. See P. Berger, "New Attack on the Legitimacy of Business," *Harvard Business Review*, September–October 1981.

4. See E. H. Schein, "The Problem of Moral Education for the Business Manager" (Paper prepared for the Seventeenth Conference on Science, Philosophy, and Religion, August 1966).

5. See G. C. Lodge, *The New American Ideology* (New York: Alfred A. Knopf, 1979).

6. See D. Bell, *The Cultural Contradictions of Capitalism* (New York: Basic Books, 1976).

7. See J. K. Galbraith, *Economics and the Public Purpose* (Boston: Houghton Mifflin, 1978).

8. See C. D. Stone, *Where the Law Ends: The Social Context of Corporate Behavior* (New York: Harper Torchbooks, 1975).

9. See C. Powers and D. Vogel, *Ethics in the Education of Business Managers* (Hastings-on-Hudson: Institute of Society, Ethics and the Life Sciences, The Hastings Institute, 1980).

10. See L. Thurow, *The Zero-Sum Society* (New York: Basic Books, 1980).

11. See J. Fletcher, *Situation Ethics: The New Morality* (Philadelphia: The Westminster Press, 1966). Dr. Fletcher is former Professor of Ethics at the Episcopal Divinity School, Cambridge, MA).

12. Ibid.

13. See D. T. Verma, "Polaroid in South Africa (A)," #9-372-624 (Boston: Intercollegiate Case Clearing House, 1971).

14. See R. A. Smith, "The Incredible Electrical Conspiracy," *Fortune*, April 1961.

15. See M. Maccoby, *The Gamesman* (New York: Bantam Books, 1976).

16. See Lodge (1979).

COST-BENEFIT ANALYSIS:
An Ethical Critique

STEVEN KELMAN*

At the broadest and vaguest level, cost-benefit analysis may be regarded simply as systematic thinking about decision-making. Who can oppose, economists sometimes ask, efforts to think in a systematic way about the consequences of different courses of action? The alternative, it would appear, is unexamined decision-making. But defining cost-benefit analysis so simply leaves it with few implications for actual regulatory decision-making. Presumably, therefore, those who urge regulators to make greater use of the technique have a more extensive prescription in mind. I assume here that their prescription includes the following views:

1. There exists a strong presumption that an act should not be undertaken unless its benefits outweigh its costs.

2. In order to determine whether benefits outweigh costs, it is desirable to attempt to express all benefits and costs in a common scale or denominator, so that they can be compared with each other, even when some benefits and costs are not traded on markets and hence have no established dollar values.

3. Getting decision-makers to make more use of cost-benefit techniques is important enough to warrant both the expense required to gather the data for improved cost-benefit estimation and the political efforts needed to give the activity higher priority compared to other activities, also valuable in and of themselves.

My focus is on cost-benefit analysis as applied to environmental, safety, and health regulation. In that context, I examine each of the above propositions from the perspective of formal ethical theory, that is, the study of what actions it is morally right to undertake. My conclusions are:

1. In areas of environmental, safety, and health regulation, there may be many instances where a certain decision might be right even though its benefits do not outweigh its costs.

2. There are good reasons to oppose efforts to put dollar values on non-marketed benefits and costs.

3. Given the relative frequency of occasions in the areas of environmental, safety, and health regulation where one would not wish to use a benefits-outweigh-costs test as a decision rule, and given the reasons to oppose the monetizing of non-marketed benefits or costs that is a prerequisite for cost-benefit analysis, it is not

Excerpted from "Cost-Benefit Analysis: An Ethical Critique," *Regulation*, January–February 1981. Reprinted by permission of the publisher.

*Kennedy School of Government, Harvard University.

justifiable to devote major resources to the generation of data for cost-benefit calculations or to undertake efforts to "spread the gospel" of cost-benefit analysis further.

I

How do we decide whether a given action is morally right or wrong and hence, assuming the desire to act morally, why it should be undertaken or refrained from? Like the Molière character who spoke prose without knowing it, economists who advocate use of cost-benefit analysis for public decisions are philosophers without knowing it: the answer given by cost-benefit analysis, that actions should be undertaken so as to maximize net benefits, represents one of the classic answers given by moral philosophers—that given by utilitarians. To determine whether an action is right or wrong, utilitarians tote up all the positive consequences of the action in terms of human satisfaction. The act that maximizes attainment of satisfaction under the circumstances is the right act. That the economists' answer is also the answer of one school of philosophers should not be surprising. Early on, economics was a branch of moral philosophy, and only later did it become an independent discipline.

Before proceeding further, the subtlety of the utilitarian position should be noted. The positive and negative consequences of an act for satisfaction may go beyond the act's immediate consequences. A facile version of utilitarianism would give moral sanction to a lie, for instance, if the satisfaction of an individual attained by telling the lie was greater than the suffering imposed on the lie's victim. Few utilitarians would agree. Most of them would add to the list of negative consequences the effect of the one lie on the tendency of the person who lies to tell other lies, even in instances when the lying produced less satisfaction for him than dissatisfaction for others. They would also add the negative effects of the lie on the general level of social regard for truth-telling, which has many consequences for future utility. A further consequence may be added as well. It is sometimes said that we should include in a utilitarian calculation the feeling of dissatisfaction produced in the liar (and perhaps in others) because, by telling a lie, one has "done the wrong thing." Correspondingly, in this view, among the positive consequences to be weighed into a utilitarian calculation of truth-telling is satisfaction arising from "doing the right thing." This view rests on an error, however, because it *assumes* what it is the purpose of the calculation to *determine*—that telling the truth in the instance in question is indeed the right thing to do. Economists are likely to object to this point, arguing that no feeling ought "arbitrarily" to be excluded from a complete cost-benefit calculation, including a feeling of dissatisfaction at doing the wrong thing. Indeed, the economists' cost-benefit calculations would, at least ideally, include such feelings. Note the difference between the economist's and the philosopher's cost-benefit calculations, however. The economist may choose to include feelings of dissatisfaction in his cost-benefit calculation, but what happens if somebody asks the economist, "Why is it right to evaluate an action on the basis of a cost-benefit test?" If an answer is to be given to that question (which does not normally preoccupy economists but which does concern both philosophers and the rest of us who need to be persuaded that cost-benefit analysis is right), then the circularity problem reemerges. And there is also another difficulty with counting feelings of dissatisfaction at doing the wrong thing in a cost-benefit calculation. It leads to the perverse result that under certain circumstances a lie, for example, might be morally right if the individual contemplating the lie felt no compunction about lying and morally wrong only if the individual felt such a compunction!

This error is revealing, however, because it begins to suggest a critique of utilitarianism. Utilitarianism is an important and powerful moral doctrine. But it is probably a minority position among contemporary moral philosophers. It is amazing that economists can proceed in unanimous endorsement of cost-benefit analysis as if unaware that their conceptual framework is highly controversial in the discipline from which it arose—moral philosophy.

Let us explore the critique of utilitarianism. The logical error discussed before appears to suggest that we have a notion of certain things being right or wrong that *predates* our calculation of costs and benefits. Imagine the case of an old man in Nazi Germany who is hostile to the regime. He is wondering whether he should speak out against Hitler. If he speaks out, he will lose his pension. And his action will have done nothing to increase the chances that the Nazi regime will be overthrown: he is regarded as somewhat eccentric by those around him, and nobody has ever consulted his views on political questions. Recall that one cannot add to the benefits of speaking out any satisfaction from doing "the right thing," because the purpose of the exercise is to determine whether speaking out *is* the right thing. How would the utilitarian calculation go? The benefits of the old man's speaking out would, as the example is presented, be nil, while the costs would be his loss of his pension. So the costs of the action would outweigh the benefits. By the utilitarians' cost-benefit calculation, it would be *morally wrong* for the man to speak out.

To those who believe that it would not be morally wrong for the old man to speak out in Nazi Germany, utilitarianism is insufficient as a moral view. We believe that some acts whose costs are greater than their benefits may be morally right and, contrariwise, some acts whose benefits are greater than their costs may be morally wrong.

This does not mean that the question whether benefits are greater than costs is morally irrelevant. Few would claim such. Indeed, for a broad range of individual and social decisions, whether an act's benefits outweigh its costs is a sufficient question to ask. But not for all such decisions. These may involve situations where certain duties—duties not to lie, break promises, or kill, for example—make an act wrong, even if it would result in an excess of benefits over costs. Or they may involve instances where people's rights are at stake. We would not permit rape even if it could be demonstrated that the rapist derived enormous happiness from his act, while the victim experienced only minor displeasure. We do not do cost-benefit analyses of freedom of speech or trial by jury. The Bill of Rights was not RARGed.* As the United Steelworkers noted in a comment on the Occupational Safety and Health Administration's economic analysis of its proposed rule to reduce worker exposure to carcinogenic coke-oven emissions, the Emancipation Proclamation was not subjected to an inflationary impact statement. The notion of human rights involves the idea that

---

*The Regulatory Analysis Review Group (RARG) was created by President Carter to improve the cost-benefit analysis of regulatory policy. It was subsequently disbanded by President Reagan. (editors' note)

people may make certain claims to be allowed to act in certain ways or to be treated in certain ways, even if the sum of benefits achieved thereby does not outweigh the sum of costs. It is this view that underlies the statement that "workers have a right to a safe and healthy work place" and the expectation that OSHA's decisions will reflect that judgment.

In the most convincing versions of nonutilitarian ethics, various duties or rights are not absolute. But each has a *prima facie* moral validity so that, if duties or rights do not conflict, the morally right act is the act that reflects a duty or respects a right. If duties or rights do conflict, a moral judgment, based on conscious deliberation, must be made. Since one of the duties non-utilitarian philosophers enumerate is the duty of beneficence (the duty to maximize happiness), which in effect incorporates all of utilitarianism by reference, a non-utilitarian who is faced with conflicts between the results of cost-benefit analysis and non-utility-based considerations will need to undertake such deliberation. But in that deliberation, additional elements, which cannot be reduced to a question of whether benefits outweigh costs, have been introduced. Indeed, depending on the moral importance we attach to the right or duty involved, cost-benefit questions may, within wide ranges, become irrelevant to the outcome of the moral judgment.

In addition to questions involving duties and rights, there is a final sort of question where, in my view, the issue of whether benefits outweigh costs should not govern moral judgment. I noted earlier that, for the common run of questions facing individuals and societies, it is possible to begin and end our judgment simply by finding out if the benefits of the contemplated act outweigh the costs. This very fact means that one way to show the great importance, or value, attached to an area is to say that decisions involving the area should not be determined by cost-benefit calculations. This applies, I think, to the view many environmentalists have of decisions involving our natural environment. When officials are deciding what level of pollution will harm certain vulnerable people—such as asthmatics or the elderly—while not harming others, one issue involved may be the right of those people not to be sacrificed on the altar of somewhat higher living standards for the rest of us. But more broadly than this, many environmentalists fear that subjecting decisions about clean air or water to the cost-benefit tests that determine the general run of decisions removes those matters from the realm of specially valued things.

II

In order for cost-benefit calculations to be performed the way they are supposed to be, all costs and benefits must be expressed in a common measure, typically dollars, including things not normally bought and sold on markets, and to which dollar prices are therefore not attached. The most dramatic example of such things is human life itself; but many of the other benefits achieved or preserved by environmental policy— such as peace and quiet, fresh-smelling air, swimmable rivers, spectacular vistas—are not traded on markets either.

Economists who do cost-benefit analysis regard the quest after dollar values for non-market things as a difficult challenge—but one to be met with relish. They have tried to develop methods for imputing a person's "willingness to pay" for such things, their approach generally involving a search for bundled goods that *are* traded on markets and that vary as to whether they include a feature that is, *by itself*, not marketed. Thus, fresh air is not marketed, but houses in different parts of Los Angeles that are similar except for the degree of smog are. Peace and quiet is not marketed, but similar houses inside and outside airport flight paths are. The risk of death is not marketed, but similar jobs that have different levels of risk are. Economists have produced many often ingenious efforts to impute dollar prices to non-marketed things by observing the premiums accorded homes in clean air areas over similar homes in dirty areas or the premiums paid for risky jobs over similar nonrisky jobs.

These ingenious efforts are subject to criticism on a number of technical grounds. It may be difficult to control for all the dimensions of quality other than the presence or absence of the non-marketed thing. More important, in a world where people have different preferences and are subject to different constraints as they make their choices, the dollar value imputed to the non-market things that most people would wish to avoid will be lower than otherwise, because people with unusually weak aversion to those things or unusually strong constraints on their choices will be willing to take the bundled good in question at less of a discount than the average person. Thus, to use the property value discount of homes near airports as a measure of people's willingness to pay for quiet means to accept as a proxy for the rest of us the behavior of those least sensitive to noise, of airport employees (who value the convenience of a near-airport location) or of others who are susceptible to an agent's assurances that "it's not so bad." To use the wage premiums accorded hazardous work as a measure of the value of life means to accept as proxies for the rest of us the choices of people who do not have many choices or who are exceptional risk-seekers.

A second problem is that the attempts of economists to measure people's willingness to pay for non-marketed things assume that there is no difference between the price a person would require for *giving up* something to which he has a preexisting right and the price he would pay to *gain* something to which he enjoys no right. Thus, the analysis assumes no difference between how much a homeowner would need to be paid in order to give up an unobstructed mountain view that he already enjoys and how much he would be willing to pay to get an obstruction moved once it is already in place. Available evidence suggests that most people would insist on being paid far more to assent to a worsening of their situation than they would be willing to pay to improve their situation. The difference arises from such factors as being accustomed to and psychologically attached to that which one believes one enjoys by right. But this creates a circularity problem for any attempt to use cost-benefit analysis to determine *whether* to assign to, say, the homeowner the right to an unobstructed mountain view. For willingness to pay will be different depending on whether the right is assigned initially or not. The value judgment about whether to assign the right must thus be made first. (In order to set an upper bound on the value of the benefit, one might hypothetically assign the right to the person and determine how much he would need to be paid to give it up.)

Third, the efforts of economists to impute willingness to pay invariably involve bundled goods exchanged in *private* transactions. Those who use figures garnered from such analysis to provide guidance for *public* decisions assume no difference between how people value certain things in private individual transactions and how they would wish those same things to be valued in public collective decisions. In making such assumptions, economists insidiously slip into their analysis an important and controversial value judgment, growing naturally out of the highly individualistic microeconomic tradition—namely, the view that there should be no difference between private behavior and the behavior we display in public social life. An alternative view—one that enjoys, I would suggest, wide resonance among citizens—would be that public, social decisions provide an opportunity to give certain things a higher valuation than we choose, for one reason or another, to give them in our private activities.

Thus, opponents of stricter regulation of health risks often argue that we show by our daily risk-taking behavior that we do not value life infinitely, and therefore our public decisions should not reflect the high value of life that proponents of strict regulation propose. However, an alternative view is equally plausible. Precisely because we fail, for whatever reasons, to give life-saving the value in everyday personal decisions that we in some general terms believe we should give it, we may wish our social decisions to provide us the occasion to display the reverence for life that we espouse but do not always show. By this view, people do not have fixed unambiguous "preferences" to which they give expression through private activities and which therefore should be given expression in public decisions. Rather, they may have what they themselves regard as "higher" and "lower" preferences. The latter may come to the fore in private decisions, but people may want the former to come to the fore in public decisions. They may sometimes display racial prejudice, but support antidiscrimination laws. They may buy a certain product after seeing a seductive ad, but be skeptical enough of advertising to want the government to keep a close eye on it. In such cases, the use of private behavior to impute the values that should be entered for public decisions, as is done by using willingness to pay in private transactions, commits grievous offense against a view of the behavior of the citizen that is deeply engrained in our democratic tradition. It is a view that denudes politics of any independent role in society, reducing it to a mechanistic, mimicking recalculation based on private behavior.

Finally, one may oppose the effort to place prices on a non-market thing and hence in effect incorporate it into the market system out of a fear that the very act of doing so will reduce the thing's perceived value. To place a price on the benefit may, in other words, reduce the value of that benefit. Cost-benefit analysis thus may be like the thermometer that, when placed in a liquid to be measured, itself changes the liquid's temperature.

Examples of the perceived cheapening of a thing's value by the very act of buying and selling it abound in everyday life and language. The disgust that accompanies the idea of buying and selling human beings is based on the sense that this would dramatically diminish human worth. Epithets such as "he prostituted himself," applied as linguistic analogies to people who have sold something, reflect the view that certain things should not be sold because doing so diminishes their value. Praise that is bought is worth little, even to the person buying it. A true anecdote is told of an economist who retired to another university community and complained that he was having difficulty making friends. The laconic response of a critical colleague—"If you want a friend why don't you buy yourself one"—illustrates in a pithy way the intuition that, for some things, the very act of placing a price on them reduces their perceived value.

The first reason that pricing something decreases its perceived value is that, in many circumstances, non-market exchange is associated with the production of certain values not associated with market exchange. These may include spontaneity and various other feelings that come from personal relationships. If a good becomes less associated with the production of positively valued feelings because of market exchange, the perceived value of the good declines to the extent that those feelings are valued. This can be seen clearly in instances where a thing may be transferred both by market and by non-market mechanisms. The willingness to pay for sex bought from a prostitute is less than the perceived value of the sex consummating love. (Imagine the reaction if a practitioner of cost-benefit analysis computed the benefits of sex based on the price of prostitute services.)

Furthermore, if one values in a general sense the existence of a non-market sector because of its connection with the production of certain valued feelings, then one ascribes added value to any non-marketed good simply as a repository of values represented by the non-market sector one wishes to preserve. This seems certainly to be the case for things in nature, such as pristine streams or undisturbed forests: for many people who value them, part of their value comes from their position as repositories of values the non-market sector represents.

The second way in which placing a market price on a thing decreases its perceived value is by removing the possibility of proclaiming that the thing is "not for sale," since things on the market by definition are for sale. The very statement that something is not for sale affirms, enhances, and protects a thing's value in a number of ways. To begin with, the statement is a way of showing that a thing is valued for its own sake, whereas selling a thing for money demonstrates that it was valued only instrumentally. Furthermore, to say that something cannot be transferred in that way places it in the exceptional category—which requires the person interested in obtaining that thing to be able to offer something else that is exceptional, rather than allowing him the easier alternative of obtaining the thing for money that could have been obtained in an infinity of ways. This enhances its value. If I am willing to say "You're a really kind person" to whoever pays me to do so, my praise loses the value that attaches to it from being exchangeable only for an act of kindness.

In addition, if we have already decided we value something highly, one way of stamping it with a cachet affirming its high value is to announce that it is "not for sale." Such an announcement does more, however, than just reflect a preexisting high valuation. It signals a thing's distinctive value to others and helps us persuade them to value the thing more highly than they otherwise might. It also expresses our resolution to safeguard that distinctive value. To state that something is not for sale is thus also a source of value for that thing, since if a thing's value is easy to affirm or protect, it will be worth more than an otherwise similar thing without such attributes.

If we proclaim that something is not for sale, we make a once-and-for-all judgment of its special value. When something is priced, the issue of its perceived value is constantly coming up, as a standing invitation to reconsider that original judgment. Were people constantly faced with questions such as "how much money could get you to give up your freedom of speech?" or "how much would you sell your vote for if you could?", the perceived value of the freedom to speak or the right to vote would soon become devastated as, in moments of weakness, people started saying "maybe it's not worth *so much* after all." Better not to be faced with the constant questioning in the first place. Something similar did in fact occur when the slogan "better red than dead" was launched by some pacifists during the Cold War. Critics pointed out that the very posing of this stark choice—in effect, "would you *really* be willing to give up your life in exchange for not living under communism?"—reduced the value people attached to freedom and thus diminished resistance to attacks on freedom.

Finally, of some things valued very highly it is stated that they are "priceless" or that they have "infinite value." Such expressions are reserved for a subset of things not for sale, such as life or health. Economists tend to scoff at talk of pricelessness. For them, saying that something is priceless is to state a willingness to trade off an infinite quantity of all other goods for one unit of the priceless good, a situation that empirically appears highly unlikely. For most people, however, the word priceless is pregnant with meaning. Its value-affirming and value-protecting functions cannot be bestowed on expressions that merely denote a determinate, albeit high, valuation. John Kennedy in his inaugural address proclaimed that the nation was ready to "pay any price [and] bear any burden . . . to assure the survival and the success of liberty." Had he said instead that we were willing to "pay a high price" or "bear a large burden" for liberty, the statement would have rung hollow.

III

An objection that advocates of cost-benefit analysis might well make to the preceding argument should be considered. I noted earlier that, in cases where various non-utility-based duties or rights conflict with the maximization of utility, it is necessary to make a deliberative judgment about what act is finally right. I also argued earlier that the search for commensurability might not always be a desirable one, that the attempt to go beyond expressing benefits in terms of (say) lives saved and costs in terms of dollars is not something devoutly to be wished.

In situations involving things that are not expressed in a common measure, advocates of cost-benefit analysis argue that people making judgments "in effect" perform cost-benefit calculations anyway. If government regulators promulgate a regulation that saves 100 lives at a cost of $1 billion, they are "in effect" valuing a life at (a minimum of) $10 million, whether or not they say that they are willing to place a dollar value on a human life. Since, in this view, cost-benefit analysis "in effect" is inevitable, it might as well be made specific.

This argument misconstrues the real difference in the reasoning processes involved. In cost-benefit analysis, equivalencies are established *in advance* as one of the raw materials for the calculation. One determines costs and benefits, one determines equivalencies (to be able to put various costs and benefits into a common measure), and then one sets to toting things up—waiting, as it were, with bated breath for the results of the calculation to come out. The outcome is determined by the arithmetic; if the outcome is a close call or if one is not good at long division, one does not know how it will turn out until the calculation is finished. In the kind of deliberative judgment that is performed without a common measure, no establishment of equivalencies occurs in advance. Equivalencies are not aids to the decision process. In fact, the decision-maker might not even be aware of what the "in effect" equivalencies were, at least before they are revealed to him afterwards by someone pointing out what he had "in effect" done. The decision-maker would see himself as simply having made a deliberative judgment; the "in effect" equivalency number did not play a causal role in the decision but at most merely reflects it. Given this, the argument against making the process explicit is the one discussed earlier in the discussion of problems with putting specific values on things that are not normally quantified—that the very act of doing so may serve to reduce the value of those things.

My own judgment is that modest efforts to assess levels of benefits and costs are justified, although I do not believe that government agencies ought to sponsor efforts to put dollar prices on non-market things. I also do not believe that the cry for more cost-benefit analysis in regulation is, on the whole, justified. If regulatory officials were so insensitive about regulatory costs that they did not provide acceptable raw material for deliberative judgments (even if not of a strictly cost-benefit nature), my conclusion might be different. But a good deal of research into costs and benefits already occurs—actually, far more in the U.S. regulatory process than in that of any other industrial society. The danger now would seem to come more from the other side.

DEFENDING COST-BENEFIT ANALYSIS:
Two Replies to Steven Kelman

JAMES V. DELONG*

Steven Kelman's "Cost-Benefit Analysis—An Ethical Critique" presents so many targets that it is difficult to concentrate one's fire. However, four points seem worth particular emphasis:

1. The decision to use cost-benefit analysis by no means implies adoption of the reductionist utilitarianism described by Kelman. It is based instead on the pragmatic conclusion that any value system one adopts is more likely to be promoted if one knows something about the consequences of the choices to be made. The effort to put dollar values on noneconomic benefits is nothing more than an effort to find some common measure for things that are not easily comparable when, in the real world, choice must be made. Its object is not to write a computer program but to improve the quality of difficult social choices under conditions of uncertainty, and no sensible analyst lets himself become the prisoner of the numbers.

2. Kelman repeatedly lapses into "entitlement" rhetoric, as if an assertion of a moral claim closes an argument. Even leaving aside the fundamental question of the philosophical basis of those entitlements, there are two major problems with this style of argument. First, it tends naturally toward all-encompassing claims.

   Kelman quotes a common statement that "workers have a right to a safe and healthy workplace," a statement that contains no recognition that safety and health are not either/or conditions, that the most difficult questions involve gradations of risk, and that the very use of entitlement language tends to assume that a zero-risk level is the only acceptable one. Second, entitlement rhetoric is usually phrased in the passive voice, as if the speaker were arguing with some omnipotent god or government that is maliciously withholding the entitlement out of spite. In the real world, one person's right is another's duty, and it often clarifies the discussion to focus more precisely on who owes this duty and what it is going to cost him or her. For example, the article posits that an issue in government decisions about acceptable pollution levels is "the right" of such vulnerable groups as asthmatics or the elderly "not to be sacrificed on the altar of somewhat higher living standards for the rest of us." This defends the entitlement by assuming the costs involved are both trivial and diffused. Suppose, though, that the price to be paid is not "somewhat higher living standards," but the jobs of a number of workers?

   Kelman's counter to this seems to be that entitlements are not firm rights, but only presumptive ones that prevail in any clash with nonentitlements, and that when two entitlements collide the decision depends upon the "moral importance we attach to the right or duty involved." So the above collision would be resolved

From *Regulation*, March–April 1981. Reprinted by permission of the publisher.
*Attorney, Washington, D.C.

by deciding whether a job is an entitlement and, if it is, by then deciding whether jobs or air have greater "moral importance."

I agree that conflicts between such interests present difficult choices, but the quantitative questions, the cost-benefit questions, are hardly irrelevant to making them. Suppose taking X quantity of pollution from the air of a city will keep one asthmatic from being forced to leave town and cost 1,000 workers their jobs? Suppose it will keep 1,000 asthmatics from being forced out and cost one job? These are not equivalent choices, economically or morally, and the effort to decide them according to some abstract idea of moral importance only obscures the true nature of the moral problems involved.

3. Kelman also develops the concept of things that are "specially valued," and that are somehow contaminated if thought about in monetary terms. As an approach to personal decision making, this is silly. There are many things one specially values—in the sense that one would find the effort to assign a market price to them ridiculous—which are nonetheless affected by economic factors. I may specially value a family relationship, but how often I phone is influenced by long-distance rates. I may specially value music, but be affected by the price of records or the cost of tickets at the Kennedy Center.

When translated to the realm of government decisions, however, the concept goes beyond silliness. It creates a political grotesquerie. People specially value many different things. Under Kelman's assumptions, people must, in creating a political coalition, recognize and accept as legitimate everyone's special value, without concern for cost. Therefore, everyone becomes entitled to as much of the thing he specially values as he says he specially values, and it is immoral to discuss vulgar questions of resource limitations. Any coalition built on such premises can go in either of two directions: It can try to incorporate so many different groups and interests that the absurdity of its internal contradictions becomes manifest. Or it can limit its membership at some point and decide that the special values of those left outside are not legitimate and should be sacrificed to the special values of those in the coalition. In the latter case, of course, those outside must be made scapegoats for any frustration of any group member's entitlement, a requirement that eventually leads to political polarization and a holy war between competing coalitions of special values.

4. The decisions that must be made by contemporary government indeed involve painful choices. They affect both the absolute quantity and the distribution not only of goods and benefits, but also of physical and mental suffering. It is easy to understand why people would want to avoid making such choices and would rather act in ignorance than with knowledge and responsibility for the consequences of their choices. While this may be understandable, I do not regard it as an acceptable moral position. To govern is to choose, and government officials—whether elected or appointed—betray their obligations to the welfare of the people who hired them if they adopt a policy of happy ignorance and nonresponsibility for consequences.

The article concludes with the judgment that the present danger is too much cost-benefit analysis, not too little. But I find it hard to believe, looking around the modern world, that its major problem is that it suffers from an excess of rationality. The world's stock of ignorance is and will remain quite large enough without adding to it as a matter of deliberate policy.

ROBERT A. NISBET*

A considerable distance separates Steven Kelman's views and mine on, first, the appositeness of cost-benefit analysis and, second, the historical context in which we live. No matter: his thoughtful and gracefully written article expresses a point of view that is widespread and must not be disregarded by those of us who see the matter somewhat differently.

1. I question Kelman's use of "utilitarianism." It seems to me that he has in mind, rather, Bentham's notable (or notorious) hedonic calculus—which does indeed posit that the morally right act is always the one that maximizes satisfaction. Granted that utilitarian theory was originated by Bentham, with the assistance of James Mill. But there is much warrant and precedent for taking it as we find it in John Stuart Mill's *Utilitarianism.*

   Mill, like Bentham and the great English utilitarians of the late nineteenth century, believes the end of government should be to accomplish the greatest possible good for the greatest possible number. But Mill will have none of the hedonic calculus. "He who saves a fellow creature from drowning does what is morally right, whether his motive be duty, or the hope of being paid for his trouble; he who betrays a friend that trusts him is guilty of a crime, even if his object be to serve another friend to whom he is under greater obligation." And there is more: "It is confessedly unjust," says Mill, "to break faith with anyone, to violate an engagement, either express or implied, or disappoint expectations raised by our own conduct. . . ." So much for Kelman's illustrations with respect to the irrelevance or impiety of cost-benefit assessment.

   In addition, the conviction that utility ought to be the ultimate standard of value is, for Mill, quite compatible with the belief that "certain social utilities . . . are vastly more important and therefore more absolute and imperative than any others are as a class"—and, further, that these utilities should be and are "guarded by a sentiment not only different in degree but in kind." Mill lists a number of such "utilities," chief among them liberty. Were he living today, he might very well—in fact, probably would—add conservation of resources to his list of overriding utilities.

2. That leads me to Kelman's worthy insistence that there are certain values in life for which cost-benefit assessment is inappropriate, even immoral or illogical. I dare

Excerpted from *Regulation*, March–April 1981. Reprinted by permission of the publisher.
*Resident scholar, American Enterprise Institute.

say there are, most of them being highly subjective and egocentric. But consider so subjective a state of mind as, say, one's love of another human being. We stipulate the crassness and venality of claiming to love another if the loved one's exclusive attraction is an abundance of worldly goods. There have been other ages, however, not without honor, and there are even now peoples whose morality must be presumed at least as elevated as ours who take a less subjective (and romantic) view of this matter than we contemporary Americans do. In many a newspaper in India we find advertisements for spouses, with everything from a Ph.D. to a given number of cows put on the negotiation counter. Marriages are not to be allowed, in such a culture, to run the risk of foundering on mere human passion—call it love—and on subjective assessment free of cost-benefit analysis. Marriage is too serious in the Hindu's mind, too sacred, too vital. I do not recommend the Hindu dogma of marriage to this generation of Americans, but from all I have been able to discover from Indian records, as many happy marriages proceed from naked cost-benefit analysis there as from whatever most marriages proceed from in the United States. In fact, I know of virtually nothing, really, in mankind's history, however sacred—birth, marriage, and death foremost—that has not been and is not today in many places subjected to cost-benefit consideration.

To take a less universal crisis of the human condition, the care of the handicapped is, I believe, an obligation of any civilized society. But are we being callous to see economic disaster ahead if we dismiss altogether cost-benefit criteria in our search for ways of increasing their mobility? Is it inhumane to look for other ways of helping wheelchair users than by spending tens of millions on ramps and lifts?

Or take the environment. As far as I am concerned, laws against pollution and resource depletion are always called for, within reasonable limits. And doubtless some parts of the wilderness should be maintained as nearly as possible in their pristine state. But not, I would argue, with such zeal that even prospecting for vital fuels and minerals is outlawed. There is no evidence in this area—or elsewhere, for that matter—of the surfeit of cost-benefit balancing Kelman seems to have observed. With memory fresh of the Alaskan wilderness bill that President Carter signed, I am obliged to conclude that proper balance lies a long way ahead of us— meaning a balance under which private industry has a great deal more leeway than it now has to explore, mine, or otherwise develop these areas. We should remember that serious environmentalism (conservation, as it was called then) began under such prescient minds as Theodore Roosevelt and Gifford Pinchot, who repeatedly declared that the purpose of conservation was *not* idle preservation but rather to prevent wanton desolation and to guarantee a future in which people could continue to rise in the scale of economy and civilization.

Unoccupied land is exactly a place where cost-benefit analysis is vital—in the sheer interest of the large numbers of underprivileged among us, including the young not yet established in a career and most emphatically blacks, Hispanics, and other minorities whose rise to middle-class status is among the highest items on our national social agenda. What they, and all others who are currently disadvantaged and in need of channels of upward mobility, require most is economic growth and increased productivity. For without the certain prospect of a vast number of new jobs in the private sector, much of the foundation for what we call the American way of life is destroyed. It is truly unfortunate that the once noble conservation movement in this country has fallen, for the most part, into the hands of those less interested in the welfare of posterity than in the preservation of a wilderness that has become an end in itself, a source of happiness for a tiny few who, I fear, love the wilderness above man. Environmentalism is rapidly becoming the socialism, not of fools, but of the middle and upper classes.

In sum, I agree with Kelman that there assuredly are considerations of the quality of life which should be free of cost-benefit analysis. But I am too avid a student of the great civilizations of past and present to believe that there are very many of these considerations.

CASES FOR PART ONE

THE GIFT RELATIONSHIP:
From Human Blood to Social Policy

RICHARD M. TITMUSS*

The starting point of this study is human blood. [It] originated, and grew over many years of introspection, from a series of value questions formulated within the context of attempts to distinguish the "social" from the "economic" in public policies and in those institutions and services with declared "welfare" goals.[1] Could, however, such distinctions be drawn and the territory of social policy at least broadly defined without raising issues about the morality of society and of man's regard or disregard for the needs of others? Why should men not contract out of the "social" and act to their own immediate advantage? Why give to strangers?—a question provoking an even more fundamental moral issue: Who is my stranger in the relatively affluent, acquisitive and divisive societies of the twentieth century? What are the connections, then, if obligations are extended, between the reciprocals of giving and receiving and modern welfare systems?

The choice of blood as an illustration and case study was no idle academic thought; it was deliberate. Short of examining humankind itself and the institution of slavery— of men and women as market commodities—blood as a living tissue may now constitute in Western societies one of the ultimate tests of where the "social" begins and the "economic" ends. If blood is considered in theory, in law, and is treated in practice as a trading commodity, then ultimately human hearts, kidneys, eyes and other organs of the body may also come to be treated as commodities to be bought and sold in the marketplace.

Profitable competition for blood "is a healthy thing," it is argued by some in the United States. It improves services, increases supplies of blood, and is the answer to a "shiftless, socialistic approach."[2] If competition for blood were eliminated, it is warned, it would "be the entering wedge for the destruction of our entire antimonopoly structure," and would threaten the interests of "great pharmaceutical companies."[3]

The payment of donors and competition for blood should be introduced in Britain, urged two economists in a publication of the Institute of Economic Affairs in London in 1968.[4] Productivity would rise; supplies of blood would increase; "a movement towards more efficiency in the economy as a whole." The Editor, Mr. Arthur Seldon,

*Professor of social administration, London School of Economics (deceased).

in a preface said that the authors "have made an unanswerable case for a trial period in which the voluntary donor is supplemented by the fee-paid donor so that the results can be judged in practice, and not prejudged by doctrinaire obfuscation."

In essence, these writers, American and British, are making an economic case against a monopoly of altruism in blood and other human tissues. They wish to set people free from the conscience of obligation. Although their arguments are couched in the language of price elasticity and profit maximization they have far-reaching implications for human values and all "social service" institutions. They legitimate, for instance, the great increase since 1967 in the number of commercial hospitals in the United States.

The moral issues that are raised extend far beyond theories of pricing and the operations of the marketplace. Moreover, they involve the foundations of professional freedom in medical care and other service relationships with people, the concept of the hospital and the university as non-profit making institutions, and the legal doctrine in the United States of charitable immunity. Charity in that country would be subject under competitive conditions to the same laws of restraint and warranty and have the same freedoms as business men in the private market.

I. THE KANSAS CITY CASE

All these issues were crystallized and debated in the now-famous Kansas City case of 1962. Before we pursue them it is instructive to review the causes and implications of this particular event. Briefly, the facts are these.[5]

In 1953 a meeting in the City of doctors, pathologists, hospital administrators and local citizens decided to form a non-profit making community blood bank. There was a need for more blood, which the local hospital blood banks were not fully supplying, and the local branch of the American Red Cross was at the time channelling the blood it collected to the Armed Forces in Korea. For the next two years there were endless disputes among the various interests involved (which need not concern us here) about power, institutional control and finance. Then, in May 1955, a commercial blood bank (calling itself the Midwest Blood Bank and Plasma Center) started operations.

The bank was owned and operated by a man and his wife. He had completed grade school, had no medical training, and had previously worked as a banjo teacher, secondhand car salesman and photographer. The blood bank procedures seem to have been actually directed by his wife. She called herself an R.N. but was not licensed as a nurse in either Kansas or Missouri, and did not show any evidence of experience or training in blood banking. Originally there had been a third partner but he had been chased out of the bank by the husband with a gun. A medical director was appointed to comply with public health regulations. He was aged 78, a general practitioner with no training in blood banking. The bank was inspected and licensed by the Federal authority, the National Institutes of Health.

It was situated in a slum area, displayed a sign reading "Cash Paid for Blood," drew blood from donors described as "Skid-Row derelicts," and was said by one witness to have "worms all over the floor." In 1958 another commercial bank, the World Blood Bank, Inc., was established in Kansas City and also began operations.

From 1955 onwards pressures of various kinds were brought to bear on relatives of hospital patients, members of associations and trade unions to provide blood on a replacement basis to these commercial banks. But local hospitals refused to accept blood from these sources to discharge patients' blood fees. These and other developments seem to have forced a solution to the disputes over the control of the non-profit community blood bank, and in April 1958 it commenced operations. Subsequently, it appears from the evidence that practically all the large local hospitals entered into blood supply contracts with the Community Bank and ceased operating their own banks. The Community Bank thus had a virtual monopoly.

The two commercial banks then complained to the Federal Trade Commission alleging restraint of trade. In July 1962, after an investigation lasting several years, the Commission issued a complaint against the Community Blood Bank and its officers, directors, administrative director and business manager; the Kansas City Area Hospital Association and its officers, directors, and executive director; three hospitals individually and as representatives of the forty members of the Hospital Association; sixteen pathologists, and two hospital administrators.

The complaint charged the respondents with having entered into an agreement or planned course of action to hamper and restrain the sale and distribution of human blood in interstate commerce. They were charged with conspiring to boycott a commercial blood bank in the sale and distribution of blood in commerce, and that the conspiracy was to the injury of the public and unreasonably restricted and restrained interstate commerce in violation of Section 5 of the Federal Trade Commission Act of 1952. This Section of the Act declares that "uniform methods of competition in commerce, and unfair or deceptive acts or practices in commerce, are declared unlawful." Violation of a Commission "cease and desist order," after it becomes final, subjects the violator to civil penalties up to $5,000 for each day that the violation continues.

The respondents appealed. After lengthy hearings before an Examiner for the Commission in 1963, a further appeal and more hearings before the full Trade Commission of five members, a ruling was issued in October 1966. By a majority of three to two the Commission decided that the Community Blood Bank and the hospitals, doctors and pathologists associated with it were illegally joined together in a conspiracy to restrain commerce in whole human blood.

In January 1969 the Federal Trade Commission's ruling of 1966 in the Kansas City case was set aside by the Eighth U.S. Circuit Court of Appeals in St. Louis.[6] Up to the end of 1969 no appeal had been made to the Supreme Court.

Though this may be the end of this particular case the fact that it happened is one illustration among many of the increasing commercialization of the blood banking system and of hospital and medical services in general. This trend must logically lead to more and more recourse to the laws and practices of the marketplace. There is no inconsistency in this development. If blood as a living human tissue is increasingly bought and sold as an article of commerce, and profit accrues from such transactions, then it follows that the laws of commerce must, in the end, prevail.

Having said this we must point out that although attempts have been made to value human life,[7] no money values can be attached to the presence or absence of a spirit of altrusim in a society. Altruism in giving to a stranger does not begin and end with blood donations. It may touch every aspect of life and affect the whole fabric of values. Its role in satisfying the biological need to help—particularly in modern societies—is another unmeasurable element. In this study we have used human blood as an indicator, perhaps the most basic and sensitive indicator of social values and human relationships that could be found for a comparative study. If dollars or pounds exchange for blood then it may be morally acceptable for a myriad of other human activities and relationships also to exchange for dollars or pounds. Economists may fragment systems and values; other people do not.

We do not know and could never estimate in economic terms the social costs to American society of the decline in recent years in the voluntary giving of blood. It is likely that a decline in the spirit of altruism in one sphere of human activities will be accompanied by similar changes in attitudes, motives and relationships in other spheres.

Once man begins to say, as he sees that dollars exchange for blood supplies from Skid Row and a poor and often coloured population of sellers, "I need no longer experience (or suffer from) a sense of responsibility (or sin) in not giving to my neighbour" then the consequences are likely to be socially pervasive. There is nothing permanent about the expression of reciprocity. If the bonds of community giving are broken the result is not a state of value neutralism. The vacuum is likely to be filled by hostility and social conflict.

II. BLOOD DISTRIBUTION IN THE UNITED STATES VERSUS BRITAIN

In comparing commercialized blood market systems in the United States with a voluntary system functioning as an integral part of the National Health Service in Britain we consider four sets of criteria. These are basic criteria which economists would themselves apply in attempting to assess the relative advantages and disadvantages of different systems. They exclude, therefore, the much wider and unquantifiable social, ethical and philosophical aspects which, as this study has demonstrated, extend far beyond the narrower confines of blood distribution systems judged simply in economic and financial terms.

These four criteria which to some extent overlap are, briefly stated: (1) economic efficiency; (2) administrative efficiency; (3) price—the cost per unit to the patient; (4) purity, potency and safety—or quality per unit.

On all four criteria, the commercialized blood market fails. In terms of economic efficiency it is highly wasteful of blood; shortages, chronic and acute, characterize the demand and supply position and make illusory the concept of equilibrium; the market also involves heavy external costs. It is administratively inefficient; the so-called mixed pluralism of the American market results in more bureaucratization, avalanches of paper and bills, and much greater administrative, accounting and computer overheads. These wastes, disequilibria and inefficiencies are reflected in the price paid by the patient (or consumer); the cost per unit of blood varying in the United States between £10 and £20 (at the official rate of exchange in 1969) compared with £1 6s. (£2 if processing costs are included) in Britain—five to fifteen times higher. And, finally, in terms of quality, commercial markets are much more likely to distribute contaminated blood; in other words, the risks for the patient of disease and death in the form of serum hepatitis are substantially higher.

Paradoxically—or so it may seem to some—the more commercialized a blood distribution system becomes (and hence more wasteful, inefficient and dangerous) the more will the gross national product be inflated. In part, and quite simply, this is the consequence of statistically "transferring" an unpaid service (voluntary blood donors, voluntary workers in the service, unpaid time) with much lower external costs to a monetary and measurable paid activity involving costlier externalities. Similar effects on the gross national product would ensue if housewives were paid for housework or childless married couples were financially rewarded for adopting children or hospital patients cooperating for teaching purposes charged medical students. The gross national product is also inflated when commercial markets accelerate "blood obsolescence"— or waste; the waste is counted because someone has paid for it.

What *The Economist* described in its 1969 survey of the American economy as the great "efficiency gap" between that country and Britain[8] clearly does not apply in the field of human blood. On the economic and technical criteria employed in this study in relation to blood distribution systems such a conclusion needs to be reversed; the voluntary socialized system in Britain is economically, professionally, administratively and qualitatively more efficient than the mixed, commercialized and individualistic American system.

Another myth, the Paretian myth of consumer sovereignty, has also to be shattered. In commercial blood markets the consumer is not king. He has less freedom to live unharmed; little choice in determining price; is more subject to shortages in supply; is less free from bureaucratization; has fewer opportunities to express altruism; and exercises fewer checks and controls in relation to consumption, quality and external costs. Far from being sovereign, he is often exploited.

Those who suffer most and have the largest bills of all to pay are haemophiliacs. It is estimated that the incidence in the United States is 1 in 10,000 of the male population (lower estimates have been made for Britain). The fact that the disease is not only hereditary but may occur as a consequence of one of the most frequent mutations in medicine, means that the incidence may be expected to increase rather than decrease throughout the world.

Modern medical treatment now consists of human plasma and a variety of concentrated blood products. A ten-day course of treatment with these substances—say for a dental extraction—may require gifts from 60 blood donors each involving a potential risk of infecting the patient with hepatitis. In Britain, these products are prepared under the auspices of the National Blood Transfusion Service and are supplied at no cost to the patient under the National Health Service. They are not sold—or priced—commercially. The blood is given by voluntary donors.[9]

In the United States, where clinically some of the products are considered to be less satisfactory, they are produced and marketed commercially. At retail prices ruling in 1966, the cost to an average adult of a ten-day course of treatment with human plasma products was about $2250. In 1969 it was reported: "Many patients require plasma or plasma concentrate therapy three times a month or more. By the end of the year, this patient has a staggering plasma bill. In families of two or more haemophiliac youngsters, the financial burden is even more acute. The financial aspects alone can cause family problems and disruption. Patients often relate guilt feelings because of the financial burden they cause their families."[10] They are also continually reminded by these market forces that for their survival from one bleeding episode to the next they are dependent on blood supplies from strangers. They are "bad risks"; noninsurable by the private market in the United States; not acceptable by profit-making hospitals.

It has been estimated that if all the needs of haemophiliac patients in the United States were fully met they would require about one-eighth of all the blood collected each year in the country—or about 1,000,000 pints.

In England, where it is estimated that there are more than 2000 patients with severe haemorrhagic disorders, the problems they face are in no way comparable to those confronting similar patients in the United States. They would not wish to emigrate. While there are serious difficulties in the technical production of adequate quantities of the appropriate blood products (which use only certain of the valuable constituents of plasma) there is no shortage of blood, and no problems for the patient in paying for the blood and medical treatment.

Let me conclude by quoting from Alexander Solzhenitsyn's great work *Cancer Ward*[11], banned in the Soviet Union. Shulubin, a cancer patient in a hospital in Central Asia, is talking to Kostoglotov, a former prisoner in a labour camp now in exile as a patient in the same hospital. "He (Shulubin) spoke very distinctly, like a master giving a lesson.

'We have to show the world a society in which all relationships, fundamental principles and laws flow directly from moral ethics, and from them *alone*. Ethical demands would determine all calculations: how to bring up children, what to prepare them for, to what purpose the work of grown-ups should be directed, and how their leisure should be occupied. As for scientific research, it should only be conducted where it doesn't damage ethical morality, in the first instance where it doesn't damage the researchers themselves.' "

Kostoglotov then raises questions. " 'There has to be an economy, after all, doesn't there? That comes before everything else.' 'Does it?' said Shulubin. 'That depends. For example, Vladimir Solovyov argues rather convincingly that an economy could and should be built on an ethical basis.'

'What's that? Ethics first and economics afterwards?' Kostoglotov looked bewildered."

NOTES

1. For an earlier attempt to define the territory of social policy and the roles and functions of the social services, see the writer's *Commitment to Welfare* (1968) and particularly Chapter 1.

2. Countless statements of such opinions have been made in the United States in recent years. See, as one example, R. E. Dice, "Paid Donor Programs," *Proc. A.M.A. Conference on Blood and Blood Banking*, Chicago, 1964. Reference should also be made to *Hearings Before the Subcommittee on Antitrust and Monopoly of the Committee of the Judiciary*, United States Senate, 88th Congress, on S. 2560 (U.S. Government Printing Office, 1964), and *Hearings Before the Subcommittee on Antitrust and Monopoly of the Committee of the Judiciary*, United States Senate, 90th Congress, S. 1945 (U.S. Government Printing Office, 1967).

3. R. Carlinger, general manager, Pioneer Blood Service, Inc., New York. Statement before the Senate Subcommittee on Antitrust and Monopoly, August 1, 1967 (*Hearings on S.* 1945, op. cit., 1967, pp. 51–56).

4. M. H. Cooper and A. J. Culyer, *The Price of Blood*, Hobart Paper 41, The Institute of Economic Affairs, 1968.

5. They are taken from: Federal Trade Commission, Washington Final Order (8519), October 26, 1966; *Hearings on S.* 2560, op. cit., 1964, and *Hearings on S.* 1945, op. cit, 1967; W. E. Whyte, "Federal Trade Commission Versus the Community Blood Bank of Kansas City et al.," *Proc. A.M.A. Conference on Blood and Blood Banking*, Chicago, 1964.

6. *A.M.A. News*, January 27, 1969.

7. See, for example, T. W. Schultz, "Investment in Human Capital," *Am. Econ. Rev.*, 51, March 1, 1961.

8. *The Economist*, U.S.A. Report, May 10, 1969.

9. R. Biggs and R. G. Macfarlane, *Treatment of Haemophilia and other Coagulation Disorders*, Blackwell, Oxford, 1966.

10. C. Taylor, "Haemophilic Center at Work," *Rehabilitation Record*, Vol. 10, No. 2, March–April 1969, pp. 1–6. A study of 177 haemophiliac patients by the university Department of Psychiatry in Sheffield in 1968 failed to confirm American findings that haemophilia is liable to cause marked psychiatric symptoms. There was also no evidence of acute financial and occupational difficulties (BBI. G. Bronks, and E. K. Blackburn, "A Socio-Medical Study of Haemophilia and Related States," *Brit. J. prev. soc. Med.*, 1968, Vol. 22, pp. 68–72).

11. Vol. 2, translated by N. Bethell and D. Burg, Bodley Head, London, 1969.

WHY SHOULD MY CONSCIENCE BOTHER ME?

KERMIT VANDIVIER*

The B. F. Goodrich Co. is what business magazines like to speak of as "a major American corporation." It has operations in a dozen states and as many foreign countries, and of these far-flung facilities, the Goodrich plant at Troy, Ohio, is not the most imposing. It is a small, one-story building, once used to manufacture airplanes. Set in the grassy flatlands of west-central Ohio, it employs only about six hundred people. Nevertheless, it is one of the three largest manufacturers of aircraft wheels and brakes, a leader in a most profitable industry. Goodrich wheels and brakes support such well-known planes as the F111, the C5A, the Boeing 727, the XB70 and many others. Its customers include almost every aircraft manufacturer in the world.

Contracts for aircraft wheels and brakes often run into millions of dollars, and ordinarily a contract with a total value of less than $70,000, though welcome, would not create any special stir of joy in the hearts of Goodrich sales personnel. But purchase order P-23718, issued on June 18, 1967, by the LTV Aerospace Corporation, and ordering 202 brake assemblies for a new Air Force plane at a total price of $69,417, was received by Goodrich with considerable glee. And there was good reason. Some ten years previously, Goodrich had built a brake for LTV that was, to say the least, considerably less than a rousing success. The brake had not lived up to Goodrich's promises, and after experiencing considerable difficulty, LTV had written off Goodrich as a source of brakes. Since that time, Goodrich salesmen had been unable to sell so much as a shot of brake fluid to LTV. So in 1967, when LTV requested bids on wheels and brakes for the new A7D light attack aircraft it proposed to build for the Air Force, Goodrich submitted a bid that was absurdly low, so low that LTV could not, in all prudence, turn it down.

Goodrich had, in industry parlance, "bought into the business." Not only did the company not expect to make a profit on the deal; it was prepared, if necessary, to lose money. For aircraft brakes are not something that can be ordered off the shelf. They are designed for a particular aircraft, and once an aircraft manufacturer buys a brake, he is forced to purchase all replacement parts from the brake manufacturer. The $70,000 that Goodrich would get for making the brake would be a drop in the bucket when compared with the cost of the linings and other parts the Air Force would have to buy from Goodrich during the lifetime of the aircraft. Furthermore, the company which manufactures brakes for one particular model of an aircraft quite naturally has the inside track to supply other brakes when the planes are updated and improved.

Thus, that first contract, regardless of the money involved, is very important, and Goodrich, when it learned that it had been awarded the A7D contract, was

*Reporter, *Daily News*, in Troy, Ohio.

determined that while it may have slammed the door on its own foot ten years before, this time, the second time around, things would be different. The word was soon circulated throughout the plant: "We can't bungle it this time. We've got to give them a good brake, regardless of the cost."

There was another factor which had undoubtedly influenced LTV. All aircraft brakes made today are of the disk type, and the bid submitted by Goodrich called for a relatively small brake, one containing four disks and weighing only 106 pounds. The weight of any aircraft part is extremely important. The lighter a part is, the heavier the plane's payload can be. The four-rotor, 106-pound brake promised by Goodrich was about as light as could be expected, and this undoubtedly had helped move LTV to award the contract to Goodrich.

The brake was designed by one of Goodrich's most capable engineers, John Warren. A tall, lanky blond and a graduate of Purdue, Warren had come from the Chrysler Corporation seven years before and had become adept at aircraft brake design. The happy-go-lucky manner he usually maintained belied a temper which exploded whenever anyone ventured to offer any criticism of his work, no matter how small. On these occasions, Warren would turn red in the face, often throwing or slamming something and then stalking from the scene. As his coworkers learned the consequences of criticizing him, they did so less and less readily, and when he submitted his preliminary design for the A7D brake, it was accepted without question.

Warren was named project engineer for the A7D, and he, in turn, assigned the task of producing the final production design to a newcomer to the Goodrich engineering stable, Searle Lawson. Just turned twenty-six, Lawson had been out of the Northrup Institute of Technology only one year when he came to Goodrich in January 1967. Like Warren, he had worked for a while in the automotive industry, but his engineering degree was in aeronautical and astronautical sciences, and when the opportunity came to enter his special field, via Goodrich, he took it. At the Troy plant, Lawson had been assigned to various "paper projects" to break him in, and after several months spent reviewing statistics and old brake designs, he was beginning to fret at the lack of challenge. When told he was being assigned to his first "real" project, he was elated and immediately plunged into his work.

The major portion of the design had already been completed by Warren, and major assemblies for the brake had already been ordered from Goodrich suppliers. Naturally, however, before Goodrich could start making the brakes on a production basis, much testing would have to be done. Lawson would have to determine the best materials to use for the linings and discover what minor adjustments in the design would have to be made.

Then, after the preliminary testing and after the brake was judged ready for production, one whole brake assembly would undergo a series of grueling, simulated braking stops and other severe trials called qualification tests. These tests are required by the military, which gives very detailed specifications on how they are to be conducted, the criteria for failure, and so on. They are performed in the Goodrich plant's test laboratory, where huge machines called dynamometers can simulate the weight and speed of almost any aircraft. After the brakes pass the laboratory tests, they are approved for production, but before the brakes are accepted for use in military service, they must undergo further extensive flight tests.

Searle Lawson was well aware that much work had to be done before the A7D brake could go into production, and he knew that LTV had set the last two weeks in June, 1968, as the starting dates for flight tests. So he decided to begin testing immediately. Goodrich's suppliers had not yet delivered the brake housing and other parts, but the brake disks had arrived, and using the housing from a brake similar in size and weight to the A7D brake, Lawson built a prototype. The prototype was installed in a test wheel and placed on one of the big dynamometers in the plant's test laboratory. The dynamometer was adjusted to simulate the weight of the A7D and Lawson began a series of tests, "landing" the wheel and brake at the A7D's landing speed, and braking it to a stop. The main purpose of these preliminary tests was to learn what temperatures would develop within the brake during the simulated stops and to evaluate the lining materials tentatively selected for use.

During a normal aircraft landing the temperatures inside the brake may reach 1000 degrees, and occasionally a bit higher. During Lawson's first simulated landings, the temperature of his prototype brake reached 1500 degrees. The brake glowed a bright cherry-red and threw off incandescent particles of metal and lining material as the temperature reached its peak. After a few such stops, the brake was dismantled and the linings were found to be almost completely disintegrated. Lawson chalked this first failure up to chance and, ordering new lining materials, tried again.

The second attempt was a repeat of the first. The brake became extremely hot, causing the lining materials to crumble into dust.

After the third such failure, Lawson, inexperienced though he was, knew that the fault lay not in defective parts or unsuitable lining material but in the basic design of the brake itself. Ignoring Warren's original computations, Lawson made his own, and it didn't take him long to discover where the trouble lay—the brake was too small. There simply was not enough surface area on the disks to stop the aircraft without generating the excessive heat that caused the linings to fail.

The answer to the problem was obvious but far from simple—the four-disk brake would have to be scrapped, and a new design, using five disks, would have to be developed. The implications were not lost on Lawson. Such a step would require the junking of all the four-disk-brake subassemblies, many of which had now begun to arrive from the various suppliers. It would also mean several weeks of preliminary design and testing and many more weeks of waiting while the suppliers made and delivered the new subassemblies.

Yet, several weeks had already gone by since LTV's order had arrived, and the date for delivery of the first production brakes for flight testing was only a few months away.

Although project engineer John Warren had more or less turned the A7D over to Lawson, he knew of the difficulties Lawson had been experiencing. He had assured the young engineer that the problem revolved around getting the right kind of lining material. Once that was found, he said, the difficulties would end.

Despite the evidence of the abortive tests and Lawson's careful computations, Warren rejected the suggestion that the four-disk brake was too light for the job. Warren knew that his superior had already told LTV, in rather glowing terms, that the preliminary tests on the A7D brake were very successful. Indeed, Warren's superiors weren't aware at this time of the troubles on the brake. It would have been difficult for Warren to admit not only that he had made a serious error in his calculations and original design but that his mistakes had been caught by a green kid, barely out of college.

Warren's reaction to a five-disk brake was not unexpected by Lawson, and, seeing that the four-disk brake was not to be abandoned so easily, he took his calculations and dismal test results one step up the corporate ladder.

At Goodrich, the man who supervises the engineers working on projects slated for production is called, predictably, the projects manager. The job was held by a short, chubby and bald man named Robert Sink. A man truly devoted to his work, Sink was as likely to be found at his desk at ten o'clock on Sunday night as ten o'clock on Monday morning. His outside interests consisted mainly of tinkering on a Model-A Ford and an occasional game of golf. Some fifteen years before, Sink had begun working at Goodrich as a lowly draftsman. Slowly, he worked his way up. Despite his geniality, Sink was neither respected nor liked by the majority of the engineers, and his appointment as their supervisor did not improve their feelings about him. They thought he had only gone to high school. It quite naturally rankled those who had gone through years of college and acquired impressive specialties such as thermodynamics and astronautics to be commanded by a man whom they considered their intellectual inferior. But, though Sink had no college training, he had something even more useful: a fine working knowledge of company politics.

Puffing upon a Meerschaum pipe, Sink listened gravely as young Lawson confided his fears about the four-disk brake. Then he examined Lawson's calculations and the results of the abortive tests. Despite the fact that he was not a qualified engineer, in the strictest sense of the word, it must certainly have been obvious to Sink that Lawson's calculations were correct and that a four-disk brake would never have worked on the A7D.

But other things of equal importance were also obvious. First, to concede that Lawson's calculations were correct would also mean conceding that Warren's calculations were incorrect. As projects manager, he not only was responsible for Warren's activities, but, in admitting that Warren had erred, he would have to admit that he had erred in trusting Warren's judgment. It also meant that, as projects manager, it would be he who would have to explain the whole messy situation to the Goodrich hierarchy, not only at Troy but possibly on the corporate level at Goodrich's Akron offices. And, having taken Warren's judgment of the four-disk brake at face value (he was forced to do this since, not being an engineer, he was unable to exercise any engineering judgment of his own), he had assured LTV, not once but several times, that about all there was left to do on the brake was pack it in a crate and ship it out the back door.

There's really no problem at all, he told Lawson. After all, Warren was an experienced engineer, and if he said the brake would work, it would work. Just keep on testing and probably, maybe even on the very next try, it'll work out just fine.

Lawson was far from convinced, but without the support of his superiors there was little he could do except keep on testing. By now, housings for the four-disk brake had begun to arrive at the plant, and Lawson was able to build up a production model of the brake and begin the formal qualification tests demanded by the military.

The first qualification attempts went exactly as the tests on the prototype had.

Terrific heat developed within the brakes and, after a few, short, simulated stops, the linings crumbled. A new type of lining material was ordered and once again an attempt to qualify the brake was made. Again, failure.

On April 11, the day the thirteenth test was completed, I became personally involved in the A7D situation.

I had worked in the Goodrich test laboratory for five years, starting first as an instrumentation engineer, then later becoming a data analyst and technical writer. As part of my duties, I analyzed the reams and reams of instrumentation data that came from the many testing machines in the laboratory, then transcribed it to a more usable form for the engineering department. And when a new-type brake had successfully completed the required qualification tests, I would issue a formal qualification report.

Qualification reports were an accumulation of all the data and test logs compiled by the test technicians during the qualification tests, and were documentary proof that a brake had met all the requirements established by the military specifications and was therefore presumed safe for flight testing. Before actual flight tests were conducted on a brake, qualification reports had to be delivered to the customer and to various government officials.

On April 11, I was looking over the data from the latest A7D test, and I noticed that many irregularities in testing methods had been noted on the test logs.

Technically, of course, there was nothing wrong with conducting tests in any manner desired, so long as the test was for research purposes only. But qualification test methods are clearly delineated by the military, and I knew that this test had been a formal qualification attempt. One particular notation on the test logs caught my eye. For some of the stops, the instrument which recorded the brake pressure had been deliberately miscalibrated so that, while the brake pressure used during the stops was recorded as 1000 psi (the maximum pressure that would be available on the A7D aircraft), the pressure had actually been 1100 psi!

I showed the test logs to the test lab supervisor, Ralph Gretzinger, who said he had learned from the technician who had miscalibrated the instrument that he had been asked to do so by Lawson. Lawson, said Gretzinger, readily admitted asking for the miscalibration, saying he had been told to do so by Sink.

I asked Gretzinger why anyone would want to miscalibrate the data-recording instruments.

"Why? I'll tell you why," he snorted. "That brake is a failure. It's way too small for the job, and they're not ever going to get it to work. They're getting desperate, and instead of scrapping the damned thing and starting over, they figure they can horse around down here in the lab and qualify it that way."

An expert engineer, Gretzinger had been responsible for several innovations in brake design. It was he who had invented the unique brake system used on the famous XB70. A graduate of Georgia Tech, he was a stickler for detail and he had some very firm ideas about honesty and ethics. "If you want to find out what's going on," said Gretzinger, "ask Lawson, he'll tell you."

Curious, I did ask Lawson the next time he came into the lab. He seemed eager to discuss the A7D and gave me the history of his months of frustrating efforts to get Warren and Sink to change the brake design. "I just can't believe this is really happening," said Lawson, shaking his head slowly. "This isn't engineering, at least not what I thought it would be. Back in school, I thought that when you were an engineer, you tried to do your best, no matter what it cost. But this is something else."

He sat across the desk from me, his chin propped in his hand. "Just wait," he warned. "You'll get a chance to see what I'm talking about. You're going to get in the act, too, because I've already had the word that we're going to make one more attempt to qualify the brake, and that's it. Win or lose, we're going to issue a qualification report!"

I reminded him that a qualification report could only be issued after a brake had successfully met all military requirements, and therefore, unless the next qualification attempt was a success, no report would be issued.

"You'll find out," retorted Lawson. "I was already told that regardless of what the brake does on test, it's going to be qualified." He said he had been told in those exact words at a conference with Sink and Russell Van Horn.

This was the first indication that Sink had brought his boss, Van Horn, into the mess. Although Van Horn, as manager of the design engineering section, was responsible for the entire department, he was not necessarily familiar with all phases of every project, and it was not uncommon for those under him to exercise the what-he-doesn't-know-won't-hurt-him philosophy. If he was aware of the full extent of the A7D situation, it meant that matters had truly reached a desperate stage—that Sink had decided not only to call for help but was looking toward that moment when blame must be borne and, if possible, shared.

Also, if Van Horn had said, "regardless what the brake does on test, it's going to be qualified," then it could only mean that, if necessary, a false qualification report would be issued! I discussed this possibility with Gretzinger, and he assured me that under no circumstances would such a report ever be issued.

"If they want a qualification report, we'll write them one, but we'll tell it just like it is," he declared emphatically. "No false data or false reports are going to come out of this lab."

On May 2, 1968, the fourteenth and final attempt to qualify the brake was begun. Although the same improper methods used to nurse the brake through the previous tests were employed, it soon became obvious that this too would end in failure.

When the tests were about half completed, Lawson asked if I would start preparing the various engineering curves and graphic displays which were normally incorporated in a qualification report. "It looks as though you'll be writing a qualification report shortly," he said.

I flatly refused to have anything to do with the matter and immediately told Gretzinger what I had been asked to do. He was furious and repeated his previous declaration that under no circumstances would any false data or other matter be issued from the lab.

"I'm going to get this settled right now, once and for all," he declared. "I'm going to see Line [Russell Line, manager of the Goodrich Technical Services Section, of which the test lab was a part] and find out just how far this thing is going to go!" He stormed out of the room.

In about an hour, he returned and called me to his desk. He sat silently for a few moments, then muttered, half to himself, "I wonder what the hell they'd do if I just quit?" I didn't answer and I didn't ask him what he meant. I knew. He had been beaten down. He had reached the point when the decision had to be made. Defy them now while there was still time—or knuckle under, sell out.

"You know," he went on uncertainly, looking down at his desk, "I've been an engineer for a long time, and I've always believed that ethics and integrity were every bit as important as theorems and formulas, and never once has anything happened to change my beliefs. Now this. . . . Hell, I've got two sons I've got to put through school and I just. . . . " His voice trailed off.

He sat for a few more minutes, then, looking over the top of his glasses, said hoarsely, "Well, it looks like we're licked. The way it stands now, we're to go ahead and prepare the data and other things for the graphic presentation in the report, and when we're finished, someone upstairs will actually write the report.

"After all," he continued, "we're just drawing some curves, and what happens to them after they leave here, well, we're not responsible for that."

He was trying to persuade himself that as long as we were concerned with only one part of the puzzle and didn't see the completed picture, we really weren't doing anything wrong. He didn't believe what he was saying, and he knew I didn't believe it either. It was an embarrassing and shameful moment for both of us.

I wasn't at all satisfied with the situation and decided that I too would discuss the matter with Russell Line, the senior executive in our section.

Tall, powerfully built, his teeth flashing white, his face tanned to a coffee-brown by a daily stint with a sun lamp, Line looked and acted every inch the executive. He was a crossword-puzzle enthusiast and an ardent golfer, and though he had lived in Troy only a short time, he had been accepted into the Troy Country Club and made an official of the golf committee. He commanded great respect and had come to be well liked by those of us who worked under him.

He listened sympathetically while I explained how I felt about the A7D situation, and when I had finished, he asked me what I wanted him to do about it. I said that as employees of the Goodrich Company we had a responsibility to protect the company and its reputation if at all possible. I said I was certain that officers on the corporate level would never knowingly allow such tactics as had been employed on the A7D.

"I agree with you," he remarked, "but I still want to know what you want me to do about it."

I suggested that in all probability the chief engineer at the Troy plant, H. C. "Bud" Sunderman, was unaware of the A7D problem and that he, Line, should tell him what was going on.

Line laughed, good-humoredly. "Sure, I could, but I'm not going to. Bud probably already knows about this thing anyway, and if he doesn't, I'm sure not going to be the one to tell him."

"But why?"

"Because it's none of my business, and it's none of yours. I learned a long time ago not to worry about things over which I had no control. I have no control over this."

I wasn't satisfied with this answer, and I asked him if his conscience wouldn't bother him if, say, during flight tests on the brake, something should happen resulting in death or injury to the test pilot.

"Look," he said, becoming somewhat exasperated, "I just told you I have no control over this thing. Why should my conscience bother me?"

His voice took on a quiet, soothing tone as he continued. "You're just getting all upset over this thing for nothing. I just do as I'm told, and I'd advise you to do the same."

He had made his decision, and now I had to make mine.

I made no attempt to rationalize what I had been asked to do. It made no difference who would falsify which part of the report or whether the actual falsification would be by misleading numbers or misleading words. Whether by acts of commission or omission, all of us who contributed to the fraud would be guilty. The only question left for me to decide was whether or not I would become a party to the fraud.

Before coming to Goodrich in 1963, I had held a variety of jobs, each a little more pleasant, a little more rewarding than the last. At forty-two, with seven children, I had decided that the Goodrich Company would probably be my "home" for the rest of my working life. The job paid well, it was pleasant and challenging, and the future looked reasonably bright. My wife and I had bought a home and we were ready to settle down into a comfortable, middle-age, middle-class rut. If I refused to take part in the A7D fraud, I would have to either resign or be fired. The report would be written by someone anyway, but I would have the satisfaction of knowing I had had no part in the matter. But bills aren't paid with personal satisfaction, nor house payments with ethical principles. I made my decision. The next morning, I telephoned Lawson and told him I was ready to begin on the qualification report.

In a few minutes, he was at my desk, ready to begin. Before we started, I asked him, "Do you realize what we are going to do?"

"Yeah," he replied bitterly, "we're going to screw LTV. And speaking of screwing," he continued, "I know now how a whore feels, because that's exactly what I've become, an engineering whore. I've sold myself. It's all I can do to look at myself in the mirror when I shave. I make me sick."

I was surprised at his vehemence. It was obvious that he too had done his share of soul-searching and didn't like what he had found. Somehow, though, the air seemed clearer after his outburst, and we began working on the report.

I had written dozens of qualification reports, and I knew what a "good" one looked like. Resorting to the actual test data only on occasion, Lawson and I proceeded to prepare page after page of elaborate, detailed engineering curves, charts, and test logs, which purported to show what had happened during the formal qualification tests. Where temperatures were too high, we deliberately chopped them down a few hundred degrees, and where they were too low, we raised them to a value that would appear reasonable to the LTV and military engineers. Brake pressure, torque values, distances, times—everything of consequence was tailored to fit the occasion.

Occasionally, we would find that some test either hadn't been performed at all or had been conducted improperly. On those occasions, we "conducted" the test— successfully, of course—on paper.

For nearly a month we worked on the graphic presentation that would be a part of the report. Meanwhile, the fourteenth and final qualification attempt had been completed, and the brake, not unexpectedly, had failed again.

During that month, Lawson and I talked of little else except the enormity of what we were doing. The more involved we became in our work, the more apparent became our own culpability. We discussed such things as the Nuremberg trials and how they related to our guilt and complicity in the A7D situation. Lawson often expressed his opinion that the brake was downright dangerous and that, once on flight tests, "anything is liable to happen."

I saw his boss, John Warren, at least twice during that month and needled him about what we were doing. He didn't take the jibes too kindly but managed to laugh the situation off as "one of those things." One day I remarked that what we were doing amounted to fraud, and he pulled out an engineering handbook and turned to a section on laws as they related to the engineering profession.

He read the definition of fraud aloud, then said, "Well, technically I don't think what we're doing can be called fraud. I'll admit it's not right, but it's just one of those things. We're just kinda caught in the middle. About all I can tell you is, do like I'm doing. Make copies of everything and put them in your SYA file."

"What's an 'SYA' file?" I asked.

"That's a 'save your ass' file." He laughed.

On June 5, 1968, the report was officially published and copies were delivered in person to the Air Force and LTV. Within a week, flight tests were begun at Edwards Air Force Base in California. Searle Lawson was sent to California as Goodrich's representative. Within approximately two weeks, he returned because some rather unusual incidents during the tests had caused them to be canceled.

His face was grim as he related stories of several near crashes during landings—caused by brake troubles. He told me about one incident in which, upon landing, one brake was literally welded together by the intense heat developed during the test stop. The wheel locked, and the plane skidded for nearly 1500 feet before coming to a halt. The plane was jacked up and the wheel removed. The fused parts within the brake had to be pried apart.

Lawson had returned to Troy from California that same day, and that evening, he and others of the Goodrich engineering department left for Dallas for a high-level conference with LTV.

That evening I left work early and went to see my attorney. After I told him the story, he advised that, while I was probably not actually guilty of fraud, I was certainly part of a conspiracy to defraud. He advised me to go to the Federal Bureau of Investigation and offered to arrange an appointment. The following week he took me to the Dayton office of the FBI, and after I had been warned that I would not be immune from prosecution, I disclosed the A7D matter to one of the agents. The agent told me to say nothing about the episode to anyone and to report any further incident to him. He said he would forward the story to his superiors in Washington.

A few days later, Lawson returned from the conference in Dallas and said that the Air Force, which had previously approved the qualification report, had suddenly rescinded that approval and was demanding to see some of the raw test data taken during the tests. I gathered that the FBI had passed the word.

Finally, early in October 1968, Lawson submitted his resignation, to take effect on October 25. On October 18, I submitted my own resignation, to take effect on November 1. In my resignation, addressed to Russell Line, I cited the A7D report and stated: "As you are aware, this report contained numerous deliberate and willful misrepresentations which, according to legal counsel, constitute fraud and expose both myself and others to criminal charges of conspiracy to defraud. . . . The events of the past seven months have created an atmosphere of deceit and distrust in which it is impossible to work . . . ."

On October 25, I received a sharp summons to the office of Bud Sunderman. As chief engineer at the Troy plant, Sunderman was responsible for the entire engineering division. Tall and graying, impeccably dressed at all times, he was capable of producing a dazzling smile or a hearty chuckle or immobilizing his face into marble hardness, as the occasion required.

I faced the marble hardness when I reached his office. He motioned me to a chair. "I have your resignation here," he snapped, "and I must say you have made some rather shocking, I might even say irresponsible, charges. This is very serious."

Before I could reply, he was demanding an explanation "I want to know exactly what the fraud is in connection with the A7D and how you can dare accuse this company of such a thing!"

I started to tell some of the things that had happened during the testing, but he shut me off saying, "There's nothing wrong with anything we've done here. You aren't aware of all the things that have been going on behind the scenes. If you had known the true situation, you would never have made these charges." He said that in view of my apparent "disloyalty" he had decided to accept my resignation "right now," and said it would be better for all concerned if I left the plant immediately. As I got up to leave he asked me if I intended to "carry this thing further."

I answered simply, "Yes," to which he replied, "Suit yourself." Within twenty minutes, I had cleaned out my desk and left. Forty-eight hours later, the B. F. Goodrich Company recalled the qualification report and the four-disk brake, announcing that it would replace the brake with a new, improved, five-disk brake at no cost to LTV.

Ten months later, on August 13, 1969, I was the chief government witness at a hearing conducted before Senator William Proxmire's Economy in Government Subcommittee of the Congress's Joint Economic Committee. I related the A7D story to the committee, and my testimony was supported by Searle Lawson, who followed me to the witness stand. Air Force officers also testified, as well as a four-man team from the General Accounting Office, which had conducted an investigation of the A7D brake at the request of Senator Proxmire. Both Air Force and GAO investigators declared that the brake was dangerous and had not been tested properly.

Testifying for Goodrich was R. G. Jeter, vice-president and general counsel of the company, from the Akron headquarters. Representing the Troy plant was Robert Sink. These two denied any wrongdoing on the part of the Goodrich Company, despite expert testimony to the contrary by Air Force and GAO officials. Sink was quick to deny any connection with the writing of the report or of directing any falsifications, claiming to be on the West Coast at the time. John Warren was the man who supervised its writing, said Sink.

As for me, I was dismissed as a high-school graduate with no technical training, while Sink testified that Lawson was a young, inexperienced engineer. "We tried to give him guidance," Sink testified, "but he preferred to have his own convictions."

About changing the data and figures in the report, Sink said: "When you take data from several different sources, you have to rationalize among those data what is the true story. This is part of your engineering know-how." He admitted that changes had been made in the data, "but only to make them more consistent with the overall picture of the data that is available."

Jeter pooh-poohed the suggestion that anything improper occurred, saying: "We have thirty-odd engineers at this plant . . . and I say to you that it is incredible that these men would stand idly by and see reports changed or falsified. . . . I mean you just do not have to do that working for anybody. . . . Just nobody does that."

The four-hour hearing adjourned with no real conclusion reached by the committee. But, the following day the Department of Defense made sweeping changes in its inspection, testing and reporting procedures. A spokesman for the DOD said the changes were a result of the Goodrich episode.

The A7D is now in service, sporting a Goodrich-made five-disk brake, a brake that works very well, I'm told. Business at the Goodrich plant is good. Lawson is now an engineer for LTV and has been assigned to the A7D project. And I am now a newspaper reporter.

At this writing, those remaining at Goodrich are still secure in the same positions, all except Russell Line and Robert Sink. Line has been rewarded with a promotion to production superintendent, a large step upward on the corporate ladder. As for Sink, he moved up into Line's old job.

SUPPLEMENTARY READING FOR PART ONE

Acton, H. B. *The Morals of Markets: An Ethical Exploration.* London: Longman Group Limited, 1971.

Arthur, John, and William H. Shaw, eds. *Justice and Economic Distribution.* Englewood Cliffs, N.J.: Prentice-Hall, 1978.

Baumhart, R. *Ethics in Business.* New York: Holt, Reinhart and Winston, 1968.

Bell, Daniel, and Irving Kristol, eds. *Capitalism Today.* New York: Basic Books, Inc., 1970.

Bowie, Norman. *Towards a New Theory of Distributive Justice.* Amherst, Mass.: University of Massachusetts Press, 1971.

Brandt, R. B. "The Concept of Welfare." In Noel Timms and David Watson (eds.), *Talking About Welfare: Readings in Philosophy and Public Policy.* London: Routledge and Kegan Paul, 1976.

Daniels, Norman, ed. *Reading Rawls: Critical Studies of a Theory of Justice.* New York: Basic Books, 1976.

Drucker, Peter. "What is 'Business Ethics'?" *The Public Interest,* **63,** Spring 1981, pp. 18–36.

Dworkin, Gerald, Gordon Bermanto, and Peter G. Brown, eds. *Markets and Morals.* Washington, D. C.: Hemisphere Publishing Corp., 1977.

Edwards, Richard C., Michael Reich, and Thomas E. Weisskopf, eds. *The Capitalist System,* 2d. ed. Englewood Cliffs, N.J.: Prentice-Hall, 1978.

Glazer, Nathan, and Irving Kristol, eds. *The American Commonwealth, 1976.* New York: Basic Books, 1976.

Hanson, Kirk. "Corporate Decision-Making and the Public Interest." In Oliver Williams and John Houck (eds.), *The Judeo-Christian Vision and the Modern Corporation.* Notre Dame, Ind.: University of Notre Dame Press, 1982, pp. 330–339.

Harrington, Michael. *Socialism.* New York: Saturday Review Press, 1974.

Hayek, F. A. *Law, Legislation and Liberty,* vols. 1–3. Chicago, Ill.: The University of Chicago Press, 1976.

Heilbroner, Robert L. *Between Capitalism and Socialism.* New York: Random House, 1970.

———. *Marxism: For and Against.* New York: W.W. Norton & Co., 1980.

Held, Virginia. *Property, Profits and Economic Justice.* Belmont, Calif.: Wadsworth Publishing Co., 1980.

Hoffman, W. Michael, and Jennifer Moore. "What is Business Ethics: A Reply to Peter Drucker." *Journal of Business Ethics,* vol. 1, **4,** 1982.

Nash, Laura. "Ethics Without the Sermon." *Harvard Business Review,* November–December 1981, pp. 79–90.

Nozick, Robert. *Anarchy, State and Utopia.* New York: Basic Books, 1974.

Phelps, E. S. *Altruism, Morality and Economic Theory.* New York: Russell Sage Foundation, 1975.

———, ed. *Economic Justice: Selected Readings.* Baltimore: Penguin Books, 1973.

Rawls, John. *A Theory of Justice.* Cambridge, Mass.: Harvard University Press, 1971.

Rescher, Nicholas. *Distributive Justice.* New York: Bobbs-Merrill, 1966.

Schein, Edgar H. "The Problem of Moral Education for the Business Manager." *Moral Education,* vol. 8, **1,** pp. 3–14.

Singer, Peter. "Rights and the Market." In Tom L. Beauchamp and Norman E. Bowie (eds.), *Ethical Theory and Business.* N.J.: Prentice-Hall, 1979, pp. 72–83.

Wuthnow, Robert. "The Moral Crisis in American Capitalism." *Harvard Business Review,* March–April. 1982, pp. 76–84.

PART TWO
THE NATURE OF THE CORPORATION

In Part One we examined the ethical dimensions of the economic system in which business operates. Here, we turn attention to the nature and role of the corporation within that system. Reflection on the nature of the corporation is important, in part, because our understanding of the corporation shapes our beliefs about the corporation's responsibilities. If we hold that a corporation is a privately owned enterprise designed to make a profit, for example, we are likely to have a narrower view of corporate responsibility than if we hold it to be a quasi-public institution. In Chapter Four we approach the problem of the nature of the corporation from the perspective of the corporate social responsibility debate.

It is not clear that we can attribute any responsibilities to corporations at all, however, unless we can look upon them as moral agents in some sense. Does it make sense to regard corporations as moral agents, analogous to individuals? Who or what is "Gulf Oil" or "Ford Motor Company?" Chapter Five explores these and other questions about the identity and agency of corporations.

Finally, we investigate the nature of the corporation from the perspective of its internal structure and governance; in particular, we focus on the corporate board of directors. Who should sit on the board? What is and what should be the relationship between the board, management, and stockholders? How far should the board's power extend? Such questions regarding the role and composition of the board of directors are taken up in Chapter Six.

THE CORPORATE SOCIAL RESPONSIBILITY DEBATE

Traditionally it has been held that the major responsibility of business in American society is to produce goods and services and to sell them for a profit. This conception of business' role has been one of the cornerstones of its legitimacy—that is, society's belief in the right of business to exist. Recently, however, the traditional view has been questioned. Increasingly, business is being asked not only to refrain from harming society, but to contribute actively and directly to public well-being; it is expected not only to obey a multitude of legal requirements, but also to go beyond the demands of the law and exercise *moral* judgment in making its decisions. The description of some of the activities of the Chase Manhattan Bank included in this part of the text presents one corporation's response to these new expectations. Over the past decade the bank has implemented a comprehensive social responsibility program which includes fostering minority economic development, sponsoring community programs, and making $5.3 million in contributions to diverse charities in areas such as housing, health, arts, and education. What are the reasons for the changing conception of corporate social responsibility?

George Cabot Lodge views the classical conception of the role and responsibility of business as part of a comprehensive ideology, and he points to a radical shift in American ideology as the source of the problem of corporate social responsibility. Traditional ideology, Lodge believes, no longer fits reality, yet it is to this ideology which we still look for legitimacy and in terms of which we still view corporate obligation. We have not yet explicitly recognized the ideology which would legitimize the modern corporation. Since ideology is the source of our ethical standards, Lodge claims, the result of the shift is a crisis of legitimacy and confusion about the responsibilities of the corporation.

The old ideology as set forth by Lodge is an individualistic one which stresses personal struggle and fulfillment and the sanctity of private property rights. It views the community as nothing more than the sum total of the individuals who make it up. Consequently, the welfare of the community is identified with the sum of the welfares of its members, and the pursuit of individual satisfaction is considered the only regulatory device needed to produce the public good. Government regulation is kept to the minimum needed to guard individual freedom.

In the context of the traditional ideology, businesses are understood as pieces of private property, instruments of their owners designed primarily to make money. Because the pressure of an "invisible hand" ensures that each entrepreneur's pursuit of his own profit will result in the good of the whole, and because businesses are the property of their owners to do with as they please, business has no other responsibility than to perform its economic function well. As economist Milton Friedman, one of the most forceful exponents of the traditional ideology, puts it, "the social responsibility of business is to increase its profits."

Why has the old ideology begun to erode and a new one begun to take its place? One answer is that today's giant corporations no longer seem to fit the old model. Usually we associate ownership with control, but the modern corporation is owned by stockholders who have little or no psychological or operational involvement in it. Some thinkers have argued that corporations can no longer accurately be viewed as private property. As ownership separates from control, corporations come to seem less like mere instruments of their owners and more like autonomous entities capable of their own goals and decisions.

The tremendous impact on and power over our society exerted by corporations also casts doubt on their private character. Some thinkers argue that social power inevitably implies social responsibility, and suggest that those who fail to exercise a responsibility commensurate with their power will lose that power. As the power of business has grown, we have become increasingly aware of the external costs—pollution, hazardous products, job dissatisfaction—corporations have passed on to society at large. These costs in turn call into question a basic assumption of the old ideology: the identity of individual and social well-being.

The corporation's evolution away from the kind of enterprise described in the traditional American ideology brings the question of corporate responsibility into sharp focus. Lodge offers us two alternatives: We can explicitly acknowledge the new, "communitarian" ideology which is already reflected in the operational realities of our institutions, and specify corporate obligations on its basis, or we can attempt to make reality fit the old ideology once again. Some, like Christopher Stone and Thomas Donaldson, take the first option, arguing that corporations are no longer merely economic institutions, but sociological institutions as well; Milton Friedman opts for the second alternative.

Although Friedman agrees with Lodge that the notion of corporate social responsibility emerges from a new ideology, he does not find this a convincing reason to support the notion. On the contrary; Friedman holds fast to the traditional values of a free market system, and rejects the idea of corporate social responsibility because he feels it is "fundamentally subversive" of these values.

It is important to realize that Friedman is not claiming that the corporation has *no* obligations. On the contrary; it is on the idea of obligation that his stand is based. Regardless of the actual relationship of ownership to control within the corporation, Friedman holds that the two *ought* not to be separate. Managers, he argues, have an obligation to carry out the desires of corporate stockholders—and, typically, these desires are to make a profit. To demand that corporate executives exercise social—as opposed to economic—responsibility is to ask them to act in some way that is not in the interest of their employers.

The businessperson who assumes social responsibility is in effect imposing taxes on consumers and stockholders, but because he or she is a private employee and not a publicly elected official, his or her action lacks legitimacy. Behind Friedman's argument lies the conviction that each social institution exists to perform a particular function. The legitimacy of corporate activity depends on its executives fulfilling and confining themselves to the role of agents serving the interests of stockholders. "Social responsibility" is the job of government, not business.

In "Why Shouldn't Corporations Be Socially Responsible?" Christoper Stone critically examines several arguments which might be used to support Friedman's position. It is often suggested that management has made a promise to maximize the profits of corporate stockholders and ought to stand by its promise but, argues Stone, this is simply not the case. There is no explicit promise or contract between managers and shareholders. Nor is it true that managers are bound by an implicit contract because they have been hired by the owners of the corporation. In reality, says Stone, shareholders have neither much power nor much interest in selecting the management of the corporation.

Even if such a contract did exist, Stone continues, it would not mean that management has an obligation to maximize profits in *every possible way*, or that the contract would supersede all other obligations. Business may have an obligation not to sell products that are dangerous to consumers, for example—such as the Ford Pinto—even if by doing so it will make a profit. A contract which required one to subordinate all moral considerations to considerations of profit would be an immoral contract, one which undermines the basis of contract itself. If such a promise had been made, argues Stone, it would be morally right to break it.

There seems to be no firm basis, Stone concludes, for the claim that management's *only* obligation is to produce a profit for corporate shareholders. To be sure, managers may have this obligation, but that does not relieve them of all other responsibilities. There are obligations more fundamental than the one Friedman describes; these may include responsibilities to consumers, employees, the surrounding community, and future generations.

In "The Social Contract: Norms for a Corporate Conscience," Thomas Donaldson calls such responsibilities "indirect obligations." He focuses on the idea of an implicit contract between business and society in an attempt to specify what such obligations might be. According to Donaldson, the very *right* of corporations to exist and operate is granted to them by society. It is society which recognizes productive organizations as single agents with special status under the law and which permits them to use natural resources and hire employees. In return, society should be permitted to demand at least that the benefits of authorizing the existence of corporations outweigh the liabilities. If Donaldson is correct, the corporation is a social entity—not merely an economic one—from the moment of its inception. His social contract theory implies that the legitimacy of corporate activity lies in the successful exercise of social responsibility.

We began our discussion of corporate social responsibility with a consideration of the decay of the traditional American ideology. And one of the cornerstones of that ideology is the notion of private property. In their article, W. Michael Hoffman and James Fisher return to the concept of property, this time in the context of corporate liability.

Friedman has argued that the corporation is a piece of private property, and that the exercise of social responsibility takes away corporate profits from those who rightfully own them—the shareholders. Lodge and others hold that corporations no longer operate as purely private institutions; therefore, one might argue that the benefits which flow from them ought to be shared collectively. Hoffman and Fisher point out that both Friedman and Lodge are assuming that property, whether private or public, is only a good; they have overlooked the fact that it can be a liability as well. Once this is understood it is no longer clear that the notion of the corporation as private property ought to be abandoned. That the corporation is private property means not only that the public may be excluded from benefiting from its profits; it also means that the public has a right to be excluded from liability for any negative effects it may cause. Thus the idea of private property allows us to hold the corporation accountable in a way in which that of public property does not.

Hoffman and Fisher also suggest that there may be some things that cannot remain private property because of the inability of individual owners to accept the liabilities. Such things, therefore, if they are to exist at all, must become public property, and all their benefits and liabilities shared collectively.

THE CORPORATION AS A MORAL AGENT

The authors included in Chapter Four examined the issue of whether the corporation ought to have moral responsibilities and offered suggestions as to what these might be. They did not, however, ask whether the corporation is the kind of entity which is capable of having responsibilities at all. Normally we associate moral responsibility with individual persons. But corporations are not individual persons; they are collections of individuals who work together to establish corporate policy, make corporate decisions, and execute corporate actions. In the 1978 *First National Bank of Boston v. Bellotti* decision the U.S. Supreme Court granted corporations the right to free speech—a right we ordinarily attribute only to individuals. It might be argued that if corporations are to receive the rights accorded persons, they should also be treated as full-fledged individuals in every way. Dissenting opinion, on the other hand, claimed that corporations are not persons, and that therefore the decision was inappropriate.

What does it mean to say that the Ford Motor Company or Gulf Oil is responsible for a particular action? Who is to blame for an immoral corporate action? Does it make sense to look at the corporation as a moral agent, analogous to a person? And if not, does this mean that we cannot judge corporate actions according to ethical standards?

Kenneth Goodpaster and John Matthews argue that there is an analogy between individual and organizational behavior, and that for this reason corporate conduct can be evaluated in moral terms. Some thinkers have claimed that only persons are capable of moral responsibility in the fullest sense, because such responsibility presupposes the ability to reason, to have intentions, and to make autonomous choices. But although the corporation is not a person in a literal sense, Goodpaster and Matthews respond, it is made up of persons. For this reason, we can project many of the attributes of individual human beings to the corporate level. We already speak of corporations having goals, values, interests, strategies. Why, ask Goodpaster and Matthews, shouldn't we also speak of the corporate conscience?

Thinkers who assume that corporations cannot exercise moral responsibility advocate trust in the "invisible hand" of the market system to "moralize" the actions of corporations. Milton Friedman is one of these. Others feel that the "hand of government" is required to ensure moral corporate behavior. Both of these views, however, fail to locate the source of responsible corporate action in the corporation itself. Both rely upon systems and forces external to the corporation. Goodpaster and Matthews argue for a third alternative: endowing the corporation with a conscience analogous to that of an individual, recognizing the ability of corporations to exercise independent moral judgment, and locating the responsibility for corporate behavior in the hands of corporate managers. This "hand of management" alternative, they admit, is not without its problems—and it requires more thorough analysis on both the conceptual and practical levels. But Goodpaster and Matthews believe that it is the best alternative of the three because it provides a framework for an inventory of corporate responsibilities and accepts corporations as legitimate members of the moral community.

Peter French develops the analogy between individual persons and corporations in detail in his article. One of the most important elements in the notion of responsibility, French points out, is that of intention. In general we do not hold persons morally responsible for unintentional acts. If we wish the idea of corporate responsibility to make sense, we must be able to discover a corporate intention. But how can a collective intend? French suggests that we make use of what he calls the Corporate Internal Decision (CID) Structure to understand the meaning of corporate intention.

The CID Structure has two major components: an organizational flowchart which indicates the "rules of the game"—the levels of responsibility within the corporate hierarchy (French calls this "the grammar of corporate decision making")—and a corporate policy which includes the beliefs, principles, and goals of the organization. Some have argued that it is precisely these characteristics that make corporations nonmoral and fundamentally different from individuals. Here French uses them in the service of corporate responsibility. A decision is a corporate decision—intended by the corporation—if it has been made in accordance with the operational flowchart and if it reflects corporate policy.

It is a crucial aspect of French's theory that a corporate intention or decision is not identical with the intentions or decisions of those within the organization. It is true that corporate action is dependent on the action of individuals in that a corporation cannot act without some human being acting. French holds that the CID Structure literally "incorporates" the actions of individuals. A corporate act is different from the acts of which it is incorporated, just as the activity of an organism is different from the activity of its parts.

If French is correct, corporations must be regarded as genuine, independent moral agents, on an equal footing with human beings. It is precisely this feature of French's position which John Danley attacks. Corporate and individual agency are *not* the same, argues Danley. The reasons in favor of "anthropological bigotry" become clear when we focus on the "moral moves" which take place after an agent has done something—especially on those of blame and punishment.

French holds that only those actions which are done in accordance with the organizational flowchart and guided by corporate policy can be counted as "corporate acts." Presumably corporate policy includes the provisions of the corporate charter, which grants corporations the right to do business as long as they obey the law. But if the members of the corporation voted to act illegally, then, Danley claims, their decision could not be described as a "corporate action" at all. It is unclear whether corporations can ever act illegally under French's theory.

Even if corporations can perform illegal acts, it is difficult to see how moral sanctions can be applied to them. Only individuals can be punished. Fines can be levied on corporations, but ultimately individuals—stockholders, consumers, employees—pay the cost. If French is correct in saying that a corporate act is not identical with the acts of individuals, however, it does not make sense to go inside the corporation to punish an individual: This is to punish a person for something he did not do. Either corporations cannot be punished at all under French's theory, Danley argues, or individuals are made to suffer in their place, and are thus relegated to the status of second-rate citizens of the moral community. French's organismic view of the corporation, concludes Danley, has some serious drawbacks. He suggests that a machine, the activities of which are dependent on persons, is a more adequate model for understanding corporate morality.

CORPORATE ACCOUNTABILITY AND THE BOARD OF DIRECTORS

Central to the issue of corporate legitimacy, responsibility, and liability taken up in Chapter Four is the issue of corporate accountability. To whom ought corporations to be accountable? How can such accountability be implemented? The authors included in Chapter Six look not to regulations imposed on the corporation from outside, but on the corporate internal structure itself for answers to these questions. Because historically the board of directors has been conceived of as one important locus of corporate accountability and because suggestions for changes in the role, election, and staffing of boards have been at the heart of several important proposals for reform, it is appropriate that they focus their attention on the nature, role, and composition of corporate boards.

Traditionally, corporate governance has been conceived on a rough analogy with the American political system. As the owners of the corporation, shareholders elect representatives—the board of directors—to establish broad objectives and direct corporate activities. The directors in turn select corporate officers to execute their policies. Management is thus accountable to the board of directors, and the board to shareholders.

But it is increasingly unclear that this picture represents the reality of corporate governance. Such thinkers as Ralph Nader, Mark Green, and Joel Seligman hold that management really controls the election of board members through its power over the machinery of proxy voting. The board, they claim, does not provide a check on the power of management; it does not really make policies or select executive officers, but routinely rubber-stamps the decisions of management.

The case of multimillion-dollar bribery by Gulf Oil executives included in this part of the text lends some credence to these claims. Gulf's board remained ignorant for more than a year after the disclosure of the payments that the company's chief executive officer and chairman of the board had been personally involved. Once aware of the payments, it seemed to be unclear about its loyalties and reluctant to exercise its authority over management.

Furthermore, as a 1978 press release from the Senate Committee on Governmental Affairs indicates, corporate boards are so tightly interlocked that what power they do have is concentrated in the hands of a small elite. The overwhelming potential for conflicts of interest further impedes boards' ability to check management power.

Nader, Green, and Seligman see an urgent need for a truly effective board which will make accountable the unbridled power of management. Their suggestions for achieving this goal include a revamping of the shareholder electoral system; the institutionalizing of a new profession, that of the professional director who devotes full time to supervising the activities of the corporation; and the prohibition of interlocking directorates.

Still other issues of corporate governance are raised by the vast power of the corporation in modern society. The traditional model of corporate governance assumes that the most important constituency of the corporation is its shareholders, and that it is primarily to shareholders that the corporation ought to be accountable. But perhaps this is not so. The view that the crucial form of corporate accountability is accountability to shareholders is based on the assumption that the corporation is a piece of private property; the shareholders are the owners of the corporation and therefore the corporation is answerable only to them. But we will see in Chapter Four that this assumption has been challenged.

Lodge has claimed that the corporation is not private property, but is really a public institution. If this is true, presumably there ought to be some way to represent all relevant constituencies of the corporation in its internal structure. Milton Freidman has argued that to ask corporations to exercise "social" power is to make them into miniature governments; but Nader, Green, and Seligman claim that corporations do in fact exert such power and that they *are* governments in a sense for this reason. To ask corporations to be accountable only to stockholders is to permit governments to exist without the consent of the governed, an idea which is fundamentally at odds with the political philosophy of the United States. The election of "public interest directors," each of whom is placed in charge of overseeing such areas as consumer protection, employee welfare, and shareholder rights, may be one way to ensure corporate accountability to those whom it affects. And Nader, Green, and Seligman propose that the board should be made up only of "outside" directors—persons who have no other relationship to the corporation.

The interpretation of the corporation as a public institution is precisely what Irving Shapiro objects to in his essay on corporate governance. Corporations are not analogous to governments, he argues. They are private enterprises formed to execute the essential task of providing goods and services—a task, Shapiro suggests, government could not perform efficiently. The corporation has an important external locus of accountability government does not: the competition engendered by the free market system. For these reasons Shapiro defends the rationale behind the present system of corporate governance; he does not believe that a radical overhaul is required.

Shapiro does not look favorably on proposals that the board contain more "outside" directors or representatives of various interest groups. Although independence of judgment is crucial in a corporate director, he fears that outside directors may lack the depth of understanding of an industry's problems necessary for informed decision making. Such directors might find themselves dependent on the explanations of the chief executive officer, and thus unable to exert adequate control over management activities. And although the presence of public interest directors on the board could generate a healthy tension, it might also lead to conflicts of interest and paralysis. A clear division of labor between boards of directors and management and a conscientious execution of their respective tasks, Shapiro concludes, are all that is necessary to produce an effective system of corporate governance that ensures accountability.

Harold William's position may be regarded as a middle way between those of Nader, Green, and Seligman and that of Shapiro. Although Williams believes that the corporation is a quasi-public institution with a far broader constituency than simply its shareholders, he holds that the existing mechanisms of corporate governance are sufficient to secure its public accountability without radical changes. He does not believe in federal chartering or in the election of "public" directors. On the other hand, Williams believes there is a need for a board of directors which is independent of management interests. He proposes that management be represented on the board only by the chief executive officer, and that the chief executive officer not be the chairman of the board as well.

chapter four
LEGITIMACY, RESPONSIBILITY, AND LIABILITY

THE ETHICAL IMPLICATIONS OF IDEOLOGY

GEORGE CABOT LODGE*

Business is said to lack a sense of social responsibility, but what is "responsibility" after all? At the least, it is, as philosopher Charles Frankel says, "the product of definite social arrangements." From such arrangements flow the do's and don'ts that constitute the more or less coercive framework by which a community assesses and controls behavior. Today the framework is in disarray. Sufficient perhaps to enable us to identify clear-cut villanies and to punish the scoundrels who perpetrate them, it is of less help in appraising the actions of many managers who in their own judgement and that of many of their peers consider their conduct justifiable and well-meaning even while large segments of public opinion believe it to be inhumane, irresponsible or corrupt.

In examining this difference of opinion it will be useful to bear in mind Frankel's "definite social arrangements." I shall call such arrangements ideology, meaning a framework of ideas which a community uses to define values and to make them explicit. Ideology is the source of legitimacy of institutions, and the justification for the authority of those who manage them. Ideology can be conveniently seen as a bridge which a community uses to get from timeless, universal, non-controversial notions such as survival, justice, economy, self-fulfillment and self-respect to the application of these notions in the real world.

The real world is made up of populations—concentrated or dispersed; of natural elements and resources—air, water, earth, oil, minerals, etc.; of institutions—General Motors, government, OPEC, the Palestine Liberation Organization. As the real world changes—either by events such as people moving to New York City or by revelation, such as of the inexorable relationships emerging between population, oil, food and money in the world—so the definition of values within the real world changes, and so ideology changes. Frequently, however, there is a lag. Communities have a propensity to linger with an old ideology after its institutions have per force departed from it. The status quo tends to use the old ideas to justify itself.

The real world of America is plainly vastly different today from what is was 20 or 50 or 100 years ago. Consequently the traditional ideology of America has also

Excerpted from "The Connection Between Ethics and Ideology" found in *Proceedings of the First National Conference on Business Ethics*, edited by W. Michael Hoffman (Waltham, Mass: The Center For Business Ethics, Bentley College, 1977). Reprinted by permission of the publisher and author.

*Department of Business Administration, Harvard Business School.

changed—for better or for worse. We are living with a new reality. Thus there are new constraints on how we define values and make them explicit. We are in transit from one ideology to another and many of the ethical dilemmas we face are the result of this transition.

Two things have happened: First, the traditional ideology of America has become inconsistent with the real world. Secondly, great institutions have departed from the traditional ideology, contributing thereby to its subversion and replacement.

We are thus looking for legitimacy and authority to ideas which are increasingly inconsistent with practice and reality. Theoretically there are two possibilities: 1) returning to the old ideology, making practice and reality conform, or 2) recognizing explicitly the new ideology and making the best of it, aligning our behavior with it, hopefully preserving what is most valuable of the old. As a practical matter, the first choice is impossible. We must do the second. Until we do so institutions will lack legitimacy; the powerful will be drained of authority; the definition of values will be unclear and what many consider unethical behavior will abound.

THE TRADITIONAL IDEOLOGY OF THE UNITED STATES

Our traditional ideology is not at all hard to identify. It is composed of five great ideas that first came to America in the eighteenth century, having been set down in seventeenth century England as "natural" laws by John Locke, among others. These ideas found fertile soil in the vast, underpopulated wilderness of America and served us well for a hundred years or so. They are now in an advanced state of erosion.
The Lockean Five are:

1. *Individualism.* This is the atomistic notion that the community is no more than the sum of the individuals in it. It is the idea that fulfillment lies in an essentially lonely struggle in what amounts to a wilderness where the fit survive—and where, if you do not survive, you are somehow unfit. Closely tied to individualism is the idea of *equality*, in the sense implied in the phrase "equal opportunity," and the idea of *contract*, the inviolate device by which individuals are tied together as buyers and sellers. In the political order in this country, individualism evolved into *interest group pluralism*, which became the preferred means of directing society.

2. *Property rights.* Traditionally, the best guarantee of individual rights was held to be the sanctity of property rights. By virtue of this concept, the individual was assured freedom from the predatory powers of the sovereign.

3. *Competition—consumer desire.* Adam Smith most eloquently articulated the idea that the uses of property are best controlled by each individual proprietor competing in an open market to satisfy individual consumer desires. It is explicit in U.S. antitrust law and practice.

4. *Limited state.* In reaction to the powerful hierarchies of medievalism, the conviction grew that the least government is the best government. We do not mind how big government may get, but we are reluctant to allow it authority or focus. And whatever happens the cry is, "Don't let it plan—particulary down there in Wash-

ington. Let it be responsive to crises and to interest groups. Whoever pays the price can call the tune."

5. *Scientific specialization and fragmentation.* This is the corruption of Newtonian mechanics which says that, if we attend to the parts, as experts and specialists, the whole will take care of itself.

There are a number of powerful American myths associated with these ideas: John Wayne as the frontiersman; rags to riches with Horatio Alger; and, most fundamentally, *the myth of material growth and progress.*

Implicit in individualsm is the notion that man has the will to acquire power, that is, to control external events, property, nature, the economy, politics or whatever. Under the concept of the limited state, the presence of this will in the human psyche meant the guarantee of progress through competition, notably when combined with the Darwinian notion that the inexorable processes of evolution are constantly working to improve on nature.

Scientific specialization has been part of this "progress," fragmenting knowledge and society while straining their adaptability. This splintering has brought us at least one hideous result: an amoral view of progress "under which nuclear ballistic missiles definitely represent progress over gunpowder and cannonballs, which in turn represent progress over bows and arrows."[1] This treacherous myth places no apparent limit on the degree to which man can gain dominion over his environment, nor does it stipulate any other ideological criteria for defining progress.

It can be argued that while the Lockean Five may be valid as ideals, in practice we have often departed from them. For example, history is replete with examples of business going to "the limited state" and seeking protection or favor. While this might be justified in the name of property rights, it had the effect of forcing the government into an active, planning mode. Or one might cite the many examples in America of ethnic communities with a high sense of interdependency, organic social constructs instead of the atomistic conglomerations of Locke. Immigrants did indeed bring a strong sense of community with them but it must be admitted that over time this sense weakened for want of nourishment from the surrounding social system. Whatever may have been our historic inconsistencies with the traditional ideology, it seems true that for most of our history it served as the principal justification for our institutional life and behavior. Departures from it were exceptional and every effort was made to minimize their significance.

Today, as I have indicated, the exceptions are overwhelming. The old ideas perform less and less well as definers of values in the real world, and many of our most important institutions have either radically departed from the old ideology or are in the process of doing so in the name of obedience to the law, efficiency, economies of scale, consumer desire, productivity, crisis and necessity.

Although many small enterprises remain comfortably and acceptably consistent with the Lockean Five and hopefully can remain so, the managers of large institutions in both the so-called private and public sectors are forced not to practice what they preach. It is this gap between the behavior of institutions and what they sometimes thoughtlessly claim as a source of authority that causes trauma. If we were to ask, what then is the ideology which would legitimize the behavior of these institutions, we would, I think, come up with five counterparts to the Lockean Five.

THE NEW IDEOLOGY

They are:

1. *Communitarianism.* The community—New York City, for example—is more than the sum of the individuals in it. It has special and urgent needs as a community, and the survival and the self-respect of the individuals in it depend on the recognition of those needs. There are few who can get their kicks à la John Wayne, although many try. Individual fulfillment for most depends on a place in a community, an identity with a whole, participation in an organic social process. And further: If the community, the factory, or the neighborhood is well designed, its members will have a sense of identity with it. They will be able to make maximum use of their capacities. If it is poorly designed, people will be correspondingly alienated and frustrated. In the complex and highly organized America of today, few can live as Locke had in mind.

Both corporations and unions have played leading roles in the creation of the circumstances which eroded the old idea of individualism and created the new. But invariably they have been ideologically unmindful of what they have done. Therefore, they have tended to linger with the old forms and assumptions even after those have been critically altered.

A central component of the old notion of individualism is the so-called protestant ethic: hard work, thrift, delayed gratification and obedience to authority. Business has extolled these virtues on the production side of things even as it has systematically undercut them on the marketing side. Advertising departments spend millions reminding us that the good life entails immediate gratification of our most lurid desires, gratification which we can buy now and pay for later. Leisure and luxury are touted as the hallmark of happiness.[2]

Our former social policy attempted to guarantee that each worker have equal opportunity. The lawyers enforcing equal employment legislation, however, have taken quite a different tack. In the case of AT&T, for example, they argued that discrimination had become institutionalized; it had become endemic to the AT&T community, and women, for example, had been slotted into certain tasks. When this kind of argument is being accepted, it is no longer necessary to prove individual discrimination in order to get redress.

The government then moved to change the makeup of the whole of AT&T so as to provide, in effect, for *equality of representation* at all levels. Without any specific charge having been brought, the company in turn agreed to upgrade 50,000 women and 6,600 minority group workers and—perhaps most significantly—to hire 4,000 men to fill traditionally female jobs such as operator and clerk. The company also agreed to pay some $15 million in compensation. Thus the issue became one of *equality of result* not of opportunity; a communitarian idea had superseded an individualistic one.

2. *Rights and duties of membership.* A most curious thing has happened to private property—it has stopped being very important. After all, what difference does it really make today whether a person *owns* or just *enjoys* property? He may get certain psychic kicks out of owning a jewel or a car or a TV set or a house—but does it really make a difference whether he owns or rents?

Even land, that most basic element of property, has gone beyond the bounds of the traditional ideology. "Land," agreed the United Nations Commission on Human Settlements in 1976, "because of the crucial role it plays in human settlements, cannot be treated as an ordinary asset controlled by individuals and subject to the pressures and inefficiencies of the market."[3]

Today there is a new right which clearly supersedes property rights in political and social importance. It is the right to survive—to enjoy income, health, and other rights associated with membership in the American community or in some component of that community, including a corporation.

These rights derive not from any individualistic action or need; they do not emanate from a contract. They are rather communitarian rights that public opinion holds to be consistent with a good community. This is a revolutionary departure from the old Lockean conception under which only the fit survive.

The utility of property as a legitimizing idea has eroded as well. It is now quite obvious that our large public corporations are not private property at all. The 1,500,000 shareholders of General Motors do not and cannot control, direct, or in any real sense be responsible for "their" company. Furthermore, the vast majority of them have not the slightest desire for such responsibility. They are investors pure and simple, and if they do not get a good return on their investment, they will put their money elsewhere.

Campaign GM and other similar attempts at stockholder agitation represent heroic but naively conservative strategies to force shareholders to behave like owners and thus to legitimize corporations as property. But such action is clearly a losing game. And it is a peculiar irony that James Roche, as GM chairman, branded such agitation as radical, as the machinations of "an adversary culture . . . antagonistic to our American ideas of private property and individual responsiblity." In truth, of course, GM is the radical; Nader et alia were acting as conservatives, trying to bring the corporation back into ideological line.

But, the reader may ask, if GM and the hundreds of other large corporations like it are not property, then what are they? The best we can say is that they are some sort of collective, floating in philosophic limbo, dangerously vulnerable to the charge of illegitimacy and to the charge that they are not amenable to community control. Consider how the management of this nonproprietary institution is selected. The myth is that the stockholders select the board of directors which in turn selects the management. This is not true, however. Management selects the board, and the board, generally speaking, blesses management.

Managers thus get to be managers according to some mystical, circular process of questionable legitimacy. Under such circumstances it is not surprising that "management's rights" are fragile and its authority waning. Alfred Sloan warned us of this trend in 1927:

There is a point beyond which diffusion of stock ownership must enfeeble the corporation by depriving it of virile interest in management upon the part of some one man or group of men to whom its success is a matter of personal and vital interest. And conversely at the same point the public interest becomes involved when the public can no longer locate some tangible personality within the ownership which it may hold responsible for the corporation's conduct.[4]

We have avoided this profound problem because of the unquestioned effectiveness of the corporate form per se. In the past, when economic growth and progress were synonymous, we preferred that managers be as free as possible from stockholder interference, in the name of efficiency. But today the definition of efficiency, the criteria for and the limitations of growth, and the general context of the corporation are all much less sure. So the myth of corporate property is becoming a vulnerability.

3. *Community need.* It was to the notion of community need that ITT appealed in 1971 when it sought to prevent the Justice Department from divesting it of Hartford Fire Insurance. The company lawyers said, in effect: "Don't visit that old idea of competition on us. The public interest requires ITT to be big and strong at home so that it can withstand the blows of Allende in Chile, Castro in Cuba, and the Japanese in general. Before you apply the antitrust laws to us, the Secretary of the Treasury, the Secretary of Commerce, and the Council of Economic Advisers should meet to decide what, in the light of our balance-of-payments problems and domestic economic difficulties, the national interest is."[5]

Note that here again it was the company arguing the ideologically radical case. The suggestion was obvious: ITT is a partner with the government—indeed with the Cabinet—in defining and fulfilling the community needs of the United States. There may be some short-term doubt about who is the senior partner, but partnership it is. This concept is radically different from the traditional idea underlying the antitrust laws—namely that the public interest emerges *naturally* from free and vigorous competition among numerous aggressive, individualistic, and preferably small companies attempting to satisfy consumer desires.

4. *Active, planning state.* It follows that the role of the state is changing radically— it is becoming the setter of our sights and the arbiter of community needs. Inevitably, it will take on unprecedented tasks of coordination, priority setting, and planning in the largest sense. It will need to become far more efficient and authoritative, capable of making the difficult and subtle tradeoffs which now confront us—for example, between environmental purity and energy supply.

Government is already big in the United States, probably bigger in proportion to our population than even in those countries which we call "socialist." Some 16 percent of the labor force now works for one or another governmental agency, and by 1980 it will be more. Increasingly, U.S. institutions live on government largess— subsidies, allowances, and contracts to farmers, corporations, and universities— and individuals benefit from social insurance, medical care, and housing allowances. The pretense of the limited state, however, means that these huge allocations are relatively haphazard, reflecting the crisis of the moment and the power of interest groups rather than any sort of coherent and objective plan.

If the role of government were more precisely and consciously defined, the government could be smaller in size. To a great extent, the plethora of bureaucracies today is the result of a lack of focus and comprehension, an ironic bit of fallout from the old notion of the limited state. With more consciousness we could also consider more fruitfully which issues are best left to local or regional planning and which, in fact, transcend the nation-state and require a more global approach.

5. *Holism—interdependence.* Finally, and perhaps most fundamentally, the old idea of scientific specialization has given way to a new consciousness of the interrelatedness of all things. Spaceship earth, the limits of growth, the fragility of our life-supporting biosphere have dramatized the ecological and philosophical truth that everything is related to everything else. Harmony between the works of man and the demand of nature is no longer the romantic plea of conservationists. It is an absolute rule of survival, and thus it is of profound ideological significance, subverting in many ways all of the Lockean ideas.

ETHICAL APPLICATIONS

Many of the ethical issues of our time can be better understood if we view them in the light of this ideological transition.

In the aftermath of Watergate came the disclosure that scores of America's most important corporations had violated the Corrupt Practices Act, making illegal contributions to political campaigns and payoffs to many politicians for presumed favors. While in general it is wrong to violate the law, there are plainly exceptions to the rule as the experience of prohibition demonstrates; there are also degrees of wrongness. Political payoffs are in a sense a perfectly natural result of the traditional ideology. If the institution of government is held in low repute, if it is indeed regarded essentially as a necessary evil and if its direction is supposed to arise from the pulling and hauling of innumerable interest groups, then it is natural that those groups will tend to use every means, fair or foul, to work their will. It is the way the system works. How do we change the system? We provide government with a more revered status, we acknowledge that it has a central role in the definition of the needs of the community and in the determination of priorities, and that this role requires a certain objective distance from special interests. We then restrict the practice of lobbying, insulate government from pressure groups and charge it with the responsibility of acting coherently in the national interest. Even as we do this we can sense the predictable threats which the Communitarian state brings: elitism, unresponsiveness and perhaps an increasing partnership between government and large corporations, replacing the adversary relationship inherent in the traditional ideology and evolving possibly into a form of corporate statism which could erode essential elements of democracy.

So without excusing the illegality of those making and receiving the payoffs or in any sense minimizing their ethical flabbiness, we must acknowledge that perhaps more important is the systemic weakness which their behavior exposed. Of equal importance is an awareness of the consequences of correcting that weakness and a precise recognition of our choices.

In this connection one of the most important uses of ideological analysis is that it helps to make explicit the full range of possibilities flowing from a change in practice. There is a propensity in any society for these possibilities to be obscured or muted by those who are seeking the change. It is perfectly possible for the United States to get the worst of Communitarianism unless we are fully alert to the choices which the transition requires of us.

Take, for example, the natural gas crisis that paralyzed the country in the winter of 1977; throwing one and a half million persons out of work and causing suffering and even death in many communities. Who and what is to blame? Some say it is regulation; others argue that it is greedy companies seeking to maximize short term profits. It is pointless and superfluous to look for villains in this matter. The problem is systemic. Sooner or later government will perceive the energy problem as the holistic one that it is and begin to offer some coherent leadership. Until it does, catastrophe will mount as will unethical behavior.

It would seem clear that the ethical corporate executive would address reality, urge government to do the coherent planning required, offer to assist—careful not to dominate or dictate—and then proceed to implement the plan with the efficiency for which U.S. corporations are justly respected. Only in this way can the investment decisions of the oil companies, for example, be both intelligent and just.

The means of achieving our energy needs can be varied. Competition in the market place may work for some of them; but clearly for others regulation and/or some sort of partnership arrangement with government will be required. Perhaps the use of a federal charter would be practical as a way of providing a broad framework for legitimate activity with a minimum of unnecessary intervention. What stands in the way of such a course of action is principally a good deal of irrelevant ideology on the part of government, business and the public in general.

The Lockheed case raises other issues of government-business relationships. In August 1975, Lockheed, a major U.S. defense contractor, admitted it had made under-the-table payments totaling at least $22 million since 1970. Part of the payments, particularly those made in Japan, were used to promote the sales of the L-1011 Tri-Star jet liner. Difficulties with both producing and selling the L-1011 had placed the company on the brink of bankruptcy in 1971 when Congress bailed it out agreeing to guarantee a $250 million loan. At the time Congress established a Loan Guarantee Board with broad powers of supervision over Lockheed. Management defended its questionable foreign payments, arguing that they were necessary to consummate foreign sales especially of the L-1011. The company also believed that such practices were "consistent with practices engaged in by numerous other companies abroad, including many of its competitors, and are in keeping with business practices in many foreign countries."[6]

Daniel J. Haughton, then chairman of Lockheed's Board, told the Senate Sub-committee on Multinational Corporations, that French competition in wide-bodied aircraft was especially serious. He submitted a newspaper article reporting that the French Defense Ministry had indulged in a variety of payments and "sweeteners" to make it the world's largest arms exporter next to the U.S. and USSR. His point was that in the interests of Lockheed's shareholders he had to do the same.

A central issue in this case is certainly the relationship between Lockheed and the U.S. Government. There are many connections. Lockheed is a major defense contractor. It is answerable to the Loan Guaranteee Board of which the Secretary of the Treasury is chairman. It is a major exporter of military aircraft. The evidence suggests that these relationships with government were and still are vague and unclear.

The government was prepared to help the company when Lockheed's banks went to bat for it in 1971 but afterwards there is little to suggest that the Loan Guarantee Board did much supervising. There is evidence that President Nixon and presumably the U.S. Government were active in persuading Japan to purchase L-1011's, but we do not know whether anyone in government knew about the $7 million paid to Yoshio Kodama for the sale of Lockheed's products there. Haughton's reference to the French is interesting. The French government obtaining business for French industry around the world in the French national interest is one matter. Lockheed bribing foreign officials in the interest of Lockheed's shareholders is clearly another. Was Lockheed acting in the national interest or its shareholder's interest? Haughton said the latter but by inference his use of the French example suggests that he was thinking of the former.

Here again clarity and explicitness are essential. The question of what U.S. business sells in the way of military equipment around the world is surely infused with the national interest. It relates to our defense posture, our diplomatic alliances and our balance of payments. Haughton's problem may well have been as much a matter of the definition of the terms of his company's partnership with government as it was of ethics.

The go-it-alone propensity of business was particularly prevalent at the end of the 1960s, manifesting itself in rampant "social responsibility" mixed with a sense of corporate omnipotence. Those were the days, for example, when powerful white urban business leaders got together supremely confident that with their wisdom and resources they could solve the problems of racism, poverty and blight that infested the cities. I heard one suggest that sending mobile libraries down through Harlem would do the trick. What these men seemed to forget or ignore was that they had neither the right nor the competence to introduce permanent irreversible changes into the social and political milieu around them. The task of renovating the ghetto was above all else a political one in which they could of course play a role but only as the political realities had been faced and dealt with. They were part of a system and it was the system which was malfunctioning.

Failure to observe this fact led to waste and bitterness. Indeed with the most ethical intentions some business leaders were downright unethical. I had a friend who owned a small paper company, employing 500 workers, located on the banks of a turgid New England stream. Seventeen paper companies dumped their effluent into this stream. In the spring of 1969 we celebrated Earth Day at Harvard. We all wore little buttons with green smiles on them. It was a beautiful day; the Charles River stunk and its banks were embroidered with beer cans and we had seminars galore. My friend came down and he really got religion—harmony with nature, holism and all the rest. He went back determined to clean up his effluent. He spent $2.5 million doing so. A few months later I read that he had gone broke, so I went up to see him. I asked him what he had learned. He was, it seemed, encased in a kind of angelic halo as he spoke of the necessity of clean water and sacrificing material things for spiritual ends. When I pointed out that the water was no cleaner, he said, "Well, that's those 17 other fellows upstream."

"How are they going to get the word?" I asked.

"Oh, they will learn from my example."

I think he thought that somehow the divinity of his image would ooze osmotically upstream.

I said, "Did it occur to you to go to the state, maybe to the several states bordering the river, perhaps even to the Environmental Protection Agency in Washington and seek strict standards, enforced, so that when you went clean everybody would go clean and the water would run clear and there would be something for your people out of work and maybe even a little something for you?"

"Oh, no," he said. "That's not the American way. Private enterprise can do the job. That's the social responsibility of business. We can't have those bureaucrats doing the job."

There is something noble, I suppose, about anyone who puts principle ahead of profits—if he knows what he is doing. That is, if my friend had said to himself, "Before I violate any one of the Lockean Five, I would rather die or go broke," we would call him a martyr. We might suggest something about the tactics of martyrdom—how it is better to have followers than not—but we would admire him. But if, on the other hand, he did what he did unmindful of the visceral control which the old ideology exerted over his perceptions and decision-making, then all we can say is that he was an ignorant, irresponsible, unethical manager who had no business managing anything.

Another problem in business leaders saying that, acting alone, they can solve our community problems is that unsophisticated people will tend to believe them, and will consequently blame business when the problems persist. Anger and violence are apt to follow.

Inside the corporation, ethical questions abound about the proper relationship between employers and employees. Work, it is said, is dehumanizing, alienating, and boring. The old notions of managerial authority rooted in property rights and contract no longer seem to be acceptable. Consequently many firms are moving away from the old notions to new ones of consensus and rights and duties of membership in which the right to manage actually comes from the managed. Consensual arrangements naturally threaten the old institutions attached to the contract both in management and labor. Trade unions are particularly anxious about the new development.

The new approaches will come easier—and more ethically—if we are mindful of the radical implications of what we are doing. The old institutions need to be treated gently so that their resistance will be minimized. There may after all be an important role for unions in the new consensual arrangements. Workers' participation in management can be made more effective by a properly functioning union. But both management and labor need to learn new techniques. Also, the new way is not without its own threats and dangers. The idea of the contract after all emerged to protect the individual from the worst abuses of ancient and medieval communitarianism. Unless we are careful, hideous injustice can be perpetrated in the name of consensus; all sorts can be excluded, for example, the weak, the black, the white, women, men, or those we merely do not like.

In conclusion, it is worth emphasizing that perhaps the most appalling ethical problems which we may face are those associated with the new ideology. How can we preserve and protect some of the most cherished attributes of the old as we move inexorably toward the new? How can we safeguard individual rights in the face of communitarianism, the rights of privacy and choice and liberty; how can we avoid the grim excesses of centralized, authoritarian, impersonal bureaucracy; how can we insure democracy at all levels of our political system; and how can we enliven efficiency as the definition of what is a cost and what is a benefit becomes increasingly obscure? The general answer to these questions is alertness, consciousness of what is happening. This is no time to sing the old hymns. Rather it is essential to compose new ones. It is after all not beyond the realm of possibility that we could find ourselves marching stolidly into a Communitarian prison lustily singing Lockean hymns.

The specific answers must flow from specific situations. The ethical manager will be realistic about both the situation and the roles and functions of business, government and other institutions in dealing with it. He will also bear in mind the long-term interests of the persons and communities which he affects, having the courage to place those interests above his own short-term preoccupations. He will see his problems in the context of all of their relationships, employing his skills as a generalist to help produce appropriately systemic solutions.

NOTES

1. Gunter Stent, *The Coming of the Golden Age: A View of the End of Progress* (Garden City, Natural History Press, 1969), p. 90.

2. See Daniel Bell, "The Cultural Contradictions of Capitalism," *The Public Interest*, Fall 1970, pp 38–39.

3. Quoted in *The New York Times*, June 7, 1976.

4. Quoted in Herman E. Drooss and Charles Gilbert, *American Business History* (Englewood Cliffs: Prentice Hall, 1972), p. 264.

5. See *Hearings Before the Committee on the Judiciary, United States Senate, 92nd Congress, Second Session on Nomination of Richard G. Kleindienst of Arizona to be Attorney General* (Washington, Government Printing Office, 1972).

6. "Lockheed Says It Paid $22 Million to Get Contracts," *The Wall Street Journal*, August 4, 1975.

THE SOCIAL RESPONSIBILITY OF BUSINESS IS TO INCREASE ITS PROFITS

MILTON FRIEDMAN*

When I hear businessmen speak eloquently about the "social responsibilities of business in a free-enterprise system," I am reminded of the wonderful line about the Frenchman who discovered at the age of 70 that he had been speaking prose all his life. The businessmen believe that they are defending free enterprise when they declaim that business is not concerned "merely" with profit but also with promoting desirable "social" ends; that business has a "social conscience" and takes seriously its responsibilities for providing employment, eliminating discrimination, avoiding pollution and whatever else may be the catchwords of the contemporary crop of reformers. In fact they are— or would be if they or anyone else took them seriously—preaching pure and unadulterated socialism. Businessmen who talk this way are unwitting puppets of the intellectual forces that have been undermining the basis of a free society these past decades.

The discussions of the "social responsibilities of business" are notable for their analytical looseness and lack of rigor. What does it mean to say that "business" has responsibilities? Only people can have responsibilities. A corporation is an artificial person and in this sense may have artificial responsibilities, but "business" as a whole cannot be said to have responsibilities, even in this vague sense. The first step toward clarity in examining the doctrine of the social responsibility of business is to ask precisely what it implies for whom.

Presumably, the individuals who are to be responsible are businessmen, which means individual proprietors or corporate executives. Most of the discussion of social responsibility is directed at corporations, so in what follows I shall mostly neglect the individual proprietors and speak of corporate executives.

In a free-enterprise, private-property system, a corporate executive is an employee of the owners of the business. He has direct responsibility to his employers. That responsibility is to conduct the business in accordance with their desires, which generally will be to make as much money as possible while conforming to the basic rules of the society, both those embodied in law and those embodied in ethical custom. Of course, in some cases his employers may have a different objective. A group of persons might establish a corporation for an eleemosynary purpose—for example, a hospital or a school. The manager of such a corporation will not have money profit as his objectives but the rendering of certain services.

In either case, the key point is that, in his capacity as a corporate executive, the manager is the agent of the individuals who own the corporation or establish the eleemosynary institution, and his primary responsibility is to them.

Needless to say, this does not mean that it is easy to judge how well he is performing his task. But at least the criterion of performance is straightforward, and the persons among whom a voluntary contractual arrangement exists are clearly defined.

*Hoover Institute on War, Revolution, and Peace, Stanford University.

Of course, the corporate executive is also a person in his own right. As a person, he may have many other responsibilities that he recognizes or assumes voluntarily—to his family, his conscience, his feelings of charity, his church, his clubs, his city, his country. He may feel impelled by these responsibilities to devote part of his income to causes he regards as worthy, to refuse to work for particular corporations, even to leave his job, for example, to join his country's armed forces. If we wish, we may refer to some of these responsibilities as "social responsibilities." But in these respects he is acting as a principal, not an agent; he is spending his own money or time or energy, not the money of his employers or the time or energy he has contracted to devote to their purposes. If these are "social responsibilities," they are the social responsibilities of individuals, not of business.

What does it mean to say that the corporate executive has a "social responsibility" in 'his capacity as businessman? If this statement is not pure rhetoric, it must mean that he is to act in some way that is not in the interest of his employers. For example, that he is to refrain from increasing the price of the product in order to contribute to the social objective of preventing inflation, even though a price increase would be in the best interests of the corporation. Or that he is to make expenditures on reducing pollution beyond the amount that is in the best interests of the corporation or that is required by law in order to contribute to the social objective of improving the environment. Or that, at the expense of corporate profits, he is to hire "hardcore" unemployed instead of better qualified available workmen to contribute to the social objective of reducing poverty.

In each of these cases, the corporate executive would be spending someone else's money for a general social interest. Insofar as his actions in accord with his "social responsibility" reduce returns to stockholders, he is spending their money. Insofar as his actions raise the price to customers, he is spending the customers' money. Insofar as his actions lower the wages of some employees, he is spending their money.

The stockholders or the customers or the employees could separately spend their own money on the particular action if they wished to do so. The executive is exercising a distinct "social responsibility," rather than serving as an agent of the stockholders or the customers or the employees, only if he spends the money in a different way than they would have spent it.

But if he does this, he is in effect imposing taxes, on the one hand, and deciding how the tax proceeds shall be spent, on the other.

This process raises political questions on two levels: principle and consequences. On the level of political principle, the imposition of taxes and the expenditure of tax proceeds are governmental functions. We have established elaborate constitutional, parliamentary and judicial provisions to control these functions, to assure that taxes are imposed so far as possible in accordance with the preferences and desires of the public—after all, "taxation without representation" was one of the battle cries of the American Revolution. We have a system of checks and balances to separate the legislative function of imposing taxes and enacting expenditures from the executive function of collecting taxes and administering expenditure programs and from the judicial function of mediating disputes and interpreting the law.

Here the businessman—self-selected or appointed directly or indirectly by stockholders—is to be simultaneously legislator, executive and jurist. He is to decide whom to tax by how much and for what purpose, and he is to spend the proceeds—all this guided only by general exhortations from on high to restrain inflation, improve the environment, fight poverty and so on and on.

The whole justification for permitting the corporate executive to be selected by the stockholders is that the executive is an agent serving the interests of his principal. This justification disappears when the corporate executive imposes taxes and spends the proceeds for "social" purposes. He becomes in effect a public employee, a civil servant, even though he remains in name an employee of a private enterprise. On grounds of political principle, it is intolerable that such civil servants—insofar as their actions in the name of social responsibility are real and not just window-dressing—should be selected as they are now. If they are to be civil servants, then they must be elected through a political process. If they are to impose taxes and make expenditures to foster "social" objectives, then political machinery must be set up to make the assessment of taxes and to determine through a political process the objectives to be served.

This is the basic reason why the doctrine of "social responsibility" involves the acceptance of the socialist view that political mechanisms, not market mechanisms, are the appropriate way to determine the allocation of scarce resources to alternative uses.

On the grounds of consequences, can the corporate executive in fact discharge his alleged "social responsibilities"? On the other hand, suppose he could get away with spending the stockholders' or customers' or employees' money. How is he to know how to spend it? He is told that he must contribute to fighting inflation. How is he to know what action of his will contribute to that end? He is presumably an expert in running his company—in producing a product or selling it or financing it. But nothing about his selection makes him an expert on inflation. Will his holding down the price of his product reduce inflationary pressure? Or, by leaving more spending power in the hands of his customers, simply divert it elsewhere? Or, by forcing him to produce less because of the lower price, will it simply contribute to shortages? Even if he could answer these questions, how much cost is he justified in imposing on his stockholders, customers and employees for this social purpose? What is his appropriate share and what is the appropriate share of others?

And, whether he wants to or not, can he get away with spending his stockholders', customers' or employees' money? Will not the stockholders fire him? (Either the present ones or those who take over when his actions in the name of social responsibility have reduced the corporation's profits and the price of its stock.) His customers and his employees can desert him for other producers and employers less scrupulous in exercising their social responsibilities.

This facet of "social responsibility" doctrine is brought into sharp relief when the doctrine is used to justify wage restraint by trade unions. The conflict of interest is naked and clear when union officials are asked to subordinate the interest of their members to some more general purpose. If the union officials try to enforce wage restraint, the consequence is likely to be wildcat strikes, rank-and-file revolts and the emergence of strong competitors for their jobs. We thus have the ironic phenomenon that union leaders—at least in the U.S.—have objected to Government interference with the market far more consistently and courageously than have business leaders.

The difficulty of exercising "social responsibility" illustrates, of course, the great virtue of private competitive enterprise—it forces people to be responsible for their own actions and makes it difficult for them to "exploit" other people for either selfish or unselfish purposes. They can do good—but only at their own expense.

Many a reader who has followed the argument this far may be tempted to remonstrate that it is all well and good to speak of Government's having the responsibility to impose taxes and determine expenditures for such "social" purposes as controlling pollution or training the hard-core unemployed, but that the problems are too urgent to wait on the slow course of political processes, that the exercise of social responsibility by businessmen is a quicker and surer way to solve pressing current problems.

Aside from the question of fact—I share Adam Smith's skepticism about the benefits that can be expected from "those who affected to trade for the public good"—this argument must be rejected on grounds of principle. What it amounts to is an assertion that those who favor the taxes and expenditures in question have failed to persuade a majority of their fellow citizens to be of like mind and that they are seeking to attain by undemocratic procedures what they cannot attain by democratic procedures. In a free society, it is hard for "evil" people to do "evil," especially since one man's good is another's evil.

I have, for simplicity, concentrated on the special case of the corporate executive, except only for the brief digression on trade unions. But precisely the same argument applies to the newer phenomenon of calling upon stockholders to require corporations to exercise social responsibility (the recent G.M. crusade for example). In most of these cases, what is in effect involved is some stockholders trying to get other stockholders (or customers or employees) to contribute against their will to "social" causes favored by the activists. Insofar as they succeed, they are again imposing taxes and spending the proceeds.

The situation of the individual proprietor is somewhat different. If he acts to reduce the returns of his enterprise in order to exercise his "social responsibility," he is spending his own money, not someone else's. If he wishes to spend his money on such purposes, that is his right, and I cannot see that there is any objection to his doing so. In the process, he, too, may impose costs on employees and customers. However, because he is far less likely than a large corporation or union to have monopolistic power, any such side effects will tend to be minor.

Of course, in practice the doctrine of social responsibility is frequently a cloak for actions that are justified on other grounds rather than a reason for those actions.

To illustrate, it may well be in the long-run interest of a corporation that is a major employer in a small community to devote resources to providing amenities to that community or to improving its government. That may make it easier to attract desirable employees, it may reduce the wage bill or lessen losses from pilferage and sabotage or have other worthwhile effects. Or it may be that, given the laws about the deductibility of corporate charitable contributions, the stockholders can contribute more to charities they favor by having the corporation make the gift than by doing it themselves, since they can in that way contribute an amount that would otherwise have been paid as corporate taxes.

In each of these—and many similar—cases, there is a strong temptation to rationalize these actions as an exercise of "social responsibility." In the present climate of opinion, with its widespread aversion to "capitalism," "profits," the "soulless corporation" and so on, this is one way for a corporation to generate goodwill as a by-product of expenditures that are entirely justified in its own self-interest.

It would be inconsistent of me to call on corporate executives to refrain from this hypocritical window-dressing because it harms the foundations of a free society. That would be to call on them to exercise a "social responsibility"! If our institutions, and the attitudes of the public make it in their self-interest to cloak their actions in this way, I cannot summon much indignation to denounce them. At the same time, I can express admiration for those individual proprietors or owners of closely held corporations or stockholders of more broadly held corporations who disdain such tactics as approaching fraud.

Whether blameworthy or not, the use of the cloak of social responsibility, and the nonsense spoken in its name by influential and prestigious businessmen, does clearly harm the foundations of a free society. I have been impressed time and again by the schizophrenic character of many businessmen. They are capable of being extremely far-sighted and clear-headed in matters that are internal to their businesses. They are incredibly short-sighted and muddle-headed in matters that are outside their businesses but affect the possible survival of business in general. This short-sightedness is strikingly exemplified in the calls from many businessmen for wage and price guidelines or controls or income policies. There is nothing that could do more in a brief period to destroy a market system and replace it by a centrally controlled system than effective governmental control of prices and wages.

The short-sightedness is also exemplified in speeches by businessmen on social responsibility. This may gain them kudos in the short run. But it helps to strengthen the already too prevalent view that the pursuit of profits is wicked and immoral and must be curbed and controlled by external forces. Once this view is adopted, the external forces that curb the market will not be the social consciences, however highly developed, of the pontificating executives; it will be the iron fist of Government bureaucrats. Here, as with price and wage controls, businessmen seem to me to reveal a suicidal impulse.

The political principle that underlies the market mechanism is unanimity. In an ideal free market resting on private property, no individual can coerce any other, all cooperation is voluntary, all parties to such cooperation benefit or they need not participate. There are no values, no "social" responsibilities in any sense other than the shared values and responsibilities of individuals. Society is a collection of individuals and of the various groups they voluntarily form.

The political principle that underlies the political mechanism is conformity. The individual must serve a more general social interest—whether that be determined by a church or a dictator or a majority. The individual may have a vote and say in what is to be done, but if he is overruled, he must conform. It is appropriate for some to require others to contribute to a general social purpose whether they wish to or not.

Unfortunately, unanimity is not always feasible. There are some respects in which conformity appears unavoidable, so I do not see how one can avoid the use of the political mechanism altogether.

But the doctrine of "social responsibility" taken seriously would extend the scope of the political mechanism to every human activity. It does not differ in philosophy from the most explicitly collectivist doctrine. It differs only by professing to believe that collectivist ends can be attained without collectivist means. That is why, in my book "Capitalism and Freedom," I have called it a "fundamentally subversive doctrine" in a free society, and have said that in such a society, "there is one and only one social responsibility of business—to use its resources and engage in activities designed to increase its profits so long as it stays within the rules of the game, which is to say, engages in open and free competition without deception or fraud."

WHY SHOULDN'T CORPORATIONS BE SOCIALLY RESPONSIBLE?

CHRISTOPHER D. STONE*

The opposition to corporate social responsibility comprises at least four related though separable positions. I would like to challenge the fundamental assumption that underlies all four of them. Each assumes in its own degree that the managers of the corporation are to be steered almost wholly by profit, rather than by what they think proper for society on the whole. Why should this be so? So far as ordinary morals are concerned, we often expect human beings to act in a fashion that is calculated to benefit others, rather than themselves, and commend them for it. Why should the matter be different with corporations?

THE PROMISSORY ARGUMENT

The most widespread but least persuasive arguments advanced by the "antiresponsibility" forces take the form of a moral claim based upon the corporation's supposed obligations to its shareholders. In its baldest and least tenable form, it is presented as though management's obligation rested upon the keeping of a promise—that the management of the corporation "promised" the shareholders that it would maximize the shareholders' profits. But this simply isn't so.

Consider for contrast the case where a widow left a large fortune goes to a broker, asking him to invest and manage her money so as to maximize her return. The broker, let us suppose, accepts the money and the conditions. In such a case, there would be no disagreement that the broker had made a promise to the widow, and if he invested her money in some venture that struck his fancy for any reason other than that it would increase her fortune, we would be inclined to advance a moral (as well, perhaps, as a legal) claim against him. Generally, at least, we believe in the keeping of promises; the broker, we should say, had violated a promissory obligation to the widow.

But that simple model is hardly the one that obtains between the management of major corporations and their shareholders. Few if any American shareholders ever put their money into a corporation upon the express promise of management that the company would be operated so as to maximize their returns. Indeed, few American shareholders ever put their money directly *into* a corporation at all. Most of the shares outstanding today were issued years ago and found their way to their current shareholders only circuitously. In almost all cases, the current shareholder gave his money to some prior shareholder, who, in turn, had gotten it from B, who, in turn, had gotten it from A, and so on back to the purchaser of the original issue, who, many years before, had bought the shares through an underwriting syndicate. In the course

*Department of Law, University of Southern California.

of these transactions, one of the basic elements that exists in the broker case is missing: The manager of the corporation, unlike the broker, was never even offered a chance to refuse the shareholder's "terms" (if they were that) to maximize the shareholder's profits.

There are two other observations to be made about the moral argument based on a supposed promise running from the management to the shareholders. First, even if we do infer from all the circumstances a "promise" running from the management to the shareholders, but not one, or not one of comparable weight running elsewhere (to the company's employees, customers, neighbors, etc.), we ought to keep in mind that as a moral matter (which is what we are discussing here) sometimes it is deemed morally justified to break promises (even to break the law) in the furtherance of other social interests of higher concern. Promises can advance moral arguments, by way of creating presumptions, but few of us believe that promises, per se, can end them. My promise to appear in class on time would not ordinarily justify me from refusing to give aid to a drowning man. In other words, even if management *had* made an express promise to its shareholders to "maximize your profits," (a) I am not persuaded that the ordinary person would interpret it to mean "maximize *in every way you can possibly get away with*, even if that means polluting the environment, ignoring or breaking the law"; and (b) I am not persuaded that, even if it were interpreted as so blanket a promise, most people would not suppose it ought—morally—to be broken in some cases.

Finally, even if, in the face of all these considerations, one still believes that there is an overriding, unbreakable, promise of some sort running from management to the shareholders, I do not think that it can be construed to be any stronger than one running to *existent* shareholders, arising from *their* expectations as measured by the price *they* paid. That is to say, there is nothing in the argument from promises that would wed us to a regime in which management was bound to maximize the income of shareholders. The argument might go so far as to support compensation for existent shareholders if the society chose to announce that henceforth management would have other specified obligations, thereby driving the price of shares to a lower adjustment level. All future shareholders would take with "warning" of, and a price that discounted for, the new "risks" of shareholding (i.e., the "risks" that management might put corporate resources to *pro bonum* ends).

THE AGENCY ARGUMENT

Related to the promissory argument but requiring less stretching of the facts is an argument from agency principles. Rather than trying to infer a promise by management to the shareholders, this argument is based on the idea that the shareholders designated the management their agents. This is the position advanced by Milton Friedman in his *New York Times* article. "The key point," he says, "is that . . . the manager is the agent of the individuals who own the corporation. . . ."[1]

Friedman, unfortunately, is wrong both as to the state of the law (the directors are *not* mere agents of the shareholders)[2] and on his assumption as to the facts of corporate life (surely it is closer to the truth that in major corporations the shareholders are *not*, in any meaningful sense, selecting the directors; management is more often using its control over the proxy machinery to designate who the directors shall be, rather than the other way around).

What Friedman's argument comes down to is that for some reason the directors ought morally to consider themselves more the agents for the shareholders than for the customers, creditors, the state, or the corporation's immediate neighbors. But why? And to what extent? Throwing in terms like "principal" and "agent" begs the fundamental questions.

What is more, the "agency" argument is not only morally inconclusive, it is embarassingly at odds with the way in which supposed "agents" actually behave. If the managers truly considered themselves the agents of the shareholders, as agents they would be expected to show an interest in determining how their principals wanted them to act—and to act accordingly. In the controversy over Dow's production of napalm, for example, one would expect, on this model, that Dow's management would have been glad to have the napalm question put to the shareholders at a shareholders' meeting. In fact, like most major companies faced with shareholder requests to include "social action" measures on proxy statements, it fought the proposal tooth and claw.[3] It is a peculiar agency where the "agents" will go to such lengths (even spending tens of thousands of dollars of their "principals' " money in legal fees) to resist the determination of what their "principals" want.

THE ROLE ARGUMENT

An argument so closely related to the argument from promises and agency that it does not demand extensive additional remarks is a contention based upon supposed considerations of *role*. Sometimes in moral discourse, as well as in law, we assign obligations to people on the basis of their having assumed some role or status, independent of any specific verbal promise they made. Such obligations are assumed to run from a captain to a seaman (and vice versa), from a doctor to a patient, or from a parent to a child. The antiresponsibility forces are on somewhat stronger grounds resting their position on this basis, because the model more nearly accords with the facts—that is, management never actually promised the shareholders that they would maximize the shareholders' investment, nor did the shareholders designate the directors their agents for this express purpose. The directors and top management are, as lawyers would say, fiduciaries. But what does this leave us? So far as the directors are fiduciaries of the shareholders in a legal sense, of course they are subject to the legal limits on fiduciaries—that is to say, they cannot engage in self-dealing, "waste" of corporate assets, and the like. But I do not understand any proresponsibility advocate to be demanding such corporate largesse as would expose the officers to legal liability; what we are talking about are expenditures on, for example, pollution control, above the amount the company is required to pay by law, but less than an amount so extravagant as to constitute a violation of these legal fiduciary duties. (Surely no court in America today would enjoin a corporation from spending more to reduce pollution than the law requires.) What is there about assuming the role of corporate officer that makes it immoral for a manager to involve a corporation in these expenditures? A father, one would think, would have stronger obligations to his children by virtue of his status than a corporate manager to the corporation's shareholders. Yet few would regard it as a compelling moral argument if a father were to distort facts about his child on a scholarship application form on the grounds that he had obligations to advance his child's career; nor would we consider it a strong moral argument if a father were to leave unsightly refuse piled on his lawn, spilling over into the street, on the plea that he had obligations to give every moment of his attention to his children, and was thus too busy to cart his refuse away.

Like the other supposed moral arguments, the one from role suffers from the problem that the strongest moral obligations one can discover have at most only prima facie force, and it is not apparent why those obligations should predominate over some contrary social obligations that could be advanced.

Then too, when one begins comparing and weighing the various moral obligations, those running back to the shareholder seem fairly weak by comparison to the claims of others. For one thing, there is the consideration of alternatives. If the shareholder is dissatisfied with the direction the corporation is taking, he can sell out, and if he does so quickly enough, his losses may be slight. On the other hand, as Ted Jacobs observes, "those most vitally affected by corporate decisions—people who work in the plants, buy the products, and consume the effluents—cannot remove themselves from the structure with a phone call."[4]

THE "POLESTAR" ARGUMENT

It seems to me that the strongest moral argument corporate executives can advance for looking solely to profits is not one that is based on a supposed express, or even implied promise to the shareholder. Rather, it is one that says, if the managers act in such fashion as to maximize profits—if they act *as though* they had promised the shareholders they would do so—then it will be best for all of us. This argument might be called the polestar argument, for its appeal to the interests of the shareholders is not justified on supposed obligations to the shareholders per se, but as a means of charting a straight course toward what is best for the society as a whole.

Underlying the polestar argument are a number of assumptions—some express and some implied. There is, I suspect, an implicit positivism among its supporters—a feeling (whether its proponents own up to it or not) that moral judgments are peculiar, arbitrary, or vague—perhaps even "meaningless" in the philosophic sense of not being amenable to rational discussion. To those who take this position, profits (or sales, or price-earnings ratios) at least provide some solid, tangible standard by which participants in the organization can measure their successes and failures, with some efficiency, in the narrow sense, resulting for the entire group. Sometimes the polestar position is based upon a related view—not that the moral issues that underlie social choices are meaningless, but that resolving them calls for special expertise. "I don't know any investment adviser whom I would care to act in my behalf in any matter except turning a profit. . . . The value of these specialists . . . lies in their limitations; they ought not allow themselves to see so much of the world that they become distracted."[5] A slightly modified point emphasizes not that the executives lack moral or social expertise per se, but that they lack the social authority to make policy choices. Thus, Friedman objects that if a corporate director took "social purposes" into account, he would become "in effect a public employee, a civil servant. . . . On grounds of political principle, it is intolerable that such civil servants . . . should be selected as they are now."[6]

I do not want to get too deeply involved in each of these arguments. That the moral judgments underlying policy choices are vague, I do not doubt—although I am tempted to observe that when you get right down to it, a wide range of actions taken by businessmen every day, supposedly based on solid calculations of "profit," are probably as rooted in hunches and intuition as judgments of ethics. I do not disagree either that, ideally, we prefer those who have control over our lives to be politically accountable; although here, too, if we were to pursue the matter in detail we would want to inspect both the premise of this argument, that corporate managers are not *presently* custodians of discretionary power over us anyway, and also its logical implications: Friedman's point that "if they are to be civil servants, then they must be selected through a political process"[7] is not, as Friedman regards it, a *reductio ad absurdum*—not, at any rate, to Ralph Nader and others who want publicly elected directors.

The reason for not pursuing these counterarguments at length is that, whatever reservations one might have, we can agree that there is a germ of validity to what the "antis" are saying. But their essential failure is in not pursuing the alternatives. Certainly, *to the extent* that the forces of the market and the law can keep the corporation within desirable bounds, it may be better to trust them than to have corporate managers implementing their own vague and various notions of what is best for the rest of us. But are the "antis" blind to the fact that there are circumstances in which the law— and the forces of the market—are simply not competent to keep the corporation under control? The shortcomings of these traditional restraints on corporate conduct are critical to understand, not merely for the defects they point up in the "antis'" position. More important, identifying where the traditional forces are inadequate is the first step in the design of new and alternative measures of corporate control.

NOTES

1. *New York Times*, September 12, 1962, sect. 6, p. 33, col. 2.

2. See, for example, *Automatic Self-Cleansing Filter Syndicate Co. Ltd. v. Cunninghame* (1906) 2 Ch. 34.

3. "Dow Shalt Not Kill," in S. Prakash Sethi, *Up Against the Corporate Wall*, Englewood Cliffs, N.J.: Prentice-Hall, 1971), pp. 236–266, and the opinion of Judge Tamm in *Medical Committee for Human Rights v. S.E.C.*, 432 F.2d 659 (D.C. Cir. 1970), and the dissent of Mr. Justice Douglas in the same case in the U.S. Supreme Court, 404 U.S. 403, 407–411 (1972).

4. Theodore J. Jacobs, "Pollution, Consumerism, Accountability," *Center Magazine* 5, 1 (January–February 1971): 47.

5. Walter Goodman, "Stocks Without Sin," *Harper's*, August 1971, p. 66.

6. *New York Times*, September 12, 1962, sec. 6, p. 122, col. 3.

7. Ibid., p. 122, cols. 3–4.

THE SOCIAL CONTRACT:
Norms for a Corporate Conscience

THOMAS DONALDSON*

In a speech to the Harvard Business School in 1969, Henry Ford II stated:

> The terms of the contract between industry and society are changing. . . . Now we are being asked to serve a wider range of human values and to accept an obligation to members of the public with whom we have no commercial transactions.

The "contract" to which Henry Ford referred concerns a corporation's *indirect* obligations. It represents not a set of formally specified obligations, but a set of binding, abstract ones. A social contract for business, if one exists, is not a typewritten contract in the real world, but a metaphysical abstraction not unlike the "social contract" between citizens and government that philosophers have traditionally discussed. Such a contract would have concrete significance, for it would help to interpret the nature of a corporation's indirect obligations, which are notoriously slippery.

The aim of this paper is to discover a corporation's indirect obligations by attempting to clarify the meaning of business's so-called "social contract." The task is challenging. Although people speak frequently of such a contract, few have attempted to specify its meaning. Although businesspeople, legislators, and academics offer examples of supposed infractions of the "contract," few can explain what justifies the contract itself.

Corporations, unlike humans, are artifacts, which is to say *we* create them. We *choose* to create corporations and we might choose either not to create them or to create different entities. Corporations thus are like political states in their need for justification.

The social contract has typically (though not always) been applied to governments. Is there any reason to suppose it is applicable to economic institutions? To productive organizations such as General Motors? One reason for doing so is that companies like General Motors are social giants. They affect the lives of millions of people, influence foreign policy, and employ more people than live in many countries of the world. Equally important is the fact that General Motors exists only through the cooperation and commitment of society. It draws its employees from society, sells its goods to society, and is given its status by society. All of this may suggest the existence of an implied agreement between it and society. If General Motors holds society responsible for providing the condition of its existence, then for what does society hold General Motors responsible? What are the terms of the social contract?

The simplest way of understanding the social contract is in the form: "We (the members of society) agree to do X, and you (the productive organizations) agree to do Y." Applying this form to General Motors (or any productive organization) means that

From *Corporations and Morality*, Copyright © 1982, pp. 36–54. Adapted by permission of Prentice-Hall, Inc., Englewood Cliffs, N.J.

*Department of Philosophy, Loyola University of Chicago.

the task of a social contract argument is to specify X, where X refers to the obligations of society to productive organizations, and to specify Y, where Y refers to the obligations of productive organizations to society.

It is relatively easy in this context to specify X, because what productive organizations need from society is:

1. Recognition as a single agent, especially in the eyes of the law.

2. The authority: (a) to own or use land and natural resources, and (b) to hire employees.

It may appear presumptuous to assume that productive organizations must be warranted by society. Can one not argue that any organization has a *right* to exist and operate? That they have this right *apart* from the wishes of society? When asking such questions, one must distinguish between claims about rights of mere organizations and claims about rights of organizations with special powers, such as productive organizations. A case can be made for the unbridled right of the Elks Club, whose members unite in fraternal activities, to exist and operate (assuming it does not discriminate against minorities or women); but the same cannot be said for Du Pont Corporation, which not only must draw on existing stores of mineral resources, but must find dumping sites to store toxic chemical by-products. Even granted that people have an inalienable right to form and operate organizations, and even granted that this right exists apart from the discretion of society, the productive organization requires special status under the law and the opportunity to use society's resources: two issues in which every member of society may be said to have a vested interest.

Conditions 1 and 2 are obviously linked to each other. In order for a productive organization to use land and hire employees (conditions of 2), it must have the authority to perform those acts as if it were an individual agent (the condition of 1). The philosophical impact of 1 should not be exaggerated. To say that productive organizations must have the authority to act as individual agents is not necessarily to affirm that they are abstract, invisible persons. Rather it is a means of stating the everyday fact that productive organizations must, for a variety of purposes, be treated as individual entities. For example, a corporation must be able to hire new employees, to sign contracts, and to negotiate purchases without getting the O.K. from *all* its employees and stockholders. The corporation *itself*, not its stockholders or managers, must be considered to be the controller of its equipment and land; for its stockholders or managers may leave, sell their shares, or die. If they do, the organization still controls its resources; it still employs its work force, and it still is obliged to honor its previous contracts and commitments.

Defining the Y side of the contract is as difficult as defining the X side is easy. It is obvious that productive organizations must be allowed to exist and act. But it is not obvious precisely why societies should allow them to exist, that is, what specific benefits society should hope to gain from the bargain. What specific functions should society expect from productive organizations? What obligations should it impose? Only one assumption can be made readily: that the members of society should demand at a minimum that the benefits from authorizing the existence of productive organizations outweigh the detriments of doing so. This is nothing other than the expectation of all voluntary agreements: that no party should be asked to conclude a contract which places him or her in a position worse than before.

Two principal classes of people stand to benefit or be harmed by the introduction of productive organizations: (1) people who consume the organizations' products, i.e., consumers; and (2) people who work in such organizations, i.e., employees. The two classes are broadly defined and not mutually exclusive. "Consumer" refers to anyone who is economically interested; hence virtually anyone qualifies as a consumer. "Employee" refers to anyone who contributes labor to the productive process of a productive organization, including managers, laborers, part-time support personnel, and (in corporations) members of the board of directors.

From the standpoint of our hypothetical consumers, productive organizations promise to *enhance the satisfaction of economic interests.* That is to say, people could hope for the introduction of productive organizations to better satisfy their interests for shelter, food, entertainment, transportation, health care, and clothing. The prima facie benefits for consumers include:

1. *Improving efficiency* through:

    a. Maximizing advantages of specialization.

    b. Improving decision-making resources.

    c. Increasing the capacity to use or acquire expensive technology and resources.

2. *Stabilizing levels of output and channels of distribution.*

3. *Increasing liability resources.*

From the standpoint of consumers, productive organizations should minimize:

1. Pollution and the depletion of natural resources.

2. The destruction of personal accountability.

3. The misuse of political power.

Productive organizations should also be viewed from the standpoint of their effects on people as workers, that is, from the standpoint of their effects upon individual laborers and craftsmen in the state of individual production who opt to work for productive organizations.

It is not difficult to discover certain prima facie benefits, such as the following:

1. Increasing income potential (and the capacity for social contributions).

2. Diffusing personal liability.

3. Adjusting personal income allocation.

From the standpoint of workers, productive organizations should minimize:

1. Worker alienation.

2. Lack of worker control over work conditions.

3. Monotony and dehumanization of the worker.

Thus the social contract will specify that these negative consequences be minimized.

Finally, a caveat must be made concerning justice. Society will grant productive organizations the conditions necessary for their existence only if they agree not to violate certain minimum standards of justice—however these are to be specified. For example, it would refuse to enact the contract if it knew that the existence of productive organizations would systematically reduce a given class of people to an inhuman existence, subsistence poverty, or enslavement.

This point, in turn, provides a clue to one of the specific tenets of the contract. Although the contract might allow productive organizations to undertake actions requiring welfare trade-offs, it would prohibit organizational acts of injustice. It might allow a corporation to lay off, or reduce the salaries of, thousands of workers in order to block skyrocketing production costs; here, worker welfare would be diminished while consumer welfare would be enhanced. But it is another matter when the company commits gross injustices in the process—for example, if it lies to workers, telling them that no layoffs are planned merely to keep them on the job until the last minute. Similarly, it is another matter when the organization follows discriminatory hiring policies, refusing to hire blacks or women, in the name of "consumer advantage." These are clear injustices of the kind that society would want to prohibit as a condition of the social contract. We may infer, then, that a tenet of the social contract will be that productive organizations are to remain within the bounds of the general canons of justice.

Determining what justice requires is a notoriously difficult task. The writings of Plato, Aristotle, and more recently, John Rawls, have shed considerable light on this subject, but unfortunately we must forego a general discussion of justice here. At a minimum, however, the application of the concept of justice to productive organizations appears to imply *that productive organizations avoid deception or fraud, that they show respect for their workers as human beings, and that they avoid any practice that systematically worsens the situation of a given group in society.* Despite the loud controversy over what justice means, most theorists would agree that justice means at least this much for productive organizations.

Our sketch of a hypothetical social contract is now complete. By utilizing the concept of rational people existing in a state of individual production, we have indicated the terms of a contract which they would require for the introduction of productive organizations. The questions asked in the beginning were: Why should corporations exist at all? What is the fundamental justification for their activities? How can we measure their performance, to say when they have performed poorly or well? A social contract helps to answer these questions. Corporations considered as productive organizations exist to enhance the welfare of society through the satisfaction of consumer and worker interests, in a way which relies on exploiting corporations' special advantages and minimizing disadvantages. This is the *moral foundation* of the corporation when considered as a productive organization. The social contract also serves as a tool to measure the performance of productive organizations. That is, when such organizations fulfill the terms of the contract, they have done well. When they do not, then society is morally justified in condemning them.

Productive organizations (whether corporations or not) that produce quality goods at low prices, that reject government favoritism, and that enhance the well-being of workers receive high marks by the standards of the social contract. Those that allow inefficiency, charge high prices, sell low-quality products, and fail to enhance the well-being of workers receive low marks. The latter organizations have violated the terms of the social contract. They must reform themselves, or lose their moral right to exist.

CORPORATE RESPONSIBILITY:
Property and Liability

W. MICHAEL HOFFMAN* and JAMES V. FISHER*

I

Daniel Bell suggested in the early seventies that the question of social responsibility would be the crux of a debate that would serve as a turning point for the corporation in modern society.[1] This thought has been echoed recently by George Lodge in his book *The New American Ideology*. Bell and Lodge are the most recent in a line of social theorists who portray our society—and particularly the world of business—as in the midst of one of the great transformations of Western civilization. Old ideas that once legitimized our institutions are eroding in the face of changing operational realities. And one of the most important of these ideas being challenged is that of private property.[2] For example Lodge says:

> A curious thing has happened to private property—it has stopped being very important. After all, *what difference* does it really make today *whether a person owns or just enjoys property?* . . . The value of property as a legitimizng idea and basis of authority has eroded as well. It is obvious that our large public corporations are not private property at all. . . . It was to (the) notion of *community need*, for example, that ITT appealed in 1971 when it sought to prevent the Justice Department from divesting it of Hartford Fire Insurance. . . . Note that here, *as so often happens, it was the company that argued the ideologically radical case.*[3] [Emphasis added]

At the heart of the entire debate is the question of the nature of the corporation. Is the corporation primarily an instrument of owners or is it an autonomous enterprise which can freely decide where its economic and moral responsibilities lie? This question arose with the advent of the megacorporation and its *de facto* separation of ownership and control. Stockholding owners today have little or no direct control over what they "own," control being for all practical purposes totally in the specially trained hands of management. With this operational shift of power to management, corporate objectives have enlarged to include at least a recognition of social obligations other than providing the greatest possible financial gain or advantage for their stockholders. But herein lie questions not only as to what these corporate social obligations are and how they are to be acted upon, but more importantly, as to what conceptually justifies and legitimizes the corporation itself now that private property theory is said to have eroded. Answers to the former clearly are dependent on answers to the latter.

Through a variety of rather slippery normative moves, corporate revisionists like Galbraith seem to argue that the great corporation must now simply be regarded as no longer a private but really a public institution. This would, presumably, provide

A longer version of this paper was presented at the Ethics and Economics Conference, University of Delaware, Nov. 12, 1977. Copyright © 1977 by W. Michael Hoffman and James V. Fisher. Reprinted by permission of the authors.

*Department of Philosophy, Bentley College.

a basis for corporate social responsibility that goes significantly beyond Friedman's "one and only one" social responsibility of business—to increase its profits.[4] Such a "corporate revolution" would appear to mean that the corporation is moving away (whether consciously or unconsciously) from legitimizing itself as *private property* to legitimizing itself as more like *common property*. In fact, perhaps the modern corporation should be seen as an exemplification of the philosophical unsoundness of private property, a strange development, to be sure, since the theory of private property has ostensibly been the essential pillar of capitalism itself.

It is important to note that the analysis which we have just sketched has focused almost exclusively on the issue of *control*. Traditionally, three elements have characterized property: the right to control, to benefit from, and to alienate (to sell or dispose of) something. An analysis of property which focuses exclusively on *control*, however, is seriously deficient, and a somewhat different picture of the question of corporate social responsibility begins to emerge when one focuses on the property rights of benefit and alienation. Clearly there are dangers to a society in the midst of radical change if it proceeds to discard basic legitimizing ideas of such social import as that of private property before it carefully considers the logic of that move.

It is an interesting fact to ponder that no fully adequate explication of a theory of justification of property acquisition has yet been achieved in modern Western social philosophy. By fully adequate is meant (a) a theory which goes beyond the "justification" that possession *is* ownership, i.e., that having an enforceable claim to something is to be understood as having the power to enforce that claim, and (b) a theory which is reasonably congruent with social realities. The lack of a fully adequate theory of property, however, does not preclude examination of the notion of property itself.

In this paper our primary interest is with the internal logic of the notion of property. The logic of *private property*, it will be argued, indicates a class of things which cannot become (or at least remain) private property, and thus the concept of private property suggests an inevitable transition from (some kinds of) private property to common property. Moreover, the theory of the "managerial revolution" will be seen to result in a gerrymandered definition of private property rather than in an innocent discarding of the idea. The social analysts who have focused on corporate control have made an important empirical observation, but, in reference to the issue of the relation of the corporation, private property, and social responsibility, they have generated serious conceptual confusion. Nor have the philosophers helped very much.

II

The property rights of control, benefit, and alienation always imply the right to exclude. Since we intend to focus on the right to benefit, the following is proposed as a working definition of *private property* in order to clarify and highlight the logic of the notion of property.[5]

> *Something (x) is the private property of someone (S) if and only if S has the right to exclude all others from the use or benefit of x.*

The right to alienate will be considered directly, though no attempt will be made in this paper to develop a satisfactory definition integrating the errant element of control.

Common property, on the other hand, must be defined in such a way as to include the individual rights of those who share ownership as well as the collective right of the owners to exclude all others.

Something (x) *is the common property of two or more people* (S_1, S_2, etc.) *if and only if S_1, S_2, etc. together have the right to exclude all others from the use or benefit of* x, *and S_1, S_2, etc. each has the right not to be excluded from the use or benefit of* x.

These definitions which emphasize the right to exclude or the right not to be excluded are, it will be argued, incomplete. There is, in fact, a *double-edged* exclusion which will become obvious when we consider the right to alienate or dispose of something.

To elaborate further the concept of common property, let us consider what it means for something to be common property. Suppose an apple tree is the common property of S_1, S_2, etc., and suppose further that it is autumn and the apple tree in question is now full of ripe apples. If S_1 were to pick one of those ripe apples and eat it, and assuming no prior agreement to refrain from eating any apples (say, for example, to save them all for pressing cider), then it would make little sense for S_2 to say to S_1: "You had no right to eat that apple since it was common property and you have now excluded the rest of us from the use or benefit of it." Here being common property would appear to mean (again in the absence of some specific agreement) that while S_1 had indeed excluded S_2 from the use or benefit of that apple, nevertheless S_2 had not been excluded from the use or benefit of the apple tree—at least as long as there is another ripe apple for S_2. The problem becomes somewhat more complicated if that autumn the apple tree in question were to have borne only one edible apple (each gets one bite?), but clearly any individual commoner's right not to be excluded cannot be taken to mean an *absolute* preclusion of any other individual commoner's actual use of the common property. What this suggests is that any notion of common property is incomplete without some (implicit or explicit) procedure for "fair-taking/using."

III

We can talk about at least three modes in which an individual makes a claim (at least a *de facto* claim) to *own* something: (1) taking possession; (2) use; and (3) alienating or *disowning* it. We will elaborate (1) briefly and then move to (3), since it is of greatest interest for the argument being developed in this paper.

Under the first category, taking possession, at least three elements can be distinguished: directly grasping something physically—what is referred to in legal contracts as "taking possession;" shaping, forming, or developing something; and taking possession by simply marking something as one's own. Note the function of the concept of intention in all three of these activities. Not only is it a necessary element in ownership, its scope extends beyond the immediate relation to the thing itself. Thus the claim to ownership extends to not only such things as unknown parts (mineral deposits, etc.) and organic results (eggs, the offspring, etc.), but also connections made by chance subsequent to the original acquisition (alluvial deposits, jetsam, etc.). This is even more explicit when I take possession by shaping or forming something. By shaping or forming it, I take more than just the immediate constituents into my possession. This applies to the organic (breeding of cattle, etc.) as well as to the reshaping of raw materials and the "forces of nature." The point that needs to be emphasized is that marking something as my own is an action that extends my intention to ownership beyond the immediate thing itself, a principle that has been long accepted in legal theory and in social practice (and in fact is at the basis of our patent laws, etc.).

It is with the third category, however, that we come to the most interesting move. In a sense when I *disown* something (e.g., by selling it) I intend the thing in its entirety (I intend, so to speak, to be rid of it) and so presuppose the claim that it is/was most completely my own.

It is at this point that we can see clearly the missing half of our definitions of property. Note that it is generally held that there are two ways of *disowning* something:

1. I may yield it to the intention (will) of another, i.e., to another's claim to ownership (usually in exchange for something I deem valuable, though it may be an outright gift as long as the recipient accepts it as his or her own); or

2. I may abandon it (as *res nullius*, the property of no one? or as now the common property of all?).

The first option is clear enough and if we pursued that discussion the questions would center around the issue of what constitutes a fair exchange. But what about the second option? Where does the logic of disowning lead us? Consider the following case:

> Suppose S, being perceptive and industrious, notes that there is a good market for tiger skins (well tanned, handsome to the eye, and luxurious to the touch). Furthermore, there are wild tigers in S's vicinity and the tigers may rightfully be appropriated by anyone and thus become the private property of the one who appropriates them (there being plenty of tigers in the vicinity relative to the number of people, etc.). By virtue of S's physical strength, cunning, and dexterity (as well as industriousness), S is able to capture several of these tigers intending to breed them in captivity for their very fine skins. Suppose further that S is successful initially in breeding the tigers, but it soon develops that they do not live long enough in captivity to grow to a size to produce sufficiently luxurious skins. But S is undaunted and eventually, by ingenuity and much hard labor, is successful in breeding stock that is long-lived, very handsome and adequately large.

> Let's suppose further that as a result of this ingenious breeding process S produces a tiger, we can call it T_n, which has two very special and advantageous characteristics: (a) T_n regularly sheds its skin, leaving each time a very fine tiger skin ready to be tanned and sold; and (b) T_n appears to be immune to the aging process and even impervious to anything which might harm or even kill it. T_n appears to be indestructible, a source, it seems, of an infinite number of fine tiger skins.

> Can it be doubted that T_n is the private property of S, that S has the right to exclude all others from the use or benefit of T_n? If anything could ever satisfy the traditional property accounts like those of Kant, Locke, and Hegel, surely S's ownership of T_n could.

Now let's imagine that one day T_n begins to show signs of a developing nasty temperament, and finally it becomes painfully clear to S that T_n is a serious danger to S (far outweighing the amazing advantages which T_n manifests), and as well a danger to those in S's immediate living unit, S's neighbors, and even S's whole community. But T_n is indestructible (or at least no one has yet found a way to do away with T_n). What is S to do? The danger is critical.

Aha! S, using what precautions are possible, takes T_n one day to the village green and in the presence of the (not too happy) villagers makes the following announcement: "I, S, who have rightfully acquired this tiger, T_n, as my private property, do here and now publicly renounce, relinquish, and abandon my property in T_n." We are assuming, of course, that S has attempted to transfer property in T_n to someone else, to yield S's property in T_n to the will of another and so into that person's possession, but understandably has found no takers.

Imagine then that the next day S's neighbor appears at S's door, cut and scratched and bearing the remains of a flock of sheep which had been destroyed during the night. "Look what your tiger has done," says the neighbor to S. "My tiger?" responds S. "I renounced and abandoned my property in that tiger yesterday. That's not *my* tiger." No doubt we would be more than a little sympathetic with the neighbor's reply: "The hell it's not *your* tiger!"

It is interesting to observe that Kant, Locke, and Hegel (to name only a few) all treat property *only* as if it were a good, i.e., as if the right to exclude all others was something always desirable (note our use of the term "goods"). Why is it that these pillars of modern Western social and political philosophy have apparently ignored what we might call the "garbage factor"? (Which is not to say that those involved with the practice of law and politics have likewise ignored this factor.) Is it because we no longer live in an age when people commonly throw their garbage out the window? Or because there are now so many of us? Or because of such things as radioactive nuclear wastes and breeder reactors? No matter. It is in any case clear that the initial definition of private property must now be revised along the following lines:

1a. *x is S's private property if and only if S has the right to exclude all others from the use or benefit of* x AND

1b. *each of these others has the right to be excluded from liability for the maleficence of* x.

The term "liability" ("responsibility" does equally as well) is chosen for etymological reasons—the root of "liability" being *ligare*, to bind. It is not intended in any technical legal sense. This is what we may call the *double-edged exclusionary definition* of private property.

What will become obvious on reflection is that *if S's property is S's in precisely the same sense and for the same reason that S's action is S's, then the discussion of morality is also a discussion of property.*

Consider for a moment the question of the relation of intention to responsibility. In one sense I cannot be held responsible for an act that was not, in some significant sense, intentional. But I doubt that we want to take this in the strictest sense, i.e., that I have a right to recognize as my action—and to accept responsibility for—only those aspects of the deed of which I was conscious in my aim and which were contained in my original purpose. Surely, even though one may intend only to bring about a single, immediate state of affairs, there are consequences which are implicit within that state of affairs or connected with it empirically of which I ought to be aware and for which I am therefore morally responsible.

There is a clear parallel between how we deal with the question of someone's liability and how we deal with the beneficial additions to someone's property (by nature, chance, etc.) which, though subsequent to the time and intention of the acquisition of that property, are judged to be *part* of that property. It is directly analogous to the distinction between having an action imputed to me and being responsible for the consequences of an action. I may be responsible for a criminal act, though it does not follow that the thing done may be directly imputed to me. To apply this to our case of T_n, we might say that on the one hand we do not want to confuse S with T_n, though on the other hand we may want to hold S responsible for the consequences that follow.

Hegel observes: "To act is to expose oneself to bad luck. Thus bad luck has a right over me and is an embodiment of my own will (intention)."[6]

It is fair, we think, to paraphrase Hegel: "To acquire property is to expose oneself to bad luck."

The case of T_n, we argue, demonstrates that we are inclined to hold T_n's owner liable for the consequences, an inclination that finds expression in positive legislation in contemporary society. If we hold S liable for T_n, it is clear that what we are saying is that not only does S have rights in reference to T_n, but all others do as well. All the story of T_n does is to make explicit that the *double-edged exclusionary definition* represents what has always been, and indeed must be, implicit in the notion of private property.

The abandonment mode of disowning makes sense, then, *only if* property is *only* considered a good. Or rather we might say, it is morally justified only if what is abandoned *is* good. If it is acknowledged that property also entails liability for maleficence, then it follows (especially where the negative consequences of something are serious) that such a mode of disowning is really tantamount to ascribing to the thing in question the *de facto* status of common property of all—and that without the express (or implied) consent of those to whom the liability is transferred. Or perhaps we should say that the thing in question *ought* to be the common property of all, since in fact the negative consequences may fall more heavily on some than on others. Note that the definition of common property must also be revised to pick up the double-edged aspect.

2a. x *is the common property of* S_1, S_2, *etc.*, *if and only if* S_1, S_2, *etc. together have the right to exclude all others from the use or benefit of* x, *and* S_1, S_2, *etc. each has the right not to be excluded from the use or benefit of* x

2b. BUT *not the right to be excluded from liability for the maleficence of* x.

IV

Given this interpretation of the logic of the notion of property, now reconsider a view which is current these days among some social theorists and popularized in Lodge's eclectic *The New American Ideology*: the view that the notion of (private) property is passé in our "post-industrial" era. Here Lodge suggests, as we have indicated above, that "(t)he value of property as a legitimizing idea and basis of authority has eroded . . . (and that it) is obvious that our large public corporations are not private property at all."

This "ideological" change, reflecting the operational changes in management practice in large "public" corporations, has been characterized as a *managerial revolution*. If we are to use a metaphor like "revolution" here, then it might be said that the managerial revolution is a revolution, to be sure, a revolution in the concept of property. That is, what seems to be implicit in the theory of the managerial revolution is not a move away from the notion of private property to some new basis of legitimation for the modern corporation, but rather a radical change in the concept of property itself. The implicit change (or revolution) is a *gerrymandering* of the concept of property out of parts of the concepts of private and common property. It would then appear to be something like the following:

1a. *S has the right to exclude all others from the use or benefit of* x BUT

2b. *these others do not have the right to be excluded from liability for the maleficence of* x.

This is, of course, a bit oversimplified, but recent cases like that of the Lockheed and Chrysler Corporations suggest that it is not far off the mark in characterizing our contemporary situation. We should entertain such (implicit) proposals for a gerrymandered definition of private property, we suggest, with considerable hesitation and even skepticism. Too easily giving up the notion of private property runs the danger of giving up the right to hold accountable for x those people who have the sole right to the use or benefit of x. What would be more rational (and not merely conceptually conservative, we are arguing) is to say that *when all others are to be held liable for S's* x, *then each of those others should also have the right not to be excluded from the use or benefit of* x—in other words, that x becomes common property. Or, one might say, logically some kind of social revolution is what is called for, not a conceptual revolution.

One of the many questions which now arise concerns the problem of symmetry (or fairness). Why should it be considered right to put a limit on liability (or to recognize a *de facto* limit, e.g., bankruptcy laws, etc.), but not to have some sort of similar limit on the use or benefits? (But would that not turn private property rights into common property rights, i.e., some procedure for fair taking/using?) The question becomes especially critical in situations where the negative consequences of something are actual while the benefits only potential. Thus, for example, S may declare the intention to assume liability for x commensurate with the potential benefits from x (or even commensurate with the total assets of S), but how does this help when the negative consequences are actual and the benefits only potential (or when the potential negative effects far outweigh the potential benefits)?

Lest one think that this a purely hypothetical situation, consider the case of the 1957 Price-Anderson Act.

> In 1954, when the government decided to encourage electric utilities to venture into nuclear power, the companies at first were enthusiastic; but after studying the consequences of a possible major nuclear accident, they and such equipment manufacturers as General Electric and Westinghouse backed off. They feared damage claims that could bankrupt them. Insurers refused then and refuse now to provide full coverage. And so the utilities told Congress they would build nuclear plants only if they first were to be immunized from full liability. Congress responded with the Price-Anderson Act of 1957. Because of this law—a law that legalized financial unaccountability—nuclear power technology exists and is growing today. . . . In 1965, when it recommended that the Price-Anderson Act be renewed, the Congressional Joint Committee on Atomic Energy "reported that one of the Act's objectives had been achieved—the deterrent to industrial participation in the atomic energy program had been removed by eliminating the threat of large liability claims." . . . In December 1975 . . . Congress voted to extend the law for ten more years.[7]

In the face of such policies we have attempted to demonstrate that the logic of property leads one from the notion of private property (the right to exclude) with a kind of inevitability to the notion of common property (the right not to be excluded)—unless one proposes gerrymandering the concept of private property. At least this is true with respect to certain kinds of things which have traditionally been seen to fall within the range of what can rightfully become (and remain) private property. A more elaborate specification of what kinds of things these might be is a topic that goes much beyond the scope of this paper. And, of course, there remains the task of filling out our incomplete notion of common property, i.e., formulating the principles for procedures for fair-taking and fair-using.

NOTES

1. Daniel Bell, *The Coming of Post-Industrial Society: A Venture in Social Forecasting* (New York: Basic Books, 1973), p. 291.

2. The classic analysis which generated much of the contemporary discussion is A. A. Berle, Jr., and G. G. Means, *The Modern Corporation and Private Property* (New York: The Macmillan Company, 1932). See also A. A. Berle, Jr., *Power Without Property* (London: Sidgwick and Jackson, 1959).

3. George C. Lodge, *The New American Ideology* (New York: Alfred A. Knopf, Inc., 1975), pp. 17–19. Also see his article "The Connection between Ethics and Ideology" delivered at Bentley College's "First National Conference on Business Ethics," published in the Conference *Proceedings*, edited by W. Michael Hoffman, Center for Business Ethics, 1977.

4. Milton Friedman, *Capitalism and Freedom* (Chicago: University of Chicago Press, 1962), p. 133.

5. These definitions are adapted from C. B. Macpherson, "A Political Theory of Property," in *Democratic Theory: Essays in Retrieval* (Oxford: Clarendon Press, 1973), p. 128.

6. Hegel, *Philosophy of Right*, trans. T. M. Knox (Oxford University Press, 1952), § 119A

7. Morton Mintz and Jerry S. Cohen, *Power, Inc.* (New York: The Viking Press, 1976), pp. 513f. Other such liability exclusionary examples could be cited.

chapter five
IDENTITY AND AGENCY

CAN A CORPORATION HAVE A CONSCIENCE?

KENNETH E. GOODPASTER* and JOHN B. MATTHEWS, JR.*

During the severe racial tensions of the 1960s, Southern Steel Company (actual case, disguised name) faced considerable pressure from government and the press to explain and modify its policies regarding discrimination both within its plants and in the major city where it was located. SSC was the largest employer in the area (it had nearly 15,000 workers, one-third of whom were black) and had made great strides toward removing barriers to equal job opportunity in its several plants. In addition, its top executives (especially its chief executive officer, James Weston) had distinguished themselves as private citizens for years in community programs for black housing, education, and small business as well as in attempts at desegregating all-white police and local government organizations.

SSC drew the line, however, at using its substantial economic influence in the local area to advance the cause of the civil rights movement by pressuring banks, suppliers, and the local government:

> As individuals we can exercise what influence we may have as citizens," James Weston said, "but for a corporation to attempt to exert any kind of economic compulsion to achieve a particular end in a social area seems to me to be quite beyond what a corporation should do and quite beyond what a corporation can do. I believe that while government may seek to compel social reforms, any attempt by a private organization like SSC to impose its views, its beliefs, and its will upon the community would be repugnant to our American constitutional concepts and that appropriate steps to correct this abuse of corporate power would be universally demanded by public opinion.

Weston could have been speaking in the early 1980s on any issue that corporations around the United States now face. Instead of social justice, his theme might be environmental protection, product safety, marketing practice, or international bribery. His statement for SSC raises the important issue of corporate responsibility. Can a corporation have a conscience?

Weston apparently felt comfortable saying it need not. The responsibilities of ordinary persons and of "artificial persons" like corporations are, in his view, separate.

Persons' responsibilities go beyond those of corporations. Persons, he seems to have believed, ought to care not only about themselves but also about the dignity and well-being of those around them—ought not only to care but also to act. Organizations, he evidently thought, are creatures of, and to a degree prisoners of, the systems of economic incentive and political sanction that give them reality and therefore should not be expected to display the same moral attributes that we expect of persons.

Others inside business as well as outside share Weston's perception. One influential philosopher—John Ladd—carries Weston's view a step further:

"It is improper to expect organizational conduct to conform to the ordinary principles of morality," he says. "We cannot and must not expect formal organizations, or their representatives acting in their official capacities, to be honest, courageous, considerate, sympathetic, or to have any kind of moral integrity. Such concepts are not in the vocabulary, so to speak, of the organizational language game."[1]

In our opinion, this line of thought represents a tremendous barrier to the development of business ethics both as a field of inquiry and as a practical force in managerial decision making. This is a matter about which executives must be philosophical and philosophers must be practical. A corporation can and should have a conscience. The language of ethics does have a place in the vocabulary of an organization. There need not be and there should not be a disjunction of the sort attributed to SSC's James Weston. Organizational agents such as corporations should be no more and no less morally responsible (rational, self-interested, altruistic) than ordinary persons.

We take this position because we think an analogy holds between the individual and the corporation. If we analyze the concept of moral responsibility as it applies to persons, we find that projecting it to corporations as agents in society is possible.

The problem is not so much power and authority has been surrendered by individuals to the corporations.

DEFINING THE RESPONSIBILITY OF PERSONS

When we speak of the responsibility of individuals, philosophers say that we mean three things: someone is to blame, something has to be done, or some kind of trustworthiness can be expected.

We apply the first meaning, what we shall call the *causal* sense, primarily to legal and moral contexts where what is at issue is praise or blame for a past action. We say of a person that he or she was responsible for what happened, is to blame for it, should be held accountable. In this sense of the word, *responsibility* has to do with tracing the causes of actions and events, of finding out who is answerable in a given situation. Our aim is to determine someone's intention, free will, degree of participation, and appropriate reward or punishment.

We apply the second meaning of *responsibility* to rule following, to contexts where individuals are subject to externally imposed norms often associated with some social role that people play. We speak of the responsibilities of parents to children, of doctors to patients, of lawyers to clients, of citizens to the law. What is socially expected and what the party involved is to answer for are at issue here.

We use the third meaning of *responsibility* for decision making. With this meaning of the term, we say that individuals are responsible if they are trustworthy and reliable, if they allow appropriate factors to affect their judgment; we refer primarily to a person's independent thought processes and decision making, processes that justify an attitude of trust from those who interact with him or her as a responsible individual.

The distinguishing characteristic of moral responsibility, it seems to us, lies in this third sense of the term. Here the focus is on the intellectual and emotional processes in the individual's moral reasoning. Philosophers call this "taking a moral point of view" and contrast it with such other processes as being financially prudent and attending to legal obligations.

To be sure, characterizing a person as "morally responsible" may seem rather vague. But vagueness is a contextual notion. Everything depends on how we fill in the blank in "vague for——————purposes."

In some contexts the term "six o'clockish" is vague, while in others it is useful and informative. As a response to a space-shuttle pilot who wants to know when to fire the reentry rockets, it will not do, but it might do in response to a spouse who wants to know when one will arrive home at the end of the workday.

We maintain that the processes underlying moral responsibility can be defined and are not themselves vague, even though gaining consensus on specific moral norms and decisions is not always easy.

What, then, characterizes the processes underlying the judgment of a person we call morally responsible? Philosopher William K. Frankena offers the following answer:

"A morality is a normative system in which judgments are made, more or less consciously, [out of a] consideration of the effects of actions . . . on the lives of persons . . . including the lives of others besides the person acting. . . . David Hume took a similar position when he argued that what speaks in a moral judgment is a kind of sympathy. . . . A little later, . . . Kant put the matter somewhat better by characterizing morality as the business of respecting persons as ends and not as means or as things. . . ."[2]

Frankena is pointing to two traits, both rooted in a long and diverse philosophical tradition:

1. *Rationality.* Taking a moral point of view includes the features we usually attribute to rational decision making, that is, lack of impulsiveness, care in mapping out alternatives and consequences, clarity about goals and purposes, attention to details of implementation.

2. *Respect.* The moral point of view also includes a special awareness of and concern for the effects of one's decisions and policies on others, special in the sense that it goes beyond the kind of awareness and concern that would ordinarily be part of rationality, that is, beyond seeing others merely as instrumental to accomplishing one's own purposes. This is respect for the lives of others and involves taking their needs and interests seriously, not simply as resources in one's own decision making but as limiting conditions which change the very definition of one's habitat from a self-centered to a shared environment. It is what philosopher Immanuel Kant meant by the "categorical imperative" to treat others as valuable in and for themselves.

It is this feature that permits us to trust the morally responsible person. We know that such a person takes our point of view into account not merely as a useful precaution (as in "honesty is the best policy") but as important in its own right.

These components of moral responsibility are not too vague to be useful. Rationality and respect affect the manner in which a person approaches practical decision making: they affect the way in which the individual processes information and makes choices. A rational but not respectful Bill Jones will not lie to his friends *unless* he is reasonably sure he will not be found out. A rational but not respectful Mary Smith will defend an unjustly treated party *unless* she thinks it may be too costly to herself. A rational *and* respectful decision maker, however, notices—and cares—whether the consequences of his or her conduct lead to injuries or indignities to others.

Two individuals who take "the moral point of view" will not of course always agree on ethical matters, but they do at least have a basis for dialogue.

PROJECTING RESPONSIBILITY TO CORPORATIONS

Now that we have removed some of the vagueness from the notion of moral responsibility as it applies to persons, we can search for a frame of reference in which, by analogy with Bill Jones and Mary Smith, we can meaningfully and appropriately say that corporations are morally responsible. This is the issue reflected in the SSC case.

To deal with it, we must ask two questions: Is it meaningful to apply moral concepts to actors who are not persons but who are instead made up of persons? And even if meaningful, is it advisable to do so?

If a group can act like a person in some ways, then we can expect it to behave like a person in other ways. For one thing, we know that people organized into a group can act as a unit. As business people well know, legally a corporation is considered a unit. To approach unity, a group usually has some sort of internal decision structure, a system of rules that spell out authority relationships and specify the conditions under which certain individuals' actions become official actions of the group.[3]

If we can say that persons act responsibly only if they gather information about the impact of their actions on others and use it in making decisions, we can reasonably do the same for organizations. Our proposed frame of reference for thinking about and implementing corporate responsibility aims at spelling out the processes associated with the moral responsibility of individuals and projecting them to the level of organizations. This is similar to, though an inversion of, Plato's famous method in the *Republic*, in which justice in the community is used as a model for justice in the individual.

Hence, corporations that monitor their employment practices and the effects of their production processes and products on the environment and human health show the same kind of rationality and respect that morally responsible individuals do. Thus, attributing actions, strategies, decisions, and moral responsibilities to corporations as entities distinguishable from those who hold offices in them poses no problem.

And when we look about us, we can readily see differences in moral responsibility among corporations in much the same way that we see differences among persons. Some corporations have built features into their management incentive systems, board structures, internal control systems, and research agendas that in a person we would call self-control, integrity, and conscientiousness. Some have institutionalized awareness and concern for consumers, employees, and the rest of the public in ways that others clearly have not.

As a matter of course, some corporations attend to the human impact of their operations and policies and reject operations and policies that are questionable. Whether the issue be the health effects of sugared cereal or cigarettes, the safety of tires or tampons, civil liberties in the corporation or the community, an organization reveals its character as surely as a person does.

Indeed, the parallel may be even more dramatic. For just as the moral responsibility displayed by an individual develops over time from infancy to adulthood,[4] so too we may expect to find stages of development in organizational character that show significant patterns.

EVALUATING THE IDEA OF MORAL PROJECTION

Concepts like moral responsibility not only make sense when applied to organizations but also provide touchstones for designing more effective models than we have for guiding corporate policy.

Now we can understand what it means to invite SSC as a corporation to be morally responsible both in-house and in its community, but *should* we issue the invitation? Here we turn to the question of advisability. Should we require the organizational agents in our society to have the same moral attributes we require of ourselves?

Our proposal to spell out the processes associated with moral responsibility for individuals and then to project them to their organizational counterparts takes on added meaning when we examine alternative frames of reference for corporate responsibility.

Two frames of reference that compete for the allegiance of people who ponder the question of corporate responsibility are emphatically opposed to this principle of moral projection—what we might refer to as the "invisible hand" view and the "hand of government" view.

The Invisible Hand

The most eloquent spokesman of the first view is Milton Friedman (echoing many philosophers and economists since Adam Smith). According to this pattern of thought, the true and only social responsibilities of business organizations are to make profits and obey the laws. The workings of the free and competitive marketplace will "moralize" corporate behavior quite independently of any attempts to expand or transform decision making via moral projection.

A deliberate amorality in the executive suite is encouraged in the name of systemic morality: the common good is best served when each of us and our economic institutions pursue not the common good or moral purpose, advocates say, but competitive advantage. Morality, responsibility, and conscience reside in the invisible hand of the free market system, not in the hands of the organizations within the system, much less the managers within the organizations.

To be sure, people of this opinion admit, there is a sense in which social or ethical issues can and should enter the corporate mind, but the filtering of such issues is thorough: they go through the screens of custom, public opinion, public relations, and the law. And, in any case, self-interest maintains primacy as an objective and a guiding star.

The reaction from this frame of reference to the suggestion that moral judgment be integrated with corporate strategy is clearly negative. Such an integration is seen as inefficient and arrogant, and in the end both an illegitimate use of corporate power and an abuse of the manager's fiduciary role. With respect to our SSC case, advocates of the invisible hand model would vigorously resist efforts, beyond legal requirements, to make SSC right the wrongs of racial injustice. SSC's responsibility would be to make steel of high quality at least cost, to deliver it on time, and to satisfy its customers and stockholders. Justice would not be part of SSC's corporate mandate.

The Hand of Government

Advocates of the second dissenting frame of reference abound, but John Kenneth Galbraith's work has counterpointed Milton Friedman's with insight and style. Under this view of corporate responsibility, corporations are to pursue objectives that are rational and purely economic. The regulatory hands of the law and the political process rather than the invisible hand of the marketplace turns these objectives to the common good.

Again, in this view, it is a system that provides the moral direction for corporate decision making—a system, though, that is guided by political managers, the custodians of the public purpose. In the case of SSC, proponents of this view would look to the state for moral direction and responsible management, both within SSC and in the community. The corporation would have no moral responsibility beyond political and legal obedience.

What is striking is not so much the radical difference between the economic and social philosophies that underlie these two views of the source of corporate responsibility but the conceptual similarities. Both views locate morality, ethics, responsibility, and conscience in the systems of rules and incentives in which the modern corporation finds itself embedded. Both views reject the exercise of independent moral judgment by corporations as actors in society.

Neither view trusts corporate leaders with stewardship over what are often called noneconomic values. Both require corporate responsibility to march to the beat of drums outside. In the jargon of moral philosophy, both views press for a rule-centered or a system-centered ethics instead of an agent-centered ethics. These frames of reference countenance corporate rule-following responsibility for corporations but not corporate decision-making responsibility.

The Hand of Management

To be sure, the two views under discussion differ in that one looks to an invisible moral force in the market while the other looks to a visible moral force in government. But both would advise against a principle of moral projection that permits or encourages corporations to exercise independent, noneconomic judgment over matters that face them in their short- and long-term plans and operations.

Accordingly, both would reject a third view of corporate responsibility that seeks to affect the thought processes of the organization itself—a sort of "hand of management" view—since neither seems willing or able to see the engines of profit regulate themselves to the degree that would be implied by taking the principle of moral projection seriously. Cries of inefficiency and moral imperialism from the right would be matched by cries of insensitivity and illegitimacy from the left, all in the name of preserving us from corporations and managers run morally amok.

Better, critics would say, that moral philosophy be left to philosophers, philanthropists, and politicians than to business leaders. Better that corporate morality be kept to glossy annual reports, where it is safely insulated from policy and performance.

The two conventional frames of reference locate moral restraint in forces external to the person and the corporation. They deny moral reasoning and intent to the corporation in the name of either market competition or society's system of explicit legal constraints and presume that these have a better moral effect than that of rationality and respect.

Although the principle of moral projection, which underwrites the idea of a corporate conscience and patterns it on the thought and feeling processes of the person, is in our view compelling, we must acknowledge that it is neither part of the received wisdom, nor is its advisability beyond question or objection. Indeed, attributing the role of conscience to the corporation seems to carry with it new and disturbing implications for our usual ways of thinking about ethics and business.

Perhaps the best way to clarify and defend this frame of reference is to address the objections to the principle found in the last pages of this article. There we see a summary of the criticisms and counterarguments we have heard during hours of discussion with business executives and business school students. We believe that the replies to the objections about a corporation having a conscience are convincing.

LEAVING THE DOUBLE STANDARD BEHIND

We have come some distance from our opening reflection on Southern Steel Company and its role in its community. Our proposal—clarified, we hope, through these objections and replies—suggests that it is not sufficient to draw a sharp line between individuals' private ideas and efforts and a corporation's institutional efforts but that the latter can and should be built upon the former.

Does this frame of reference give us an unequivocal prescription for the behavior of SSC in its circumstances? No, it does not. Persuasive arguments might be made now and might have been made then that SSC should not have used its considerable economic clout to threaten the community into desegregation. A careful analysis of the realities of the environment might have disclosed that such a course would have been counterproductive, leading to more injustice than it would have alleviated.

The point is that some of the arguments and some of the analyses are or would have been moral arguments, and thereby the ultimate decision that of an ethically responsible organization. The significance of this point can hardly be overstated, for it represents the adoption of a new perspective on corporate policy and a new way of thinking about business ethics. We agree with one authority, who writes that "the business firm, as an organic entity intricately affected by and affecting its environment, is as appropriately adaptive . . . to demands for responsible behavior as for economic service."[5]

The frame of reference here developed does not offer a decision procedure for corporate managers. That has not been our purpose. It does, however, shed light on the conceptual foundations of business ethics by training attention on the corporation as a moral agent in society. Legal systems of rules and incentives are insufficient, even though they may be necessary, as frameworks for corporate responsibility. Taking conceptual cues from the features of moral responsibility normally expected of the person in our opinion deserves practicing managers' serious consideration.

The lack of congruence that James Weston saw between individual and corporate moral responsibility can be, and we think should be, overcome. In the process, what a number of writers have characterized as a double standard—a discrepancy between our personal lives and our lives in organizational settings—might be dampened. The principle of moral projection not only helps us to conceptualize the kinds of demands that we might make of corporations and other organizations but also offers the prospect of harmonizing those demands with the demands that we make of ourselves.

IS A CORPORATION A MORALLY RESPONSIBLE "PERSON"?

Objection 1 to the Analogy

Corporations are not persons. They are artifical legal constructions, machines for mobilizing economic investments toward the efficient production of goods and services. We cannot hold a corporation responsible. We can only hold individuals responsible.

Reply

Our frame of reference does not imply that corporations are persons in a literal sense. It simply means that in certain respects concepts and functions normally attributed to persons can also be attributed to organizations made up of persons. Goals, economic values, strategies, and other such personal attributes are often usefully projected to the corporate level by managers and researchers. Why should we not project the functions of conscience in the same way? As for holding corporations responsible, recent criminal prosecutions such as the case of Ford Motor Company and its Pinto gas tanks suggest that society finds the idea both intelligible and useful.

Objection 2

A corporation cannot be held responsible at the sacrifice of profit. Profitability and financial health have always been and should continue to be the "categorical imperatives" of a business operation.

Reply

We must of course acknowledge the imperatives of survival, stability, and growth when we discuss corporations, as indeed we must acknowledge them when we discuss the life of an individual. Self-sacrifice has been identified with moral responsibility in only the most extreme cases. The pursuit of profit and self-interest need not be pitted against the demands of moral responsibility. Moral demands are best viewed as containments—not replacements—for self-interest.

This is not to say that profit maximization never conflicts with morality. But profit maximization conflicts with other managerial values as well. The point is to coordinate imperatives, not deny their validity.

Objection 3

Corporate executives are not elected representatives of the people, nor are they anointed or appointed as social guardians. They therefore lack the social mandate that a democratic society rightly demands of those who would pursue ethically or socially motivated policies. By keeping corporate policies confined to economic motivations, we keep the power of corporate executives in its proper place.

Reply

The objection betrays an oversimplified view of the relationship between the public and the private sector. Neither private individuals nor private corporations that guide their conduct by ethical or social values beyond the demands of law should be constrained merely because they are not elected to do so. The demands of moral responsibility are independent of the demands of political legitimacy and are in fact presupposed by them.

To be sure, the state and the political process will and must remain the primary mechanisms for protecting the public interest, but one might be forgiven the hope that the political process will not substitute for the moral judgment of the citizenry or other components of society such as corporations.

Objection 4

Our system of law carefully defines the role of agent or fiduciary and makes corporate managers accountable to shareholders and investors for the use of their assets. Management cannot, in the name of corporate moral responsibility, arrogate to itself the right to manage those assets by partially noneconomic criteria.

Reply

First, it is not so clear that investors insist on purely economic criteria in the management of their assets, especially if some of the shareholders' resolutions and board reforms of the last decade are any indication. For instance, companies doing business in South Africa have had stockholders question their activities, other companies have instituted audit committees for their boards before such auditing was mandated, and mutual funds for which "socially responsible behavior" is a major investment criterion now exist.

Second, the categories of "shareholder" and "investor" connote wider time spans than do immediate or short-term returns. As a practical matter, considerations of stability and long-term return on investment enlarge the class of principals to which managers bear a fiduciary relationship.

Third, the trust that managers hold does not and never has extended to "any means available" to advance the interests of the principals. Both legal and moral constraints must be understood to qualify that trust—even, perhaps, in the name of a larger trust and a more basic fiduciary relationship to the members of society at large.

Objection 5

The power, size, and scale of the modern corporation—domestic as well as international—are awesome. To unleash, even partially, such power from the discipline of the marketplace and the narrow or possibly nonexistent moral purpose implicit in that discipline would be socially dangerous. Had SSC acted in the community to further racial justice, its purposes might have been admirable, but those purposes could have led to a kind of moral imperialism or worse. Suppose SSC had thrown its power behind the Ku Klux Klan.

Reply

This is a very real and important objection. What seems not to be appreciated is the fact that power affects when it is used as well as when it is not used. A decision by SSC not to exercise its economic influence according to "noneconomic" criteria is inevitably a moral decision and just as inevitably affects the community. The issue in the end is not whether corporations (and other organizations) should be "unleashed" to exert moral force in our society but rather how critically and self-consciously they should choose to do so.

The degree of influence enjoyed by an agent, whether a person or an organization, is not so much a factor recommending moral disengagement as a factor demanding a high level of moral awareness. Imperialism is more to be feared when moral reasoning is absent than when it is present. Nor do we suggest that the "discipline of the marketplace" be diluted; rather, we call for it to be supplemented with the discipline of moral reflection.

Objection 6

The idea of moral projection is a useful device for structuring corporate responsibility only if our understanding of moral responsibility at the level of the person is in some sense richer than our understanding of moral responsibility on the level of the organization as a whole. If we are not clear about individual responsibility, the projection is fruitless.

Reply

The objection is well taken. The challenge offered by the idea of moral projection lies in our capacity to articulate criteria or frameworks of reasoning for the morally responsible person. And though such a challenge is formidable, it is not clear that it cannot be met, at least with sufficient consensus to be useful.

For centuries, the study and criticism of frameworks have gone on, carried forward by many disciplines, including psychology, the social sciences, and philosophy. And though it would be a mistake to suggest that any single framework (much less a decision mechanism) has emerged as the right one, it is true that recurrent patterns are discernible and well enough defined to structure moral discussion.

In the body of the article, we spoke of rationality and respect as components of individual responsibility. Further analysis of these components would translate them into social costs and benefits, justice in the distribution of goods and services, basic rights and duties, and fidelity to contracts. The view that pluralism in our society has undercut all possibility of moral agreement is anything but self-evident. Sincere moral disagreement is, of course, inevitable and not clearly lamentable. But a process and a vocabulary for articulating such values as we share is no small step forward when compared with the alternatives. Perhaps in our exploration of the moral projection we might make some surprising and even reassuring discoveries about ourselves.

Objection 7

Why is it necessary to project moral responsibility to the level of the organization? Isn't the task of defining corporate responsibility and business ethics sufficiently discharged if we clarify the responsibilities of men and women in business as individuals? Doesn't ethics finally rest on the honesty and integrity of the individual in the business world?

Reply

Yes and no. Yes, in the sense that the control of large organizations does finally rest in the hands of managers, of men and women. No, in the sense that what is being controlled is a cooperative system for a cooperative purpose. The projection of responsibility to the organization is simply an acknowledgment of the fact that the whole is more than the sum of its parts. Many intelligent people do not an intelligent organization make. Intelligence needs to be structured, organized, divided, and recombined in complex processes for complex purposes.

Studies of management have long shown that the attributes, successes, and failures of organizations are phenomena that emerge from the coordination of persons' attributes and that explanations of such phenomena require categories of analysis and description beyond the level of the individual. Moral responsibility is an attribute that can manifest itself in organizations as surely as competence or efficiency.

Objection 8

Is the frame of reference here proposed intended to replace or undercut the relevance of the "invisible hand" and the "government hand" views, which depend on external controls?

Reply

No. Just as regulation and economic competition are not substitutes for corporate responsibility, so corporate responsibility is not a substitute for law and the market. The imperatives of ethics cannot be relied on—nor have they ever been relied on—without a context of external sanctions. And this is true as much for individuals as for organizations.

This frame of reference takes us beneath, but not beyond, the realm of external systems of rules and incentives and into the thought processes that interpret and respond to the corporation's environment. Morality is more than merely part of that environment. It aims at the projection of conscience, not the enthronement of it in either the state or the competitive process.

The rise of the modern large corporation and the concomitant rise of the professional manager demand a conceptual framework in which these phenomena can be accommodated to moral thought. The principle of moral projection furthers such accommodation by recognizing a new level of agency in society and thus a new level of responsibility.

Objection 9

Corporations have always taken the interests of those outside the corporation into account in the sense that customer relations and public relations generally are an integral part of rational economic decision making. Market signals and social signals that filter through the market mechanism inevitably represent the interests of parties affected by the behavior of the company. What, then, is the point of adding respect to rationality?

Reply

Representing the affected parties solely as economic variables in the environment of the company is treating them as means or resources and not as ends in themselves. It implies that the only voice which affected parties should have in organizational decision making is that of potential buyers, sellers, regulators, or boycotters. Besides, many affected parties may not occupy such roles, and those who do may not be able to signal the organization with messages that effectively represent their stakes in its actions.

To be sure, classical economic theory would have us believe that perfect competition in free markets (with modest adjustments from the state) will result in all relevant signals being "heard," but the abstractions from reality implicit in such theory make it insufficient as a frame of reference for moral responsibility. In a world in which strict self-interest was congruent with the common good, moral responsibility might be unnecessary. We do not, alas, live in such a world.

The element of respect in our analysis of responsibility plays an essential role in ensuring the recognition of unrepresented or underrepresented voices in the decision making of organizations as agents. Showing respect for persons as ends and not mere means to organizational purposes is central to the concept of corporate moral responsibility.

NOTES

1. See John Ladd, "Morality and the Ideal of Rationality in Formal Organizations," *The Monist*, October 1970, p. 499.

2. See William K. Frankena, *Thinking About Morality* (Ann Arbor: University of Michigan Press, 1980), p. 26.

3. See Peter French, "The Corporation as a Moral Person," *American Philosophical Quarterly*, July 1979, p. 207.

4. A process that psychological researchers from Jean Piaget to Lawrence Kohlberg have examined carefully; see Jean Piaget, *The Moral Judgement of the Child* (New York: Free Press, 1965) and Lawrence Kohlberg, *The Philosophy of Moral Development* (New York: Harper & Row, 1981).

5. See Kenneth R. Andrews, *The Concept of Corporate Strategy*, revised edition (Homewood, Ill.: Dow Jones–Irwin, 1980), p. 99.

CORPORATE MORAL AGENCY*

PETER A. FRENCH†

1. In one of his *New York Times* columns of not too long ago Tom Wicker's ire was aroused by a Gulf Oil Corporation advertisement that "pointed the finger of blame" for the energy crisis at all elements of our society (and supposedly away from the oil company). Wicker attacked Gulf Oil as the major, if not the sole, perpetrator of that crisis and virtually every other social ill, with the possible exception of venereal disease. I do not know if Wicker was serious or sarcastic in making all of his charges; I have a sinking suspicion that he was in deadly earnest, but I have doubts as to whether Wicker understands or if many people understand what sense such ascriptions of moral responsibility make when their subjects are corporations. My interest is to argue for a theory that accepts corporations as members of the moral community, of equal standing with the traditionally acknowledged residents—biological human beings—and hence treats Wicker-type responsibility ascriptions as unexceptionable instances of a perfectly proper sort without having to paraphrase them. In short, I shall argue that corporations should be treated as fullfledged moral persons and hence that they can have whatever privileges, rights, and duties as are, in the normal course of affairs, accorded to moral persons.

2. There are at least two significantly different types of responsibility ascriptions that I want to distinguish in ordinary usage (not counting the laudatory recommendation, "He is a responsible lad.") The first type pins responsibility on someone or something, the who-dun-it or what-dun-it sense. Austin has pointed out that it is usually used when an event or action is thought by the speaker to be untoward. (Perhaps we are more interested in the failures rather than the successes that punctuate our lives.)

    The second type of responsibility ascription, parasitic upon the first, involves the notion of accountability.[1] "Having a responsibility" is interwoven with the notion "Having a liability to answer," and having such a liability or obligation seems to imply (as Anscombe has noted[2]) the existence of some sort of authority relationship either between people, or between people and a deity, or in some weaker versions between people and social norms. The kernel of insight that I find intuitively compelling is that for someone to legitimately hold someone else responsible for some event, there must exist or have existed a responsibility relationship between them such that in regard to the event in question the latter was answerable to the former. In other words, a responsibility ascription of the second type is properly

From "The Corporation as a Moral Person" by Peter A. French. Paper presented at the Ethics and Economics Conference, University of Delaware, November 11, 1977. Copyright © 1977 by Peter A. French. Reprinted by permission of the author.

*I am grateful to Professors Donald Davidson, J. L. Mackie, Howard Wettstein, and T. E. Uehling for their helpful comments on earlier versions of this paper. I wish also to acknowledge the support of the University of Minnesota Graduate School.

†Department of Philosophy, University of Minnesota, Morris.

uttered by someone Z if he or she can hold X accountable for what he or she has done. Responsibility relationships are created in a multitude of ways, e.g., through promises, contracts, compacts, hirings, assignments, appointments, by agreeing to enter a Rawlsian original position, etc. The "right" to hold responsible is often delegated to third parties; but importantly, in the case of moral responsibility, no delegation occurs because no person is excluded from the relationship: moral responsibility relationships hold reciprocally and without prior agreements among all moral persons. No special arrangement needs to be established between parties for anyone to hold someone morally responsible for his or her acts or, what amounts to the same thing, every person is a party to a responsibility relationship with all other persons as regards the doing or refraining from doing of certain acts: those that take descriptions that use moral notions.

Because our interest is in the criteria of moral personhood and not the content or morality, we need not pursue this idea further. What I have maintained is that moral responsibility, although it is neither contractual nor optional, is not a class apart but an extension of ordinary, garden-variety responsibility. What is needed in regard to the present subject, then, is an account of the requirements in *any* responsibility relationship.[3]

3. A responsibility ascription of the second type amounts to the assertion that the person held responsible is the cause of an event (usually an untoward one) and that the action in question was intended by the subject or that the event was the direct result of an intentional act of the subject. In addition to what it asserts, it implies that the subject is liable to account to the speaker (who the speaker is or what the speaker is, a member of the "moral community," a surrogate for that aggregate). The primary focus of responsibility ascriptions of the second type is on the subject's intentions rather than, though not to the exclusion of, occasions.[4]

4. For a corporation to be treated as a responsible agent it must be the case that some things that happen, some events, are describable in a way that makes certain sentences true, sentences that say that some of the things a corporation does were intended by the corporation itself. That is not accomplished if attributing intentions to a corporation is only a shorthand way of attributing intentions to the biological persons who comprise, for example, its board of directors. If that were to turn out to be the case, then on metaphysical if not logical grounds there would be no way to distinguish between corporations and mobs. I shall argue, however, that a corporation's CID Structure (the Corporate Internal Decision Structure) is the requisite redescription device that licenses the predication of corporate intentionality.

It is obvious that a corporation's doing something involves or includes human beings' doing things and that the human beings who occupy various positions in a corporation usually can be described as having reasons for *their* behavior. In virtue of those descriptions they may be properly held responsible for their behavior, *ceteris paribus*. What needs to be shown is that there is sense in saying that corporations, and not just the people who work in them, have reasons for doing what they do. Typically, we will be told that it is the directors, or the managers, etc. that really have the corporate reasons and desires, etc. and that although corporate actions may not be reducible without remainder, corporate intentions are always reducible to human intentions.

5. Every corporation must have an internal decision structure. The CID Structure has two elements of interest to us here: (1) an organizational or responsibility flow chart that delineates stations and levels within the corporate power structure and (2) corporate decision recognition rule(s) (usually embedded in something called "corporate policy"). The CID Structure is the personnel organization for the exercise of the corporation's power with respect to its ventures, and as such its primary function is to draw experience from various levels of the corporation into a decision-making and ratification process. When operative and properly activated, the CID Structure accomplishes a subordination and synthesis of the intentions and acts of various biological persons into a corporate decision. When viewed in another way the CID Structure licenses the descriptive transformation of events seen under another aspect as the acts of biological persons (those who occupy various stations on the organizational chart) as corporate acts by exposing the corporate character of those events. A functioning CID Structure *incorporates* acts of biological persons. For illustrative purposes, suppose we imagine that an event E has at least two aspects, that is, can be described in two nonidentical ways. One of those aspects is "Executive X's doing y" and one is "Corporation C's doing z." The corporate act and the individual act may have different properties: indeed they have different causal ancestors though they are causally inseparable.[5]

Although I doubt he is aware of the metaphysical reading that can be given to this process, J. K. Galbraith rather neatly captures what I have in mind when he writes in his recent popular book on the history of economics:

> From [the] interpersonal exercise of power, the interaction . . . of the participants, comes the *personality* of the corporation.[6]

I take Galbraith here to be quite literally correct, but it is important to spell out how a CID Structure works this "miracle."

In philosophy in recent years we have grown accustomed to the use of games as models for understanding institutional behavior. We all have some understanding of how rules of games make certain descriptions of events possible that would not be so if those rules were nonexistent. The CID Structure of a corporation is a kind of constitutive rule (or rules) analogous to the game rules with which we are familiar. The organization chart of, for example, the Burlington Northern Corporation distinguishes "players" and clarifies their rank and the interwoven lines of responsibility within the corporation. The Burlington chart lists only titles, not unlike King, Queen, Rook, etc. in chess. What it tells us is that anyone holding the title "Executive Vice President for Finance and Administration" stands in a certain relationship to anyone holding the title "Director of Internal Audit" and to anyone holding the title "Treasurer," etc. Also it expresses, or maps, the interdependent and dependent relationships that are involved in determinations of corporate decisions and actions. In effect, it tells us what anyone who occupies any of the positions is vis-à-vis the decision structure of the whole. The organizational chart provides what might be called the grammar of corporate decision-making. What I shall call internal recognition rules provide its logic.[7]

Recognition rules are of two sorts. Partially embedded in the organizational chart are the procedural recognitors: we see that decisions are to be reached collectively at certain levels and that they are to be ratified at higher levels (or at inner circles, if one prefers the Galbraithean model). A corporate decision is recognized internally not only by the procedure of its making, but by the policy it instantiates. Hence every corporation creates an image (not to be confused with its public image) or a general policy, what G. C. Buzby of the Chilton Company has called the "basic belief of the corporation,"[8] that must inform its decisions for them to be properly described as being those of that corporation. "The moment policy is side-stepped or violated, it is no longer the policy of that company."[9]

Peter Drucker has seen the importance of the basic policy recognitors in the CID Structure (though he treats matters rather differently from the way I am recommending). Drucker writes:

> Because the corporation is an institution it must have a basic policy. For it must subordinate individual ambitions and decisions to the *needs* of the corporation's welfare and survival. That means that it must have a set of principles and a rule of conduct which limit and direct individual actions and behavior.[10]

6. Suppose, for illustrative purposes, we activate a CID Structure in a corporation, Wicker's favorite, the Gulf Oil Corporation. Imagine then that three executives X, Y, and Z have the task of deciding whether or not Gulf Oil will join a world uranium cartel (I trust this may catch Mr. Wicker's attention and hopefully also that of Jerry McAfee, current Gulf Oil Corporation president). X, Y, and Z have before them an Everest of papers that have been prepared by lower echelon executives. Some of the reports will be purely factual in nature, some will be contingency plans, some will be in the form of position papers developed by various departments, some will outline financial considerations, some will be legal opinions, and so on. Insofar as these will all have been processed through Gulf's CID Structure system, the personal reasons, if any, individual executives may have had when writing their reports and recommendations in a specific way will have been diluted by the subordination of individual inputs to peer group input even before X, Y, and Z review the matter. X, Y, and Z take a vote. Their taking of a vote is authorized procedure in the Gulf CID Structure, which is to say that under these circumstances the vote of X, Y, and Z can be redescribed as the corporation's making a decision: that is, the event "X Y Z voting" may be redescribed to expose an aspect otherwise unrevealed, that is quite different from its other aspects, e.g., from X's voting in the affirmative.

But the CID Structure, as already suggested, also provides the grounds in its nonprocedural recognitor for such an attribution of corporate intentionality. Simply, when the corporate act is consistent with the implementation of established corporate policy, then it is proper to describe it as having been done for corporate reasons, as having been caused by a corporate desire coupled with a corporate belief and so, in other words, as corporate intentional.

An event may, under one of its aspects, be described as the conjunctive act "X did a (or as X intentionally did a) and Y did a (or as Y intentionally did a) and Z did a (or as Z intentionally did a)" (where a = voted in the affirmative on the question of Gulf Oil joining the cartel). Given the Gulf CID Structure—formulated in this instance as the conjunction of rules: when the occupants of positions A, B, and C on the organizational chart unanimously vote to do something and if doing that something is consistent with an implementation of general corporate policy, other things being equal, then the corporation has decided to do it for corporate reasons—the event is redescribable as "the Gulf Oil Corporation did j for corporate reasons f" (where j is "decided to join the cartel" and f is any reason [desire + belief] consistent with basic policy of Gulf Oil, e.g., increasing profits) or simply as "Gulf Oil Corporation intentionally did j." This is a rather technical way of saying that in these circumstances the executives voting are, given its CID Structure, also the corporation deciding to do something, and that regardless of the personal reasons the executives have for voting as they do, and even if their reasons are inconsistent with established corporate policy or even if one of them has no reason at all for voting as he does, the corporation still has reasons for joining the cartel; that is, joining is consistent with the inviolate corporate general policies as encrusted in the precedent of previous corporate actions and its statements of purpose as recorded in its certificate of incorporation, annual reports, etc. The corporation's only method of achieving its desires or goals is the activation of the personnel who occupy its various positions. However, if X voted affirmatively purely for reasons of personal monetary gain (suppose he had been bribed to do so), that does not alter the fact that the corporate reason for joining the cartel was to minimize competition and hence pay higher dividends to its shareholders. Corporations have reasons because they have interests in doing those things that are likely to result in realization of their established corporate goals regardless of the transient self-interest of directors, managers, etc. If there is a difference between corporate goals and desires and those of human beings, it is probably that the corporate ones are relatively stable and not very wide ranging, but that is only because corporations can do relatively fewer things than human beings, being confined in action predominately to a limited socioeconomic sphere. It is, of course, in a corporation's interest that its component membership view the corporate purposes as instrumental in the achievement of their own goals. (Financial reward is the most common way this is achieved.)

It will be objected that a corporation's policies reflect only the current goals of its directors. But that is certainly not logically necessary nor is it in practice totally true for most large corporations. Usually, of course, the original incorporators will have organized to further their individual interests and/or to meet goals which they shared. But even in infancy the melding of disparate interests and purposes gives rise to a corporate long-range point of view that is distinct from the intents and purposes of the collection of incorporators viewed individually. Also corporate basic purposes and policies, as already mentioned, tend to be relatively stable when compared to those of individuals and not couched in the kind of language that would be appropriate to individual purposes. Furthermore, as histories of corporations will show, when policies are amended or altered it is usually only peripheral issues and matters of style that are involved. Radical policy alteration constitutes

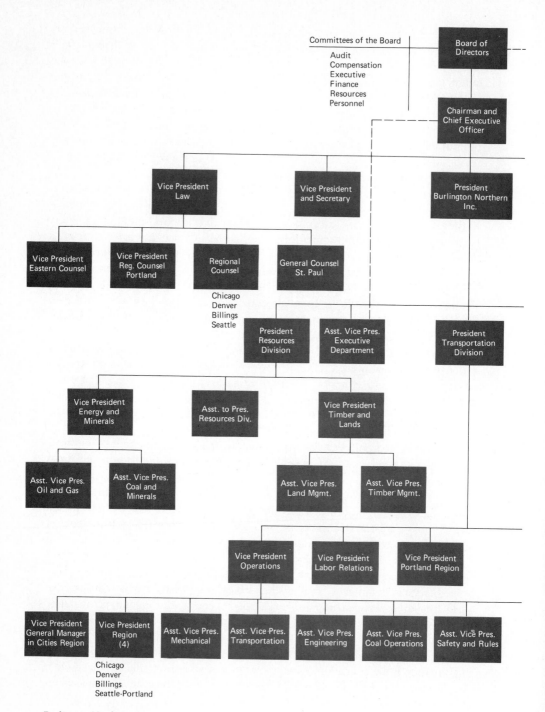

Committees of the Board
- Audit
- Compensation
- Executive
- Finance
- Resources
- Personnel

Board of Directors

Chairman and Chief Executive Officer

Vice President Law

Vice President and Secretary

President Burlington Northern Inc.

Vice President Eastern Counsel

Vice President Reg. Counsel Portland

Regional Counsel
Chicago
Denver
Billings
Seattle

General Counsel St. Paul

President Resources Division

Asst. Vice Pres. Executive Department

President Transportation Division

Vice President Energy and Minerals

Asst. to Pres. Resources Div.

Vice President Timber and Lands

Asst. Vice Pres. Oil and Gas

Asst. Vice Pres. Coal and Minerals

Asst. Vice Pres. Land Mgmt.

Asst. Vice Pres. Timber Mgmt.

Vice President Operations

Vice President Labor Relations

Vice President Portland Region

Vice President General Manager in Cities Region

Vice President Region (4)
Chicago
Denver
Billings
Seattle-Portland

Asst. Vice Pres. Mechanical

Asst. Vice Pres. Transportation

Asst. Vice Pres. Engineering

Asst. Vice Pres. Coal Operations

Asst. Vice Pres. Safety and Rules

Burlington Northern top management organization chart, January 1, 1977.

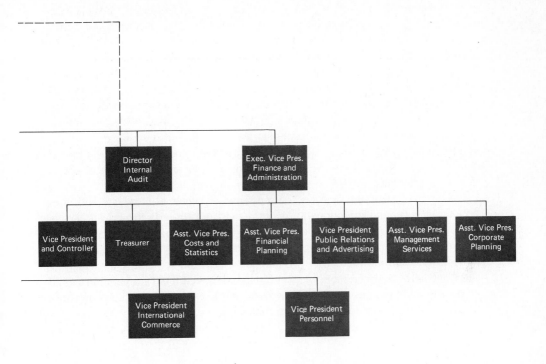

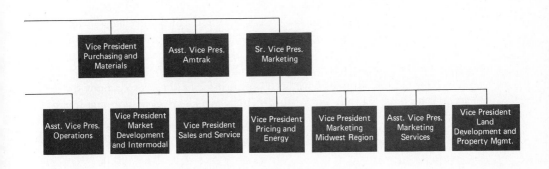

a new corporation. This point is captured in the incorporation laws of such states as Delaware. ("Any power which is not enumerated in the charter or which cannot be inferred from it is *ultra vires*[11] of the corporation.") Obviously underlying the objection is an uneasiness about the fact that corporate intent is dependent upon policy and purpose that is but an artifact of the sociopsychology of a group of biological persons. Corporate intent seems somehow to be a tarnished, illegitimate, offspring of human intent. But this objection is a form of the anthropocentric bias that pervades traditional moral theory. By concentrating on possible descriptions of events and by acknowledging only that the possibility of describing something as an agent depends upon whether or not it can be properly described as having done something for a reason, we avoid the temptation of trying to reduce all agents to human referents.

The CID Structure licenses redescriptions of events as corporate and attributions of corporate intentionality while it does not obscure the private acts of executives, directors, etc. Although X voted to support the joining of the cartel because he was bribed to do so, X did not join the cartel: Gulf Oil Corporation joined the cartel. Consequently, we may say that X did something for which he should be held morally responsible, yet whether or not Gulf Oil Corporation should be held morally responsible for joining the cartel is a question that turns on issues that may be unrelated to X's having accepted a bribe.

Of course Gulf Oil Corporation cannot join the cartel unless X or somebody who occupies position A on the organization chart votes in the affirmative. What that shows, however, is that corporations are collectivities. That should not, however, rule out the possibility of their having metaphysical status and being thereby full-fledged moral persons.

This much seems to me clear: We can describe many events in terms of certain physical movements of human beings and we also can sometimes describe those events as done for reasons by those human beings, but further we also can sometimes describe those events as corporate and still further as done for corporate reasons that are qualitatively different from whatever personal reasons, if any, component members may have for doing what they do.

Corporate agency resides in the possibility of CID Structure licensed redescription of events as corporate intentional. That may still appear to be downright mysterious, although I do not think it is, for human agency, as I have suggested, resides in the possibility of description as well. On the basis of the foregoing analysis, however, I think that grounds have been provided for holding corporations *per se* to account for what they do, for treating them as metaphysical persons *qua* moral persons.

A. A. Berle has written:

The medieval feudal power system set the "lords spiritual" over and against the "lords temporal." These were the men of learning and of the church who in theory were able to say to the greatest power in the world: "You have committed a sin; therefore either you are excommunicated or you must mend your ways." The lords temporal could reply: "I can kill you." But the lords spiritual could retort: "Yes that you can, but you cannot change the philosophical fact." In a sense this is the great lacuna in the economic power system today.[12]

I have tried to fill that gap by providing reasons for thinking that the moral world is not necessarily composed of homogeneous entities. It is sobering to keep in mind that the Gulf Oil Corporation certainly knows what "You are held responsible for payment in full of the amount recorded on your statement" means. I hope I have provided the beginnings of a basis for an understanding of what "The Gulf Oil Corporation should be held responsible for destroying the ecological balance of the bay" means.

NOTES

1. For which there are good lexical grounds. See *Oxford English Dictionary*, especially entry, Accountability.

2. G. E. M. Anscombe, "Modern Moral Philosophy," *Philosophy* 33, 1958, pp. 1–19.

3. For a more detailed discussion, see my *Foundations of Corporate Responsibility*, forthcoming. In that book I show that the notion of the juristic person does not provide a sufficient account. For example, the deceased in a probate case cannot be *held* responsible in the relevant way by anyone, even though the deceased is a juristic person, a subject of rights.

4. L. Austin, "Three Ways of Spilling Ink," in *Philosophical Papers* (Oxford: Clarendon Press, 1970), p. 273. "In considering responsibility, few things are considered more important than to establish whether a man *intended* to do A, or whether he did A intentionally." Moreover, to be the subject of a responsibility ascription of the second type, to be a party in responsibility relationships, hence to be a moral person, the subject must be, at minimum, what I shall call a Davidsonian agent. If corporations are moral persons, they will be noneliminatable Davidsonian agents. See, for example, Donald Davidson, "Agency," in *Agent, Action, and Reason*, ed. Binkley, Bronaugh and Marros (Toronto: University of Toronto Press, 1971).

5. The causal inseparability of these acts I hope to show is a product of the CID Structure, X's doing y is not the cause of C's doing z nor is C's doing z the cause of X's doing y, although if X's doing y causes Event E then C's doing z causes E and vice versa.

6. John Kenneth Galbraith, *The Age of Uncertainty* (Boston: Houghton Mifflin, 1977), p. 261.

7. By "recognition rule(s)" I mean what Hart, in another context, calls "conclusive affirmative indication" that a decision on an act has been made or performed for corporate reasons. H. L. A. Hart, *The Concept of Law* (Oxford: Clarendon Press, 1961), Chap. VI.

8. G. C. Buzby, "Policies—A Guide to What a Company Stands For," *Management Record* (March 1962), p. 5.

9. Ibid.

10. Peter Drucker, *Concept of the Corporation* (New York: John Day Co., 1946/1972), pp. 36–37.

11. Beyond the legal competence.

12. A. A. Berle, "Economic Power and the Free Society," *The Corporate Take-Over*, ed. Andrew Hacker (Garden City, N.Y.: Doubleday, 1964), p. 99.

CORPORATE MORAL AGENCY:
The Case for Anthropological Bigotry

JOHN R. DANLEY*

In "Corporate Moral Agency,"[1] Peter A. French argues for a position, increasingly popular, which would accept "corporations as members of the moral community, of equal standing with the traditionally acknowledged residents—biological human beings." This is but one implication of accepting the claim that one can legitimately ascribe moral responsibility to corporations. To put the matter somewhat differently, again in French's words, "corporations should be treated as full-fledged moral persons and hence . . . have whatever privileges, rights, and duties as are, in the normal course of affairs, accorded to moral persons."

Unwilling to rest content with the usual assaults on prejudices against real persons based on race, creed, sex, religion, or national origin, French is among those[2] seeking to open yet another new front. The struggle is now being extended beyond real persons to eliminate discrimination against a particular class of *personae fictae*, fictitious persons, namely the corporation. Before too hastily endorsing this new "corporate" liberation movement let us pause for reflection. If after serious consideration we do vote to admit these peculiar entities into our rather exclusivist and elitist community of moral beings, we should insist on their having equal standing with the rest of us run-of-the-mill featherless bipeds. After all, what moral neighborhood worthy of the name would allow second-class citizens? After examining the case for admission, however, I find myself driven to the uncomfortable position of defending apartheid, biological apartheid that is, of defending anthropological bigotry. I contend that corporations should not be included in the moral community; they should not be granted full-fledged moral status. Within this emotionally charged atmosphere it is tempting to employ the standard *ad hominems* of bigotry ("Think of the value of your property"; or, "Before you know it your daughter will bring a corporation home to dinner"; "What about the children?"; and so forth), but I will attempt to ward off these temptations. My claim is that the corporatist programs of the kind represented by French would seriously disturb the logic of our moral discourse. Indeed, the corporatist position, while offering no substantial advantages, would entail the reduction of biological persons to the status of second-class citizens. Let us turn now to the dispute.

I

There is little doubt that we often speak of corporations as being responsible for this or that sin or charitable act, whether of microscopic or cosmic proportions. The question is what we mean when we speak in that way. Sometimes all we mean is that the corporation is the cause of such and such. In these instances we are isolating a cause for an event or state of affairs, an exercise not much more (or less) troublesome

From *Action and Responsibility: Bowling Green Studies in Applied Philosophy*, vol. II, 1980. Reprinted by permission of the publisher.

*Department of Philosophy, Southern Illinois University.

than saying "The icy pavement caused the accident." The debate revolves around a fuller sense of "responsibility," a sense which includes more than the idea of "causing to happen." In this richer sense, we ascribe responsibility only if the event or state of affairs caused was also intended by the agent.

When the concept of responsibility is unpacked in this fashion, the traditionalists appear to have victory already in hand. Whatever else we may say of them, collective entities are surely not the kinds of things capable of intending. Individuals within the corporation can intend, lust, have malice aforethought, and so forth, but the corporation cannot. Traditionalists, like myself, maintain that only persons, i.e., entities with particular physical and mental properties, can be morally responsible. Corporations lack these. For the traditionalists, to speak of corporations being responsible is simply elliptical for speaking of certain individuals within the corporation being responsible. On this point, and perhaps this one alone, I do not believe Milton Friedman[3] to be in error.

Undaunted by this venerable line of reasoning, the corporatists proceed to press their case. Although it is French's view that I am treating, I am concerned not so much with the details of his argument as with the general outlines of the corporatist position. Using French's theory as representative, however, provides us with one of the most forceful, sophisticated theories developed. French has worked for years in the area of collective responsibility.[4] His strategy is to accept the traditionalists' analysis of "responsibility," and then to attempt to show that some sense can be made of ascribing "intentions" to a corporation.

The key to making some sense of corporate "intentions" is what French calls the Corporate Internal Decision Structure, the CID. The CID is that which allows one, "licenses" one, to redescribe the actions of certain individuals within a corporation as actions of the corporation. Although the notion is complicated, a CID contains two elements which are particularly relevant:

1. an organization or responsibility flow chart delineating stations and levels within the corporate power structure and

2. corporate decision recognition rules.

As French puts it, the organizational chart provides the grammar for corporate decision making; the recognition rules provide the logic. The purpose of the organizational chart is to locate which procedures will count as decisions for the corporation, and who may or must participate in those procedures. The recognition rules, we are informed, are of two sorts. The first sort are procedural recognitors, "partially embedded in the organizational chart." What these amount to, it seems, are directives more explicit than those contained in the chart, expanding upon it. The second sort of recognition rules are expressed primarily in corporate policy.

Employing the cumbersome apparatus of the CID, some acts may now be described in two non-identical ways, or so it is claimed.

> One of these . . . is 'Executive X's doing y' and one is 'Corporation C's doing z.' The corporate act, and the individual act may have different properties; indeed, they have different causal ancestors though they are causally inseparable.

The effect of this, of course, is that when certain individuals as specified by the organizational chart, engage in certain procedures as specified by the organizational chart and some recognition rules, and act in accordance with other recognition rules (corporate policy), then French claims we can redescribe the action as a corporate act, an intentional corporate act. It is critical to the corporatist position that the two descriptions are non-identical. Saying that "Corporation C did z" is not reducible to the statement that "Executives X, Y, and Z, voted to do y," even though y and z are the same. Since they are non-identical the traditionalist is supposedly prevented from ascribing responsibility only to these individuals. The acts of the individuals are necessary for a corporate act but not identical with it.

Like a child with a new toy, one is strongly inclined by the glitter of this technical hardware to dismantle it, to try to find out how it all works, to see whether it really fits together, to see how and whether it can handle hard cases. To be sure, there are some problems which one can detect immediately. Let me mention two. First of all, it is unclear what French means by an organizational chart. Since his examples are those of nice neat black lines and boxes on a page, like the ones found in business textbooks and corporate policy manuals, one is left with the impression that this is what he has in mind. If so, there are severe difficulties. Most everyone is aware of the extent to which corporate reality departs from the ethereal world of black lines and boxes. Will French maintain that any decisions made by the managers of corporations which do not conform to the organizational chart are not decisions of the corporation? Biting the bullet here may be the best course but it is probable that most decisions are not strictly corporate decisions then. Few corporations act at all, if this criterion is used. French needs a more positivistic interpretation[5] of the organizational chart, one which would insure that the flow chart realistically captured the actual procedures and personages holding the powers. The difficulty with this modification, however, is that the CID begins to lose its function as a normative criterion by which to determine which acts are corporate acts and which are not. The positivistic interpretation would mean that a corporate act is whatever some powerful person within the corporation manages to get others in the corporation to perform, or gets others outside to accept as a corporate act. That will not work at all. The CID appears nestled upon the familiar horns of a dilemma. At least more work is necessary here.

There is a second difficulty. A basic component of the CID must be the corporate charter. Recently the general incorporation charters have become little more than blank tablets for the corporation to engage in business for "any lawful purpose," although some aspects of the organizational chart and a few recognition rules are delineated. Even these permissive rules of recognition have pertinence for French. Suppose every aspect of the CID was followed except that the board of directors voted unanimously to engage the corporation in some unlawful activity. According to the charter, a part of the CID, this is not possible. One could not redescribe such an act as a corporate act. This result of this is that corporations can never act illegally. Unlike the Augustinian doctrine that for fallen man it is not possible not to sin, the French doctrine appears to be that for the corporation it is not possible to sin at all.

These are but two of many queries which might be addressed to French's proposal. However, it is not my concern to dwell on such technical points here, lest we be distracted from the larger issue. Suppose, for the sake of argument, that we accept some mode of redescribing individual acts such that one could identify these acts as constituting a corporate intentional act. Accept French's. Would that establish the corporatist case? I think not. French tips his hand, for instance, when he writes that what "needs to be shown is that there is sense in saying that corporations, and not just the people who work in them, have reasons for doing what they do." But, obviously, French needs to show much more. All that is established by a device which redescribes, is that there is *a sense* in saying that corporations have intentions. The significant question is whether that sense of "intend" is the one used by the traditionalists when explicating "responsibility," and when denying that corporations can have intentions. The traditionalists can easily, and quite plausibly, claim that the corporatist is equivocating on "intend." The sense in which a corporation intends is much different from that in which a biological person intends. The corporatist has further laid the foundation for this charge by finding it necessary to construct the apparatus so that the sense of "intend" involved can be made clear. The more clearly this sense of "intend" is articulated, the more clearly it diverges from what we usually mean by "intend." The arbitrariness of constructing a sense of "intend" should be evident when we consider the possibility of ascribing intentions to numerous other entities, such as plants, animals, or machines. One could go to extraordinary lengths to provide a sense for attributing intentionally to many of these. Yet, few would contend that it was very similar to what we mean in attributing "intention" to humans.

Consider a computer programmed to play chess which learns from previous mistakes. There is a sense in which the computer intends to respond P-K4 to my king pawn opening, but is this the same sense of "intend" as when I intended P-K4? Furthermore, even ascribing an intention to the computer by no means entails that we would be ready to ascribe responsibility to it. The point is that it remains for the corporatist to demonstrate the relationship between the sense of "intend" and the sense involved in ascriptions of responsibility to humans. Hence, a rather difficult task remains for the corporatist before the case is made.

II

Thus far I have established only that the corporatist has failed to establish the position. I must admit that I am not entirely enamored of the preceding line of argument. The dispute smacks of the theological controversies concerning whether "wisdom" or "goodness" when attributed to God have the same sense as when predicated of humans. Nonetheless, the corporatist has moved the debate in that direction by attempting to equate two markedly different senses. There are, fortunately, other factors to be considered in evaluating the corporatist position. These factors appear when one expands the focus of attention beyond the narrow conditions for ascribing "responsibility," and begins to examine the concept as it functions in the broader context of moral discourse.

Much hangs in the balance when ascribing "responsibility." Affixing responsibility is a prelude to expressing approbation or disapprobation—praise or blame. When the agent responsible is praised, that is the final move in the moral game. (Morality never pays very well.) But, when the responsibility is affixed and the agent in question is blame worthy, that is far from the end of the matter. In this case, affixing responsibility and expressing disfavor is itself a prelude to many further permissible or obligatory moves. Minimally, the blameworthy party is expected to express regret or remorse. More importantly, the agent may be required to pay compensation or be subject to punishment. Ascribing responsibility opens the door for these major moral moves. (There are other door openers as well, for example, the notion of cause in strict liability.) Any understanding of the concept of responsibility is incomplete without incorporating the role it plays in relation to these other moral moves. It is this which is lacking from the previous discussion of "intend." Such an analysis cannot be provided here. What can be done, however, is to sketch briefly how ascribing responsibility to corporations effectively blocks these moves, sundering many of the threads which tie "responsibility" so intimately with concepts like remorse, regret, compensation, or punishment. Let me elaborate.

An indication of the consequences of admitting the corporation into the moral community have been foreshadowed by admission into the legal corpus as a person. That legacy is an odious one, marred by an environment within which the corporation has enjoyed nearly all of the benefits associated with personhood while shouldering but few of the burdens or risks. Much the same would result from admission into the moral world. That legacy is not solely to be explained by jaundiced justices or bad judicial judgments, but is a natural consequence of attempting to pretend that the corporation is just another pretty face. While the law early began holding the corporation liable (read: responsible) for certain specified acts, and the scope of things for which it was liable has dramatically increased over the years, there has been a hesitancy to judge that corporations could be subject to most criminal statutes. One of the major stumbling blocks was just the one which is the subject of this paper. It was clear that many of the criminal statutes required criminal intent, or a criminal state of mind, and unable to locate the corporate mind, it was judged that the corporation was not subject to these. The relevance of proposals such as French's is that the justices would now have a method for determining when the corporation acts with intent, with malice aforethought, with premeditation or out of passion. What I am anxious to bring to light, however, is that these proposals offer no advantage over the traditionalist view and in fact create further problems. Consider now the moral moves involved in extracting compensation from, or punishing, a guilty person. How is one to make these moral moves against a corporate person? One cannot. An English jurist put the point well in an often quoted quip to the effect that corporations have no pants to kick, no soul to damn. We may concur with the sentiment of that jurist who concluded that "by God they ought to have both," but they have neither, although French has given them a surrogate soul, the CID.

The corporation cannot be kicked, whipped, imprisoned, or hanged by the neck until dead. Only individuals of the corporation can be punished. What of punishment through the pocketbook, or extracting compensation for a corporate act? Here too, the corporation is not punished, and does not pay the compensation. Usually one punishes the stockholders who in the present corporate climate have virtually no control over corporate actions. Or, if the corporation can pass on the cost of a fiscal punishment or compensation, it is in the end the consumer who pays for the punishment or compensation. If severe enough, hitting the pocketbook may result in the reduction of workforce, again resting the burden on those least deserving, more precisely, on those not responsible at all. Sooner or later, usually sooner, someone hits upon the solution of punishing those individuals of the corporation most directly responsible for the corporate act. There are also moral difficulties associated with this alternative. For example, many top executives are protected through insurance policies, part of the perks of the job. That would be satisfactory if the intent is simply to compensate, but it neutralizes any deterrent or retributive effect. But let us pass over these considerations and examine more closely these recommendations to "go inside" the corporation to punish an individual, whether stockholder, employee, agent, manager, or director of the corporation.

For the traditionalist there is little difficulty. The traditionalist recognizes the corporation as a legal fiction which for better or worse may have equal protection under the law of other persons, but the traditionalist may accept those legal trappings as at best a useful way of treating the corporation for legal purposes. For the traditionalist it makes moral sense for the law to go inside the corporation. After all, morally the corporation is not responsible; only individuals are. As long as those within the corporation pay for the deed, there is no theoretical difficulty.

What of the corporatist's position? The single advantage is that the adoption of that position would mean that some sense could be made of pointing an accusing finger or raising a fist in moral outrage at a fictitious person, a behavior which might otherwise appear not only futile but ridiculous. In the new corporatist scheme the behavior would no longer be ridiculous, only futile. The disadvantages, on the other hand, are apparent when one attempts to follow the responsibility assignment with the normally attendant moral moves as I have just shown. Either those moves are blocked entirely, since one may find no method by which to punish, or the moves are diverted away from the genuine culprit (the fictitious moral agent) and directed toward someone inside the corporation (non-fictitious moral agent). Either alternative is unacceptable. The former would entail that some citizens of the moral community, namely corporate persons, were not subject to the full obligations of membership. That reduces biological members to the status of second-class citizens, shouldering as they do all the burdens. The latter alternative, "going inside," is equally offensive. This alternative means that biological agents are sacrificed vicariously for the sins of the corporation. This solution not only reduces the biological agents to second-class citizens, but would make scapegoats or worse, sacrificial lambs, of them. Thus would the admission of the corporation into the moral community threaten to disturb the logic associated with the ascription of responsibility.

In addition to these problems, the corporatists face other theoretical obstacles. It is not clear that "going inside" a corporation is often, if ever, intelligible, given the analysis of a corporate act. To counter the traditionalist's claim that only individuals are responsible, French claims that the corporate act is not identical with the acts of individuals in the corporation. Given this, how is it possible now to reverse that claim and hold individuals responsible for something which they did not do? All they did at most was to vote for the corporation to do something, or to pay for something to be done on behalf of the corporation. The claim that individual acts and corporate acts are not identical opens the door to criminalless crime, a possibility admitted openly by French in another earlier paper. French there notes that a collective entity may be responsible yet no individual in that collectivity be responsible. Far from being an extreme case, that outcome may include all corporate acts. As mentioned above, such an alternative is unacceptable. But, again, can one make intelligible going inside to make one or more individuals responsible? In order to do so the corporatist must shift ground and concede that the individual acts and the corporate acts are identical, or perhaps that the individuals, by voting on a course of illegal or immoral action, coerced the hapless corporation to go along with the deed.

III

Although I have offered what I take to be a satisfactory defense of the traditionalist position, I would like to close by suggesting an alternative model for viewing the corporation. An alternative is needed because the corporatist's model has largely succeeded in warping many of our intuitions and is reinforced not only by legal idioms, but by managerial vocabulary. In many a corporatist's eye the corporation is an organism, and perhaps even much like a biological person. It has a brain, nerve receptors, muscle, it moves, reproduces, expands, develops, grows, in some periods the "fat is cut off," processes information, makes decisions, and so on. It adjusts to the environment. Such a metaphor may be useful but we have now begun to be victimized by the metaphorical model. Unfortunately, reformers have found it useful to accept that language and that model. It is useful to personify and then to vilify. The model, I fear, stands behind many attempts to endow the corporation with moral agency and personhood.

A more adequate model, especially for those who are reform minded, I would maintain provides a different perspective from which to view contemporary trends. The corporation is more like a machine than an organism.[6] Like machines they are human inventions, designed by humans, modified by humans, operated by humans. Like many machines they are controlled by the few for the benefit of the few. They are no longer simple, easily understandable, organizations, but as complicated as the latest piece of electronic hardware. It takes years of training to learn how to operate and direct one. Like machines they are created, yet they create and shape humans.

If a complicated machine got out of hand and ravaged a community, there seems something perverse about expressing our moral outrage and indignation to the machine. More appropriately, our fervor should be addressed to the operators and to the designers of the machine. They, not the machines, are morally responsible. To ascribe responsibility to such machines, no matter how complicated, is tantamount to mistaking the created for the creator. This mystification is a contemporary form of animism. Such is the case for anthropological bigotry.

NOTES

1. The basic argument of the article appears in a more detailed version in French's forthcoming book *Foundations of Corporate Responsibility*. I have not had the opportunity to consult that book. See also his article in the *American Philosophical Quarterly*, Vol. 13, No. 3, 1976.

2. Of those who apparently espouse this view to some degree are Norman Bowie and Tom L. Beauchamp in *Ethical Theory and Business* (Englewood Cliffs, N.J., Prentice-Hall, Inc., 1979) e.g. Chapter 1 and comments on page 128 and Christopher Stone in *Where The Law Ends* (Harper Colophon, New York, 1975).

3. See *Capitalism and Freedom*, (Chicago, IL, University of Chicago Press, 1962), pp. 133–136.

4. One of French's earliest works is "Morally Blaming Whole Populations," which appears in *Philosophy, Morality, and International Affairs* (New York, Oxford University Press, 1974) edited by Virginia Held et al., pp. 266–285.

5. The positivistic interpretation is suggested by, among other things, French's references to Austin and H. L. A. Hart. The distinction between organizational chart and recognition rules also resembles the positivistic distinction between secondary and primary rules.

6. Although I do not follow Ladd's argument, one good example of taking this alternative model seriously is demonstrated in his "Morality and the Ideal of Rationality in Formal Organizations," in *The Monist*, Vol. 54 (October 1970), pp. 488–516.

chapter six
GOVERNANCE

WHO RULES THE CORPORATION?

RALPH NADER*, MARK GREEN†, and JOEL SELIGMAN‡

All modern state corporation statutes describe a common image of corporate governance, an image pyramidal in form. At the base of the pyramid are the shareholders or owners of the corporation. Their ownership gives them the right to elect representatives to direct the corporation and to approve fundamental corporate actions such as mergers or bylaw amendments. The intermediate level is held by the board of directors, who are required by a provision common to nearly every state corporation law "to manage the business and affairs of the corporation." On behalf of the shareholders, the directors are expected to select and dismiss corporate officers; to approve important financial decisions; to distribute profits; and to see that accurate periodic reports are forwarded to the shareholders. Finally, at the apex of the pyramid are the corporate officers. In the eyes of the law, the officers are the employees of the shareholder owners. Their authority is limited to those responsibilities which the directors delegate to them.

In reality, this legal image is virtually a myth. In nearly every large American business corporation, there exists a management autocracy. One man—variously titled the President, or the Chairman of the Board, or the Chief Executive Officer—or a small coterie of men rule the corporation. Far from being chosen by the directors to run the corporation, this chief executive or executive clique chooses the board of directors and, with the acquiescence of the board, controls the corporation.

The common theme of many instances of mismanagement is a failure to restrain the power of these senior executives. A corporate chief executive's decisions to expand, merge, or even violate the law can often be made without accountability to outside scrutiny. There is, for example, the detailed disclosures of the recent bribery cases. Not only do these reports suggest how widespread corporate foreign and domestic criminality has become; they also provide a unique study in the pathology of American corporate management.

At Gulf Corporation, three successive chief executive officers were able to pay

Excerpted from Ralph Nader, Mark Green, and Joel Seligman, *Taming the Giant Corporation* (New York: W.W. Norton, 1976). Copyright © 1976 by Ralph Nader. Reprinted by permission.

*Founder of Public Citizen, Inc.

†Director, Corporate Accountability Research Group.

‡Department of Law, Northeastern University.

out over $12.6 million in foreign and domestic bribes over a 15-year period without the knowledge of "outside" or non-employee directors on the board. At Northrop, chairman Thomas V. Jones and vice president James Allen were able to create and fund the Economic and Development Corporation, a separate Swiss company, and pay $750,000 to Dr. Hubert Weisbrod, a Swiss attorney, to stimulate West German jet sales without the knowledge of the board or, apparently, other senior executives. At 3M, chairman Bert Cross and finances vice president Irwin Hansen ordered the company insurance department to pay out $509,000 for imaginary insurance and the bookkeeper to fraudulently record the payments as a "necessary and proper" business expense for tax purposes. Ashland Oil Corporation's chief executive officer, Orwin E. Atkins, involved at least eight executives in illegally generating and distributing $801,165 in domestic political contributions, also without question.

The legal basis for such a consolidation of power in the hands of the corporation's chief executive is the proxy election. Annually the shareholders of each publicly held corporation are given the opportunity of either attending a meeting to nominate and elect directors or returning proxy cards to management or its challengers signing over their right to vote. Few shareholders personally attend meetings. Sylvan Silver, a Reuters correspondent who covers over 100 Wilmington annual meetings each year, described representative 1974 meetings in an interview: At Cities Service Company, the 77th largest industrial corporation with some 135,000 shareholders, 25 shareholders actually attended the meeting; El Paso Natural Gas with 125,000 shareholders had 50 shareholders; at Coca Cola, the 69th largest corporation with 70,000 shareholders, 25 shareholders attended the annual meeting; at Bristol Meyers with 60,000 share-holders a like 25 shareholders appeared. Even "Campaign GM," the most publicized shareholder challenge of the past two decades, attracted no more than 3,000 of General Motors' 1,400,000 shareholders, or roughly two-tenths of one percent.

Thus, corporate directors are almost invariably chosen by written proxies. Yet management so totally dominates the proxy machinery that corporate elections have come to resemble the Soviet Union's euphemistic "Communist ballot"—that is, a ballot which lists only one slate of candidates. Although federal and state laws require the annual performance of an elaborate series of rituals pretending there is "corporate democracy," in 1973, 99.7 percent of the directorial elections in our largest corporations were uncontested.

THE BEST DEMOCRACY MONEY CAN BUY

The key to management's hegemony is money. Effectively, only incumbent management can nominate directors—because it has a nearly unlimited power to use corporate funds to win board elections while opponents must prepare separate proxies and campaign literature entirely at their own expense.

There is first management's power to print and post written communications to shareholders. In a typical proxy contest, management will "follow up" its initial proxy solicitation with a bombardment of five to ten subsequent mailings. As attorneys Edward Aranow and Herb Einhorn explain in their treatise, *Proxy Contests for Corporate Control*:

Perhaps the most important aspect of the follow-up letter is its role in the all-important efforts of a soliciting group to secure the *latest-dated* proxy from a stockholder. It is characteristic of every proxy contest that a large number of stockholders will sign and return proxies to one faction and then change their minds and want to have their stock used for the opposing faction.

The techniques of the Northern States Power Company in 1973 are illustrative. At that time, Northern States Power Company voluntarily employed cumulative voting, which meant that only 7.2 percent of outstanding shares was necessary to elect one director to Northern's 14-person board. Troubled by Northern's record on environmental and consumer issues, a broadly based coalition of public interest groups called the Citizens' Advocate for Public Utility Responsibility (CAPUR) nominated Ms. Alpha Snaby, a former Minnesota state legislator, to run for director. These groups then successfully solicited the votes of over 14 percent of all shareholders, or more than twice the votes necessary to elect her to the board.

Northern States then bought back the election. By soliciting proxies a second, and then a third time, the Power Company was able to persuade (or confuse) the shareholders of 71 percent of the 2.8 million shares cast for Ms. Snaby to change their votes.

Larger, more experienced corporations are usually less heavyhanded. Typically, they will begin a proxy campaign with a series of "build-up" letters preliminary to the first proxy solicitation. In Campaign GM, General Motors elevated this strategy to a new plateau by encasing the Project on Corporate Responsibility's single 100-word proxy solicitation within a 21-page booklet specifically rebutting each of the Project's charges. The Project, of course, could never afford to respond to GM's campaign. The postage costs of soliciting GM's 1,400,000 shareholders alone would have exceeded $100,000. The cost of printing a document comparable to GM's 21-page booklet, mailing it out, accompanied by a proxy statement, a proxy card, and a stamped return envelope to each shareholder might have run as high as $500,000.

Nor is it likely that the Project or any other outside shareholder could match GM's ability to hire "professional" proxy solicitors such as Georgeson & Company, which can deploy up to 100 solicitors throughout the country to personally contact shareholders, give them a campaign speech, and urge them to return their proxies. By daily tabulation of returned proxies, professional solicitors are able to identify on a day-by-day basis the largest blocks of stock outstanding which have yet to return a favorable vote.

THE STATE OF THE BOARD

But does not the board of directors with its sweeping statutory mandate "to manage the business and affairs of every corporation" provide an internal check on the power of corporate executives? No. Long ago the grandiloquent words of the statutes ceased to have any operative meaning. "Directors," William O. Douglas complained in 1934, "do not direct." "[T]here is one thing all boards have in common, regardless of their legal position," Peter Drucker has written. *"They do not function."* In Robert Townsend's tart analysis, "[M]ost big companies have turned their boards of directors into nonboards. . . . In the years that I've spent on various boards I've never heard a single suggestion from a director (made as a director *at* a board meeting) that produced any result at all."

Recently these views are corroborated by Professor Myles Mace of the Harvard Business School, the nation's leading authority on the performance of boards of directors. In *Directors—Myth and Reality*, Mace summarized the results of hundreds of interviews with corporate officers and directors.

Directors do not establish the basic objectives, corporate strategies or broad policies of large and medium-size corporations, Mace found. Management creates the policies. The board has a right of veto but rarely exercises it. As one executive said, "Nine hundred and ninety-nine times out of a thousand, the board goes along with management. . . . " Or another, "I can't think of a single time when the board has failed to support a proposed policy of management or failed to endorse the recommendation of management."

The board does not select the president or other chief executive officers. "What is perhaps the most common definition of a function of the board of directors— namely, to select the president—was found to be the greatest myth," reported Mace. "The board of directors in most companies, except in a crisis, does not select the president. The president usually chooses the man who succeeds him to that position, and the board complies with the legal amenities in endorsing and voting his election." A corporate president agreed: "The former company president tapped me to be president, and I assure you that I will select my successor when the time comes." Even seeming exceptions such as RCA's 1975 ouster of Robert Sarnoff frequently turn out to be at the instigation of senior operating executives rather than an aroused board.

The board's role as disciplinarian of the corporation is more apparent than real. As the business-supported Conference Board conceded, "One of the most glaring deficiencies attributed to the corporate board . . . is its failure to monitor and evaluate the performance of the chief executive in a concrete way." To cite a specific example, decisions on executive compensation are made by the president—with perfunctory board approval in most situations. In the vast majority of corporations, Professor Mace found, the compensation committee, and the board which approves the recommendations of the compensation committee, "are not decision-making bodies."

Exceptions to this pattern become news events. In reporting on General Motors' 1971 annual shareholders' meeting, the *Wall Street Journal* noted that, "The meeting's dramatic highlight was an impassioned and unprecedented speech by the Rev. Leon Sullivan, GM's recently appointed Negro director, supporting the Episcopal Church's efforts to get the company out of South Africa. It was the first time that a GM director had ever spoken against management at an annual meeting." Now Rev. Sullivan is an unusual outside director, being General Motor's first black director and only "public interest" director. But what makes Leon Sullivan most extraordinary is that he was the first director in *any* major American corporation to come out publicly against his own corporation when its operations tended to support apartheid.

REVAMPING THE BOARD

The modern corporation is akin to a political state in which all powers are held by a single clique. The senior executives of a large firm are essentially not accountable to any other officials within the firm. These are precisely the circumstances that, in a democratic political state, require a separation of powers into different branches of authority. As James Madison explained in the *Federalist No. 47*:

> The accumulation of all powers, legislative, executive, and judiciary, in the same hands, whether of one, a few or many, and whether hereditary, self-appointed, or elective, may justly be pronounced the very definition of tyranny. Were the federal constitution, therefore, really chargeable with this accumulation of power, or with a mixture of powers, having a dangerous tendency to such an accumulation, no further arguments would be necessary to inspire a universal reprobation of the system.

A similar concern over the unaccountability of business executives historically led to the elevation of a board of directors to review and check the actions of operating management. As a practical matter, if corporate governance is to be reformed, it must begin by returning the board to this historical role. The board should serve as an internal auditor of the corporations, responsible for constraining executive management from violations of law and breach of trust. Like a rival branch of government, the board's function must be defined as separate from operating management. Rather than pretending directors can "manage" the corporation, the board's role as disciplinarian should be clearly described. Specifically, the board of directors should:

- establish and monitor procedures that assure that operating executives are informed of and obey applicable federal, state, and local laws;

- approve or veto all important executive management business proposals such as corporate by-laws, mergers, or dividend decisions;

- hire and dismiss the chief executive officer and be able to disapprove the hiring and firing of the principal executives of the corporation; and

- report to the public and the shareholders how well the corporation has obeyed the law and protected the shareholders' investment.

It is not enough, however, to specify what the board should do. State corporations statutes have long provided that "the business and affairs of a corporation shall be managed by a board of directors," yet it has been over a century since the boards of the largest corporations have actually performed this role. To reform the corporation, a federal chartering law must also specify the manner in which the board performs its primary duties.

First, to insure that the corporation obeys federal and state laws, the board should designate executives responsible for compliance with these laws and require periodic signed reports describing the effectiveness of compliance procedures. Mechanisms to administer spot checks on compliance with the principal statutes should be created. Similar mechanisms can insure that corporate "whistle blowers" and nonemployee sources may communicate to the board—in private and without fear of retaliation—knowledge of violations of law.

Second, the board should actively review important executive business proposals to determine their full compliance with law, to preclude conflicts of interest, and to assure that executive decisions are rational and informed of all foreseeable risks and costs. But even though the board's responsibility here is limited to approval or veto of executive initiatives, it should proceed in as well-informed a manner as practicable. To demonstrate rational business judgment, the directorate should require management "to prove its case." It should review the studies upon which management relied to make a decision, require management to justify its decision in terms of costs or rebutting dissenting views, and, when necessary, request that outside experts provide an independent business analysis.

Only with respect to two types of business decisions should the board exceed this limited review role. The determination of salary, expense, and benefit schedules inherently possesses such obvious conflicts of interest for executives that only the board should make these decisions. And since the relocation of principal manufacturing facilities tends to have a greater effect on local communities than any other type of business decision, the board should require management to prepare a "community impact statement." This public report would be similar to the environmental impact statements presently required by the National Environmental Policy Act. It would require the corporation to state the purpose of a relocation decision; to compare feasible alternative means; to quantify the costs to the local community; and to consider methods to mitigate these costs. Although it would not prevent a corporation from making a profit-maximizing decision, it would require the corporation to minimize the costs of relocation decisions to local communities.

To accomplish this restructuring of the board requires the institutionalization of a new profession: the full-time "professional" director. Corporate scholars frequently identify William O. Douglas' 1940 proposal for "salaried, professional experts [who] would bring a new responsibility and authority to directorates and a new safety to stockholders" as the origin of the professional director idea. More recently, corporations including Westinghouse and Texas Instruments have established slots on their boards to be filled by full-time directors. Individuals such as Harvard Business School's Myles Mace and former Federal Reserve Board chairman William McChesney Martin consider their own thoroughgoing approach to boardroom responsibilities to be that of a "professional" director.

To succeed, professional directors must put in the substantial time necessary to get the job done. One cannot monitor the performance of Chrysler's or Gulf's management at a once-a-month meeting; those firms' activities are too sweeping and complicated for such ritual oversight. The obvious minimum here is an adequate salary to attract competent persons to work as full-time directors and to maintain the independence of the board from executive management.

The board must also be sufficiently staffed. A few board members alone cannot oversee the activities of thousands of executives. To be able to appraise operating management, the board needs a trim group of attorneys, economists, and labor and consumer advisors who can analyze complex business proposals, investigate complaints, spot-check accountability, and frame pertinent inquiries.

The board also needs timely access to relevant corporate data. To insure this, the board should be empowered to nominate the corporate financial auditor, select the corporation's counsel, compel the forwarding and preservation of corporate records, require all corporate executives or representatives to answer fully all board questions respecting corporate operations, and dismiss any executive or representative who fails to do so.

This proposed redesign for corporate democracy attempts to make executive management accountable to the law and shareholders without diminishing its operating efficiency. Like a judiciary within the corporation, the board has ultimate powers to judge and sanction. Like a legislature, it oversees executive activity. Yet executive management substantially retains its powers to initiate and administer business operations. The chief executive officer retains control over the organization of the executive hierarchy and the allocation of the corporate budget. The directors are given ultimate control over a narrow jurisdiction: Does the corporation obey the law, avoid exploiting consumers or communities, and protect the shareholders' investment? The executive contingent retains general authority for all corporate operations.

No doubt there will be objections that this structure is too expensive or that it will disturb the "harmony" of executive management. But it is unclear that there would be any increased cost in adopting an effective board. The true cost to the corporation could only be determined by comparing the expense of a fully paid and staffed board with the savings resulting from the elimination of conflicts of interest and corporate waste. In addition, if this should result in a slightly increased corporate expense, the appropriateness must be assessed within a broader social context: should federal and state governments or the corporations themselves bear the primary expense of keeping corporations honest? In our view, this cost should be placed on the corporations as far as reasonably possible.

It is true that an effective board will reduce the "harmony" of executive management in the sense that the power of the chief executive or seniors executives will be subject to knowledgeable review. But a board which monitors rather than rubber-stamps management is exactly what is necessary to diminish the unfettered authority of the corporate chief executive or ruling clique. The autocratic power these individuals presently possess has proven unacceptably dangerous: it has led to recurring violations of law, conflicts of interest, productive inefficiency, and pervasive harm to consumers, workers, and the community environment. Under normal circumstances there should be a healthy friction between operating executives and the board to assure that the wisest possible use is made of corporate resources. When corporate executives are breaking the law, there should be no "harmony" whatsoever.

ELECTION OF THE BOARD

Restructuring the board is hardly likely to succeed if boards remain as homogeneously white, male, and narrowly oriented as they are today. Dissatisfaction with current selection of directors is so intense that analysts of corporate governance, including Harvard Laws School's Abram Chayes, Yale political scientist Robert Dahl, and University of Southern California Law School Professor Christopher Stone, have each separately urged that the starting point of corporate reform should be to change the way in which the board is elected.

Professor Chayes, echoing John Locke's principle that no authority is legitimate except that granted "the consent of the governed," argues that employees and other groups substantially affected by corporate operations should have a say in its governance:

Shareholder democracy, so-called, is misconceived because the shareholders are not the governed of the corporations whose consent must be sought. . . . Their interests are protected if financial information is made available, fraud and overreaching are prevented, and a market is maintained in which their shares may be sold. A priori, there is no reason for them to have any voice, direct or representational, in [corporate decision making]. They are no more affected than nonshareholding neighbors by these decisions. . . .

A more spacious conception of 'membership,' and one closer to the facts of corporate life, would include all those having a relation of sufficient intimacy with the corporation or subject to its powers in a sufficiently specialized way. Their rightful share in decisions and the exercise of corporate power would be exercised through an institutional arrangement appropriately designed to represent the interests of a constituency of members having a significant common relation to the corporation and its power.

Professor Dahl holds a similar view: "[W]hy should people who own shares be given the privileges of citizenship in the government of the firm when citizenship is denied to other people who also make vital contributions to the firm?" he asks rhetorically. "The people I have in mind are, of course, employees and customers, without whom the firm could not exist, and the general public, without whose support for (or acquiescence in) the myriad protections and services of the state the firm would instantly disappear. . . . " Yet Dahl finds proposals for interest group representation less desirable than those for worker self-management. He also suggests consideration of co-determination statutes such as those enacted by West Germany and ten other European and South American countries under which shareholders and employees separately elect designated portions of the board.

From a different perspective, Professor Stone has recommended that a federal agency appoint "general public directors" to serve on the boards of all the largest industrial and financial firms. In certain extreme cases such as where a corporation repeatedly violates the law, Stone recommends that the federal courts appoint "special public directors" to prevent further delinquency.

There are substantial problems with each of those proposals. It seems impossible to design a general "interest group" formula which will assure that all affected constituencies of large industrial corporations will be represented and that all constituencies will be given appropriate weight. Even if such a formula could be designed, however, there is the danger that consumer or community or minority or franchisee representatives would become only special pleaders for their constituents and otherwise lack the loyalty or interest to direct generally. This defect has emerged in West Germany under codetermination. Labor representatives apparently are indifferent to most problems of corporate management that do not directly affect labor. They seem as deferential to operating executive management as present American directors are. Alternatively, federally appointed public directors might be frozen out of critical decision-making by a majority of "privately" elected directors, or the appointing agency itself might be biased.

Nonetheless, the essence of the Chayes-Dahl-Stone argument is well taken. The boards of directors of most major corporations are, as CBS's Dan Rather criticized the original Nixon cabinet, too much like "twelve grey-haired guys named George." The quiescence of the board has resulted in important public and, for that matter, shareholder concerns being ignored.

An important answer is structural. The homogeneity of the board can only be ended by giving to each director, in addition to a general duty to see that the corporation is profitably administered, a separate oversight responsibility, a separate expertise, and a separate constituency so that each important public concern would be guaranteed at least one informed representative on the board. There might be nine corporate directors, each of whom is elected to a board position with one of the following oversight responsibilities:

1. Employee welfare

2. Consumer protection

3. Environmental protection and community relations

4. Shareholder rights

5. Compliance with law

6. Finances

7. Purchasing and marketing

8. Management efficiency

9. Planning and research

By requiring each director to balance responsibility for representing a particular social concern against responsibility for the overall health of the enterprise, the problem of isolated "public" directors would be avoided. No individual director is likely to be "frozen out" of collegial decision-making because all directors would be of the same character. Each director would spend the greater part of his or her time developing expertise in a different area; each director would have a motivation to insist that a different aspect of a business decision be considered. Yet each would simultaneously be responsible for participating in all board decisions, as directors now are. So the specialized area of each director would supplement but not supplant the director's general duties.

To maintain the independence of the board from the operating management it reviews also requires that each federally chartered corporation shall be directed by a purely "outside" board. No executive, attorney, representative, or agent of a corporation should be allowed to serve simultaneously as a director of that same corporation. Directorial and executive loyalty should be furthered by an absolute prohibition of interlocks. No director, executive, general counsel, or company agent should be allowed to serve more than one corporation subject to the Federal Corporate Chartering Act.

Several objections may be raised. First, how can we be sure that completely outside boards will be competent? Corporate campaign rules should be redesigned to emphasize qualifications. This will allow shareholder voters to make rational decisions based on information clearly presented to them. It is also a fair assumption that shareholders, given an actual choice and role in corporate governance, will want to elect the men and women most likely to safeguard their investments.

A second objection is that once all interlocks are proscribed and a full-time outside board required, there will not be enough qualified directors to staff all major firms. This complaint springs from that corporate mentality which, accustomed to 60-year-old white male bankers and businessmen as directors, makes the norm a virtue. In fact, if we loosen the reins on our imagination, America has a large, rich, and diverse pool of possible directorial talent from academics and public administrators and community leaders to corporate and public interest lawyers.

But directors should be limited to four two-year terms so that boards do not become stale. And no director should be allowed to serve on more than one board at any one time. Although simultaneous service on two or three boards might allow key directors to "pollinize" directorates by comparing their different experiences, this would reduce their loyalty to any one board, jeopardize their ability to fully perform their new directorial responsibilities, and undermine the goal of opening up major boardrooms to as varied a new membership as is reasonable.

The shareholder electoral process should be made more democratic as well. Any shareholder or allied shareholder group which owns .1 percent of the common voting stock in the corporation or comprises 100 or more individuals and does not include a present executive of the corporation, nor act for a present executive, may nominate up to three persons to serve as directors. This will exclude executive management from the nomination process. It also increases the likelihood of a diverse board by preventing any one or two sources from proposing all nominees. To prevent frivolous use of the nominating power, this proposal establishes a minimum shareownership condition.

Six weeks prior to the shareholders' meeting to elect directors, each shareholder should receive a ballot and a written statement on which each candidate for the board sets forth his or her qualifications to hold office and purposes for seeking office. All campaign costs would be borne by the corporation. These strict campaign and funding rules will assure that all nominees will have an equal opportunity to be judged by the shareholders. By preventing directorates from being bought, these provisions will require board elections to be conducted solely on the merit of the candidates.

Finally, additional provisions will require cumulative voting and forbid "staggered" board elections. Thus any shareholder faction capable of jointly voting approximately 10 percent of the total number of shares cast may elect a director.

A NEW ROLE FOR SHAREHOLDERS

The difficulty with this proposal is the one that troubled Juvenal two millennia ago: *Quis custodiet ipsos custodes*, or Who shall watch the watchmen? Without a full-time body to discipline the board, it would be so easy for the board of directors and executive management to become friends. Active vigilance could become routinized into an uncritical partnership. The same board theoretically elected to protect shareholder equity and internalize law might instead become management's lobbyist.

Relying on shareholders to disipline directors may strike many as a dubious approach. Historically, the record of shareholder participation in corporate governance has been an abysmal one. The monumental indifference of most shareholders is worse than that of sheep; sheep at least have some sense of what manner of ram they follow. But taken together, the earlier proposals—an outside, full-time board, nominated by rival shareholder groups and voted on by beneficial owners—will increase involvement by shareholders. And cumulative voting insures that an aroused minority of shareholders—even one as small as 9 or 10 percent of all shareholders—shall have the opportunity to elect at least one member of the board.

But that alone is hardly sufficient. At a corporation the size of General Motors, an aggregation of 10 percent of all voting stock might require the allied action of over 200,000 individuals—which probably could occur no more than once in a generation. To keep directors responsive to law and legitimate public concerns requires surer and more immediate mechansims. In a word, it requires arming the victims of corporate abuses with the powers to swiftly respond to them. For only those employees, consumers, racial or sex minorities, and local communities harmed by corporate depradations can be depended upon to speedily complain. By allowing any victim to become a shareholder and by permitting any shareholder to have an effective voice, there will be the greatest likelihood of continuing scrutiny of the corporation's directorate.

Shareholders are not the only ones with an incentive to review decisions of corporate management; nor, as Professors Chayes and Dahl argue, are shareholders the only persons who should be accorded corporate voting rights. The increasing use by American corporations of technologies and materials that pose direct and serious threats to the health of communities surrounding their plants requires the creation of a new form of corporate voting right. When a federally chartered corporation engages, for example, in production or distribution of nuclear fuels or the emission of toxic air, water, or solid waste pollutants, citizens whose health is endangered should not be left, at best, with receiving money damages after a time-consuming trial to compensate them for damaged property, impaired health, or even death.

Instead, upon finding of a public health hazard by three members of the board of directors or 3 percent of the shareholders, a corporate referendum should be held in the political jurisdiction affected by the health hazard. The referendum would be drafted by the unit triggering it—either the three board members or a designate of the shareholders. The affected citizens by majority vote will then decide whether the hazardous practice shall be allowed to continue. This form of direct democracy has obvious parallels to the initiative and referendum procedures familiar to many states— except that the election will be paid for by a business corporation and will not necessarily occur at a regular election.

This type of election procedure is necessary to give enduring meaning to the democratic concept of "consent of the governed." To be sure, this proposal goes beyond the traditional assumption that the only affected or relevant constituents of the corporation are the shareholders. But no longer can we accept the Faustian bargain that the continued toleration of corporate destruction of local health and property is the cost to the public of doing business. In an equitable system of governance, the perpetrators should answer to their victims.

POWER AND ACCOUNTABILITY:
The Changing Role of the Corporate Board of Directors

IRVING S. SHAPIRO*

The proper direction of business corporations in a free society is a topic of intense and often heated discussion. Under the flag of corporate governance there has been a running debate about the performance of business organizations, together with a flood of proposals for changes in the way corporate organizations are controlled.

It has been variously suggested that corporate charters be dispensed by the Federal Government as distinct from those of the states (to tighten the grip on corporate actions); that only outsiders unconnected to an enterprise be allowed to sit on its board of directors or that, as a minimum, most of the directors should qualify as "independent"; that seats be apportioned to constituent groups (employees, women, consumers and minorities, along with stockholders); that boards be equipped with private staffs, beyond the management's control (to smoke out facts the hired executives might prefer to hide or decorate); and that new disclosure requirements be added to existing ones (to provide additional tools for outside oversight of behavior and performance).

Such proposals have come from the Senate Judiciary Committee's antitrust arm; from regulatory agency spokesmen, most notably the current head of the Securities and Exchange Commission, Harold Williams, and a predecessor there, William Cary; from the professoriat in schools of law and business; from the bench and bar; and from such observers of the American scene as Ralph Nader and Mark Green.[1]

Suggestions for change have sometimes been offered in sympathy and sometimes in anger. They have ranged from general pleas for corporations to behave better, to meticulously detailed reorganization charts. The span in itself suggests part of the problem: "Corporate Governance" (like Social Responsibility before it) is not a subject with a single meaning, but is a shorthand label for an array of social and political as well as economic concerns. One is obliged to look for a way to keep discussion within a reasonable perimeter.

There appears to be one common thread. All of the analyses, premises, and prescriptions seem to derive in one way or another from the question of accountability: Are corporations suitably controlled, and to whom or what are they responsible? This is the central public issue, and the focal point for this paper.

One school of opinion holds that corporations cannot be adequately called to account because there are systemic economic and political failings. In this view, nothing short of a major overhaul will serve. What is envisioned, at least by many in this camp, are new kinds of corporate organizations constructed along the lines of democratic political institutions. The guiding ideology would be communitarian, with the needs and rights of the community emphasized in preference to profit-seeking goals now pursued by corporate leaders (presumably with Darwinian abandon, with

Excerpted from a paper presented in the Fairless Lecture Series, Carnegie-Mellon University, Oct. 24, 1979. Reprinted by permission.

*Chairman of the finance committee of the board and former chairman of the board, E.I. du Pont Nemours & Company, Incorporated.

natural selection weeding out the weak, and with society left to pick up the external costs).

BOARDS CHANGING FOR BETTER

Other critics take a more temperate view. They regard the present system as sound and its methods of governance as morally defensible. They concede, though, that changes are needed to reflect new conditions. Whether the changes are to be brought about by gentle persuasion, or require the use of a two-by-four to get the mule's attention, is part of the debate.

This paper sides with the gradualists. My position, based on a career in industry and personal observation of corporate boards at work, is that significant improvements have been made in recent years in corporate governance, and that more changes are coming in an orderly way; that with these amendments, corporations are accountable and better monitored than ever before; and that pat formulas or proposals for massive "restructuring" should be suspect. The formula approach often is based on ignorance of what it takes to run a large enterprise, on false premises as to the corporate role in society, or on a philosophy that misreads the American tradition and leaves no room for large enterprises that are both free and efficient.

The draconian proposals would almost certainly yield the worst of all possibilities, a double-negative tradeoff: They would sacrifice the most valuable qualities of the enterprise system to gain the least attractive features of the governmental system. Privately owned enterprises are geared to a primary economic task, that of joining human talents and natural resources in the production and distribution of goods and services. That task is essential, and two centuries of national experience suggest these conclusions: The United States has been uncommonly successful at meeting economic needs through reliance on private initiative; and the competitive marketplace is a better course-correction device than governmental fiat. The enterprise system would have had to have failed miserably before the case could be made for replacing it with governmental dictum.

Why should the public have any interest in the internal affairs of corporations? Who cares who decides? Part of the answer comes from recent news stories noting such special problems as illegal corporate contributions to political campaigns, and tracking the decline and fall of once-stout companies such as Penn Central. Revelations of that kind raise questions about the probity and competence of the people minding the largest stores. There is more to it than this, though. There have always been cases of corporate failures. Small companies have gone under too, at a rate far higher than their larger brethren.[2] Instances of corruption have occurred in institutions of all sizes, whether they be commercial enterprises or some other kind.

Corporate behavior and performance are points of attention, and the issue attaches to size, precisely because people do not see the large private corporation as entirely private. People care about what goes on in the corporate interior because they see themselves as affected parties whether they work in such companies or not.

There is no great mystery as to the source of this challenge to the private character of governance. Three trends account for it. First is the growth of very large corporations. They have come to employ a large portion of the workforce, and have become key factors in the nation's technology, wealth and security. They have generated admiration for their prowess, but also fear of their imputed power.

The second contributing trend is the decline of owner-management. Over time, corporate shares have been dispersed. The owners have hired managers, entrusted them with the power to make decisions, and drifted away from involvement in corporate affairs except to meet statutory requirements (as, for example, to approve a stock split or elect a slate of directors).

That raises obvious practical questions. If the owners are on the sidelines, what is to stop the managers from remaining in power indefinitely, using an inside position to control the selection of their own bosses, the directors? Who is looking over management's shoulder to monitor performance?

The third element here is the rise in social expectations regarding corporations. It is no longer considered enough for a company to make products and provide commercial services. The larger it is, the more it is expected to assume various obligations that once were met by individuals or communities, or were not met at all.

With public expectations ratcheting upward, corporations are under pressure to behave more like governments and embrace a universe of problems. That would mean, of necessity, that private institutions would focus less on problems of their own choice.

If corporations succumbed to that pressure, and in effect declared the public's work to be their own, the next step would be to turn them into institutions accountable to the public in the same way that units of government are accountable.

But the corporation does not parallel the government. The assets in corporate hands are more limited and the constituents have options. There are levels of appeal. While the only accountability in government lies within government itself—the celebrated system of checks and balances among the executive, legislative, and judicial branches—the corporation is in a different situation: It has external and plural accountability, codified in the law and reinforced by social pressure. It must "answer" in one way or another to all levels of government, to competitors in the marketplace who would be happy to have the chance to increase their own market share, to employees who can strike or quit, and to consumers who can keep their wallets in their pockets. The checks are formidable even if one excludes for purposes of argument the corporation's initial point of accountability, its stockholders (many of whom do in fact vote their shares, and do not just use their feet).

The case for major reforms in corporate governance rests heavily on the argument that past governmental regulation of large enterprises has been impotent or ineffectual. This is an altogether remarkable assertion, given the fact that the nation has come through a period in which large corporations have been subjected to an unprecedented flood of new legislation and rule making. Regulation now reaches into every corporate nook and cranny—including what some people suppose (erroneously) to be the sanctuary of the boardroom.

Market competition, so lightly dismissed by some critics as fiction or artifact, is in fact a vigorous force in the affairs of almost all corporations. Size lends no immunity to its relentless pressures. The claim that the largest corporations somehow have set themselves above the play of market forces or, more likely, make those forces play for themselves, is widely believed. Public opinion surveys show that. What is lacking is any evidence that this is so. Here too, the evidence goes the other way. Objective studies of concentrated industries (the auto industry, for instance) show that corporate size does not mean declining competitiveness, nor does it give assurance that the products will sell.

Everyday experience confirms this. Consider the hard times of the Chrysler Corporation today, the disappearance of many once-large companies from the American scene, and the constant rollover in the membership list of the "100 Largest," a churning process that has been going on for years and shows no signs of abating.[3]

If indeed the two most prominent overseers of corporate behavior, government and competition, have failed to provide appropriate checks and balances, and if that is to be cited as evidence that corporations lack accountability, the burden of proof should rest with those who so state.

The basics apply to Sears Roebuck as much as to Sam's appliance shop. Wherever you buy the new toaster, it should work when it is plugged in. Whoever services the washing machine, the repairman should arrive at the appointed time, with tools and parts.

Special expectations are added for the largest firms, however. One is that they apply their resources to tasks that invite economies of scale, providing goods and services that would not otherwise be available, or that could be delivered by smaller units only at considerable loss of efficiency. Another is that, like the elephant, they watch where they put their feet and not stamp on smaller creatures through clumsiness or otherwise.

A second set of requirements can be added, related not to the markets selected by corporations individually, but to the larger economic tasks that must be accomplished in the name of the national interest and security. In concert with others in society, including big government, big corporations are expected to husband scarce resources and develop new ones, and to foster strong and diverse programs of research and development, to the end that practical technological improvements will emerge and the nation will be competitive in the international setting.

Beyond this there are softer but nonetheless important obligations: To operate with respect for the environment and with careful attention to the health and safety of people, to honor and give room to the personal qualities employees bring to their jobs, including their need to make an identifiable mark and to realize as much of their potential as possible; to lend assistance in filling community needs in which corporations have some stake; and to help offset community problems which in some measure corporations have helped to create.

This is not an impossible job, only a difficult one. Admitting that the assignment probably is not going to be carried out perfectly by any organization, the task is unlikely to be done even half well unless some boundary conditions are met. Large corporations cannot fulfill their duties unless they remain both profitable and flexible. They must be able to attract and hold those volunteer owners; which is to say, there must be the promise of present or future gain. Companies must have the wherewithal to reinvest significant amounts to revitalize their own capital plants, year after year in unending fashion. Otherwise, it is inevitable that they will go into decline versus competitors elsewhere, as will the nation.

Flexibility is no less important. The fields of endeavor engaging large business units today are dynamic in nature. Without an in-and-out flow of products and services, without the mobility to adapt to shifts in opportunities and public preferences, corporations would face the fate of the buggywhip makers.

Profitability and flexibility are easy words to say, but in practice they make for hard decisions. A company that would close a plant with no more than a passing thought for those left unemployed would and should be charged with irresponsibility; but a firm that vowed never to close any of its plants would be equally irresponsible, for it might be consigning itself to a pattern of stagnation that could ultimately cost the jobs of the people in all of its plants.

The central requirement is not that large corporations take the pledge and bind themselves to stated actions covering all circumstances, but that they do a thoughtful and informed job of balancing competing (and ever changing) claims on corporate resources, mediating among the conflicting (also changing) desires of various constituencies, and not giving in to any one-dimensional perspective however sincerely felt. It is this that describes responsible corporate governance.

Certainly, corporations do not have the public mandate or the resources to be what Professor George Lodge of the Harvard Business School would have them be, which is nationally chartered community-oriented collectives.[4] Such a mission for corporations would be tolerable to society only if corporations were turned into mini-governments—but that takes us back to the inefficiency problem noted earlier. The one task governments have proven they almost always do badly is to run production and distribution organizations. The only models there are to follow are not attractive. Would anyone seriously argue that the public would be ahead if General Motors were run along the lines of Amtrak, or Du Pont were managed in the manner of the U.S. Postal System?

Once roles are defined, the key to success in running a large corporation is to lay out a suitable division of labor between the board and the management, make that division crystal clear on both sides, and staff the offices with the right people. Perhaps the best way to make that split is to follow the pattern used in the U.S. Constitution, which stipulates the powers of the Federal Government and specifies that everything not covered there is reserved to the states or the people thereof. The board of directors should lay claim to five basic jobs, and leave the rest to the paid managers.

The duties the board should not delegate are these:

1. The determination of the broad policies and the general direction the efforts of the enterprise should take.

2. The establishment of performance standards—ethical as well as commercial—against which the management will be judged, and the communication of these standards to the management in unambiguous terms.

3. The selection of company officers, and attention to the question of succession.

4. The review of top management's performance in following the overall strategy and meeting the board's standards as well as legal requirements.

5. The communication of the organization's goals and standards to those who have a significant stake in its activities (insiders and outsiders both) and of the steps being taken to keep the organization responsive to the needs of those people.

The establishment of corporate strategy and performance standards denotes a philosophy of active stewardship, rather than passive trusteeship. It is the mission of directors to see that corporate resources are put to creative use, and in the bargain subjected to calculated risks rather than simply being tucked into the countinghouse for safekeeping.

That in turn implies certain prerequisites for board members of large corporations which go beyond those required of a school board member, a trustee of a charitable organization, or a director of a small, local business firm. In any such assignments one would look for personal integrity, interest and intelligence, but beyond these there is a dividing line that marks capability and training.

The stakes are likely to be high in the large corporation, and the factors confronting the board and management usually are complex. The elements weighing heavily in decisions are not those with which people become familiar in the ordinary course of day-to-day life, as might be the case with a school board.

Ordinarily the management of a corporation attends to such matters as product introductions, capital expansions, and supply problems. This in no way reduces the need for directors with extensive business background, though. With few exceptions, corporate boards involve themselves in strategic decisions and those involving large capital commitments. Directors thus need at least as much breadth and perspective as the management, if not as much detailed knowledge.

If the directors are to help provide informed and principled oversight of corporate affairs, a good number of them must provide windows to the outside world. That is at least part of the rationale for outside directors, and especially for directors who can bring unique perspective to the group. There is an equally strong case, though, for directors with an intimate knowledge of the company's business, and insiders may be the best qualified to deliver that. What is important is not that a ratio be established, but that the group contain a full range of the competences needed to set courses of action that will largely determine the long-range success of the enterprise.

BOARDS NEED WINDOWS

The directors also have to be able and willing to invest considerable time in their work. In this day and age, with major resources on the line and tens of thousands of employees affected by each large corporation, there should be no seat in the boardroom for people willing only to show up once a month to pour holy water over decisions already made. Corporate boards need windows, not window dressing!

There are two other qualities that may be self-evident from what has been said, but are mentioned for emphasis. Directors must be interested in the job and committed to the overall purpose of the organization. However much they may differ on details of accomplishment, they must be willing to work at the task of working with others on the board. They ought to be able to speak freely in a climate that encourages open discussion, but to recognize the difference between attacking an idea and attacking the person who presents it. No less must they see the difference between compromising tactics to reach consensus and compromising principles.

Structures and procedures, which so often are pushed to the fore in discussions of corporate governance, actually belong last. They are not unimportant, but they are subordinate.

Structure follows purpose, or should, and that is a useful principle for testing some of the proposals for future changes in corporate boards. Today, two-thirds to three-quarters of the directors of most large corporations are outsiders, and it is being proposed that this trend be pushed still farther, with the only insider being the chief executive officer, and with a further stipulation that he not be board chairman. This idea has surfaced from Harold Williams, and variations on it have come from other sources.

The idea bumps into immediate difficulties. High-quality candidates for boards are not in large supply as it is. Conflicts of interest would prohibit selection of many individuals close enough to an industry to be familiar with its problems. The disqualification of insiders would reduce the selection pool to a still smaller number, and the net result could well be corporate boards whose members were less competent and effective than those now sitting.

Experience would also suggest that such a board would be the most easily manipulated of all. That should be no trick at all for a skillful CEO, for he would be the only person in the room with a close, personal knowledge of the business.

The objective is unassailable: Corporate boards need directors with independence of judgment; but in today's business world, independence is not enough. In coping with such problems as those confronting the electronics corporations beset by heavy foreign competition, or those encountered by international banks which have loans outstanding in countries with shaky governments, boards made up almost entirely of outsiders would not just have trouble evaluating nuances of the management's performance; they might not even be able to read the radar and tell whether the helmsman was steering straight for the rocks.

If inadequately prepared individuals are placed on corporate boards, no amount of sincerity on their part can offset the shortcoming. It is pure illusion to suppose that complex business issues and organizational problems can be overseen by people with little or no experience in dealing with such problems. However intelligent such people might be, the effect of their governance would be to expose the people most affected by the organization—employees, owners, customers, suppliers—to leadership that would be (using the word precisely) incompetent.

It is sometimes suggested that the members of corporate boards ought to come from the constituencies—an employee-director, a consumer-director, an environmentalist-director, etc. This Noah's Ark proposal, which is probably not to be taken seriously, is an extension of the false parallel between corporations and elected governments. The flaw in the idea is all but self evident: People representing specific interest groups would by definition be committed to the goals of their groups rather than any others; but it is the responsibility of directors (not simply by tradition but as a matter of law as well) to serve the organization as a whole. The two goals are incompatible.

If there were such boards they would move at glacial speed. The internal political maneuvering would be Byzantine, and it is difficult to see how the directors could avoid an obvious challenge of accountability. Stockholder suits would pop up like dandelions in the spring.

One may also question how many people of ability would stand for election under this arrangement. Quotas are an anathema in a free society, and their indulgence here would insult the constituencies themselves—a woman on the board not because she is competent but only because she is female; a black for black's sake; and so on ad nauseam.

A certain amount of constituency pleading is not all bad, as long as it is part of a corporate commitment. There is something to be said for what Harold Williams labels "tension," referring to the divergence in perspective of those concerned primarily with internal matters and those looking more at the broader questions. However, as has been suggested by James Shepley, the president of Time, Inc., "tension" can lead to paralysis, and is likely to do so if boards are packed with groups known to be unsympathetic to the management's problems and business realities.

As Shepley commented, "The chief executive would be out of his mind who would take a risk-laden business proposition to a group of directors who, whatever their other merits, do not really understand the fine points of the business at hand, and whose official purpose is to create 'tension.' "[5]

Students of corporate affairs have an abundance of suggestions for organizing the work of boards, with detailed structures in mind for committees on audit, finance, and other areas; plus prescriptions for membership. The danger here is not that boards will pick the wrong formula—many organization charts could be made to work—but that boards will put too much emphasis on the wrong details.

The idea of utilizing a committee system in which sub-groups have designated duties is far more important than the particulars of their arrangement. When such committees exist, and they are given known and specific oversight duties, it is a signal to the outside world (and to the management) that performance is being monitored in a no-nonsense fashion.

It is this argument that has produced the rule changes covering companies listed on the New York Stock Exchange, calling for audit committees chaired by outside directors, and including no one currently active in management. Most large firms have moved in that direction, and the move makes sense, for an independently minded audit committee is a potent instrument of corporate oversight. Even a rule of that kind, though, has the potential of backfiring.

Suppose some of the directors best qualified to perform the audit function are not outsiders? Are the analytical skills and knowledge of career employees therefore to be bypassed? Are the corporate constituencies well served by such an exclusionary rule, keeping in mind that all directors, insiders or outsiders, are bound by the same legal codes and corporate books are still subject to independent, outside audit? It is scarcely a case of the corporate purse being placed in the hands of the unwatched.

Repeatedly, the question of structure turns on the basics: If corporations have people with competence and commitment on their boards, structure and process fall into line easily; if people with the needed qualities are missing or the performance standards are unclear, corporations are in trouble no matter whose guidebook they follow. Equally, the question drives to alternatives: The present system is surely not perfect, but what is better?

By the analysis presented here the old fundamentals are still sound, no alternative for radical change has been defended with successful argument, and the best course appears to be to stay within the historical and philosophical traditions of American enterprise, working out the remaining problems one by one.

NOTES

1. U.S. Senate, Committee on the Judiciary Subcommittee on Antitrust, Monopoly & Business Rights; Address by Harold M. Williams, *Corporate Accountability*, Fifth Annual Securities Regulation Institute, San Diego, California (January 18, 1978); W. Cary, *A Proposed Federal Corporate Minimum Standards Act*, 29 Bus. Law. 1101 (1974) and W. Cary, *Federalism & Corporate Law: Reflections Upon Delaware*, 83 Yale L.J., 663 (1974); D. E. Schwartz, *A Case for Federal Chartering of Corporations*, 31 Bus. Law. 1125 (1976); M. A. Eisenberg, *Legal Modes of Management Structure in the Modern Corporation; Officers, Directors & Accountants*, 63 Calif. L. Rev. 375 (1975); A. J. Goldberg, *Debate on Outside Directors*, *New York Times*, October 29, 1972 (§3, p. 1); Ralph Nader & Mark Green, *Constitutionalizing the Corporation: The Case for Federal Chartering of Giant Corporations* (1976).

2. *See* "Sixty Years of Corporate Ups, Downs & Outs," *Forbes*, September 15, 1977, p. 127 et seq.

3. *See* Dr. Betty Bock's Statement before Hearings on S.600, Small and Independent Business Protection Act of 1979, April 25, 1979.

4. G. Lodge, *The New American Ideology* (1975).

5. Shepley, *The CEO Goes to Washington*, Remarks to Fortune Corporation Communications Seminar, March 28, 1979.

CORPORATE ACCOUNTABILITY:
The Board of Directors

HAROLD M. WILLIAMS*

I personally do not look forward with any pleasure to the possibility of federal chartering, federal incorporation, or similar measures designed to bring in their wake a body of federal corporation law directed at the structure and governance of the corporation. In my judgment, the emphasis should be on fostering private accountability—the process by which corporate managers are held responsible for the results of their stewardship—rather than on devising ways of intervening in the mechanism of corporate governance in an effort to legislate a sort of federal "corporate morality." Indeed, I question whether there can, over time, be such a thing as *corporate* morality or *corporate* ethics, as distinct from that of the society of which it is a part, and the people who make up that society. I believe there is only a corporate environment that responds to, and impacts upon, the individual behavior, morality, and ethics of those who inhabit that environment. Government may have a role in creating an environment which facilitates and encourages accountability. It should not, as a general matter, dictate the way in which managerial decisions are reached or demand that a certain balance be struck between the conflicting groups affected by corporate action.

The implications of the accelerating rush to federal corporate governance legislation are far-reaching. I fear this as the beginning of an effort which will not be successful and, when the effort fails, that failure will, in turn, serve as the predicate for yet more intensive and profound efforts to constrict the latitude of private decision-making. The eventual painful lesson may be that it is one thing for the federal government to legislate on discrete socially impacting issues, such as safety standards; it is another for it to begin to deal directly with the process by which private economic activity is directed and controlled.

I want to outline an alternative to federal intervention—the development of a corporate structure which compels that those who exercise corporate power are held accountable for the consequences of their stewardship.

In considering the state of corporate accountability and the balance of corporate power, it is traditional to begin—and end—with the proposition that management is accountable to the board of directors and the board of directors is in turn, elected by and accountable to, the shareholders. Unfortunately, as we know, those propositions are often more in the nature of myths. The truth is that shareholder elections are almost invariably routine affirmations of management's will and that the historic and traditional shareholder is now a vanishing breed. Most stock today is purchased by people and institutions whose sole intention is to hold for a relatively brief period and

Excerpted from "Corporate Accountability: The Board of Directors" published in *Vital Speeches of the Day*, vol. XLIV, no. 15, May 15, 1978, pp. 468–472. Delivered at the Securities Regulation Institution, San Diego, California, January 18, 1978. Reprinted by permission of the publisher.

*Former chairman of Securities and Exchange Commission; presently with J. Paul Getty Museum in California.

to sell at a profit. They do not perceive themselves as owners of the company, but rather as investors—or speculators—in its income stream and the stock market assessment of its securities. Perhaps one of the starkest illustrations of this fact is that securities analysts, even for major institutions, rarely involve themselves with corporate governance issues; in fact, they typically do not even make recommendations on proxy voting of securities purchased on their recommendation.

Despite efforts, such as the Commission's current inquiry, to enhance the quality of shareholder information and to revitalize shareholder democracy, I believe it is unrealistic to expect that the shareholder constituency will of itself prove an effective vehicle to keep corporate power accountable. Because of the nature of the majority of these shareholders, they are fully protected if adequate information is made available, if fraud and over-reaching are prevented in securities trading, and if a fair and orderly securities market is maintained. To some extent, the decline in ownership of equities may indicate that even this function is not being well discharged. It is vital that individuals and institutions be willing to invest in a system they trust and in which they perceive they have a reasonably inviting opportunity for gain. However, many companies do not seem to appreciate that their cavalier treatment of shareholders is alienating them from what should be one of their strongest natural constituencies against government intervention.

The second traditional assumption regarding corporate accountability is also open to question. Many boards of directors, although by no means all, cannot truly be said to exercise the accountability function. The board itself is a mini-society, with all the forces of cooption and cooperation, desire for compatibility, and distaste for divisiveness, which characterize any group. Moreover, the board environment is not particularly conducive to nurturing challenge when the majority of directors are beholden—as employees, suppliers of goods or services, or due to other conflicting roles—to the chairman and chief executive. Even friendship itself often inhibits vigorous directorship, although a strong independent director, asking hard questions, in my judgment, performs an act of true friendship. Dissenting directors are, however, rare, and for some reason, they often seem to have short tenure. Thus, the board, in effect, often insulates management rather than holding it accountable.

With this perspective on corporate accountability and the existing mechanisms of corporate governance in mind, I will turn to the core question—whether we can improve the existing process and make it work better, or whether we should take steps to modify or replace it.

Let me dispose of the second set of alternatives first. I have not heard any proposals for structural change which I am prepared to accept today. And, perhaps because I die hard, I believe the existing system can be made substantially more effective. I believe we are dealing with a delicate mechanism—one which can and should function more effectively. Yet I am concerned with suggestions for what appear to be simple solutions—suggestions which are too often lacking in full appreciation for the consequences, including the unpredicted consequences. We need to understand what gets splashed on when we make waves. I believe that the superior economic achievement of our private enterprise system and our unequalled political and personal freedom are three closely intertwined and mutually reinforcing characteristics of our society.

We need to be cautious in tampering with their balance. Direct intervention, through corporate governance legislation, into how business is run may, over time, seriously disturb that balance.

If, on the other hand, corporations are to preserve the power to control their own destiny, the larger corporations need to be able to assure the public that they are capable of self-discipline and that they will appropriately contain and channel their economic power—both real and perceived—in a fashion which is consistent with both the discipline of the marketplace and the noneconomic aspects of the public interest. Mechanisms which provide that assurance must become effective structural components of the process of governance and accountability of the American corporation. The major part of the responsibility for the effectiveness of those structures, and for assuring the public of the corporation's responsibility and accountability, rests with the leaders of the corporate sector and with the lawyers who counsel them.

The first requirement, if government involvement in the mechanisms of corporate decisionmaking is to be obviated, is that those in business understand and recognize the gap which much of the public perceives. The Commission's own hearings on shareholder participation in corporate governance and shareholder rights can make an important contribution to this educative process. Heightened awareness of the problems and obstacles to effective accountability can stimulate self-help in reaching solutions. Shareholder proposals and shareholder litigation will also have a constructive effect in stimulating companies to recognize the problem of accountability.

Second, effective accountability depends on identifying certain tension-producing forces and putting them to work in the corporate environment. We need to support the creation and institutionalization of pressures which operate to balance the natural forces that otherwise exist. For example, management quite naturally is the source of pressure for a totally compatible, comfortable, and supportive board. We need to create a countervailing force that works against that tendency toward comfort. Certainly, the relationship between management and the board should not, by any means, be antagonistic, but tension is essential.

In concrete terms, how can this environment be created? The ideal board, in my opinion, would be constructed as follows: First, since the board guards two thresholds—that between ownership and management and that separating the corporation from the larger society—it must be recognized that there are some people who do not belong on boards—members of management, outside counsel, investment bankers, commercial bankers, and others who might realistically be thought of as suppliers hired by management. Some of these, as individuals, can and do make excellent directors. Yet all must be excluded unless a mechanism can be designed whereby they can establish their ability to function on a basis independent of their management-related role.

Second, ideally, management should not be represented on the board by other than the chief executive. Such a board environment would not preclude other members of management, counsel, and bankers from being present to contribute their expertise to the deliberations in an uncontentious context. Yet, when it comes to the discussion and vote, the independent director would not be faced with, and discouraged or worn down over time by, what is so often a stacked majority against him.

Third, I believe that the chief executive should not be the chairman of the board. Control of the agenda process is a powerful tool, and the issues presented at board meetings should be determined by a chairman who is not a member of management. The substance and process of board deliberations, and the priority which the board assigns to the matters before it, should not be management's prerogatives. And this also means that hard decisions concerning what the board will take up when time is short and the issues are many should not be dictated by management. Finally, the intimidating power of the chair, when occupied by a chief executive in situations where the majority of the board are indebted to him for their directorship, is avoided.

The type of board I have described is an ideal. I recognize that many companies cannot immediately adopt it in all its aspects, but at the same time, there are few public corporations which cannot utilize some of these concepts. For example, it should be apparent by now that I favor a board of independent directors. In this context, committees of independent directors remain important, but primarily as a vehicle for organizing and dividing up the work of the board. Given a lesser number of independent directors, then committees composed exlusively of independent directors for audit, nomination of directors, executive compensation, public policy, and conflict of interest, becomes essential. But even this will not be adequate unless the board, as structured, understands and accepts its responsibility and concerns itself with the corporate environment and its compatibility with the essential corporate responsibilities.

The key point is to create a type of board which builds into the corporate structure and turns to advantage some natural elements of human behavior. My suggestions make it less likely that the board members will succumb to the very human tendency to simply follow along with management's recommendations, management's agenda, and management's attitudes. This is not inconsistent with the true role and responsibilities of the chief executive, and nothing substitutes for a relationship of mutual trust between the chief executive and the board. By suggesting the institutionalization of certain countervailing tensions, I am not proposing anything contrary to, or destructive of, that mutual trust. Indeed, my most important rule for board membership is trust in the chief executive. If that is lacking, the directors should either replace him or get off the board.

Aside from changes in board structure, I believe that the concept of corporate accountability requires that new mechanisms must be created to judge management based on the full range of its responsibilities; that is, its responsibility to both ownership and society to balance short-term and long-term profitability, taking into full account the political and social expectations of the firm, specifically and as part of the larger corporate community. Holding management accountable can enhance economic performances—let alone other aspects. For purposes of this discussion, I will concentrate on the latter.

The quality of an organization's performance is vitally affected by its systems of measurements and control—the lenses through which it views and evaluates itself. The typical manager functions with a high level of confidence that, if he meets his short-term economic targets, he will be rewarded—and certainly not criticized, let alone severely punished, for failure to perform adequately in other areas. Unfortunately, however, much of what we characterize today as sophisticated management control encourages and rewards conduct often contrary to the long-term best interests of socially accountable business.

Corporate control systems need to assure that what is being measured and what is being rewarded conform to what is expected of business. The longer term and the social and political impacts of current decisions must be both visible and consciously accepted. Reward systems need to make those concerns worthwhile. I am not advocating elimination of incentive compensation or options; I fully support them. I am urging that we understand the behavior that these systems encourage and reinforce, and that we design them to include appropriate countervailing pressures, rewards, and penalties. Absent measurement and control systems which recognize explicitly the long-term and noneconomic aspects of managerial responsibility, executives on the firing line, charged with implementation, may not believe that the board and the chief executive mean what they say when they promulgate codes of ethics or talk about high standards of corporate conduct or that they are doing anything more than making a public relations statement for the record and external consumption. When it comes to conduct which makes a manager's life more complicated, or does not seem to be consistent with profits, many managers are inclined to ignore or disbelieve, to delay action and to implement with little enthusiasm, unless there is some tangible evidence that that conduct will form a real part of the evaluation of that manager's performance. This is not a condemnation of corporate ethics—it is a recognition of human behavior. In order to be effective, the mechanisms of corporate accountability must also incorporate that recognition.

A well-known legal historian and scholar, Professor Willard Hurst, has observed:

> [W]e feel very strongly that there should be in the society no significant center of power, which is not somehow accountable to external checks outside of the immediate power holders . . . [F]rom the 18th century on, the idea was that we would check and legitimize entrepreneurial will by holding it accountable to owners. But if the owners cease to be interested as managing owners, if they become interested simply as participants in flows of income, then where does one find the basis for legitimizing the entrepreneurial will which the society so highly prizes?

I have tried to set forth some of the reasons why I believe that, in part at least, the answer to that question lies in creating an environment in which managers are subject to meaningful scrutiny, by an independent board of directors, of the manner in which they discharge their stewardship responsibilities. Our goal should be to create processes which encourage that scrutiny, not to draw lines which confine or restrain it. Holding corporate management accountable in more effective ways will also have collateral benefits—such as strengthened management and improved allocations of scarce resources and profitability. But we can't expect management to lead the way alone—because it would make life less comfortable and secure for it and is contrary to its short-term, day-to-day interests.

Government has a role to play in this process. That role is, however, in many ways very limited. Government—and I expressly include the Securities and Exchange

Commission—does not have the requisite wisdom to be prescriptive, and, as I have indicated, the area does not, in any event, lend itself to solution by prescription. Instead, the Commission's role—and the role of government generally—is to help create an environment which encourages corporate accountability and to stimulate the private sector to take advantage of the opportunity which that environment affords to earn and maintain public trust.

CASES FOR PART TWO

CHASE MANHATTAN BANK, N.A.:
A Case Narrative in Company Values

P. V. PUMPHREY*

CORPORATE RESPONSIBILITY: THE PRO AND CON OF A MORAL DIMENSION

Today the American public demands "corporate responsibility"—the exercise by commercial and industrial organizations of "social awareness," of values that go beyond the bottom line and stockholders' return on capital. To a large extent, either formally or informally, business and industry have responded. The particular values held within an *industry group* (for example, how mineral resources companies see virgin territory) and the evolution of a corporate responsibility program in an individual organization within that group (for example, Company X's commitment to reforesting mined terrain) and the implementation of that policy within the program may well be of interest. The more pronounced the contrast between the traditional outlook of the corporation and that reflected by its corporate responsibility program, the more interesting the case.

Important to any consideration of corporate responsibility is some background knowledge of the rise of—and also the opposition to—this burgeoning movement. Without such a background, neither the general nor the individual business response can be critically measured.

Historically, strong opposition has been voiced in influential quarters to any demand for corporate "social" responsibility: corporations have only an "economic" responsibility.

Adam Smith is perhaps the most noted of a long line of economic thinkers and public figures who have held the view expressed above. His dictum, expressed in moderate terms, "Each individual, left to pursue his own selfish interest, is guided by an unseen hand to promote the public good" has given much comfort to corporations who have demurred at making any tangible commitment to a social commitment. Commodore Vanderbilt expressed himself and his robber baron generation more succinctly: "The public be damned." A leading contemporary conservative economist,

Excerpted from "Chase Manhattan Bank, N.A.: A Case Narrative in Company Values," found in *Case Narratives: Values in Business Management* (C. W. Post Center: Long Island University, 1980). Updated for this volume by the author. Reprinted by permission of Long Island University and the author.

*Department of Finance, C. W. Post Center, Long Island University.

Milton Friedman, has chosen to say much the same thing, though he has given his words a somewhat more palatable flavor:

> Most of the talk of corporate responsibility is utter hogwash. In the first place, the only entities who can have responsibility are individuals; a business cannot have responsibility. So the question is this: Do corporate executives—provided they stay within the law—have any responsibilities within their business activities other than to make money for their stockholders? My answer to that is, No, they do not. Take the corporate executive who says: "I have responsibility over and above that of making profits." If he feels he has such a responsibility, he is going to spend money in ways not in the interest of the stockholders. The crucial question is: What right do executives have to spend their stockholders' money? If "socially responsible" executives would stop and think, they would recognize that they are acting irresponsibly.

The case for corporate responsibility can be summarized equally forcefully. Society and business are inter-dependent; the corporation cannot realistically or rationally divorce itself from social concerns and constraints. Socially constructive corporate action in the long run benefits the whole society. Irresponsible social action—or lack of social action—boomerangs to harm business as well as society.

Business in general has adopted this view. The Corporate Annual Report, Inc. notes that an increasing number of companies are taking strong stands on issues of social importance, and are making statements about such issues in their annual and quarterly reports. Another source reported that pronouncements about social responsibility issue forth so abundantly from corporations that it is hard for anyone to get a decent play in the press. Everyone is in on the act, so to speak, and everyone means what he says. Thus the specific philosophy underlying a corporate responsibility program, the particular aims of that program, the extent of implementation, and the quality of the results are of great importance in any attempt to assess the level of responsibility exercised by a corporation.

THE BANKING INDUSTRY

Since World War II, major banks in the United States have enjoyed substantial growth in capital assets and, in most years, significant increases in the volume of banking business done. These facts have not gone unnoticed: banks are now seen not only as catalysts in the development of the national economy but also as forces shaping daily life in the nation. The quality of daily life has come under critical examination. Maslow's hierarchy of need fulfillment has often been quoted: after physical needs have been fulfilled and after basic personal security (financial and other) has been established, people become concerned about the fulfillment of broader, public social needs. In the early 1970's Fortune Magazine reported that over two-thirds of the population expected business to devote some portion of its profits to the alleviation of social problems; many felt that business was the best equipped and managed category of organization to take on such tasks.

Even in the course of ordinary operations, the impact of banks upon society and their role in shaping the quality of life is immense. This can be easily illustrated:

- commercial loan policies can "favor" certain industries, thus affecting competition and growth rates;

- mortgage and home improvement loans can be made to or withheld from specific residential areas, thus affecting stability and values in the area;

- new construction can be encouraged or discouraged by availability of financing, with long-term impact on an area's tax base;

- municipal financial stability can be encouraged or jeopardized by banks' willingness or unwillingness to purchase notes and bonds;

- personal loan policies can favor or exclude certain population groups, promoting or restricting social mobility; and

- international loans can support oppressive foreign regimes; they can support the internal controls exercised over populations.

The size and range of activities of any major bank are such that each is a significant force in shaping daily life in its operating area. In essence, a bank is a citizen of preponderant strength in its community. Having such strength, the bank must remain aware that its use of it will have permanent effects—good, less good, or bad. Since no nationwide code exists to promote the social awareness of banks or to govern their social conduct, each must develop its own. This report details the activities of the Chase Manhattan Bank in developing and implementing such a code.

THE CHASE MANHATTAN BANK: THE FORMULATION AND IMPLEMENTATION OF A CORPORATE RESPONSIBILITY PROGRAM

The Chase Manhattan Bank is the second largest bank in New York and the third largest in the nation. In 1980, it employed 16,500 people in New York City. The bank is the largest source of consumer credit in the New York area, with $2 billion outstanding. It operates the largest credit card system in the New York area, with 1.5 million Visa card customers. Clearly then, the Chase Manhattan's retail policies affect a significant proportion of New York City's population. Since the bank, like most of its competitors, experienced a personnel turnover in excess of 25 percent per year in the 1960's, every fourth year more Chase Manhattan ex-employees were working elsewhere than there were current employees working at the bank. These ex-employees took the social awareness and values prevalent at Chase Manhattan with them when working at other jobs and in other firms. Thus, whatever policies Chase Manhattan developed for its employees have an effect far beyond the confines of the bank. The development of a corporate responsibility policy has to be seen as one which will be identified with the bank throughout the business community: as one in which the balance between private and public goods can be assessed.

Though the Chase Manhattan Bank today has a comprehensive and clearly stated corporate responsibility policy, this did not come into being fully fledged on the first day of the bank's existence. Rather, the current policy and program reflect a consideration of observed social needs and a concern for broad-based and ongoing responses.

Highly visible commitments to widely publicized causes will attract headlines, but such commitments do not usually involve a significant number of employees for any substantial length of time: they do not create a company-wide sense of purpose at the individual level.

In the 1940's and early 1950's, various departments of the Chase Manhattan were sponsoring a number of uncoordinated charitable or socially responsible activities. In the mid-1950's, the bank took steps to consolidate and focus these activities. Management established a policy whereby a percentage of pre-tax earnings was set aside to be distributed for charitable purposes. A Contributions Committee was formed to supervise distribution. Made up of senior officers, it screened requests for donations and determined what organizations would receive them.

This system centralized the bank's charitable giving: it did not in any way specify a code of conduct to govern the bank's operating procedures as a competitive financial organization.

The urban crises of the 1960's played an important role in the development of a more conscious social policy and a more clearly focussed set of values at Chase Manhattan. The bank began to see itself as a healthy citizen in a far from healthy environment—New York City. The bank began to explore ways in which it could bring some part of its corporate resources to bear upon social problems, and to ascertain how its conduct of daily operations could be shaped to ensure fair and nondiscriminatory dealings with all populations within the city.

In 1968, Chase Manhattan set up its Urban Affairs Advisory Board. This group of appointed senior officers prepared a report entitled: "Chase Manhattan and the Urban Crisis." This was a broad policy document. In 1970, the chairman and president of the bank appointed an Urban Affairs Task Force to examine the future direction and goals of the bank's urban affairs activities. The task force produced a comprehensive 120 page report. The key recommendation was that the bank centralize and coordinate its diverse charitable endeavors to focus resources on areas of greatest importance. At this time, the Urban Affairs Advisory Board was named the Corporate Responsibility Committee.

In 1980, this committee consisted of 21 of the bank's top executives. [It] included a top-level officer from each of the bank's major functional areas; it did not include any of the Chase Manhattan's outside directors. The reason for this is clear: if corporate responsibility is to be "an integral part of normal business operations," then full-time executives of the bank rather than part-time consultants or outside directors must formulate and implement the necessary policies.

The appointment of a committee and the announcement of its purpose do not ensure that policy is carried out. To avoid the trap of nonperformance as instructions were passed down, the Corporate Responsibility Committee set up a number of subcommittees, each one covering a defined program area. In all, the Corporate Responsibility Committee and its subcommittees involved 40 top-level officers. Through this broad-based executive participation the Chase Manhattan sought to ensure real participation and support from all departments of the bank and to ensure that no executives dismissed the corporate responsibility program as "PR eyewash" or "management's pet projects."

THE CORPORATE RESPONSIBILITY POLICY: GENERAL PRINCIPLES

The Chase Manhattan Corporate Responsibility Committee based its policy upon five general principles:

- Responsible and constructive delivery of services and products,

- Equal access to all,

- Enhancement of the communities Chase Manhattan serves,

- Balanced assessment of environmental and energy issues, and

- Concerted cooperation with others in public and private sectors.

Each of these major principles had to be translated into action. The steps that Chase Manhattan took to achieve this translation require consideration.

(1) Responsible and Constructive Delivery of Services and Products

In February 1977, the bank issued the *Chase Manhattan Code of Ethics*, a booklet distributed to all employees. Chairman David Rockefeller described the development of the *Code* as the outcome of a struggle between coming up with "moral generalities too broad to be meaningful" and "laying down a list of 'thou shalts' and 'thou shalt nots' designed to cover every situation." A Chase staff member compared the process to "nailing a custard pie to the wall."

That the *Chase Manhattan Code of Ethics* provides applicable guidelines for bankers is more important than whether or not it is a definitive code which every business or bank would endorse. Mr. Rockefeller described the code as "an evolutionary undertaking" and encouraged each department to discuss, clarify, and amplify the code.

Four key principles were emphasized:

- honesty and candor in all banking activities

- integrity in the use of resources

- avoidance of conflict of interest

- fairness to all

In summing up the Chase Manhattan's publication of its *Code of Ethics*, Mr. Rockefeller stressed that it was a working code for a profitmaking institution: "Establishing a specific Code of Ethics for a particular corporation will not in itself convince the dubious to believe in the free enterprise system. But it is a *logical* and, I would add, a *critical* first step toward the ultimate realization of that goal."

(2) Equal Treatment for All

America in theory affords equal rights and equal treatment for all; however, the daily experience of millions of minority citizens clearly demonstrates that practice does not bear out theory.

Chase Manhattan management recognized that in one important activity, the purchasing of services, products and supplies, to offer equal treatment to minority vendors would require more than merely welcoming those who presented themselves to the bank. Since minority vendors were usually in the small business category, lacking in resources and experience, the bank accepted that any meaningful effort to purchase from them would mean putting them in a position to do business with the bank—and slowly becoming competitive with other, larger mainstream firms.

Since 1970, the Chase Manhattan had attempted to foster minority economic development by encouraging all departments of the bank to purchase goods and services from minority vendors capable of meeting the bank's needs.

The Chase Manhattan's management set up a Minority Purchasing Advisory Council, staffed by representatives of each department in the bank that had purchased goods or services from minority vendors. This committee was charged with two responsibilities: (1) to seek out minority vendors, and (2) implement an incentive system to enable them to do business with the bank. The incentive system allowed for purchases to be made from minority vendors even if quoted prices were 10 percent in excess of the lowest price asked by any other vendor. In the following year, this 10 percent margin was cut to 7 percent; in the third year, the vendor was required to be fully competitive.

The success of this approach to minority purchasing is demonstrated by a fourfold increase in the dollar volume of purchases from minority vendors, from $290,000 in 1975 to over $1,351,000 in 1980.

Another aspect of "equal treatment for all" is the bank's efforts to ensure that this ideal is a reality for those who seek employment and careers with Chase Manhattan. In 1973 Chase Manhattan had two female vice presidents; now there are over 90. The total number of female officers has risen from 155 in 1973 to over 600 in 1980. In 1973 Chase Manhattan had 75 minority officers; now there are over 200. Overall in 1980 more than 18 percent of Chase Manhattan's managerial and professional staff were minority and almost 32 percent were women.

(3) Enhancement of the Communities Chase Manhattan Serves

Chase Manhattan implements this facet of its corporate responsibility policy through its corporate philanthropic budget and through its assistance in community development.

During 1980, Chase increased total contributions to $5.3 million or 1.7 percent of corporate after-tax earnings. In 1981, the philanthropic budget was set at $6.6 million dollars. Chase has not only increased the dollar amount of contributions, but has also increased the percentage of after-tax earnings allocated for philanthropic purposes. The corporate philanthropic budget increased from 1.5 percent of after-tax earnings in 1977 to 1.7 percent in 1980. An increase to 2.0 percent is planned by

1983. In contrast, the seven largest New York City banks (including Chase Manhattan) allocated 1.2 percent of after-tax income to charitable purposes.

More striking than the size of the Chase Manhattan's philanthropic budget is the range and diversity of the grants. The Chase supports activities in housing, health, free enterprise, youth programs, the arts, public management and general societal issues, education, and regional business development. In addition to the 21 senior officers on the Corporate Responsibility Committee, some 40 Chase officers worked on special subcommittees to develop strategies for supporting each of these areas. The net result was over 557 separate grants, many for as little as $500 or $1,000.

As the corporate philanthropy budget expands the Chase is exerting an extra effort to channel the money into the smaller community organizations. In an unusual "outreach" program, the Chase mailed applications for grants forms to every not-for-profit organization in the five boroughs of New York City. The program of Neighborhood Grants, which provides for smaller grants to neighborhood organizations, such as a youth center or block association, was expanded from $55,000 in 1979 to $200,000 in 1980. This enabled the Chase to fund 150 neighborhood groups. As Chase community development officer, Arthur Humphrey says, "If you need $500 to fence a vacant lot so that it doesn't fill up with trash, how many foundations or major corporations would even consider making a $500 grant?"

In the words of David Rockefeller, chairman of the board:

> We have to expand our social consciousness as we expand our range of technical conquests unless we are to conclude that all progress is bound to founder on the shoals of democracy. Profit must remain the yardstick because it is the measure of our efficiency, but profit must be based more and more on calculations of social costs and benefits. We must accept the fact that economic growth is not an end in itself, but rather a means to a greater number of social as well as private ends.

In making the investments that the listed programs have called for, Chase Manhattan has risen to the challenge laid down in Mr. Rockefeller's remarks. It should be noted that the bank maintained its commitments to the programs it had undertaken despite the New York City crisis of 1975, when the bank faced the difficult challenge of balancing its responsibilities to its stockholders, to its depositors, and to the community in which it carries on a major portion of its operations—all of which are interrelated to a significant degree.

(4) Balanced Assessment of Environmental and Energy Issues

Attempts to balance the conservation of resources against the need to develop jobs, products, and revenues are akin to efforts to walk a tight rope spanning an abyss. Banks cannot escape involvement: their primary role is to finance large scale industrial growth and thereby guarantee the social stabilization brought about by expanding economies and rising living standards.

Many projects banks are called upon to finance are far from being environmentally sound or energy-efficient. The exhaustion of raw resources, the production of polluting industrial goods, and the excessive consumption of energy characterize many industrial projects—all of which are shown by their sponsors to offer short-term benefits to the nation or region. Long-term costs and irreversible environmental damage are factors often absent from consideration.

The Chase Manhattan believes that "It is folly to suggest that our society can exist or prosper on a strict 'no growth' policy. Such an approach permanently handicaps the poor and undermines the continual rejuvenation necessary to the health of any entity." Rather, the bank believes that "energy development and economic growth must be compatible with protecting the environment." This policy carries no criteria governing implementation: just how is "compatibility" established?

Each development project is analyzed separately and exhaustively. The bank takes environmental factors into account when considering requests to finance major developments, and to this end trained environmental specialists work with the Corporate Responsibility Division to assist bank officers.

Thus, in supporting growth—whether urban, industrial, or other, the bank is concerned that proper consideration be given to all environmental factors, and that the best anti-pollution technology available be incorporated in any industrial project. People and business thrive best in livable and attractive environments.

(5) Concerted Cooperation with Others in the Public and Private Sectors

The Chase Manhattan's opportunities for concerted cooperation with other organizations in the public and private sectors is unlimited: it is far beyond the bank's capacity to respond to more than a small number. To decide which shall receive time, energy, or funds is indeed difficult; the line between overemphasis and undue neglect is finely drawn, and each of the bank's service constituencies has public and private economic, social, and educational projects for which they seek support. Four of the several hundred programs in which the bank is involved are briefly described below. They cannot fully represent the range of the bank's concerns; they do, however, indicate areas considered to be of primary and continuing importance.

Blackout Emergency Fund. After the 1977 blackout, Chase Manhattan immediately contributed to the Emergency Aid Commission, established to dispense almost $3 million in vital cash aid to businesses that were in danger of being unable to reopen without prompt assistance.

The Business Experience Training Program. For more than a dozen years the Chase Manhattan has run this program which provides a range of entry-level banking jobs for low-income high school students. Since the early 1970's the Bank has also run the High School Summer Intern Program. This places disadvantaged youth in summer jobs in various community-based social agencies.

The Bedford Hills Program. The Chase Manhattan has worked with the State of New York to set up training and employment programs for female inmates. Upon release from the facility, these women, many of whom are New York City residents, have greatly enhanced chances of re-entering the mainstream of society and becoming self-dependent.

New York Educational Institutions. The bank is acutely aware that both public and private educational institutions, at all levels, are facing acute shortages of operating funds. In many cases such situations lead to curtailment of programs and educational opportunity. In 1980, the bank made contributions totaling $1.5 million to universities and colleges.

CONCLUSION

The programs presented above are representative of a far wider range in which the bank is involved.

Some of the programs described are "seed" money programs, in which a community, after receipt of initial grants, must chart its own future course. Other programs involve human catalysts, the skilled bank expert who can guide the layman. Still others offset emergencies or provide a vital bridge for displaced persons who seek to re-enter society. Others pertain to the vital work of education.

No range of programs, however great or however enlightened, will protect a bank from all criticism about its business philosophy or practices. In the case of the Chase Manhattan, three issues have proved to be of public concern: policies in South Africa; policies for trade with the Soviet Union, and employment practices pertaining to women and minorities.

As regards investments in South Africa, the bank has stated its guiding policy: To make no loans which, in the bank's judgment, would support the South African government's apartheid policies or reinforce discriminatory business practices. Chase is willing to support projects of a productive nature which it believes will result in social and economic benefits for all South Africans, namely, private industry projects.

The bank's policy on trade with the Soviet Union is as follows: Though the Soviet Union violates many principles of human rights in dealing with its dissidents, trade keeps the channels of communication open. Through trade it is at times possible to bring Western thoughts and ideas into the country.

In response to suit brought by 10 managerial employees, the bank came to an out-of-court settlement under which a special $2 million, 3-year program will be implemented to further qualify women and minority persons for higher-skill jobs.

This narrative should illustrate a primary point: no philanthropic or corporate responsibility program will meet with equal approval by all who review it. In fact, it is the nature of the business and society relation that the level of mutual criticism remains high, with the former seeing the maximum social good being achieved through reinvestment of earnings and expansion of operations and the latter favoring a diversion of earnings into the direct funding of socially oriented programs.

CORPORATE FREE SPEECH IS UPHELD:
First National Bank of Boston v. Bellotti

*If the speakers here were not corporations, no one would suggest that the state could silence
their proposed speech. It is the type of speech indispensable to decision making in a
democracy, and this is no less true because the speech comes from a corporation rather than
from an individual.*

Justice Lewis F. Powell, Jr.

*Ideas which are not a product of individual choice are entitled to less First Amendment
protection. Indeed, what some have considered to be the principal function of the First
Amendment, the use of communication as a means of self-expression, self-realization and
self-fulfillment, is not at all furthered by corporate speech.*

Justice Byron R. White

WASHINGTON—The U.S. Supreme Court yesterday struck down a Massachusetts
law that prohibited banks and business corporations from spending corporate funds to
publicize political views not related to their companies' business purposes.

In a 5–4 decision defining the free-speech rights of corporations for the first time,
the high court overturned a Massachusetts Supreme Judicial Court decision against
the First National Bank of Boston and four other businesses in the state that wanted
to spend money in 1976 to express their opposition to a referendum proposal to amend
the state constitution.

The proposed amendment, which was defeated, would have authorized the legislature to enact a graduated personal income tax.

Justice Lewis Powell, writer for the majority, said yesterday that the First Amendment to the Constitution was not meant to abridge "speech indispensable to decision
making in a democracy" simply because "the speech comes from a corporation rather
than an individual."

In the main dissenting opinion, Justice Byron R. White said the decision raises
"considerable doubt" that the Court would uphold laws in 31 states that restrict corporate political activities. Most of the laws ban corporate contributions to candidates
for state offices.

White said the ruling also "clearly raises great doubt" that the Court would uphold
the Corrupt Practices Act, the 1907 law with which Congress made it a crime for a
corporation, a national bank, or a labor union to contribute money in connection
with congressional or presidential elections.

States should be free to draw distinctions between corporations and individuals,
White said. "Ideas which are not a product of individual choice are entitled to less
First Amendment protection," he said.

Powell was joined by Chief Justice Warren F. Burger and Justices Potter Stewart,
Harry A. Blackmun, and John Paul Stevens.

White's dissent was joined by Justices Thurgood Marshall and William J. Brennan, Jr. Justice William H. Rehnquist wrote his own dissenting opinion, emphasizing
states' regulatory rights over corporations.

Excerpted from United Press International and AP newsfeatures. "Reaction" from *The Boston Globe* (April
27, 1978). Reprinted by permission of UPI, AP, and *The Boston Globe*.

"A state grants to a business corporation the blessings of potentially perpetual life and limited liability to enhance its efficiency as an economic entity," Rehnquist wrote.

"It might reasonably be concluded that those properties, so beneficial in the economic sphere, pose special dangers in the political sphere," he said.

Joining First National in the court challenge were the New England Merchants National Bank, the Gillette Co., Digital Equipment Corp., and Wyman-Gordon Co.

The statute involved prohibited corporations from making contributions or expenditures to influence the vote on any referendum unless it "materially" affects any of the companies' property, business or assets. When the five firms announced plans in 1976 to spend money to make their opposition known to the income tax, the state attorney general's office announced it would prosecute.

Violation of the law carried a possible corporation fine of up to $50,000 and a one-year prison sentence or $10,000 fine to individual company officers.

Yesterday's ruling was the first to confront the issue whether a corporation—defined by Chief Justice John Marshall in 1819 as "an artificial being, invisible, intangible and existing only in contemplation of law"—has a protected liberty to engage in political activities.

Reaction: "It's a Major Blow to Consumers"

JAMES B. AYRES* and LAWRENCE COLLINS*

The Supreme Court decision upholding the right of corporations to spend their money to speak out on political issues will make it harder for citizens' groups to win referendum questions involving corporate interests, a spokesman for the Massachusetts Public Interest Research Group (MassPIRG) said yesterday.

Peter S. Rider, MassPIRG staff counsel, said the bottle industry spent more than $5 million to kill the bottle referendum last year, permissible under the state law which allows a corporation with a direct interest in a referendum to advertise.

"But," said Rider, "What happens on a broad-reaching referendum such as a proposal to classify property tax levies according to business or residential use? You have the potential for virtually unlimited spending."

Rep. Lois G. Pines (D–Newton), who has led a drive for six years to ban nondeposit bottles and cans in Massachusetts and who last year saw a statewide referendum on the issue defeated by 21,000 votes, expressed shock at the high court's decision.

"This is a major disappointment," Pines said. "I think it has a potentially devastating effect on government. It will mean that big business interests will have more clout than ever before. It's a major blow to consumers or just ordinary people."

First Asst. Atty. Gen. Thomas R. Kiley, who argued the Commonwealth's case before the Supreme Court last November, yesterday said he "naturally is disappointed."

"We haven't seen the full decision yet, so I couldn't even speculate on the possible

*Boston Globe staff.

impact it might have on the state's political scene," said Kiley. "But it is a very significant case."

The U.S. Chamber of Commerce, however, hailed the decision as a great victory for the business community.

"The opinion clears business of the charge that the appearance or possibility of corruption will inevitably result if business speaks out on public issues," Chamber President Richard Lesher said.

The "decision also casts doubt about the legality of lobby reform proposals which single out activities of business for special treatment and regulation," Lesher contended.

On the other hand, Common Cause Senior Vice President Fred Wertheimer called the court's decision "just plain wrong."

Wertheimer said the decision "sets the stage for massive corporate expenditures in initiative campaigns throughout the country and seriously undermines the integrity of the initiative process."

More bluntly, an AFL-CIO spokesman termed the decision, "a victory for the best freedom of speech that money can buy."

Excerpts from High Court Opinions

FROM MAJORITY OPINION BY JUSTICE POWELL

In sustaining a state criminal statute that forbids certain expenditures by banks and business corporations for the purpose of influencing the vote on referendum proposals, the Massachusetts Supreme Judicial Court held that the First Amendment rights of a corporation are limited to issues that materially affect its business, property, or assets. The Court rejected appellants' claim that this statute abridged freedom of speech in violation of the First and Fourteenth Amendments. . . .

The Court below framed the principal question in this case as whether and to what extent corporations have First Amendment rights. We believe that the Court posed the wrong question. The Constitution often protects interests broader than those of the party seeking their vindication. The First Amendment, in particular, serves significant social interests. The proper question therefore is not whether corporations have First Amendment rights and, if so, whether they are co-extensive with those of natural persons. Instead, the question must be whether [the statute in question] abridges expression that the First Amendment was meant to protect. We hold that it does. . . .

In appellants' view the enactments of a graduated personal income tax, as proposed to be authorized by constitutional amendment, would have a seriously adverse effect on the economy of the state. The importance of the referendum issue to the people and government of Massachusetts is not disputed. Its merits, however, are the subject of sharp disagreement. . . .

If the speakers here were not corporations, no one would suggest that the state could silence their proposed speech. It is the type of speech indispensable to decision making in a democracy, and this is no less true because the speech comes from a corporation rather than from an individual.

Nor do our recent commercial speech cases lend support to appellee's business interest theory. They illustrate that the First Amendment goes beyond the protection of the press and the self-expression of individuals to prohibit government from limiting the stock of information from which members of the public may draw. A commercial advertisement is constitutionally protected not so much because it pertains to the seller's business as because it furthers the social interest in the free flow of commercial information.

We thus find no support in the First or Fourteenth Amendments, or in the decisions of this Court, for the proposition that speech that otherwise would lie within the protection of the First Amendment loses that protection simply because its source is a corporation that cannot prove, to the satisfaction of a court, a material effect on its business or property. . . .

If a legislature may direct business corporations to stick to business, it also may limit other corporations—religions, charitable, or civic—to their respective business when addressing the public. Such power in government to channel the expression of views is unacceptable under the First Amendment. . . .

If appellee's arguments were supported by record or legislative findings that corporate advocacy threatened imminently to undermine democratic processes, thereby denigrating, rather than serving First Amendment interest, these arguments would merit our consideration. But there has been no showing that the relative voice of corporations has been overwhelming or even significant in influencing referendums in Massachusetts or that there has been any threat to the confidence of the citizenry in government.

Nor are appellee's arguments inherently persuasive or supported by the precedents of this Court. Referendums are held on issues, not candidates for public office. The risk of corruption perceived in cases involving candidate elections simply is not present in a popular vote on a public issue.

FROM CONCURRING MAJORITY BY CHIEF JUSTICE BURGER

I joined the opinion and judgment of the Court but write separately to raise some questions likely to arise in this area in the future.

A disquieting aspect of Massachusetts' position is that it may carry the risk of infringing on the First Amendment rights of those who employ the corporate form— as most do—to carry on the business of mass communications, particularly the large media conglomerates. This is because of the difficulty, and perhaps impossibility, of distinguishing, either as a matter of fact or constitutional law, media corporations from corporations such as the appellants in this case.

Making traditional use of the corporate form, some media enterprises have amassed vast wealth and power and conduct many activities, some directly related—and some not—to their publishing and broadcasting activities. Today, a corporation might own the dominant newspaper in one or more large metropolitan centers, television and radio stations in those same centers and others, a newspaper chain, news magazines with nationwide circulation, national or worldwide wire news services, and substantial interests in book publishing and distribution enterprises. Corporate ownership may extend vertically, to pulp timberlands to insure an adequate continuing supply of newsprint and to trucking and steamship lines for the purpose of transporting the newsprint to the presses.

Such activities would be logical economic auxiliaries to a publishing conglomerate. Ownership also may extend beyond to business activities unrelated to the task of publishing newspapers and magazines or broadcasting radio and television programs. Obviously, such far-reaching ownership would not be possible without the state-provided corporate form and its "special rules relating to such matters as limited liability, perpetual life, and the accumulation, distribution, and taxation of assets. . . ."

The meaning of the Press Clause, as a provision separate and apart from the Speech Clause, is implicated only indirectly by this case. Yet Massachusetts' position poses serious questions. The evolution of traditional newspapers into modern corporate conglomerates in which the daily dissemination of news by print is no longer the major part of the whole enterprise suggests the need for caution in limiting the First Amendment rights of corporations as such. Thus, the tentative probings of this brief inquiry are wholly consistent, I think, with the Court's refusal to sustain [a] serious and potentially dangerous restriction on the freedom of political speech.

FROM DISSENTING OPINION BY JUSTICE WHITE

. . . the issue is whether a state may prevent corporate management from using the corporate treasury to propagate views having no connection with the corporate business. The Court commendably enough squarely faces the issue but unfortunately errs in deciding it. The Court invalidates the Massachusetts statute and holds that the First Amendment guarantees corporate managers the right to use not only their personal funds but also those of the corporation to circulate fact and opinion, irrelevant to the business placed in their charge and necessarily representing their own personal or collective views about political and social questions. I do not suggest for a moment that the First Amendment requires a state to forbid such use of corporate funds, but I do strongly disagree that the First Amendment forbids state interference with managerial decisions of this kind.

By holding that Massachusetts may not prohibit corporate expenditures or contributions made in connection with referendums involving issues having no material connection with the corporate business the Court not only invalidates the statute, which has been on the books in one form or another for many years, but also casts considerable doubt upon the constitutionality of legislation passed by some states restricting corporate political activity as well as upon the federal Corrupt Practices Act. The Court's fundamental error is its failure to realize that the state's regulatory interests, in terms of which the alleged curtailment of First Amendment rights accomplished by the statute must be evaluated, are themselves derived from the First Amendment. . . . Although in my view the choice made by the state would survive even the most exacting scrutiny, perhaps a rational argument might be made to the contrary. What is inexplicable is for the Court to substitute its judgment as to the proper balance for that of Massachusetts where the state has passed legislation reasonably designed to further First Amendment interests in the context of the political arena where the expertise of legislation is at its peak and that of judges is at its very lowest. Moreover, the result reached today in critical respects marks a drastic departure from the Court's prior decisions which have protected against governmental infringement the very First Amendment interests which the Court now deems inadequate to justify the Massachusetts statute.

. . . Indeed, what some have considered to be the principal function of the First Amendment, the use of communication as a means of self-expression, self-realization, and self-fulfillment, is not at all furthered by corporate speech.

The state has not interfered with the prerogatives of corporate management to communicate about matters that have material impact on the business affairs entrusted to them, however much individual stockholders may disagree on economic or ideological grounds.

Nor has the state forbidden management from formulating and circulating its views at its own expense or at the expense of others, even where the subject at issue is irrelevant to corporate business affairs. But Massachusetts has chosen to forbid corporate management from spending corporate funds in referendum elections absent from demonstrable effect of the issue on the economic life of the company. In short, corporate management may not use corporate monies to promote what does not further corporate affairs but in the last analysis are purely personal views of the management, individually or as a group.

This is not only a policy which a state may adopt consistent with the First Amendment but one which protects the very freedoms that the court has held to be guaranteed by the First Amendment. In *Board of Education v. Barnette* the Court struck down a West Virginia statute which compelled children enrolled in public school to salute the flag and pledge allegiance to it on the grounds that the First Amendment prohibits public authorities from requiring an individual to express support for or agreement with the cause with which he disagrees or concerning which he prefers to remain silent. Subsequent cases have applied this principle to prohibit organizations to which individuals are compelled to belong as a condition of employment from using compulsory dues to support candidates, political parties, or other forms of political expression with which members disagree or do not wish to support.

I would affirm the judgment of the Supreme Judicial Court of the Commonwealth of Massachusetts.

FROM DISSENTING OPINION BY JUSTICE REHNQUIST

This Court decided at an early date with neither argument nor discussion that a business corporation is a "person" entitled to the protection of the Equal Protection clause of the Fourteenth Amendment. Likewise it soon became accepted that the property of a corporation was protected under the Due Process Clause of that same amendment. . . . I can see no basis for concluding that the liberty of the corporation to engage in political activity with regard to matters having no material effect on its business is necessarily incidental to the purpose for which the Commonwealth permitted these corporations to be organized or submitted within its boundaries. Nor can I disagree with the Supreme Judicial Court's factual finding that no such effect has been shown by these appellants. Because the statute as construed provides at least as much protection as the Fourteenth Amendment requires, I believe it is constitutionally valid.

It is true, as the Court points out, that recent decisions of this Court have emphasized the interest of the public in receiving the information offered by the speaker seeking protection. The free flow of information is in no way diminished by the Commonwealth's decision to permit the operation of business corporations with limited rights of political expression. All natural persons who owe their existence to a higher sovereign than the Commonwealth remain as free as before to engage in political activity.

I would affirm the judgment of the Supreme Judicial Court.

DIRECTORSHIPS OF MAJOR U.S. CORPORATIONS TIGHTLY INTERLOCKED

SENATE COMMITTEE ON GOVERNMENTAL AFFAIRS

For the first time in over a decade, a Congressional committee has taken a comprehensive look at interlocking directorships among the Nation's largest corporations.

Initiated by the late Sen. Lee Metcalf (D–Mont.) as chairman of the Subcommittee on Reports, Accounting and Management, the study, prepared by the subcommittee's staff, identifies and analyzes 530 direct and 12,193 indirect interlocks among 130 of the nation's top industrials, financial institutions, retailing organizations, transportation companies, utilities, and broadcasting companies. The companies in the study represented about 25 percent of the assets of all U.S. corporations.

The study disclosed an extraordinary pattern of directorate concentration:

- 123 of these major firms each connected on an average with half of the other major companies in the study.

- The 13 largest firms not only were linked together, but accounted for 240 direct and 5,547 indirect interlocks, reaching an average of more than 70 percent of the other 117 corporations. The 13 largest corporations ranked by assets were: American Telephone and Telegraph, BankAmerica, Citicorp, Chase Manhattan, Prudential, Metropolitan Life, Exxon, Manufacturers Hanover, J.P. Morgan, General Motors, Mobil, Texaco, and Ford.

- The leading competitors in the fields of automotives, energy, telecommunications, and retailing met extensively on boards of America's largest financial institutions, corporate customers, and suppliers.

- The largest commercial bankers clustered on major insurance company boards and insurance directors joined on the banking company boards.

- A direct interlock occurs when two companies have a common director. An indirect interlock occurs when two companies each have a director on the board of a third company.

- The nation's largest airlines and electric utilities were substantially interlocked with major lending institutions.

- The boardrooms of four of the largest banking companies (Citicorp, Chase Manhattan, Manufacturers Hanover, and J.P. Morgan), two of the largest insurance companies (Prudential and Metropolitan Life) and three of the largest nonfinancial companies (AT&T, Exxon, and General Motors) looked like virtual summits for leaders in American business.

Press release, April 23, 1978.

These patterns of director interrelationships imply an overwhelming potential for antitrust abuse and possible conflicts of interest which could affect prices, supply and competition, and impact on the shape and direction of the American economy, said the staff.

Use of the Senate Computer Center enabled the staff to compile master lists of the direct and indirect interlocks among the major companies studied for the year 1976. These lists and accompanying computer analyses are included in the study, along with directorships of officials of the Business Council, Conference Board and Business Roundtable. The study also identifies 256 directors who each sat on the boards of from six to thirteen corporations and the 74 persons who each sat on from three to six of the 130 major corporations.

The subcommittee staff recommended, among other things, that Congress consider:

1. Prohibiting interlocking directorates between corporations with over $1 billion in sales or assets. The proscription would apply to all lines of business, including regulated and nonregulated enterprises. It would be a flat prohibition against multiple management representation involving two or more companies above the $1 billion threshold. Such legislation, said the staff, may be more palatable to both the business and the political sectors since it seeks to reach concentration by restructuring the composition of corporate boards rather than the corporate organizations themselves.

2. Amending the Clayton Act to prohibit all types of horizontal interlocks between actual and potential competitors and vertical interlocks between a company and its customers, suppliers and sources of credit and capital. Such prohibitions, said the staff, may have to be specially tailored to meet the interlock problems within regulatory jurisdictions, but in the nonregulated areas, they should be given sweeping effect.

3. In cooperation with regulatory agencies, legislate a Business in the Sunshine Act requiring open corporate board meetings, subject to closure when trade secrets, privileged and/or special financial information or personnel matters are to be discussed.

Regulatory agencies, the staff proposed, should

1. adopt rules requiring public representation on the boards of large corporations, and

2. collect and make public current and complete reports on interlocking directorships of companies under their jurisdiction.

Commenting on the disarray of Federal records regarding corporate ownership and control, the staff said that prosecutors and the average citizen should "no longer have to hunt and pick their way through incomplete and inaccurate Government and private information sources. Computerization is far enough advanced to provide a central and up-to-date source for that information."

The Securities and Exchange Commission should take a lead role in collecting and disseminating such data, the staff suggested, adding that the executive branch could require such action under the Federal Reports Act if cooperation among regulatory agencies was not forthcoming.

THE DIRECTORS WOKE UP TOO LATE AT GULF

WYNDHAM ROBERTSON*

Sister Jane Scully had just returned from a winter visit to Florida. It had not been altogether a pleasure trip. The Roman Catholic nun, president of Carlow College in Pittsburgh, had also been, since April of 1975, a member of the board of directors of Gulf Oil Corp., the eighth-largest industrial company in the nation and for a time one of the most troubled companies anywhere. For her trip, Sister Jane had taken along a 364-page volume—a detailed account of how Gulf had handed out more than $12 million to national and international political figures.

The report was written after a nine-month investigation demanded by the Securities and Exchange Commission as part of a consent judgment settling a suit against Gulf last year. The investigation was headed by John J. McCloy, eighty-one, the distinguished lawyer and public servant, and two outside directors. Sister Jane had felt she needed to get away for a while to ponder the McCloy report and, as she puts it, borrowing from campus vernacular, "to get my head together." She came home to Pittsburgh with "strong feelings." So, forthrightly, last January 11, she paid a Sunday visit to Bob Rawls Dorsey, sixty-three, the man who had invited her to join Gulf's board and of whom she remains "very fond."

At that point Dorsey was the chairman and chief executive officer of Gulf, but his days in the job were numbered. The polished Texan was not yet resigned to his fate, but Sister Jane, whose head was by now thoroughly together, knew precisely where she stood. "I told him," she said recently, "that I felt there had to be some management changes—and that would certainly include him—in order to restore a sense of rectitude to the corporation." Asked how Dorsey responded, she replied, "He didn't say anything. Just, 'Thank you for your views.'"

At an emotional six-hour meeting on the following day, Gulf's board of directors decided, without ever taking a vote, that Dorsey and three other officers of the company should resign their positions. As Sister Jane recalls the session, "Most of that meeting was devoted to philosophical speculation about the role of the corporate citizen." She believes the board took strong action in the conviction that it had "an obligation to society" to restore the credibility of the company. As the discussion wore on into the evening, she says, "People were speaking from the heart and expressing their deepest values."

Perhaps. But it can be argued that the board had been slow to summon those values. Two and a half years had passed since August of 1973, when Dorsey called a special meeting to tell the board that Gulf's Washington lobbyist, Claude Wild Jr., had given $100,000 in corporate cash to Richard Nixon's 1972 campaign. During that long hiatus, the directors displayed questionable judgment. For example, there is no evidence that, until the SEC stepped in, the directors pressed very hard to find

Abridged from *Fortune*, June 1976. Copyright © 1976 Time, Inc. All rights reserved. Reprinted by permission of the publisher.

*Assistant managing editor, *Fortune* magazine.

out who in management was responsible for authorizing the illegal payments. And they released a principal culprit—Claude Wild himself—from all liability to the corporation in what may have been, at least partly, an effort to keep the dimensions of the scandal hidden.

THE VEIL OF POLITENESS

Why did the directors behave as they did? In part, because they were led astray by the management. Gulf's general counsel and lawyers retained by the company withheld from the board some devastating details that they had turned up while looking into the company's transgressions. And Dorsey kept secret from the board, for more than a year and a half after the scandal broke, the fact that he had personally authorized the largest political payments—$4 million to the party backing President Park Chung Hee of Korea.

Beyond that, the board's temporizing seems to have flowed from the inherently ambiguous relationship between the directors and the chief executive whose actions they were supposed to oversee. There is nothing disreputable about Gulf's directors—the nine outsiders include such men as James Higgins, chairman of the Mellon Bank, the archetype of the hardworking, conscientious businessman. But most of the outside directors were personal friends of Dorsey, and the three insiders on the board were dependent upon him for their advancement.

Under these conditions, familiar in many corporations large and small, the directors found it difficult to pierce the veil of politeness by aggressively questioning the chief executive or usurping his reins. And for a long time, Gulf's directors seemed not to sense that their interests and those of management might be at odds. They traveled a long and rutted road with Dorsey, generally following his lead—until it took them into litigious territory that threatened their own reputations and fortunes. As a result, the effects of the scandal have been dragged out, the corporation is still struggling to clean itself up, and the directors have exposed themselves to serious personal liability.

Gulf's initial investigation began in July, 1973, soon after Claude Wild owned up to Dorsey that he had given that $100,000 to the Nixon campaign. Wild was compelled to confess after Common Cause, the "citizens' lobby," won its fight to spring "Rose Mary's Baby"—a previously undisclosed list of campaign contributors held by Nixon's secretary, Rose Mary Woods. Dorsey says this was the first he had learned about Gulf's illegal political activities in the U.S. To this day, however, no one but Dorsey and his closest confidants can be sure whether that is true.

THE FIRST REVELATIONS

Shortly after Wild delivered his news, Gulf retained a Pittsburgh law firm, Eckert, Seamans, Cherin & Mellott, to represent the corporation before the Watergate Special Prosecution, which was investigating illegal contributions. At the board meeting on August 1, after Dorsey revealed the $100,000 contribution, the directors ordered a partner in the firm, Cloyd Mellott, to make a "thorough investigation" and report back at their meeting the following month. For reasons that are not clear, Mellott didn't report back until four months later.

But throughout August, both he and, presumably, Dorsey learned plenty—mainly from Claude Wild. Wild, fifty-two, is the son of a former Humble Oil lobbyist in Austin who was himself well connected politically.

On August 2, 1973, the day after the special board meeting, Mellott, one of his partners, Thomas Wright, and Gulf's general counsel, Merle Minks, met with Wild. According to Wright, Wild said he had been receiving $300,000 or $400,000 every year in cash from one William Viglia, who brought the funds from the Bahamas. Wild sent about half of this to subordinates in Pennsylvania, Louisiana, Texas, California, and other states for distribution to politicians there.

He did not give details of the contributions made by the subordinates, but he gave the lawyers an earful about what he did with *his* share. His first assignment was to funnel $50,000 to Lyndon Johnson in the early Sixties, and after that he passed money along to such well-known politicians as Hugh Scott, Henry Jackson, Wilbur Mills, and Hubert Humphrey. He also told the lawyers, according to Wright, that because politicians did not like their names showing up on expense accounts, he used some of the cash for entertaining.

IT HAPPENED IN A WATER CLOSET

On the following day, the same three lawyers and a second in-house counsel found out a little more from William Viglia. A small, elderly, and nervous man, Viglia had lived in Nassau since 1959 and kept the books for Bahamas Exploration Ltd., a largely dormant Gulf subsidiary that held a few exploration licenses and paid annual fees to keep them, but hadn't explored for years.

Every year, Bahamas Ex, as it was called, got an average of $400,000 from another subsidiary, Gulf Petroleum, S.A. Viglia said he took this money out in cash, and at intervals of about three weeks carried $25,000, often in his pocket, for delivery to Wild. Viglia assumed that the transfers of money between the two subsidiaries had been requested over the years by the various Gulf controllers. The transfers were made to a Bahamian bank account in the name of Bahamas Ex, but this account was kept secret, and deposits and withdrawals were never reflected on the internal records of the company. Viglia told the lawyers that he was instructed to destroy the bank statements and canceled checks after examining them for accuracy. As the McCloy report later described the process, in a phrase that appears to have sprung from the quill of its octogenarian editor, Viglia "tore [the records] up and flushed them in a water closet."

All of this, it should be remembered, the lawyers learned a mere two days after the board's August 1 meeting. Yet the first time the directors knew that the payments exceeded $100,000 was more than three months later, and at that time they learned only of an additional $25,000. In November, after a series of meetings with the Watergate Special Prosecution, Gulf and Wild pleaded guilty in U.S. District Court to violations of the federal Corrupt Practices Act. Gulf was charged with making the Nixon contribution, plus payments of $10,000 to Senator Jackson and $15,000 to Congressman Mills for their 1972 presidential campaigns. The company requested the return of the payments and got the money back. Gulf was fined $5,000 and Wild, $1,000.

THE BAD NEWS CAME SLOWLY

Though Mellott had been asked to report to the board in September, 1973, he didn't get around to it until December. When he finally appeared, his prepared remarks—which he says he read "practically verbatim"—show that he confined himself mainly to a description of the 1972 presidential-campaign payments, which were already public knowledge. But he also revealed that he had turned up "various other contributions in connection with federal elections since January 1, 1968," and that other political contributions may have been made from corporate funds "possibly beginning as early as 1960." He disclosed no details about these payments other than to say that "the amounts involved were substantial."

Mellott apparently volunteered very little of what he knew. For example, his written remarks don't mention that the contributions passed through a systematic mechanism, nor do they reveal recipients other than the three whose names were already well known. Two months later, in February, 1974, Mellott made a second report, and it was only under questioning from the board that he disclosed that "the total amount involved since 1960 would be approximately $4.8 million."

Mellott made a third and, apparently, final report to the board on June 11. At that time he repeated the figure of $4.8 million, told of 1968 contributions to Nixon's and Humphrey's presidential campaigns, and ran through a list of dollar amounts expended since 1968 for various political cocktail parties and fund-raising dinners. This was, almost exactly, the same accounting of illegal payments that he had given the Watergate Special Prosecution *eight months earlier*. These contributions to federal elections added up to only $345,000. As for the rest, he said, "we are advised by Mr. Wild" that it went to candidates in the states, other political dinners and cocktail parties, business and charitable gifts, entertainment, and expenses of delivering the funds. Wild had received and dispensed $4.1 million, either to federal officials or to bagmen in the states. But according to Mellott, Wild had no records to account for it.

Dorsey himself, during all this time, kept from the directors the biggest political payments of all—that $4 million in Korea. It is still unclear whether these payments to President Park's political party were legal or illegal under Korean law, but the McCloy committee said that Dorsey did not even consider the question at the time. In any case, they were obviously something the directors ought to have been told about in order to help them determine who was responsible for Gulf's political payments and what should be done about them.

As it happened, the money for Korea, like the payments in the U.S., had been charged to the books of Bahamas Ex, and one of the lawyers at Eckert, Seamans, saw an entry about it early in the investigation. He didn't know what the money was for, however, and Viglia told him that the actual funds—as opposed to the bookkeeping entry itself—never passed through the subsidiary. Mellott apparently never brought any of this to the board's attention. Nor did the lawyers, or anyone in Gulf's management, call in Price Waterhouse, the company's auditors, who could have tracked down that payment in short order. Moreover, the directors apparently didn't share with the auditors what Mellott *had* told them. Although the board's audit committee met with Price Waterhouse five times in 1974, the partner in charge of the account says the firm didn't know that the illegal payments exceeded $125,000 until "early 1975."

The board had to wait until May, 1975—or nearly two years—to find out about the Korean payments. Dorsey told the directors just before he was forced to tell the world, in testifying before the Senate subcommittee on multinational corporations. As a footnote to history, it is instructive to observe that Dorsey's self-assured bearing and straightforward testimony to the committee obviously impressed the Senators. One of them, Charles Percy, was moved to make a statement that is today heavy with irony. Said Percy: "I think if President Nixon had done what you have done, originally, and just owned up to everything, and laid it on the line . . . I think he would have finished his term." Of course, one of Dorsey's problems, and one of the problems facing his directors, was that he *hadn't* laid it on the line, originally.

WAS A DIRECTOR DOZING?

While a lot was withheld from the directors, it is at least clear that they were told, as early as December of 1973, that the $125,000 was only the tip of an iceberg. And by the following June they had learned the scope, if not the details, of the domestic payments. What is far less clear is how closely the directors were paying attention. One who apparently missed a lot was James Walton, forty-five, a graduate of Yale and the Harvard Business School. Walton worked for Gulf for ten years before becoming president of the Carnegie Institute, the Pittsburgh cultural center. His mother was the daughter of one of Gulf's founders, and he is the only member of the founding family now on the board.

Last fall Walton testified under oath in connection with a shareholders' suit and insisted that Eckert, Seamans had never reported any payments beyond the $125,000. A portion of his testimony went like this:

Q. Did you at some point learn that there was more than had been reported to you by Eckert, Seamans?
A. Than the $125,000?
Q. Yes.
A. Yes.
Q. When?
A. The spring of 1975.

The testimony is more than a little puzzling, because over a year earlier, Mellott had told the board that the payments were substantially greater. Moreover, Walton said that when the board finally did learn of the larger payments, it was Dorsey, not Mellott, who told them. Perhaps the kindest interpretation that can be put on Walton's answers is that he was woefully confused.

When Mellott reported to the directors in December of 1973 and again in February, he advised them that they had to decide what action to take, if any, with respect to the illegal payments. He told them they could seek recovery from both the recipients and from any officer or employee who participated. He also advised that they had no "absolute duty" to bring a lawsuit. So long as they acted "honestly, in good faith, and for what they believed to be in the best interests of Gulf," he believed a business judgment not to litigate could be successfully defended against a shareholder's derivative action. (By February this was no hypothetical matter, as several shareholders' lawyers had written threatening letters demanding action from the board.)

THE BOARD FACES THE FULL DISCLOSURES

The SEC started to investigate Gulf in October and quickly turned up the off-the-books account and the Korean payments. On March 13 of last year, the SEC issued an injunction that ordered the McCloy investigation, and on the same day Gulf admitted publicly that it had spent more than $10 million of corporate funds on political activities. With that, shareholders began to sue and the directors awakened to the idea that their interests and those of management could be quite different. Sister Jane, who joined the board in April of 1975, described her experience almost a year later: "I was aware throughout his last year of a growing tension—almost a paranoia—among the board members. There was increasing uneasiness from the time I joined until January, when we did something about it."

Several board members—most notably Nathan Pearson, financial adviser to the Paul Mellon family—became extremely cautious about authorizing seemingly routine corporate actions. They may have felt that management had led them astray once and they weren't going to let it happen again. Pearson, a towering man of sixty-four, was a member of the McCloy committee and was presumably learning things that offended what one longtime friend calls his "New England conscience." While he and others picked nits with management, Dorsey became increasingly testy. Not a reflective man by nature, and often given to arrogance, Dorsey was impatient with what he regarded as the directors' growing preoccupation with details he felt were the prerogative of management.

At the two board meetings following the SEC injunction, the directors started second-guessing a lot of decisions. The board had been enjoined against filing proxy or registration statements that failed to disclose material information about unlawful payments. Not knowing how much they still *didn't* know, the directors worried that the McCloy investigation would turn up information that could later be used to prove they hadn't made full disclosure. So in the spring of last year, despite Dorsey's urging, they refused to sign the SEC registration statement necessary to effect a new stock-option plan. And some of them argued for canceling the 1975 annual meeting for fear that the proxy statement could be challenged for failing to make adequate disclosure.

The McCloy report concluded that since 1960 Gulf and its subsidiaries had made payments to politicians and government officials in the U.S. and abroad, both legal and illegal, of more than $12 million. The committee said the figure was "subject to some increase." For example, it was "possible that for a number of years as much as $1,000,000 annually" may have found its way to Korean political figures and parties. Gulf's chief financial officer, Harold Hammer, argued strenuously in early 1975 that an additional $2 million paid out in Italy, ostensibly for nonpolitical purposes, should be added in. (The McCloy report, citing a lack of evidence, disagreed with Hammer.)

Hammer thinks his criticism was the reason Dorsey later stripped him of virtually all of his corporate responsibilities. This year, after Dorsey left, Hammer again became Gulf's principal financial officer.

The shareholders' lawyers are pushing for restitution, of course, and they say they don't care where the money comes from, so long as it flows back into Gulf. They occasionally point out that some of the directors who are defendants in the suits are themselves very well-to-do. All together, the lawyers are asking for some $14.8 million in restitution—plus the more than $3 million that Gulf says it has spent on all its investigations. Jerry McAfee, Dorsey's successor, calls the litigation a "sword of Damocles." He says the directors "have been through hell."

In some ways it is easy to sympathize and to conclude that, but for the grace of God, any well-meaning director could find himself in the same position. Gulf's directors—who incidentally are paid more than $20,000 annually to do their jobs—erred, as others might have, by treating as a routine matter something that was anything but.

In discussing the problem of illegal campaign contributions, the McCloy committee said: "It is hard to escape the conclusion that a sort of 'shut-eye sentry' attitude prevailed upon the part of both the responsible corporate officials and the recipients as well as on the part of those charged with enforcement responsibilities." The key phrase is from a Kipling poem, "The Shut-Eye Sentry," which contains these lines:

> But I'd shut my eyes in the sentry-box,
> So I didn't see nothin' wrong.

If there is a lesson for directors in the Gulf episode, it is that, as surrogate sentries for the shareholders, they must be alert at the watch. And if they doze, they are apt to be rudely awakened by unfriendly lawyers rapping loudly on the box.

SUPPLEMENTARY READING FOR PART TWO

Anshen, Melvin. *Corporate Strategies for Social Performance.* New York: MacMillan, 1980.

Berger, Peter L. "New Attack on the Legitimacy of Business." *Harvard Business Review,* September–October 1981, pp. 82–89.

Blumberg, Phillip I. "Reflections on Proposals for Corporate Reform Through Change in the Composition of the Board of Directors: 'Special Interest' or 'Public Directors'." In S. Prakash Sethi (ed.), *The Unstable Ground: Corporate Social Policy in a Dynamic Society.* Los Angeles: Melville Publishing Co., 1974.

Brown, Courtney. *Putting the Corporate Board to Work.* New York: MacMillan, 1976.

Carroll, Archie S., ed. *Managing Corporate Social Responsibility.* Boston: Little, Brown and Company, 1977.

Dill, William R., ed. *Running the American Corporation.* Englewood Cliffs, N.J.: Prentice-Hall, 1978.

Donaldson, Thomas. "Moral Change in the Corporation." In W. Michael Hoffman (ed.), *Proceedings of the Second National Conference on Business Ethics.* Washington, D.C.: University Press of America, 1979.

Eisenberg, Melvin Aron. *The Structure of the Corporation.* Boston: Little, Brown and Company, 1976.

Friedman, Milton. *Capitalism and Freedom.* Chicago: University of Chicago Press, 1962.

Goodpaster, Kenneth E. "Morality and Organizations." In W. Michael Hoffman (ed.), *Proceedings of the Second National Conference on Business Ethics.* Washington, D.C.: University Press of America, 1979.

Green, Mark, et al. "The Case for a Corporate Democracy Act." *Business and Society Review,* **34,** Summer 1980.

Hastings Law Journal Symposium on Corporate Social Responsibility, **30,** 5, May 1979.

Ladd, John. "Is 'Corporate Responsibility' a Coherent Notion?" In W. Michael Hoffman (ed.), *Proceedings of the Second National Conference on Business Ethics.* Washington, D.C.: University Press of America, 1979.

———. "Morality and the Ideal of Rationality in Formal Organizations." *Monist,* **54,** 1970.

Levitt, Theodore. "The Dangers of Corporate Social Responsibility." *Harvard Business Review,* September–October 1958, pp. 41–50.

Lodge, George C. *The New American Ideology.* New York: Alfred A. Knopf, 1979.

Nader, Ralph, Mark Green, and Joel Seligman. *Taming the Giant Corporation.* New York: W.W. Norton & Co., 1976.

Schwartz, Donald C. "The Case for Federal Chartering of Corporations." *Business and Society Review,* Winter 1973–1974, pp. 52–58.

Stone, Christopher D. "Public Directors Merit a Try." *Harvard Business Review,* March–April 1976, pp. 20–39.

The Role and Composition of the Board of Directors of the Large Publicly Owned Corporation. Statement of the Business Roundtable, January 1978.

PART THREE
WORK IN THE CORPORATION

In Part Two we examined the notion that business organizations have obligations not only, or even primarily, to their stockholders, but also to other "stakeholders" in the firm. One of the most important of these groups of stakeholders is the corporation's employees. They provide the productive and decision-making power of the business; in a very real sense, they *are* the corporation.

What obligations hold between a business and its employees? Traditionally, the primary duty of business to those who work in it has been to pay fair wages. Employees in turn have been expected to perform their jobs well and to be loyal and obedient to their employer. Like the traditional understanding of the corporation itself, however, this simple model of employer–employee relations has been challenged. Some thinkers argue that employees are virtually rightless during working hours. In the past decade a strong interest has emerged in securing more extensive rights for employees to protect them from potential abuses of power by employers. The increasing frequency of "whistle-blowing" incidents—cases in which employees reveal corporate wrongdoing to the public—is another indication of the changing conception of the relationship between employers and employees. In Chapter Seven of this part we examine the rights and duties of employees, with a special focus on the employee rights movement and the issue of whistle blowing.

Vast numbers of Americans spend part or all of their working lives in business. Business, then, is one of the most powerful forces shaping work today, in a position to provide work that is rewarding—or work that is empty, meaningless, alienating. A 1971 study on work in America commissioned by the Department of Health, Education and Welfare reported that Americans are increasingly dissatisfied with their jobs. Since then other studies have supported these findings, and issues surrounding work have received a growing amount of attention. The selections included in Chapter Eight address questions of job satisfaction and the quality of working life.

In Chapter Nine we turn to an area of business–employee relations that has already been the subject of much legislation—that of discrimination in the workplace. As a major social institution, business can play a significant role in the perpetuation or termination of discrimination in American society. But how should it exercise this role? Do those who have been discriminated against in the past deserve compensation in the form of preferential treatment today? Does such treatment infringe on the rights of others to equal consideration? If so, does this mean that it is unjustified?

EMPLOYEE RIGHTS AND DUTIES

Until recently, employee rights have been restricted to those specified in the contract between employee and employer; generally, these had to do with wages, job description, hours, pension, and other benefits. If an employee did not like the treatment he or she received at the hands of an employer, did not wish to carry out an order, or disagreed with company policy, he or she could leave the job. Conversely, employers were permitted to fire employees for any reason or for no reason at all. Both parties, then, were free to terminate their contract at any time; but because jobs have usually been harder to find than employees, many felt that employers held the power and that employees were relatively powerless and required protection.

Today corporations are subject to laws governing minimum wages and maximum hours, specifying health and safety standards, and forbidding discrimination in hiring, firing, and promotion. An employer cannot fire an employee for union activity. But within these limits, argues David Ewing in his "An Employee Bill of Rights," corporations retain a great deal of power over their employees. The structure of most business organizations is still an authoritarian one. The relationship of employer to employee remains that of a superior to a subordinate.

According to Ewing, employees in the workplace lack many of the most basic civil liberties guaranteed by the Constitution. A number of corporations give their employees lie detector tests, collect extensive information about them, and attempt to dictate their behavior off the job. For the most part, employees are permitted little control over matters that directly affect their work lives. They can be fired for dissenting from company views or for refusing to execute an order, even if they believe that the order is immoral or illegal. Frequently there is no grievance procedure within the organization and no means of ensuring that employees receive just treatment. In effect, Ewing holds, the workplace represents a "black hole" in American rights; most citizens are virtually rightless from nine to five.

The civil liberties specified in the Bill of Rights were designed to protect citizens against possible abuses of power by government. But many corporations today have bigger "populations" than the largest of the original thirteen colonies, Ewing points out. The gross annual income of some of the largest conglomerates exceeds the gross national product of such countries as Austria, Norway, and Greece. When corporate power reaches the magnitude of a mini-government, argues Ewing, it is necessary to protect those subject to that power by an explicit recognition of their rights. His proposed employee bill of rights, which would guarantee employees the rights of free speech, dissent, privacy, and due process, represents one way in which this task might be accomplished.

The argument for more extensive employee rights has not gone unchallenged. It is pointed out that there has been no widespread agitation for such rights among workers themselves. Unions have not spent much time negotiating for them. Some believe that creating a legal base for such rights will increase employee complaints, encourage litigation, and foster an atmosphere of hostility between employer and employee. In addition, it further restricts the freedom of the private sector. Explicit recognition and enforcement of the rights discussed by Ewing may well decrease efficiency and increase the costs of business organizations. These costs could be passed on to society at large in the form of higher prices. Finally, it is argued, recognition of civil liberties in the workplace could undermine the authority necessary for the smooth, successful operation of a private enterprise.

Particularly controversial have been the rights of free speech and dissent. Concern over these has been heightened by the increasingly frequent occurrence of incidents of whistle blowing. In the Bay Area Rapid Transit (BART) case included in this part of the text, for example, three engineers employed to build San Francisco's automated subway system expressed their concerns about safety to the public after they failed to get a response from within their firm. Did the engineers have the right, or perhaps even the obligation, to blow the whistle on their employer? Should they receive legal protection from such retaliations by the company as firing, blackballing, or attacks on professional integrity? Some, such as Ralph Nader, recommend not only that whistle blowing receive protection, but that it be actively encouraged as a means of improving corporate responsibility. Others are violently opposed to whistle blowing, feeling that excessive concern for employee rights has eclipsed concern for employee duties, which are just as important. States James M. Roche, chairman of General Motors Corporation:

> Some of the enemies of business now encourage an employee to be disloyal to the enterprise. They want to create suspicion and disharmony and pry into the proprietary interests of the business: However this is labeled—industrial espionage, whistle blowing, or professional responsibility—it is another tactic for spreading disunity and creating conflict.

Legally, an employee is regarded as the agent of the corporation for which he or she works. Agency law states that employees have a duty to obey the directions of their employers; to act solely in their employers' interests in all matters related to their jobs; and to refrain from disclosing confidential information that, if revealed, might harm their employers. The law does not require employees to carry out commands which are illegal or immoral, but neither does it authorize them to reveal such commands to the public or protect them from reprisals if they do so.

Even though employees owe their employers loyalty, obedience, and confidentiality, however, these duties may not be absolute. In his "In Defense of Whistle Blowing," Gene James suggests that employees have other duties—such as a duty to protect society from harm—which may override their loyalty to their employers. Both Kermit Vandivier in the B.F. Goodrich case included in Part One and the three BART engineers, for example, felt that they could not permit serious harm to come to the public in the name of loyalty to the corporation. James argues that employees are not only permitted to disclose corporate wrongdoing they are unable to prevent, but positively obligated to do so. This obligation increases with the seriousness and extent of the harm expected to result from the wrongdoing. Employees who are aware of the potentially harmful consequences of a corporate act and who fail to blow the whistle, James holds, bear part of the responsibility for those consequences. The duty to reveal corporate practices that seriously threaten the public holds even if the employee's own job is at stake.

It is not always clear that a dissenting employee *is* being disloyal to the corporation.

In many cases corporations could have saved themselves thousands of dollars in lawsuits and a tarnished public image by responding to dissenting employees. In part, whether a dissenting employee is acting in the interest of the corporation depends upon how broadly we interpret the nature, function, and goals of business. If the function of business is to produce a reliable product and to refrain from harming the public as well as to make a profit, it could be argued that top management—and not Kermit Vandivier or the BART engineers—acted against the interests of their companies.

The practice of whistle blowing is not without its problems, however. Employee loyalty and obedience are necessary to the functioning of a business organization. Workers cannot be permitted to question every management decision or to evaluate every company policy independently before deciding to carry it out. Employee free speech is not always appropriate. Not all employees are competent to judge the potential harm resulting from a corporate decision; they may lack the information which puts their concern in perspective. If it is actively encouraged, the widespread practice of whistle blowing could foster an atmosphere of hostility and distrust. Employees could blow the whistle out of revenge or a desire to escape sanctions for their own unsatisfactory performance. Finally, if the practice is buttressed by a legal apparatus to protect whistle blowers from reprisal, it could interfere with the autonomy of the private sector.

Although these objections do not entirely rule out whistle blowing, they do suggest that not all whistle blowing is justified, and they point to the need for guidelines for responsible whistle blowing. James offers a set of such guidelines in his article. Perhaps the ideal solution to the problems raised by whistle blowing is to encourage channels of communication and response inside corporations so that employees are not forced to make their concerns public. James offers some suggestions for undertaking this task. Those who are interested in pursuing such ideas further might examine some of the internal mechanisms of regulation suggested by Norman Bowie in Chapter Eleven.

THE QUALITY OF WORKING LIFE

> I start the automobile, the first welds . . . the welding gun's got a square handle with a button on the top for high voltage and a button on the bottom for low. . . . I stand in one spot, about a two- or three-feet area, all night. The only time a person stops is when the line stops. We do about thirty-two jobs per car, per unit. Forty-eight units an hour, eight hours a day. Thirty-two times forty-eight times eight. Figure it out. That's how many times I push that button. . . . Repetition is such that if you were to think about the job itself, you'd slowly go out of your mind. . . . I don't understand why more guys don't flip. Because you're nothing but a machine when you hit this type of thing. They give better care to that machine than they will to you. They'll have more respect, give more attention to that machine. . . . If that machine breaks down, there's somebody out there to fix it right away. If I break down, I'm just pushed over to the other side until another man takes my place. The only thing they have in their mind is to keep that line running.

The feelings of this spot welder at a Ford assembly plant are not unique. Thousands of Americans hold jobs in which they experience fragmentation, repetition, the feeling of being a mere cog in a machine. Most statistics indicate that job dissatisfaction in America is increasing. The 1971 task force report to the secretary of Health, Education and Welfare reported that only 24 percent of all blue-collar workers would choose the same type of work if they could make the choice again.

Nor is the dissatisfaction confined to blue-collar workers, although they are the primary focus of the readings included in this chapter. One executive describes his job:

> I don't know of any situation in the corporate world where an executive is completely free and sure of his job from moment to moment. . . . The danger starts as soon as you become a district manager. You have men working for you and you have a boss above —you're caught in a squeeze. . . . There's always the insecurity. You bungle a job. You're fearful of losing a big customer. You're fearful so many things will appear on your record, stand against you. You're always fearful of the big mistake. You've got to be careful when you go to corporation parties. Your wife, your children have got to behave properly. You've got to fit in the mold. You've got to be on guard. . . . The executive is a lonely animal in the jungle who doesn't have a friend. . . .
>
> I left that world because suddenly the power and the status were empty. I'd been there, and when I got there it was nothing. . . . So when the corporation was sold, my share of the sale was such . . . I didn't have to go back into the jungle. I don't have to fight to the top. I've been to the mountain top. . . . It isn't worth it.

Richard Walton groups such feelings of meaninglessness, powerlessness, and repetitiveness under the heading of "alienation." Alienation occurs when workers have no control over their work processes, when they lack a sense of purpose and a sense of the finished product of their work, and when work ceases to be a means of self-expression and becomes merely the task of carrying out the purposes of another. When we hire someone to perform a task for us, we are treating that person as a means to accomplish our end. The fact that we offer payments in return for the job, however, is a recognition of the fact that the person we have hired is also what Kant would call an end in himself or herself, a person with his or her own goals, purposes, and desires. Designing jobs so that employees can achieve self-expression and self-fulfillment is another, perhaps equally important, way of recognizing employees' intrinsic value as people. The major complaint of the spot welder quoted above is that he is treated not as a person, but as an object.

Although it begins at the workplace, explains Walton, alienation places a heavy toll on society at large in the form of mental health problems, absenteeism, high turnover rates, frequent strikes, sabotage, lack of commitment to work and a decline in the quality of services and products. As characterized by Walton, alienation is a deep-rooted and pervasive problem which requires thoughtful, systematic solutions.

Walton sees the search for innovations to reduce alienation, however, as an opportunity not only to enhance the quality of working life but also to increase productivity. His conviction that overcoming alienation in the workplace can be rewarding both to workers and to business is supported by statistics from the HEW Work in America study mentioned above. At Corning Glass, for example, changes which gave workers more autonomy decreased rejects from 28 to 1 percent, decreased absenteeism from 8 to 1 percent, and increased productivity. Redesign of work at Norway's *Norsk Hydro* fertilizer company decreased production costs per ton by 30 percent and decreased absenteeism from 7 to 4 percent. The percentage of workers expressing satisfaction rose from 58 to 100 percent.

How do we go about conquering alienation and improving the quality of working life? Proposed solutions include structuring jobs to give workers more challenge, more mobility, more variety, and a greater sense of accomplishment. Often this involves decreasing specialization and replacing assembly lines with teams of three or four workers who assemble an entire unit of machinery. Union leader Irving Bluestone suggests that worker participation is the key to improving the quality of working life. Echoing some of the themes touched upon by Ewing, Bluestone argues for a more democratic working environment. He believes that workers ought to have more control over decisions which affect their work. They need to be able to exercise some autonomy and to feel that their views have a significant impact on the business of the company for which they work. Some corporations, especially in Europe, have broadened the notion of employee participation to include participation in ownership and profits as well as decision making. The Harman Auto Plant in Bolivar, Tennessee, described by Michael Maccoby, is an American example of an experiment in workplace democracy.

Like the argument for employee rights, projects to improve the quality of working life are not without their opponents. Mitchell Fein questions the assumption of thinkers like Walton, Bluestone, and Maccoby that the opportunity for personal fulfillment is an essential component of a satisfying job. Not all workers want more autonomy, more challenge, and more variety in their work, he argues. If they did, unions would agitate for quality-of-working-life programs instead of concentrating on issues of wages, hours, safety, and health. In fact, he believes, most workers are satisfied with their jobs. Fein fears that workers will suffer because sociologists will impose preconceived ideas upon them about what makes work satisfying, and he suggests that quality-of-working-life programs represent an exploitation of workers' job satisfaction for gains in productivity.

Maccoby's discoveries during the development of the Bolivar project support Fein's claim that not all workers demand the same kind of satisfaction from their jobs. But quality-of-working-life programs need not be implemented without regard to the individual preference of workers, Maccoby argues. To avoid this pitfall the Bolivar project embraced the goal of *individuation* and incorporated a high degree of participation to allow workers to structure jobs in the way most satisfying to them. The Bolivar project also received strong support from the United Auto Workers Union, an indication that unions are taking an interest in improving the quality of working life.

PREFERENTIAL HIRING

Few people take issue with the goal of equality of opportunity for all Americans. The workplace is one of the most important areas in which to reach this goal. When applicants are denied jobs because of some characteristic—such as sex or race—which is irrelevant to their capacity to perform satisfactorily, they are not receiving an equal opportunity, but are being discriminated against. More subtly, even if applicants are selected on the basis of their qualifications alone, past discriminations may mean that members of some groups have been denied the chance to develop the relevant qualifications and thus lack equal opportunity in a different sense. Comparisons of annual income, proportional representation in the highest economic positions, and proportional representation in the lowest economic positions between white males and women and minorities show that racial and sexual discrimination is being practiced in our society in many firms, and that this discrimination has not decreased significantly in recent years.

Title VII of the Civil Rights Act of 1964 prohibits discrimination on the basis of race, color, religion, sex, or national origin. The act also established the Equal Employment Opportunity Commission, which has the power to enforce compliance with Title VII. Business has responded with a range of strategies, from what has been termed "passive nondiscrimination" to the establishment of hard quotas specifying the number of women or minorities which must be hired. Under a policy of passive nondiscrimination, organizations commit themselves to making personnel decisions without regard to race, sex, color, and so on. But it has been argued that this approach does nothing to rectify unfair patterns of job distribution which are a result of past injustices. A more active approach is that of affirmative action, in which employers attempt to publicize opportunities widely and make efforts to seek out female or minority applicants. Still another suggestion for ending job discrimination is preferential hiring, in which preference is given to women and members of minority groups.

Because preferential hiring involves giving preference to certain applicants *because* they are female or members of minority groups, some feel that it is a form of reverse discrimination—that is, that it deprives applicants who are *not* members of disadvantaged groups to their right to equal consideration on the basis of qualifications alone.

Supporters of preferential hiring policies like Judith Jarvis Thomson hold that compensatory justice requires that we adopt policies of preferential hiring. In the past, members of disadvantaged groups were denied what they were owed—an equal opportunity. We can best compensate for this injustice by making it easier for members of those groups to acquire jobs now. This compensatory argument is reminiscent of Nozick's claim that if present distribution has been shaped by past injustice, some redistribution is necessary to make amends. Thomson acknowledges that the preferential hiring of blacks and women will deprive the white male of his right to equal consideration. But, she argues, this is not inappropriate, since even those white males who have not individually harmed blacks or women have benefited, directly or indirectly, from past discriminatory policies.

In his reply to Thomson, Robert K. Fullinwider challenges the claim that the right of disadvantaged groups to compensation justifies our setting aside the white male's right to equal consideration. He agrees with Thomson that victims of past discrimination deserve compensation; but it is only fair to make white males bear the burden of compensation, he holds, if it can be shown that they themselves were responsible for the injustice, and Thomson has failed to do this. She has argued that white males benefited from past discrimination but, claims Fullinwider, it is possible to benefit from a wrong without being responsible for it or owing the victim compensation.

The arguments discussed above focus on the deontological concerns of justice and the right to equal opportunity. There are also important consequentialist arguments for and against preferential hiring. Some thinkers hold that even if they are unjust, preferential hiring and/or reverse discrimination policies are justified because they are the only effective means of eliminating present discrimination, a goal which is desirable from the point of view of business and also of society as a whole. This is essentially a utilitarian argument which justifies the method for achieving a desirable end on the basis of the end it is designed to achieve. One might interpret the United States Supreme Court's decision in *Weber v. U.S. Steel*, a decision some feel contradicts the court's traditional stand on equality, as a version of this argument. In that case the preferential admission of minorities into a U.S. Steel training program was declared not to be in violation of Title VII because its intention was to eliminate discrimination in the workplace.

Although they agree in wishing to promote the general welfare, not all utilitarians believe that preferential hiring or reverse discrimination will accomplish this goal. In "Reverse Discrimination and Compensatory Justice," William Blackstone offers a utilitarian argument against reverse discrimination. Blackstone fears that a focus on race or sex in hiring as opposed to ability or training could result in lowering the quality of job performance, which would be bad for society as a whole. More importantly, he believes that such a strategy could foster strife and resentment and could set in motion an endless series of injustices, each of which would have to be compensated for by another injustice.

chapter seven
EMPLOYEE RIGHTS AND DUTIES

AN EMPLOYEE BILL OF RIGHTS

DAVID EWING*

For nearly two centuries Americans have enjoyed freedom of press, speech, and assembly, due process of law, privacy, freedom of conscience, and other important rights—in their homes, churches, political forums, and social and cultural life. But Americans have not enjoyed these civil liberties in most companies, government agencies, and other organizations where they work. Once a U.S. citizen steps through the plant or office door at 9 A.M., he or she is nearly rightless until 5 P.M., Monday through Friday. The employee continues to have political freedoms, of course, but these are not the significant ones now. While at work, the important relationships are with bosses, associates, and subordinates. Inequalities in dealing with these people are what really count for an employee.

To this generalization there are important exceptions. In some organizations, generous managements have seen fit to assure free speech, privacy, due process, and other concerns as privileges. But there is no guarantee the privileges will survive the next change of chief executive. As former Attorney General Ramsey Clark once said in a speech, "A right is not what someone gives you; it's what no one can take from you." Defined in this manner, rights are rare in business and public organizations.

In effect, U.S. society is a paradox. The Constitution and Bill of Rights light up the sky over political campaigners, legislators, civic leaders, families, church people, and artists. But not so over employees. The employee sector of our civil liberties universe is more like a black hole, with rights so compacted, so imploded by the gravitational forces of legal tradition, that, like the giant black stars in the physical universe, light can scarcely escape.

Perhaps the most ironic thing is that only in recent years have Americans made many noises about this paradox. It is as if we took it for granted and assumed there was no alternative. "Organizations have always been this way and always have to be," we seem to say. One is reminded of an observation attributed to Marshall McLuhan: "Anybody's total surround, or environment, creates a condition of nonperception."

To put the situation in focus, let us make a brief review of rights in the workplace.

Speech In many private and public organizations there is a well-oiled machinery for providing relief to an employee who is discharged because of his or her race,

*Executive editor, *Harvard Business Review*.

religion, or sex. But we have no mechanisms for granting similar relief to an employee who is discharged for exercising the right of free speech. The law states that all employers "may dismiss their employees at will . . . for good cause, for no cause, or even for cause morally wrong, without being thereby guilty of legal wrong."[1]

Of course, discharge is only the extreme weapon; many steps short of discharge may work well enough—loss of a raise in pay, demotion, assignment to the boondocks, or perhaps simply a cutback of normal and expected benefits.

Consider the case of a thirty-five-year-old business executive whom I shall call "Mike Z." He was a respected research manager in a large company. He believed that his company was making only superficial efforts to comply with newly enacted pollution laws. In a management meeting and later in social groups he spoke critically of top management's attitude. Soon strange things began to happen to him, different only in degree from what happens to a political dissenter in the Soviet Union. First, his place in the company parking lot was canceled. Then his name was "accidentally" removed from the office building directory inside the main entrance. Soon routine requests he made to attend professional meetings began to get snarled up in red tape or were "lost." Next he found himself harassed by directives to rewrite routine reports. Then his budget for clerical service was cut, followed by a drastic slash in his research budget. When he tried to protest this treatment, he met a wall of top management silence. Rather than see his staff suffer further for his dissidence, he quit his job and moved his family to another city.

Mike Z. could be almost anyone in thousands of companies, government agencies, and other organizations. It should not be surprising, therefore, that when it comes to speaking out on issues of company policy or management practice, employees make about as much noise as fish swimming.

So well-established is the idea that any criticism of the company is "ratting" or "finking" that some companies hang out written prohibitions for all to see. For instance, a private bus company on the West Coast puts employees on notice with this rule:

> The company requires its employees to be loyal. It will not tolerate words or acts of hostility to the company, its officers, agents, or employees, its services, equipment or its condition, or . . . criticisms of the company to others than . . . superior officers.

Conscientious Objection

There is very little protection in industry for employees who object to carrying out immoral, unethical, or illegal orders from their superiors. If the employee doesn't like what he or she is asked to do, the remedy is to pack up and leave. This remedy seems to presuppose an ideal economy, where there is another company down the street with openings for jobs just like the one the employee left. But what about the real world? Here resignation may mean having to uproot one's family and move to a strange city in another state. Or it may mean, for an employee in the semifinals of a career, or for an employee with a specialized competence, not being able to find another suitable job anywhere.

In 1970 Shirley Zinman served as a secretary in a Philadelphia employment agency called LIB Services. One day she was instructed by her bosses to record all telephone conversations she might have with prospective clients. This was to be done for "training purposes," she was told, although the callers were not to be told that their words were being taped. The office manager would monitor the conversations on an extension in her office. Ms. Zinman refused to play along with this game, not only because it was unethical, in her view, but illegal as well—the telephone company's regulations forbade such unannounced telephone recordings.

So Ms. Zinman had to resign. She sought unemployment compensation. The state unemployment pay board refused her application. It reasoned that her resignation was not "compelling and necessitous." With the help of attorneys from the American Civil Liberties Union, she appealed her case to the Pennsylvania Commonwealth Court. In a ruling hailed by civil rights leaders, the court in 1973 reversed the pay board and held that Ms. Zinman was entitled to unemployment compensation because her objection to the unethical directive was indeed a "compelling" reason to quit her job.[2]

What this interesting case leaves unsaid is as important as what it does say: Resignation continues to be the accepted response for the objecting employee. The Pennsylvania court took a bold step in favor of employee rights, for prior to this decision there was little reason to think that the Shirley Zinmans of industry could expect any help at all from the outside world. But within the organization itself, an employee is expected to sit at the feet of the boss's conscience.

Security and Privacy

When employees are in their homes, before and after working hours, they enjoy well-established rights to privacy and to protection from arbitrary search and seizure of their papers and possessions. But no such rights protect them in the average company, government agency, or other organization; their superiors need only the flimsiest pretext to search their lockers, desks, and files. The boss can rummage through an employee's letters, memoranda, and tapes looking for evidence that (let us say) he or she is about to "rat" on the company. "Ratting" might include reporting a violation of safety standards to the Occupational Safety and Health Administration (which is provided for by law), or telling Ralph Nader about a product defect, or giving the mayor's office requested information about a violation of energy-use regulations.

Choice of Outside Activities and Associations

In practice, most business employees enjoy no right to work after hours for the political, social, and community organizations of their choice. To be sure, in many companies an enlightened management will encourage as much diversity of choice in outside activities as employees can make. As noted earlier, however, this is an indulgence which can disappear any time, for most states do not mandate such rights, and even in those that do, the rights are poorly protected. An employee who gets fired for his or her choice of outside activities can expect no damages for his loss even if he or she wins a suit against the employer. The employee may only "secure the slight satisfaction of seeing his employer suffer the statutory penalties."[3]

Ironically, however, a company cannot discriminate against people whose politics it dislikes when it *hires* them.[4] It has to wait a few days before it can exercise its prerogatives.

Due Process

"Accidents will occur in the best-regulated families," said Mr. Micawber in *David Copperfield*. Similarly, accidents of administration occur even in the best-managed companies, with neurotic, inept, or distracted supervisors inflicting needless harm on subordinates. Many a subordinate who goes to such a boss to protest would be well-advised to keep one foot in the stirrups, for he is likely to be shown to the open country for his efforts.

This generalization does not hold for civil service employees in the federal government, who can resort to a grievance process. Nor does it hold for unionized companies, which also have grievance procedures. But it holds for *most* other organizations. A few organizations voluntarily have established a mechanism to ensure due process.

The absence of a right to due process is especially painful because it is the second element of constitutionalism in organizations. As we shall think of it in this book, employee constitutionalism consists of a set of clearly defined rights, and a means of protecting employees from discharge, demotion, or other penalties imposed when they assert their rights.

Why bother about rightlessness in corporations, government agencies, and other organizations? They are much smaller than state and federal governments, are they not? Must an organization that "rules" an employee only for forty or so hours per week be treated as a government?

For one answer, let us turn to the Founding Fathers. Of course, they did not know or conceive of the modern corporation and public agency, so we cannot read what their thoughts about all this might have been. Perhaps we can make a reasonable guess, however, by comparing some numbers.

If the original thirteen colonies were large and powerful enough to concern the Founding Fathers, it seems likely that those men, if here today, would want to extend their philosophy to other assemblages of equivalent size and magnitude. In the writings of James Madison, Thomas Jefferson, George Mason, Jonas Phillips, Richard Henry Lee, Elbridge Gerry, Luther Martin, and others, there is no inference that human rights were seen as a good thing only some of the time or for some places. Instead, the Fathers saw rights as a universal need.[5]

In 1776, and in 1789, when the Bill of Rights (first ten amendments to the Constitution) was passed by Congress and sent to the states for ratification, trading companies and government agencies were tiny organizations incapable of harboring bureaucracy. Indeed, to use Mr. Micawber's phrase, there was hardly room in them to swing a cat, much less create layer on layer of hierarchy and wall after wall of departmental structure.

Today all that has changed. Some of our corporate and public organizations have larger "populations" than did the thirteen colonies. And a truly vast number of organizations have large enough "populations" to rank as real powers in people's everyday lives. For instance:

- AT&T has more than 939,000 employees, nearly twice the size of the largest colony, Virginia, which had about 493,000 inhabitants in 1776.

- General Motors, with 681,000 employees, is nearly two and one-half times the size of the second largest colony, Pennsylvania, which had a population of about 284,000 people in 1776.

- Westinghouse, the thirteenth largest corporate employer today with 166,000 employees, is four times the size of the thirteenth largest colony, Delaware, which had a population of 41,400. Westinghouse's "population" is also larger than that in 1776 of South Carolina, New Jersey, New Hampshire, Rhode Island, and Georgia.

In fact, 125 corporations have larger "populations" than did Delaware, the smallest colony, in 1776. But can employee workforces legitimately be compared with state populations? Of course, there are important differences—the twenty-four-hours-per-day jurisdiction of the state as opposed to only eight hours per day for an employer, the fact that the state has courts and military forces while the employer does not, and others. Yet it is not an apples-and-oranges comparison. Decades ago, and long before corporations and public agencies achieved anything like their current size, political scientists were noting many important similarities between the governments of organizations and political governments. In 1908, for example, Arthur Bentley wrote:

> A corporation is government through and through . . . Certain technical methods which political government uses, as, for instance, hanging, are not used by corporations, generally speaking, but that is a detail.[6]

In numerous ways, sizable corporations, public agencies, and university administrations qualify as "minigovernments." They pay salaries and costs. They have medical plans. They provide for retirement income. They offer recreational facilities. They maintain cafeterias. They may assist an employee with housing, educational loans, personal training, and vacation plans. They schedule numerous social functions. They have "laws," conduct codes, and other rules. Many have mechanisms for resolving disputes. A few even keep chaplains on the payroll or maintain facilities for religious worship.

Accordingly, it seems foolish to dismiss minigovernments as possible subjects of rights, or to exclude employees from discussions of civil liberties. We have assumed that rights are not as important for employees as for political citizens. Our assumption is in error.

The bill of rights that follows is one person's proposal, a "working paper" for discussion, not a platform worked out in committee.

1. *No organization or manager shall discharge, demote, or in other ways discriminate against any employee who criticizes, in speech or press, the ethics, legality, or social responsibility of management actions.*

    Comment: What this right does not say is as important as what it does say. Protection does not extend to employees who make nuisances of themselves or who balk, argue, or contest managerial decisions on normal operating and planning matters, such as the choice of inventory accounting method, whether to diversify the product line or concentrate it, whether to rotate workers on a certain job or specialize them, and so forth. "Committing the truth," as Ernest Fitzgerald called it, is protected only for speaking out on issues where we consider an average citizen's judgment to be as valid as an expert's—truth in advertising, public safety standards, questions of fair disclosure, ethical practices, and so forth.

2. *No employee shall be penalized for engaging in outside activities of his or her choice after working hours, whether political, economic, civic, or cultural, nor for buying products and services of his or her choice for personal use, nor for expressing or encouraging views contrary to top management's on political, economic, and social issues.*

   Comment: Many companies encourage employees to participate in outside activities, and some states have committed this right to legislation. Freedom of choice of products and services for personal use is also authorized in various state statutes as well as in arbitrators' decisions. The third part of the statement extends the protection of the First Amendment to the employee whose ideas about government, economic policy, religion, and society do not conform with the boss's.

   Note that this provision does not authorize an employee to come to work "beat" in the morning because he or she has been moonlighting. Participation in outside activities should enrich employees' lives, not debilitate them; if on-the-job performance suffers, the usual penalties may have to be paid.

3. *No organization or manager shall penalize an employee for refusing to carry out a directive that violates common norms of morality.*

   Comment: The purpose of this right is to afford job security to subordinates who cannot perform an action because they consider it unethical or illegal. It is important that the conscientious objector in such a case hold to a view that has some public acceptance. Fad moralities—messages from flying saucers, mores of occult religious sects, and so on—do not justify refusal to carry out an order. Nor in any case is the employee entitled to interfere with the boss's finding another person to do the job requested.

4. *No organization shall allow audio or visual recordings of an employee's conversations or actions to be made without his or her prior knowledge and consent. Nor may an organization require an employee or applicant to take personality tests, polygraph examinations, or other tests that constitute, in his opinion, an invasion of privacy.*

   Comment: This right is based on policies that some leading organizations have already put into practice. If an employee doesn't want his working life monitored, that is his privilege so long as he demonstrates (or, if an applicant, is willing to demonstrate) competence to do a job well.

5. *No employee's desk, files, or locker may be examined in his or her absence by anyone but a senior manager who has sound reason to believe that the files contain information needed for a management decision that must be made in the employee's absence.*

   Comment: The intent of this right is to grant people a privacy right as employees similar to that which they enjoy as political and social citizens under the "searches and seizures" guarantee of the Bill of Rights (Fourth Amendment to the Constitution). Many leading organizations in business and government have respected the principle of this rule for some time.

6. *No employer organization may collect and keep on file information about an employee that is not relevant and necessary for efficient management. Every employee shall have the right to inspect his or her personnel file and challenge the accuracy, relevance, or necessity of data in it, except for personal evaluations and comments by other employees which could not reasonably be obtained if confidentiality were not promised. Access to an employee's file by outside individuals and organizations shall be limited to inquiries about the essential facts of employment.*

   Comment: This right is important if employees are to be masters of their employment track records instead of possible victims of them. It will help to eliminate surprises, secrets, and skeletons in the clerical closet.

7. *No manager may communicate to prospective employers of an employee who is about to be or has been discharged gratuitous opinions that might hamper the individual in obtaining a new position.*

   Comment: The intent of this right is to stop blacklisting. The courts have already given some support for it.

8. *An employee who is discharged, demoted, or transferred to a less desirable job is entitled to a written statement from management of its reasons for the penalty.*

   Comment: The aim of this provision is to encourage a manager to give the same reasons in a hearing, arbitration, or court trial that he or she gives the employee when the cutdown happens. The written statement need not be given unless requested; often it is so clear to all parties why an action is being taken that no document is necessary.

9. *Every employee who feels that he or she has been penalized for asserting any right described in this bill shall be entitled to a fair hearing before an impartial official, board, or arbitrator. The findings and conclusions of the hearing shall be delivered in writing to the employee and management.*

   Comment: This very important right is the organizational equivalent of due process of law as we know it in political and community life. Without due process in a company or agency, the rights in this bill would all have to be enforced by outside courts and tribunals, which is expensive for society as well as time-consuming for the employees who are required to appear as complainants and witnesses. The nature of a "fair hearing" is purposely left undefined here so that different approaches can be tried, expanded, and adapted to changing needs and conditions.

Note that the findings of the investigating official or group are not binding on top management. This would put an unfair burden on an ombudsperson or "expedited arbitrator," if one of them is the investigator. Yet the employee is protected. If management rejects a finding of unfair treatment and then the employee goes to court, the investigator's statement will weigh against management in the trial. As a practical matter, therefore, employers will not want to buck the investigator-referee unless they fervently disagree with the findings.

Every sizable organization, whether in business, government, health, or another field, should have a bill of rights for employees. Only small organizations need not have such a statement—personal contact and oral communications meet the need for them. However, companies and agencies need not have identical bills of rights. Industry custom, culture, past history with employee unions and associations, and other considerations can be taken into account in the wording and emphasis given to different provisions.

NOTES

1. See Lawrence E. Blades, "Employment at Will vs. Individual Freedom: On Limiting the Abusive Exercise of Employer Power," *Columbia Law Review* 67 (1967):1405.

2. 8 Pa. Comm. Ct. Reports 649,304 A. 2nd 380 (1973). Also see *New York Times*, August 26, 1973.

3. Blades, 1412.

4. See 299 F. Supp. 1100, cited in *Employee Relations in Action*, August 1971 (New York, N.Y., Man & Manager), pp. 1–2.

5. See, for example, Bernard Schwartz, *The Bill of Rights: A Documentary History*. Vol. 1 (Toronto and New York: Chelsea House Publishers in association with McGraw-Hill Book Company, 1971), pp. 435 ff.

6. Arthur Bentley, *The Process of Government*, cited in Arthur Selwyn Miller, *The Modern Corporate State* (Westport, Conn.: Greenwood Press, 1976), p. 188.

IN DEFENSE OF WHISTLE BLOWING

GENE G. JAMES*

Whistle blowing may be defined as the attempt by an employee or former employee of an organization to disclose what he or she believes to be wrongdoing in or by the organization. Like blowing a whistle to call attention to a thief, whistle blowing is an effort to make others aware of practices one considers illegal, unjust, or harmful. Whenever someone goes over the head of immediate supervisors to inform higher management of wrongdoing, the whistle blowing is *internal* to the organization. Whenever someone discloses wrongdoing to outside individuals or groups such as reporters, public interest groups, or regulatory agencies, the whistle blowing is *external*.

Most whistle blowing is done by people presently employed by the organization. However, people who have left the organization may also blow the whistle. The former may be referred to as *current* whistle blowers; the latter as *alumni* whistle blowers. If the whistle blower discloses his or her identity, the whistle blowing may be said to be *open*; if the person's identity is not disclosed, the whistle blowing is *anonymous*.

Whistle blowers differ from muckrakers because the latter do not have any ties to the organizations whose wrongdoing they seek to disclose. They differ from informers and stool pigeons because the latter usually have self-interested reasons for their disclosures, such as obtaining prosecutorial immunity. The term *whistle blower*, on the other hand, usually refers to people who disclose wrongdoing for moral reasons. However, unless whistle blowing is *defined* as disclosing wrongdoing for moral reasons, the distinction between whistle blowing and informing cannot be a sharp one. Thus, although most whistle blowers do it for moral reasons, one cannot take for granted that their motives are praiseworthy.

Whistle blowers almost always experience retaliation. If they work for private industry, they are likely to be fired. They also receive damaging letters of recommendation and may be blacklisted so they cannot find work in their profession. If they are not fired, or work for government agencies, they are still likely to be transferred, demoted, given less interesting work, and denied salary increases and promotions. Their professional competence is usually attacked. They are said to be unqualified to judge, misinformed, and so forth. Since their actions seem to threaten both the organization and their fellow employees, attacks on their personal lives are also frequent. They are called traitors, rat finks, and other names. They are also said to be disgruntled, known troublemakers, people who make an issue out of nothing, self-serving, and publicity-seekers. Their life-styles, sex lives, and mental stability may be questioned. Physical assaults, abuse of their families, and even murder are not unknown as retaliation to whistle blowing.

Original essay. Copyright © 1984 by Gene James. Reprinted by permission of the author.

*Department of Philosophy, Memphis State University.

WHISTLE BLOWING AND THE LAW[1]

The law does not at present offer whistle blowers very much protection. Agency law, the area of common law which governs relations between employees and employers, imposes a duty on employees to keep confidential any information learned through their employment which might be detrimental to their employers. However, this duty does not hold if the employee has knowledge that the employer either has committed or is about to commit a felony. In this case the employee has a positive obligation to report the offense. Failure to do so is known as misprision and makes one subject to criminal penalties.

The problem with agency law is that it is based on the assumption that unless there are statutes or agreements to the contrary, contracts between employees and employers can be terminated at will by either party. It therefore grants employers the right to discharge employees at any time for any reason or even for no reason at all. The result is that most employees who blow the whistle on their employers, even those who report felonies, are fired or suffer other retaliation. One employee of thirty years was even fired the day before his pension became effective for testifying under subpoena against his employer, without the courts doing anything to aid him.

This situation has begun to change somewhat in recent years. In *Pickering v. Board of Education* in 1968 the Supreme Court ruled that government employees have the right to speak out on policy issues affecting their agencies provided doing so does not seriously disrupt the agency. A number of similar decisions have followed and the right of government employees to speak out on policy issues now seems firmly established. But employees in private industry do not have the right to speak out on company policies without being fired. In one case involving both a union and a company doing a substantial portion of its business with the federal government, federal courts did award back pay to an employee fired for criticizing the union and the company, but did not reinstate him or award him punitive damages.

A few state courts have begun to modify the right of employers to dismiss employees at will. Courts in Oregon and Pennsylvania have awarded damages to employees fired for serving on juries. A New Hampshire court granted damages to a woman fired for refusing to date her foreman. A West Virginia court reinstated a bank employee who reported illegal interest rates. The Illinois Supreme Court upheld the right of an employee to sue when fired for reporting and testifying about criminal activities of a fellow employee. However, a majority of states still uphold the right of employers to fire employees at will unless there are statutes or agreements to the contrary. Only one state, Michigan, has passed a law prohibiting employers from retaliating against employees who report violations of local, state, or federal laws.

A number of federal statutes contain provisions intended to protect whistle blowers. The National Labor Relations Act, Fair Labor Standards Act, Title VII of the 1964 Civil Rights Act, Age Discrimination Act, and Occupational Safety and Health Act all have sections prohibiting employers from taking retaliatory actions against employees who report or testify about violations of the acts.

Although these laws seem to encourage and protect whistle blowers, to be effective they must be enforced. A 1976 study[2] of the Occupational Safety and Health Act showed that only about 20 percent of the 2300 complaints filed in fiscal years 1975 and 1976 were judged valid by OSHA investigators. About half of these were settled out of court. Of the sixty cases taken to court at the time of the study in November 1976, one had been won, eight were lost, and the others were still pending. A more recent study[3] showed that of the 3100 violations reported in 1979, only 270 were settled out of court and only sixteen litigated.

Since the National Labor Relations Act guarantees the right of workers to organize and bargain collectively and most collective bargaining agreements contain a clause requiring employers to have just cause for discharging employees, these agreements would seem to offer some protection for whistle blowers. In fact, however, arbitrators have tended to agree with employers that whistle blowing is an act of disloyalty which disrupts business and injures the employer's reputation. Their attitude seems to be summed up in a 1972 case in which the arbitrator stated that one should not "bite the hand that feeds you and insist on staying for future banquets."[4] One reason for this, pointed out by David Ewing, is that unions are frequently as corrupt as the organizations on which the whistle is being blown. Such unions, he says, "are not likely to feed a hawk that comes to prey in their own barnyard."[5] The record of professional societies is not any better. They generally have failed to come to the defense of members who have attempted to live up to their professional codes of ethics by blowing the whistle on corrupt practices.

THE MORAL JUSTIFICATION OF WHISTLE BLOWING

Under what conditions, if any, is whistle blowing morally justified? Some people have argued that it is always justified because it is an exercise of free speech. But the right to free speech, like most other rights, is not absolute. Thus, even if whistle blowing is a form of free speech, that does not mean it is justified in every case. Others have argued that whistle blowing is never justified because employees have obligations of absolute loyalty and confidentiality to the organization for which they work. However, because the actions of organizations often harm or violate the rights of others, and one has an obligation to prevent harmful actions if one can, a universal prohibition against whistle blowing is not justifiable.

Assuming that we reject such extreme views, what conditions must be satisfied for whistle blowing to be morally justified? Richard De George believes that whistle blowing is morally permissible if it meets the following three conditions:

1. The company must be engaged in a practice or about to release a product which does *serious* harm to individuals or to society in general. The more serious the harm, the more serious the obligation.

2. The employee should report his concern or complaint to his immediate superior.

3. If no appropriate action is taken, the employee should take the matter up the managerial line. Before he or she is obliged to go public, the resources for remedy within the company should be exhausted.[6]

For whistle blowing to be morally obligatory De George thinks two other conditions must be satisfied:

4. The employee should have documentation of the practice or defect. . . . Without adequate evidence his chances of being successful . . . are slim.

5. The employee must have good reason to believe that by going public he will be able to bring about the necessary changes.[7]

De George believes that because of the almost certain retaliation whistle blowers experience, whistle blowing is frequently morally permissible but not morally obligatory. He holds that this is true even when the person involved is a professional whose code of ethics requires him or her to put the public good ahead of personal good. He argues, for example:

> The myth that ethics has no place in engineering has . . . at least in some corners of the engineering profession . . . been put to rest. Another myth, however, is emerging to take its place—the myth of the engineer as moral hero. . . . The zeal . . . however, has gone too far, piling moral responsibility upon moral responsibility on the shoulders of the engineer. This emphasis . . . is misplaced. Though engineers are members of a profession that holds public safety paramount, we cannot reasonably expect engineers to be willing to sacrifice their jobs each day for principle and to have a whistle ever at their sides. . . . [8]

He contends that engineers only have an obligation to do their jobs as best they can. This includes reporting observations about safety to management. But engineers do not have an "obligation to insist that their perceptions or their standards be accepted. They are not paid to do that, they are not expected to do that, and they have no moral or ethical obligation to do that."[9]

There are a number of problems with this analysis of whistle blowing.

The first condition is far too strong because it requires de facto wrongdoing instead of extremely probable evidence of wrongdoing before whistle blowing is morally justified. All that should be required of whistle blowers in this regard is that they be diligent in gathering evidence and act on the basis of the best evidence available to them. They should not be held to a more rigid standard than is usually applied to moral actions.

What constitutes serious and considerable harm? Must the harm be physical? Since De George was writing on business ethics, it is understandable that he only discussed whistle blowing involving corporations. But businesses, like governments, can be guilty of wrongs other than physically harming people. Should one, for example, never blow the whistle on such things as invasions of privacy?

If the harm is physical, how many people's health or safety must be endangered before the harm can be said to be considerable? And do professionals not have an obligation to inform the public of dangerous products and practices even if they will lose their jobs? Even though some Ford engineers had serious misgivings about the safety of Pinto gas tanks and several people were killed when tanks exploded after rear-end crashes, De George says that Ford engineers did not have an obligation to make their misgivings public. He maintains that although engineers are better qualified than other people to calculate cost versus safety, decisions about acceptable risk are not primarily engineering but managerial decisions. He believes that under ideal conditions the public itself would make this kind of decision. "A panel of informed people, not necessarily engineers, should decide . . . acceptable risk and minimum standards."[10] This information should then be relayed to car buyers who, he believes, are entitled to it.

One of the reasons it is difficult to decide when employees have an obligation to blow the whistle is that this is part of the larger problem of the extent to which people are responsible for actions by organizations of which they are members. The problem arises because it is extremely difficult to determine when a given individual in an organization is responsible for a particular decision or policy. Decisions are often the product of committees rather than single individuals. Since committee members usually serve temporary terms, none of the members who helped make a particular decision may be on the committee when it is implemented. Implementation is also likely to be the responsibility of others. Since committee membership is temporary, decisions are often made that contradict previous decisions. Even when decisions are made by individuals, these individuals seldom have control over the outcome of the decisions.

The result is that no one feels responsible for the consequences of organizational decisions. Top management does not because it only formulates policy; it does not implement it. Those in the middle and at the bottom of the chain of authority do not, because they simply carry out policy. If challenged to assume moral responsibility for their actions, they reply "I'm not responsible, I was simply carrying out orders" or "I was just doing my job." But, as De George points out, absence of a feeling of obligation does not mean absence of obligation.

Whenever one acts in such a way as to harm or violate the rights of others, one is justly held accountable for those actions. This is true regardless of one's occupation or role in society. Acting as a member of an institution or corporation does not relieve a person of moral obligations. To the contrary. Because most of the actions we undertake in such settings have more far-reaching consequences than those we undertake in our personal lives, our moral obligation is *increased*. The amount of responsibility one bears for organizational actions is dependent on the extent to which (a) one could foresee the consequences of the organizational action, and (b) one's own acts or failures to act are a cause of those consequences. It is important to include failures to act here because frequently it is easier to determine what will happen if we don't act than if we do and because we are morally responsible for not preventing evil as well as for causing it.

Although the foregoing discussion is brief and the ideas not fully worked out, if the criteria which are presented are applied to the engineers in the Pinto case, I think one must conclude that they had an obligation to blow the whistle. They knew the gas tanks were likely to explode, injuring or killing people, if Pintos were struck from behind by cars traveling thirty miles per hour. They knew that if they did not blow the whistle, Ford would market the cars. They were also members of a profession that, because of its special knowledge and skills, has a particular obligation to be concerned about public safety.

De George thinks that the Ford engineers would have had an obligation to blow the whistle only if they had also known that doing so would have been likely to prevent the deaths. But we have an obligation to warn others of danger even if we believe they will ignore our warnings. This is especially true if the danger will come about partly because we did not speak out. De George admits that the public has a right to know about dangerous products. If that is true, it would seem that those who have knowledge about such products have an obligation to inform the public. This is not usurping the public's right to decide acceptable risk; it is supplying it with the information necessary to exercise the right.

De George also believes we are not justified in asking engineers to blow the whistle if it would threaten their jobs. It is true that we would not be justified in demanding that they blow the whistle if that would place their or their families' lives in danger. But this is not true if only their jobs are at stake. Engineers are recognized as professionals and accorded respect and high salaries, not only because of their specialized knowledge and skills, but also because of the special responsibilities we entrust to them. All people have a prima facie obligation to blow the whistle on practices that are illegal, unjust, or harmful to others. But engineers who have special knowledge about, and are partially responsible for, dangerous practices or products have an especially strong obligation to blow the whistle if they are unsuccessful in getting the practices or products modified. Indeed, if they do not have an obligation to blow the whistle in such situations, no one ever has such an obligation.

A number of people have argued that for external whistle blowing to be justified the whistle blower must first make his or her concern known within the organization. "Surely," says Arthur S. Miller, "an employee owes his employer enough loyalty to try to work, first of all, within the organization to attempt to effect change."[11] De George even states that for whistle blowing to be morally justified one must first have informed one's immediate supervisor and exhausted all possible avenues of change within the organization. The problems with this kind of advice are: (1) It may be one's immediate supervisor who is responsible for the wrongdoing. (2) Organizations differ considerably in both their mechanisms for reporting and how they respond to wrongdoing. (3) Not all wrongdoing is of the same type. If the wrongdoing is one which threatens people's health or safety, exhausting all channels of protest within the organization could result in unjustified delay in correcting the problem. Exhausting internal channels of protest can also give people time to destroy evidence needed to substantiate one's allegations. Finally, it may expose the employee to possible retaliation that he or she would have some protection against if the wrongdoing were reported to an external agency.

It has also been argued that anonymous whistle blowing is never justified. It is said, for example, that anonymous whistle blowing violates the right of people to face their accusers. The fact that the whistle blower's identity is unknown also raises questions about his or her motives. But, as Frederick Elliston points out, anonymous whistle blowing can both protect whistle blowers from unjust retaliation and prev . ' those on whom the whistle is blown from engaging in an ad hominem attack to draw attention away from their wrongdoing. As he also points out, people should be protected from false accusations, but it is not necessary for the identity of whistle blowers to be known to accomplish this. "It is only necessary that accusations be properly investigated, proven true or false, and the results widely disseminated."[12] Discovering the whistle blower's motive is also irrelevant as far as immediate public policy is concerned. All that matters is whether wrongdoing has taken place and, if so, what should be done about it.

It has also been argued that anonymous whistle blowing should be avoided because it is ineffective. In fact, if anonymous whistle blowing is ineffective, it is more likely to be a function of lack of documentation and follow-up testimony than of its anonymity. Moreover, anonymity is a matter of degree. For whistle blowing to be anonymous, the whistle blower's identity does not have to be unknown to everyone, only to those on whom the whistle is blown and the general public. A few key investigators may know his or her identity. It should also not be forgotten that one of the most dramatic and important whistle-blowing incidents in recent years, Deep Throat's disclosure of Richard Nixon's betrayal of the American people, was an instance of anonymous whistle blowing.

FACTORS TO CONSIDER IN WHISTLE BLOWING

I have argued that because we have a duty to prevent harm and injustice to others, which holds even though we are members of organizations, we have a prima facie obligation to disclose organizational wrongdoing we are unable to prevent. The degree of the obligation depends on the extent to which we are capable of foreseeing the consequences of organizational actions and our own acts or failures to act are causes of those consequences. It also depends on the kind and extent of the wrongdoing. Even a part-time or temporary employee has an obligation to report serious or extensive wrongdoing. But, in general, professionals who occupy positions of trust and special responsibilities have a stronger obligation to blow the whistle than ordinary workers.

Although we have an obligation to document wrongdoing as thoroughly as possible, we can only act on the basis of probability, so it is possible for the whistle blower to be in error about the wrongdoing and the whistle blowing still be justified. Whether we have an obligation to express our concern within the organization before going outside depends on the nature of the wrongdoing, the kind of organization involved, and the likelihood of retaliation. Whether we have an obligation to blow the whistle openly rather than anonymously depends on the extent to which it helps us avoid unfair retaliation and is effective in exposing the wrongdoing. The same is true of alumni as opposed to current whistle blowing.

Since whistle blowing usually involves conflicting obligations and a wide range of variables and has far-reaching consequences for all people involved, decisions to blow the whistle are not easily made. Like all complicated moral actions, whistle blowing cannot be reduced to a how-to-do list. However, some of the factors whistle blowers should take into consideration, if they are to act prudently and morally, can be stated. The following is an attempt to do this.

- *Make sure the situation is one that warrants whistle blowing.*

    Make sure the situation involves illegal actions, harm to others, or violation of people's rights, and is not one in which you would be disclosing personal matters, trade secrets, customer lists, or similar material. If disclosure of the wrongdoing would involve the latter, make sure that the harm to be avoided is great enough to offset the harm from the latter.

- *Examine your motives.*

  Although it is not necessary for the whistle blower's motive to be praiseworthy for the action to be justified in terms of the public interest, examination of your motives will help in deciding whether the situation warrants whistle blowing.

- *Verify and document your information.*

  If at all possible, try to obtain evidence that would stand up in court or regulatory hearings. If the danger to others is so great that you believe you are justified in obtaining evidence by surreptitious methods such as eavesdropping or recording telephone calls, examine your motives thoroughly, weigh carefully the risks you are taking, and try to find alternative and independent sources for any evidence you uncover. In general, it is advisable to avoid surreptitious methods.

- *Determine the type of wrongdoing you are reporting and to whom it should be reported.*

  Determining the exact nature of the wrongdoing can help you decide both what kind of evidence to obtain and to whom it should be reported. For example, if the wrongdoing consists of illegal actions such as the submission of false test reports to government agencies, bribery of public officials, racial or sexual discrimination, or violation of safety, health, or pollution laws, then determining the nature of the laws being violated will also indicate which agencies have authority to enforce those laws. If, on the other hand, the wrongdoing consists of actions which are legal but contrary to the public interest, determining this will help you decide whether you have an obligation to publicize the actions and, if so, in what way. The best place to report this type of wrongdoing is usually a public interest group. Such an organization is more likely than the press to: (1) be concerned about and advise the whistle blower regarding retaliation, (2) maintain confidentiality, (3) investigate the whistle blower's allegations to try to substantiate them rather than sensationalize them by turning the issue into a "personality dispute." If releasing information to the press is the best way to remedy the situation, the public interest group can help with or do this.

- *State your allegations in an appropriate way.*

  Be as specific as possible without being unintelligible. If you are reporting violation of a law to a government agency and it is possible for you to do so, include information and technical data necessary for experts to verify the wrongdoing. If you are disclosing wrongdoing which does not require technical information to substantiate it, still be as specific as possible in stating the type of illegal or immoral action involved, who is being injured, and in what ways.

- *Stick to the facts.*

  Avoid name calling, slander, and being drawn into a mud-slinging contest. As Peter Raven-Hansen wisely points out: "One of the most important points . . . is to focus on the disclosure. . . . This rule applies even when the whistle blower believes that certain individuals are responsible. . . . The disclosure itself usually leaves a trail for others to follow to the miscreants."[13] Sticking to the facts also helps the whistle blower minimize retaliation.

- *Decide whether the whistle blowing should be internal or external.*

    Familiarize yourself with all available internal channels for reporting wrong-doing and obtain as many data as you can both on how people who have used these channels were treated by the organization and on what was done about the problems they reported. If you are considering blowing the whistle on an immediate supervisor, find out what has happened in the past in this kind of situation. If people who report wrongdoing have been treated fairly and problems corrected, use internal channels to report the wrongdoing. If not, decide to what external agencies you should report the wrongdoing.

- *Decide whether the whistle blowing should be open or anonymous.*

    If you intend to remain anonymous, decide whether partial or total anonymity is required. Also, make sure your documentation is as thorough as possible. Finally, since anonymity may be difficult to preserve, anticipate what you will do if your identity becomes known.

- *Decide whether current or alumni whistle blowing is required.*

    Sometimes it is advisable to resign your present position and obtain another before blowing the whistle. This protects you from being fired, receiving damaging letters of recommendation, or even being blacklisted from your profession. Alumni whistle blowing may also be advisable if you are anticipating writing a book about the wrongdoing. Since this can be profitable, anyone planning to take this step has a particularly strong obligation to examine his or her motives to make sure they are morally praiseworthy.

- *Find out how much protection is available for whistle blowers in your industry, state, or federal agency.*

    Follow any guidelines that have been established and make sure you meet all qualifications, deadlines, and so on for filing reports.

- *Anticipate and document retaliation.*

    Although it is not as certain as Newton's law of motion that for every action there is an equal reaction, whistle blowers whose identities are known can expect retaliation. Thus whether you decide to work within the organization or go outside, document every step with letters, records, tape recordings of meetings, and so forth. Unless you do this, you may find that regulatory agencies and the courts are of no help.

- *Consult a lawyer.*

    Lawyers are advisable at almost every stage of whistle blowing. They can help you determine if the wrongdoing violates the law, aid you in documenting infor-mation about it, inform you of any laws you might be breaking in documenting it, assist you in deciding to whom to report it, make sure reports are filed on time, and help you protect yourself against retaliation. However, since lawyers tend to view problems within a narrow legal framework and decisions to blow the whistle are moral decisions, in the final analysis you must rely on your conscience.

BEYOND WHISTLE BLOWING

What can be done to eliminate the wrongdoing which gives rise to whistle blowing? One solution would be to give whistle blowers greater legal protection. Another would be to try to change the nature of organizations so as to diminish the need for whistle blowing. These solutions of course are not mutually exclusive.

Many people are opposed to legislation protecting whistle blowers because they think it is unwarranted interference with the right to freedom of contract. However, if the right to freedom of contract is to be consistent with the public interest, it cannot serve as a shield for wrongdoing. It does this when threat of dismissal prevents people from blowing the whistle. The right of employers to dismiss at will has been restricted previously by labor laws which prevent employers from dismissing employees for union activities. It is ironic that we have restricted the right of employers to fire employees who are pursuing their economic self-interest, but allowed employers to fire employees acting in behalf of the public interest. The right of employers to dismiss employees in the interest of efficiency should be balanced against the right of the public to know about illegal, dangerous, and unjust practices of organizations. The most effective way to achieve the latter goal would be to pass a federal law protecting whistle blowers.

Laws protecting whistle blowers have also been opposed on the grounds that (1) employees would use them as an excuse to mask poor performance, (2) they would create an "informer ethos" within organizations, and (3) they would take away the autonomy of business, strangling it in red tape.

The first objection is illegitimate because only those employees who could show that an act of whistle blowing preceded their being dismissed or penalized and that their employment records were adequate up to the time of the whistle blowing could seek relief under the law.

The second objection is more formidable. A society that encourages snooping, suspicion, and mistrust is not most people's idea of the good society. Laws which encourage whistle blowing for self-interested reasons, such as the federal tax law, which pays informers part of any money that is collected, could help bring about such a society. However, laws protecting whistle blowers from being penalized or dismissed are quite different. They do not reward the whistle blower; they merely protect him or her from unjust retaliation. It is unlikely that federal or state laws of this sort would promote an informer society.

The third objection is also unfounded. Laws protecting whistle blowers would not require any positive duties on the part of organizations—only the negative duty of not retaliating against employees who speak out in the public interest. However, not every act of apparent whistle blowing should be protected. Only people who can show they had probable reasons for believing wrongdoing existed should be protected. Furthermore, the burden of proof should be on the individual. People who cannot show they had good cause to suspect wrongdoing may justly be penalized or dismissed. If the damage to the organization is serious, it should also be allowed to sue. Since these conditions would impose some risks on potential whistle blowers, they would reduce the possibility of frivolous action.

If, on the other hand, someone who has probable reasons for believing wrongdoing exists blows the whistle and is fired, the burden of proof should be on the organization to show that he or she was not fired for blowing the whistle. If the whistle blowing is found to be the reason for the dismissal, the whistle blower should be reinstated and awarded damages. If there is further retaliation after reinstatement, additional damages should be awarded.

What changes could be made in organizations to prevent the need for whistle blowing? Some of the suggestions which have been made are that organizations develop effective internal channels for reporting wrongdoing, reward people with salary increases and promotions for using these channels, and appoint senior executives, board members, ombudspersons, and so on whose primary obligations would be to investigate and eliminate organizational wrongdoing. These changes could be undertaken by organizations on their own or mandated by law. Other changes which might be mandated are requiring that certain kinds of records be kept, assessing larger fines for illegal actions, and making executives and other professionals personally liable for filing false reports, knowingly marketing dangerous products, failing to monitor how policies are being implemented, and so forth. Although these reforms could do much to reduce the need for whistle blowing, given human nature it is highly unlikely that this need can ever be totally eliminated. Therefore, it is important to have laws which protect whistle blowers and for us to state as clearly as we can both the practical problems and moral issues pertaining to whistle blowing.

NOTES

1. For discussion of the legal aspects of whistle blowing see Lawrence E. Blades, "Employment at Will vs. Individual Freedom: On Limiting the Abusive Exercise of Employer Power," *Columbia Law Review*, vol. 67 (1967); Philip Blumberg, "Corporate Responsibility and the Employee's Duty of Loyalty and Obedience: A Preliminary Inquiry," *Oklahoma Law Review*, vol. 24 (1971); Clyde W. Summers, "Individual Protection Against Unjust Dismissal: Time for a Statute," *Virginia Law Review*, vol. 62 (1976); Arthur S. Miller, "Whistle Blowing and the Law," in Ralph Nader, Peter J. Petkas, and Kate Blackwell, *Whistle Blowing*, New York: Grossman Publishers, 1972; Alan F. Westin, *Whistle Blowing!*, New York: McGraw-Hill, 1981; Martin H. Marlin, "Current Status of Legal Protection for Whistleblowers," paper delivered at the Second Annual Conference on Ethics in Engineering, Illinois Institute of Technology, 1982. See also Gene G. James, "Whistle Blowing: Its Nature and Justification," *Philosophy in Context*, vol. 10, (1980).

2. For a discussion of this study which was by Morton Corn see Frank von Hipple, "Professional Freedom and Responsibility: The Role of the Professional Society," *Newsletter on Science, Technology and Human Values*, vol. 22, January 1978.

3. See Westin, op. cit.

4. See Marlin, op. cit.

5. David W. Ewing, *Freedom Inside the Organization*, New York: E. P. Dutton, 1977, pp. 165–166.

6. Richard T. De George, *Business Ethics*, New York: Macmillan, 1982, p. 161. See also De George, "Ethical Responsibilities of Engineers in Large Organizations," *Business and Professional Ethics Journal*, vol. 1, no. 1, Fall 1981, pp. 1–14. He formulates the first criterion in a slightly different way in the last work, saying that the harm must be both serious and considerable before whistle blowing is justified.

7. Ibid.

8. De George, "Ethical Responsibilities of Engineers in Large Organizations," op. cit., p. 1.

9. Ibid., p. 5.

10. Ibid., p. 7.

11. Miller, op. cit., p. 30.

12. Frederick A. Elliston, "Anonymous Whistleblowing," *Business and Professional Ethics Journal*, vol. 1, no. 2, Winter 1982.

13. Peter Raven-Hansen, "Dos and Don'ts for Whistleblowers: Planning for Trouble," *Technology Review*, May 1980, p. 30. My discussion in the present section is heavily indebted to this article.

chapter eight
THE QUALITY OF WORKING LIFE

ALIENATION AND INNOVATION IN THE WORKPLACE

RICHARD E. WALTON*

Managers don't need anyone to tell them that employee alienation exists. Terms such as "blue-collar blues" and "salaried dropouts" are all too familiar. But are they willing to undertake the major innovations necessary for redesigning work organizations to deal effectively with the root causes of alienation? My purpose in this article is to urge them to do so, for two reasons: (1) The current alienation is not merely a phase that will pass in due time. (2) The innovations needed to correct the problem can simultaneously enhance the quality of work life (thereby lessening alienation) and improve productivity. I shall risk covering terrain already familiar to some readers in order to establish the fact that alienation is a basic, long-term, and mounting problem.

ANATOMY OF ALIENATION

There are two parts to the problem of employee alienation: (1) the productivity output of work systems and (2) the social costs associated with employee inputs. Regarding the first, U.S. productivity is not adequate to the challenges posed by international competition and inflation; it cannot sustain impressive economic growth. (I do not refer here to economic growth as something to be valued merely for its own sake—it is politically a precondition for the income redistribution that will make equality of opportunity possible in the United States.) Regarding the second, the social and psychological costs of work systems are excessive, as evidenced by their effects on the mental and physical health of employees and on the social health of families and communities.

Employee alienation *affects* productivity and *reflects* social costs incurred in the workplace. Increasingly, blue- and white-collar employees and, to some extent, middle managers tend to dislike their jobs and resent their bosses. Workers tend to rebel against their union leaders. They are becoming less concerned about the quality of the product of their labor and more angered about the quality of the context in which they labor.

Reprinted by permission of the *Harvard Business Review*. Excerpts from "Alienation and Innovation in the Workplace" by Richard E. Walton (November–December 1972). This paper appeared first under the title "How to Counter Alienation in the Plant." Copyright © 1972 by the president and fellows of Harvard College; all rights reserved.

*Department of Business Administration, Harvard Business School.

In some cases, alienation is expressed by passive withdrawal—tardiness, absenteeism and turnover, and inattention on the job. In other cases, it is expressed by active attacks—pilferage, sabotage, deliberate waste, assaults, bomb threats, and other disruptions of work routines. Demonstrations have taken place and underground newspapers have appeared in large organizations in recent years to protest company policies. Even more recently, employees have cooperated with newsmen, congressional committees, regulatory agencies, and protest groups in exposing objectionable practices.

These trends all have been mentioned in the media, but one expression of alienation has been underreported: pilferage and violence against property and persons. Such acts are less likely to be revealed to the police and the media when they occur in a private company than when they occur in a high school, a ghetto business district, or a suburban town. Moreover, dramatic increases in these forms of violence are taking place at the plant level. This trend is not reported in local newspapers, and there is little or no appreciation of it at corporate headquarters. Local management keeps quiet because violence is felt to reflect unfavorably both on its effectiveness and on its plant as a place to work.

ROOTS OF CONFLICT

The acts of sabotage and other forms of protest are overt manifestations of a conflict between changing employee attitudes and organizational inertia. Increasingly, what employees expect from their jobs is different from what organizations are prepared to offer them. These evolving expectations of workers conflict with the demands, conditions, and rewards of employing organizations in at least six important ways:

- Employees want challenge and personal growth, but work tends to be simplified and specialties tend to be used repeatedly in work assignments. This pattern exploits the narrow skills of a worker, while limiting his or her opportunities to broaden or develop.

- Employees want to be included in patterns of mutual influence; they want egalitarian treatment. But organizations are characterized by tall hierarchies, status differentials, and chains of command.

- Employee commitment to an organization is increasingly influenced by the intrinsic interest of the work itself, the human dignity afforded by management, and the social responsibility reflected in the organization's products. Yet organization practices still emphasize material rewards and employment security and neglect other employee concerns.

- What employees want from careers, they are apt to want *right now*. But when organizations design job hierarchies and career paths, they continue to assume that today's workers are as willing to postpone gratifications as yesterday's workers were.

- Employees want more attention to the emotional aspects of organization life, such as individual self-esteem, openness between people, and expressions of warmth. Yet organizations emphasize rationality and seldom legitimize the emotional part of the organizational experience.

- Employees are becoming less driven by competitive urges, less likely to identify competition as the "American way." Nevertheless, managers continue to plan career patterns, organize work, and design reward systems as if employees valued competition as highly as they used to.

The foregoing needs and desires that employees bring to their work are but a local reflection of more basic, and not readily reversible, trends in U.S. society. These trends are fueled by family and social experience as well as by social institutions, especially schools. Among the most significant are:

- *The rising level of education.* Employees bring to the workplace more abilities and, correspondingly, higher expectations than in the past.

- *The rising level of wealth and security.* Vast segments of today's society never have wanted for the tangible essentials of life: thus they are decreasingly motivated by pay and security, which are taken for granted.

- *The decreased emphasis given by churches, schools, and families to obedience to authority.* These socialization agencies have promoted individual initiative, self-responsibility and self-control, the relativity of values, and other social patterns that make subordinacy in traditional organizations an increasingly bitter pill to swallow for each successive wave of entrants to the U.S. work force.

- *The decline in achievement motivation.* For example, whereas the books my parents read in primary school taught them the virtues of hard work and competition, my children's books emphasize self-expression and actualizing one's potential. The workplace has not yet fully recognized this change in employee values.

- *The shifting emphasis from individualism to social commitment.* This shift is driven in part by a need for the direct gratifications of human connectedness (for example, as provided by communal living experiments). It also results from a growing appreciation of our interdependence, and it renders obsolete many traditional workplace concepts regarding the division of labor and work incentives.

I believe that protests in the workplace will mount even more rapidly than is indicated by the contributing trends postulated here. The latent dissatisfaction of workers will be activated as (1) the issues receive public attention and (2) some examples of attempted solutions serve to raise expectations (just as the blacks' expressions of dissatisfaction with social and economic inequities were triggered in the 1950s and women's discontent expanded late in the 1960s).

REVITALIZATION AND REFORM

It seems clear that employee expectations are not likely to revert to those of an earlier day. And the conflicts between these expectations and traditional organizations result in alienation. This alienation, in turn, exacts a deplorable psychological and social cost as well as causes worker behavior that depresses productivity and constrains growth.

In short, we need major innovative efforts to redesign work organizations, efforts that take employee expectations into account.

Over the past two decades we have witnessed a parade of organization development, personnel, and labor relations programs that promised to revitalize organizations:

- *Job enrichment* would provide more varied and challenging content in the work.

- *Participative decision making* would enable the information, judgments, and concerns of subordinates to influence the decisions that affect them.

- *Management by objectives* would enable subordinates to understand and shape the objectives toward which they strive and against which they are evaluated.

- *Sensitivity training* or *encounter groups* would enable people to relate to each other as human beings with feelings and psychological needs.

- *Productivity bargaining* would revise work rules and increase management's flexibility with a quid pro quo whereby the union ensures that workers share in the fruits of the resulting productivity increases.

Each of the preceding programs by *itself* is an inadequate reform of the workplace and has typically failed in its more limited objectives. While application is often based on a correct diagnosis, each approach is only a partial remedy; therefore, the organizational system soon returns to an earlier equilibrium.

The lesson we must learn in the area of work reform is similar to one we have learned in another area of national concern. It is now recognized that a health program, a welfare program, a housing program, or an employment program alone is unable to make a lasting impact on the urban-poor syndrome. Poor health, unemployment, and other interdependent aspects of poverty must be attacked in a coordinated or systemic way.

So it is with meaningful reform of the workplace: we must think "systemically" when approaching the problem. We must coordinate into the redesign the way tasks are packaged into jobs, the way workers are required to relate to each other, the way performance is measured and rewards are made available, the way positions of authority and status symbols are structured, and the way career paths are conceived. Moreover, because these types of changes in work organizations imply new employee skills and different organizational cultures, transitional programs must be established.

WORKER PARTICIPATION IN DECISION MAKING

IRVING BLUESTONE*

The history of mankind has been marked by struggle between those who govern and those who are governed. In each major conflict, regardless of time, place, and circumstances, the voice of rebellion against authority has manifested itself in the cry for freedom, liberty, human rights, and human dignity. The underlying motivation is the desire for the right to participate in the decisions that affect one's welfare.

AUTHORITARIAN RULE IN THE WORKPLACE

In a society that prides itself on its democratic system of freedom for the individual and rejection of dictatorial rule, the workplace still stands as an island of authoritarianism. The organizational mold of business, especially big business, and the material objective of maximizing profits serve to obstruct, or at least deter, the fulfillment of democracy in the workplace. In fact, the workplace is probably the most authoritarian environment in which the adult finds himself in a free society. Its rigidity leads people to live a kind of double life: at home, they enjoy a reasonable measure of autonomy and self-fulfillment; at work, they are subject to regimentation, supervision, and control by others.

A society anchored in democratic principles should ensure each individual the dignity, respect, and liberty worthy of free people; it should afford opportunity for self-expression and participation in the shaping of one's own life. At work, however, personal freedom is severely curtailed, each worker having to adapt himself to tasks, work speeds, and behavior decided upon by others or by machines.

The American way of life rests on the concept that in public life the "governors" are subject to the will of the "governed." In the private life of business, however, leadership does not stem from the confidence of the "governed" (the workers); rather, it is directed toward protection of the interests of the firm, most often against the "governed," whose activities and patterns of life at work are organized, directed, and dominated by the "governors."

In a democracy, the rules of society are fashioned with the consent of those who must live by them, and the individual is guaranteed a fair trial and is "innocent until proved guilty." In the workplace, management decides the rules to be lived by, then exercises its authority to impose sanctions in cases of individual transgression.

The argument used to support authoritarianism in the workplace is that the organization of production and the goal of maximizing profit make it mandatory. Ownership means control. Ownership means rule by decree. Thus, the pattern of relations between the "governors" and the "governed" in business is contradictory to democracy.

Excerpted from "Worker Participation in Decision Making," published in *The Humanist*, September–October 1973, pp. 50–61. Reprinted by permission of the publisher.

*Former vice-president and director of General Motors Department of United Auto Workers; presently professor at Wayne State University.

Present-day industrialized society holds to certain economic precepts. Among them are: (1) technological progress is inevitable and desirable; (2) a better living standard for all depends on increased productivity and an expanding gross national product; (3) the purpose of business is to make and maximize profit.

Thus, the underlying thrust of our economic system, anchored in these precepts, has motivated management to develop a production system that is maximally advanced technologically, with maximum production at the lowest possible unit cost, and with maximum profitability.

The pursuit of maximum profit received remarkable stimulus with the advent of industrial organization and its system of production. Very soon, individuals and their needs became extensions of that tool. Skills were broken down to the least common denominator so that humans became as interchangeable as machine parts. Specialization through fractioning the job into the simplest, most repetitive acts of performance reduced skill requirements to the minimum. This production process evolved into scientific management.

The granddaddy of the principles of scientific management, Frederick Taylor, once observed that the average workingman is "so stupid and so phlegmatic that he more resembles the ox in his mental makeup than any other type." Obviously, this is more than mere exaggeration. It is a cynical expression concerning human beings who happen to be workers.

Over the years, scientific management evolved refinements that have robotized workers, removing to the greatest degree possible requirements of education, knowledge, skill, creativity, brain power, and muscle power. The assembly line, with its repetitive, monotonous sameness, developed into the ultimate symbol of scientific management. Taylor's principles have served industry well as a guide toward ever increasing productivity, lower unit costs, and higher profits. They also dovetailed neatly into the concept of "profits before people."

WINDS OF CHANGE IN THE PRODUCTION SYSTEM

Times and circumstances are now beginning to modify the eighty-year-old practices of refined technology—in part because workers' attitudes toward the meaning of work are changing, but also because society as a whole is paying closer attention to the total environment and the quality of life.

About the time that Henry Ford announced the "five-dollar day," he remarked, "The assembly line is a haven for those who haven't got the brains to do anything else." Mr. Ford's hiring practices were strict and stifling. No women were to work in his factories; they belonged at home in the kitchen and with their children. Men who failed to support their dependents would find no work at Ford, nor would divorced men or others who were "living unworthily"—those who smoked or drank hard liquor. Once hired, the workers were subjected to a spy system. "Social workers" on the Ford payroll visited workers' homes and reported on living habits: Did the man raise his own garden as instructed? Did his family house male boarders (which was taboo)? Did the worker complain to his family about his job and factory conditions? And so forth.

Today, the employer no longer has control of the worker outside the workplace, and unionization has wrested from the employer a measure of the control he exercises at the workplace. The next step is to provide the worker with a more meaningful measure of control over his job through participation in decisions affecting the job.

Contrast Henry Ford's stifling authoritarianism with the words of Richard Gerstenberg, chairman of the board of directors of General Motors Corporation, in 1972: "Productivity is not a matter of making employees work longer or harder. . . . We must improve working conditions and take out the boredom from routine jobs. . . . We must increase an employee's satisfaction with his job, heightening pride of workmanship, and, as far as is feasible, involve the employee personally in decisions that relate directly to his job. . . ."[1]

Mr. Gerstenberg's statement hopefully represents a conscious departure from the historic trickle-down theory that profits come first, that profits exemplify good in themselves and can only redound to the benefit of all society. Yet, more income and more material wealth, in and of themselves, do not guarantee a life of satisfaction or worth, and certainly cannot compensate for lives converted into deadened extensions of the tools of production.

New directions emerge as new problems arise. Cracks are occurring in the traditional discipline of the workplace. Absenteeism has been increasing. The Monday and Friday absentee is more commonplace. Tardiness also shows a generally upward trend. Labor turnover increases. Job boredom and repetitiveness are accompanied by "job alienation." Departure from the "work ethic" in turn results in a deterioration of production and quality. Workers feel a loss of individuality, dignity, and self-respect. Job dissatisfaction grows, and workers question the current ways of doing things as they seek to change the inflexible restrictions the production process puts upon them.

In 1969, the Survey Research Center of the University of Michigan reported the results of a study of 1,533 workers at various occupational levels. It concluded that workers ranked interesting work and enough equipment, information, and authority to get the job done ahead of good pay and job security.

An extensive study by Harold Sheppard and Neal Herrick, *Where Have All the Robots Gone?* concluded that job dissatisfaction is indeed widespread—and not only among blue-collar workers; that workers entering the labor force are increasingly anti-authoritarian, better educated, less income oriented than past generations of workers, and more resistant to meaningless, repetitive, and boring job assignments. They expect to enhance the quality of their working lives.

Each year, the Gallup organization has been taking a poll aimed at determining "job satisfaction." Between 1969 and 1971, those indicating satisfaction with their work dropped by seven points, from eighty-eight to eighty-one. Still further, the Bureau of Labor Statistics indicates that absentee rates have increased an average of 35 percent since 1961.

One significant aspect of American life that has been undergoing rapid change relates to freedom to enjoy the autonomy of self-employment. In 1950, 16 percent of the labor force was self-employed. This figure dropped to about 12 percent in 1960, and to 8 percent in 1970. Thus, the percentage of the self-employed dropped by half in two decades. Increasingly, people have been losing even this bastion of control over their working lives.

A study undertaken by HEW, published in 1973 as *Work in America*, leaves no doubt that worker dissatisfaction with jobs, both blue-collar and white-collar, is widespread, is on the rise, and presents an urgent problem for management, union, and government. The report notes: "And significant numbers of American workers are dissatisfied with the quality of their working lives. Dull, repetitive, seemingly meaningless tasks, offering little challenge or autonomy, are causing discontent among workers at all occupational levels."[2]

It is axiomatic that people respond more affirmatively to their role in society as they share in the opportunity to participate significantly in decisions affecting their welfare. History teaches, moreover, that at some point people who are denied this opportunity will reach out to grasp it.

This is equally true in the workplace. The stirrings of job dissatisfaction, in my judgment, relate in large measure to denial of participation in the decision-making process, denial of the opportunity to be creative and innovative and to control the machine, instead of being controlled by it.

The ferment of union activity in the 1930s and 1940s consolidated the organizing strength of industrial workers. It was the first stage toward accomplishment of a larger goal: industrial democracy. It provided the base on which workers were then able to improve their standard of living, win better working conditions, and achieve a greater measure of dignity and security as important members of society. Every gain constituted an incursion into the traditional authority wielded by management. The vast array of benefits won in collective bargaining over the years relates essentially to protecting the worker and his family against the hazards of economic insecurity. Workers, young and old, continue to aspire toward a better life, to be won at the bargaining table and through legislation. Their unions will, of course, persist in innovative collective-bargaining efforts as well as in improving upon already established benefit programs. They mobilize politically, cognizant of the intimate relationship between the bread box and the ballot box.

There is little need to spell out the enormously important progress workers have made through their unions. In *quantitative* terms, organized workers have won, and continue to win, a larger share of economic well-being. Unorganized workers have, of course, reaped the advantages of the gains made by unionized workers. Working conditions have also been vastly improved under the pressure of collective bargaining. Yet in *qualitative* terms, workers have not made as marked progress and are still struggling to play a more meaningful role in the decisions that affect their welfare in the business enterprise. Emphasis on qualitative improvement of life on the job is, I believe, the next step on the road toward industrial democracy.

WHITHER WORKER PARTICIPATION?

Two distinct, somewhat overlapping directions are indicated. One relates to "managing the enterprise"; the other relates to "managing the job." The latter is part and parcel of the former, but it is of more immediate concern to the worker.

Experiments with worker participation in "managing the enterprise" are under way in Yugoslavia (worker control of management), Germany (*Mitbestimmung*— codetermination established by law), Sweden (voluntary acceptance of worker representation on a company's board of directors), and Israel (union owned and operated cooperative enterprises). But in the United States, labor contracts, with their hundreds of provisions establishing and protecting workers' rights, leave substantially to management the "sole responsibility" to determine the products to be manufactured, the location of plants, production schedules, the methods, processes, and means of manufacture, as well as administrative decisions governing finances, marketing, purchasing, pricing, and the like. Unions traditionally have moved in the direction of improving wages, benefits, and working conditions. Generally, they have left "managing the enterprise" to management, only *reacting* to managerial acts objectionable to the workers. They have not embraced a political philosophy to motivate their overall policies and programs. This is not to say that American unions have no socioeconomic-political concepts. Quite the contrary; but they are not married to an "ism" governing and directing their behavior.

Rather, American unions move to meet practical problems with practical solutions. It is highly improbable that they will approach the problem of worker participation in decision making via fierce ideological struggle founded in socioeconomic theory. They are not prone to beat their wings in ideological or doctrinaire frustration. Where workers feel victimized, they combine their forces to correct the situation, case by case, problem by problem. Gradual persistent change, not revolutionary upheaval, has marked the progress of the American worker. When explosions occur, as in the 1930s, they are responses to specific problems and are searches for specific solutions. We can anticipate that worker participation in managing the enterprise or job will manifest itself in a similar way.

Decisions regarding purchasing, advertising, selling, and financing, for instance, are far more remote from the immediate problems facing the worker than are decisions concerning his or her job. In the vast range of managerial decisions, the immediacy of impact on the worker varies enormously. Thus, the average worker in a gigantic enterprise usually displays less interest in the selection of the chairman of the board than in the amount of overtime he receives.

What direction, then, will the drive toward worker participation in decision making take? To begin with, it seems safe to say that any further encroachment on so-called management prerogatives will spell "revolution" to management, while to the worker it will simply represent a nonideological effort to resolve a bothersome problem.

Certain areas of possible confrontation come to mind. By way of example, management makes a decision to shut down a plant or move all or part of it to another location, often hundreds of miles away. The union bargains for severance pay, early retirement, the right of the worker to transfer with the job and to receive moving allowance, and so forth. But the worker, often with long years of service, is the victim of such a decision. He is permanently thrown out of work, or even if he is given the right to transfer with the job, he must pull up stakes, cut his roots in the community, leave friends, perhaps break family ties, and begin a new life in a strange place, with no assurance of permanence. Management wields the decision-making authority; the workers and the community dangle at the end of that decision.

Similarly, management generally controls the final decision to subcontract work or to shuffle work among its facilities in a multiplant corporation. The worker faces the ultimate insecurity. Management also holds the authority to discipline. All places of work (as in society at large) require rules and regulations for people to live by; but discipline can be a fearful weapon in the hands of a ruthless employer, even when subject to a collectively bargained grievance procedure.

Production scheduling can be a serious source of friction. In an auto-assembly plant, for instance, changes in line speed to meet changes in production schedules or changes in model mix require rebalancing of jobs and operations. This in turn gives rise to disputes over production standards and manpower. Frequent changes in line speed or model mix disturb agreed-upon settlements about production standards and manpower agreements, often resulting in crisis bargaining and, on occasion, strike action.

The never ending yet necessary introduction of technological innovation and the concomitant alteration of jobs, cutbacks in manpower, and effect on skill requirements are a constant source of new problems, emphasizing the concern workers naturally have for their job security. Furthermore, the call for excessive overtime is a constant source of unhappiness and discontent.

These are but a handful of the kinds of confrontation issues that directly affect workers and that are increasingly subject to "worker participation" bargaining.

Other types of issues, also relating directly to life in the workplace, will command attention, for democratizing the workplace carries considerations beyond the worker's immediate job. The double standard for managers and workers is being questioned. Symbols of elitism, traditionally taken for granted in industrial society, are challenged: salaries and their normally recognized advantages (versus hourly payment and the punching of time clocks), paneled dining rooms (versus spartan cafeterias), privileged parking facilities nearest the plant entrance, and so forth.

Democratizing the workplace may entail organizing the work schedule to enable the worker to manage his personal chores: visiting the dentist or doctor, getting his car repaired, visiting his children's school during teaching and conference hours, for example.

Worker participation in decision making will be demanded more often with regard to those aspects of working life most immediately and noticeably affected. "Managing the job" is more immediate and urgent. Worker concern for "managing the enterprise" is more variable and is best measured by the immediacy of impact on the worker's welfare.

Increasing attention is currently being devoted to this problem of "managing the job." Rising rates of absenteeism, worker disinterest in the quality and quantity of production, job alienation, and the insistence on unit-cost reduction are motivating some employers to re-evaluate current practices and customs governing management-worker relationships. Concurrently, workers rebel against the authoritarian atmosphere of the workplace and the subordination of their personal dignity, desires, and aspirations to the drive for more production at lower cost; they find little challenge, satisfaction, or interest in their work. While the worker's rate of pay may dominate his relationship to the job, he can be responsive to the opportunity for playing an innovative, creative, and imaginative role in the production process.

One of the essential tasks of the union movement is to "humanize the workplace." A pleasant, decent management is desirable but does not alter the basic managerial design. "Human engineering" concepts may make for more comfortable employer-employee relationships, but here, too, managerial administration of the workplace remains fundamentally unchanged. "Humanizing the workplace" not only must include the normally recognized amenities of life in the workplace but it also must move to a higher plateau and relate to job satisfaction—a closing of the widening gap between the mechanization of production by scientific management and the worker's participation in the production and decision-making process. "Humanizing the workplace" in this sense represents one additional step toward the fulfillment of industrial democracy.

But humanizing the workplace must not become simply another gimmick designed essentially to "fool" the worker by having as its primary goal or hidden agenda an increase in worker productivity. Manipulation of the worker will be recognized for what it is—another form of exploitation; it will breed suspicion and distrust.

In this regard, Delmar Landan, an expert in personnel development for General Motors, has said: ". . . where we have to aim is participation—it is the only way to work in this increasingly complex society. The man at the top can't have all the answers. The man doing the job will have some of them."[3]

Worker participation in decision making about his job is one means of achieving democratization of the workplace. It should result in a change from the miniaturization and oversimplification of the job to the evolution of a system embracing broader distribution of authority, increasing rather than diminishing responsibility and accountability. It should combine the imaginative creation of more interesting jobs with the opportunity to exercise a meaningful measure of autonomy and utilization of more varied skills. It requires tapping the creative and innovative ingenuity of the worker to the maximum.

Hundreds of experiments have been and are being undertaken in American industry, following the European lead. They are directed toward opening up opportunities for meaningful worker participation. The HEW report describes some of them. In the auto industry, the industry with which I am most closely associated, a myriad of demonstration projects are under way. They cover innumerable facets of the problem and some are a sharp departure from the assembly-line concept.

It is too early to describe precisely what form or forms humanizing the workplace will take. Certain criteria, however, deserve serious consideration.

1. The worker should genuinely feel that he or she is not simply an adjunct to the tool, but that his or her bent toward being creative, innovative, and inventive plays a significant role in the production (or service) process.

2. The worker should be assured that his or her participation in decision making will not erode job security or that of fellow workers.

3. Job functions should be adapted to the worker; the current system is designed to make the worker fit the job, on the theory that this is a more efficient production system and that, in any event, economic gain is the worker's only reason for working. This theory may be proved wrong on both counts.

4. The worker should be assured the widest possible latitude of self-management, responsibility, and opportunity to use her or his brain. Gimmickery and manipulation of the worker must be ruled out.

5. Changes in job content and the added responsibility and involvement in decision making should be accompanied by upgrading pay rates.

6. The worker should be able to foresee opportunities for growth in his or her work and for promotion.

7. The worker's role in the business should enable her or him to relate to the product or services rendered, as well as to their meanings in society; in a broader sense, it should also enable her or him to relate constructively to her or his role in society.

The union, as the workers' representative, will naturally share with management in implementing these and other criteria. But crisis negotiating—settling a wage dispute before a midnight strike deadline— is not the time to seek precise means of humanizing the workplace. This task requires careful experiment and analysis. While issues of economic security (wages, fringe benefits) and continuing encroachment on what management terms its sole prerogatives will remain adversary in nature, there is every reason why humanizing the workplace should be undertaken as a joint, cooperative, constructive, nonadversary effort by management and the union. The initial key to achieving this goal may well be open, frank, and enlightened discussion between the parties, recognizing that democratizing the workplace and humanizing the job need not be matters of confrontation but of mutual concern for the worker, the enterprise, and the welfare of society.

NOTES

1. Richard C. Gerstenberg, speech to the Annual Meeting of the American Publishers Association, New York, April 26, 1972.

2. *Work in America*, Report of a Special Task Force to the Secretary of Health, Education, and Welfare (Cambridge, Mass.: MIT Press, 1973), p. xv.

3. Delmar Landan in Judson Gooding, *The Job Revolution* (New York: Walker Publishing Co., 1972), p. 111.

THE MYTH OF JOB ENRICHMENT

MITCHELL FEIN*

Practically all writing that deals with worker boredom and frustration starts with the idea that the nature of work in industry and offices degrades the human spirit, is antithetical to workers' needs and damages their mental health, and that the redesign of work is socially desirable and beneficial to workers. Curiously, however, this view is not supported by workers or their unions. If workers faced the dire consequences of deprivation projected by the behaviorists, they should be conscious of the need to redesign and enrich their jobs. (The term "behaviorist" is used in this article to include psychologists, social scientists, and others who favor the redesign of work and job enrichment as a way to enhance the quality of working life. Many behaviorists, in fact, may not hold these views. Still, there is a sharp difference of opinion between what workers say they want and what behaviorists say workers want.)

WHO SPEAKS FOR WORKERS?

Workers' feelings about their work and what goes on at the workplace are expressed quite freely by workers themselves and their spokesmen in the unions. Since no union has yet raised the issue of work boredom and the redesign of jobs, is it not reasonable to assume that the question is not important to workers? Workers are not bashful in their demands, and worker representatives are quite vocal in championing workers' needs. One might argue that workers do not comprehend the harm that is done to them by their work and that they must be shown that many of their problems and troubles really stem from the nature of their jobs. But that assumes that workers are naive or stupid, which is not the case.

The judgments of those advocating job changes derive from people whom Abraham Maslow would characterize as "superior people (called self-actualizers) who are also superior perceivers, not only of facts but of values, . . . their ultimate values [are then used] as possibly the ultimate values for the whole species."[1] These advocates of change maintain that healthy progress for people is toward self-fulfillment through work, and they see most jobs as dull, repetitive, seemingly meaningless tasks, offering little challenge or autonomy. They view the nature of work as the main deterrent to more fulfilling lives for the workers and the redesign of jobs as the keystone of their plans for accomplishing the desired changes.

Paul Kurtz has stated: "Humanists today attack all those social forces which seek to destroy man: they deplore the dehumanization and alienation of man within the industrial and technological society. . . . and the failure of modern man to achieve the full measure of his potential excellence. The problem for the humanist is to create the conditions that would emancipate man from oppressive and corruptive social organization, and from the denigration and perversion of his human talents . . . ."[2]

From *The Humanist*, September–October 1973, pp. 71–77. Reprinted by permission of the publisher.
*Former professor of industrial engineering, New York University.

Humanists' goals and behaviorists' objectives appear similar. Both accept Maslow's self-actualization concepts as the preferred route to fulfillment. But by what divine right does one group assume that its values are superior to others and should be accepted as normal? Both the selection of goals and attitudes toward work are uniquely personal. The judges of human values have no moral right to press their normative concepts on others as preferable.

SATISFACTION AND ACHIEVEMENT

The fundamental question is whether or not the nature of work prevents people from achieving the full measure of their potential. When behaviorists view people at work, they see two main groups: those who are satisfied and those who are not. They examine the satisfied and like what they see. These are eager, energetic people, who are generally enthusiastic about their jobs and life in general. The behaviorists hold them up as ideal and prepare to convert the dissatisfied.

In contrasting the satisfied workers with the dissatisfied ones, behaviorists see the nature of the work performed as the main difference. So they propose to change the work of the dissatisfied to more closely resemble that performed by the satisfied. But there is a large "if" in this approach: What if the nature of the work is not the reason for the satisfaction?

It could very well be that the satisfied have more drive, which creates greater material wants and higher goals, which in turn motivates them to make more effective efforts in the workplace and to bid for more highly skilled jobs, and so on. Restructuring the work and creating new opportunities may make some people enthusiastic, but to what extent is the nature of the work the determinant of a person's drive?

There are no data that definitively show that restructuring and enriching jobs will increase the will to work or give workers greater satisfaction. Similarly, I have not seen any research data that show that a person with drive is deterred from reaching his potential by the nature of the work.

I believe that ethical considerations alone should keep behaviorists from setting up their values as the ideals for society. In addition, I will attempt to demonstrate that the behaviorists' views on redesigning jobs are misguided; they do not understand the work process in plants, and they misjudge workers' attitudes toward their jobs.

WORKERS' ATTITUDES TOWARD THEIR WORK

A 1972 Gallup Poll found that 80 to 90 percent of American workers are satisfied with their jobs. A 1973 poll by Thomas C. Sorenson found that from 82 to 91 percent of blue- and while-collar workers like their work. He asked, "If there were one thing you could change about your job, what would it be?" He found that "Astonishingly, very few mentioned making their jobs 'less boring' or 'more interesting.' "[3]

Behaviorists and humanists find it difficult to understand how workers can possibly say they like their work when it appears so barren to intellectuals. This view was recently expressed by the behavioral scientist David Sirota, after making a study in a garment plant. He was surprised to find that most sewing-machine operators found their work interesting. Since the work appeared highly repetitive to him, he had expected that they would say that they were bored and that their talents were not fully utilized. These workers' views are supported in a study by Emanuel Weintraub of 2,535 female sewing-machine operators in seventeen plants from Massachusetts to Texas. He found that "most of the operators like the nature of their work."[4] What the behaviorists find so difficult to comprehend is really quite simply explained: Workers have similar attitudes toward their work because *they are not a cross-section of the population, but rather a select group.*

There is greater choice in the selection of jobs by workers than is supposed. The selection process in factories and offices goes on without conscious direction by either workers or management. The data for white- and blue-collar jobs show that there is tremendous turnover in the initial employment period but that the turnover drops sharply with time on the job. What occurs is that a worker comes onto a new job, tries it out for several days or weeks, and decides whether or not the work suits his needs and desires. Impressions about a job are a composite of many factors: pay, proximity to home, nature of work, working conditions, attitude of supervision, congeniality of fellow workers, past employment history of the company, job security, physical demands, possibilities for advancement, and many others. Working conditions may be bad, but if the pay and job security are high, the job may be tolerable. To a married woman, the pay may be low, but if the job is close to home and working conditions are good, it may be desirable. There are numerous combinations of factors that influence a worker's disposition to stay on the job or not.

There is a dual screening process that sifts out many of those who will be dissatisfied with the work. The process operates as follows: The worker in the first instance decides whether or not to stay on the job; management then has the opportunity to determine whether or not to keep him beyond the trial period. The combination of the worker's choice to remain and management's decision regarding the worker's acceptability screens out many workers who might find the job unsatisfying.

Some workers find highly repetitive work in factories intolerable, so they become truck drivers, where they can be out on the road with no supervisor on their back all day. Others prefer to work in gas stations, warehouses, retail stores, and other such places. Increasingly workers are taking white-collar jobs that in many ways are similar to repetitive factory jobs but which have cleaner physical surroundings and better working conditions. In times of high unemployment, workers stay in safe jobs for continuity of income; but, as the job market improves, the rate of turnover increases and selection of jobs resumes.

There would undoubtedly be much greater dissatisfaction among workers if they were not free to make changes and selections in the work they do. Some prefer to remain in highly repetitive, low-skilled work even when they have an opportunity to advance to more highly skilled jobs through job bidding. A minority of workers strive to move into the more skilled jobs, such as machinists, maintenance mechanics, setup men, group leaders, and utility men, where work is discretionary and the workers have considerable autonomy in the tasks they perform.

The continued evaluation of workers by management and the mobility available to workers in the job market refine the selection process. A year or two after entering a plant, most workers are on jobs or job progressions that suit them or which they find tolerable.

However, the work force in the plant is not homogeneous. There are two main groups, the achievers and the nonachievers. Their attitudes toward work and their goals are vastly different. A minority of the work force, which I find to be 15 percent, have a drive for achievement and identify with their work. These workers' attitudes match the ideal projected by behaviorists. They dislike repetitive work and escape from it by moving into more skilled jobs, which have the autonomy and interest they look for in their work. Only a minority of jobs in industry and offices are in the skilled category, and fortunately only a minority of workers aspire to these jobs. About 85 percent of workers do not identify with their work, do not prefer more complicated and restructured jobs, and simply work in order to eat. Yet they, too, like their work and find it interesting.[5]

For different reasons, both groups of workers find their work interesting and satisfying. The work of the 85 percent who are nonachievers is interesting to them though boring to the other 15 percent. And the 15 percent who are achievers find their work interesting, though it is not sufficiently appealing for the majority to covet it. The selection process does amazingly well in matching workers and jobs.

What blinds behaviorists to this process is their belief that the achievement drive is an intrinsic part of human nature, that fulfillment at work is essential to sound mental health, and that, given the opportunity, workers would choose to become more involved in their work and take on larger and more complicated tasks. Once behaviorists take this view, they cannot understand what really happens on the plant floor or why workers do one thing rather than another.

WHY DO BEHAVIORISTS CLAIM TO SPEAK FOR WORKERS?

Behaviorists' insistence that they know more about what workers want than workers themselves is largely based on a number of job-enrichment case histories and studies of workers over the past decade. It is claimed that these studies show that workers really want job enrichment and benefit from it. But when these studies are examined closely, four things are found. (1) What actually occurred was quite different from what was reported by the behaviorists. (2) Most of the studies were conducted with hand-picked employees, usually working in areas or plants isolated from the main operation, and they do not reflect a cross-section of the working population. Practically all are in nonunion plants. (3) Only a handful of job-enrichment cases have been reported in the past ten years, despite the behaviorists' claims of gains for employees and management obtained through job changes. (4) In all instances, the experiments were initiated by management, never by workers or unions.

The *Survey of Working Conditions*, conducted for the United States Department of Labor by the Survey Research Center of the University of Michigan, contained serious errors.[6] The General Foods-Topeka case reported by Richard E. Walton[7] omits important information that shows that the sixty-three workers for this plant were handpicked from seven hundred applicants. Texas Instruments, which conducted the longest and broadest experiments, only attracted 10 percent of its employees to the program.[8] The Texas Instruments cleaning-employees case, as well as others, was grossly misreported in HEW's *Work in America*.

There are no job-enrichment successes that bear out the predictions of the behaviorists, because the vast majority of workers reject the concept. A small proportion of workers who desire job changes are prevented from participating by the social climate in the plant. They find involvement by moving into skilled jobs. Perhaps behaviorists do not recognize the moral issues raised by their proposals to redesign work—for example: intrusion upon a person's right to personal decisions; exploitation of workers' job satisfaction for company gains; distortion of the truth.

The boundless wisdom of this country's founders in separating religion from government and public practices has been revealed in countless ways. But along comes a new faith that proclaims that people should derive satisfaction from their work. When up to 90 percent of workers are reported to be satisfied with their work, the behaviorists say that workers do not really know what satisfaction is and that they will lead them to a superior kind. This sounds oddly like the proselytizing of a missionary. If behaviorists called for making enriched work available for those who want it, I would support them because I believe a minority of workers do want it. But I oppose foisting these practices on workers who do not call for it. In any case, I believe the minority has all the enrichment they want.

Exploiting workers' job satisfaction for management's gain can backfire dangerously. Workers expect management to develop new approaches and production processes to increase productivity; they are prepared for continuous pressure for more output. But when these changes are designed primarily to create a more receptive worker attitude toward greater productivity, they may see that they have been "had." If management's gains are real, while workers' benefits are only in their minds, who has really benefited? The behaviorists now say that workers should also share in productivity gains. But these statements have come late and are couched in such vague terms as to be meaningless.

When a supposedly good thing must be put into fancy wrappings to enhance it, something is amiss. Why must the job-enrichment cases be distorted to make the final results appealing? Why must behaviorists use phrases such as "work humanization" to describe their proposals, as though work were now inhuman? Workers understand the meaning of money, job security, health benefits, and retirement without fancy explanations. If the enrichment and redesign of work is such a good thing, why is it rejected by those who would benefit from it? The so-called new industrial democracy is not really democracy but a new autocracy of "we know better than you what's good for you."

NOTES

1. Abraham Maslow, *The Farther Reaches of Human Nature* (New York: Viking, 1971), p. 10.

2. Paul Kurtz, "What Is Humanism?" in *Moral Problems in Contemporary Society: Essays in Humanistic Ethics*, ed. P. Kurtz (Buffalo: Prometheus Books, 1973), p. 11.

3. Thomas C. Sorenson, "Do Americans Like Their Jobs?" *Parade*, June 3, 1973.

4. Emanuel Weintraub, "Has Job Enrichment Been Oversold?" an address to the 25th annual convention of the American Institute of Industrial Engineers, May 1973, *Technical Papers*, p. 349.

5. A more complete discussion and supporting data for the 15/85 worker composition is contained in M. Fein's "Motivation for Work," in *Handbook of Work Organization and Society*, ed. Robert Dubin (Skokie, Ill.: Rand-McNally, 1973).

6. *Survey of Working Conditions* (Washington, D.C.: U.S. Dept. of Labor, 1971). These errors were disclosed in my analysis in "The Real Needs and Goals of Blue Collar Workers," *The Conference Board Record*, Feb. 1973.

7. Richard E. Walton, "How To Counter Alienation in the Plant," *Harvard Business Review*, Nov.–Dec. 1972, pp. 70–81.

8. Fein, "Motivation for Work."

chapter nine
HIRING PRACTICES: PREFERENTIAL HIRING AND REVERSE DISCRIMINATION

PREFERENTIAL HIRING

JUDITH JARVIS THOMSON*

Many people are inclined to think preferential hiring an obvious injustice.[1] I should have said "feel" rather than "think": it seems to me the matter has not been carefully thought out, and that what is in question, really, is a gut reaction.

I am going to deal with only a very limited range of preferential hirings: that is, I am concerned with cases in which several candidates present themselves for a job, in which the hiring officer finds, on examination, that all are equally qualified to hold that job, and he then straightway declares for the black, or for the woman, because he or she *is* a black or woman. And I shall talk only of hiring decisions in the universities, partly because I am most familiar with them, partly because it is in the universities that the most vocal and articulate opposition to preferential hiring is now heard—not surprisingly, perhaps, since no one is more vocal and articulate than a university professor who feels deprived of his rights.

I suspect that some people may say, Oh well, in *that* kind of case it's all right, what we object to is preferring the less qualified to the better qualified. Or again, What we object to is refusing even to consider the qualifications of white males. I shall say nothing at all about these things. I think that the argument I shall give for saying that preferential hiring is not unjust in the cases I do concentrate on can also be appealed to to justify it outside that range of cases. But I won't draw any conclusions about cases outside it. Many people do have that gut reaction I mentioned against preferential hiring in *any* degree or form; and it seems to me worthwhile bringing out that there is good reason to think they are wrong to have it. Nothing I say will be in the slightest degree novel or original. It will, I hope, be enough to set the relevant issues out clearly.

From *Philosophy & Public Affairs*, vol. 2, no. 4 (Summer 1973). Copyright © 1973 by Princeton University Press, Princeton, N.J. Excerpt reprinted by permission of Princeton University Press.

*Department of Philosophy, Massachusetts Institute of Technology.

I

But first, something should be said about qualifications.

I said I would consider only cases in which the several candidates who present themselves for the job are equally qualified to hold it; and there plainly are difficulties in the way of saying precisely how this is to be established, and even what is to be established. Strictly academic qualifications seem at a first glance to be relatively straight-forward: the hiring officer must see if the candidates have done equally well in courses (both courses they took, and any they taught), and if they are recommended equally strongly by their teachers, and if the work they submit for consideration is equally good. There is no denying that even these things are less easy to establish than first appears: for example, you may have a suspicion that Professor Smith is given to exaggeration, and that his "great student" is in fact less strong than Professor Jones's "good student"—but do you *know* that this is so? But there is a more serious difficulty still: as blacks and women have been saying, strictly academic indicators may themselves be skewed by prejudice. My impression is that women, white and black, may possibly suffer more from this than black males. A black male who is discouraged or down-graded for being black is discouraged or down-graded out of dislike, repulsion, a desire to avoid contact; and I suspect that there are very few teachers nowadays who allow themselves to feel such things, or, if they do feel them, to act on them. A woman who is discouraged or down-graded for being a woman is not discouraged or down-graded out of dislike, but out of a conviction she is not serious.

II

Suppose two candidates for a civil service job have equally good test scores, but that there is only one job available. We could decide between them by coin-tossing. But in fact we do allow for declaring for A straightway, where A is a veteran, and B is not.[2] It may be that B is a nonveteran through no fault of his own: perhaps he was refused induction for flat feet, or a heart murmur. That is, those things in virtue of which B is a nonveteran may be things which it was no more in his power to control or change than it is in anyone's power to control or change the color of his skin. Yet the fact is that B is not a veteran and A is. On the assumption that the veteran has served his country,[3] the country owes him something. And it seems plain that giving him preference is a not unjust way in which part of that debt of gratitude can be paid.

And now, finally, we should turn to those debts which are incurred by one who wrongs another. It is here we find what seems to me the most powerful argument for the conclusion that the preferential hiring of blacks and women is not unjust.

I obviously cannot claim any novelty for this argument: it's a very familiar one. Indeed, not merely is it familiar, but so are a battery of objections to it. It may be granted that if we have wronged A, we owe him something: we should make amends, we should compensate him for the wrong done him. It may even be granted that if we have wronged A, we must make amends, that justice requires it, and that a failure to make amends is not merely callousness, but injustice. But (a) are the young blacks and women who are amongst the current applicants for university jobs amongst the blacks and women who were wronged? To turn to particular cases, it might happen that the black applicant is middle class, son of professionals, and has had the very best in private schooling; or that the woman applicant is plainly the product of feminist upbringing and encouragement. Is it proper, much less required, that the black or woman be given preference over a white male who grew up in poverty, and has to make his own way and earn his encouragements? Again, (b), did we, the current members of the community, wrong any blacks or women? Lots of people once did; but then isn't it for them to do the compensating? That is, if they're still alive. For presumably nobody now alive owned any slaves, and perhaps nobody now alive voted against women's suffrage. And (c) what if the white male applicant for the job has never in any degree wronged any blacks or women? If so, *he* doesn't owe any debts to them, so why should *he* make amends to them?

These objections seem to me quite wrong-headed.

Obviously the situation for blacks and women is better than it was a hundred and fifty, fifty, twenty-five years ago. But it is absurd to suppose that the young blacks and women now of an age to apply for jobs have not been wronged. Large-scale, blatant, overt wrongs have presumably disappeared; but it is only within the last twenty-five years (perhaps the last ten years in the case of women) that it has become at all widely agreed in this country that blacks and women must be recognized as having, not merely this or that particular right normally recognized as belonging to white males, but all of the rights and respect which go with full membership in the community. Even young blacks and women have lived through down-grading for being black or female: they have not merely not been given that very equal chance at the benefits generated by what the community owns which is so firmly insisted on for white males, they have not until lately even been felt to have a right to it.

And even those who were not themselves down-graded for being black or female have suffered the consequences of the down-grading of other blacks and women: lack of self-confidence, and lack of self-respect. For where a community accepts that a person's being black, or being a woman, are right and proper grounds for denying that person full membership in the community, it can hardly be supposed that any but the most extraordinarily independent black or woman will escape self-doubt. All but the most extraordinarily independent of them have had to work harder—if only against self-doubt—than all but the most deprived white males, in the competition for a place amongst the best qualified.

If any black or woman has been unjustly deprived of what he or she has a right to, then of course justice does call for making amends. But what of the blacks and women who haven't actually been deprived of what they have a right to, but only made to suffer the consequences of injustice to other blacks and women? *Perhaps* justice doesn't require making amends to them as well; but common decency certainly does. To fail, at the very least, to make what counts as public apology to all, and to take positive steps to show that it is sincerely meant, is, if not injustice, then anyway a fault at least as serious as ingratitude.

Opting for a policy of preferential hiring may of course mean that some black or woman is preferred to some white male who as a matter of fact has had a harder life than the black or woman. But so may opting for a policy of veterans' preference mean that a healthy, unscarred, middle class veteran is preferred to a poor, struggling, scarred, nonveteran. Indeed, opting for a policy of settling who gets the job by having all equally qualified candidates draw straws may also mean that in a given case the candidate with the hardest life loses out. Opting for any policy other than hard-life preference may have this result.

I have no objection to anyone's arguing that it is precisely hard-life preference that we ought to opt for. If all, or anyway all of the equally qualified, have a right to an equal chance, then the argument would have to draw attention to something sufficiently powerful to override that right. But perhaps this could be done along the lines I followed in the case of blacks and women: perhaps it could be successfully argued that we have wronged those who have had hard lives, and therefore owe it to them to make amends. And then we should have in more extreme form a difficulty already present: how are these preferences to be ranked? shall we place the hard-lifers ahead of blacks? both ahead of women? and what about veterans? I leave these questions aside. My concern has been only to show that the white male applicant's right to an equal chance does not make it unjust to opt for a policy under which blacks and women are given preference. That a white male with a specially hard history may lose out under this policy cannot possibly be any objection to it, in the absence of a showing that hard-life preference is not unjust, and, more important, takes priority over preference for blacks and women.

Lastly, it should be stressed that to opt for such a policy is not to make the young white male applicants themselves make amends for any wrongs done to blacks and women. Under such a policy, no one is asked to give up a job which is already his; the job for which the white male competes isn't his, but is the community's, and it is the hiring officer who gives it to the black or woman in the community's name. Of course the white male is asked to give up his equal chance at the job. But that is not something he pays to the black or woman by way of making amends; it is something the community takes away from him in order that *it* may make amends.

Still, the community does impose a burden on him: it is able to make amends for its wrongs only by taking something away from him, something which, after all, we are supposing he has a right to. And why should *he* pay the cost of the community's amends-making?

If there were some appropriate way in which the community could make amends to its blacks and women, some way which did not require depriving anyone of anything he has a right to, then that would be the best course of action for it to take. Or if there were anyway some way in which the costs could be shared by everyone, and not imposed entirely on the young white male job applicants, then that would be, if not best, then anyway better than opting for a policy of preferential hiring. But in fact the nature of the wrongs done is such as to make jobs the best and most suitable form of compensation. What blacks and women were denied was full membership in the community; and nothing can more appropriately make amends for that wrong than precisely what will make them feel they now finally have it. And that means jobs. Financial compensation (the cost of which could be shared equally) slips through the fingers; having a job, and discovering you do it well, yield—perhaps better than anything else—that very self-respect which blacks and women have had to do without.

But of course choosing this way of making amends means that the costs are imposed on the young white male applicants who are turned away. And so it should be noticed that it is not entirely inappropriate that those applicants should pay the costs. No doubt few, if any, have themselves, individually, done any wrongs to blacks and women. But they have profited from the wrongs the community did. Many may actually have been direct beneficiaries of policies which excluded or down-graded blacks and women—perhaps in school admissions, perhaps in access to financial aid, perhaps elsewhere; and even those who did not directly benefit in this way had, at any rate, the advantage in the competition which comes of confidence in one's full membership, and of one's rights being recognized as a matter of course.

Of course it isn't only the young white male applicant for a university job who has benefited from the exclusion of blacks and women: the older white male, now comfortably tenured, also benefited, and many defenders of preferential hiring feel that he should be asked to share the costs. Well, presumably we can't demand that he give up his job, or share it. But it seems to me in place to expect the occupants of comfortable professional chairs to contribute in some way, to make some form of return to the young white male who bears the cost, and is turned away. It will have been plain that I find the outcry now heard against preferential hiring in the universities objectionable; it would also be objectionable that those of us who are now securely situated should placidly defend it, with no more than a sigh of regret for the young white male who pays for it.

III

One final word: "discrimination." I am inclined to think we so use it that if anyone is convicted of discriminating against blacks, women, white males, or what have you, then he is thereby convicted of acting unjustly. If so, and if I am right in thinking that preferential hiring in the restricted range of cases we have been looking at is *not* unjust, then we have two options: (a) we can simply reply that to opt for a policy of preferential hiring in those cases is not to opt for a policy of discriminating against white males, or (b) we can hope to get usage changed—e.g., by trying to get people to allow that there is discriminating against and discriminating against, and that some is unjust, but some is not.

Best of all, however, would be for that phrase to be avoided altogether. It's at best a blunt tool: there are all sorts of nice moral discriminations [sic] which one is unable to make while occupied with it. And that bluntness itself fits it to do harm: blacks and women are hardly likely to see through to what precisely is owed them while they are being accused of welcoming what is unjust.

NOTES

1. This essay is an expanded version of a talk given at the Conference on the Liberation of Female Persons, held at North Carolina State University at Raleigh, on March 26–28, 1973, under a grant from the S & H Foundation. I am indebted to James Thomson and the members of the Society for Ethical and Legal Philosophy for criticism of an earlier draft.

2. To the best of my knowledge, the analogy between veterans' preference and the preferential hiring of blacks has been mentioned in print only by Edward T. Chase, in a Letter to the Editor, *Commentary*, February 1973.

3. Many people would reject this assumption, or perhaps accept it only selectively, for veterans of this or that particular war. I ignore this. What interests me is what follows if we make the assumption—as, of course, many other people do, more, it seems, than do not.

PREFERENTIAL HIRING AND COMPENSATION:
A Reply to Thomson

ROBERT K. FULLINWIDER*

Persons have rights, but sometimes a right may justifiably be overridden. Can we concede to all job applicants a right to equal consideration, and yet support a policy of preferentially hiring female over white male applicants?

Judith Thomson, in her article "Preferential Hiring,"[1] appeals to the principle of compensation as a ground which justifies us in sometimes overriding a person's rights. She applies this principle to a case of preferential hiring of a woman in order to defend the claim that such preferential hiring is not unjust. Her defense rests upon the contention that a debt of compensation is owed to women, and that the existence of this debt provides us with a justification of preferential hiring of women in certain cases even though this involves setting aside or overriding certain rights of white male applicants.

Although she is correct in believing that the right to compensation sometimes allows us or requires us to override or limit other rights, I shall argue that Thomson has failed to show that the principle of compensation justifies preferential hiring in the case she constructs. Thus, by implication, I argue that she has failed to show that preferential hiring of women in such cases is not unjust.

Thomson asks us to imagine the following case. Suppose for some academic job a white male applicant (WMA) and a female applicant (FA) are under final consideration.[2] Suppose further that we grant that WMA and FA each has a *right to equal consideration* by the university's hiring officer. This means that each has a right to be evaluated for the job solely in terms of his or her possession of job-related qualifications. Suppose, finally, that the hiring officer hires FA because she is a woman. How can the hiring officer's choice avoid being unjust.

Since being a woman is, by hypothesis, not a job-related qualification in this instance, the hiring officer's act of choosing FA because she is a woman seems to violate WMA's right to equal consideration. The hiring officer's act would not be unjust only if in this situation there is some sufficient moral ground for setting aside or overriding WMA's right.

I offer the following as a fair construction of the argument Thomson intends.

Women, as a group, are owed a debt of compensation. Historically women, because they were women, have been subject to extensive and damaging discrimination, socially approved and legally supported. The discriminatory practices have served to limit the opportunities for fulfillment open to women and have put them at a disadvantage in the competition for many social benefits. Since women have been the victims of injustice, they have a moral right to be compensated for the wrongs done to them.

The compensation is owed by the community. The community as a whole is

Excerpted from "Preferential Hiring and Compensation," published in *Social Theory and Practice*, Vol. 3, no. 3 (Spring 1975). Reprinted by permission of publisher and author.

*Center for Philosophy and Public Policy, University of Maryland.

responsible, since the discriminatory practices against women have not been limited to isolated, private actions. These practices have been widespread, and public as well as private. Nowhere does Thomson argue that the case for preferring FA over WMA lies in a debt to FA *directly incurred by* WMA. In fact, Thomson never makes an effort to show any direct connection between FA and WMA. The moral relationship upon which Thomson's argument must rely exists between women and the community. The sacrifice on WMA's part is exacted from him by the community so it may pay its debt to women. This is a crucial feature of Thomson's case, and creates the need for the next premise: The right to compensation on the part of women justifies the community in overriding WMA's right to equal consideration.

In short, Thomson's argument contains the following premises:

1. Women, as a group, are owed a debt of compensation.

2. The compensation is owed to women by the community.

3. The community exacts a sacrifice from WMA (that is, sets aside his right to equal consideration) in order to pay its debt. [3]

4. The right to compensation on the part of women against the community justifies the community in setting aside WMA's right.

I shall not quarrel with premises 1 to 3, nor with the assumption that *groups* can be wronged and have rights. [4] My quarrel here is with premise 4. I shall show that Thomson offers no support for 4, and that it does not involve a correct application of the principle of compensation as used by Thomson.

Imagine a thirty-six–hole, two-round golf tournament among FA, WMA, and a third party, sanctioned and governed by a tournament-organizing committee. In previous years FA switched to a new model club, which improved her game. Before the match the third player surreptitiously substitutes for FA's clubs a set of the old type. This is discovered after eighteen holes have been played. If we suppose that the match cannot be restarted or canceled, then the committee is faced with the problem of compensating FA for the unfair disadvantage caused her by the substitution. By calculating her score averages over the years, the committee determines that the new clubs have yielded FA an average two-stroke improvement per eighteen holes over the old clubs. The committee decides to compensate FA by penalizing the third player by two strokes in the final eighteen holes.

But the committee must also penalize WMA two strokes. If FA has been put at a disadvantage by the wrongful substitution, she has been put at a disadvantage with respect to every player in the game. She is in competition with all the players; what the third player's substitution has done is to deprive her of a fair opportunity to defeat all the other players. That opportunity is not restored by penalizing the third player alone. If the committee is to rectify in midmatch the wrong done to FA, it must penalize WMA as well, even though WMA had no part in the wrong done to FA.

Now, if it is right for the committee to choose this course of action, then this example seems promising for Thomson's argument. Perhaps in it can be found a basis for defending premise 4. This example seems appropriately similar to Thomson's case:

In it an orgnization penalizes WMA to compensate FA, even though WMA is innocent of any wrong against FA. If the two situations are sufficiently alike and in the golfing example it is not unjust for the committee to penalize WMA, then by parity of reasoning it would seem that the community is not unjust in setting aside WMA's right.

Are the committee's action and the community's action to be seen in the same light? Does the committee's action involve setting aside any player's rights? The committee constantly monitors the game, and intervenes to balance off losses or gains due to infractions or violations. Unfair gains are nullified by penalties; unfair losses are offset by awards. In the end no player had a complaint because the interventions ensure that the outcome has not been influenced by illegitimate moves or illegal actions. Whatever a player's position at the end of the game, it is solely the result of his own unhindered efforts. In penalizing WMA two strokes (along with the third player), the committee does him no injustice and overrides none of his rights.

The community, or its government, is responsible for preserving fair employment practices for its members. It can penalize those who engage in unfair discrimination; it can vigorously enforce fair employment rules; and, if FA has suffered under unfair practices, it may consider some form of compensation for FA. However, compensating FA by imposing a burden on WMA, when he is not culpable, is not like penalizing WMA in the golf match. The loss imposed by the community upon WMA is not part of a gamelike scheme, carefully regulated and continuously monitored by the community. The community does not intervene continually to offset unfair losses and gains by distributing penalties and advantages, ensuring that over their lifetimes WMA's and FA's chances at employment are truly equal. WMA's loss may endure; and there is no reason to believe that his employment position at the end of his career reflects only his unhindered effort. If the community exacts a sacrifice from WMA to pay FA, *it merely distributes losses and gains without balancing them.*

Since Thomson never explicitly expresses premise 4 in her paper, she never directly addresses the problem of its defense. In the one place in which she seems to take up the problem raised by premise 4, she says:

> Still, the community does impose a burden upon him (WMA): it is able to make amends for its wrongs only by taking something away from him, something which, after all, we are supposing he has a right to. And why should *he* pay the cost of the community's amends-making?
>
> If there were some appropriate way in which the community could make amends to its . . . women, some way which did not require depriving anyone of anything he has a right to, then that would be the best course of action to take. Or if there were anyway some way in which the costs could be shared by everyone, and not imposed entirely on the young white male applicants, then that would be, if not the best, then anyway better than opting for a policy of preferential hiring. But in fact *the nature of the wrongs done is such as to make jobs the best and most suitable form of compensation (emphasis added).*[5]

How does this provide an answer to our question? Is this passage to be read as suggesting, in support of premise 4, the principle that a group may override the rights of its (nonculpable) members in order to pay the "best" form of compensation?[6] If WMA's right to equal consideration stood in the way of the community's paying best compensation to FA, then this principle would entail premise 4. This principle, however, will not withstand scrutiny.

Consider an example: Suppose that you have stolen a rare and elaborately engraved hunting rifle from me. Before you can be made to return it, the gun is destroyed in a fire. By coincidence, however, your brother possesses one of the few other such rifles in existence; perhaps it is the only other model in existence apart from the one you stole from me and which was destroyed.

From my point of view, having my gun back, or having one exactly like it, is the best form of compensation I can have from you. No other gun will be a suitable replacement, nor will money serve satisfactorily to compensate me for my loss. I prized the rifle for its rare and unique qualities, not for its monetary value. You can pay me the best form of compensation by giving me your brother's gun. However, this is clearly not a morally justifiable option. I have no moral title to your brother's gun, nor are you (solely by virtue of your debt to me) required or permitted to take your brother's gun to give to me. The gun is not yours to give; and nothing about the fact that you owe me justifies you in taking it.

In this example it is clear that establishing what the best compensation is (what makes up for the wrongful loss) does not determine the morally appropriate form of compensation. Thus, as a defense of premise 4, telling us that preferential hiring is the best compensation begs the question.

The case of preferential hiring seems to me more like the case of the stolen rifle than like the case of the golfing match. If WMA has a right to equal consideration, then he, not the community, owns the right. In abridging his right in order to pay FA, the community is paying in stolen coin, just as you would be if you were to expropriate your brother's rifle to compensate me. The community is paying with something that does not belong to it.

WMA has not been shown by Thomson to owe anybody anything. Nor has Thomson defended or made plausible premise 4, which on its face ill fits her own expression of the principle of compensation. If we reject the premise, then Thomson has not shown what she claimed—that it is not unjust to engage in preferential hiring of women. I fully agree with her that it would be appropriate, if not obligatory, for the community to adopt measures of compensation to women.[7] I cannot agree, on the basis of her argument, that it may do so by adopting a policy of preferential hiring.

Thomson seems vaguely to recognize that her case is unconvincing without a demonstration of culpability on the part of WMA. At the end of her paper, after having made her argument without assuming WMA's guilt, she assures us that after all WMA is not so innocent, and it is not unfitting that he should bear the sacrifice required in preferring FA.

> . . . it is not entirely inappropriate that those applicants (like WMA) should pay the cost. No doubt few, if any, have themselves, individually, done any wrongs to . . . women. But they have profited from the wrongs the community did. Many may actually have been direct beneficiaries of policies which excluded or downgraded . . . women—perhaps in school admissions, perhaps in access to financial aid, perhaps elsewhere; and even those who did not directly benefit in this way had, at any rate, the advantage in the competition which comes of confidence in one's full membership, and of one's rights being recognized as a matter of course.[8]

Does this passage make a plausible case for WMA's diminished "innocence" and the appropriateness of imposing the costs of compensation on him? The principle implied in the passage is, "He who benefits from a wrong shall pay for the wrong." Perhaps Thomson confuses this principle with the principle of compensation itself ("He who wrongs another shall pay for the wrong"). At any rate, the principle, "He who benefits from a wrong shall pay for the wrong," is surely suspect as an acceptable moral principle.

Consider the following example. While I am away on vacation, my neighbor contracts with a construction company to repave his driveway. He instructs the workers to come to his address, where they will find a note describing the driveway to be repaired. An enemy of my neighbor, aware somehow of this arrangement, substitutes for my neighbor's instructions a note describing *my* driveway. The construction crew, having been paid in advance, shows up on the appointed day while my neighbor is at work, finds the letter, and faithfully following its instructions paves my driveway.

In this example my neighbor has been wronged and damaged. He is out a sum of money, and his driveway is unimproved. I benefited from the wrong, for my driveway is considerably improved. But am I morally required to compensate my neighbor for the wrong done him? Is it appropriate that the costs of compensating my neighbor fall on me? I cannot see why. My paying the neighbor the cost he incurred in hiring the construction company would be an act of supererogation on my part, not a discharge of an obligation to him. If I could afford it, it would be a decent thing to do; but it is not something I *owe* my neighbor. I am not less than innocent in this affair because I benefited from my neighbor's misfortune; and no one is justified in exacting compensation from me.

Though young white males like WMA have undeniably benefited in many ways from the sexist social arrangements under which they were reared, to a large extent, if not entirely, these benefits are involuntary. From an early age the male's training and education inculcate in him an advantage over women in later life. Such benefits are unavoidable (by him) and ineradicable. Most especially is this true of "that advantage . . . which comes of confidence in one's full membership [in the community] and of one's rights being recognized as a matter of course."

The principle, "He who *willingly* benefits from a wrong must pay for the wrong," may have merit as a moral principle. To show a person's uncoerced and knowledgeable complicity in wrongdoing is to show him less than innocent, even if his role amounts to no more than ready acceptance of the fruits of wrong. Thomson makes no effort to show such complicity on WMA's part. The principle she relies upon, "He who benefits from a wrong must pay for the wrong," is without merit. So, too, is her belief that "it is not entirely inappropriate" that WMA (and those like him) should bear the burden of a program of compensation to women. What Thomson ignores is the moral implication of the fact that the benefits of sexism received by WMA may be involuntary and unavoidable. This implication cannot be blinked, and it ruins Thomson's final pitch to gain our approval of a program which may violate the rights of some persons.[9]

NOTES

1. Judith Thomson, "Preferential Hiring," *Philosophy and Public Affairs,* vol. 2 (Summer 1973): pp. 364–384.

2. Thomson asks us to imagine two such applicants *tied* in their qualifications. Presumably, preferring a less qualified teacher would violate students' rights to the best available instruc-

tion. If the applicants are equally qualified, the students' rights are satisfied whichever one is picked. In some cases where third-party rights are not involved, there would seem to be no need to include the stipulation, for if the principle of compensation is strong enough to justify preferring a woman over a man, it is strong enough whether the woman is equally qualified or not so long as she is minimally qualified. (Imagine hiring a librarian instead of a teacher.) Thus, I leave out the requirement that the applicants be tied in their qualifications. Nothing in my argument turns on whether the applicants are equally qualified. The reader may, if he or she wishes, mentally reinstate this feature of Thomson's example.

3. The comments from which propositions 1 to 3 are distilled occur on pp. 381–382.

4. For a discussion of these issues, see Robert Simon, "Preferential Hiring: A Reply to Judith Jarvis Thomson," *Philosophy and Public Affairs*, vol. 3 (Spring 1974): pp. 312–320.

5. Thomson, p. 383.

6. In the passage quoted, Thomson is attempting to justify morally the community's imposing a sacrifice on WMA. Thus, her reference to "best" compensation cannot be construed to mean "morally best," since morally best means morally justified. By best compensation Thomson means that compensation which will best make up the loss suffered by the victim. This is how I understand the idea of best compensation in the succeeding example and argument.

7. And there are many possible modes of compensation open to the community which are free from any moral taint. At the worst, monetary compensation is always an alternative. This may be second- or third-best compensation for the wrongs done, but when the best is not available, second-best has to do. For the loss of my gun, I am going to have to accept cash from you (assuming you have it), and use it to buy a less satisfactory substitute.

8. Thomson, pp. 383–384.

9. But if FA is *not* given preferential treatment in hiring (the best compensation), are *her* rights violated? In having a right to compensation, FA does not have a right to anything at all that will compensate her. She has a right to the best of the morally available options open to her debtor. Only if the community refuses to pay her this is her right violated. We have seen no reason to believe that setting aside the putative right of white male applicants to equal consideration is an option morally available to the community.

REVERSE DISCRIMINATION AND COMPENSATORY JUSTICE

WILLIAM T. BLACKSTONE*

Is reverse discrimination justified as a policy of compensation or of preferential treatment for women and racial minorities?[1] That is, given the fact that women and racial minorities have been invidiously discriminated against in the past on the basis of the irrelevant characteristics of race and sex—are we now justified in discriminating in their favor on the basis of the same characteristics? This is a central ethical and legal question today, and it is one which is quite unresolved. Philosophers, jurists, legal scholars, and the man-in-the-street line up on both sides of this issue.

I will argue that reverse discrimination is improper. However, I do this with considerable ambivalence, even "existential guilt." Several reasons lie behind that ambivalence. First, there are moral and constitutional arguments on both sides. The ethical waters are very muddy and I simply argue that the balance of the arguments are against a policy of reverse discrimination.[2] My ambivalence is further due not only to the fact that traditional racism is still a much larger problem than that of reverse discrimination but also because I am sympathetic to the *goals* of those who strongly believe that reverse discrimination as a policy is the means to overcome the debilitating effects of past injustice. Compensation and remedy are most definitely required both by the facts and by our value commitments. But I do not think that reverse discrimination is the proper means of remedy or compensation.

Let us examine the possibility of a utilitarian justification of reverse discrimination and to the possible conflict of justice-regarding reasons and those of social utility on this issue. The category of morally relevant reasons is broader, in my opinion, than reasons related to the norm of justice. It is broader than those related to the norm of utility. Also it seems to me that the norms of justice and utility are not reducible one to the other. We cannot argue these points of ethical theory here.[3] But, if these assumptions are correct, then it is at least possible to morally justify injustice or invidious discrimination in some contexts. A case would have to be made that such injustice, though regrettable, will produce the best consequences for society and that this fact is an overriding or weightier moral reason than the temporary injustice. Some arguments for reverse discrimination have taken this line. Professor Thomas Nagel argues that such discrimination is justifiable as long as it is "clearly contributing to the eradication of great social evils."[4]

Another example of what I would call a utilitarian argument for reverse discrimination was recently set forth by Congressman Andrew Young of Georgia. Speaking specifically of reverse discrimination in the context of education, he stated: "While that may give minorities a little edge in some instances, and you may run into the danger of what we now commonly call reverse discrimination, I think the educational system needs this. Society needs this as much as the people we are trying to help . . . a

Excerpted from "Reverse Discrimination and Compensatory Justice," published in *Social Justice and Preferential Treatment*, edited by William T. Blackstone and Robert D. Heslep. Copyright © 1977 by The University of Georgia Press, Athens, Ga. Reprinted by permission of the publisher.

*Department of Philosophy, University of Georgia (deceased).

society working toward affirmative action and inclusiveness is going to be a stronger and more relevant society than one that accepts the limited concepts of objectivity . . . I would admit that it is perhaps an individual injustice. But it might be necessary in order to overcome an historic group injustice or series of group injustices."[5] Congressman Young's basic justifying grounds for reverse discrimination, which he recognizes as individual injustice, are the results which he thinks it will produce: a stronger and more relevant education system and society, and one which is more just overall. His argument may involve pitting some justice-regarding reasons (the right of women and racial minorities to be compensated for past injustices) against others (the right of the majority to the uniform application of the same standards of merit to all). But a major thrust of his argument also seems to be utilitarian.

Just as there are justice-regarding arguments on both sides of the issue of reverse discrimination, so also there are utilitarian arguments on both sides. In a nutshell, the utilitarian argument in favor runs like this: Our society contains large groups of persons who suffer from past institutionalized injustice. As a result, the possibilities of social discord and disorder are high indeed. If short-term reverse discrimination were to be effective in overcoming the effects of past institutionalized injustice and if this policy could alleviate the causes of disorder and bring a higher quality of life to millions of persons, then society as a whole would benefit.

There are moments in which I am nearly convinced by this argument, but the conclusion that such a policy would have negative utility on the whole wins out. For although reverse discrimination might appear to have the effect of getting more persons who have been disadvantaged by past inequities into the mainstream quicker, that is, into jobs, schools, and practices from which they have been excluded, the cost would be invidious discrimination against majority group members of society. I do not think that majority members of society would find this acceptable, i.e., the disadvantaging of themselves for past inequities which they did not control and for which they are not responsible. If such policies were put into effect by government, I would predict wholesale rejection or non-cooperation, the result of which would be negative not only for those who have suffered past inequities but also for the justice-regarding institutions of society. Claims and counter-claims would obviously be raised by other ethnic or racial minorities—by Chinese, Chicanos, American Indians, Puerto Ricans— and by orphans, illegitimate children, ghetto residents, and so on. Literally thousands of types or groups could, on similar grounds as blacks or women, claim that reverse discrimination is justified on their behalf. What would happen if government attempted policies of reverse discrimination for all such groups? It would mean the arbitrary exclusion or discrimination against all others relative to a given purpose and a given group. Such a policy would itself create an injustice for which those newly excluded persons could then, themselves, properly claim the need for reverse discrimination to offset the injustice to them. The circle is plainly a vicious one. Such policies are simply self-destructive. In place of the ideal of equality and distributive justice based on relevant criteria, we would be left with the special pleading of self-interested power groups, groups who gear criteria for the distribution of goods, services, and opportunities to their special needs and situations, primarily. Such policies would be those of special privilege, not the appeal to objective criteria which apply to all.[6] They would lead to social chaos, not social justice.

Furthermore, in cases in which reverse discrimination results in a lowering of quality, the consequences for society, indeed for minority victims of injustice for which reverse discrimination is designed to help, may be quite bad. It is no easy matter to calculate this, but the recent report sponsored by the Carnegie Commission on Higher Education points to such deleterious consequences.[7] If the quality of instruction in higher education, for example, is lowered through a policy of primary attention to race or sex as opposed to ability and training, everyone—including victims of past injustice—suffers. Even if such policies are clearly seen as temporary with quite definite deadlines for termination, I am sceptical about their utilitarian value.

NOTES

1. There are wide differences between the kinds and degrees of injustice suffered by blacks and by women. Women have not literally been slaves. But these differences are not my concern here. Primarily I am concerned with any possible grounds for reverse discrimination, and women and blacks are the classes for whom such treatment is generally pressed. Also this question could be broken down into two distinct ones: (1) Is reverse discrimination justified as a policy of compensation? (2) Is reverse discrimination justified as a policy of preferential treatment? One could answer affirmatively to (2) without answering affirmatively to (1), seeing preferential treatment as a means of assuring social justice but not as a mode of compensation in the strict sense of "compensation."

2. I hasten to add a qualification—more ambivalence!—resulting from discussion with Tom Beauchamp of Georgetown University. In cases of extreme recalcitrance to equal employment by certain institutions or businesses some quota requirement (reverse discrimination) may be justified. I regard this as distinct from a general policy of reverse discrimination.

3. For discussion, see William Frankena, *Ethics* (Englewood Cliffs, N.J., 1963).

4. *New York University Law Review*, 43, pt. 2 (1968).

5. The Atlanta Journal and Constitution, Sept. 22, 1974, p. 20-A6.

6. For similar arguments see Lisa Newton, "Reverse Discrimination as Unjustified," *Ethics*, 83, (1973).

7. Richard A. Leska, *Antibias Regulation of Universities* (New York, 1974); discussed in *Newsweek*, July 15, 1974, p. 78.

CASES FOR PART THREE

THE BAY AREA RAPID TRANSIT (BART) WHISTLE-BLOWING INCIDENT [1]

LEA P. STEWART*

BACKGROUND

Whistle-blowing incidents do not occur in a vacuum, nor do they occur instantaneously. They develop over time, even though they may appear to occur suddenly and without warning.[2] The Bay Area Rapid Transit (BART) whistle-blowing incident is not atypical in this respect.

On November 6, 1962 voters in Alameda, Contra Costa, and San Francisco counties in California approved a $792-million bond issue and authorized construction of a 71.5-mile rapid transit system which included a Transbay tube under the bay between San Francisco and Oakland, subways under Oakland and Market streets in San Francisco, and a tunnel through the Berkely Hills. The voters were promised an ultra-modern, computer-controlled, streamlined, and soundless transportation system. In 1962, the total cost of the system was estimated to be $996 million.

The board of directors of the Bay Area Rapid Transit District (BARTD) hired a consortium of three engineering firms (Parsons, Brinckerhoff, Quade and Douglas; Tudor Engineering Company; and Bechtel Corporation) to engineer and manage the design and construction of the BART system. This consortium became known as PBTB, and received a contract that was described at the time as "probably . . . the largest contract ever let for engineering services."[3]

In the original contracts, full operation of the BART system was scheduled for late 1970.[4] At that time, however, construction of the system was not complete, and the transit cars were still being tested. Construction of the system was not completed until July 1971. Because BART was not an ordinary railroad, completion of construction did not mean the system was ready to operate. The BART system was designed to be controlled automatically, so the computer control system had to be tested thoroughly before the first passenger could ride the trains.

By 1972, BARTD management was under tremendous financial pressure. In 1969, the California state legislature had approved a 0.5 percent district sales tax to provide an additional $150 million to complete the system. Nevertheless, BART's

*Department of Communications, Rutgers University.

293

costs continued to increase. The completion of the system was behind schedule and the money was running out.

BART also faced engineering problems. The BART system was to be run by a computer system which would regulate the speed of trains, stop them at the proper stations, and open and close train doors to let passengers in and out. Unfortunately, the development of this Automatic Train Control (ATC) system by Westinghouse did not proceed as smoothly as planned. The first successful test of the ATC software was not completed until October 1971, almost three years after the BART system was originally scheduled to open. As one local newspaper reported in January 1972: "Hailed many years ago when BART was just a dream as one of the innovative mass transit systems in the country, some fear the system will be outdated and plagued with problems within a year after it starts operation."[5]

This was the state of the BARTD organization preceding the 1972 whistle-blowing incident.

THE ENGINEERS

In September 1966, Holger Hjortsvang saw a help-wanted advertisement for engineers for the BART system. He had been looking for work for several months, so he applied for a position and was hired as a train control engineer. He wanted to specialize in the central control of the BART system, so eleven months after he was hired he was sent to Pittsburgh for ten months to work with the system's designers at Westinghouse. When BARTD, PBTB, and Westinghouse began to coordinate the start-up of the system, Hjortsvang's "essential function" was to "specify and write maintenance procedures" and give "assistance to the technicians and maintenance foremen." He continued to monitor the development of the train control system as his "personal duty."[6] His direct supervisor was E. F. Wargin, superintendent of BARTD's Maintenance Engineering Division. (An abbreviated version of the BARTD organizational chart is included at the end of this case.)

In late 1969, Robert Bruder saw a want ad in the *San Francisco Chronicle*, applied for employment, and was hired by BARTD as an electrical and electronic engineer. His duties included coordinating the train control and communication contracts with the consultants in BARTD's operations group, PBTB and Westinghouse. He monitored the schedules to ensure that the contracts were being complied with. He reported directly to Frank Wagner, supervisor of Systemwide Contracts in BARTD's Construction Division.

In 1971, Max Blankenzee worked as a temporary programmer-analyst for Westinghouse Electric Corporation. Among other things, he worked on the computer programming to be used in the BART system's central control and, through this experience, became interested in working for BARTD. He met Holger Hjortsvang while working for Westinghouse and asked him if BARTD had any openings. Hjortsvang brought him an application form and took his resumé and completed application to E. F. Wargin. Wargin interviewed Blankenzee and hired him in May 1971 as a senior programmer and analyst. He worked on the "development, installation, operation and maintenance of the train control and central control system."[7] In the organizational hierarchy Blankenzee was considered subordinate to Hjortsvang.

Hjortsvang and Blankenzee shared an office in the basement of the Lake Merritt station in Oakland, California. They were physically separated from Wargin and BARTD upper management, whose offices were located in BARTD headquarters in San Francisco. Bruder contacted Hjortsvang and Blankenzee as a routine part of his work verifying the status of the train control contract. Hjortsvang and Blankenzee were involved primarily with the train and yard control computers and Bruder's job was to check the train control contract. In 1972, Hjortsvang was 60 years old, Bruder was 51, and Blankenzee was 30.

THE WHISTLE-BLOWING INCIDENT

During early or middle 1971 Hjortsvang invited Bruder and Bruder's co-worker Jay Burns to lunch. Hjortsvang expressed concern that the BART project was not proceeding as it should. According to Bruder, Hjortsvang wanted the support of other professionals to "somehow get information up to upper management that things weren't being taken care of."[8] Bruder claimed Hjortsvang "was blocked in his own channels . . . and wanted to see if we could go up through our channels and get some solution to the general problem of the contractor not complying."[9] Hjortsvang suggested they go outside normal management channels of communication, possibly to a member of the BARTD board of directors, because "nobody inside is listening."[10] Burns and Bruder discouraged him. Burns told him it would be better to work within normal lines of command and communication. Bruder refused to get involved.

During the middle of 1971 Hjortsvang spoke to Gilbert Ortiz, a BARTD employee who was also a union organizer. Ortiz said he could arrange a meeting for Hjortsvang with any of the labor-supported members of BARTD's board of directors. Hjortsvang reported: "After thinking about that . . . for a while, I decided that I did not want to . . . start anything, anything that could be dangerous for me personally."[11]

Several months later, on September 8–10, 1971, Hjortsvang and Blankenzee attended a seminar given by the Advanced Institute of Technology on standards in program development. During September, October, November, and December, Blankenzee sent his supervisor, Ed Wargin, a series of memoranda criticizing various aspects of the ATC system and offering to give BARTD management a half-day presentation on what was wrong with the system and how to correct the problems. He was never given permission to make the presentation.

Hjortsvang also wrote a series of memoranda between April 1969 and December 1971 which pointed out problems in the train control system and called for the creation of a Systems and Programming Division of the Department of Operations to coordinate operating procedures, train control, and computer programming. As with Blankenzee's memoranda, BARTD management did not act upon the suggestions in Hjortsvang's memoranda. Nonetheless, an unsigned memorandum titled "BART System Engineering" and dated "Nov. 18, 1971" played a key role in the whistle-blowing incident. Although the memorandum was unsigned, Hjortsvang acknowledged that he was the author.

According to E. F. Wargin, Hjortsvang's supervisor, the November 18, 1971, memorandum was "circulated to a large number of employees on the BART technical staff, including most, if not all, of the engineers under my supervision."[12] Wargin's supervisor, General Superintendent of Power and Way C. O. Kramer, sent a copy to his supervisor, Director of Operations E. J. Ray, and one to Assistant General Manager D. G. Hammond. Kramer claimed he discussed the memorandum with Hammond, and they disagreed with its proposal to restructure the BARTD organization to include a systems engineering group. Kramer claimed he did not make an effort to find out who wrote it. Because of the writing style, Wargin believed it was written by Hjortsvang.

According to Bruder's supervisor, Frank Wagner, in late 1971 Bruder spoke to him and several other BARTD managers about forming a systems engineering group to provide a better method of coordinating operations. Wagner and the other BARTD managers with whom Bruder talked did not recommend the formation of such a group.

Thus, during 1971, the three engineers became increasingly concerned about the BART system. Each engineer communicated his concerns to his supervisor, but did not receive an answer he felt answered his questions satisfactorily.

Each of the three engineers was concerned about somewhat different problems affecting the BART system. Hjortsvang was concerned, first, about the ability of the ATC system to control the trains in the way the specifications required because, in his opinion, the train control components were inadequate and were not being tested properly, the Westinghouse design deviated from good engineering practice, and the friction he perceived within the Westinghouse organization could cause trouble getting the system coordinated properly. In addition, he believed BARTD's internal management structure was not adequate to monitor the progress of the ATC system to ensure the development of a "satisfactory system."[13]

Blankenzee also had two main concerns about the development of the BART system. First, he believed the system was not being tested adequately. Second, he felt that BARTD engineers would be unable to maintain the system because they lacked documentation which would allow them to understand the "internal workings of the system."[14] Bruder believed that BARTD management, made up mostly of nonengineers, did not have the technical expertise to supervise development of the train control system adequately and that it was publicly announcing unrealistic opening dates.

By late 1971, Hjortsvang and Blankenzee were both concerned about the development of the BART system and frustrated in their attempts to receive answers from their supervisors. Hjortsvang spoke to Ortiz again, and Ortiz reported he could put Hjortsvang and Blankenzee in contact with members of the board of directors to open up a line of communication with BARTD's top management.

Several days later Ortiz told Hjortsvang and Blankenzee that he had tried to set up a meeting for them with BARTD directors William C. Blake and Nello J. Bianco, but was unsuccessful. He suggested Blankenzee phone Blake personally. Blankenzee phoned Blake and told him several engineers were concerned about problems in the development of the BART system and would like to present their concerns to him so he could talk to BARTD's upper management about the problems. According to Blankenzee, Blake told him to set up a meeting which Blake would attend. In addition, Blankenzee claimed he told Blake the engineers did not have anyone to back up their story, but that Blake could hire a consultant to confirm their concerns. According to Blankenzee: "We wanted him to get the independent consultant, but since he did not have the time we said we would get it."[15] Blankenzee attempted to set up a meeting but was unable to reach Blake again.

While he was attempting to set up this meeting, Blankenzee searched for an independent consultant to verify his and Hjortsvang's concerns. He contacted an acquaintance who recommended Edward Burfine. Blankenzee contacted Burfine and asked him "on behalf of the directors" to visit the BART system and "pass judgment on our statement of BART."[16] According to Burfine, Blankenzee told him he wanted a short study of the ATC system to be given to the board of directors, and that a group of directors was seeking the report.[17] Burfine spent one day in November 1971 at the Lake Merritt station talking to Blankenzee, Hjortsvang, and Bruder and looking at specifications for the system, computer hardware, and various documentations.

Shortly after his visit to the BART system, Burfine sent a draft of a report to Hjortsvang and Blankenzee. They corrected some errors in the report, and Burfine wrote a corrected version with a cover letter addressed to the BARTD board of directors. Blankenzee, Hjortsvang, and Bruder all received a copy of the final "Burfine Report." Since Blankenzee and Hjortsvang had been unable to meet with directors Blake and Bianco, Ortiz told them Director Daniel Helix, who had just become a board member in October 1971, was interested in talking with them. According to Helix: "I asked both directors Bianco and Blake about this prior to my meeting with the engineers. They confirmed that they were aware of the problem and encouraged me to meet with the engineers and with Gil Ortiz."[18] (Later, both Blake and Bianco adamantly denied ordering the Burfine Report.)

According to Hjortsvang, the contact with Helix was a "last-ditch attempt" to attract BARTD management's attention to a situation which they felt was threatening the successful completion of the system.[19] Blankenzee, Hjortsvang, Ortiz, and Helix met in early January 1972 in the local union office in Oakland. The engineers told Helix the BART system would not be ready to open as scheduled; Helix became concerned about the safety of the system after listening to them. He asked them why they came to him instead of going to Assistant General Manager Hammond or General Manager Stokes, and they told him they tried to go through their supervisors but could get no response.

Hjortsvang gave Helix a copy of the November 18, 1971, memorandum. According to Blankenzee, he and Hjortsvang told Helix that they had retained Burfine to provide independent verification of their concerns.

On January 9, 1972 Hjortsvang's November 18, 1971, memorandum appeared in an article in the *Contra Costa Times*, a local newspaper. The article described Helix's concerns about the safety of the BART system and labeled the anonymous memorandum a "memo to the board of directors."[20] Later on, Hjortsvang claimed he gave copies of the memorandum to Helix "to hand to the members of the board, but it was certainly not intended for further distribution, or publication."[21]

According to Blankenzee, the second meeting with Helix was held in Concord, California, and was attended by Blankenzee, Bruder, Hjortsvang, Helix, and a computer specialist brought by Helix. Helix read the Burfine Report and asked questions. Following this meeting, Helix gave a copy of the Burfine Report to General Manager Stokes without disclosing the names of the three engineers.

While waiting for a response from Stokes, Helix, who was the vice mayor of Concord, California, talked about the BART system after a Concord city council meeting and mentioned the Burfine Report. Justin Roberts, an investigative reporter for the *Contra Costa Times*, overheard Helix's remark and questioned him about the report. Helix said the report was about the BART system and that he had given a copy of the report to the BARTD general manager. Roberts asked for a copy; Helix gave it to him after Roberts promised not to release it until Helix received a response from General Manager Stokes.

Stokes arranged a meeting for Helix and representatives of PBTB which Helix later felt was "a royal snow job." According to Helix, the PBTB representatives said "not to worry about anything, that there were no problems that they were not aware of or couldn't handle, that things were going along just fine and that the system was going to open in March or April 1972 on schedule."[22] After the meeting, Helix told Roberts he could release the Burfine Report because the situation was "shaping up to be a massive cover-up."[23]

The Burfine Report appeared in the *Contra Costa Times* on January 20, 1972, and the story was picked up by other local papers. According to Bruder, the Burfine Report had already been given to all BARTD board members and top management, but nothing was done about it until it appeared in the press.

Once the Burfine Report appeared in the press, BARTD management attempted to find out who was responsible for it. According to Blankenzee, Wargin called him into his office and asked Blankenzee if he knew who the "ring-leader" of the group of engineers speaking to Helix was. Wargin asked if Hjortsvang was the leader and explained that he wanted to know "because BART couldn't tolerate that type of person in its organization."[24] Blankenzee denied knowing the ringleader. On February 7, 1972, Director of Operations Ray met with Hjortsvang and asked him if he had been talking to Helix. Hjortsvang said he had not.

The BARTD board of directors met on February 24, 1972. Board of Directors' President George Silliman began the meeting by suggesting that the engineers who had been speaking to Helix speak with General Manager Stokes. Silliman said he had been assured that Stokes' "office was open to any complaints by staff members and that if there are any 'corrective measures' to be taken, Stokes would see they are taken."[25] During the meeting Stokes said "his door was always open" to employees who wanted to discuss problems concerning the BART system.[26] The issue was closed, and a vote of confidence was given to Stokes.

In reference to the engineers who had been speaking to Helix, one of the other directors declared: "I have very little sympathy for the people involved at this point. If I was running the organization, I think I'd fire them."[27] Another director noted: "The unnamed employees went behind the back of their supervisors. Put yourself in that position and you suffer the consequences."[28] After the meeting, L. A. Kimball, assistant general manager for administration, said there were no plans to fire the engineers who asked Burfine to study the computer system.

Up to this point, BARTD management did not know the names of the engineers who had supplied information to Helix. Apparently the engineers' identity was discovered almost accidentally. In late February 1972 Bruder visited his supervisor, F. H. Wagner, in his home and told Wagner he had participated in a conference call with Helix, Hjortsvang, and Blankenzee, in which they discussed appearing before

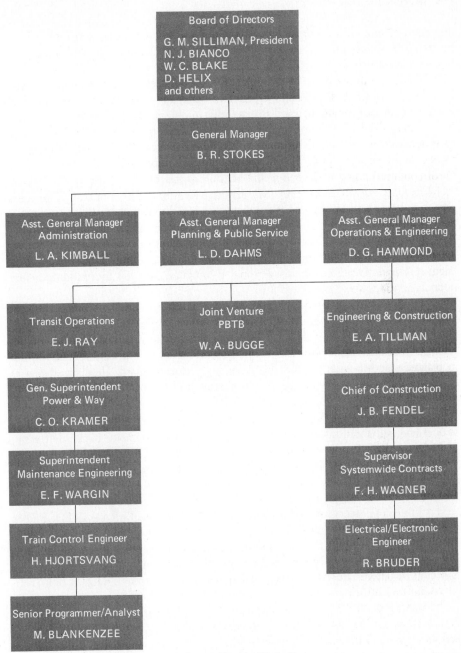

Board of Directors

G. M. SILLIMAN, President
N. J. BIANCO
W. C. BLAKE
D. HELIX
and others

General Manager

B. R. STOKES

**Asst. General Manager
Administration**

L. A. KIMBALL

**Asst. General Manager
Planning & Public Service**

L. D. DAHMS

**Asst. General Manager
Operations & Engineering**

D. G. HAMMOND

Transit Operations

E. J. RAY

**Joint Venture
PBTB**

W. A. BUGGE

Engineering & Construction

E. A. TILLMAN

**Gen. Superintendent
Power & Way**

C. O. KRAMER

Chief of Construction

J. B. FENDEL

**Superintendent
Maintenance Engineering**

E. F. WARGIN

**Supervisor
Systemwide Contracts**

F. H. WAGNER

Train Control Engineer

H. HJORTSVANG

**Electrical/Electronic
Engineer**

R. BRUDER

Senior Programmer/Analyst

M. BLANKENZEE

Other Persons Mentioned in the Case
(Identification as of 1972)

Edward Burfine — Consultant, Beckers, Burfine and Associates, Palo Alto, California.
Jay Burns — Engineering department employee, BARTD.
Jerome C. Dougherty — Attorney, Pillsbury, Madison and Sutro, attorneys for the San Francisco Bay Area Rapid
    Transit District.
Gilbert Ortiz — Employee, BARTD.
Justin Roberts — Reporter, *Contra Costa Times,* Walnut Creek, California.

the board of directors. After Bruder left, Wagner phoned his own supervisor, J. B. Fendel, and reported the conversation. The next day he reported the conversation to Fendel's supervisor, E. A. Tillman.

During the week of February 28, General Manager Stokes, Assistant General Manager Hammond, Director of Operations Ray, and General Superintendent of Power and Way Kramer met and decided that problems with the ATC system had been misrepresented to persons outside the BARTD organization. According to a memorandum written after the meeting by Ray, they agreed to discharge the participating employees because the employees supplied information to external parties directly contrary to BARTD policy and because of the severity of the action.

On March 2, 1972, at 9:30 A.M., Ray and Kramer called Hjortsvang into Ray's office, and Ray told Hjortsvang that for the good of the district his employment was being terminated. He was given the option of resignation or termination. Hjortsvang again claimed he had not participated in the dealings with Burfine and had met with Helix only once. Hjortsvang was escorted to his office by a person from BARTD's Security Division, picked up his personal belongings, and left the building before noon.

Blankenzee saw Hjortsvang before he left, and Hjortsvang told him he was fired. Ten to twenty minutes later, Blankenzee was called into Ray's office. Ray told Blankenzee he would have to resign or he would be terminated by order of the general manager. Blankenzee asked to talk to the general manager, and Ray said he was not in. Blankenzee was then taken to his office by a security guard. He claimed that as he went through his files an assistant to Kramer and the head of security told him what he could take with him.

The next morning, March 3, 1972, Tillman told Kimball he was satisfied that Bruder had lied about his participation in the Burfine–Helix incident. At 11:40 A.M., Tillman met with Bruder and Fendel in Tillman's office. Tillman asked Bruder if he was involved with Helix; Bruder denied involvement. Tillman said he had evidence that Bruder was involved, but Bruder continued to deny it. Tillman offered Bruder the opportunity to resign. Bruder refused and was fired.

All three engineers suffered personally after their dismissal from BARTD. Bruder went on welfare and received food stamps. He sold his house and could not find professional employment for eight months. Blankenzee was separated from his wife for forty-five days, lost his house, and was unable to find employment for four and a half months. Hjortsvang became "agitated and tense" and required sleeping pills.[29] He could not find full-time employment for fourteen months.

On May 21, 1973, the three engineers filed a lawsuit which charged BARTD management with breach of contract, interference with prospective business relations, and deprivation of First and Fourteenth Amendment rights guaranteed by the United States Constitution and asked for $875,000 in damages. The lawsuit was scheduled for jury trial on February 3, 1975; however, on January 29, 1975, the engineers and BARTD settled out of court for $75,000 minus 40 percent for lawyers' fees. The engineers were advised by their attorney that they could not win the lawsuit in court because they had denied hiring an outside consultant when questioned by BARTD management.

NOTES

1. For a complete discussion of the whistle-blowing incident and a history of the Bay Area Rapid Transit District see Lea P. Stewart, "The Ethnography of a Whistle Blowing Incident: Implications for Organizational Communication," Diss. Purdue University 1979, and R. M. Anderson, R. Perrucci, D. E. Schendel and L. E. Trachtman, *Divided Loyalties: Whistle-Blowing at BART* (West Lafayette, Indiana: Purdue University Press, 1980). Funding for these studies was provided by National Science Foundation Grant No. OSS76-14230, "An In-Depth Case Study of Ethical Problems of Professional Engineers: The BART (Bay Area Rapid Transit) Engineers."

2. Richard Austin Smith, *Corporations in Crisis* (Garden City, New York: Anchor Books, 1966), p. 3.

3. Francis B. O'Gara, "Sharp Fight on Transit Engineers," *San Francisco Examiner*, Nov. 29, 1962, p. 17, col. 2.

4. Joseph H. Wujek, Jr., "Bart: Electronics Aids Rapid Transit," *Electronics World*, January 1969, p. 36.

5. "BART Depot Construction: The Beat Goes On," *Contra Costa Times*, Jan. 7, 1972, p. 2A, col. 3.

6. *Holger Hjortsvang v. San Francisco Bay Area Rapid Transit District*, Cal. Sup. Ct. 1973, No. 436443, Deposition of Holger Hjortsvang, p. 99.

7. *Holger Hjortsvang v. San Francisco Bay Area Rapid Transit District*, Cal. Sup. Ct. 1974, No. 436443, Answer of Plaintiff Max Blankenzee to Interrogatories of Defendant, p. 9.

8. Telephone interview with Robert Bruder conducted by Robert Perrucci, June 15, 1977.

9. *Robert Bruder v. San Francisco Bay Area Rapid Transit District*, Cal. Sup. Ct. 1973, No. 436444, Deposition of Robert Bruder, p. 25.

10. Telephone interview with Robert Bruder conducted by Robert Perrucci, June 15, 1977.

11. Hjortsvang Deposition, p. 124.

12. *Holger Hjortsvang v. San Francisco Bay Area Rapid Transit District*, Cal. Sup. Ct. 1974, No. 436443, Declaration of E. Wargin, p. 2.

13. Hjortsvang Deposition, p. 77.

14. Telephone interview with Max Blankenzee conducted by Robert Perrucci, Feb. 21, 1977.

15. *Max Blankenzee v. San Francisco Bay Area Rapid Transit District*, Cal. Sup. Ct. 1973, No. 436445, Deposition of Max Leopold Blankenzee, p. 88.

16. Blankenzee Deposition, p. 89.

17. *Holger Hjortsvang v. San Francisco Bay Area Rapid Transit District*, Cal. Sup. Ct. 1974, No. 436443, Declaration of Jerome C. Dougherty, Exhibit F, p. 5.

18. Letter received by R. M. Anderson from Daniel Helix, Aug. 14, 1978.

19. Gordon G. Friedlander, "The Case of the Three Engineers vs. BART," *IEEE Spectrum*, October 1974, p. 70.

20. Rick Vogt, "Local BART Director Checking Into Reasons for System Delays," *Contra Costa Times*, Jan. 9, 1972, Sec. A, p. 7, col. 1.

21. Letter received by R. M. Anderson from H. Hjortsvang, July 28, 1978.

22. *Holger Hjortsvang v. San Francisco Bay Area Rapid Transit District*, Cal. Sup. Ct. 1974, No. 436443, Declaration of Daniel Helix, p. 4.

23. Personal interview with Daniel Helix conducted by Dan E. Schendel, July 26, 1977.

24. *Holger Hjortsvang v. San Francisco Bay Area Rapid Transit District*, Cal. Sup. Ct. 1974, No. 436443, Supplemental Answers of Plaintiff Max Blankenzee, p. 3.

25. Rick Vogt, "Helix Loses as BART Supports Staff," *Contra Costa Times*, Feb. 25, 1972, Sec. A, p. 1, col. 3.

26. Justin Roberts, "3 BART Engineers Fired for Aiding Burfine Inquiries," *Contra Costa Times*, Mar. 7, 1972, Sec. A, p. 1.

27. Harre W. Demoro, "BART Train Control Issue Ends," *Oakland Tribune*, Feb. 25, 1972, p. 13.

28. Demoro, p. 13.

29. *Holger Hjortsvang v. San Francisco Bay Area Rapid Transit District*, Cal. Sup. Ct. 1974, No. 436443, Points and Authorities, p. 29.

CHANGING WORK:
The Bolivar Project

MICHAEL MACCOBY*

Attempts to reorganize industrial work are not new. Particularly in recent years, numerous experiments involving job enrichment, "work humanization," and even some measures of worker self-management on the job have been carried out. The Bolivar project, which involves workers at an automobile mirror factory in southwest Tennessee, is an experiment in this tradition.

But the outcome of Bolivar may be more significant than the results of most such projects. The goal of the Bolivar project is to create an American model of industrial democracy, a model that is acceptable to unions and that might stimulate further union efforts. The project is based on the view that a national movement to improve the quality of work is unlikely to succeed without union support—and that union leaders are practical people who can't be expected to struggle for abstract concepts like "humanized work" or self-management without something concrete to point to. If the project is successful, the workers and managers at Harman International Industries in Bolivar, Tennessee, will develop practices that not only change the character of their work but also can be adopted by unions as goals for collective bargaining.

It's unusual for a work-reorganization experiment to have such far-reaching objectives, but—in the case of the Bolivar project—it's not accidental. The project originated with officials of the United Auto Workers, notably Vice-President Irving Bluestone, who were interested in relating the humanization of work to union concerns. For his part, the idealistic president of Harman International Industries, Sidney Harman, wanted to create a progressive example for businessmen. Like the Norwegian Industrial Democracy Project, but unlike most American attempts to improve work, the Bolivar project thus began with the active involvement of the union as well as management. Our staff of social scientists was invited in jointly by the union and management as an independent third party, and we accepted because we shared the project's goals.

Some aspects of the project that distinguish it from others naturally flowed from this fact of joint sponsorship. For one thing, the project includes the whole Harman auto mirror factory at Bolivar, Tennessee, rather than a single department as is often the case with projects to restructure work (such as at Corning Glass, Motorola, and Texas Instruments). (The plant, and the project, includes industrial processes such as die cast, polishing, painting, plating, assembly, and packing; and indirect departments such as data processing and inspection.) Also, Harman is an established factory with an existing unionized workforce. It's not a plant designed from scratch and manned with carefully selected nonunion workers, like the General Foods plant in Topeka (where another well-known work reorganization experiment was carried out).

Excerpted from "Changing Work: The Bolivar Project," published in *Working Papers*, Summer 1975. Reprinted by permission of the author.

*Director, Harvard Project on Technology, Work and Character, Harvard University.

The project's goals for changing the working environment are similarly ambitious. Often, quality-of-work experiments attempt simply to enlarge jobs, raise employee morale, decrease turnover or absenteeism, or increase productivity. With the Bolivar project, the objective has been to reorganize the way the company itself operates. To this end, we began by spelling out the principles that everyone agreed should govern the work life of hourly employees and managers alike.

Every organization, of course, is based on principles; they may either be stated explicitly as corporate ideology or remain hidden. Principles determine the practices of both individuals and organizations. Where the main principles are maximum profit and corporate growth, changes in the technology of production are likely to serve the goal of increasing productivity by strengthening centralized control over the worker. The worker becomes a standardized replaceable part of the process, and anger, hostility, depression, and stifled creativity are often the result. This was the case at the factory in Bolivar, where the economics of the auto parts industry, fierce competition, and fluctuating demand intensified insecurity and the dehumanizing conditions of work.

When they first pledged to support the project, both Harman's managers and the UAW officials understood that new principles would be needed to reconstruct the system in a more humane way. New principles would be a yardstick for measuring new programs, a basis for making critical decisions, and an impetus for developing a new spirit.

Four principles were agreed on: security, equity, democracy, and an objective we termed "individuation." How are these principles defined and how do they determine practice?

Security refers to job security, health, and safety. Working for an auto parts manufacturer is not the most secure job, especially right now. Sudden upturns in auto sales require more workers, and downturns produce layoffs. The company cannot change the market. But it is now pursuing a policy that maximizes worker security, both by providing as many jobs as possible and by offering an educational program that prepares workers for other employment.

During the past year, for example, workers in experimental programs began to meet standards established by time study according to the contract in less than the full eight hours. The Working Committee, composed of five representatives from management and five from the union, decided not to allow them to produce more for extra pay, because in the present economic situation this would have meant loss of jobs. Instead, the workers could use the time to go home early, to go to meetings, or to go to classes at the new school that has developed from the program. Many workers are farmers or mothers for whom time may be more important than money. In making this decision, some members of the committee also argued that if they had allowed workers to increase production and earnings, they would have been stimulating the kind of materialistic attitude that contrasts to the principle of individuation.[1]

Equity refers to fair rules, regulations, and compensation—and to overcoming discrimination because of race, sex, or age. Equity means fair pay differentials. If changes in the work place lead to higher productivity, the workers and managers contributing to these profits should share them equitably.

At Bolivar, the agreement signed by the plant management and union in 1974 begins by emphasizing the goal of the project and affirming the principle of equity in relation to any gains in productivity that might result:

> The purpose of the joint management-labor Work Improvement Program is to make work better and more satisfying for all employees, salaried and hourly, while maintaining the necessary productivity for job security.
> The purpose is *not* to increase productivity. If increased productivity is a by-product of the program, ways of rewarding the employees for increased productivity will become legitimate matters for inclusion in the program.

The ideal of fairness is deeply rooted in the character of the Bolivar workers, most of whom come from farm backgrounds. As in most rural farming societies, independence, self-reliance, frugality, and hard work are all valued highly. With these values goes the belief that each person should receive a just reward for his or her efforts, and that no one is entitled to a free ride in life.

A survey carried out by the staff at the start of the project showed that many workers at the factory resented unfairness in a number of areas. A majority stated that the employees' share of earnings was not fair, that the method of promotion was not fair, and that workers were not rewarded equitably for doing their jobs well. Almost half felt that the grievance procedure was not used enough. And a significant number of black and women workers complained about discrimination against them.

As the project developed, some of these fairness issues were faced and steps taken toward greater equity. In February 1974, for example, just as the first seminar on methods of developing workshop democracy was beginning, workers rejected a contract after management and the union had shaken hands on it. Workers argued that the contract did not protect them adequately from the rising cost of living. Management and union leaders were astonished by the rejection. But all parties decided to proceed with the seminar while continuing to bargain over the contract.

The demand for equity also forced the program to expand—from volunteer experiments in three departments to the whole plant—more quickly than planned. Once the experiments proved rewarding for the participants, the majority of workers demanded to be let in, threatening to end the project if they weren't. (In contrast to the situation at Bolivar, workers at Hunsfos Fabrikker in Norway have for ten years maintained an industrial democracy project in which no more than 40 percent of the workers have had their work restructured.)

Principles of security and equity can be viewed as traditional union goals that compensate the worker for submitting to the industrial system and protect him from extreme exploitation. Principles of democracy and individuation go beyond this. Here the objective is transforming the hierarchical organization to one based on concern for human development and mutual support.

Democracy in the project has been defined by the participants as "giving each worker more opportunities to have a say in the decisions that affect his life, including his work life." Although the union has maintained democratic procedures in the election of stewards and officers, for the most part workers had no say about methods of production and the organization of work. The development of new democratic practices at the plant began, in a way, with the initial interview-survey of 300 workers and 50 managers. The survey stimulated people to think critically in a new way about their jobs, supervision, working conditions, fairness, and so forth.[2] Until then, management and workers had freely criticized each other, but neither questioned the work structure and the roles that put both sides at each other's throats. Managers were policemen, and the main creative outlet for many workers was to figure out how to avoid work or how to infuriate the foreman. But in the survey, 70 percent of the workers told us they had ideas on how to improve work that they had never conveyed to anyone, either because no one would listen or because others would take the credit. The process of thinking critically about work began to spark hope that it might be possible to improve conditions.

The survey showed that the most pressing issues were working conditions such as heat, cold, and poor ventilation. However, a majority of workers also wanted a greater say in deciding matters such as how fast the work should be done, setting pay standards, taking breaks, job assignments, promotions, work methods, selecting supervisors, discipline, and deciding when the workday begins and ends. At that time there was no mechanism for instituting new democratic procedures.

In the fall of 1973, the project's staff—an independent group invited in by management and the union—suggested the formation of an ad hoc management-union committee. The committee would try to resolve the problems of improving the working environment by exploring alternative solutions. The staff suggested this might develop a relationship and a process for deciding how to solve problems. The idea was accepted, and the new Working Committee was formed, composed of five management representatives and five union members (the local president and four members appointed by him subject to review by the bargaining committee).[3] For the first few months, the Working Committee dealt with ventilation and other problems such as parking, traffic jams at the change of shift, congestion in punching the time clock, and keeping bill collectors out of the factory. The group then organized a credit union. But a process for creating democracy on the shop floor was still lacking.

At this point, we invited Einar Thorsrud, director of the Norwegian Industrial Democracy Project, to conduct a seminar on ways of analyzing and changing work democratically. He came for three days, and together with the project staff and Working Committee developed a methodology and strategy of inviting volunteer groups to experiment with changes in the assembly and buff-and-polish departments. The method begins by bringing a work group together (including the supervisor) to analyze work processes according to human and social criteria (such as work satisfaction, chances for learning, fairness in assignments) as well as technical and economic criteria. Possible variations are discussed, and the group can propose to experiment with changes.

This process is quite different from job enrichment, in which experts may enlarge a job for workers. The workers at Harman may decide to make changes similar to those made for job enrichment (such as job rotation or a longer work cycle), but they have made the changes and reserve the right to modify them. The goal is to institute a process of democratic decision making and evaluation rather than any specific changes in tasks.

The right to experiment and the evaluation of results are determined by the Working Committee, under the guidelines established by collective bargaining. The success of the first experiments (involving sixty people in four departments over a period of nine months) led the Working Committee to decide to expand the project to include all workers in this democratic process.

Early on, too, Sidney Harman concluded that the growth of democratic process on the shop floor could not proceed without a change in the hierarchical relationship among managers at all levels, and he instituted a companywide process aimed at this goal. Sanford Berlin, executive vice president of Harman, took the lead in developing a new collegial managerial decision-making process at the plant, and both he and Harman maintain that if the project has done nothing else for the company, it has resulted in much more effective management.

The project has served two educational functions. The first, through the survey and study, was to help people learn about themselves and to stimulate critical, independent thinking about alternatives. The second was to provide models for improving work that the participants could use and develop, including decision-making structures like the Working Committee, and methods of analyzing and evaluating work.

One result of the first experiments was that workers asked for training in how standards are set and in other industrial engineering subjects; they have begun to request classes in business subjects such as pricing and accounting. In 1974, a group of workers and managers traveled to Sweden and Norway, visiting Volvo's Kalmar plant and Hunsfos. The main value of the trip to many people was their conclusion that they had to develop their own model, different from any they had seen in Scandinavia.

The full development of democracy, of course, depends not just on education and the development of independent, critical thinking, but also on cooperative attitudes. Otherwise, the traditional individualistic attitude tends to limit democracy to mutual self-protectiveness and defense of shared interests. A spirit of "what's mine is mine and yours is yours" or "don't tread on me" can control exploitation. But it can't develop community. If people are to go beyond self-protectiveness to a spirit of mutuality, they need to develop a concern for others' needs. The principle of *individuation* expresses the goal of stimulating the fullest possible development of each individual's creative potential.

In the simplest sense, individuation means that no one should be treated as a standardized machine part, and that work should not rob people of the opportunity to perfect their skills, use their minds, and participate in decisions. It implies, furthermore, that different people have legitimate needs which must be met if they are to develop their creative potential.

For some people, this seems utopian. "Of course everyone is different," they say, "but how can any organization support a separate program for everyone?" The answer is that while individual programs may not be possible, to say "everyone is different" is to conclude that everyone is the same as far as the organization is concerned, and that there can be but one program for all. In fact, there is a middle ground. The staff began to discover this ground by identifying significant numbers of workers who share particular needs and goals.

In describing different types of workers, we focus on the *human reality* of the factory, which is what is missing in so many standard sociological accounts. From our point of view, the ultimate evaluation of the project must be in terms of its success in stimulating the human development of the different types of people involved.

The knowledge of different types also has served practical purposes, besides helping to make sense of the various attitudes and feelings expressed in the survey. Above all, it cut off the kind of fruitless debate so common among managers in which each speaks in terms of his personal needs, experiences, and prejudices about what the workers "really" want ("to get away with little or no work," "a chance to make more money," "opportunity for advancement," and so on). From the start we could show that everyone didn't have the same goals or want exactly the same kind of program. When some workers stood back from beginning experiments, our reaction was not to consider them as "negative" or "uncooperative," but to try to understand why their needs were not being met. Understanding of character types also provided knowledge for developing different kinds of educational programs that moved beyond improving the work environment to a concern with stimulating human development.

Most of us are a mixture of sometimes conflicting attitudes. Which attitudes are dominant depends on how we lead our lives. Probably some Bolivar managers figured that if cooperation was the way to please Sidney Harman, then ambition required a democratic attitude. However, others welcomed the chance to be less ambitious and more helpful to other people. One manager who had left the company a few years earlier returned because the program allowed him to act in a way that made him happy with himself. The new knowledge about different kinds of people and their needs helped these managers to have greater compassion toward those they had previously characterized as lazy or hostile.

The Bolivar project has offered both workers and managers an alternative through which they can become less alienated from themselves and from others. The newest development in the program has been the establishment of a school at the factory. This grew out of experimental improvements in work methods. The courses given now are also those requested by workers and range from welding, sewing, and crafts to courses on black studies and how the business is run. In some cases, workers and managers are the teachers. The school has the cooperation of the Hardeman County vocational education program, which pays some of the teachers. A new full-time school coordinator, Loren Farmer, has been approved by the Education Committee, which is composed of representatives of management, the union, and the project staff.

Ambitious workers were among the first volunteers in an experiment in which a group agreed to pool its work and was able to leave the factory if it finished early. One woman in the group was slower than the others and, sensing their annoyance that they had to help her out in order to finish, she asked to withdraw from the experiment. The others met and decided to ask her to stay. They were demonstrating that character can change for the better if a democratic work place supports cooperation and stimulates the development of the individual's talents, compassion, and capacity for reasoning.

NOTES

1. Before the experiments, many workers considered the standards unfair, and worked on the average at about 85 percent of standard. The only penalty received by failure to meet standards was a reprimand. Some of the first meetings with workers in polish and buff brought out the fact that there were many variables affecting standards. Where they felt the standard was unfair, workers often spent time arguing with the foreman, or their anger led to a slowdown. On their own, they came up with the idea of forming groups with a joint standard and they

developed a process for reevaluating the fairness of the standard on any part. Now, by allowing them use of time remaining after the standard is reached, the company also benefits. Other company benefits may be in quality, less absenteeism, less turnover, and above all a more cooperative environment.

2. Harold Sheppard directed the survey. Others who took part in the interviewing and participant observation included Bob and Maggie Duckles, Rolando Weissman, Mac Greene, Cynthia Elliott, Katherine A. Terzi, Sue Thrasher, Leah Wise, Barry Macy, Esther Leonelli, Josh Alper, and myself.

3. We originally suggested that the union members should be the elected bargaining committee, but some of them refused to join the Working Committee. Therefore, some of the elected union officials feel threatened by the program as it has gained support. On the other hand, the program has allowed the development of new leaders who are interested in cooperative rather than adversary relationships.

HIGH COURT BACKS A PREFERENCE PLAN
FOR BLACKS IN JOBS:
United Steelworkers of America v. Weber

LINDA GREENHOUSE*

WASHINGTON, June 27, 1979—The Supreme Court ruled today that private employers can legally give special preferences to black workers to eliminate "manifest racial imbalance" in traditionally white-only jobs.

In a 5-to-2 decision that was greeted as an important victory by civil rights leaders, the Court held that voluntary affirmative action plans, even those containing numerical quotas, do not automatically violate the Civil Rights Acts of 1964. Title VII of that act bars discrimination in employment on the basis of race.

The majority opinion, written by Associate Justice William J. Brennan Jr., reversed two lower Federal courts, which had held that Title VII outlawed a special training program designed to increase the number of blacks in skilled craft jobs in a Louisiana steel mill.

WHITE WORKER'S ARGUMENT

The majority rejected the argument of a white worker, Brian F. Weber, that the training program constituted illegal "reverse discrimination" against whites by reserving half the places for black workers.

"It would be ironic indeed," Justice Brennan wrote, "if a law triggered by a nation's concern over centuries of racial injustice and intended to improve the lot of those who had 'been excluded from the American dream for so long' constituted the first legislative prohibition of all voluntary, private, race-conscious efforts to abolish traditional patterns of racial segregation and hierarchy."

The majority was joined by Associate Justices Potter Stewart, Byron R. White, Thurgood Marshall and Harry A. Blackmun, who also filed a concurring opinion. Chief Justice Warren E. Burger and Associate Justice William H. Rehnquist both filed dissenting opinions.

A CLEAR MAJORITY

The decision in *United Steelworkers of America v. Weber* (No. 78-432) stopped short of giving blanket approval of any conceivable affirmative action plan. Nevertheless, it commanded a clear, if narrow, majority, without the confusion and ambiguity engendered by the six opinions in last year's case of Allan P. Bakke. In that decision, handed down a year ago tomorrow, the Court struck down a rigid quota system for admission to a California state medical school but also suggested that affirmative action programs could be justified under other circumstances.

*Reporter, *New York Times*.

The Bakke case turned on the Court's analysis of the equal protection clause of the Fourteenth Amendment to the United States Constitution. Today's opinion did not involve the Constitution at all. The Court viewed the affirmative action plan as a voluntary agreement between private parties whose behavior is not regulated by the Constitution. The Justices therefore addressed only the question of whether Congress meant to bar this kind of voluntary action when it outlawed discrimination in employment on the basis of race.

Justice Brennan conceded that the literal language of Title VII would seem to outlaw racial preferences as well as race discrimination in hiring. That argument, he said, "is not without force." But such a literal interpretation, he continued, "is misplaced," and ignores both the historical context in which Congress enacted the law and the intention of the legislators who voted for it to improve the economic condition of blacks in America.

An interpretation of Title VII that "forbade all race-conscious affirmative action," Justice Brennan wrote, "would bring about an end completely at variance with the purpose of the statute and must be rejected."

The two dissenters sharply disputed this conclusion. Chief Justice Burger called it "contrary to the explicit language of the statute and arrived at by means wholly incompatible with long-established principles of separation of powers."

In enacting Title VII, the Chief Justice said, "Congress expressly *prohibited* the discrimination against Brian Weber the Court approves now." In unusually acerbic language, Chief Justice Burger accused the majority of "totally rewriting a crucial part of Title VII to reach a desirable result."

Justice Rehnquist, frequently the Court's most rhetorically flamboyant member, was even more biting in a 37–page dissent also signed by the Chief Justice. The majority opinion itself ran 13 pages.

Justice Rehnquist quoted at length from the floor debates, committee reports, and other legislative history of Title VII to show that "Congress meant to outlaw *all* racial discrimination, recognizing that no discrimination based on race is benign, that no action disadvantaging a person because of his color is affirmative."

He wrote that the majority opinion "introduces into Title VII a tolerance for the very evil that the law was intended to eradicate, without offering even a clue as to what the limits on that tolerance may be."

The challenged affirmative action program was part of a nationwide agreement reached in 1974 through collective bargaining between Kaiser and the United Steelworkers. It covered 15 Kaiser plants around the country and was designed to remedy the almost complete absence of black workers from skilled jobs in the aluminum industry.

AGREEMENT ON TRAINING

The agreement called for the creation of special training programs, open to blacks and whites on a 50-50 basis and remaining in operation until the number of blacks in skilled jobs reached the proportion of blacks in the labor force from which the individual plants recruited.

At Kaiser's plant in Gramercy, Louisiana, where Mr. Weber works, the area's work force was 39 percent black. But blacks made up less than 2 percent—five out of 273—of the skilled workers at the plant.

There were 13 openings in the new training program at the Gramercy plant. Mr. Weber had insufficient seniority to get one of the six places reserved for whites. However, two of the blacks accepted had less seniority than he did, and he brought a lawsuit in Federal District Court charging violation of Title VII.

The district court held that the training program was unlawful under Title VII because the black workers whom it benefited had not themselves been the victims of illegal discrimination by Kaiser.

On appeal, the United States Court of Appeals for the Fifth Circuit affirmed. In a 2-to-1 opinion, that court held that Title VII made affirmative action programs permissible only to remedy discrimination against individual employees, not as a response to a perception of general societal discrimination.

That opinion was viewed by the federal Government and the civil rights movement as a serious threat to all voluntary affirmative action plans. In order to satisfy the Fifth Circuit's requirement that an affirmative action plan be a remedy for past discrimination, an employer would have to admit that it had discriminated and thereby invite Title VII lawsuits from blacks.

Failure to admit past discrimination, on the other hand, would invite "reverse discrimination" suits from whites. Given such a dilemma, employers could be expected to abandon the effort and wait for the Government to sue them.

The Supreme Court agreed to take the case last December and heard arguments in March. The union, the company and the Federal government all argued for reversal, but the union and the government were in nearly total disagreement about the approach the Court should take.

The union contended that Title VII, while prohibiting the government from ordering affirmative action plans, nonetheless permitted voluntary action. The government argued that Title VII did authorize the Federal courts to impose affirmative action plans, and that employers could therefore legally devise their own whenever the low numbers of blacks on their employment rolls raised the possibility of a government enforcement suit.

Excerpts from High Court's Opinions

FROM MAJORITY OPINION BY JUSTICE BRENNAN

We emphasize at the outset the narrowness of our inquiry. Since the Kaiser-USWA plan does not involve state action, this case does not present an alleged violation of the Equal Protection Clause of the Constitution. Further, since the Kaiser-USWA plan was adopted voluntarily, we are not concerned with what Title VII requires or with what a court might order to remedy a past proven violation of the act. The only question before us is the narrow statutory issue of whether Title VII forbids private employers and unions from voluntarily agreeing upon bona fide affirmative action plans that accord racial preferences in the manner and for the purpose provided in the Kaiser-USWA plan. That question was expressly left open in *McDonald v. Santa*

Fe Trail Trans. Co., which held, in a case not involving affirmative action, that Title VII protects whites as well as blacks from certain forms of racial discrimination.

Respondent argues that Congress intended in Title VII to prohibit all race-conscious affirmative action plans. Respondent's argument rests upon a literal interpretation of Sec. 703 (a) and (d) of the Act. Those sections make it unlawful to "discriminate . . . because of . . . race" in hiring and in the selection of apprentices for training programs. Since, the argument runs, *McDonald v. Santa Fe Trans. Co.*, supra, settled that Title VII forbids discrimination against whites as well as blacks, and since the Kaiser-USWA affirmative action plan operates to discriminate against white employees solely because they are white, it follows that the Kaiser-USWA plan violates Title VII.

Affirmative Action Plan

Respondent's argument is not without force. But it overlooks the significance of the fact that the Kaiser-USWA plan is an affirmative action plan voluntarily adopted by private parties to eliminate traditional patterns of racial segregation. In this context respondent's reliance upon a literal construction of Sec. 703 (a) and (d) and upon McDonald is misplaced. The prohibition against racial discrimination in Sec. 703 (a) and (d) of Title VII must therefore be read against the background of the legislative history of Title VII and the historical context from which the Act arose. Examination of those sources makes clear that an interpretation of the sections that forbade all race-conscious affirmative action would "bring about an end completely at variance with the purpose of the statute" and must be rejected.

Congress' primary concern in enacting the prohibition against racial discrimination in Title VII of the Civil Rights Act of 1964 was with "the plight of the Negro in our economy" (remarks of Senator Humphrey). Before 1964, blacks were largely relegated to "unskilled and semiskilled jobs." Because of automation the number of such jobs was rapidly decreasing. As a consequence "the relative position of the Negro worker (was) steadily worsening. In 1947 the nonwhite unemployment rate was only 64 percent higher than the white rate; in 1962 it was 124 percent higher." Congress considered this a serious social problem.

Congress feared that the goals of the Civil Rights Act—the integration of blacks into the mainstream of American society—could not be achieved unless this trend were reversed. And Congress recognized that that would not be possible unless blacks were able to secure jobs "which have a future."

Title VII Prohibition

Accordingly, it was clear to Congress that "the crux of the problem [was] to open employment opportunities for Negroes in occupations which have been traditionally closed to them," and it was to this problem that Title VII's prohibition against racial discrimination in employment was primarily addressed.

It plainly appears from the House Report accompanying the Civil Rights Act that Congress did not intend wholly to prohibit private and voluntary affirmative action efforts as one method of solving this problem.

Given this legislative history, we cannot agree with respondent that Congress intended to prohibit the private sector from taking effective steps to accomplish the goal that Congress designed Title VII to achieve. The very statutory words intended as a spur or catalyst to cause "employers and unions to self-examine and to self-evaluate their employment practices and to endeavor to eliminate, so far as possible, the last vestiges of an unfortunate and ignominious page in this country's history," *Albemarle v. Moody*, cannot be interpreted as an absolute prohibition against all private, voluntary, race-conscious affirmative action efforts to hasten the elimination of such vestiges. It would be ironic indeed if a law triggered by a Nation's concern over centuries of racial injustice and intended to improve the lot of those who had "been excluded from the American dream for so long" constituted the first legislative prohibition of all voluntary, private, race-conscious efforts to abolish traditional patterns of racial segregation and hierarchy.

History Of Section 703

Our conclusion is further reinforced by examination of the language and legislative history of Section 703 (j) of Title VII. Opponents of Title VII raised two related arguments against the bill. First, they argued that the Act would be interpreted to require employers with racially imbalanced work forces to grant preferential treatment to racial minorities in order to integrate. Second, they argued that employers with racially imbalanced work forces would grant preferential treatment to racial minorities, even if not required to do so by the Act. Had Congress meant to prohibit all race-conscious affirmative action, as respondent urges, it easily could have answered both objections by providing that Title VII would not require or permit racially preferential integration efforts. But Congress did not choose such a course. Rather, Congress added Section 703 (j), which addresses only the first objection. The section provides that nothing contained in Title VII "shall be interpreted to require any employer . . . to grant preferential treatment . . . to any group because of the race . . . of such . . . group on account of" a de facto racial imbalance in the employer's work force. The section does not state that "nothing in Title VII shall be interpreted to permit" voluntary affirmative efforts to correct racial imbalances. The natural inference is that Congress chose not to forbid all voluntary race-conscious affirmative action.

The reasons for this choice are evident from the legislative record. Title VII could not have been enacted into law without substantial support from legislators in both Houses who traditionally resisted federal regulation of private business. Those legislators demanded as a price for their support that "management prerogatives and union freedoms . . . be left undisturbed to the greatest extent possible." Section 703 (j) was proposed by Senator Dirksen to allay any fears that the Act might be interpreted in such a way as to upset this compromise. In view of this legislative history and in view of Congress' desire to avoid undue federal regulation of private businesses, use of the word "require" rather than the phrase "require or permit" in Section 703 (j) fortifies the conclusion that Congress did not intend to limit traditional business freedom to such a degree as to prohibit all voluntary, race-conscious affirmative action.

Limits Of Prohibition

We therefore hold that Title VII's prohibition in Sec. 703 (a) and (d) against racial discrimination does not condemn all private, voluntary, race-conscious affirmative action plans.

We need not today define in detail the line of demarcation between permissible and impermissible affirmative action plans. It suffices to hold that the challenged Kaiser-USWA affirmative action plan falls on the permissible side of the line. The purposes of the plan mirror those of the statute. Both were designed to break down old patterns of racial segregation and hierarchy. Both were structured to "open employment opportunities for Negroes in occupations which have been traditionally closed to them."

At the same time the plan does not unnecessarily trammel the interests of the white employees. The plan does not require the discharge of white workers and their replacement with new black hirees. Nor does the plan create an absolute bar to the advancement of white employees; half of those trained in the program will be white. Moreover, the plan is a temporary measure; it is not intended to maintain racial balance, but simply to eliminate a manifest racial imbalance. Preferential selection of craft trainees at the Gramercy plant will end as soon as the percentage of black skilled craft workers in the Gramercy plant approximates the percentage of blacks in the local labor force.

We conclude, therefore, that the adoption of the Kaiser-USWA plan for the Gramercy plant falls within the area of discretion left by Title VII to the private sector voluntarily to adopt affirmative action plans designed to eliminate conspicuous racial imbalance in traditionally segregated job categories. Accordingly, the judgment of the Court of Appeals for the Fifth Circuit is reversed.

FROM DISSENTING OPINION BY JUSTICE REHNQUIST

We have never wavered in our understanding that Title VII "prohibits all racial discrimination in employment, without exception for any particular employees."

Today, however, the Court behaves as if it had been handed a note indicating that Title VII would lead to a result unacceptable to the Court if interpreted here as it was in our prior decisions. Accordingly, without even a break in syntax, the Court rejects "a literal construction of Sec. 703 (a)" in favor of newly discovered "legislative history," which leads it to a conclusion directly contrary to that compelled by the "uncontradicted legislative history" unearthed in McDonald and our other prior decisions.

Thus, by a tour de force reminiscent not of jurists such as Hale, Holmes, and Hughes, but of escape artists such as Houdini, the Court eludes clear statutory language, "uncontradicted" legislative history, and uniform precedent in concluding that employers are, after all, permitted to consider race in making employment decisions.

Were Congress to act today specifically to prohibit the type of racial discrimination suffered by Weber, it would be hard pressed to draft language better tailored to the task than that found in Sec. 703 (d) of Title VII:

"It shall be an unlawful employment practice for any employers, labor organization, or joint labor-management committee controlling apprenticeship or other training or retraining, including on-the-job training programs to discriminate against any individual because of his race, color, religion, sex, or national origin in admission to, or employment in, any program established to provide apprenticeship or other training." 43 U.S.C. Sec. 2000e-2 (d). Equally suited to the task would be Sec. 703

(a) (2), which makes it unlawful for an employer to classify his employees "in any way which would deprive or tend to deprive any individual of employment opportunities or otherwise adversely affect his status as an employee, because of such individual's race, color, religion, sex, or national origin."

Entirely consistent with these two express prohibitions is the language of Sec. 703 (j) of Title VII, which provides that the Act is not to be interpreted "to require any employer . . . to grant preferential treatment to any individual or to any group because of the race . . . of such individual or group" to correct a racial imbalance in the employer's work force. Seizing on the word "require," the Court infers that Congress must have intended to "permit" this type of racial discrimination. Not only is this reading of Sec. 703 (j) outlandish in the light of the flat prohibitions of Sec. 703 (a) and (d), but it is totally belied by the Act's legislative history.

Quite simply, Kaiser's racially discriminatory admission quota is flatly prohibited by the plain language of Title VII.

FROM DISSENTING OPINION BY CHIEF JUSTICE BURGER

The Court reaches a result I would be inclined to vote for were I a member of Congress considering a proposed amendment of Title VII. I cannot join the Court's judgment, however, because it is contrary to the explicit language of the statute and arrived at by means wholly incompatible with long-established principles of separation of powers. Under the guise of statutory "construction," the Court effectively rewrites Title VII to achieve what it regards as a desirable result.

Often we have difficulty interpreting statutes either because of imprecise drafting or because legislative compromises have produced genuine ambiguities. But here there is no lack of clarity, no ambiguity. The quota embodied in the collective-bargaining agreement between Kaiser and the Steelworkers unquestionably discriminates on the basis of race against individual employees seeking admission to on-the-job training programs. And, under the plain language of Section 703 (d), that is "an unlawful employment practice."

Oddly, the Court seizes upon the very clarity of the statute almost as a justification for evading the unavoidable impact of its language. The Court blandly tells us that Congress could not really have meant what it said, for a "literal construction" would defeat the "purpose" of the statute—at least the Congressional "purpose" as five Justices divine it today.

Arguably, Congress may not have gone far enough in correcting the effects of past discrimination when it enacted Title VII. But that statute was conceived and enacted to make discrimination against any individual illegal, and I fail to see how "voluntary compliance" with the no-discrimination principle that is the heart and soul of Title VII as currently written will be achieved by permitting employers to discriminate against some individuals to give preferential treatment to others.

It is often observed that hard cases make bad law. I suspect there is some truth to that adage, for the "hard" cases always tempt judges to exceed the limits of their authority, as the Court does today by totally rewriting a crucial part of Title VII to reach a desirable result.

SUPPLEMENTARY READING FOR PART THREE

Blackstone, William T., and Robert D. Heslep, eds. *Social Justice and Preferential Treatment.* Athens: University of Georgia Press, 1977.

Blumberg, Phillip I. "Corporate Responsibility and the Employee's Duty of Loyalty and Obedience: A Preliminary Inquiry." *Oklahoma Law Review,* vol. 24, **3,** August 1971.

Cohen, Marshall, Thomas Nagel, and Thomas Scanlon, eds. *Equality and Preferential Treatment.* Princeton, N.J.: Princeton University Press, 1977.

Davis, Louis E., and Albert Cherns, eds. *The Quality of Working Life,* vols. 1 and 2. New York: Free Press, 1975.

De George, Richard T. "Ethical Responsibilities of Engineers in Large Organizations." *Business and Professional Ethics Journal,* vol. 1, **1,** Fall 1981, pp. 1–14.

Ewing, David W. *Freedom Inside the Organization.* New York: Dutton, 1977.

Fairfield, Roy P., ed. *Humanizing the Workplace.* New York: Prometheus Books, 1974.

Fullinwider, Robert K. *The Reverse Discrimination Controversy.* Totowa, N.J.: Rowman and Littlefield, 1980.

Gross, Barry R., ed. *Reverse Discrimination.* Buffalo, N.Y.: Prometheus Books, 1977.

Heisler, W. J., and John W. Houck, eds. *A Matter of Dignity: Inquiries into the Humanization of Work.* Notre Dame and London: University of Notre Dame Press, 1977.

Hoffman, W. Michael, and Thomas J. Wyly, eds. *The Work Ethic in Business: Proceedings of the Third National Conference on Business Ethics.* Cambridge, Mass.: Oelgeschlager, Gunn & Hain, 1981.

Nader, Ralph, Peter J. Petkas, and Kate Blackwell, eds. *Whistle Blowing.* New York: Grossman Publishers, 1972.

Peters, Charles, and Taylor Branch, eds. *Blowing the Whistle.* New York: Praeger Publishers, 1972.

Schappe, Robert H. "Twenty-Two Arguments Against Job Enrichment." *Personnel Journal,* vol. 53, **2,** February 1974, pp. 116–123.

Terkel, Studs. *Working.* New York: Pantheon Books, 1974.

Westin, Alan F. *Whistle Blowing!* New York: McGraw-Hill, 1981.

Westin, Alan F., and Stephen Salisbury, eds. *Individual Rights in the Corporation.* New York: Pantheon Books, 1980.

Whyte, William H., Jr. *The Organization Man.* New York: Simon and Schuster, 1956.

Work in America: Report of a Special Task Force to the Secretary of Health, Education and Welfare. Cambridge, Mass.: The MIT Press, 1973.

Work. The Philosophical Forum, vol. X, **2, 3,** Winter/Summer, 1978/1979. A special issue edited in cooperation with the Society for Philosophy and Public Affairs.

PART FOUR
THE CORPORATION IN SOCIETY

In Part Three we examined some aspects of the relationship of business to one of its most important internal constituencies, its employees. Here we turn attention to the relationship between business and its external constituencies—that is, between business and the environment in which it operates. In Chapter Ten we examine the relationship between business and consumers through a look at some of the ethical aspects of marketing and production; Chapter Eleven explores some ethical dimensions of the relationship of business to the natural environment; in Chapter Twelve we raise questions about the appropriate roles of government and business in the regulation of corporate behavior; and Chapter Thirteen takes up some of the ethical problems raised by multinational business operations.

BUSINESS AND CONSUMERS

Business organizations exist by selling goods and services to consumers. Consumers, then, are one of business' most important constituencies, literally essential for its survival. Traditionally, the relationship between business and consumers in American society has been defined by the free market, which links the two together in what is intended to be a mutually beneficial relationship. Business is free to make as large a profit as possible on its transactions with consumers; but business succeeds only by giving consumers what they want. Both consumer and business interests, then, are protected by the market itself. Presumably an unsatisfactory product or one offered at an unreasonable price will not sell. In such a system the consumer is king, and sellers must serve the consumer or go out of business.

This system can work in practice, however, only if two conditions are met: (1) There is no deception, and the consumer receives adequate and accurate enough information about products on the market to make rational market decisions; and (2) the consumer is free to choose what to buy. Do these really characterize the relation between business and consumers, however? The attempt to answer this question is the takeoff point for some of the most important consumer-related issues in business ethics.

One aspect of business activity which has led thinkers to question the accuracy of the traditional picture of relations between business and consumers is that of advertising and marketing. Advertising of some kind is necessary to convey information to consumers and to make them aware of what products are available. But how much information is really conveyed in such slogans as "Coke is the real thing." or "When you've said Budweiser, you've said it all."?

Observers of advertising might conclude that its primary purpose is not to inform, but to persuade. Advertisers have been accused not only of failing to inform the public, but of actively deceiving it as well, through techniques such as "puffery" or exaggeration, failure to tell the whole truth about a product, misleading packaging, and misuse of statistics. These accusations are important, because if the consumer has been led by a deceptive advertisement to buy a product, he or she has purchased that product on a false basis, and the system has failed to protect the consumer's interests. Because the product is not what the consumer intended to buy when he or she made the purchase, the consumer's freedom has been violated.

Another way of violating consumer freedom that advertising has been accused of is by the creation of needs and desires which the consumer would not otherwise have had. This is the charge made by John Kenneth Galbraith in his article, "The Dependence Effect." Galbraith argues that in America the manufacture of consumer demands is as important as, if not more important than, the manufacture of products which satisfy those demands. The same companies which satisfy wants, he claims, also *create* those wants by advertising, establishing a self-perpetuating cycle of desire and satisfaction. Galbraith believes that to be genuine and urgent, desires must originate with the person who has them, and not be instilled in that person from without.

If Galbraith is correct, consumers are being manipulated into buying things they do not really want or need. The consumer is not the king in this picture, but a pawn. Recalling Kant, we might say that if Galbraith is correct then consumers are being treated by producers as means to an end rather than as ends in themselves. For rather than responding to consumer needs, producers are creating needs and viewing the consumer as nothing more than an instrument for making profits. Creation of consumer needs is also bad, according to Galbraith, because it encourages the excessive consumption of private goods which are not really essential, and diverts spending away from public goods, which are not advertised. Galbraith feels that although our society is rich in private goods, it is poor in public goods such as clean air, livable cities, and public transportation.

But is it true that advertising literally creates needs in us? Robert Arrington does not believe so. We may have no direct desire for many of the products on the market, Arrington holds, but we do have basic, often hidden desires such as those for security, power, sex, or adventure. It is to these independent desires which we already have that advertising appeals. And even if advertising does make us aware of needs and desires we never knew we had, Arrington argues, it does not follow that these needs are not urgent and legitimate. We would not desire many of those products of civilization we value most—art, music, and literature, for example—if the culture in which we live had not made us aware of our desire for them.

Another important issue raised by the relationship between business and consumers is that of product safety. If a manufacturer has a responsibility to consumers not to market unsafe products, how far does this responsibility extend? Who should assume the liability if a customer is injured by a defective product? Here, as in the case of advertising, it is unclear whether the market system by itself really protects the interests of the consumers. If they had adequate information consumers could freely choose the risks they wish to run, and products considered too risky would be driven off the market. But in most cases manufacturers need not make explicit the potential hazards of what they sell. Most consumers lack the expertise to assess the safety of today's technologically sophisticated products, and must rely at least to some extent on the impression they are given by sellers. Many purchases are "one-shot" deals, which means that the consumer has no opportunity to benefit from his or her experience in the future. And although we are likely to hear about seriously dangerous products, their danger does not attract attention until some consumers are injured.

Our growing lack of confidence in the market system to protect consumer safety is demonstrated by the increase in consumer protection legislation, and by the establishment of two major consumer protection agencies in the last decade—the Consumer Product Safety Commission and the National Highway Traffic Safety Administration. Some observers of this trend claim that we have moved from a stance of "let the buyer beware" to one of "let the manufacturer/seller beware." Moreover, many feel that the responsibility of manufacturers to consumers goes beyond obedience to federal safety regulations. Ford, for example, was asked to pay substantial amounts in settlements for accidents due to the placement of the Pinto's gas tank, even though there were no federal standards for fuel-system integrity at the time the Pinto was produced. One might argue that the manufacturer has an obligation to the consumer to make a product that can be used safely for the purposes for which the consumer has been led to believe it can be used, regardless of federal standards.

No product can be absolutely risk-free, however; some theorists hold that the most that can be demanded of manufacturers is that they exercise "due care" to make all products "reasonably" safe. The National Commission on Product Safety (NCPS) has suggested that risks are reasonable when consumers are aware of them, able to assess their probability and severity, know how to cope with them if they do arise, and voluntarily accept them to receive benefits they could not get otherwise. Risks which could easily be prevented, or which consumers would be willing to pay to prevent if given the choice, the NCPS concluded, are not reasonable. In part, it was the failure of Ford to exercise due care in making a safe product which is at issue in the Pinto case included in this book. But the case is an unusual one because in it Ford is accused of *criminal* homicide—of knowingly choosing not to exercise due care and trading human lives for profit.

It may seem fair that manufacturers should assume liability for consumer injuries caused by failure to exercise due care. But in recent years the courts have extended the liability of manufacturers to include all cases in which injuries result from defects in the manufacturing process, even if the manufacturer could not have foreseen or prevented the injury. This doctrine is called "strict products liability." Proponents of the doctrine argue that manufacturers are best able to bear the costs of injuries because they can distribute them to others, and that forcing manufacturers to assume liability is likely to reduce the frequency of accidents in the future. These are essentially utilitarian arguments. But do they constitute a justification for strict products liability? George Brenkert is one thinker who does not find them convincing, although he supports the doctrine of strict products liability.

Brenkert questions whether holding manufacturers strictly liable really will reduce the number of accidents and, if it will, whether it is the only way or the best way to do so. And even if a policy of strict products liability would reduce accidents, Brenkert argues, it does not follow that the doctrine is just. Similarly, that manufacturers are best able to bear the costs of injuries does not mean that it is just that they pay those costs.

Nevertheless, Brenkert believes that in the context of a free enterprise system, the doctrine of strict products liability is a just one. Essential to the functioning of a free enterprise system, he argues, is equal opportunity. However unintentionally, a manufacturer whose defective product has injured a consumer has interfered with that consumer's equal opportunity to participate in the system. Just as a team may be penalized for hurting an opposing player's ability to compete, even if the injury was an accident, a manufacturer may be required to compensate a consumer injured by a defective product, whether the defect was foreseen or not. Brenkert concludes that for this reason it is just to place the burden of liability on the manufacturer.

BUSINESS AND THE ENVIRONMENT

Some of the most urgent questions faced by society today are those raised by the increasing contamination and depletion of our natural resources. The air pollution which is present in all major United States cities increases the incidence of respiratory disease, heart disease, and lung cancer. Toxic wastes like those dumped in Love Canal by Hooker Chemical Company find their way into drinking water and pose serious threats to human life and health. The earth's protective ozone layer is deteriorating, leaving us vulnerable to harmful effects from beyond the atmosphere. Researchers predict that if the exponentially rising rate of use of fossil fuels continues, estimated reserves will be depleted in about a hundred years.

In Chapter Eleven we look at some environmental problems raised by the activities of commercial and industrial enterprises. Business is by no means the sole polluter, nor is it the sole consumer of natural resources. But there are several important reasons for focusing on business-related environmental issues.

One reason is that the structure of the free enterprise system itself has been accused of encouraging pollution. At one time air and water were thought of as unlimited and "free" goods, available for anyone's use without charge. The effects—in terms of pollution—of any particular business' use of air or water were negligible, and we were confident of the ability of the environment to absorb them.

Business itself has not paid for all the costs of production, then, but has "externalized" some of them—that is, passed them on to society as a whole. Market forces encourage this conversion of private to public costs. However, as increasing pollution and the depletion of natural resources force us to adopt what Kenneth Boulding has called a "spaceship earth" mentality, it seems clear that pollution must be made less desirable by forcing polluters to internalize environmental costs. It is not surprising that business is resisting such attempts, and that some businesspeople view environmental protection measures as contrary to their interests.

A second reason for examining business' role in the environmental crisis is the pervasiveness of the value placed on consumption, which is an integral part of our business society. Although Americans comprise only 6 percent of the world's population, we consume 35 percent of the world's annual energy resources. We also have the highest gross national product of any country in the world. The link between standard of living, economic growth as measured by the GNP, and high levels of pollution and consumption of natural resources cannot be denied. Business has developed into a powerful force in our society because of its ability to satisfy the appetite for consumption. Whether business is responsible for the pervasiveness of consumption as a social value, as Galbraith would suggest, is not clear. But it is clear that the environmental protection movement presents a challenge to private consumption, and therefore to a very important aspect of business activity.

Some thinkers hold that pollution is wrong because it violates the rights of nature to be respected. They argue that these rights ought to be protected by the recognition of legal rights for natural entities such as forests, lakes, and streams. Others, like William T. Blackstone in this text, claim that pollution is wrong because it violates the *human* right to a livable environment. Blackstone claims that each of us possesses the basic rights necessary for us to live human lives and to fulfill our capacities as rational and free beings. Such inalienable rights have traditionally included equality, liberty, happiness, life, and property.

But these basic rights cannot be exercised, Blackstone argues, without a livable environment. He concludes that the right to a livable environment, a right which has emerged as a result of changing environmental conditions, is also an inalienable right on an equal footing with the rights to life, liberty, and property. One might argue along Blackstone's lines that the violation of Niagara Falls residents' right to a livable environment is part of what is at issue in the Love Canal case. Recognition of the right to a livable environment as a legal as well as a moral right, Blackstone suggests, could be an important tool in solving some of our environmental problems.

But what constitutes a livable environment, and how far ought we to go to protect people's rights to one? As we noted above, it seems clear that pollution control and conservation of natural resources will have a significant cost. The Council on Environmental Quality reported a 78 percent decrease in carbon monoxide levels from 1972 to 1975, and dramatic improvements in water quality. By 1977, 30 percent of our air quality regions had met clean air goals. But in 1977 $40.6 billion was spent by consumers, government, and private enterprise to control pollution—$187 per person. The Council on Environmental Quality estimates that $290 billion will be spent between 1976 and 1985 in bringing about compliance with environmental standards. Other, indirect costs, some argue, include lower standards of living, higher rates of unemployment, and the slowdown or cessation of economic growth.

In his article, Wilfred Beckerman argues that we should not reduce pollution and the consumption of natural resources at the expense of economic growth. Pollution should only be cut to a point at which the benefits no longer outweigh the costs of doing so, he claims. We need not do away with *all* pollution. Beckerman's argument seems to imply that the economic growth of a society is essential for its well-being.

Is economic growth a true measurement of the well-being of society, however? In his article Kenneth Boulding challenges the usefulness of the GNP as a social indicator. When the environment becomes polluted, Boulding explains, the cost of cleaning it up is added to the national product but the pollution is not subtracted, so that the gross national product is higher than it would have been had there been no pollution at all. But the increased GNP does not reflect an increase in social well-being. This and other examples, Boulding argues, indicate that the GNP is not an accurate measure of the welfare of society. He suggests that economic growth may have to be curtailed to enhance the quality of life on "spaceship earth."

BUSINESS AND GOVERNMENT

Thus far we have explored the notion that business has obligations to its multiple "stakeholders," and we have examined some of the specific responsibilities of business toward its employees, consumers, and society at large. How can we best ensure that business discharges these obligations? This question inevitably raises issues regarding the relationship between business and government. In the Pinto case, for example, part of the strength of Ford's defense was the fact that the company did not violate any government regulations in producing the Pinto. And we might indict not only Niagara Falls' Board of Education and Hooker Chemical Company, but also the state of New York and the United States government for their part in the Love Canal tragedy.

Should we use extensive government regulations to enforce responsible business behavior? Or can and should business organizations regulate themselves? Although there are a number of important issues surrounding the relationship between business and government, we focus here on the so-called social regulations which are designed to make business carry out ethical obligations to its various constituencies.

American business has never been unregulated; but in recent years the "invisible hand" of market forces has been increasingly supported by the visible—and sometimes heavy—hand of government. As George Steiner explains in his article, the past two decades have seen a shift from industry-oriented regulations designed mainly to promote competition to regulations which cut across industry lines and are intended to improve the quality of life.

The new regulations are concerned with one function of corporate activity, such as product safety, environmental protection, or worker health and safety, and not with the organization as a whole. They are numerous, specific, and detailed. Important benefits can be and have been produced by the new regulations. Some of them are cited by Steven Kelman in his article: significant improvements in the quality of air in major urban areas, a 50 percent reduction in accidental workplace deaths, decreases in racial and sexual discriminations in the workplace.

But substantial costs have resulted as well. Steiner, a critic of the new regulatory policies, believes that the costs of the policies outweigh their benefits. He points out that they are expensive to implement and enforce, that they reduce efficiency, and that the high costs of conforming to them must be passed on to society as a whole in the form of higher prices. Much of the new regulation is cumbersome and contradictory. And Steiner believes that the extensive government regulation has upset the balance of power between government and business, interfering with the freedom of private enterprise.

Steven Kelman claims that Steiner and other opponents of the new regulation have vastly exaggerated its costs and failed to consider the savings it can provide. But even if this were not true, he argues, many of the new regulations ought to remain in force. The regulations are directed at preventing serious harms, and thus far they have been effective in doing so. Persons have a right to safe products, a clean environment, and humane working conditions, Kelman argues, and this right should be protected even if it is expensive to do so. Readers will recognize some of Kelman's arguments from his article on cost-benefit analysis in Chapter Three.

Because government regulation is costly and undesirable to most businesspeople, some thinkers have pointed to forms of self-regulation as a possible key to responsible business behavior. Others are skeptical of self-regulation, claiming that corporations will not regulate themselves for fear of putting themselves at a competitive disadvantage. For this reason Norman Bowie suggests industrywide codes of ethics as an alternative to government regulation. Such codes could protect businesses from unethical acts on the part of competitors as well as enhance the public confidence which is necessary for business survival. If they are supplemented by procedures for interpreting their requirements and adequate enforcement processes, and if they are truly taken seriously by top management, Bowie believes that industrywide codes can be effective.

Other means of self-regulation have also been suggested. One of the most important of these is the corporate social audit, a tool for measuring the ethical status of a business organization just as traditional accounting and audit procedures measure its financial status. Although they pose some problems in implementation, social audit and reporting procedures have increased in sophistication and are now in use in a number of major business organizations.

Advocates of self-regulation do not argue that there should be *no* government regulation of business. While we expect individual persons to regulate their behavior, we also back up our expectations with legal statutes and sanctions. But when government does not bear the sole responsibility for corporate behavior, regulations can be less numerous and less specific, and business can be given more freedom. What the self-regulation proposals of Bowie and others do is to shift the emphasis in corporate responsibility from controls imposed from outside the organization to changes from within, from what Goodpaster and Matthews (Chapter Five) have called the "hand of government" to the "hand of management." They are attempts to internalize ethical values in the organization and to establish a moral corporate ethos. We take up the development of such an ethos in more detail in Chapter Seventeen.

BUSINESS IN A MULTINATIONAL SETTING

Multinational corporations are business organizations which maintain extensive operations in more than one country. Multinational business faces many of the same ethical issues as domestic business, but the fact that multinationals conduct business across national and cultural lines raises special problems. Practices which are benign in the United States may be inappropriate or unethical in other contexts. Because they are so extensive, multinational corporations do not come under the complete control of any one government.

Extensive investment by multinational corporations can help the economies of developing nations, but as Louis Turner points out in his article on multinationals and the Third World, it can have harmful effects as well. Multinational investment can lead to extensive dependence on foreign involvement, leaving the developing nation powerless and vulnerable. Many multinationals establish foreign operations in order to get cheap labor, or to engage in hazardous production processes without the expense of conforming to United States worker health and safety regulations. Multinational industry can stifle local enterprise and submerge the characteristic culture of the nations in which it operates. Successful private enterprise, as we have seen, does not always lead to the satisfaction of social needs, which in developing countries may be urgent.

Are multinational corporations obligated to use their power to correct injustice in the countries in which they operate—in effect, to exercise global social responsibility? How much care should they exercise in the production and marketing of consumer products? Bribery, which we discuss in Part Five under the heading of questionable practices, is another issue often faced by members of multinational corporations. Here we focus on ethical problems raised by the presence of United States firms in South Africa and by the marketing of infant formula in developing countries.

South Africa has been condemned by many throughout the world for its policy of racial segregation and repression known as *apartheid*. Although there are 19 million blacks and only 4.5 million whites in the country, blacks are permitted to live on only 13 percent of the land and earn less than 20 percent of national income. Blacks are not permitted to vote, own property, or organize politically. They hold only low-paying, low-status jobs and are forced to use segregated facilities. It seems clear that the involvement of United States firms in South Africa strengthens the economy, thus indirectly preserving the stability of the government. If this is so, is it possible for United States multinationals to operate ethically in South Africa, or should they pull out altogether? Precisely this issue was faced by Polaroid Corporation in its attempt to decide whether to continue to do business in South Africa.

Proponents of the involvement of United States firms in South Africa, like Robert Moss, point to the strategic importance of the country to the United States. Moss also argues that improvement in the position of South African blacks is more likely to come about in an expanding than in a faltering economy. The damage to the South African economy which would follow withdrawal of United States investment would harm blacks more than whites, he claims. Moss believes that United States multinationals have effected and can continue to effect beneficial changes from within by setting an enlightened example. He cites the Sullivan principles, formulated by General Motors director Leon Sullivan and endorsed by a large number of United States firms with South African operations, as appropriate guidelines for conducting business ethically in South Africa.

Other thinkers, such as John Payton, claim that the Sullivan principles have failed to bring about any significant changes in South African society. Investment in South African operations only strengthens the repressive regime, he argues, and the presence of United States firms in South Africa indicates our acceptance of and willingness to cooperate with the policies of the South African government. Payton calls for legislation prohibiting United States firms from doing business in South Africa either directly or indirectly.

S. Prakash Sethi's and James Post's article on marketing infant formula in the Third World provides a focal point for a discussion of issues surrounding advertising and product safety as well as those raised by multinational operations. Sold in the United States and in developed countries, infant formula provides a safe and nutritious alternative to breast-feeding. But when used under unsanitary conditions, diluted with contaminated water, and prepared by illiterate mothers unable to follow the directions for its use, the formula can result in malnutrition and even death. Marketing practices which fail to take into account the context in which the formula will be used have been condemned severely, and it has been suggested that cross-cultural operations demand a more stringent set of obligations of manufacturers to customers.

chapter ten
THE CONSUMER

THE DEPENDENCE EFFECT

JOHN KENNETH GALBRAITH*

The theory of consumer demand, as it is now widely accepted, is based on two broad propositions, neither of them quite explicit but both extremely important for the present value system of economists. The first is that the urgency of wants does not diminish appreciably as more of them are satisfied or, to put the matter more precisely, to the extent that this happens it is not demonstrable and not a matter of any interest to economists or for economic policy. When man has satisfied his physical needs, then psychologically grounded desires take over. These can never be satisfied or, in any case, no progress can be proved. The concept of satiation has very little standing in economics. It is neither useful nor scientific to speculate on the comparative cravings of the stomach and the mind.

The second proposition is that wants originate in the personality of the consumer or, in any case, that they are given data for the economist. The latter's task is merely to seek their satisfaction. He has no need to inquire how these wants are formed. His function is sufficiently fulfilled by maximizing the goods that supply the wants.

The notion that wants do not become less urgent the more amply the individual is supplied is broadly repugnant to common sense. It is something to be believed only by those who wish to believe. Yet the conventional wisdom must be tackled on its own terrain. Intertemporal comparisons of an individual's state of mind do rest on doubtful grounds. Who can say for sure that the deprivation which afflicts him with hunger is more painful than the deprivation which afflicts him with envy of his neighbour's new car? In the time that has passed since he was poor his soul may have become subject to a new and deeper searing. And where a society is concerned, comparisons between marginal satisfactions when it is poor and those when it is affluent will involve not only the same individual at different times but different individuals at different times. The scholar who wishes to believe that with increasing affluence there is no reduction in the urgency of desires and goods is not without points for debate. However plausible the case against him, it cannot be proved. In the defence of the conventional wisdom this amounts almost to invulnerability.

However, there is a flaw in the case. If the individual's wants are to be urgent they must be original with himself. They cannot be urgent if they must be contrived

*Former Paul M. Warburg Professor of Economics, Harvard University.

for him. And above all they must not be contrived by the process of production by which they are satisfied. For this means that the whole case for the urgency of production, based on the urgency of wants, falls to the ground. One cannot defend production as satisfying wants if that production creates the wants.

Were it so that man on arising each morning was assailed by demons which instilled in him a passion sometimes for silk shirts, sometimes for kitchenware, sometimes for chamber-pots, and sometimes for orange squash, there would be every reason to applaud the effort to find the goods, however odd, that quenched this flame. But should it be that his passion was the result of his first having cultivated the demons, and should it also be that his effort to allay it stirred the demons to ever greater and greater effort, there would be question as to how rational was his solution. Unless restrained by conventional attitudes, he might wonder if the solution lay with more goods or fewer demons.

So it is that if production creates the wants it seeks to satisfy, or if the wants emerge *pari passu* with the production, then the urgency of the wants can no longer be used to defend the urgency of the production. Production only fills a void that it has itself created.

The even more direct link between production and wants is provided by the institutions of modern advertising and salesmanship. These cannot be reconciled with the notion of independently determined desires, for their central function is to create desires—to bring into being wants that previously did not exist.[1] This is accomplished by the producer of the goods or at his behest. A broad empirical relationship exists between what is spent on production of consumers' goods and what is spent in synthesizing the desires for that production. A new consumer product must be introduced with a suitable advertising campaign to arouse an interest in it. The path for an expansion of output must be paved by a suitable expansion in the advertising budget. Outlays for the manufacturing of a product are not more important in the strategy of modern business enterprise than outlays for the manufacturing of demand for the product. None of this is novel. All would be regarded as elementary by the most retarded student in the nation's most primitive school of business administration. The cost of this want formation is formidable. In 1956 total advertising expenditure—though, as noted, not all of it may be assigned to the synthesis of wants—amounted to about ten thousand million dollars. For some years it had been increasing at a rate in excess of a thousand million dollars a year. Obviously, such outlays must be integrated with the theory of consumer demand. They are too big to be ignored.

But such integration means recognizing that wants are dependent on production. It accords to the producer the function both of making the goods and of making the desires for them. It recognizes that production, not only passively through emulation, but actively through advertising and related activities, creates the wants it seeks to satisfy.

The businessman and the lay reader will be puzzled over the emphasis which I give to a seemingly obvious point. The point is indeed obvious. But it is one which, to a singular degree, economists have resisted. They have sensed, as the layman does not, the damage to established ideas which lurks in these relationships. As a result, incredibly, they have closed their eyes (and ears) to the most obtrusive of all economic phenomena, namely modern want creation.

This is not to say that the evidence affirming the dependence of wants on advertising has been entirely ignored. It is one reason why advertising has so long been regarded with such uneasiness by economists. Here is something which cannot be accommodated easily to existing theory. More pervious scholars have speculated on the urgency of desires which are so obviously the fruit of such expensively contrived campaigns for popular attention. Is a new breakfast cereal or detergent so much wanted if so much must be spent to compel in the consumer the sense of want? But there has been little tendency to go on to examine the implications of this for the theory of consumer demand and even less for the importance of production and productive efficiency. These have remained sacrosanct. More often the uneasiness has been manifested in a general disapproval of advertising and advertising men, leading to the occasional suggestion that they shouldn't exist. Such suggestions have usually been ill received.

And so the notion of independently determined wants still survives. In the face of all the forces of modern salesmanship it still rules, almost undefiled, in the textbooks. And it still remains the economist's mission—and on few matters is the pedagogy so firm—to seek unquestioningly the means for filling these wants. This being so, production remains of prime urgency. We have here, perhaps, the ultimate triumph of the conventional wisdom in its resistance to the evidence of the eyes. To equal it one must imagine a humanitarian who was long ago persuaded of the grievous shortage of hospital facilities in the town. He continues to importune the passers-by for money for more beds and refuses to notice that the town doctor is deftly knocking over pedestrians with his car to keep up the occupancy.

And in unravelling the complex we should always be careful not to overlook the obvious. The fact that wants can be synthesized by advertising, catalysed by salesmanship, and shaped by the discreet manipulations of the persuaders shows that they are not very urgent. A man who is hungry need never be told of his need for food. If he is inspired by his appetite, he is immune to the influence of Messrs. Batten, Barton, Durstine and Osborn. The latter are effective only with those who are so far removed from physical want that they do not already know what they want. In this state alone men are open to persuasion.

The general conclusion of these pages is of such importance for this essay that it had perhaps best be put with some formality. As a society becomes increasingly affluent, wants are increasingly created by the process by which they are satisfied. This may operate passively. Increases in consumption, the counterpart of increases in production, act by suggestion or emulation to create wants. Or producers may proceed actively to create wants through advertising and salesmanship. Wants thus come to depend on output. In technical terms it can no longer be assumed that welfare is greater at an all-round higher level of production than at a lower one. It may be the same. The higher level of production has, merely, a higher level of want creation necessitating a higher level of want satisfaction. There will be frequent occasion to refer to the way wants depend on the process by which they are satisfied. It will be convenient to call it the Dependence Effect.

The final problem of the productive society is what it produces. This manifests itself in an implacable tendency to provide an opulent supply of some things and a niggardly yield of others. This disparity carries to the point where it is a cause of social discomfort and social unhealth. The line which divides our area of wealth from our area of poverty is roughly that which divides privately produced and marketed goods and services from publicly rendered services. Our wealth in the first is not only in startling contrast with the meagreness of the latter, but our wealth in privately produced goods is, to a marked degree, the cause of crisis in the supply of public services. For we have failed to see the importance, indeed the urgent need, of maintaining a balance between the two.

This disparity between our flow of private and public goods and services is no matter of subjective judgment. On the contrary, it is the source of the most extensive comment which only stops short of the direct contrast being made here. In the years following World War II, the papers of any major city—those of New York were an excellent example—told daily of the shortages and shortcomings in the elementary municipal and metropolitan services. The schools were old and overcrowded. The police force was under strength and underpaid. The parks and playgrounds were insufficient. Streets and empty lots were filthy, and the sanitation staff was under-equipped and in need of men. Access to the city by those who work there was uncertain and painful and becoming more so. Internal transportation was overcrowded, un-healthful, and dirty. So was the air. Parking on the streets had to be prohibited, and there was no space elsewhere. These deficiencies were not in new and novel services but in old and established ones. Cities have long swept their streets, helped their people move around, educated them, kept order, and provided horse rails for vehicles which sought to pause. That their residents should have a non-toxic supply of air suggests no revolutionary dalliance with socialism.

The contrast was and remains evident not alone to those who read. The family which takes its mauve and cerise, air-conditioned, power-steered, and power-braked car out for a tour passes through cities that are badly paved, made hideous by litter, blighted buildings, billboards, and posts for wires that should long since have been put underground. They pass on into a countryside that has been rendered largely invisible by commercial art. (The goods which the latter advertise have an absolute priority in our value system. Such aesthetic considerations as a view of the countryside accordingly come second. On such matters we are consistent.) They picnic on ex-quisitely packaged food from a portable icebox by a polluted stream and go on to spend the night at a park which is a menace to public health and morals. Just before dozing off on an air-mattress, beneath a nylon tent, amid the stench of decaying refuse, they may reflect vaguely on the curious unevenness of their blessings. Is this, indeed, the American genius?

The case for social balance has, so far, been put negatively. Failure to keep public services in minimal relation to private production and use of goods is a cause of social disorder or impairs economic performance. The matter may now be put affirmatively. By failing to exploit the opportunity to expand public production we are missing opportunities for enjoyment which otherwise we might have had. Presumably a com-munity can be as well rewarded by buying better schools or better parks as by buying bigger cars. By concentrating on the latter rather than the former it is failing to maximize its satisfactions. As with schools in the community, so with public services over the country at large. It is scarcely sensible that we should satisfy our wants in private goods with reckless abundance, while in the case of public goods, on the evidence of the eye, we practice extreme self-denial. So, far from systematically exploiting the opportunities to derive use and pleasure from these services, we do not supply what would keep us out of trouble.

The conventional wisdom holds that the community, large or small, makes a decision as to how much it will devote to its public services. This decision is arrived at by democratic process. Subject to the imperfections and uncertainties of democracy, people decide how much of their private income and goods they will surrender in order to have public services of which they are in greater need. Thus there is a balance, however rough, in the enjoyments to be had from private goods and services and those rendered by public authority.

It will be obvious, however, that this view depends on the notion of independently determined consumer wants. In such a world one could with some reason defend the doctrine that the consumer, as a voter, makes an independent choice between public and private goods. But given the dependence effect—given that consumer wants are created by the process by which they are satisfied—the consumer makes no such choice. He is subject to the forces of advertising and emulation by which production creates its own demand. Advertising operates exclusively, and emulation mainly, on behalf of privately produced goods and services.[2] Since management and emulative effects operate on behalf of private production, public services will have an inherent tendency to lag behind. Car demand which is expensively synthesized will inevitably have a much larger claim on income than parks or public health or even roads where no such influence operates. The engines of mass communication, in their highest state of development, assail the eyes and ears of the community on behalf of more beer but not of more schools. Even in the conventional wisdom it will scarcely be contended that this leads to an equal choice between the two.

The competition is especially unequal for new products and services. Every corner of the public psyche is canvassed by some of the nation's most talented citizens to see if the desire for some merchantable product can be cultivated. No similar process operates on behalf of the nonmerchantable services of the state. Indeed, while we take the cultivation of new private wants for granted we would be measurably shocked to see it applied to public services. The scientist or engineer or advertising man who devotes himself to developing a new carburetor, cleanser, or depilatory for which the public recognizes no need and will feel none until an advertising campaign arouses it, is one of the valued members of our society. A politician or a public servant who dreams up a new public service is a wastrel. Few public offences are more reprehensible.

So much for the influences which operate on the decision between public and private production. The calm decision between public and private consumption pictured by the conventional wisdom is, in fact, a remarkable example of the error which arises from viewing social behaviour out of context. The inherent tendency will always be for public services to fall behind private production. We have here the first of the causes of social imbalance.

NOTES

1. Advertising is not a simple phenomenon. It is also important in competitive strategy and want creation is, ordinarily, a complementary result of efforts to shift the demand curve of the individual firm at the expense of others or (less importantly, I think) to change its shape

by increasing the degree of product differentiation. Some of the failure of economists to identify advertising with want creation may be attributed to the undue attention that its use in purely competitive strategy has attracted. It should be noted, however, that the competitive manipulation of consumer desire is only possible, at least on any appreciable scale, when such need is not strongly felt.

2. Emulation does operate between communities. A new school or a new highway in one community does exert pressure on others to remain abreast. However, as compared with the pervasive effects of emulation in extending the demand for privately produced consumers' goods there will be agreement, I think, that this intercommunity effect is probably small.

ADVERTISING AND BEHAVIOR CONTROL

ROBERT L. ARRINGTON*

Consider the following advertisements:

1. "A woman in *Distinction Foundations* is so beautiful that all other women want to kill her."

2. Pongo Peach color from Revlon comes "from east of the sun . . . west of the moon where each tomorrow dawns." It is "succulent on your lips" and "sizzling on your finger tips (And on your toes, goodness knows)." Let it be your "adventure in paradise."

3. "Increase the value of your holdings. Old Charter Bourbon Whiskey—The Final Step Up."

4. Last Call Smirnoff Style: "They'd never really miss us, and it's kind of late already, and it's quite a long way, and I could build a fire, and you're looking very beautiful, and we could have another martini, and its awfully nice just being home . . . you think?"

5. A Christmas Prayer. "Let us pray that the blessings of peace be ours—the peace to build and grow, to live in harmony and sympathy with others, and to plan for the future with confidence." New York Life Insurance Company.

These are instances of what is called puffery—the practice by a seller of making exaggerated, highly fanciful or suggestive claims about a product or service. Puffery, within ill-defined limits, is legal. It is considered a legitimate, necessary, and very successful tool of the advertising industry. Puffery is not just bragging; it is bragging carefully designed to achieve a very definite effect. Using the techniques of so-called motivational research, advertising firms first identify our often hidden needs (for security, conformity, oral stimulation) and our desires (for power, sexual dominance and dalliance, adventure) and then they design ads which respond to these needs and desires. By associating a product, for which we may have little or no direct need or desire, with symbols reflecting the fulfillment of these other, often subterranean interests, the advertisement can quickly generate large numbers of consumers eager to purchase the product advertised. What woman in the sexual race of life could resist a foundation which would turn other women envious to the point of homicide? Who can turn down an adventure in paradise, east of the sun where tomorrow dawns? Be at the pinnacle of success—drink Old Charter. Or stay at home and dally a bit—with Smirnoff. And let us pray for a secure and predictable future, provided for by New York Life, God willing. It doesn't take very much motivational research to see the

Excerpted from "Advertising and Behavior Control," published in *Journal of Business Ethics*, vol. 1, no. 1 (February 1982), pp. 3–12. Copyright © 1982 by D. Reidel Publishing Company, Dordrecht, Holland.
*Department of Philosophy, Georgia State University.

point of these sales pitches. Others are perhaps a little less obvious. The need to feel secure in one's home at night can be used to sell window air conditioners, which drown out small noises and provide a friendly, dependable companion. The fact that baking a cake is symbolic of giving birth to a baby used to prompt advertisements for cake mixes which glamorized the 'creative' housewife. And other strategies, for example involving cigar symbolism, are a bit too crude to mention, but are nevertheless very effective.

Don't such uses of puffery amount to manipulation, exploitation, or downright control? In his very popular book *The Hidden Persuaders*, Vance Packard points out that a number of people in the advertising world have frankly admitted as much:

> As early as 1941 Dr. Dichter (an influential advertising consultant) was exhorting ad agencies to recognize themselves for what they actually were—"one of the most advanced laboratories in psychology". He said the successful ad agency "manipulates human motivations and desires and develops a need for goods with which the public has at one time been unfamiliar—perhaps even undesirous of purchasing". The following year *Advertising Agency* carried an ad man's statement that psychology not only holds promise for understanding people but "ultimately for controlling their behavior."[1]

Such statements lead Packard to remark: "With all this interest in manipulating the customer's subconscious, the old slogan 'let the buyer beware' began taking on a new and more profound meaning."[2]

B. F. Skinner, the high priest of behaviorism, has expressed a similar assessment of advertising and related marketing techniques. Why, he asks, do we buy a certain kind of car?

> Perhaps our favorite TV program is sponsored by the manufacturer of that car. Perhaps we have seen pictures of many beautiful or prestigeful persons driving it—in pleasant or glamorous places. Perhaps the car has been designed with respect to our motivational patterns: the device on the hood is a phallic symbol; or the horsepower has been stepped up to please our competitive spirit in enabling us to pass other cars swiftly (or, as the advertisements say, 'safely'). The concept of freedom that has emerged as part of the cultural practice of our group makes little or no provision for recognizing or dealing with these kinds of control.[3]

In purchasing a car we may think we are free, Skinner is claiming, when in fact our act is completely controlled by factors in our environment and in our history of reinforcement. Advertising is one such factor.

A look at some other advertising techniques may reinforce the suspicion that Madison Avenue controls us like so many puppets. T.V. watchers surely have noticed that some of the more repugnant ads are shown over and over again, *ad nauseum*. My favorite, or most hated, is the one about A-1 Steak Sauce which goes something like this: Now, ladies and gentlemen, what *is* hamburger? It has succeeded in destroying my taste for hamburger, but it has surely drilled the name of A-1 Sauce into my head. And that is the point of it. Its very repetitiousness has generated what ad theorists call *information*. In this case it is indirect information, information derived not from the content of what is said but from the fact that it is said so often and so vividly that it sticks in one's mind—i.e., the information yield has increased. And not only do I always remember A-1 Sauce when I go to the grocers, I tend to assume that any product advertised so often has to be good—and so I usually buy a bottle of the stuff.

Still another technique: On a recent show of the television program 'Hard Choices' it was demonstrated how subliminal suggestion can be used to control customers. In a New Orleans department store, messages to the effect that shoplifting is wrong, illegal, and subject to punishment were blended into the Muzak background music and masked so as not to be consciously audible. The store reported a dramatic drop in shoplifting. The program host conjectured whether a logical extension of this technique would be to broadcast subliminal advertising messages to the effect that the store's $15.99 sweater special is the "bargain of a lifetime." Actually, this application of subliminal suggestion to advertising has already taken place. Years ago in New Jersey a cinema was reported to have flashed subthreshold ice cream ads onto the screen during regular showings of the film—and, yes, the concession stand did a landslide business.[4]

Puffery, indirect information transfer, subliminal advertising—are these techniques of manipulation and control whose success shows that many of us have forfeited our autonomy and become a community, or herd, of packaged souls?[5] The business world and the advertising industry certainly reject this interpretation of their efforts. *Business Week*, for example, dismissed the charge that the science of behavior, as utilized by advertising, is engaged in human engineering and manipulation. It editorialized to the effect that "it is hard to find anything very sinister about a science whose principle conclusion is that you get along with people by giving them what they want."[6] The theme is familiar: businesses just give the consumer what he/she wants; if they didn't they wouldn't stay in business very long. Proof that the consumer wants the products advertised is given by the fact that he buys them, and indeed often returns to buy them again and again.

The techniques of advertising we are discussing have had their more intellectual defenders as well. For example, Theodore Levitt, Professor of Business Administration at the Harvard Business School, has defended the practice of puffery and the use of techniques dependent on motivational research.[7] What would be the consequences, he asks us, of deleting all exaggerated claims and fanciful associations from advertisements? We would be left with literal descriptions of the empirical characteristics of products and their functions. Cosmetics would be presented as facial and bodily lotions and powders which produce certain odor and color changes; they would no longer offer hope or adventure. In addition to the fact that these products would not then sell as well, they would not, according to Levitt, please us as much either. For it is hope and adventure we want when we buy them. We want automobiles not just for transportation, but for the feelings of power and status they give us. Quoting T. S. Eliot to the effect that "Human kind cannot bear very much reality," Levitt argues that advertising is an effort to "transcend nature in the raw," to "augment what nature has so crudely fashioned." He maintains that "everybody everywhere wants to modify, transform, embellish, enrich and reconstruct the world around him." Commerce takes the same liberty with reality as the artist and the priest—in all three instances the purpose is "to influence the audience by creating illusions, symbols, and implications that promise more than pure functionality." For example, "to amplify the temple in men's eyes, (men of cloth) have, very realistically, systematically sanctioned the embellishment of the houses of the gods with the same kind of luxurious design and expensive decoration that Detroit puts into a Cadillac." A poem, a temple, a Cadillac—they all elevate our spirits, offering imaginative promises and symbolic interpretations of our mundane activities. Seen in this light, Levitt claims, "Embellishment and distortion are among advertising's legitimate and socially desirable purposes." To reject these techniques of advertising would be "to deny man's honest needs and values."

Phillip Nelson, a Professor of Economics at SUNY-Binghamton, has developed an interesting defense of indirect information advertising.[8] He argues that even when the message (the direct information) is not credible, the fact that the brand is advertised, and advertised frequently, is valuable indirect information for the consumer. The reason for this is that the brands advertised most are more likely to be better buys—losers won't be advertised a lot, for it simply wouldn't pay to do so. Thus even if the advertising claims made for a widely advertised product are empty, the consumer reaps the benefit of the indirect information which shows the product to be a good buy.

I don't know of any attempt to defend the use of subliminal suggestion in advertising, but I can imagine one form such an attempt might take. Advertising information, even if perceived below the level of conscious awareness, must appeal to some desire on the part of the audience if it is to trigger a purchasing response. Just as the admonition not to shoplift speaks directly to the superego, the sexual virtues of TR-7's, Pongo Peach, and Betty Crocker cake mix present themselves directly to the id, bypassing the pesky reality principle of the ego. With a little help from our advertising friends, we may remove a few of the discontents of civilization and perhaps even enter into the paradise of polymorphous perversity.[9]

The defense of advertising which suggests that advertising simply is information which allows us to purchase what we want, has in turn been challenged. Does business, largely through its advertising efforts, really make available to the consumer what he/she desires and demands? John Kenneth Galbraith has denied that the matter is as straightforward as this.[10] In his opinion the desires to which business is supposed to respond, far from being original to the consumer, are often themselves created by business. The producers make both the product and the desire for it, and the "central function" of advertising is "to create desires." Galbraith coins the term 'The Dependence Effect' to designate the way wants depend on the same process by which they are satisfied.

David Braybrooke has argued in similar and related ways.[11] Even though the consumer is, in a sense, the final authority concerning what he wants, he may come to see, according to Braybrooke, that he was mistaken in wanting what he did. The statement 'I want x,' he tells us, is not incorrigible but is "ripe for revision." If the consumer had more objective information than he is provided by product puffing, if his values had not been mixed up by motivational research strategies (e.g., the confusion of sexual and automotive values), and if he had an expanded set of choices instead of the limited set offered by profit-hungry corporations, then he might want something quite different from what he presently wants. This shows, Braybrooke thinks, the extent to which the consumer's wants are a function of advertising and not necessarily representative of his real or true wants.

The central issue which emerges between the above critics and defenders of advertising is this: do the advertising techniques we have discussed involve a violation of human autonomy and a manipulation and control of consumer behavior, *or* do they simply provide an efficient and cost-effective means of giving the consumer information on the basis of which he or she makes a free choice. Is advertising information, or creation of desire?

To answer this question we need a better conceptual grasp of what is involved in the notion of autonomy. This is a complex, multifaceted concept, and we need to approach it through the more determinate notions of (a) autonomous desire, (b) rational desire and choice, (c) free choice, and (d) control or manipulation. In what follows I shall offer some tentative and very incomplete analyses of these concepts and apply the results to the case of advertising.

(a) Autonomous Desire

Imagine that I am watching T.V. and see an ad for Grecian Formula 16. The thought occurs to me that if I purchase some and apply it to my beard, I will soon look younger—in fact I might even be myself again. Suddenly I want to be myself! I want to be young again! So I rush out and buy a bottle. This is our question: was the desire to be younger manufactured by the commercial, or was it 'original to me' and truly mine? Was it autonomous or not?

F. A. von Hayek has argued plausibly that we should not equate nonautonomous desires, desires which are not original to me or truly mine, with those which are culturally induced.[12] If we did equate the two, he points out, then the desires for music, art, and knowledge could not properly be attributed to a person as original to him, for these are surely induced culturally. The only desires a person would really have as his own in this case would be the purely physical ones for food, shelter, sex, etc. But if we reject the equation of the nonautonomous and the culturally induced, as von Hayek would have us do, then the mere fact that my desire to be young again is caused by the T.V. commercial—surely an instrument of popular culture transmission—does not in and of itself show that this is not my own, autonomous desire. Moreover, even if I never before felt the need to look young, it doesn't follow that this new desire is any less mine. I haven't always liked 1969 Aloxe Corton Burgundy or the music of Satie, but when the desires for these things first hit me, they were truly mine.

This shows that there is something wrong in setting up the issue over advertising and behavior control as a question whether our desires are truly ours *or* are created in us by advertisements. Induced and autonomous desires do not separate into two mutually exclusive classes. To obtain a better understanding of autonomous and nonautonomous desires, let us consider some cases of a desire which a person does not *acknowledge* to be his own even though he *feels* it. The kleptomaniac has a desire to steal which in many instances he repudiates, seeking by treatment to rid himself of it. And if I were suddenly overtaken by a desire to attend an REO concert, I would immediately disown this desire, claiming possession or momentary madness. These are examples of desires which one might have but with which one would not identify. They are experienced as foreign to one's character or personality. Often a person will have what Harry Frankfurt calls a second-order desire, that is to say, a desire *not* to have another desire.[13] In such cases, the first-order desire is thought of as being nonautonomous, imposed on one. When on the contrary a person has a second-order desire to maintain and fulfill a first-order desire, then the first-order desire is truly his own, autonomous, original to him. So there is in fact a distinction between desires which are the agent's own and those which are not, but this is not the same as the distinction between desires which are innate to the agent and those which are externally induced.

If we apply the autonomous/nonautonomous distinction derived from Frankfurt to the desires brought about by advertising, does this show that advertising is responsible for creating desires which are not truly the agent's own? Not necessarily, and indeed not often. There may be some desires I feel which I have picked up from advertising and which I disown—for instance, my desire for A-1 Steak Sauce. If I act on these desires it can be said that I have been led by advertising to act in a way foreign to my nature. In these cases my autonomy has been violated. But most of the desires induced by advertising I fully accept, and hence most of these desires are autonomous. The most vivid demonstration of this is that I often return to purchase the same product over and over again, without regret or remorse. And when I don't, it is more likely that the desire has just faded than that I have repudiated it. Hence, while advertising may violate my autonomy by leading me to act on desires which are not truly mine, this seems to be the exceptional case.

Note that this conclusion applies equally well to the case of subliminal advertising. This may generate subconscious desires which lead to purchases, and the act of purchasing these goods may be inconsistent with other conscious desires I have, in which case I might repudiate my behavior and by implication the subconscious cause of it. But my subconscious desires may not be inconsistent in this way with my conscious ones; my id may be cooperative and benign rather than hostile and malign.[14] Here again, then, advertising may or may not produce desires which are 'not truly mine.'

What are we to say in response to Braybrooke's argument that insofar as we might choose differently if advertisers gave us better information and more options, it follows that the desires we have are to be attributed more to advertising than to our own real inclinations? This claim seems empty. It amounts to saying that if the world we lived in, and we ourselves, were different, then we would want different things. This is surely true, but it is equally true of our desire for shelter as of our desire for Grecian Formula 16. If we lived in a tropical paradise we would not need or desire shelter. If we were immortal, we would not desire youth. What is true of all desires can hardly be used as a basis for criticizing some desires by claiming that they are nonautonomous.

(b) Rational Desire and Choice

Braybrooke might be interpreted as claiming that the desires induced by advertising are often irrational ones in the sense that they are not expressed by an agent who is in full possession of the facts about the products advertised or about the alternative products which might be offered him. Following this line of thought, a possible criticism of advertising is that it leads us to act on irrational desires or to make irrational choices. It might be said that our autonomy has been violated by the fact that we are prevented from following our rational wills or that we have been denied the 'positive freedom' to develop our true, rational selves. It might be claimed that the desires induced in us by advertising are false desires in that they do not reflect our essential, i.e., rational, essence.

The problem faced by this line of criticism is that of determining what is to count as rational desire or rational choice. If we require that the desire or choice be the product of an awareness of *all* the facts about the product, then surely every one of us is always moved by irrational desires and makes nothing but irrational choices. How could we know all the facts about a product? If it be required only that we possess all of the *available* knowledge about the product advertised, then we still have to face the problem that not all available knowledge is *relevant* to a rational choice. If I am purchasing a car, certain engineering features will be, and others won't be, relevant, *given what I want in a car.* My prior desires determine the relevance of information. Normally a rational desire or choice is thought to be one based upon relevant information, and information is relevant if it shows how other, prior desires may be satisfied. It can plausibly be claimed that it is such prior desires that advertising agencies acknowledge, and that the agencies often provide the type of information that is relevant in light of these desires. To the extent that this is true, advertising does not inhibit our rational wills or our autonomy as rational creatures.

(c) Free Choice

It might be said that some desires are so strong or so covert that a person cannot resist them, and that when he acts on such desires he is not acting freely or voluntarily but is rather the victim of an irresistible impulse or an unconscious drive. Perhaps those who condemn advertising feel that it produces this kind of desire in us and consequently reduces our autonomy.

This raises a very difficult issue. How do we distinguish between an impulse we *do* not resist and one we *could* not resist, between freely giving in to a desire and succumbing to one? A person acts or chooses freely if he does so for a reason, that is, if he can adduce considerations which justify in his mind the act in question. Many of our actions are in fact free because this condition frequently holds. Often, however, a person will act from habit, or whim, or impulse, and on these occasions he does not have a reason in mind. Nevertheless he often acts voluntarily in these instances, i.e., he could have acted otherwise. And this is because if there *had been* a reason for acting otherwise of which he was aware, he would in fact have done so. Thus acting from habit or impulse is not necessarily to act in an involuntary manner. If, however, a person is aware of a good reason to do x and still follows his impulse to do y, then he can be said to be impelled by irresistible impulse and hence to act involuntarily. Many kleptomaniacs can be said to act involuntarily, for in spite of their knowledge that they likely will be caught and their awareness that the goods they steal have little utilitarian value to them, they nevertheless steal. Here their 'out of character' desires have the upper hand, and we have a case of compulsive behavior.

Applying these notions of voluntary and compulsive behavior to the case of behavior prompted by advertising, can we say that consumers influenced by advertising act compulsively? The unexciting answer is: sometimes they do, sometimes not. I may have an overwhelming, T.V. induced urge to own a Mazda Rx-7 and all the while realize that I can't afford one without severely reducing my family's caloric intake to a dangerous level. If, aware of this good reason not to purchase the car, I nevertheless do so, this shows that I have been the victim of T.V. compulsion. But if I have the urge, as I assure you I do, and don't act on it, or if in some other possible world I could afford an Rx-7, then I have not been the subject of undue influence by Mazda advertising. Some Mazda Rx-7 purchasers act compulsively; others do not. The Mazda advertising effort *in general* cannot be condemned, then, for impairing its customers' autonomy in the sense of limiting free or voluntary choice. Of course the question remains what should be done about the fact that advertising may and does *occasionally* limit free choice.

(d) Control or Manipulation

Briefly let us consider the matter of control and manipulation. Under what conditions do these activities occur? In a recent paper on 'Forms and Limits of Control' I suggested the following criteria:[15]

A person C controls the behavior of another person P *iff*

1. C intends P to act in a certain way A;

2. C's intention is causally effective in bringing about A; and

3. C intends to ensure that all of the necessary conditions of A are satisfied.

These criteria may be elaborated as follows. To control another person it is not enough that one's actions produce certain behavior on the part of that person; additionally one must intend that this happen. Hence control is the intentional production of behavior. Moreover, it is not enough just to have the intention; the intention must give rise to the conditions which bring about the intended effect. Finally, the controller must intend to establish by his actions any otherwise unsatisfied necessary conditions for the production of the intended effect. The controller is not just influencing the outcome, not just having input; he is as it were guaranteeing that the sufficient conditions for the intended effect are satisfied.

Let us apply these criteria of control to the case of advertising and see what happens. Conditions 1 and 3 are crucial. Does the Mazda manufacturing company or its advertising agency intend that I buy an Rx-7? Do they intend that a certain number of people buy the car? *Prima facie* it seems more appropriate to say that they *hope* a certain number of people will buy it, and hoping and intending are not the same. But the difficult term here is 'intend.' Some philosophers have argued that to intend A it is necessary only to desire that A happen and to believe that it will. If this is correct, and if marketing analysis gives the Mazda agency a reasonable belief that a certain segment of the population will buy its product, then, assuming on its part the desire that this happen, we have the conditions necessary for saying that the agency intends that a certain segment purchase the car. If I am a member of this segment of the population, would it then follow that the agency intends that I purchase an Rx-7? Or is control referentially opaque? Obviously we have some questions here which need further exploration.

Let us turn to the third condition of control, the requirement that the controller intend to activate or bring about any otherwise unsatisfied necessary conditions for the production of the intended effect. It is in terms of this condition that we are able to distinguish brainwashing from liberal education. The brainwasher arranges all of the necessary conditions for belief. On the other hand, teachers (at least those of liberal persuasion) seek only to influence their students—to provide them with information and enlightenment which they may absorb *if they wish*. We do not normally think of teachers as controlling their students, for the students' performances depend as well on their own interests and inclinations.

Now the advertiser—does he control, or merely influence, his audience? Does he intend to ensure that all of the necessary conditions for purchasing behavior are met, or does he offer information and symbols which are intended to have an effect only *if* the potential purchaser has certain desires? Undeniably advertising induces some desires, and it does this intentionally, but more often than not it intends to induce a desire for a particular object, *given* that the purchaser already has other desires. Given a desire for youth, or power, or adventure, or ravishing beauty, we are led to desire Grecian Formula 16, Mazda Rx-7's, Pongo Peach, and Distinctive Foundations. In this light, the advertiser is influencing us by appealing to independent desires we already have. He is not creating those basic desires. Hence it seems appropriate to deny that he intends to produce all of the necessary conditions for our purchases, and appropriate to deny that he controls us.

Let me summarize my argument. The critics of advertising see it as having a pernicious effect on the autonomy of consumers, as controlling their lives and manufacturing their very souls. The defense claims that advertising only offers information and in effect allows industry to provide consumers with what they want. After developing some of the philosophical dimensions of this dispute, I have come down tentatively in favor of the advertisers. Advertising may, but certainly does not always or even frequently, control behavior, produce compulsive behavior, or create wants which are not rational or are not truly those of the consumer. Admittedly it may in individual cases do all of these things, but it is innocent of the charge of intrinsically or necessarily doing them or even, I think, of often doing so. This limited potentiality, to be sure, leads to the question whether advertising should be abolished or severely curtailed or regulated because of its potential to harm a few poor souls in the above ways. This is a very difficult question, and I do not pretend to have the answer. I only hope that the above discussion, in showing some of the kinds of harm that can be done by advertising and by indicating the likely limits of this harm, will put us in a better position to grapple with the question.

NOTES

1. Vance Packard, *The Hidden Persuaders* (Pocket Books, New York, 1958), pp. 20–21.

2. *Ibid.*, p. 21.

3. B. F. Skinner, 'Some Issues Concerning the Control of Human Behavior: A Symposium', in Karlins and Andrews (eds.), *Man Controlled* (The Free Press, New York, 1972).

4. For provocative discussion of subliminal advertising, see W. B. Key, *Subliminal Seduction* (The New American Library, New York, 1973), and W. B. Key, *Media Sexploitation* (Prentice-Hall, Inc., Englewood Cliffs, N.J., 1976).

5. I would like to emphasize that in what follows I am discussing these techniques of advertising from the standpoint of the issue of control and not from that of deception. For a good and recent discussion of the many dimensions of possible deception in advertising, see Alex C. Michalos, 'Advertising: Its Logic, Ethics, and Economics' in J. A. Blair and R. H. Johnson (eds.), *Informal Logic: The First International Symposium* (Edgepress, Pt. Reyes, Calif., 1980).

6. Quoted by Packard, *op. cit.*, p. 220.

7. Theodore Levitt, 'The Morality (?) of Advertising', *Harvard Business Review* 48 (1970), 84–92.

8. Phillip Nelson, 'Advertising and Ethics', in Richard T. De George and Joseph A. Pichler (eds.), *Ethics, Free Enterprise, and Public Policy* (Oxford University Press, New York, 1978), pp. 187–198.

9. For a discussion of polymorphous perversity, see Norman O. Brown, *Life Against Death* (Random House, New York, 1969), Chapter III.

10. John Kenneth Galbraith, *The Affluent Society*; reprinted in Tom L. Beauchamp and Norman E. Bowie (eds.), *Ethical Theory and Business* (Prentice-Hall, Englewood Cliffs, 1979), pp. 496–501.

11. David Braybrooke, 'Skepticism of Wants, and Certain Subversive Effects of Corporations on American Values', in Sidney Hook (ed.), *Human Values and Economic Policy* (New York University Press, New York, 1967); reprinted in Beauchamp and Bowie (eds.), *op. cit.*, pp. 502–508.

12. F. A. von Hayek, 'The *Non Sequitur* of the "Dependence Effect,'" *Southern Economic Journal* (1961); reprinted in Beauchamp and Bowie (eds.), *op. cit.*, pp. 508–512.

13. Harry Frankfurt, 'Freedom of the Will and the Concept of a Person', *Journal of Philosophy* **LXVIII** (1971), 5–20.

14. For a discussion of the difference between a malign and a benign subconscious mind, see P. H. Nowell-Smith, 'Psycho-analysis and Moral Language,' *The Rationalist Annual* (1954); reprinted in P. Edwards and A. Pap (eds), A *Modern Introduction to Philosophy*, Revised Edition (The Free Press, New York, 1965), pp. 86–93.

15. Robert L. Arrington, 'Forms and Limits of Control', delivered at the annual meeting of the Southern Society for Philosophy and Psychology, Birmingham, Alabama, 1980.

STRICT PRODUCTS LIABILITY AND COMPENSATORY JUSTICE

GEORGE G. BRENKERT*

I

Strict products liability is the doctrine that the seller of a product has legal responsibilities to compensate the user of that product for injuries suffered because of a defective aspect of the product, even when the seller has not been negligent in permitting that defect to occur.[1] Thus, even though a manufacturer, for example, has reasonably applied the existing techniques of manufacture and has anticipated and cared for nonintended uses of the product, he may still be held liable for injuries a product user suffers if it can be shown that the product was defective when it left the manufacturer's hands.[2]

To say that there is a crisis today concerning this doctrine would be to utter a commonplace which few in the business community would deny. The development of the doctrine of strict products liability, according to most business people, threatens many businesses financially.[3] Furthermore, strict products liability is said to be a morally questionable doctrine, since the manufacturer or seller has not been negligent in permitting the injury-causing defect to occur. On the other hand, victims of defective products complain that they deserve full compensation for injuries sustained in using a defective product whether or not the seller is at fault. Medical expenses and time lost from one's job are costs no individual should have to bear by himself. It is only fair that the seller share such burdens.

In general, discussions of this crisis focus on the limits to which a business ought to be held responsible. Much less frequently, discussions of strict products liability consider the underlying question of whether the doctrine of strict products liability is rationally justifiable. But unless this question is answered it would seem premature to seek to determine the limits to which businesses ought to be held liable in such cases. In the following paper I discuss this underlying philosophical question and argue that there is a rational justification for strict products liability which links it to the very nature of the free enterprise system.

II

It should be noted at the outset that strict products liability is not absolute liability. To hold a manufacturer legally (and morally) responsible for any and all injuries which product users might sustain would be morally perverse. First, it would deny the product user's own responsibility to take care in his actions and to suffer the consequences when he does not. It would therefore constitute an extreme form of moral and legal paternalism.

Original article. Copyright © 1984 by George Brenkert. Reprinted by permission of the author.

*Department of Philosophy, The University of Tennessee.

Second, if the product is not defective, there is no significant moral connection between anything the manufacturer has done or not done and the user's injuries other than the production and sale of the product. This provides no basis for holding the manufacturer responsible for the user's injuries. If, because of my own carelessness, I cut myself with my new pocket knife, the fact that I just bought my knife from Blade Manufacturing Company provides no moral reason to hold Blade Manufacturing responsible for my injury.

Finally, though the manufacturer's product might be said to have harmed the person,[4] it is wholly implausible, when the product is not defective and the manufacturer not negligent, to say that the manufacturer has harmed the user. Thus, there would seem to be no moral basis upon which to maintain that the manufacturer has any liability to the product user. Strict products liability, on the other hand, holds that the manufacturer can be held liable when the product can be shown to be defective, even though the manufacturer himself has not been negligent.[5]

Two justifications of strict products liability are predominant in the literature. Both, I believe, are untenable. They are:

1. To hold producers strictly liable for defective products will cut down on the number of accidents and injuries which occur by forcing manufacturers to make their products safer.[6]

2. The manufacturer is best able to distribute to others the costs of injuries which users of his defective products suffer.[7]

There are several reasons why the first justification is unacceptable. First, it has been argued plausibly that almost everything that can be attained through the use of strict liability to force manufacturers to make their products safer can also be attained in other ways through the law.[8] Hence, to hold manufacturers strictly liable will not necessarily help reduce the number of accidents. The incentive to produce safer products already exists, without invoking the doctrine of strict products liability.

Second, at least some of the accidents which have been brought under strict liability have been caused by features of the products which the manufacturers could not have foreseen or controlled. At the time the product was designed and manufactured, the technological knowledge required to discover the hazard and take steps to minimize its effects was not available. It is doubtful that in such cases the imposition of strict liability upon the manufacturer could reduce accidents.[9] Thus, again, this justification for strict products liability fails.[10]

Third, the fact that the imposition of legal restraints and/or penalties would have a certain positive effect—for example, reduce accidents—does not show that the imposition of those penalties would be just. It has been pointed out before that the rate of crime might be cut significantly if the law would imprison the wives and children of men who break the law. Regardless of how correct that claim may be, to use these means in order to achieve a significant reduction in the crime rate would be unjust. Thus, the fact—if fact it be—that strict liability would cut down on the amount of dangerous and/or defective products placed on the market, and thus reduce the number of accidents and injuries, does not justify the imposition of strict liability on manufacturers.

Finally, the above justification is essentially a utilitarian appeal which emphasizes the welfare of the product users. It is not obvious, however, that those who use this justification have ever undertaken the utilitarian analysis which would show that greater protection of the product user's safety would further the welfare of product users. If emphasis on product user safety would cut down on the number and variety of products produced, the imposition of strict liability might not enhance product user welfare; rather, it might lower it. Furthermore, if the safety of product users is the predominant concern, massive public and private education safety campaigns might do as much or more to lower the level of accidents and injuries as strict products liability.

The second justification given for strict products liability is also utilitarian in nature. Among the factors cited in favor of this justification are the following:

1. "An individual harmed by his or her use of a defective product is often unable to bear the loss individually."

2. "Distribution of losses among all users of a product would minimize both individual and aggregate loss."

3. "The situation of producers and marketers in the marketplace enables them conveniently to distribute losses among all users of a product by raising prices sufficiently to compensate those harmed (which is what in fact occurs where strict liability is in force)."[11]

This justification is also defective.

First, the word "best" in the phrase "best able to distribute to others the cost" is usually understood in a nonmoral sense; it is used to signify that the manufacturer can most efficiently pass on the costs of injuries to others. Once this use of "best" is recognized, surely we may ask why these costs ought to be passed on to other consumers and/or users of the same product or line of products. Even if the imposition of strict liability did maximize utility, it might still be unjust to use the producer as the distributor of losses.[12] Indeed, some have objected that to pass along the costs of such accidents to other consumers of a manufacturer's products is unjust to them.[13] The above justification is silent with regard to these legitimate objections.

Second, manufacturers may not always be in the best (that is, most efficient and economical) position to pass costs on to customers. Even in monopoly areas, there are limitations. Furthermore, some products are subject to an elastic demand, preventing the manufacturer from passing along the costs.[14] Finally, the present justification could justify far more than is plausible. If the reason for holding the manufacturer liable is that the manufacturer is the "best" administrator of costs, one might plausibly argue that the manufacturer should pay for injuries suffered not only when he is not negligent but also when the product is not defective. Theoretically, at least, this argument could be extended from cases of strict liability to that of absolute liability.

Whether this argument holds up depends upon contingent facts concerning the nature and frequency of injuries people suffer using products, the financial strength of businesses, and the kinds and levels of products liability insurance available to them. It does not depend on any morally significant elements in the relationship between the producer and the product user. Such an implication, I believe, undercuts the purported moral nature of this justification and reveals it for what it is: an economic, not a moral, justification.

Accordingly, neither of the major current justifications for the imposition of strict liability appears to be acceptable. If this is the case, is strict products liability a groundless doctrine, willfully and unjustly imposed on manufacturers?

III

This question can be asked in two different ways. On the one hand, it can be asked within the assumptions of the free enterprise system. On the other hand, it could be raised with the premise that the fundamental assumptions of that socioeconomic system are also open to revision and change. In the following, I will discuss the question *within* the general assumptions of the free enterprise system. Since these assumptions are broadly made in legal and business circles it is interesting to determine what answer might be given within these constraints. Indeed, I suggest that only within these general assumptions can strict products liability be justified.

To begin with, it is crucial to remember that what we have to consider is the relationship between an entity doing business and an individual.[15] The strict liability attributed to business would not be attributed to an individual who happened to sell some product he had made to his neighbor or a stranger. If Peter sold an article he had made to Paul and Paul hurt himself because the article had a defect which occurred through no negligence of Peter's, we would not normally hold Peter morally responsible to pay for Paul's injuries.

Peter did not claim, we may assume, that the product was absolutely risk-free. Had he kept it, he himself might have been injured by it. Paul, on the other hand, bought it. He was not pressured, forced, or coerced to do so. Peter mounted no advertising campaign. Though Paul might not have been injured if the product had been made differently, he supposedly bought it with open eyes. Peter did not seek to deceive Paul about its qualities. The product, both its good and bad qualities, became his when he bought it.

In short, we assume that both Peter and Paul are morally autonomous individuals capable of knowing their own interests, that such individuals can legitimately exchange their ownership of various products, that the world is not free of risks, and that not all injuries one suffers in such a world can be blamed on others. To demand that Peter protect Paul from such dangers and/or compensate him for injuries resulting from such dangers is to demand that Peter significantly reduce the risks of the product he offers to Paul and to protect Paul from encountering those risks. However, this demand smacks of paternalism and undercuts our basic moral assumptions about such relations. Hence, in such a case, Peter is not morally responsible for Paul's injuries or, because of this transaction, obligated to aid him. Perhaps Peter owes Paul aid because Paul is an injured neighbor or person. Perhaps for charitable reasons Peter ought to help Paul. But Peter has no moral obligation stemming from the sale itself to provide aid.

It is different for businesses. They have been held to be legally and morally obliged to pay the victim for his injuries. Why? What is the difference? The difference is that when Paul is hurt by a defective product from corporation X, he is hurt by something produced in a socioeconomic system purportedly embodying free enterprise. In other words, among other things:

1. Each business and/or corporation produces articles or services it sells for profit.

2. Each member of this system competes with other members of the system in trying to do as well as it can for itself not simply in each exchange, but through each exchange for its other values and desires.

3. Competition is to be "open and free, without deception or fraud."

4. Exchanges are voluntary and undertaken when each party believes it can benefit thereby. One party provides the means for another party's ends if the other party will provide the first party the means to its ends.[16]

5. The acquisition and disposition of ownership rights—that is, of private property—is permitted in such exchanges.

6. No market or series of markets constitutes the whole of a society.

7. Law, morality, and government play a role in setting acceptable limits to the nature and kinds of exchange in which people may engage.[17]

What is it about such a system which would justify claims of strict products liability against businesses? Calabresi has suggested that the free enterprise system is essentially a system of strict liability.[18] Thus the very nature of the free enterprise system justifies such liability claims. His argument has two parts. First, he claims that "bearing risks is both the function of, and justification for, private enterprise in a free enterprise society."[19] "Free enterprise is prized, in classical economics, precisely because it fosters the creation of entrepreneurs who will take such uninsurable risks, who will, in other words, gamble on uncertainty and demonstrate their utility by surviving—by winning more than others."[20]

Accordingly, the nature of private enterprise requires individual businesses to assume the burden of risk in the production and distribution of its products. However, even if we grant that this characterization of who must bear the risks "in deciding what goods are worthy of producing and what new entrants into an industry are worth having" is correct, it would not follow that individual businesses ought to bear the burden of risk in cases of accidents.

Calabresi himself recognizes this. Thus in the second part of his argument he maintains that there is a close analogy which lets us move from the regular risk-bearing businesses must accept in the marketplace to the bearing of risks in accidents: "although . . . [the above characterization] has concerned *regular* entrepreneurial-product risks, not accident risks, the analogy is extremely close."[21] He proceeds to draw the analogy, however, in the following brief sentence: "As with product-accident risks, our society starts out by allocating ordinary product-production risks in ways which try to maximize the chances that incentives will be placed on those most suited to 'manage' these risks."[22] In short, he asserts that the imposition of strict products liability on business will be the most effective means of reducing such risks.

But such a view does not really require, as we have seen in the previous section, any assumptions about the nature of the free enterprise system. It could be held independently of such assumptions. Further, this view is simply a form of the first justificatory argument we discussed and rejected in the previous section. We can hardly accept it here just by attaching it to the nature of free enterprise.

Nevertheless, Calabresi's initial intuitions about a connection between the assumptions of the free enterprise system and the justification of strict products liability are correct. However, they must be developed in the following, rather different, manner. In the free enterprise system, each person and/or business is obligated to follow the rules and understandings which define this socioeconomic system. Following the rules is expected to channel competition among individuals and businesses to socially positive results. In providing the means to fulfill the ends of others, one's own ends also get fulfilled.

Though this does not happen in every case, it is supposed to happen most of the time. Those who fail in their competition with others may be the object of charity, but not of other duties. Those who succeed, qua members of this socioeconomic system, do not have moral duties to aid those who fail. Analogously, the team which loses the game may receive our sympathy but the winning team is not obligated to help it to win the next game or even to play it better. Those who violate the rules, however, may be punished or penalized, whether or not the violation was intentional and whether or not it redounded to the benefit of the violator. Thus, a team may be assessed a penalty for something that a team member did unintentionally to a member of the other team but which injured the other team's chances of competition in the game by violating the rules.

This point may be emphasized by another instance involving a game that brings us closer to strict products liability. Imagine that you are playing table tennis with another person in his newly constructed table tennis room. You are both avid table tennis players and the game means a lot to both of you. Suppose that after play has begun, you are suddenly and quite obviously blinded by the light over the table—the light shade has a hole in it which, when it turned in your direction, sent a shaft of light unexpectedly into your eyes. You lose a crucial point as a result. Surely it would be unfair of your opponent to seek to maintain his point because he was faultless— after all, he had not intended to blind you when he installed that light shade. You would correctly object that he had gained the point unfairly, that you should not have to give up the point lost, and that the light shade should be modified so that the game can continue on a fair basis. It is only fair that the point be played over.

Businesses and their customers in a free enterprise system are also engaged in competition with each other.[23] The competition here, however, is multifaceted as each tries to gain the best agreement he can from the other with regard to the buying and selling of raw materials, products, services, and labor. Such agreements must be voluntary. The competition which leads to them cannot involve coercion. In addition, such competition must be fair and ultimately result in the benefit of the entire society through the operation of the proverbial invisible hand.

Crucial to the notion of fairness of competition are not simply the demands that the competition be open, free, and honest, but also that each person in a society be given an equal opportunity to participate in the system in order to fulfill his or her own particular ends. Friedman formulates this notion in the following manner:

> . . . the priority given to equality of opportunity in the hierarchy of values . . . is manifested particularly in economic policy. The catchwords were free enterprise, competition, laissez-faire. Everyone was to be free to go into any business, follow any occupation, buy any property, subject only to the agreement of the other parties to the transaction. Each was to have the opportunity to reap the benefits if he succeeded, to suffer the costs if he failed. There were to be no arbitrary obstacles. Performance, not birth, religion, or nationality, was the touchstone.[24]

What is obvious in Friedman's comments is that he is thinking primarily of a person as a producer. Equality of opportunity requires that one not be prevented by arbitrary obstacles from participating (by engaging in a productive role of some kind or other) in the system of free enterprise, competition, and so on in order to fulfill one's own ends ("reap the benefits"). Accordingly, monopolies are restricted, discriminatory hiring policies have been condemned, and price collusion is forbidden.

However, each person participates in the system of free enterprise *both* as a worker/producer *and* as a consumer. The two roles interact; if the person could not consume he would not be able to work, and if there were no consumers there would be no work to be done. Even if a particular individual is only (what is ordinarily considered) a consumer, he or she plays a theoretically significant role in the competitive free enterprise system. The fairness of the system depends upon what access he or she has to information about goods and services on the market, the lack of coercion imposed on that person to buy goods, and the lack of arbitrary restrictions imposed by the market and/or government on his or her behavior.

In short, equality of opportunity is a doctrine with two sides which applies both to producers and to consumers. If, then, a person as a consumer or a producer is injured by a defective product—which is one way his activities might arbitrarily be restricted by the action of (one of the members of) the market system—surely his free and voluntary participation in the system of free enterprise will be seriously affected. Specifically, his equal opportunity to participate in the system in order to fulfill his own ends will be diminished.

Here is where strict products liability enters the picture. In cases of strict liability the manufacturer does not intend for a certain aspect of his product to injure someone. Nevertheless, the person is injured. As a result, he is at a disadvantage both as a consumer and as a producer. He cannot continue to play either role as he might wish. Therefore, he is denied that equality of opportunity which is basic to the economic system in question just as surely as he would be if he were excluded from employment by various unintended consequences of the economic system which nevertheless had racially or sexually prejudicial implications. Accordingly, it is fair for the manufacturer to compensate the person for his losses before proceeding with business as usual. That is, the user of a manufacturer's product may justifiably demand compensation from the manufacturer when its product can be shown to be defective and has injured him and harmed his chances of participation in the system of free enterprise.

Hence, strict liability finds a basis in the notion of equality of opportunity which plays a central role in the notion of a free enterprise system. That is why a business which does *not* have to pay for the injuries an individual suffers in the use of a defective article made by that business is felt to be unfair to its customers. Its situation is analogous to that of a player's unintentional violation of a game rule which is intended to foster equality of competitive opportunity.

A soccer player, for example, may unintentionally trip an opposing player. He did not mean to do it; perhaps he himself had stumbled. Still, he has to be penalized. If the referee looked the other way, the tripped player would rightfully object that he had been treated unfairly. Similarly, the manufacturer of a product may be held strictly liable for a product of his which injures a person who uses that product. Even if he is faultless, a consequence of his activities is to render the user of his product less capable of equal participation in the socioeconomic system. The manufacturer should be penalized by way of compensating the victim. Thus, the basis upon which manufacturers are held strictly liable is compensatory justice.

In a society which refuses to resort to paternalism or to central direction of the economy and which turns, instead, to competition in order to allocate scarce positions and resources, compensatory justice requires that the competition be fair and losers be protected.[25] Specifically, no one who loses should be left so destitute that he cannot reenter the competition. Furthermore, those who suffer injuries traceable to defective merchandise or services which restrict their participation in the competitive system should also be compensated.

Compensatory justice does not presuppose negligence or evil intentions on the part of those to whom the injuries might ultimately be traced. It is not perplexed or incapacitated by the relative innocence of all parties involved. Rather, it is concerned with correcting the disadvantaged situation an individual experiences due to accidents or failures which occur in the normal working of that competitive system. It is on this basis that other compensatory programs which alleviate the disabilities of various minority groups are founded. Strict products liability is also founded on compensatory justice.

An implication of the preceding argument is that business is not morally obliged to pay, as such, for the physical injury a person suffers. Rather, it must pay for the loss of equal competitive opportunity—even though it usually is the case that it is because of a (physical) injury that there is a loss of equal opportunity. Actual legal cases in which the injury which prevents a person from going about his or her daily activities is emotional or mental, as well as physical, supports this thesis. If a person were neither mentally nor physically harmed, but still rendered less capable of participating competitively because of a defective aspect of a product, there would still be grounds for holding the company liable.

For example, suppose I purchased and used a cosmetic product guaranteed to last a month. When used by most people it is odorless. On me, however, it has a terrible smell. I can stand the smell, but my co-workers and most other people find it intolerable. My employer sends me home from work until it wears off. The product has not harmed me physically or mentally. Still, on the above argument, I would have reason to hold the manufacturer liable. Any cosmetic product with this result is defective. As a consequence my opportunity to participate in the socioeconomic system is curbed. I should be compensated.

IV

There is another way of arriving at the same conclusion about the basis of strict products liability. To speak of business or the free enterprise system, it was noted above, is to speak of the voluntary exchanges between producer and customer which take place when each party believes he has an opportunity to benefit. Surely customers and producers may miscalculate their benefits; something they voluntarily agreed to buy or sell may turn out not to be to their benefit. The successful person does not have any moral responsibilities to the unsuccessful person—at least as a member of this economic system. If, however, fraud is the reason one person does not benefit, the system is, in principle, undermined. If such fraud were universalized, the system would collapse. Accordingly, the person committing the fraud does have a responsibility to make reparations to the one mistreated.

Consider once again the instance of a person who is harmed by a product he bought or used, a product that can reasonably be said to be defective. Has the nature of the free enterprise system also been undermined or corrupted in this instance? Producer and consumer have exchanged the product but it has not been to their mutual benefit; the manufacturer may have benefited, but the customer has suffered because of the defect. Furthermore, if such exchanges were universalized, the system would also be undone.

Suppose that whenever people bought products from manufacturers the products turned out to be defective and the customers were always injured, even though the manufacturers could not be held negligent. Though one party to such exchanges might benefit, the other party always suffered. If the rationale for this economic system— the reason it was adopted and is defended—were that in the end both parties share the equal opportunity to gain, surely it would collapse with the above consequences. Consequently, as with fraud, an economic system of free enterprise requires that injuries which result from defective products be compensated. The question is: Who is to pay for the compensation?

There are three possibilities. The injured party could pay for his own injuries. However, this is implausible since what is called for is compensation and not merely payment for injuries. If the injured party had simply injured himself, if he had been negligent or careless, then it is plausible that he should pay for his own injuries. No compensation is at stake here. But in the present case the injury stems from the actions of a particular manufacturer who, albeit unwittingly, placed the defective product on the market and stands to gain through its sale.

The rationale of the free enterprise system would be undermined, we have seen, if such actions were universalized, for then the product user's equal opportunity to benefit from the system would be denied. Accordingly, since the rationale and motivation for an individual to be part of this socioeconomic system is his opportunity to gain from participation in it, justice requires that the injured product user receive compensation for his injuries. Since the individual can hardly compensate himself, he must receive compensation from some other source.

Second, some third party—such as government—could compensate the injured person. This is not wholly implausible if one is prepared to modify the structure of the free enterprise system. And, indeed, in the long run this may be the most plausible course of action. However, if one accepts the structure of the free enterprise system, this alternative must be rejected because it permits the interference of government into individual affairs.[26]

Third, we are left with the manufacturer. Suppose a manufacturer's product, even though the manufacturer wasn't negligent, always turned out to be defective and injured those using his products. We might sympathize with his plight, but he would either have to stop manufacturing altogether (no one would buy such products) or else compensate the victims for their losses. (Some people might buy and use his products under these conditions.) If he forced people to buy and use his products he would corrupt the free enterprise system. If he did not compensate the injured users, they would not buy and he would not be able to sell his products. Hence, he could partake of the free enterprise system—that is, sell his products—only if he compensated his user/victims. Accordingly, the sale of this hypothetical line of defective products would be voluntarily accepted as just or fair only if compensation were paid the user/victims of such products by the manufacturer.

The same conclusion follows even if we consider a single defective product. The manufacturer put the defective product on the market. Because of his actions others who seek the opportunity to participate on an equal basis in this system in order to benefit therefrom are unable to do so. Thus, a result of his actions, even though unintended, is to undermine the system's character and integrity. Accordingly, when a person is injured in his attempt to participate in this system, he is owed compensation by the manufacturer. The seller of the defective article must not jeopardize the equal opportunity of the product user to benefit from the system. The seller need not guarantee that the buyer/user will benefit from the purchase of the product; after all, the buyer may miscalculate or be careless in the use of a nondefective product. But if he is not careless or has not miscalculated, his opportunity to benefit from the system is illegitimately harmed if he is injured in its use because of the product's defectiveness. He deserves compensation.

It follows from the arguments in this and the preceding section that strict products liability is not only compatible with the system of free enterprise but that if it were not attributed to the manufacturer the system itself would be morally defective. And the justification for requiring manufacturers to pay compensation when people are injured by defective products is that the demands of compensatory justice are met.[27]

NOTES

1. This characterization of strict products liability is adapted from Alvin S. Weinstein et al., *Products Liability and the Reasonably Safe Product* (New York: John Wiley & Sons, 1978), ch. 1. I understand the seller to include the manufacturer, the retailer, distributors, and wholesalers. For the sake of convenience, I will generally refer simply to the manufacturer.

2. Cf. John W. Wade, "On Product 'Design Defects' and Their Actionability," 33 *Vanderbilt Law Review* 553 (1980); Weinstein et al., *Products Liability and the Reasonably Safe Product*, pp. 8, 28–32; Reed Dickerson, "Products Liability: How Good Does a Product Have to Be?" 42 *Indiana Law Journal* 308–316 (1967). Section 402A of the Restatement (Second) of Torts characterizes the seller's situation in this fashion: "the seller has exercised all possible care in the preparation and sale of his product."

3. Cf. John C. Perham, "The Dilemma in Product Liability," *Dun's Review*, 109 (1977), pp. 48–50, 76; W. Page Keeton, "Products Liability–Design Hazards and the Meaning of

Defect," 10 *Cumberland Law Review* 293–316 (1979); Weinstein et al., *Products Liability and the Reasonably Safe Product*, ch. 1.

4. More properly, of course, the person's use of the manufacturer's product harmed the product user.

5. Clearly one of the central questions confronting the notion of strict liability is what is to count as "defective." With few exceptions, it is held that a product is defective if and only if it is unreasonably dangerous. There have been several different standards proposed as measures of the defectiveness or unreasonably dangerous nature of a product. However, in terms of logical priorities, it really does not matter what the particular standard for defectiveness is unless we know whether we may justifiably hold manufacturers strictly liable for defective products. That is why I concentrate in this paper on the justifiability of strict products liability.

6. Michel A. Coccia, John W. Dondanville, and Thomas R. Nelson, *Product Liability: Trends and Implications* (New York: American Management Association, 1970), p. 13; W. Page Keeton, "The Meaning of Defect in Products Liability Law—A Review of Basic Principles," 45 *Missouri Law Review* 580 (1980); William L. Prosser, "The Assault Upon the Citadel (Strict Liability to the Consumer)," 69 *The Yale Law Journal* 119 (1960).

7. Coccia, Dondanville, and Nelson, *Product Liability: Trends and Implications*, p. 13; Keeton, "The Meaning of Defect in Products Liability Law—A Review of Basic Principles," pp. 580–581; David G. Owen, "Rethinking the Policies of Strict Products Liability," 33 *Vanderbilt Law Review* 686 (1980); Prosser, "The Assault Upon the Citadel (Strict Liability to the Consumer)," p. 1120.

8. Marcus L. Plant, "Strict Liability of Manufacturers for Injuries Caused by Defects in Products—An Opposing View," 24 *Tennessee Law Review* 945 (1957); Prosser, "The Assault Upon the Citadel (Strict Liability to the Consumer)," pp. 1114, 1115, 1119.

9. Keeton, "The Meaning of Defect in Products Liability—A Review of Basic Principles," pp. 594–595; Weinstein et al., *Products Liability and the Reasonably Safe Product*, p. 55.

10. An objection might be raised that such accidents ought not to fall under strict products liability and hence do not constitute a counterexample to the above justification. This objection is answered in Sections III and IV.

11. These three considerations are formulated by Michael D. Smith, "The Morality of Strict Liability in Tort," *Business and Professional Ethics Newsletter*, 3(1979), p. 4. Smith himself, however, was drawing upon Guido Calabresi, "Some Thoughts on Risk Distribution and the Law of Torts," 70 *Yale Law Journal* 499–553 (1961).

12. Smith, "The Morality of Strict Liability in Tort," p. 4. Cf. George P. Fletcher, "Fairness and Utility in Tort Theory," 85 *Harvard Law Review* 537–573 (1972).

13. Rev. Francis E. Lucey, S. J., "Liability Without Fault and the Natural Law," 24 *Tennessee Law Review* 952–962 (1957); Perham, "The Dilemma in Product Liability," pp. 48–49.

14. Plant, "Strict Liability of Manufacturers for Injuries Caused by Defects in Products—An Opposing View," pp. 946–947. By "elastic demand" is meant "a slight increase in price will cause a sharp reduction in demand or will turn consumers to a substitute product" (pp. 946–947).

15. Cf. Prosser, "The Assault Upon the Citadel (Strict Liability to the Consumer)," pp. 1140–1141; Wade, "On Product 'Design Defects' and Their Actionability," p. 569; Coccia, Dondanville, and Nelson, *Product Liability: Trends and Implications*, p. 19.

16. F. A. Hayek emphasizes this point in "The Moral Element in Free Enterprise," in *Studies in Philosophy, Politics, and Economics* (New York: Simon and Schuster, 1967), p. 229.

17. Several of these characteristics have been drawn from Milton Friedman and Rose Friedman, *Free to Choose* (New York: Avon Books, 1980).

18. Calabresi, "Product Liability: Curse or Bulwark of Free Enterprise," 27 *Cleveland State Law Review* 325 (1978).

19. *Ibid.*, p. 321.

20. *Ibid.*

21. *Ibid.*, p. 324.

22. *Ibid.*

23. Cf. H. B. Acton, *The Morals of Markets* (London: Longman Group Limited, 1971), pp. 1–7, 33–37; Milton Friedman and Rose Friedman, *Free to Choose.*

24. Milton Friedman and Rose Friedman, *Free to Choose*, pp. 123–124.

25. I have drawn heavily, in this paragraph, on the fine article by Bernard Boxhill, "The Morality of Reparation," reprinted in *Reverse Discrimination*, ed. Barry R. Gross (Buffalo, New York: Prometheus Books, 1977), pp. 270–278.

26. Cf. Calabresi, "Product Liability: Curse or Bulwark of Free Enterprise, pp. 315–319.

27. I would like to thank the following for providing helpful comments on earlier versions of this paper: Betsy Postow, Jerry Phillips, Bruce Fisher, John Hardwig, and Sheldon Cohen.

chapter eleven
THE ENVIRONMENT

ETHICS AND ECOLOGY

WILLIAM T. BLACKSTONE*

Much has been said about the right to a decent or livable environment. In his 22 January 1970 state of the union address, President Nixon stated: "The great question of the seventies is, shall we surrender to our surroundings, or shall we make our peace with Nature and begin to make the reparations for the damage we have done to our air, our land, and our water? . . . Clean air, clean water, open spaces—these would once again be the birthright of every American; if we act now, they can be." It seems, though, that the use of the term *right* by President Nixon, under the rubric of a "birthright" to a decent environment, is not a strict sense of the term. That is, he does not use this term to indicate that one has or should have either a legal right or a moral right to a decent environment. Rather he is pointing to the fact that in the past our environmental resources have been so abundant that all Americans did in fact inherit a livable environment, and it would be *desirable* that this state of affairs again be the case. Pollution and the exploitation of our environment is precluding this kind of inheritance.

Few would challenge the desirability of such a state of affairs or of such a "birthright." What we want to ask is whether the right to a decent environment can or ought to be considered a right in a stricter sense, either in a legal or moral sense. In contrast to a merely desirable state of affairs, a right entails a correlative duty or obligation on the part of someone or some group to accord one a certain mode of treatment or to act in a certain way.[1] Desirable states of affairs do not entail such correlative duties or obligations.

THE RIGHT TO A LIVABLE ENVIRONMENT AS A HUMAN RIGHT

Let us first ask whether the right to a livable environment can properly be considered to be a human right. For the purposes of this paper, however, I want to avoid raising the more general question of whether there are any human rights at all. Some phi-

Excerpted from "Ethics and Ecology" in *Philosophy and Environmental Crisis*, edited by William T. Blackstone. Copyright © 1974 by the University of Georgia Press, Athens, Ga. Reprinted by permission of the publisher.

*Department of Philosophy, University of Georgia (deceased).

losophers do deny that any human rights exist.[2] In two recent papers I have argued that human rights do exist (even though such rights may properly be overridden on occasion by other morally relevant reasons) and that they are universal and inalienable (although the actual exercise of such rights on a given occasion is alienable).[3] My argument for the existence of universal human rights rests, in the final analysis, on a theory of what it means to be human, which specifies the capacities for rationality and freedom as essential, and on the fact that there are no relevant grounds for excluding any human from the opportunity to develop and fulfill his capacities (rationality and freedom) as a human.

If the right to a livable environment were seen as a basic and inalienable human right, this could be a valuable tool (both inside and outside of legalistic frameworks) for solving some of our environmental problems, both on a national and on an international basis. Are there any philosophical and conceptual difficulties in treating this right as an inalienable human right? Traditionally we have not looked upon the right to a decent environment as a human right or as an inalienable right. Rather, inalienable human or natural rights have been conceived in somewhat different terms; equality, liberty, happiness, life, and property. However, might it not be possible to view the right to a livable environment as being entailed by, or as constitutive of, these basic human or natural rights recognized in our political tradition? If human rights, in other words, are those rights which each human possesses in virtue of the fact that he is human and in virtue of the fact that those rights are essential in permitting him to live a human life (that is, in permitting him to fulfill his capacities as a rational and free being), then might not the right to a decent environment be properly categorized as such a human right? Might it not be conceived as a right which has emerged as a result of changing environmental conditions and the impact of those conditions on the very possibility of human life and on the possibility of the realization of other rights such as liberty and equality? Let us explore how this might be the case.

Given man's great and increasing ability to manipulate the environment, and the devastating effect this is having, it is plain that new social institutions and new regulative agencies and procedures must be initiated on both national and international levels to make sure that the manipulation is in the public interest. It will be necessary, in other words, to restrict or stop some practices and the freedom to engage in those practices. Some look upon such additional state planning, whether national or international, as unnecessary further intrusion on man's freedom. Freedom is, of course, one of our basic values, and few would deny that excessive state control of human action is to be avoided. But such restrictions on individual freedom now appear to be necessary in the interest of overall human welfare and the rights and freedoms of *all* men. Even John Locke with his stress on freedom as an inalienable right recognized that this right must be construed so that it is consistent with the equal right to freedom of others. The whole point of the state is to restrict unlicensed freedom and to provide the conditions for equality of rights for all. Thus it seems to be perfectly consistent with Locke's view and, in general, with the views of the founding fathers of this country to restrict certain rights or freedoms when it can be shown that such restriction is necessary to insure the equal rights of others. If this is so, it has very important implications for the rights to freedom and to property. These rights, perhaps properly seen as inalienable (though this is a controversial philosophical question), are not properly seen as unlimited or unrestricted. When values which we hold dear conflict (for example, individual or group freedom and the freedom of all, individual or group rights and the rights of all, and individual or group welfare and the welfare of the general public) something has to give; some priority must be established. In the case of the abuse and waste of environmental resources, less individual freedom and fewer individual rights for the sake of greater public welfare and equality of rights seem justified. What in the past had been properly regarded as freedoms and rights (given what seemed to be unlimited natural resources and no serious pollution problems) can no longer be so construed, at least not without additional restrictions. We must recognize both the need for such restrictions and the fact that none of our rights can be realized without a livable environment. Both public welfare and equality of rights now require that natural resources not be used simply according to the whim and caprice of individuals or simply for personal profit. This is not to say that all property rights must be denied and that the state must own all productive property, as the Marxist argues. It is to insist that those rights be qualified or restricted in the light of new ecological data and in the interest of the freedom, rights, and welfare of all.

The answer then to the question, Is the right to a livable environment a human right? is yes. Each person has this right *qua* being human and because a livable environment is essential for one to fulfill his human capacities. And given the danger to our environment today and hence the danger to the very possibility of human existence, access to a livable environment must be conceived as a right which imposes upon everyone a correlative moral obligation to respect.

THE RIGHT TO A LIVABLE ENVIRONMENT AS A LEGAL RIGHT

If the right to a decent environment is to be treated as a legal right, then obviously what is required is some sort of legal framework which gives this right a legal status. Such legal frameworks have been proposed. Sen. Gaylord Nelson, originator of Earth Day, proposed a Constitutional Amendment guaranteeing every American an inalienable right to a decent environment.[4] Others want to formulate an entire "environmental bill of rights" to assist in solving our pollution problems. Such a bill of rights or a constitutional revision would provide a legal framework for the enforcement of certain policies bearing on environmental issues. It would also involve the concept of "legal responsibility" for acts which violate those rights. Such legal responsibility is beginning to be enforced in the United States.

Others propose that the right to a decent environment also be a cardinal tenet of international law. Pollution is not merely a national problem but an international one. The population of the entire world is affected by it, and a body of international law, which includes the right to a decent environment and the accompanying policies to save and preserve our environmental resources, would be an even more effective tool than such a framework at the national level. Of course, one does not have to be reminded of the problems involved in establishing international law and in eliciting obedience to it. Conflicts between nations are still settled more by force than by law or persuasion. The record of the United Nations attests to this fact. In the case of international conflict over environmental interests and the use of the environment, the possibility of international legal resolution, at least at this stage of history, is somewhat remote; for the body of enforceable international law on this topic is meager indeed. This is not to deny that this is the direction in which we should (and must) move.

A good case can be made for the view that not all moral or human rights should be legal rights and that not all moral rules should be legal rules. It may be argued that any society which covers the whole spectrum of man's activities with legally enforceable rules minimizes his freedom and approaches totalitarianism. There is this danger. But just as we argued that certain traditional rights and freedoms are properly restricted in order to insure the equal rights and welfare of all, so also it can plausibly be argued that the human right to a livable environment should become a legal one in order to assure that it is properly respected. Given the magnitude of the present dangers to the environment and to the welfare of all humans, and the ingrained habits and rules, or lack of rules, which permit continued waste, pollution, and destruction of our environmental resources, the legalized status of the right to a livable environment seems both desirable and necessary.

It is essential that government step in to prevent the potentially dire consequences of industrial pollution and the waste of environmental resources. Such government regulations need not mean the death of the free enterprise system. The right to private property can be made compatible with the right to a livable environment, for if uniform antipollution laws were applied to all industries, then both competition and private ownership could surely continue. But they would continue within a quite different set of rules and attitudes toward the environment. This extension of government would not be equivalent to totalitarianism. In fact it is necessary to insure equality of rights and freedom, which is essential to a democracy.

ECOLOGY AND ECONOMIC RIGHTS

We suggested above that it is necessary to qualify or restrict economic or property rights in the light of new ecological data and in the interest of the freedom, rights, and welfare of all. In part, this suggested restriction is predicated on the assumption that we cannot expect private business to provide solutions to the multiple pollution problems for which they themselves are responsible. Some companies have taken measures to limit the polluting effect of their operations, and this is an important move. But we are deluding ourselves if we think that private business can function as its own pollution police. This is so for several reasons: the primary objective of private business is economic profit. Stockholders do not ask of a company, "Have you polluted the environment and lowered the quality of the environment for the general public and for future generations?" Rather they ask, "How high is the annual dividend and how much higher is it than the year before?" One can hardly expect organizations whose basic norm is economic profit to be concerned in any great depth with the long-range effects of their operations upon society and future generations or concerned with the hidden cost of their operations in terms of environmental quality to society as a whole. Second, within a free enterprise system companies compete to produce what the public wants at the lowest possible cost. Such competition would preclude the spending of adequate funds to prevent environmental pollution, since this would add tremendously to the cost of the product—unless all other companies would also conform to such antipollution policies. But in a free enterprise economy such policies are not likely to be self-imposed by businessmen. Third, the basic response of the free enterprise system to our economic problems is that we must have greater economic growth or an increase in gross national product. But such growth many ecologists look upon with great alarm, for it can have devastating long-range effects upon our environment. Many of the products of uncontrolled growth are based on artificial needs and actually detract from, rather than contribute to, the quality of our lives. A stationary economy, some economists and ecologists suggest, may well be best for the quality of man's environment and of his life in the long run. Higher GNP does not automatically result in an increase in social well-being, and it should not be used as a measuring rod for assessing economic welfare. This becomes clear when one realizes that the GNP

> aggregates the dollar value of all goods and services produced—the cigarettes as well as the medical treatment of lung cancer, the petroleum from offshore wells as well as the detergents required to clean up after oil spills, the electrical energy produced and the medical and cleaning bills resulting from the air-pollution fuel used for generating the electricity. The GNP allows no deduction for negative production, such as lives lost from unsafe cars or environmental destruction perpetrated by telephone, electric and gas utilities, lumber companies, and speculative builders.[5]

To many persons, of course, this kind of talk is not only blasphemy but subversive. This is especially true when it is extended in the direction of additional controls over corporate capitalism. (Some ecologists and economists go further and challenge whether corporate capitalism can accommodate a stationary state and still retain its major features.[6]) The fact of the matter is that the ecological attitude forces one to reconsider a host of values which have been held dear in the past, and it forces one to reconsider the appropriateness of the social and economic systems which embodied and implemented those values. Given the crisis of our environment, there must be certain fundamental changes in attitudes toward nature, man's use of nature, and man himself. Such changes in attitudes undoubtedly will have far-reaching implications for the institutions of private property and private enterprise and the values embodied in these institutions. Given the crisis we can no longer look upon water and air as free commodities to be exploited at will. Nor can the private ownership of land be seen as a lease to use that land in any way which conforms merely to the personal desires of the owner. In other words, the environmental crisis is forcing us to challenge what had in the past been taken to be certain basic rights of man or at least to restrict those rights. And it is forcing us to challenge institutions which embodied those rights.

ETHICS AND TECHNOLOGY

I have been discussing the relationship of ecology to ethics and to a theory of rights. Up to this point I have not specifically discussed the relation of technology to ethics, although it is plain that technology and its development is responsible for most of our pollution problems. This topic deserves separate treatment, but I do want to briefly relate it to the thesis of this work.

It is well known that new technology sometimes complicates our ethical lives and our ethical decisions. Whether the invention is the wheel or a contraceptive pill, new technology always opens up new possibilities for human relationships and for society, for good and ill. The pill, for example, is revolutionizing sexual morality, for its use can preclude many of the bad consequences normally attendant upon premarital intercourse. *Some* of the strongest arguments against premarital sex have been shot down by this bit of technology (though certainly not all of them). The fact that the use of the pill can prevent unwanted pregnancy does not make premarital sexual intercourse morally right, nor does it make it wrong. The pill is morally neutral, but its existence does change in part the moral base of the decision to engage in premarital sex. In the same way, technology at least in principle can be neutral—neither necessarily good nor bad in its impact on other aspects of the environment. Unfortunately, much of it is bad—very bad. But technology can be meshed with an ecological attitude to the benefit of man and his environment.

I am not suggesting that the answer to technology which has bad environmental effects is necessarily more technology. We tend too readily to assume that new technological developments will always solve man's problems. But this is simply not the case. One technological innovation often seems to breed a half-dozen additional ones which themselves create more environmental problems. We certainly do not solve pollution problems, for example, by changing from power plants fueled by coal to power plants fueled by nuclear energy, if radioactive waste from the latter is worse than pollution from the former. Perhaps part of the answer to pollution problems is less technology. There is surely no real hope of returning to nature (whatever that means) or of stopping *all* technological and scientific development, as some advocate. Even if it could be done, this would be too extreme a move. The answer is not to stop technology, but to guide it toward proper ends, and to set up standards of anti-pollution to which all technological devices must conform. Technology has been and can be used to destroy and pollute an environment, but it can also be used to save and beautify it.

NOTES

1. This is a dogmatic assertion in this context. I am aware that some philosophers deny that rights and duties are correlative. Strictly interpreted this correlativity thesis is false, I believe. There are duties for which there are no correlative rights. But space does not permit discussion of this question here.

2. See Kai Nielsen's "Scepticism and Human Rights," *Monist*, 52, no. 4 (1968): 571–594.

3. See my "Equality and Human Rights," *Monist*, 52, no. 4 (1968): 616–639; and my "Human Rights and Human Dignity," in Laszlo and Gotesky, eds., *Human Dignity*.

4. *Newsweek*, 4 May 1970, p. 26.

5. See Melville J. Ulmer, "More Than Marxist," *New Republic*, 26 December 1970, p. 14.

6. See Murdock and Connell, "All about Ecology," *Center Magazine*, 3, no. 1 (January–February 1970): 63.

THE CASE FOR ECONOMIC GROWTH

WILFRED BECKERMAN*

For some years now it has been very unfashionable to be in favor of continued long-run economic growth. Unless one joins in the chorus of scorn for the pursuit of continued economic growth, one is in danger of being treated either as a coarse Philistine, who is prepared to sacrifice all the things that make life really worth living for vulgar materialist goods, or as a shortsighted, complacent Micawber who is unable to appreciate that the world is living on the edge of a precipice. For it is widely believed that if growth is not now brought to a halt in a deliberate orderly manner, either there will be a catastrophic collapse of output when we suddenly run out of key raw materials, or we shall all be asphyxiated by increased pollution. In other words, growth is either undesirable or impossible, or both. Of course, I suppose this is better than being undesirable and inevitable, but the antigrowth cohorts do not seem to derive much comfort from the fact.

Hence it is not entirely surprising that the antigrowth movement has gathered so much support over the past few years even though it is 99 per cent nonsense. Not 100 per cent nonsense. There does happen to be a one per cent grain of truth in it.

This is that, in the absence of special government policies (policies that governments are unlikely to adopt if not pushed hard by communal action from citizens), pollution will be excessive. This is because—as economists have known for many decades—pollution constitutes what is known in the jargon as an "externality." That is to say, the costs of pollution are not always borne fully—if at all—by the polluter. The owner of a steel mill that belches smoke over the neighborhood, for example, does not usually have to bear the costs of the extra laundry, or of the ill-health that may result. Hence, although he is, in a sense, "using up" some of the environment (the clean air) to produce his steel he is getting this particular factor of production free of charge. Naturally, he has no incentive to economize its use in the same way as he has for other factors of production that carry a cost, such as labor or capital. In all such cases of "externalities," or "spillover effects" as they are sometimes called, the normal price mechanism does not operate to achieve the socially desirable pattern of output or of exploitation of the environment. This defect of the price mechanism needs to be corrected by governmental action in order to eliminate excessive pollution.

But, it should be noted that the "externality" argument, summarized above, only implies that society should cut out "excessive" pollution; not *all* pollution. Pollution should only be cut to the point where the benefits from reducing it further no longer offset the costs to society (labor or capital costs) of doing so.

Mankind has always polluted his environment, in the same way that he has always used up some of the raw materials that he has found in it. When primitive man cooked his meals over open fires, or hunted animals, or fashioned weapons out of rocks and stones, he was exploiting the environment. But to listen to some of the

From *Public Utilities Fortnightly* (Sept. 26, 1972). Reprinted by permission of the publisher.

*Department of Political Economy, University of London.

extreme environmentalists, one would imagine that there was something immoral about this (even though God's first injunction to Adam was to subdue the earth and every living thing that exists in it). If all pollution has to be eliminated we would have to spend the whole of our national product in converting every river in the country into beautiful clear-blue swimming pools for fish. Since I live in a town with 100,000 population but without even a decent swimming pool for the humans, I am not prepared to subscribe to this doctrine.

Anyway, most of the pollution that the environmentalists make such a fuss about, is not the pollution that affects the vast mass of the population. Most people in industrialized countries spend their lives in working conditions where the noise and stench cause them far more loss of welfare than the glamorous, fashionable pollutants, such as PCB's or mercury, that the antigrowth lobby makes such a fuss about. Furthermore, such progress as has been made over the decades to improve the working conditions of the mass of the population in industrialized countries has been won largely by the action of working-class trade unions, without any help from the middle classes that now parade so ostentatiously their exquisite sensibilities and concern with the "quality of life."

The extreme environmentalists have also got their facts about pollution wrong. In the Western world, the most important forms of pollution are being reduced, or are being increasingly subjected to legislative action that will shortly reduce them. In my recently published book *("In Defense of Economic Growth")*[1] I give the facts about the dramatic decline of air pollution in British cities over the past decade or more, as well as the improvement in the quality of the rivers. I also survey the widespread introduction of antipollution policies in most of the advanced countries of the world during the past few years, which will enable substantial cuts to be made in pollution. By comparison with the reductions already achieved in some cases, or envisaged in the near future, the maximum pollution reductions built into the computerized calculations of the Club of Rome[2] can be seen to be absurdly pessimistic.

The same applies to the Club of Rome's assumption that adequate pollution abatement would be so expensive that economic growth would have to come to a halt. For example, the dramatic cleaning up of the air in London cost a negligible amount per head of the population of that city. And, taking a much broader look at the estimates, I show in my book that reductions in pollution many times greater than those which the Club of Rome purports to be the upper limits over the next century can, and no doubt will, be achieved over the next decade in the advanced countries of the world at a cost of only about one per cent to 2 per cent of annual national product.

When confronted with the facts about the main pollutants, the antigrowth lobby tends to fall back on the "risk and uncertainty" argument. This takes the form, "Ah yes, but what about all these new pollutants, or what about undiscovered pollutants? Who knows, maybe we shall only learn in a 100 years' time, when it will be too late, that they are deadly." But life is full of risk and uncertainty. Every day I run the risk of being run over by an automobile or hit on the head by a golf ball. But rational conduct requires that I balance the probabilities of this happening against the costs of insuring against it. It would only be logical to avoid even the minutest chance of some catastrophe in the future if it were costless to do so. But the cost of stopping economic growth would be astronomic. This cost does not merely comprise the loss of any hope of improved standards of living for the vast mass of the world's population, it includes also the political and social costs that would need to be incurred. For only a totalitarian regime could persist on the basis of an antigrowth policy that denied people their normal and legitimate aspirations for a better standard of living.

But leaving aside this political issue, another technical issue which has been much in the public eye lately has been the argument that growth will be brought to a sudden, and hence catastrophic, halt soon on account of the impending exhaustion of raw material supplies. This is the "finite resources" argument; i.e., that since the resources of the world are finite, we could not go on using them up indefinitely.

Now resources are either finite or they are not. If they are, then even zero growth will not save us in the longer run. Perhaps keeping Gross National Product at the present level instead of allowing it to rise by, say, 4 per cent per annum, would enable the world's resources to be spread out for 500 years instead of only 200 years. But the day would still come when we would run out of resources. (The Club of Rome's own computer almost gave the game away and it was obliged to cut off the printout at the point where it becomes clear that, even with zero growth, the world eventually begins to run out of resources!) So why aim only at zero growth? Why not cut output? If resources are, indeed, finite, then there must be some optimum rate at which they should be spread out over time which will be related to the relative importance society attaches to the consumption levels of different generations. The "eco-doomsters" fail to explain the criteria that determine the optimum rate and why they happen to churn out the answer that the optimum growth rate is zero.

And if resources are not, after all, finite, then the whole of the "finite resources" argument collapses anyway. And, in reality, resources are not finite in any meaningful sense. In the first place, what is now regarded as a resource may not have been so in the past decades or centuries before the appropriate techniques for its exploitation or utilization had been developed. This applies, for example, to numerous materials now in use but never heard of a century ago, or to the minerals on the sea bed (e.g., "manganese nodules"), or even the sea water itself from which unlimited quantities of certain basic minerals can eventually be extracted.

In the second place, existing known reserves of many raw materials will never appear enough to last more than, say, twenty or fifty years at current rates of consumption, for the simple reason that it is rarely economically worthwhile to prospect for more supplies than seem to be salable, at prospective prices, given the costs of exploitation and so on. This has always been the case in the past, yet despite dramatic increases in consumption, supplies have more or less kept pace with demand. The "finite resource" argument fails to allow for the numerous ways that the economy and society react to changes in relative prices of a product, resulting from changes in the balance between supply and demand.

For example, a major United States study in 1929 concluded that known tin resources were only adequate to last the world ten years. Forty years later, the Club of Rome is worried because there is only enough to last us another fifteen years. At this rate, we shall have to wait another century before we have enough to last us another thirty years. Meanwhile, I suppose we shall just have to go on using up that ten years' supply that we had back in 1929.

And it is no good replying that demand is growing faster now than ever before, or that the whole scale of consumption of raw materials is incomparably greater than before. First, this proposition has also been true at almost any time over the past few thousand years, and yet economic growth continued. Hence, the truth of such propositions tells us nothing about whether the balance between supply and demand is likely to change one way or the other. And it is this that matters. In other words, it may well be that demand is growing much faster than ever before, or that the whole scale of consumption is incomparably higher, but the same applies to supply. For example, copper consumption rose about fortyfold during the nineteenth century and demand for copper was accelerating, around the turn of the century, for an annual average growth rate of about 3.3 per cent per annum (over the whole century) to about 6.4 per cent per annum during the period 1890 to 1910. Annual copper consumption had been only about 16,000 tons at the beginning of the century, and was about 700,000 tons at the end of it; i.e., incomparably greater. But known reserves at the end of the century were greater than at the beginning.

And the same applies to the postwar period. In 1946 world copper reserves amounted to only about 100 million tons. Since then the annual rate of copper consumption has trebled and we have used up 93 million tons. So there should be hardly any left. In fact, we now have about 300 million tons!

Of course, it may well be that we shall run out of some individual materials; and petroleum looks like one of the most likely candidates for exhaustion of supplies around the end of this century—if the price did not rise (or stay up at its recent level). But there are two points to be noted about this. First, insofar as the price does stay up at its recent level (i.e., in the $10 per barrel region) substantial economies in oil use will be made over the next few years, and there will also be a considerable development of substitutes for conventional sources, such as shale oil, oil from tar sands, and new ways of using coal reserves which are, of course, very many times greater than oil reserves (in terms of common energy units).

Secondly, even if the world did gradually run out of some resources it would not be a catastrophe. The point of my apparently well-known story about "Beckermonium" (the product named after my grandfather who failed to discover it in the nineteenth century) is that we manage perfectly well without it. In fact, if one thinks about it, we manage without infinitely more products than we manage with! In other words, it is absurd to imagine that if, say, nickel or petroleum had never been discovered, modern civilization would never have existed, and that the eventual disappearance of these or other products must, therefore, plunge us back into the Dark Ages.

The so-called "oil crisis," incidentally, also demonstrates the moral hypocrisy of the antigrowth lobby. For leaving aside their mistaken interpretation of the technical reasons for the recent sharp rise in the oil price (i.e., it was not because the world suddenly ran out of oil), it is striking that the antigrowth lobby has seized upon the rise in the price of oil as a fresh argument for abandoning economic growth and for rethinking our basic values and so on. After all, over the past two or three years the economies of many of the poorer countries of the world, such as India, have been hit badly by the sharp rise in the price of wheat. Of course, this only means a greater threat of starvation for a few more million people in backward countries a long way away. That does not, apparently, provoke the men of spiritual and moral sensibility to righteous indignation about the values of the growth-oriented society as much as does a rise in the price of gasoline for our automobiles!

The same muddled thinking is behind the view that mankind has some moral duty to preserve the world's environment or supplies of materials. For this view contrasts strangely with the antigrowth lobby's attack on materialism. After all, copper, oil, and so on are just material objects, and it is difficult to see what moral duty we have to preserve indefinitely the copper species from extinction.

Nor do I believe that we have any overriding moral duty to preserve any particular animal species from extinction. After all, thousands of animal species have become extinct over the ages, without any intervention by mankind. Nobody really loses any sleep over the fact that one cannot now see a live dinosaur. How many of the people who make a fuss about the danger that the tiger species may disappear even bother to go to a zoo to look at one? And what about the web-footed Beckermanipus, which has been extinct for about a million years?

In fact, I am not even sure that the extinction of the human race would matter. The bulk of humanity lead lives full of suffering, sorrow, cruelty, poverty, frustration, and loneliness. One should not assume that because nearly everybody has a natural animal instinct to cling to life they can be said, in any meaningful sense, to be better off alive than if they had never been born. Religious motivations apart, it is arguable that since, by and large (and present company excepted, of course), the human race stinks, the sooner it is extinct the better.

Whilst economic growth alone may never provide a simple means of solving any of these problems, and it may well be that, by its very nature, human society will always create insoluble problems of one kind or another, the absence of economic growth will only make our present problems a lot worse.

NOTES

1. Jonathan Cape, London. The U.S.A. edition, under the title *"Two Cheers for the Affluent Society,"* was published by the St. Martins Press in the fall of 1974.

2. The Club of Rome is an informal international organization of educators, scientists, economists, and others which investigates what it conceives to be the overriding problems of mankind. Its study, "The Limits to Growth," has become the bible of no-growth advocates (Potomac Associates, 1707 L Street, N.W., Washington, D.C.). The study assembled data on known reserves of resources and asked a computer what would happen if demand continued to grow exponentially. Of course, the computer replied everything would break down. The theory of "Beckermonium" lampoons this. Since the author's grandfather failed to discover "Beckermonium" by the mid-1800's, the world has had no supplies of it at all. Consequently, if the club's equations are followed, the world should have come to a halt many years ago. "Beckermonium's" foundation is that the things man has not yet discovered are far more numerous and of greater importance than what has been discovered. (Editor's of *Public Utilities Fortnightly* Note.)

FUN AND GAMES WITH THE GROSS NATIONAL PRODUCT:
The Role of Misleading Indicators in Social Policy

KENNETH E. BOULDING*

The Gross National Product is one of the great inventions of the twentieth century, probably almost as significant as the automobile and not quite so significant as TV. The effect of *physical* inventions is obvious, but social inventions like the GNP change the world almost as much.

The idea of the total product of society is fairly old, certainly dating back to Adam Smith, but the product's measurement is very much a matter of the second half of the 1900s, which I suppose we can call the fortieth half-century. Before 1929 we did not really have any adequate measure of Gross National Product, although its measurement was pioneered by Simon Kuznets and others at the National Bureau of Economic Research from 1919 on. We began to get theories which used it in the '30s, and the cumulative effect has been substantial.

The danger of measures is precisely that they become ideals. You see it even in the thermostat. If we had no Fahrenheit, we would not be stabilizing our room temperature too high. There is a magic about the number 70, and we tend to stabilize the temperature at it, when for the sake of health it might be better at 64 degrees. Certainly, one should never underestimate the power of magic numbers. We are really all Pythagoreans. Once we get a number, we sit down and worship it.

This may seem to be a long way from the GNP. Actually, I am trying to illustrate this: when you measure something, you inevitably affect people's behavior; and as a measure of the total gross output of the economy, the GNP has had an enormous impact on behavior.

A fascinating book, *The Fiscal Revolution in America* (University of Chicago Press, 1969), has been written by Herbert Stein. Stein has done an extremely interesting study, an intellectual history explaining the great change in economic policy from the administration of Herbert Hoover to that of John F. Kennedy.

In the depths of the depression, Hoover engineered a tax increase which exacerbated the depression. That dark hour in the global economy contributed to the rise of Adolf Hitler who precipitated World War II. Had it not been for all those developments we might not have had today's Russian problem; we might not even have had Vietnam. Hoover never knew what hit him because he did not have a Council of Economic Advisers. We did not know much economics in those days. We did not know about the GNP.

Kennedy, in a much milder situation, fostered a tax cut which was an enormous success. As a result, we have had the bloated '60s, the decade without a depression. That should go down in the history books as something spectacular. It is the longest

*Department of Economics, University of Colorado.

boom ever enjoyed in the United States. Economics has had something to do with it. So has the GNP.

These days, if the GNP starts to go down, an economic adviser will go to the President and say, "Oh, look, Mr. President. The GNP dropped half a point. We have to do something about this." This is the beauty of having social cybernetics, an information system that we can use to our advantage.

I suspect that without economics we might have had a Great Depression in the 1950s and '60s. The rate of return on investment in economics may be at least 10,000 percent per annum, because we have not put much into it and we have gotten a lot out of it. On the other hand, this very success worries me. I have revised some folk wisdom lately; one of my edited proverbs is "Nothing fails like success," because you do not learn anything from it. The only thing we ever learn from is failure. Success only confirms our superstitions.

For some strange reason which I do not understand at all a small subculture arose in western Europe which legitimated failure. Science is the only subculture in which failure is legitimate. When astronomers Albert A. Michelson and Edward W. Morley did an experiment which proved to be a dud (in some eyes), they did not just bury it the way the State Department does. Instead, they shouted the results from the housetops, and revised the whole image of the universe. In political life—and to a certain extent in family life—when we make an Edsel, we bury it. We do not learn from our mistakes. Only in the scientific community is failure legitimated. The very success of the GNP and the success of economics should therefore constitute a solemn warning.

I am something of an ecologist at heart, mainly because I am really a preacher, and we know that all ecologists are really preachers under the skin. They are great viewers with alarm. Is there any more single-minded, simple pleasure than viewing with alarm? At times it is even better than sex.

I propose, then, to view the GNP with alarm.

The Gross National Product is supposed to be a measure of economic success, or economic welfare, or something like that. Of course, it is not. So we have to modify it.

In the first place, the Gross National Product is too gross. It includes a number of things which should be netted out. If we are going to get the net benefit of our economic activity, we have to net the national product, and the real question is how net can we make it? We get first what we call the Net National Product, which technically is the Gross National Product minus depreciation.

The GNP is like the Red Queen in *Alice Through the Looking Glass*: it runs as fast as it can to stay where it is. It includes all the depreciation of capital, so we net that out.

We really ought to net out all sorts of other things such as the military, which is also in the GNP and does not produce much. The world war industry is really a self-contained exercise in mutual masochism. The war industry of each country depends on the other's war industry, and it is a largely self-contained system. It has little to do with defense. It is extremely expensive and very dangerous, and we certainly ought to net it out of the product. That takes out about 10 percent.

Things like commuting and pollution also should be netted out. When somebody pollutes something and somebody else cleans it up, the cleanup is added to the national product and the pollution is not subtracted; that, of course, is ridiculous. In fact, I have been conducting a mild campaign to call the GNP the Gross National Cost rather than the product. It really represents what we have to produce, first to stay where we are and second to get a little farther along.

I have been arguing for years (and nobody has paid the slightest attention) that the real measure of economic welfare is not income at all. It is the state or condition of the person, or of the society. Income is just the unfortunate price that we have to pay because the state is corruptible. We have breakfast, and breakfast depreciates; so we must have lunch. The sole reason for lunch is metabolism, and metabolism is decay. Most change is truly decay. Consumption is decay—your automobile wearing out, your clothes becoming threadbare. It is burning up the gasoline. It is eating up the food. Consumption is a bad, not a good thing; production is what we must undergo because of consumption. Things will not stay as they are because of a reality which I sometimes call the Law of Moth and Rust. What causes our illusion that welfare is measured by the Gross National Product or anything else related to income (that is, any flow variable)? The more there is, the more is consumed; therefore, the more we must produce to replace what has been consumed. The bigger the capital stock, the more it will be consumed; hence, the more you have to produce to replace it and, of course, add to it if you want to increase it. In this sense the GNP has a kind of rough relationship with the stock or state, but I think it should always be regarded as a cost rather than a product.

All of economics, the whole GNP mentality, assumes that economic activity is a throughput, a linear process from the mine to the garbage dump.

The ultimate physical product of economic life is garbage. The system takes ores and fossil fuels (and in a boom the unemployed) out of the earth, chews them up in the process of production, and eventually spews them out into sewers and garbage dumps. We manage to have a state or condition in the middle of the throughput in which we are well fed and well clothed, in which we can travel, in which we have buildings in which we are protected from the atrocious climate and enabled to live in the temperate zone. Just imagine how the GNP would fall and welfare would rise if man abandoned the temperate zone and moved into the tropics. An enormous amount of the GNP is heating this building because the plain truth is that nature is very disagreeable. It is cold, damp, and miserable, and the main effort of human activity is to get away from it. As a matter of fact, we do not even like pure air. Otherwise we would not smoke. All of this indicates that a great deal of man's activity is directed toward what we might call desired pollution.

The throughput is going to come to an end. We are approaching the end of an era. People have been saying it for a long time, but nobody has ever believed them. Very often they were wrong in their forecasts, but this time I suspect they are right. We really are approaching the end of the era of expanding man.

Up to now, man has psychologically lived on a flat earth—a great plain, in fact a "darkling plain" where "ignorant armies clash by night," as Matthew Arnold says. Man has always had somewhere to go. There has always been a Kansas somewhere to beckon him as a virgin land of promise. There is no longer any Kansas. The photographs of the earth by astronauts in lunar orbit symbolize the end of this era.

Clearly the earth is a beautiful little spaceship, all blue and green and white, with baroque cloud patterns on it, and its destination unknown. It is getting pretty crowded and its resources rather limited.

The problem of the present age is that of the transition from the Great Plains into the spaceship or into what Barbara Ward and I have been calling spaceship earth. We do not have any mines and we do not have any sewers in a spaceship. The water has to go through the algae to the kidneys to the algae to the kidneys, and so on, and around and around and around. If the earth is to beome a spaceship, we must develop a cyclical economy within which man can maintain an agreeable state.

Under such circumstances the idea of the GNP simply falls apart. We need a completely different set of concepts for that eventuality, and we are still a long way from it technologically because we never had to worry about it. We always have had an unlimited Schmoo, Al Capp's delightful cartoon creature that everlastingly gets its kicks from being the main course for gluttonous man. We could just rip the earth apart and sock it away. We used to think Lake Erie was a great lake; now it smells like the Great Society. We used to think the oceans were pretty big, but events like the oil leakage in California have spotlighted that fallacy. Suddenly, it is becoming obvious that the Great Plains has come to an end and that we are in a very crowded spaceship. This is a fundamental change in human consciousness, and it will require an adjustment of our ethical, religious, and national systems which may be quite traumatic.

On the whole, human society has evolved in response to a fairly unlimited environment. That is not true of all societies, of course. It is not so true of the Indian village, but the societies that are mainly cyclical are almost uniformly disagreeable. Even the societies which are cyclical (where you return the night soil to the farms) are not really circular. They rely on water and solar energy coming down from somewhere and going out to somewhere. There is some sort of an input-output.

Up to now we have not even begun to solve the problem of a high-level circular economy. In fact, we have not even been interested in it. We did not have to be, because it was so far off in the future. Now it is still a fair way off. Resources for the Future says, "We're all right, Jack. We've got a hundred years." Its report points to our fossil fuels and our ores, and reassures us that they will be adequate for a century. After that, the deluge. I would not be a bit surprised if we run out of pollutable reservoirs before our mines and ores are exhausted. There are some signs of this happening in the atmosphere, in the rivers, and in the oceans.

My IBM spies tell me that a fundamental doctrine applied to computers is called the Gigo Principle, standing for "garbage in, garbage out." It is a basic law that what you put in you have to take out. This is throughput. Otherwise, we have to recycle everything, and we have not begun to consider the problems of a high-level, recycled economy. I am pretty sure there is no nonexistence theorem about it. I am certain that a recycling technology is possible which, of course, must have an input of energy. Nobody is going to repeal the second law of thermodynamics, not even the Democrats. This means that if we are to avoid the increase of material entropy, we must have an input of energy into the system. The present system has an enormous input of energy in fossil fuels which cannot last very long unless we go to nuclear fusion. In that case there is an awful lot of water around, and it would last a long time.

Fission is not any good; it is just messy. I understand that if we began using uranium to produce all our power requirements in this country, we would run out of it in ten years. So actually nuclear energy is not a great source of energy; this planet's coal probably has more. Nuclear energy is not a great new field opened up. I suspect it could turn out to be rather dangerous nonsense.

What does this leave us with? The good old sun. At the most pessimistic, you might say we have to devise a basic economy which relies on the input of solar energy for all its energy requirements. As we know, there is a lot of solar energy.

On the other hand, what we do not know is how many people this spaceship earth will support at a high level. We do not know this even to order of magnitude. I suggest that this is one of the major research projects for the next generation, because the whole future of man depends on it. If the optimum population figure is 100 million, we are in for a rough time. It could be as low as that if we are to have a really high-level economy in which everything is recycled. Or it could be up to 10 billion. If it is up to 10 billion, we are okay, Jack—at least for the time being. A figure somewhere between 100 million and 10 billion is a pretty large area of ignorance. I have a very uneasy feeling that it may be towards the lower level, but we do not really know that.

We do not really know the limiting factor. I think we can demonstrate, for instance, that in all probability the presently underdeveloped countries are not going to develop. There is not enough of anything. There is not enough copper. There is not enough of an enormous number of elements which are essential to the developed economy. If the whole world developed to American standards overnight, we would run out of everything in less than 100 years.

Economic development is the process by which the evil day is brought closer when everything will be gone. It will result in final catastrophe unless we treat this interval in the history of man as an opportunity to make the transition to the spaceship earth.

When we get to $10,000 per capita, what does it really mean? Does it simply mean that we are exhausting the resources of the earth at a much more rapid rate? Of course, we have a process here of increased efficiency in exploitation of the earth, not exploitation of man. We go on, we become terribly rich, and suddenly it is all gone. We may have a process of this sort.

What may happen is that we are going to have to face something of this sort in the next 500 years. Unquestionably, we will have to aim for much lower levels of growth, because the cyclical process costs more than the throughput does. However, if we devote our knowledge industries to solution of the problem of the cyclical economy, maybe it will turn out all right.

The idea that we are moving into a world of absolutely secure and effortless abundance is nonsense. This is an illusion of the young who are supported by their parents. Once they have children of their own, they realize that abundance is an illusion. It is a plausible illusion, because we have had an extraordinary two centuries. We have had an extraordinary period of economic growth and of the discovery of new resources.

But this is not a process that can go on forever, and we do not know how abundant this spaceship is going to be. Nobody here now is going to live to see the spaceship, because it is certainly 100 years—perhaps 500 years—off. I am sure it will be no longer than 500 years off, and that is not a tremendously long period of historic time.

An extraordinary conference was held in December [1968] on the Ecological Consequences of International Development. It was an antidevelopment gathering of ecologists, who presented 60 developmental horror stories, among them predictions that the Aswan Dam is going to ruin Egypt, the Kariba Dam will ruin central Africa, DDT will ruin us all, insecticides will ruin the cotton crops, thallium will ruin Israel, and so on all down the line. Some of these forecasts I take with a little grain of ecological salt. The cumulative effect, however, is significant, and suggests that no engineer should be allowed into the world without an ecologist in attendance as a priest. The most dangerous thing in the world is the completely untrammeled engineer. A friend of mine was at the Aswan Dam talking to the Russian engineer in charge. He asked him about all the awful ecological consequences: snails, erosion, evaporation, and such. The engineer replied, "Well, that is not my business. My job is just to build the dam."

We are all like that, really. I have recently discovered the real name of the devil, which is something terribly important to know. The real name of the devil is *suboptimization*, finding out the best way to do something which should not be done at all. The engineers, the military, the governments, and the corporations are all quite busy at this. Even professors try to find the best way of giving a Ph.D. degree, which to my mind should not be done at all. We are all suboptimizers.

The problem of how to prevent suboptimization is, I think, the great problem of social organization. The only people who have thought about it are the economists, and they have the wrong answer, which was perfect competition. Nobody else has any answer at all. Obviously, the deep, crucial problem of social organization is how to prevent people from doing their best when the best in the particular, in the small, is not the best in the large.

The answer to this problem lies mainly in the ecological point of view, which is perhaps the most fundamental thing we can teach anybody. I am quite sure that it has to become the basis of our educational system.

I have added a verse to a long poem I wrote at that ecological conference. There are some who may still shrug off its somber tone, but the wise man—and nation— will take heed.

> With development extended to the whole of planet earth
> What started with abundance may conclude in dismal dearth.
> And it really will not matter then who started it or ran it
> If development results in an entirely plundered planet.

chapter twelve
REGULATION

BUSINESS CODES OF ETHICS:
Window Dressing or Legitimate Alternative to Government Regulation?

NORMAN E. BOWIE*

The problem is to find some mechanism for ensuring that *all* corporations adhere to the minimum conditions of business ethics. Most corporations believe that it is clearly in the enlightened self-interest of the free enterprise system to ensure adherence to ethical standards through self-regulation. Unethical conditions should not be allowed to develop to the point where government regulation takes over. Government regulation of corporate ethics is viewed on a scale from distrust to horror. There are several reasons why government regulation is opposed. These include:

1. A recognition that government regulation would diminish the power and the prestige of corporate officials.

2. A fear that government officials would interfere with incentives and efficiency and hence reduce profit.

3. A judgment that government officials do not understand business and hence that its regulations would be unrealistic and hence unworkable.

4. A judgment that government officials are in no position to comment on the ethics of others.

5. A judgment that the federal government is already too powerful in a pluralistic society so that it is inappropriate to increase the power of government in this way.

6. A judgment that government regulation violates the legitimate freedom and moral rights of corporations.

When compared to the spectre of government regulations, codes of ethics at least deserve a second look. Codes of good business practice do serve a useful function and are not new. After all, one of the purposes of the Better Business Bureau is to protect

From *Ethical Theory and Business*, edited by Tom L. Beauchamp and Norman E. Bowie (Englewood Cliffs, N.J.: Prentice-Hall, 1979). Reprinted by permission of the author and publisher.

*Department of Philosophy, University of Delaware; Director, Center for the Study of Values.

both the consumer and the legitimate business operator from the "fly-by-night operator." The lesson we learn from the Better Business Bureau is that business ethics is not simply in the interest of the consumer, it is in the vital interest of the business community as well. Business activity depends on a high level of trust and confidence. If a firm or industry loses the confidence of the public, it will have a difficult time in selling its products. An important result follows from the argument that business codes are in the general interest of business. To be effective, codes of business ethics must be adopted industry-wide. Otherwise, it is not to the competitive advantage of the individual firm to follow them. For example, it would not make sense for Bethlehem Steel to initiate the installation of anti-pollution devices for their own plants. In the absence of similar initiatives on the part of other steel companies, Bethlehem's steel would become more expensive and hence Bethlehem would suffer at the hands of its competitors.

An industry-wide code based on rational self-interest would help rebut a frequent criticism of the codes of individual firms. Often the cynical reaction of the public to any individual code is that it is a mere exercise in public relations. An individual code by a particular firm on matters of industry-wide significance runs the danger of being nothing but window dressing if the firm is not to be at a competitive disadvantage. However an industry-wide code designed to protect legitimate businesses from the unethical acts of their competitors is not mere public relations; it is designed to preserve the trust and confidence of the public which is necessary for the survival of the industry itself. For the purpose of protecting the consumer and hence ultimately for the protection of industry itself, industry-wide codes of ethics are in theory a viable alternative to government regulation.

If industry-wide codes of ethics make sense on grounds of self-interest, why don't we have more successful examples? Two factors explain the basic situation. The first has to do with the scope of the regulations, and the second has to do with enforcement.

First, it is hard to make regulations flexible enough to meet a wide variety of situations, especially new situations, and yet simple enough to guide people's behavior in ways that will hold them accountable. Many criticize professional codes of ethics because they are too broad and amorphous. For example, consider four of the first six standards of the Public Relations Society of America.

1. A member has a general duty of fair dealing towards his clients or employees, past and present, his fellow members and the general public.

2. A member shall conduct his professional life in accord with the public welfare.

3. A member has the affirmative duty of adhering to generally accepted standards of accuracy, truth, and good taste.

6. A member shall not engage in any practice which tends to corrupt the integrity of channels of public communication.

By using such terms as "fair dealing," "public welfare," "generally accepted standards," and "corrupt the integrity" the code of standards of the PRSA could be charged with being too general and vague.

Before giving up on codes on this account, a few comments about the nature of language are in order. Except in the use of proper names, language is always general and is always in need of interpretation. Consider a municipal law: "No vehicles are allowed in the park." What counts as a vehicle? A bicycle? A skateboard? A baby carriage? Moreover, whenever we have a definition, there are certain borderline cases. When is a person bald or middle-aged? I used to think 35 was middle-aged. Now I am not so sure. The point of these comments is to show that some of the criticisms of business codes are really not criticisms of the codes but of language itself.

One should note, however, that none of these remarks refutes the criticism that business codes of ethics are too general and amorphous. Indeed these codes must be supplemented by other forms of self-regulation. First, the codes must provide procedures for interpreting what the code means and what it requires. Just as the Constitution needs the Supreme Court, a code of business ethics needs something similar. A serious code of business ethics can have its vagueness and generality corrected in ways not dissimilar from the mechanisms used by the law to correct vagueness problems in statutes and precedents. Perhaps a professional association could serve as the necessary analogue. Business codes of ethics do not have unique problems here.

Now we come to the second basic factor underlying the lack of successful existing codes of ethics: the difficulty of adequate enforcement procedures. There is a validity to the saying that a law which is unenforceable is really not a law at all. Any code of ethics worth having is worth enforcing and enforcing effectively.

First, the codes must be taken seriously in the sense that failure to follow them will carry the same penalties that failure to meet other company objectives carries. The trouble with many corporate codes of ethics is that employees see the codes as peripheral to their main concerns. After all, what is important is the bottom line. Experience demonstrates that when the crunch comes, ethics takes a back seat.

If they were philosophers, the employees could put their point in the form of a syllogism. (1) If management is serious about a policy, management will enforce it; (2) management doesn't enforce its codes of ethics; (3) therefore management isn't really serious about its codes of ethics.

If codes of ethics are to work they must be enforced, and the first step in getting them enforced is to get them taken seriously by the management. How is that to be done? Phillip T. Drotning of Standard Oil of Indiana puts it this way:

> Several generations of corporate history have demonstrated that any significant corporate activity must be locked into the mainstream of corporate operations or it doesn't get done. Social policies will remain placebos for the tortured executive conscience until they are implemented with the same iron fisted management tools that are routinely employed in other areas of activity to measure performance, secure accountability, and distribute penalties and rewards.[1]

In a home where discipline is taken seriously a certain atmosphere pervades. I submit that in a company where ethics is taken seriously, a certain atmosphere will also pervade. Since I do not work in a business corporation, I cannot identify all the signs which indicate that the right atmosphere exists, but I can mention some possibilities discussed in the literature. These include:

1. Recognition that ethical behavior transcends the requirements of the law. The attitude that if it's not illegal it's okay is wrong. It's wrong first because at most the law prescribes minimum standards of ethical behavior. The public desires higher standards and the desire of the public is legitimate although I will not argue for this point here. Moreover, the attitude "if it's not illegal, it's okay" is wrong because it is ultimately self-defeating. By depending upon the law, one is encouraging the government regulations most business persons strongly object to. The American Institute for Certified Public Accountants recognizes this point when it describes its code of professional ethics as a voluntary assumption of self-discipline above and beyond the requirements of law.

2. A high level officer, presumably a vice-president, with suitable staff support, being empowered to interpret and enforce the code. This vice-president should have the same status as the vice-presidents for marketing, production, personnel, etc. The vice-president should also be responsible for measuring performance.

3. Utilization of the device of the corporate social audit as part of the measurement of performance. The corporate social audit has come to have a number of different meanings. What I have in mind, however, is a revision of the corporation's profit and loss statement and balance sheet. Following the ideas of David Linowes, on the credit side all voluntary expenditures not required by law aimed at improving the employees and the public would be entered. On the debit side would be known expenditures which a reasonably prudent socially aware management would make, but didn't make. Such debit entries represent lost opportunities which the company should not have lost.

I recognize that many of these suggestions are highly controversial and I do not want the discussion to shift away from our main topic. This discussion does reiterate, however, an important point made before. Codes of ethics by themselves are not sufficient devices to provide the climate for a desirable record on business ethics. Codes of ethics must be buttressed by internal mechanisms within the corporation if they are to be effective. They must be adequately interpreted and effectively enforced.

Given these criticisms, we should remind ourselves why written codes, both legal and moral, are viewed as desirable despite their inadequacies. Laws or codes of conduct provide more stable permanent guides to right or wrong than do human personalities. As you recall, God recognized that the charismatic leadership of Moses needed to be replaced by the Ten Commandments. Codes of ethics or rules of law provide guidance especially in ethically ambiguous situations. When one is tempted to commit a wrong act, laws also provide the basis for appeal in interpersonal situations. Professor Henry P. Sims, Jr., Professor of Organizational Behavior at Penn State, has done some research with graduate students confronted with decision-making opportunities. His results show that a clear company policy forbidding kickbacks lowers the tendency of the graduate students to permit kickbacks. A business code of ethics can provide an independent ground of appeal when one is urged by a friend or associate to commit an unethical act. "I'm sorry, but company policy strictly forbids it," is a gracious way of ending a conversation about a "shady" deal.

Codes of ethics have another advantage. They not only guide the behavior of average citizens or employees, they control the power of the leaders and employers. For Plato, questions of political morality were to be decided by philosopher kings. Plato had adopted this approach after observing the bad decisions of the Athenian participatory democracy. Aristotle, however, saw the danger that Plato's elitism could easily lead to tyranny. The actions of human beings needed to be held in check by law. The English and American tradition is similar. One means for controlling the king or other governing officials is through a constitution. The Bill of Rights of our own Constitution protects the individual from the tyranny of the majority. A strict company code of ethics would help provide a needed defense for an employee ordered by a superior to do something immoral. "I'm sorry but company regulations forbid that" does have some bite to it.

Finally, during the time when conflicting standards of ethics are being pushed on the business community, a code of ethics would help clarify the ethical responsibilities of business. One of the most frustrating aspects of the current debate about business ethics is that no one knows what the rules are. Most business leaders recognize that the social responsibilities of business must expand and that businessmen and women will be held to higher ethical standards than in the past. However there are some obvious limits. A blanket ethical demand that business solve all social problems is arbitrary and unrealistic. Business codes of ethics acceptable both to the business community and to the general public would help bring some order out of the chaos.

Let me conclude by providing some suggestions for writing an effective code of ethics. I am taking these suggestions directly from an article by Neil H. Offen, Senior Vice-President and Legal Counsel of the Direct Selling Association.

1. Be clear on your objectives, and make sure of your constitutent's support. It is important to get the commitment from the president of each company.

2. Set up a realistic timetable for developing and implementing your code.

3. Know the costs of running a code program, and be sure you have long-term as well as short-term funding.

4. Make sure to provide for changing the code to meet new situations and challenges. It should be a living document.

5. Gear your code to the problems faced by your industry or profession.

6. Be aware of the latest developments and trends in the area of self-regulation. Pay particular attention to FTC, Justice Department, and Congressional activities.

7. Make sure legal counsel is consulted and the code is legally defensible.

8. Get expert advice on how to promote the code and how to go about educating the public.

9. Watch your rhetoric. Don't promise more than you can deliver.

10. Write it as simply as possible. Avoid jargon and gobbledygook.

11. Be totally committed to being responsive and objective.

12. Select an independent administrator of unquestionable competence and integrity.

13. Be patient, maintain your perspective, and don't lose your sense of humor.[2]

NOTES

1. Phillip T. Drotning, "Organizing the Company for Social Action," in S. Prakash Sethi, *The Unstable Ground: Corporate Social Policy in a Dynamic Society* (Los Angeles: Melville Publishing Co., 1974), p. 259.

2. Neil H. Offen, "Commentary on Code of Ethics of Direct Selling Association," in *The Ethical Basis of Economic Freedom* (Chapel Hill, N.C.: American Viewpoint, Inc., 1976), pp. 274–75.

NEW PATTERNS IN GOVERNMENT REGULATION
OF BUSINESS

GEORGE A. STEINER*

A new wave of government regulation of business began in 1962. The purpose of this article is primarily to illustrate the dimensions of this new wave and their significance to individual businesses and the evolution of the business institution. These dimensions are not presented in any particular order of importance. They are not mutually exclusive. All are interrelated.

Not only has the volume of regulation grown dramatically during the past sixteen years but also, when aggregated with past governmental regulations, the result is an extraordinary total body of federal regulations affecting business.[1] So huge is this body of regulation that one executive lamented, and probably correctly: "The volume of laws and regulations is such that no one can comply faithfully with all rules. No large organization can effectively police all its employees."[2]

It is not easy to portray the sheer volume of regulations to which business is subject. One dimension, of course, is federal expenditure for regulatory activities, most of which goes to pay employees to regulate business. From 1974 to 1978, federal expenditures (for consumer safety and health; job safety and other working conditions; energy; financial reporting and other financial controls; and industry-specific regulation) increased 85 percent, from $2.030 billion to $3.764 billion.[3]

In 1975 there appeared in the *Federal Register* 177 proposed rules and 2,865 proposed amendments to existing rules. During the same period, the *Federal Register* printed 309 final rules and 7,305 final rule amendments. In 1975, therefore, federal agencies had under consideration more than 10,000 regulations. This was an increase of 14 percent over 1974. The number of pages in the *Federal Register* rose from more than 20,000 in 1970 to more than 60,000 in 1975, an increase of more than 200 percent.[4]

As late as the mid-1950s, the federal government assumed major regulatory responsibility in only four areas: antitrust, financial institutions, transportation, and communications. In 1976, 83 federal agencies were involved in regulating private business activity. Of these, 34 had been created after 1960.[5] Included in the former group are agencies such as the Interstate Commerce Commission, Civil Aeronautics Board, Federal Trade Commission, Federal Communications Commission, Federal Reserve Board, and Securities and Exchange Commission. In the latter group are the newer agencies, such as the Environmental Protection Agency, Equal Employment Opportunity Commission, Consumer Product Safety Commission, and Occupational Safety and Health Administration.

Excerpted from "New Patterns in Government Regulation of Business," published in *MSU Business Topics*, Autumn 1978. Reprinted by permission of publisher.

*Department of Management, University of California, Los Angeles.

THE GROWING COSTS OF REGULATION

Federal expenditures for regulatory employees, noted above, are merely the tip of the iceberg of the total cost of these regulations. There is, of course, no reliable single measure of cost; a number of types of cost must be considered.

In 1975 the Ford administration made an official estimate that the annual cost to consumers of unnecessary and wasteful regulatory policies was $2,000 per family. The total cost, therefore, was estimated to be $130 billion. The Center for the Study of American Business, Washington University, St. Louis, Missouri, calculated that in fiscal 1979 the aggregate cost of government regulation would be $102.7 billion. By comparison, the total costs in fiscal 1977 were $79.1 billion.[6] While these numbers cannot, of course, be exact, they do reveal the magnitude of the cost.

There are many cost estimates of particular types of regulations. For example, the Federal Council on Environmental Quality has calculated that pollution control for the 1970s will cost more than $287 billion.[7] A more recent estimate of the ten-year cost of pollution control for the 1974–1983 decade is $217.7 billion.[8]

Murray Weidenbaum has calculated that federally mandated safety and environmental features increase the price of the average passenger car by $666.[9] General Motors has reported that in 1977 it spent $1.258 billion on research, development, and administrative expenses in response to government regulations. This figure did not include installation of federally mandated parts, such as emission-control systems and safety devices. Beyond these costs, GM states that the fuel economy standards coming into effect between now and the early 1980s could add another $800 or more to the average retail price of cars.[10]

Also to be considered are expenses incurred to comply with data requirements. The Office of Management and Budget, in its first report to the Congress on President Carter's effort to cut paperwork, calculated that Americans now spend 785 million hours a year filling out about 4,000 federal forms at a cost of $100 billion.[11] This is not all, of course, carried on by business. To illustrate the impact on one company, which probably is reasonably typical, Standard Oil of Indiana says it files 1,000 forms annually with 35 federal agencies. To do this work the company employs 100 persons at a cost of about $3 million a year.[12] Even small companies must bear heavy reporting burdens.[13]

Foundries have closed down because they could not meet costs imposed by the Environmental Protection Agency, OSHA, and other government agency regulations. The cost of meeting pollution standards has weakened the competitive position of heavy industries in foreign markets. Costs added to products to meet government regulations have been inflationary. According to Paul MacAvoy, the reallocation of investment from productivity increasing projects to projects meeting government regulations has probably reduced overall GNP growth by one-quarter to one-half of a percentage point per year. This means, to him, that our economy is operating at 6 to 7 percent below its capacity potential because of controls.[14] A major cost of regulation is its contribution to inflation, reduced productivity, and a slower GNP rate of growth.[15]

A primary and unanswered question concerns the justification for these regulatory costs. There are, of course, offsetting benefits, a point which will be discussed later, but there are also many illustrations of costs being incurred which exceed benefits.

To illustrate, Irving Shapiro, chairman of the board of Du Pont, says that his company spent $1.2 million to reduce particulate emissions in one plant by 94 percent. He said this was a justified expenditure. However, federal regulations required an additional reduction of particulates by 3 percent. The costs of meeting this standard totaled $1.8 million. According to Shapiro, there was no detectable difference in air quality between the 94 and 97 percent reduction. This was equivalent, he said, to paying 80 cents for a dozen eggs and an additional $1.20 for a piece of eggshell.[16]

A recent government-sponsored poll of 57 chief executive officers and top government liaison staff officers found that 86 percent believed that government regulations added more to product and service costs than the benefits they supposedly provided were worth.[17]

OLD AND NEW REGULATION

It is important to observe that there are major differences between the old and new models of regulation. The new model might be called *functional social* regulation in contrast to the older *industrial* regulation. All regulation, of course, is social in that it is ultimately concerned with social welfare, but there are basic distinctions between the models.

The old style of regulation was concerned with one industry, such as railroads, airlines, drugs, and so on. The focus was on such matters as markets, rates, and obligations to serve the public. There were regulations that cut across industry lines but the main focus was on industrial segments. In contrast, the newer functional regulations cut across industrial lines. They are broader in scope and are concerned with one function in an organization, not the entirety of the organization. As a result, of course, the newer regulations affect far more industries and companies than older regulations and, therefore, more customers.

Several important implications for business exist in this new pattern, aside from the number of regulations which must be followed. The old cliché about an industry capturing the agency that regulates it is obsolete. What industry is going to capture OSHA? It would be impractical for an industry to try to dominate a functional regulatory agency such as the Consumer Product Safety Commission or EPA. On the contrary, these agencies can dominate a company's affairs in their realm of functional authority and do so with limited understanding of their impact on the total operation of the company. Older industry regulatory agencies are more or less concerned with the total operation of an industry and the companies in it. Newer functional regulatory agencies are only concerned with a specific part of an industry's operations. Weidenbaum concludes that, far from being dominated by an industry, the newer type of regulatory activity is more likely to ignore the needs of various industries, including their service to the public, to further the agency's objectives.[18]

PURPOSES, POLICIES, AND METHODS OF NEWER REGULATIONS

Newer regulations have different purposes and apply different policies and methods. There are several aspects of this dimension. First, in a simplistic way, the purposes of the new legislation differ from the older regulatory agencies. For example, the older independent regulatory agencies, such as the Civil Aeronautics Board, the Federal Trade Commission, and so on, were designed to prevent monopoly; increase competition; save free enterprise from big business; establish uniform standards of safety, security, communications, and financial practice; and prevent abuses of managerial practices.

The newer regulations are the results of pressures to improve the quality of life. The purposes of the newer regulations are to clean up the environment, employ minorities, assure greater safety and health of workers, provide more information to consumers, protect consumers from shoddy products, and so on.

Second, in the achievement of their purposes the newer agencies do not establish policy to guide private industry in its operations, but specify in detail what shall be done. The National Highway Traffic Safety Administration, which now administers the Motor Vehicle Safety Standards Act of 1966, is very specific about safety features which automobiles must have. This is what Charles Schultze calls a "command and control" method of regulation. He points out that once a decision is made to intervene in the market, the current pattern of regulation is not to seek to alter incentives in the marketplace, modify information flows, or change institutional structures. Rather, direct intervention, the command and control technique, is almost always chosen. Seldom do we try other alternatives, "regardless of whether that mode of response fits the problem."[19]

A third dimension of the new regulations is that legislation is lengthy and specific. Government regulatory legislation in the past established broad policies, with comparatively little specific guidance, and gave the regulatory agency wide powers to set detailed regulations in conformance with the public interest and the policy guidelines drawn by the Congress. Today's legislation tends to be lengthy and detailed. The EPA, for example, administers statutes that run into hundreds of pages of detailed specifications. The Clean Air Act sets specific pollution-reduction targets and timetables and leaves the EPA little discretion.

Two significant results ensue. First, government today is an active managerial partner with business executives. This partnership extends all the way from the governance of corporations to the specific ways in which products are produced and distributed. Many business managers today are in fact acting as agents of the government without being under contract.[20] Second, government is losing the power of motivated individuals in the decentralized market process. As Schultze has put it:

> Regardless of the circumstances . . . new social intervention has almost always been output-oriented, giving short shrift to the process-oriented alternative. And this has proven a costly bias. It has, with no offsetting gain, forfeited the strategic advantages of market-like arrangements. It has led to ineffective and inefficient solutions to important social problems. It has taxed, well beyond its limit, the ability of government to make complex output decisions. And it has stretched thin the delicate fabric of political consensus by unnecessarily widening the scope of activities it must cover.[21]

NONSENSE REGULATIONS

One significant dimension of federal regulation is the growth of nonsense regulations.[22] OSHA regulates trivia in exquisite detail, as the following examples from the *Code of Federal Regulations* of 1 July 1975 reveal:

Section 1910.35(b): Exit access is that portion of a means of egress which leads to the entrance to an exit.

Section 1910.25(d)(vii): [out of 21 pages of fine print devoted to ladders] when ascending or descending, the user should face the ladder; . . . (d)(2)(xx): The bracing on the back leg of step ladders is designed solely for increasing stability and not for climbing.

Section 1910.244(a)(2)(vii): Jacks which are out of order shall be tagged accordingly, and shall not be used until repairs are made.

Such trivia has little to do with the important causes of industrial accidents and worker illness. Many silly rules on worker safety have been eliminated or modified, but many remain.[23]

Nonsense regulations are not, of course, confined to OSHA. Other regulatory agencies are just as guilty of this shortcoming.

CONFLICTS AMONG REGULATIONS

There have always been conflicts among government regulations, but the number, intensity, and incidence have been mounting. Cases have arisen in which the EPA has demanded that a plant convert from coal to oil to reduce atmospheric pollution. At the same time, power plants have been ordered to convert from oil to coal by the Department of Energy to reduce oil consumption. Antipollution requirements have forced some companies to abandon marginal plants, a policy which conflicts with federal goals of reduced unemployment.[24]

NEW TECHNOLOGICAL ISSUES

The new policy regulations are raising significant and controversial technological issues. For example, we all want clean air, clean water, less noise, and protection of workers from carcinogens. In dealing with such matters the question of standards arises. Generally speaking, the costs of eliminating 90 percent of hazardous effluent from a belching smokestack are not great in light of total costs of production. Each additional percentage point of air purification, however, can be achieved only by accelerating costs, until the last few percentage points become prohibitively expensive.

Extremely sensitive issues arise with respect to equating statistical loss of life with costs of controls. Sam Peltzman, for instance, concluded that Federal Drug Administration regulations which delay the introduction of new drugs on the market save fewer lives than would a quicker introduction of the drugs.[25] Of course, different lives are involved. How should the cost-benefit equation be balanced?

With growing scientific knowledge, more and more hazards to life are becoming apparent. Decisions about technical matters, such as whether to put fluorocarbons or another substance in spray-propelled fluids, no longer are being left to private industry. No one knows in all cases what a rational decision is or how it should be made.

New biological, chemical, and other findings are continuously raising difficult technical questions. They reflect, of course, a growing awareness of hazards to human life and a national policy to reduce them. The policy is not a question here, but the fact is that new regulations do become embroiled in controversial technical issues undreamed of in the past.

BUREAUCRATIC IMPERIALISM

Bureaucrats tend to be arbitrary, authoritarian, arrogant, and uncompromising in making and applying rules. Furthermore, a certain antipathy toward business exists in the U.S. federal bureaucracy, and in recent years this tendency seems to have increased. Irving Kristol, who has been observing the scene for some time, has concluded:

> Here we must be candid as well as careful. Though officialdom will deny it—sometimes naively, sometimes not—it is a fact that most of those holding career jobs in EPA, OSHA, and other newer regulatory agencies have an ideological animus against the private economic sector. . . . They are not in those jobs because they could not find any others. Most of them, in truth, are sufficiently educated and intelligent to find better-paying jobs in the world of business. But they are not much interested in money. They are idealistic— that is, they are concerned with exercising power so as to create "a better world."[26]

Another characteristic of some officials is a reluctance, if not lack of interest, to consider the cost of their regulations. Weidenbaum quotes a member of the CPSC: "When it involves a product that is unsafe, I don't care how much it costs the company to correct the problem."[27] Such an attitude can lead not only to ignoring alternative solutions to a problem but also to severe injury to the regulated. Weidenbaum cites the example of an offending company that had not pasted a label on its product bearing the correct statement required by a regulation ("cannot be made nonpoisonous"). The company was forced to destroy the contents. "If you do not care about costs," noted Weidenbaum, "apparently you do not think about such economical solutions as pasting a new label on the can."[28]

A more serious illustration of the unfortunate results of such an attitude concerns the Marlin Toy Products Company of Horicon, Wisconsin. The CPSC mistakenly put the company's toy on its ban list. When the error was called to its attention, the agency refused to issue a retraction, and the company was forced out of business.[29]

INCREASING BUSINESS DISRESPECT FOR LAW

Regulations that are trivial, seemingly contrary to common sense, arbitrarily imposed and administered, and difficult to understand tend to erode respect for the law and willingness to comply with it. This trend is exacerbated when those to whom a rule applies do not know of its existence. The chief executive of Citicorp expresses deep concern about the latter situation in these words:

> What worries me is that General Motors and Citibank have a fighting chance of obeying all the new regulatory laws because we have the staff and the big-time lawyers to do so. But most small business people do not. They cannot even find out what the law is. There are, for example, 1,200 interpretations by the Federal Reserve staff of the Truth in Lending Act. Now 90% of the more than 14,000 commercial banks in the country have fewer than 100 employees. If you gave every staff member those regulations and started them reading, they wouldn't be finished by next year.[30]

Declining respect for the law, if such is really present in the United States today, is the result of a great many forces. The regulatory experience is one of those forces.

The great volume of penetrating, detailed, and often petty regulations lays a fertile groundwork for the development of some form of payoff, both large and small, to government officials either to get needed action or to avoid paying the costs of regulation.

Thomas Ehrlich, dean of the Law School at Stanford University, has used the term *legal pollution* to describe what he calls the growing feeling that it is virtually impossible to move "without running into a law or a regulation or a legal problem."[31]

CONFLICTS AMONG ECONOMIC, LEGAL, AND POLITICAL RATIONALITY

A major pattern in federal regulation is the significant shift which has taken place from market to political-legal decisions. More and more governmental regulatory decisions are supplanting market decisions, and less reliance is being placed on the market mechanism in achieving the objectives of society.

Associated with this phenomenon is the conflict which often occurs among economic, political, and legal rationality. What is politically rational may not be, and frequently is not, economically rational. The obvious result, therefore, is the injection of more and more irrationality into the private market mechanism. A theme discussed by Schultze is the tendency of government to intervene in resource allocation decisions in order to achieve equity and income distribution goals.[32] The failure to disentangle the two may lead to irrational economic decisions because of what politicians see as politically rational actions. The problem in devising an energy program is a case in point.

As implementation and adjudication of regulations move into courts of law, a further potential conflict with economic rationality arises. Courts have their own rationality rooted, of course, in the law. Rationality concerns adherence to legal precedents, seeking a balance among many competing values and interests, and a bias toward exploration of all matters in a case with equal thoroughness and diligence, irrespective of their relative importance in economic life.[33] It is not at all surprising, therefore, that many legal decisions may not square with the logic of the economic market mechanism.

Within a particular government regulatory agency the rationality of politics and law may collide with economic rationality. A former U.S. tariff commissioner, a trained economist, has lamented the difficulties in behaving like an economist in a government agency.[34]

THE REGULATORY COST-BENEFIT EQUATION

Regulations have protected and subsidized business interests as well as consumer and general public interests. Regulation has helped society achieve economic and social goals. It has helped to improve the position of minorities, achieve cleaner air, hold business accountable, prevent abuses of the market mechanism, prevent monopoly, reduce industrial accidents, and so on. The list of pluses of government regulation is long.

On the other hand, there are substantial costs of regulation, using cost in a broad sense. Many, but by no means all, have been discussed here.

In the aggregate, the costs of today's government regulations seem greater than the benefits. Twenty-five years ago the power scale between business and government was balanced reasonably well.[35] Five years ago, the balance seemed to be reasonable.[36] Today, the overall balance is significantly upset in favor of government.

NOTES

1. It is recognized, of course, that there is a vast and growing volume of state and local regulation of business. Limited space forces me to deal only with federal controls.

2. Eleanore Carruth, "The 'Legal Explosion' Has Left Business Shell-Shocked" *Fortune* 87 (April 1973): 65.

3. Murray L. Weidenbaum, "A Fundamental Reform of Government Regulation," in George A. Steiner, ed., *Business and Its Changing Environment* (Los Angeles: UCLA Graduate School of Management, 1978), p. 189.

4. William Lilley III and James C. Miller III, "The New Social Regulation," *Public Interest* 45 (Spring 1977): 5–51.

5. Charles L. Schultze, The *Public Use of Private Interest* (Washington, D.C.: The Brookings Institution, 1977), p. 7.

6. Reported in the *New York Times*, 13 April 1978.

7. Council on Environmental Quality, *Environmental Quality* (Washington, D.C.: U.S. Government Printing Office, 1972), pp. 277–78.

8. Ibid., p. 534.

9. If 11 million cars are sold this year, as expected, the compliance cost to American consumers will be $7 billion. In addition, weight added to cars by such equipment is increasing fuel consumption by $3 billion annually. Murray Weidenbaum, quoted in the *New York Times*, 13 April 1978.

10. Reported in *Time*, 5 June 1978.

11. *Time*, 10 July 1978, p. 26. See also Paul H. Weaver, "That Crusade against Federal Paperwork Is a Paper Tiger," *Fortune* 94 (November 1976): 118–21, 206–10.

12. Don Dedera, "Paperwork! It's Costing Us All a Bundle!" *Exxon USA*, Fourth Quarter 1977.

13. The owner of a small automobile repair shop in California reported that last year he spent 270 hours completing 548 government mandated forms at a conservatively calculated cost of $3,904. A California legislative survey calculated that each small business in California spends an average of $4,000 a year completing government forms. Ibid.

14. Paul W. MacAvoy, "The Existing Condition of Regulation and Regulatory Reform," in Chris Argyris et al., *Regulating Business: The Search for an Optimum* (San Francisco: Institute for Contemporary Studies, 1978), p. 3.

15. See John G. Myers, Leonard I. Nakamura, and Normal R. Madrid, "The Impact of OPEC, FEA, EPA, and OSHA on Productivity and Growth," *Conference Board Record* 13 (April 1976): 61–64. By presidential order, initiated in 1974, the executive branch of the federal government now must evaluate the effects of all major legislation on regulatory proposals in the areas of prices and costs. This is called an Inflationary Impact Statement. See Robert F. Kamm, Stephen F. Nagy, and Joseph Nemec, "Complying with Proposed Regulations: Estimating Industry's Costs," *Business Horizons* 20 (August 1977): 86–91. I have seen no studies relating to the effects of such statements.

16. Irving S. Shapiro, an excerpt of remarks presented at the Southern Governors' Conference, San Antonio, Texas, 29 August 1977, found in *Across the Board* 15 (January 1978): 37.

17. John F. Steiner, "Government Regulation of Business: An Overview," *Los Angeles Business and Economics* 3 (Fall 1977): 7.

18. Weidenbaum, "Business, Government, and the Public," in *Business and Its Changing Environment*, pp. 14–15.

19. Schultze, *Public Use of Private Interest*, p. 13.

20. Weidenbaum, "Business, Government, and the Public."

21. Schultze, *Public Use of Private Interest*.

22. Ibid.

23. "Interview with Eula Bingham, Head of the Occupational Safety and Health Administration," *U.S. News & World Report*, 16 January 1978, p. 65.

24. Murray L. Weidenbaum, "The Costs of Government Regulation," Publication No. 12, Center for the Study of American Business, Washington University (St. Louis: February 1977).

25. Sam Peltzman, "An Evaluation of Consumer Protection Legislation: The 1962 Drug Amendments," *Journal of Political Economy* 81 (September/October 1973): 1049–91.

26. Irving Kristol, "A Regulated Society?" *Regulation* 1 (July/August 1977): 13.

27. Murray L. Weidenbaum, "The Case for Economizing on Government Controls," *Journal of Economic Issues* 11 (June 1975): 207.

28. Ibid.

29. Comptroller General of the United States, *Banning of Two Toys and Certain Aerosol Spray Adhesives*, MWD-75-65 (Washington, D.C.: U.S. General Accounting Office, 1975).

30. Walter B. Wriston, quoted in *Time*, 1 May 1978, p. 44.

31. "Complaints about Lawyers," interview with Thomas Ehrlich, *U.S. News & World Report*, 21 July 1975, p. 46.

32. Schultze, *Public Use of Private Interest*.

33. Norman Kangun and R. Charles Moyer, "The Failings of Regulation," *MSU Business Topics* 24 (Spring 1976): 5–14.

34. Penelope Hartland-Thunberg, "Tales of a One-time Tariff Commissioner," *Challenge* 19 (July-August 1977): 6–12.

35. George A. Steiner, *Government's Role in Economic Life* (New York: John Wiley & Sons, 1953).

36. George A. Steiner, *Business and Society*, 1st ed. (New York: Random House, 1971).

REGULATION THAT WORKS

STEVEN KELMAN*

The last decade has seen dramatic restrictions in the freedom of action society chooses to allow to business firms. A series of laws in areas like environmental protection, occupational safety and health, consumer product safety and equal opportunity has restricted the prerogatives of business firms to pursue production, hiring and marketing practices that would have continued without these laws. Business and conservatives have now launched a counterattack against these changes. Cleverly exploiting various popular resentments, the counterattacking forces seek to lump "excessive government regulation" together with themes as diverse as high taxes and school busing to generate an all-embracing demand to "get the government out of our hair." To hear the critics of the new government regulatory programs tell it, nothing less fundamental than our very freedom is at stake in the battle against meddlesome bureaucrats. And now, with national concern over inflation growing, we are being told that the new regulatory programs are an important cause of the increased cost of living, and must be reduced for that reason as well.

One fact it is important to get clear from the beginning is that the alleged popular ground swell against government regulation of business does not exist. A recent Louis Harris survey asked Americans, "In the future, do you think there should be more government regulation of business, less government regulation, or the same amount there is now?" By 53 percent to 30 percent, those polled favored either more regulation or the same amount as now, over less regulation. In fact, almost as many respondents (24 percent) favored more regulation as favored less regulation (30 percent). Repeated polls have shown wide popular support for measures to make workplaces safe, and to clean up the environment.

This absence of any ground swell against the new regulatory thrust of the last decade is reassuring, because the conservative and business counterattack is, I believe, largely wrong. New regulatory programs neither threaten freedom nor contribute significantly to inflation. On the whole, the new regulation is a good thing. Certainly there have been excesses by bureaucrats, but what is more impressive than these excesses is the unfinished work the new agencies still have before them to deal with the injustices that prompted their creation in the first place.

There are two kinds of activities often lumped together as "government regulation." When denouncing the "costs of government regulation," opponents of the new regulatory agencies tend to forget this distinction. An older generation of liberals, fond of asserting that regulatory agencies always get captured by those they regulate, also ignore this distinction.

Most of the regulatory agencies established before the last decade were set up to regulate prices and conditions of entry in various industries. The grandfather of such

*Kennedy School of Government, Harvard University.

agencies was the Interstate Commerce Commission, established in 1887 to regulate railroads. There is a lively dispute among historians about whether the ICC, when it was established, was an attempt to tame a powerful and oppressive industry, or a government-sanctioned effort by the railroads themselves to set up a cartel to avoid price competition. It is much clearer, however, that other agencies regulating market conditions in various industries, such as the Civil Aeronautics Board and the Federal Communications Commission, *were* originally established at the behest of industries seeking to avoid "excessive" competition. These agencies, by maintaining artificially high prices in various industries, have been very costly to consumers and to the economy as a whole. But you do not hear the voices of business complaining about them. Indeed, when proposals are made to deregulate surface transportation, airlines, or television, the main opponents of such proposals have been the industries being "regulated."

The situation is very different, both politically and conceptually, for the regulatory agencies—which have blossomed especially during the last decade—intended to regulate non-market behavior by business firms. Usually they regulate acts that injure third parties. These "social" regulatory agencies include the Environmental Protection Agency, the Occupational Safety and Health Administration, the National Highway Transportation Safety Board, the Consumer Product Safety Commission, and the Equal Employment Opportunity Commission. These agencies generally came into being despite genuine business resistance. Business representatives certainly have ample opportunity to participate in developing the regulations these agencies promulgate, but there are other organized constituencies interested in their work as well (environmentalists at EPA, trade unions at OSHA, civil rights and women's groups at EEOC, for instance). Few reasonable people believe the social regulatory agencies have been "captured" by business—least of all, as the current attacks demonstrate, business itself.

The conceptual basis for the social regulatory agencies also is different from that of agencies intended to limit or replace the free market. In any society, one of the basic tasks of government and the legal system is to decide which acts of individuals are so harmful to others that they cannot be freely permitted (and which harmful acts may rightfully be performed, even though others are indeed harmed). The social regulatory agencies are engaged in this age-old task. There is nothing conceptually new about their activities. What *is* new is that they have redefined certain acts by business firms previously regarded as acceptable, and determined that they are henceforth unacceptable.

Government has never left businessmen "unregulated," as business spokesmen now wistfully, but erroneously, imagine. The voluminous case and statute law of property, contracts and torts along with large chunks of the criminal law, comprise an elaborate system—far more complex and intricate than any OSHA standard—regulating acts that injure property holders, as well as acts by property holders that injure others. A starving person does not have the freedom to injure a rich man by appropriating the rich man's money in order to buy food. People do not have the freedom to injure a landowner by trespassing on his land. Furthermore, the process by which these older rules were elucidated and enforced through litigation was much more cumbersome and arbitrary than the rulemaking of today's regulatory agencies.

The plethora of regulations regarding property that has grown up over the centuries is not some sort of natural order, onto which new regulations of business behavior in areas like safety, health, environmental protection, consumer fraud, and discrimination represent an unnatural intrusion. As long as the regulations were restricting the freedom of non-property-holders to injure *them*, businessmen raised no chorus of complaints about an oppressive government stifling freedom. The chorus of complaints from business has begun only as regulations have begun increasingly to restrict the freedom of business firms to injure others.

The harms that social regulations of the last decade were intended to curb were not insignificant. Urban air had become unhealthy as well as unpleasant to breathe. Rivers were catching on fire. Many working people were dying from exposure to chemicals on their jobs. Firms were selling products of whose hazards consumers were ignorant. And the nation faced a legacy of racial and sexual discrimination. Frequently the harm was borne disproportionately by the more disadvantaged members of society, while the more advantaged produced the harm. The social regulation of the past decade grew largely, then, out of a sense of fairness—a view that people, frequently disadvantaged people, were being victimized by others in unacceptable ways.

The impact of the new agencies in alleviating these injuries has begun to be felt. Racial and sexual discrimination have decreased, partly thanks to broader social trends, but partly thanks to government efforts. There has been a vast increase in the amount of information manufacturers are required to tell consumers about their products, and surveys indicate that many consumers use this information in making purchasing decisions.

Since the much-maligned OSHA and its sister agency regulating coal mining safety have come into existence, the number of accidental workplace deaths has been cut almost in half. Worker exposures to harmful amounts of coal dust and chemicals like vinyl chloride, asbestos and lead have been reduced, and this will reduce the toll of occupational sickness and death in the years to come. Improvements in emergency medical care and some changes in workforce composition since 1970 may be partially responsible for the dramatic reduction in workplace deaths. But today's figures don't even reflect the reduction in deaths due to occupational disease, which will be felt mainly in future years because of the frequently lengthy period separating exposure to harmful levels of chemical and death or illness due to that exposure.

Environmental regulation has produced significant improvements in the quality of air in the United States. Without regulation the situation would have gotten worse because economic growth tends to increase the level of pollution. Carbon monoxide levels in eight representative cities declined 46 percent between 1972 and 1976. Carbon monoxide levels that had been found in urban air were enough to increase the incidence of heart attacks and of painful angina attacks among people with heart disease. There has been a major decline in heart attack deaths in the United States during the 1970s. No one yet knows why, but I predict that studies will show that improvement in air quality has played a role in this decline. Another common air pollutant, sulfur dioxide, which definitely causes respiratory illness and death and is suspected of causing cancer, has now declined to a point where almost every place in the country is in compliance with EPA standards.

The critics ask: have the benefits outweighed the costs? Are they feeding inflation, for example? Allegations that health, safety, environmental and antidiscrimination regulations are a major cause of inflation are little short of grotesque. Much of the business thunder about regulation begins by citing some overall figure for the "cost of regulation," and then goes on to zero in on agencies like OSHA and EPA. These agencies are chosen, however, only because business dislikes them especially, not because they are major contributors to the "cost of regulation." Most of the cost of regulation is imposed by the market-fixing agencies, like the ICC, that the business world likes. Murray Weidenbaum, director of the Center for the Study of American Business and an adjunct scholar at the American Enterprise Institute, estimated that in 1976 federal regulation in the areas he examined cost $62.3 billion to comply with. But of this sum, approximately $26 billion—or 42 percent—was the estimated impact on consumer prices of tariff protection against imports and of price and entry regulations by the ICC, CAB and FCC. (The largest figure in this category was the cost of ICC regulation of transportation). Another $18 billion—29 percent of the estimated total cost—represented the alleged cost of federal paperwork. Certainly there are plenty of pointless federal paperwork requirements. But few of these relate to what would normally be thought of as "government regulation." Much federal paperwork takes the form of reports for statistical purposes and of requirements for federal contractors or other citizens receiving federal benefits.

Only five percent of Weidenbaum's estimated total—$3.2 billion in 1976—was spent on complying with OSHA regulations. Another $7.8 billion allegedly was spent to comply with EPA regulations—less than 13 percent of the total. (Weidenbaum also estimated a $3.7 billion retail cost for auto safety and emissions requirements.)

Even these modest figures do not reflect the direct savings that result from some of these regulations. The actual monetary cost of pollution abatement measures, for example, is the cost to firms of capital equipment, energy and maintenance, *minus* the savings in medical bills, damaged crops, premature corrosion of property, laundering expenses and so forth, that would otherwise be borne by victims of pollution. Most accounts of the "inflationary impact" of government regulation do not calculate such savings.

More fundamentally, these estimates of the "cost" of regulation ignore widespread benefits that do not have a direct monetary value, but are real nonetheless. In the case of pollution control, for example, the air smells a bit better for five million people; 100,000 people get to see mountains in the distance which they would not have seen had the air not been as clean; and 50 lives are saved. There is no way of objectively determining whether these non-priced benefits justify the net monetary costs.

The costs and benefits of the business behavior now coming under regulation have not been distributed randomly. Much of the new social regulation benefits more disadvantaged groups in society. To put it somewhat simply—but not, in my view, unfairly—those who argue, say, that OSHA should "go soft" on its health regulations in order to spare the country the burden of additional costs, are saying that some workers should die so that consumers can pay a few bucks less for the products they purchase, and stockholders can make a somewhat higher return on their investments. It is hard to see why workers exposed to health hazards should be at the front line of the battle against inflation, however the overall costs and benefits tally up.

There are, to be sure, those sudden friends of the poor who allege that environmental regulation has significantly added to unemployment, or who point out that regulation-induced price increases weigh most heavily on the poor. But studies have concluded that, on balance, environmental legislation has probably created many more jobs than it has cost. And one must wonder whether there aren't more direct ways to help the poor than to eliminate the health, safety, and environmental regulations that slightly increase the costs of goods they buy.

None of this means that every regulation promulgated by social regulatory agencies in the last few years is justified. In some instances, as with some affirmative action requirements, regulations may have gone beyond their conceptual justifications. In other instances the administrative burden, the paperwork requirements or the monetary costs of regulating may be too great to justify the benefits, however real, received by those whom the regulations are intended to protect. Offhand, for example, it appears to me that the costs of retrofitting older urban subway systems to accommodate the handicapped, only a small number of whom could be expected to use those systems anyway, appear unjustified, even though failure to retrofit does indeed injure some disadvantaged people. Questions like this should be considered case-by-case, but with sympathy for those people injured by the failure to regulate.

The thrust of the current movement against social regulation in the United States is a wish by the strong to regain prerogatives whose disappearance, for the most part, is one of the most welcome events of the past decade. Individual regulations can and should be criticized. But the assault on the concept of regulation must be resisted if we are to continue to be a decent people living in a decent society.

chapter thirteen
MULTINATIONAL BUSINESS

THERE'S NO LOVE LOST BETWEEN MULTINATIONAL COMPANIES AND THE THIRD WORLD

LOUIS TURNER*

Managers of multinational corporations excel at such tasks as transferring products, technology, and advanced management thinking to all quarters of the globe. In doing so, they tend to assume that the problems of New Delhi, Lagos, or Rio de Janeiro can be solved by hardware and concepts developed in Frankfurt or Detroit. Critics deny this. They argue that the impact of such corporations in the Third World is, in fact, harmful in that they exacerbate the tensions found within such societies and help create the kind of tragically polarized societies which we can see throughout Latin America. What is good for General Motors is probably, in the long run, not so good for Gabon and Guatemala.

To take a simple example: The Swiss company, Nestlé, introduced powdered milk as a baby food into West Africa as an alternative to breast feeding. Emulating Western fashion, local mothers adopted bottle feeding wholeheartedly. The result was increased infant mortality: To combat their extreme poverty, mothers were diluting the milk to the point that a bottle had virtually no nutrition.

In earlier times, few managers worried about such niceties. The bulk of corporations in the Third World were looking for minerals or tropical produce which they would ship back to the industrialized world as fast as possible. Rather than contribute to the wider development of the societies in which they found themselves, they created "enclaves," virtual states-within-states, in which their rule was law. Due to their influence, some countries with diversified agricultural economies became dependent on single crops; the Central American "banana republics" and the rubber economies of Malaya and Liberia are examples. Even if such countries were formally independent, they were in fact shackled by their nearly total dependence on the benevolence of companies such as Firestone and United Fruit. Political leaders and local entrepreneurs either flourished or were overthrown at the whim of these companies, thus stifling the development of local economic and political initiative. On occasions, the companies even tried to redraw political boundaries, as when the Belgian mining company,

*Research scholar, Royal Institute of International Affairs, London.

Union Minière, helped finance the attempted breakaway of Katanga soon after the ex-Belgian Congo (now Zaire) attained independence.

Today, despite the abortive coup attempts of ITT in Chile, the situation is less stark. As Third World economies have grown, they have become more diversified, reducing their dependence on single companies and forcing managements to become more circumspect in their outward behaviour. In the aftermath of the Independence Era, governments have been growing in self-confidence and experience, and they are now willing to attack corporations which get out of line. Obviously the example of OPEC (Organization of Petroleum Exporting Countries) has been extremely important, as it has shown how relatively powerless the oil giants actually are. Since the oil producers began their onslaught, the bauxite producers have started to follow suit, with significant actions also coming from the governments of Malaysia (rubber) and Morocco (phosphates). However, despite this Third World militancy, the multinationals remain formidable adversaries.

SQUEEZING OUT LOCAL ENTREPRENEURS

For one thing, the multinationals are still very large by Third World standards. They possess the technical and marketing skills that countries trying to industrialize desperately need. The result is often a dependence on foreign companies to a degree embarrassing to see. Take the case of Unilever's subsidiary in Nigeria, the United Africa Co. (UAC), which originally entered that country to produce palm oil needed for the manufacture of margarine. By natural expansion it diversified into shipping and a general import-export trade aimed at the Nigerian market. As the country grew, so did the UAC, establishing itself in all the new markets created by Nigeria's fledgling industrialization. By the mid-1960s, it was four times the size of the next largest company, and one could almost claim that the industrialization of Nigeria was the industrialization of UAC. From its start as an agricultural and trading company, it moved into textiles, sugar, beer, cement, cigarettes, building contracting, radio assembly, plastic products, bicycle and truck assembly, etc. In any sector which mattered, the company was involved.

UAC is generally credited with having used its power responsibly; but, in microcosm, its history reflects what has been happening throughout the Third World. In the case of Latin America, foreign industrialists were squeezing local competitors out of all key industries as early as the nineteenth century. Every time there was a slump, it would be the undercapitalized local businessmen who would go to the wall, leaving the multinationals to emerge ever more dominant. Only during the two world wars, when European and American companies had other things on their minds, did local entrepreneurs have a chance to flourish—but this was not enough. Today, it is virtually meaningless to talk of Third World entrepreneurship in the sense in which Carnegie or Rockefeller were entrepreneurs. What we find instead is Third World planners and businessmen passively accepting technologies which have been developed by the multinationals, perhaps modifying them slightly for local needs, but certainly not trying to produce innovations which might challenge the foreigners' sway. This approach has probably contributed to the long-term political stagnation found in many Third

World countries. Furthermore, it is culturally dangerous in that it assumes that products produced by the multinationals are suitable for Third World needs. In many cases, this is blatantly untrue.

The vast majority of multinationals are just not interested in the Third World except as a convenient residual market in which extra profits can be made once a product has proved itself in the American and European arenas. I once tested this belief by reading a couple of hundred company reports, looking for examples of involvement with the Third World which the companies might want to emphasize. It was a depressing experience. The majority of companies gave Third World activities no coverage at all, instead stressing things like the companies' contribution to the American space program. Otherwise, apart from CPC (the Corn Products Corp.), which had its chairman pictured knee-deep in a paddy field, the reports boasted of products like refrigerator fronts of Formica-based laminate (American Cyanamid in Argentina), car radios (Bosch in Brazil), or the lighting, traffic lights, and illustrated fountains along eighteen miles of road in the oil-rich Trucial States (Philips). Nothing about searches for nutritionally enriched forms of tropical fruits and vegetables; virtually nothing about the search for cures for tropical diseases; nothing about the search for labor-intensive industries which might well mop up the vast armies of the unemployed found everywhere in the poor countries. Instead, the companies listed trivial products which can contribute nothing to the long-term development of the Third World, but which are symptomatic of the overall corrupting effect which the multinationals tend to have on Third World elites.

CORRUPTING THE ELITE

These elites should be concerned with the majority of their countrymen who are still in the countryside working outside the market economy (if working at all—only some 2 percent of Nigeria's 63 million population is earning a wage or salary). They ought to be thinking of ways to cope with spiraling urban unemployment (some estimates suggest that 20 percent of the world's potential work force is without a job). Above all, they ought to be preaching austerity, since the task of pulling the world's poorest 40 percent above their current near-starvation level is one which will take decades, if not centuries.

The multinationals have very little constructive to offer. What they are good at is identifying and filling gaps in the markets of industrialized consumer societies; but, as Galbraith has pointed out, private enterprise does not lead automatically to the satisfaction of wider social needs. A dynamic auto industry, for instance, does not guarantee a good educational or health system; in the Third World, such an industry may even harm the interests of the bottom 40 percent of the population, since the elites will divert precious resources to building the roads and importing the gasoline which a flourishing auto industry demands. Thus the inequality of such societies increases, precisely the danger which the World Bank is starting to warn against. It contends that social inequality is growing noticeably within the Third World, even within rapidly growing economies like Brazil's. And it is starting to argue that the classic measurement of growth, G.N.P., is (by itself) a misleading indicator of development, that slower growing countries which put more stress on reducing social inequalities may well produce stabler societies in the long run.

The multinationals, whether they know it or not, are firmly on the side of inequality, forming a deadly alliance with corruptible Third World elites. The latter have been brought up to believe that one should envy the slick consumer society of the West, and they see the multinationals as the organizations which will deliver the goods. The elites want record players, refrigerators, cars, television, telephones, etc., and the multinationals are only too happy to deliver them. There are some managers who are aware that none of this is helping the starving and unemployed at the bottom of the pile. Sometimes they make token protests, but the elites prevail, since national pride tells them that their country is not modern unless it has things like an airport, an airline, a car industry, and a Hilton hotel. They can be extremely insistent on getting them. For instance, a Fiat manager once told me of the efforts they made in the late 1960s to persuade various national governments that truck plants were far better investments than car plants for countries at a low level of development. The technologies involved in assembling trucks are simpler, less import-intensive and more labor-intensive, and produce products which are of direct use in activities like farming and civil engineering. Their arguments were to no avail; the government officials insisted on having a car plant.

While the multinationals are not all to blame, clearly they are a vital part of the process which corrupts the elites. Hollywood films, television programs, and advertising are all instrumental in creating a certain image of Western society. The expatriate managers of multinational subsidiaries are a flesh and blood demonstration of this way of life. Highly paid (by local standards), they provide a model to the indigenous managers (who are increasingly replacing them) and to local officials. Their replacement can cause problems. In Africa, for instance, local replacements have been expecting not only similar levels of pay to those of the expatriate managers, but even some of the latters' "perks," like the free trip to Europe every eighteen months. From the start, local managers have expectations which can be satisfied only at the expense of the less powerful in their societies. In East Africa they have coined the name *Wa-Benzi* for the African elite which rides about in Mercedes-Benzes while the peasants and unemployed starve.

Another insidious effect arises from tourism, an industry in which multinationals are playing an increasing role. Tourists are flying more and more to exotic (i.e., poor) Third World destinations like the Pacific Islands, the Caribbean, and North and East Africa. Although many tourist resorts are "golden ghettos," located away from the centers of population, the social harm done by this industry is extraordinarily difficult to avoid. The local population learns to despise and cheat tourists, whose wealth appears limitless and who normally have no clear idea how much anything costs. Prostitution springs up, as seen in the Boys' towns, like Tijuana, along the U.S.-Mexican border. Even more grotesque are government attempts to build an image of friendliness toward tourists, launching "Be-Nice" campaigns and going so far as to have school children taught that tourists are friends who must be smiled at and treated well. Such campaigns are necessary in the sense that expressions of hostility may keep tourists from returning. But there is something intensely degrading about nations like Jamaica, Barbados, and the Bahamas launching such programs, particularly when they are part of a culture steeped deeply in the slave trade, with all its connotations of black servitude.

REAL DEVELOPMENT DOES NOT PAY

Despite everything, we should not be too harsh on the multinationals, since they are merely symbols for the general capitalist system, of which most of us are just as much a part. Asking them to contribute positively to the development of the Third World is to ask them to perform a task for which they were not designed. They are motivated by money, and yet we critics are asking them to develop goods for part of the world which is still predominantly outside the market economy. A bank, the Barclay's, lost $4.2 million in the early 1960s when its managers in West Africa were instructed to lend much more adventurously in rural areas. They managed to pull in small savings, but the amounts were so small, and so expensive to collect, that normal banking practices seemed almost irrelevant. Undoubtedly there was an overall social gain for Nigeria in the attempts to attract rural savings into productive investments, but a profit-oriented institution was obviously not the right vehicle for extending the experiment. Likewise, tractor manufacturers are searching for a mini-tractor which can compete effectively with the traditional ox and plough. Ford, for instance, spent at least six years trying to develop a simple, one-speed, seven-horse-power, rope-started model which could be easily assembled by local dealers, but after field-testing in Jamaica, Mexico, and Peru, and market-testing in Jamaica, they finally concluded that the returns were not going to be enough to justify their utilizing a disproportionately high number of their executives on this product.

One is tempted to argue that there is little that the multinationals can do in key fields like population control, tropical diseases, and tropical agriculture—just the areas which would do most for that bottom 40 percent of the Third World. This is simply because on the scale on which most multinationals work, there just is not sufficient money to be made, and the risks are horrendous. So a pharmaceutical company will always choose to investigate a possible cure for arthritis, rather than a simple, self-administered, long-action contraceptive using materials indigenous, say, to India. A cure for arthritis would be an instant gold mine; a long-action contraceptive for India would run the risk that the company might have to sell to the Indian government at a loss, or might have its patents ignored. Either way, the product aimed at the Third World is just not an acceptable risk.

The multinationals play safe. They develop products for the U.S. and Europe and are pleasantly surprised if they find Third World markets as well. Obviously, the formula sometimes works well for the poor. The discovery of DDT, for instance, did, with all its side effects, eradicate malaria. On balance, though, the multinationals are happiest doing business with urbanized, westernized elites—the soldiers who will buy their weapons, the managers who will buy their consumer goods. It would be nice if all the people of the Third World were as rich as those of Rio de Janeiro and Sao Paulo; unfortunately, they are not. Multinationals have a lot to contribute to these cities, but virtually nothing for the peasants living in grinding poverty in Brazil's northeast.

THE EVILS OF "DEPENDENCIA"

Finally, if we are looking at the cultural impact of multinationals, we must examine arguments stemming from Latin America about "Dependencia"—the contention that many of the ills of that continent can be blamed on the polarization of societies by overdependence on foreign markets, technology and culture. If this is indeed true of Latin America, what chance have the less developed continents of Africa and Asia?

This argument is difficult to substantiate conclusively, but it is not dissimilar to the charges raised by Ralph Nader and Mark Green about the effect of corporate domination of U.S. communities. They have written that when a community's economy is controlled by national or multinational conglomerates, the overall well-being of the community is threatened. Civic leadership suffers since corporate officials do not identify with communities which are merely one step on the career ladder. The independent middle classes are eliminated and income becomes less equitably distributed. Local society becomes more polarized. They cite the words of C. Wright Mills: "Big business tends to depress, while small business tends to raise the level of civic welfare."

On the international level, one can make a similar argument. Multinationals certainly prefer to do business with authoritarian regimes, which can guarantee a "secure" investment climate. They are happier investing in Brazil or Spain than in radical states like Allende's Chile or Nyerere's Tanzania. Nor do they show much sympathy toward democracies like Italy and India where underlying social tensions interfere with the smooth running of the economy. Governments encourage multinationals to invest by repressing potential troublemakers. Taiwan, Singapore, and Malaysia vie with each other by guaranteeing foreign investors freedom from trade union activities.

On a deeper level, reliance on multinationals saps a nation's vitality. Multinationals do not encourage indigenous research and development, almost always choosing to locate these facilities in North America or Europe. Local businessmen become mere intermediaries, adapting foreign technologies (if at all) to local conditions. Where countries are industrializing, multinationals move in to snuff out local competition before it has any chance of getting established.

THE AMERICAN LESSON

The degree of dominance exercised, however benevolently, by companies like UAC in Nigeria is a phenomenon which no Western commentator is entitled to gloss over. It is totally unlike anything in the history of the United States or Europe. To begin to comprehend it, imagine the United States as a Third World country winning its independence from a technically sophisticated Great Britain whose per capita GNP was ten times as great as that of ours, and which possessed companies fully capable of operating in the American market. The first result would have been that the incredible flowering of American entrepreneurial talent in the nineteenth century would have been nipped in the bud. Cyrus McCormick, Francis Cabot Lowell, Cornelius Vanderbilt, John D. Rockefeller, and J.P. Morgan would, at best, have ended up as talented managers for some British conglomerate. After all, who would need to design an American reaper when perfectly adequate British designs already existed and could be imported or assembled under license? Public ire in the late nineteenth century would not have focused on "the trusts," but would have vented itself against a handful of British giants, one of which might well have owned not just the oil industry, but the key American railroads and transatlantic shipping lines as well. Congress would have been in the pay of the British, and independent presidents would have invited bombardment by the British navy or coups from the British intelligence service.

This is a fair picture of what multinational investment has meant to many Third World countries. Clearly, the American political tradition would have been totally different had it sprung from such a background. For one thing, political divisions would have been far deeper than they are. Labor disputes and left-wing politics would be tinged with greater intensity, for there would be a xenophobic element to all controversies. Radical critics would face a much less powerful middle class, since the entrepreneurial element of U.S. society would be much smaller. Above all, the unifying belief in the American dream would not exist. How could there be a feeling of hope and optimism in a society where material "success" means working for some giant foreign company? The forces of the left would thus be relatively strong, forcing foreign corporate interests into relatively extreme defensive action. The likelihood of coups, armed repression, and terrorist tactics would be high.

So, we come to the harsh conclusion that multinational investment in the Third World has long-term harmful social and cultural effects. The multinational managers who complain about political chaos in Latin America are deluding themselves, since they are an integral part of the problem. This is not to claim that the majority of such managers are not perfectly well-meaning citizens; nor is it to deny that many of the products of their companies are of vital importance in the Third World. But we would do well to look more sympathetically at alternative approaches to development, while agreeing sadly with the words of George Bernard Shaw:

> "Capitalism is not an orgy of human villainy, but a utopia that has dazzled and misled very amiable and public spirited men. The upholders of capitalism are dreamers and visionaries who, instead of doing good with evil intentions like Mephistopheles, do evil with the best of intentions."

WHY UNITED STATES CORPORATIONS SHOULD GET OUT OF SOUTH AFRICA

JOHN PAYTON*

We are here today to testify on behalf of the National Bar Association, founded over 50 years ago to represent the interests of black lawyers in this country. Historically, the National Bar Association has been concerned with numerous domestic and international civil rights issues. In recent years the National Bar Association has been actively involved in the dialogue concerning the crisis in Southern Africa. We welcome this opportunity to discuss United States corporate involvement in South Africa. At your request, we will comment on the Sullivan Principles, a code of conduct voluntarily adopted by some United States corporations doing business in South Africa. Before discussing the Sullivan Principles, we will review the political and economic context in which they exist. With a full appreciation of the magnitude of the political, economic and social oppression of black people in South Africa, the inadequacy and hollow symbolism of the Sullivan Principles are clearly revealed.

I. THE REALITY OF APARTHEID

Black South Africans have no rights.

They have no right to citizenship. Under South African law, blacks must be citizens of the so-called "homelands." These homelands were established to accommodate the 72 percent of the country that is black, yet they constitute only 13 percent of the total land area of South Africa. Blacks are forcibly relocated to these generally barren, worthless areas. By 1978, over 2,115,000 blacks had been relocated and such mass relocations are planned to continue until substantially all Africans have been removed from the "white areas."

Blacks have no right to own land outside the homelands. Only a limited number of blacks may lease land. The natural desire of people to own their own property is rendered meaningless by laws of South Africa.

Blacks have no right to vote.

Blacks have no freedom of movement. Absolute physical segregation of the races is ensured by influx control laws by which all blacks must carry with them special identification and must observe rigid curfews.

Blacks have no right to free association or free expression. For even a murmur of dissent or an effort at political organization, they are subject to indefinite detention without charges, beating, banning, torture or death.

Blacks have no right to maintain the integrity of their families. Families are uprooted by the forced relocation of people to the homelands areas. Husbands often must live in all male hostels near their employment while their families live in the homelands.

Excerpted from the statement of the National Bar Association Before the House Committee on Foreign Affairs Subcommittee on Africa, May 22, 1980. Reprinted by permission of the National Bar Association.

*Attorney, Wilmer, Cutler and Pickering law firm.

South Africa's public relations managers would lead us to believe that, in recent years, the government has undertaken measures designed to improve the living conditions of black South Africans and to reform the apartheid system. The truth is that the quality of life for black South Africans has not improved in the last several years— it has significantly deteriorated.

During this time, the denial of political and civil rights has become more systematic, if more refined in its public presentation. Last week, Prime Minister Botha's government dramatically announced its plan for a new constitution. However, in the words of the *Washington Post*, blacks are intended to play only a "walk-on part." The black majority will have no meaningful role in the creation of the new constitution. Affirming the policy of separate development in the new constitution, Botha stated: "I do not believe in a unitary state or in a unitary society." As the *New York Times* stated in an editorial yesterday:

> The sad truth is that the new "reform" further confirms Prime Minister P. W. Botha's retreat from his early promises to bring South Africa's blacks to a position of greater economic and political influence. Without such an evolution, no peaceful development seems conceivable.

The response of the South African system to black protest has also grown more repressive. In 1976, when thousands of blacks demonstrated in the streets of Soweto, the South African regime responded by killing at least 700 demonstrators and arresting hundreds more. Police killed at least 26 of those arrested while they were in detention centers. In late 1977, Steve Biko, a prominent black leader, was killed while in police custody. His death, and the failure of the South African government adequately to explain the circumstances of his death, shocked the conscience of the world.

In 1979, a labor strike erupted in Port Elizabeth over the treatment of the black employees. The government's response to the nonviolent strike was to arrest and detain or ban the labor leadership. In recent weeks, thousands of colored students have been arrested and detained for their protests against the inferior educational system for nonwhites.

In fact, just last week, the government announced proposed legislation relating to arrest and detention. The new proposal provides that no person shall disclose to any person the fact that any particular person has been arrested or is being detained . . . or anything purporting to be such information.

The logic of apartheid dictates that racial oppression, and indeed, oppression of all people critical of the system, will intensify rather than become ameliorated. This is because the South African Government is unwilling to make the only concession that will satisfy the legitimate demands of the blacks: political equality and full civil rights.

II. UNITED STATES CORPORATE INVOLVEMENT IN SOUTH AFRICA

As racial oppression in South Africa has intensified, United States corporate involvement in South Africa has increased. This involvement has strengthened the South African economy and government by providing key assistance in the most strategic sectors of the economy and contributing to the efforts of the South African regime to become self-sufficient. From 1966 to 1978 direct investment by United States corporations increased from $490 million to $1.8 billion, and presently accounts for 17 percent of the foreign investment in South Africa. Over 75 percent of the total United States investment in South Africa is attributable to a dozen corporations, and the operations of those corporations are concentrated in the most crucial areas of the economy. United States businesses account for 33 percent of the motor vehicle market; 44 percent of the petroleum products market; and 70 percent of the computer market.

Automobiles, oil, and computers are essential components of the South African economy, and the United States corporations dominating these sectors have demonstrated a willingness to cooperate with and to do business with the South African Government.

Both Ford and General Motors sell vehicles to the South African military avoiding United States Commerce Department regulations prohibiting such sales by manufacturing the vehicles in South Africa without using any parts made in the United States. GM has developed a contingency plan, to be activated in the case of civil unrest or national emergency, to cooperate fully with the South African Ministry of Defense, including actual surrender of the company's facilities to the military, manufacturing vehicles directly for the military, and even encouraging its white employees to form and join local defense units.

South Africa has no domestic oil production. Because of its racist policies, every member of OPEC has refused to sell oil to South Africa. There is strong evidence that United States oil companies assist South Africa in obtaining its oil needs despite these boycotts. More disturbing is the fact that South Africa is relying on the Fluor Corporation, a California based engineering and construction company, to become energy self-sufficient. Fluor has signed a $4.2 billion contract to design and supervise the expansion of the South African Coal, Oil and Gas Corporation's coal to oil conversion plant (SASOL II). This is the largest economic undertaking in South African history, and by 1983, is projected to provide 30–50 percent of South Africa's energy needs.

Of the United States computer companies in South Africa, IBM, Control Data, Hewlett-Packard, NCR, Sperry Rand, Burroughs, and Honeywell each include the South African government among their major clients. Computers supplied by these companies are used by the South African Government to implement the pass laws, control the law of migratory labor, and to create an information bank that keeps the government informed on the entire adult black population. Furthermore, all of South Africa's key industries rely on United States computers.

III. THE SULLIVAN PRINCIPLES

Faced with a rising tide of sentiment against doing business with a country whose existence is based on a political system totally repugnant to the world community, United States corporations have sought to justify their continued presence in South Africa and to protect billions of dollars in investment by embracing the Sullivan Principles. The Sullivan Principles were quickly adopted not only by a significant portion of United States corporations doing business in South Africa, but by the South African Government which reviewed, revised and approved the Principles.

The Sullivan Principles have failed to promote peaceful change in South Africa. Moreover, the Principles have failed to achieve their more limited purpose, to "contribute greatly to the general economic welfare of all the people of the Republic of South Africa." We will examine the effect or non-effect of each principle on the lot of black workers—three years after the promulgation of the code.

Principle 3. Equal pay for all employees doing equal or comparable work for the same period of time.

This principle has no effect for the great majority of black workers; 71 percent of black workers employed in United States corporations work in job categories that employ no whites. Ninety-nine percent of the workers employed in the top job categories are white; one percent is black.

Principle 1. Nonsegregation of the races in all eating, comfort and work facilities.

While some United States corporations no longer post signs that segregate their facilities according to race, the majority of the facilities are *still* segregated through the use of more subtle but equally effective means of discrimination. Initially, some companies substituted color-keyed signs for explicitly racial signs. Currently, the discriminatory effect is maintained by assigning separate plant facilities to hourly workers and salaried workers, when the overwhelming majority of wage workers are black and the overwhelming majority of salaried workers are white.

Principle 2. Equal and fair employment practices for all employees.

This principle has been amplified to contain an ambiguous statement encouraging companies to "support" the elimination of discrimination against black trade unions and to "acknowledge generally" the right of blacks to join or form their own trade unions. There is no requirement that the companies recognize or negotiate with unions. In fact, an overwhelming majority of signatories do not negotiate with *any* union—white or black. Only two companies recognize a black trade union, and only one has actually signed a contract.

Principle 4. Initiation and development of training programs that will prepare, in substantial numbers, blacks and other nonwhites for supervisory, administrative, clerical and technical jobs.

South African law cripples this principle by reserving skilled positions for whites. For example, black artisan-trainees are ineligible for certificates of competency, without which they cannot be employed. Closed shop agreements between white unions and their employers reserve skilled positions for members of white trade unions.

Principle 5. Increasing the number of blacks and other nonwhites in management and supervisory positions.

Approximately half the United States companies responding to the most recent Sullivan questionnaire employed no blacks in managerial or supervisory positions.

Even the successful completion by all blacks presently enrolled in training programs of responding companies would result in the employment of blacks in only 3 percent of the managerial and 6 percent of the professional positions.

> Principle 6. Improving the quality of employees' lives outside the work environment in such areas as housing, transportation, schooling, recreation and health.

Unlike the first five principles which purport to improve the work environment of blacks, the sixth principle holds out the nebulous promise of improving the quality of black employees' lives. As we have demonstrated earlier in this testimony, apartheid controls the quality of black South African lives. Token philanthropy is a palliative that does not address the pervasive tyranny of apartheid.

IV. NATIONAL BAR ASSOCIATION POSITION AND RECOMMENDATIONS

The National Bar Association has thus far attempted to set forth the grim reality of the South African experience in order to point out the negligible consequences which the "Sullivan Principles"—even if mandatory—would have on the prospects for ameliorating the condition of South African blacks.

The National Bar Association takes the position that the President and the Congress must take decisive and uncompromised action by prohibiting United States companies from directly or indirectly doing business in South Africa. This would require disinvestment of all current commercial interests of United States companies in South Africa, a ban on all new investments, and the immediate termination of all exportation to and importation from South Africa.

The National Bar Association does not cry wolf. Ours is the calm judgment that the situation in South Africa is deteriorating and, absent fundamental changes, will ultimately explode into racial warfare. Such a circumstance could not but help to tear at the seams of our own multiracial society if we remain ambivalent or non committal.

Arguments will be heard that continued economic intercourse with South Africa benefits blacks thereby providing them with jobs and income. Slavery in the United States was rationalized in a similar way.

The stark fact is that the United States Government policy regarding United States corporate involvement in South Africa feeds apartheid. Thus, African nations, including those which are greatly dependent upon trade with South Africa, have strongly advocated the imposition of mandatory economic sanctions. Within South Africa moderate spokespersons now almost without exception advocate disinvestment, even though such advocacy is illegal and punishable by imprisonment or death in South Africa. At the same time, with increasing incidents of guerilla activity, the nature of the debate within South Africa has changed. In the absence of efforts directed toward the achievement of full political equality, significant numbers of blacks appear committed to a violent solution as the only viable alternative. It is ludicrous to contend that the Sullivan Principles can have a meaningful impact on this situation.

The American black community is unanimous in calling for comprehensive economic sanctions against South Africa. Recently, more than one thousand black leaders and elected officials, representing over three hundred organizations, and millions of constituents across the country, met to adopt a national political, social, economic, and international agenda for the decade of the eighties. That agenda, to which the National Bar Association subscribed, called for the immediate cessation of all economic, diplomatic, political and cultural relations with South Africa.

FRIENDS IN NEED:
Five Good Reasons for Standing by South Africa

ROBERT MOSS*

A strident chorus is now urging Western governments and corporations to commit a destructive act of folly: cut business ties with South Africa. We have heard that demand, on and off, for the best part of two decades. But lately it has become a bull roar. Under a thunder of rhetoric likening South Africa to Nazi Germany, church groups have disinvested in companies with big South African holdings. Universities are being pressured to follow suit. Newspapers and TV networks are lobbied not to run advertisements for Krugerrands. Nigeria threatens to boycott corporations that are heavily involved in South Africa and, with the backing of the Communists, third world radicals and sun-dry Arabs, pushes for a UN oil embargo and other sanctions. And David Rockefeller feels obliged to put out a statement that Chase Manhattan will not make loans that tend to support apartheid. For all the clamor, the advocates of disinvestment have not yet succeeded in persuading any large Western company with a significant stake in South Africa to pull out.

I can readily understand that, in the wake of Steve Biko's tragic death and the clampdown on the South African press, passions are running high. I can also understand that the system of apartheid—which I personally abhor—has singled South Africa out, in many people's eyes, as a uniquely repressive society—which it is not. But what the campaigners for disinvestment should understand is that, if Western governments and corporations succumbed to their demands, the immediate effect would be to push many more South African blacks in penury and unemployment and to drive white South Africans in overwhelming numbers to support the most inflexible, *verkrampte* policies.

In a condition of economic as well as political isolation, South Africa would become the complete fortress-state, quelling beneath an iron heel the social revolt that would stem from the loss of hundreds of thousands of jobs in the cities. All hope of liberalization, for which foreign business in South Africa is a primary catalyst, would be lost. Instead, two grim alternatives would face the country. Either the Afrikaners, whose stamina, military prowess and sheer determination to survive is equal to that of the Israelis, would manage to hold out—perhaps at terrible cost—until the West changed its mind. Or a combination of civil war and foreign invasion would eventually drive them into the sea and bring about a black dictatorship of "Azania" closely aligned with the Soviet bloc and able, if it suited Soviet strategy, to deny the West access to vital raw materials and the strategic cape route.

Such a prospect is unlikely to trouble Marxists who want a revolutionary outcome, inverted radicals who don't care what sort of government South Africa has as long as

---

Excerpted from "Friends in Need: Five Good Reasons for Standing by South Africa," published in *Politics Today*, May/June 1978.

*Former editor of *The Economist's Foreign Report*.

it's black, or the voyeur liberal who simply gets a thrill out of seeing anti-Communist countries kicked in the ribs. But it should worry anyone who hopes for liberal reform.

There are five major reasons for opposing economic sanctions against South Africa. I will briefly explore each of these arguments.

THE MORAL ARGUMENT

Everyone knows the name of Steve Biko, and the terrible story of his death. But how many people know the name of Ijegayehu Asfa-Wossen, the late Emperor Haile Selassie's daughter, who died under almost identical conditions in a prison hospital in Ethiopia on January 31 last year? According to an Amnesty International report, her death "was possibly due to bad detention conditions and lack of proper medical treatment."

South Africa's crimes are writ large, while those of other African countries are completely ignored. South Africa's government is described as a repressive regime, but how repressive is it compared to the other governments of Africa? Western nations were rightly shocked by the banning of editors and the forcible closure of black newspapers. Yet the African director of the International Press Institute has observed, with reason, that "there is more press freedom in South Africa than in the rest of Africa put together." Only whites can vote in South Africa, but *no one* can vote in much of black Africa. Of the 49 member states of the Organization of African Unity (OAU) only four can boast anything resembling democratic institutions.

The abuses of the security police in South Africa are kindergarten fun compared to the tribal and political massacres that have been executed since independence in such countries as Uganda, Nigeria, Zaire or Equatorial Guinea. Yet the documented slaughter of thousands, the murder of an archbishop and the mass expulsion of the local Asian community by Uganda's crazed dictator did not prevent him from being elected president of the OAU. And no one is calling for economic sanctions against Uganda.

So why is South Africa singled out for special punishment? The answer is not that South Africa is "uniquely racist," as is often claimed. Idi Amin praised Hitler for his treatment of the Jews. What is the expulsion of Asians from Uganda or the expropriation of their property in Mozambique if not racism?

No, South Africa is not being hounded because it is racist, but because its rulers are white and, to compound their offense, anti-Communist. Harry Oppenheimer, the leader of the Liberal opposition party in South Africa, put his finger on it when he declared in an address to the Foreign Policy Association in New York last November that "the American attitude towards Southern Africa begins to appear to be based neither on defense of human rights nor on majority rule, but on a policy of supporting blacks against whites."

So let's be done with the moralistic claptrap that the boycott campaigners use to justify their demands. South Africa's blacks live in greater security, comfort and free-dom than blacks in most other African countries. They are ruled by a white tribe rather than a black one, which is considered by some to be unforgivable. Because the United States has a higher proportion of black voters than any other Western country, it is peculiarly susceptible to radically based appeals to act against South Africa, and is in serious danger of allowing its foreign policy toward Africa to shrink to nothing more than a function of US domestic politics.

I am not denying the force of the moral case against apartheid, which amounts to a denial of individual freedom. But I would insist on the basic point: Selective morality is no morality at all. Those who call for economic sanctions against South Africa on moral grounds should remember that the same argument applies, with just as much force, to countries as diverse as the Soviet Union and Iran, China and South Korea, Mozambique and Zaire, Cuba and Chile. If the boycott campaigners want us to stop trading and investing in more than half the world, I admire their consistency, but I am afraid they are holy idiots.

THE SECURITY FACTOR

While the UN was debating the arms embargo against South Africa last year, the Egyptians decided not to permit a British nuclear submarine, the *Dreadnought*, to pass through the Suez Canal on its way to naval exercises in the Pacific. The incident was a timely reminder of the critical importance of the cape route. Last year, about half of America's oil imports were supplied by tankers using this route (supertankers cannot get through the canal anyway) and the proportion is rising. Some 25,000 ships use the cape route every year.

South Africa's strategic importance lies in its mineral wealth as well as in its geographical position astride one of the world's major sea roads. South Africa has been aptly described as "the world's metal bin." The country produces 99 percent of the Western world's platinum, 84 percent of its chrome and manganese, 61 percent of its gold and 40 percent of its titanium. Chrome, of which South Africa is the world's second largest producer, is of singular importance to the United States, since it has almost no chrome of its own, and the mineral is essential in producing alloys for jet engines. Significantly, the Red Army's Major General Lagovskiy drew attention to this vulnerability more than 20 years ago in a book entitled *Strategy and Economics*. He suggested that lack of chrome was a weak link in American defenses that the Soviets should seek to exploit.

Why, given this risk and South Africa's evident strategic importance, should Western governments and corporations participate in a campaign to undermine the South African economy, particularly when that campaign is explicitly intended to achieve political destabilization, whose outcome would be wholly unpredictable?

BENEFITS TO BLACK AFRICA

Whatever their official line on South Africa, many black African countries are heavily dependent on it to provide jobs, revenue, technical help and a wide range of imported goods. The shrinkage of the South African economy that would result from major disinvestment could deal some of these states a body blow. The most ironic example is that of Marxist Mozambique, which sends more than 100,000 migrant workers to South Africa's gold mines each year.

South Africa has a thriving trade—overtly or covertly—with most of Africa. At least a dozen black African states would face economic ruin if they were compelled to respect a total trade embargo with South Africa. Who would pick up the bill? Even without a total embargo, these states stand to suffer badly from the deepening recession in South Africa that would result from a cutoff of Western investment.

BUSINESS BRINGS REFORM

According to the advocates of disinvestment, putting money into South Africa means "investing in apartheid," i.e., helping to shore up a system whose economic *raison d'être* (in their view) is to ensure a permanent supply of cheap labor. Now there is no doubt that cheap labor rates—compared to wage levels in Western countries—are a major attraction to foreign investors, as is true in any developing country. But wage rates are considerably higher for industrial workers in South Africa than in the black African states to the north. The living standards of black South African families are, on average, from two to five times higher than the norm in other African countries.

Foreign business in South Africa has demonstrably been a catalyst for beneficial change. Allegations about corporations that pay their workers at levels below the poverty line get massive exposure in the media. Less attention is paid to initiatives like General Motors' statement of principles, drawn up last year by a black director, Reverend Leon Sullivan. It called for American firms in South Africa to abandon racial segregation in the workplace, to provide equal pay for equal work and to follow fair practices in making promotions. The Sullivan declaration has been endorsed by 56 American companies.

Apart from initiatives of this kind, there is a logic in the growth of manufacturing industry in South Africa that is helping to advance the social position, as well as the living standards, of blacks and to show up the economic absurdity of racial discrimination. The white community cannot supply all the skilled labor that is required, especially given the inroads of military conscription. As a result, blacks are being brought into positions of greater responsibility. It is in the context of an expanding economy, not the siege economy into which South Africa would be driven by trade or investment embargoes, that equality on the job is most likely to come about. This may appear a frustratingly slow process to outsiders, but peaceful reforms come about through short steps, not giant leaps.

THE BLACKS WOULD SUFFER FIRST

Any approach to the South African problem must begin with the recognition that the whites have every right to be there and that their nationalism, which runs strong, is as valid as anyone else's. The Afrikaner pioneers did not steal the land of black nations; the area that they settled was for the most part uninhabited. South Africa is a multinational state, where the divide is not simply between black and white, but between a white nationalism and a number of black nationalisms including those of the Zulu nation, the Xhosa nation, the Tswana and Sotho peoples. Above all, South Africa is not, and has never been, a colonial problem, as was recognized even by the black African leaders who issued the Lusaka Declaration against colonialism and racialism in 1969.

South Africa's political establishment is seeking a solution for the problem of rival white and black nationalism in the policy of separate development. Some 13 percent of the country's land, including almost half of the most fertile agricultural land, has been designated as black "homelands." The homelands, or Bantustans, have either become independent states, or are destined to become so.

"Separate development" in its present form may be no solution for South Africa's problems, but neither is the simplistic demand for majority rule now. The United States, after all, only began to solve its racial problems after a hundred years and a bloody civil war. Outside the Communist party of South Africa (which doesn't believe in "bourgeois democracy" anyway), no serious figure in the white community believes that one man, one vote will be possible in this country anytime soon. The fundamentalism with which most Afrikaners adhere to the ideology of apartheid makes it certain that the more strongly the demand for majority rule is voiced, the more firmly it will be resisted.

The West must come to terms with the fact that it *needs* South Africa, as do many black African countries. A friendly South Africa is a vital ally in the struggle to contain Soviet expansionism, as we saw in Angola. Try telling any moderate black leader in Africa that racism, not communism, is the problem and he will laugh in your face. Men like Kenyatta, and Kaunda, and Mobutu and most of the French-African leaders are not threatened by South Africa; they are threatened by the protégés of Moscow. Most of them were secretly begging the South Africans to go into Angola in response to the invasion by the Cubans, Russia's proxy troops.

Boycott or no boycott, my own hunch is that South Africa is going to survive. I cannot explain my confidence purely in terms of South Africa's self-sufficiency in every major commodity except oil (and it has enough oil stockpiled to last three or four years) or its highly professional and well-equipped armed forces, or the probability that it already has nuclear weapons, or even its vital defense relationship with Israel, France, West Germany and Iran.

The primary reason for my confidence lies in the character of the Afrikaners. They are, in fact, a white tribe in Africa. They owe nothing to anyone: They didn't steal their lands from any existing culture; they fought the British for independence; they are not colonial settlers who will meekly depart with a retreating colonial power. They have no place to run to, and their nationalism runs strong and deep. Like the Jews of the Bible, they are a "stiff-necked people." Like the Israelis, they mean to survive.

CASES FOR PART FOUR

THE FORD PINTO

W. MICHAEL HOFFMAN*

I

On August 10, 1978, a tragic automobile accident occurred on U.S. Highway 33 near Goshen, Indiana. Sisters Judy and Lynn Ulrich (ages 18 and 16, respectively) and their cousin Donna Ulrich (age 18) were struck from the rear in their 1973 Ford Pinto by a van. The gas tank of the Pinto ruptured, the car burst into flames, and the three teenagers were burned to death.

Subsequently an Elkhart County grand jury returned a criminal homicide charge against Ford, the first ever against an American corporation. During the following twenty-week trial, Judge Harold R. Staffeldt advised the jury that Ford should be convicted of reckless homicide if it were shown that the company had engaged in "plain, conscious and unjustifiable disregard of harm that might result (from its actions) and the disregard involves a substantial deviation from acceptable standards of conduct."[1]

The key phrase around which the trial hinged, of course, is "acceptable standards." Did Ford knowingly and recklessly choose profit over safety in the design and placement of the Pinto's gas tank? Elkhart County prosecutor Michael A. Cosentino and chief Ford attorney James F. Neal battled dramatically over this issue in a rural Indiana courthouse. Meanwhile, American business anxiously awaited the verdict which could send warning ripples through boardrooms across the nation concerning corporate responsibility and product liability.

II

As a background to this trial some discussion of the Pinto controversy is necessary. In 1977 the magazine *Mother Jones* broke a story by Mark Dowie, general manager of *Mother Jones* business operations, accusing Ford of knowingly putting on the road an unsafe car—the Pinto—in which hundreds of people have needlessly suffered burn deaths and even more have been scarred and disfigured from burns. In his article "Pinto Madness" Dowie charges that:

Original essay. Copyright © 1984 by Michael Hoffman.
*Department of Philosophy, Bentley College, Waltham, Mass.

- Fighting strong competition from Volkswagen for the lucrative small-car market, the Ford Motor Company rushed the Pinto into production in much less than the usual time.

- Ford engineers discovered in preproduction crash tests that rear-end collisions would rupture the Pinto's fuel system extremely easily.

- Because assembly-line machinery was already tooled when engineers found this defect, top Ford officials decided to manufacture the car anyway—exploding gas tank and all— even though Ford owned the patent on a much safer gas tank.

- For more than eight years afterward, Ford successfully lobbied, with extraordinary vigor and some blatant lies, against a key government safety standard that would have forced the company to change the Pinto's fire-prone gas tank.

By conservative estimates Pinto crashes have caused 500 burn deaths to people who would not have been seriously injured if the car had not burst into flames. The figure could be as high as 900. Burning Pintos have become such an embarrassment to Ford that its advertising agency, J. Walter Thompson, dropped a line from the ending of a radio spot that read "Pinto leaves you with that warm feeling."

Ford knows that the Pinto is a firetrap, yet it has paid out millions to settle damage suits out of court, and it is prepared to spend millions more lobbying against safety standards. With a half million cars rolling off the assembly lines each year, Pinto is the biggest-selling subcompact in America, and the company's operating profit on the car is fantastic. Finally, in 1977, new Pinto models have incorporated a few minor alterations necessary to meet that federal standard Ford managed to hold off for eight years. Why did the company delay so long in making these minimal, inexpensive improvements?

- Ford waited eight years because its internal "cost-benefit analysis," which places a dollar value on human life, said it wasn't profitable to make the changes sooner.[2]

Several weeks after Dowie's press conference on the article, which had the support of Ralph Nader and auto safety expert Byron Bloch, Ford issued a news release attributed to Herbert T. Misch, vice president of Environmental and Safety Engineering, countering points made in the *Mother Jones* article. Their statistical studies conflict significantly with each other. For example, Dowie states that more than 3,000 people were burning to death yearly in auto fires; he claims that, according to a National Highway Traffic Safety Administration (NHTSA) consultant, although Ford makes 24 percent of the cars on American roads, these cars account for 42 percent of the collision-ruptured fuel tanks.[3] Ford, on the other hand, uses statistics from the Fatality Analysis Reporting System (FARS) maintained by the government's NHTSA to defend itself, claiming that in 1975 there were 848 deaths related to fire-associated passenger-car accidents and only 13 of these involved Pintos; in 1976, Pintos accounted for only 22 out of 943. These statistics imply that Pintos were involved in only 1.9 percent of such accidents, and Pintos constitute about 1.9 percent of the total registered passenger cars. Furthermore, fewer than half of those Pintos cited in the FARS study were struck in the rear.[4] Ford concludes from this and other studies that the Pinto was never an unsafe car and has not been involved in some 70 burn deaths annually, as *Mother Jones* claims.

Ford admits that early-model Pintos did not meet rear-impact tests at 20 mph but denies that this implies that they were unsafe compared with other cars of that type and era. In fact, according to Ford, some of its tests were conducted with experimental rubber "bladders" to protect the gas tank, in order to determine how best to have its future cars meet a 20-mph rear-collision standard which Ford itself set as an internal performance goal. The government at that time had no such standard. Ford also points out that in every model year the Pinto met or surpassed the government's own standards, and

> it simply is unreasonable and unfair to contend that a car is somehow unsafe if it does not meet standards proposed for future years or embody the technological improvements that are introduced in later model years.[5]

Mother Jones, on the other hand, presents a different view of the situation. If Ford was so concerned about rear-impact safety, why did it delay the federal government's attempts to impose standards? Dowie gives the following answer:

> The particular regulation involved here was Federal Motor Vehicle Safety Standard 301. Ford picked portions of Standard 301 for strong opposition way back in 1968 when the Pinto was still in the blueprint stage. The intent of 301, and the 300 series that followed it, was to protect drivers and passengers after a crash occurs. Without question the worst post-crash hazard is fire. So Standard 301 originally proposed that all cars should be able to withstand a fixed barrier impact of 20 mph (that is, running into a wall at that speed) without losing fuel.
>
> When the standard was proposed, Ford engineers pulled their crash-test results out of their files. The front ends of most cars were no problem—with minor alterations they could stand the impact without losing fuel. "We were already working on the front end," Ford engineer Dick Kimble admitted. "We knew we could meet the test on the front end." But with the Pinto particularly, a 20 mph rear-end standard meant redesigning the entire rear end of the car. With the Pinto scheduled for production in August of 1970, and with $200 million worth of tools in place, adoption of this standard would have created a minor financial disaster. So Standard 301 was targeted for delay, and with some assistance from its industry associates, Ford succeeded beyond its wildest expectations: the standard was not adopted until the 1977 model year.[6]

Ford's tactics were successful, according to Dowie, not only due to their extremely clever lobbying, which became the envy of lobbyists all over Washington, but also because of the pro-industry stance of NHTSA itself.

Furthermore, it is not at all clear that the Pinto was as safe as comparable cars with regard to the positioning of its gas tank. Unlike the gas tank in the Capri, which rode over the rear axle, a "saddle-type" fuel tank on which Ford owned the patent, the Pinto tank was placed just behind the rear bumper. According to Dowie,

> Dr. Leslie Ball, the retired safety chief for the NASA manned space program and a founder of the International Society of Reliability Engineers, recently made a careful study of the Pinto. "The release to production of the Pinto was the most reprehensible decision in the

history of American engineering," he said. Ball can name more than 40 European and Japanese models in the Pinto price and weight range with safer gas-tank positioning.

Los Angeles auto safety expert Byron Bloch has made an in-depth study of the Pinto fuel system. "It's a catastrophic blunder," he says. "Ford made an extremely irresponsible decision when they placed such a weak tank in such a ridiculous location in such a soft rear end. It's almost designed to blow up—premeditated. [7]

Although other points could be brought out in the debate between *Mother Jones* and Ford, perhaps the most intriguing and controversial is the cost-benefit analysis study that Ford did entitled "Fatalities Associated with Crash-Induced Fuel Leakage and Fires" released by J. C. Echold, director of automotive safety for Ford. This study apparently convinced Ford and was intended to convince the federal government that a technological improvement costing $11 per car which would have prevented gas tanks from rupturing so easily was not cost effective for society. The costs and benefits are broken down in the following way:

BENEFITS

Savings:	180 burn deaths, 180 serious burn injuries, 2,100 burned vehicles
Unit Cost:	$200,000 per death, $67,000 per injury, $700 per vehicle
Total Benefit:	$180 \times (\$200,000) + 180 \times (\$67,000) + 2,100 \times (\$700) = \$49.5 \text{ million}$

COSTS

Sales:	11 million cars, 1.5 million light trucks
Unit Cost:	$11 per car, $11 per truck
Total Cost:	$11,000,000 \times (\$11) + 1,500,000 \times (\$11) = \$137 \text{ million}$

And where did Ford come up with the $200,000 figure as the cost per death? This came from a NHTSA study which broke down the estimated social costs of a death as follows:

COMPONENT	1971 COSTS
Future Productivity Losses	
Direct	$132,000
Indirect	41,300
Medical Costs	
Hospital	700
Other	425
Property Damage	1,500
Insurance Administration	4,700
Legal and Court	3,000
Employer Losses	1,000
Victim's Pain and Suffering	10,000
Funeral	900
Assets (Lost Consumption)	5,000
Miscellaneous	200
Total per fatality	$200,725

(Although this analysis was on all Ford vehicles, a breakout of just the Pinto could be done.) *Mother Jones* reports it could not find anybody who could explain how the $10,000 figure for "pain and suffering" had been arrived at.[8]

Although Ford does not mention this point in its news release defense, one might have replied that it was the federal government, not Ford, that set the figure for a burn death. Ford simply carried out a cost-benefit analysis based on that figure. *Mother Jones*, however, in addition to insinuating that there was industry-agency (NHTSA) collusion, argues that the $200,000 figure was arrived at under intense pressure from the auto industry to use cost-benefit analysis in determining regulations. *Mother Jones* also questions Ford's estimate of burn injuries: "All independent experts estimate that for each person who dies by an auto fire, many more are left with charred hands, faces and limbs." Referring to the Northern California Burn Center, which estimates the ratio of burn injuries to deaths at ten to one instead of one to one, Dowie states that "the true ratio obviously throws the company's calculations way off."[9] Finally, *Mother Jones* claims to have obtained "confidential" Ford documents which Ford did not send to Washington, showing that crash fires could largely be prevented by installing a rubber bladder inside the gas tank for only $5.08 per car, considerably less than the $11 per car Ford originally claimed was required to improve crashworthiness.[10]

Instead of making the $11 improvement, installing the $5.08 bladder, or even giving the consumer the right to choose the additional cost for added safety, Ford continued, according to *Mother Jones*, to delay the federal government for eight years in establishing mandatory rear-impact standards. In the meantime, Dowie argues, thousands of people were burning to death and tens of thousands more were being badly burned and disfigured for life, while many of these tragedies could have been prevented for only a slight cost per vehicle. Furthermore, the delay also meant that millions of new unsafe vehicles went on the road, "vehicles that will be crashing, leaking fuel and incinerating people well into the 1980s."[11]

In concluding his article Dowie broadens his attack beyond just Ford and the Pinto.

> Unfortunately, the Pinto is not an isolated case of corporate malpractice in the auto industry. Neither is Ford a lone sinner. There probably isn't a car on the road without a safety hazard known to its manufacturer. . . .
> Furthermore, cost-valuing human life is not used by Ford alone. Ford was just the only company careless enough to let such an embarrassing calculation slip into public records. The process of willfully trading lives for profits is built into corporate capitalism. Commodore Vanderbilt publicly scorned George Westinghouse and his "foolish" air brakes while people died by the hundreds in accidents on Vanderbilt's railroads.[12]

Ford has paid millions of dollars in Pinto jury trials and out-of-court settlements, especially the latter. *Mother Jones* quotes Al Slechter in Ford's Washington office as saying: "We'll never go to a jury again. Not in a fire case. Juries are just too sentimental. They see those charred remains and forget the evidence. No sir, we'll settle."[13] But apparently Ford thought such settlements would be less costly than the safety improvements. Dowie wonders if Ford would continue to make the same decisions "were Henry Ford II and Lee Iacocca serving twenty-year terms in Leavenworth for consumer homicide."[14]

III

On March 13, 1980, the Elkhart County jury found Ford not guilty of criminal homicide in the Ulrich case. Ford attorney Neal summarized several points in his closing argument before the jury. Ford could have stayed out of the small-car market, which would have been the "easiest way," since Ford would have made more profit by sticking to bigger cars. Instead, Ford built the Pinto "to take on the imports, to save jobs for Americans and to make a profit for its stockholders."[15] The Pinto met every fuel-system standard of any federal, state, or local government, and was comparable to other 1973 subcompacts. The engineers who designed the car thought it was a good, safe car and bought it for themselves and their families. Ford did everything possible to recall the Pinto quickly after NHTSA ordered it to do so. Finally, and more specifically to the case at hand, Highway 33 was a badly designed highway, and the girls were fully stopped when a 4,000-pound van rammed into the rear of their Pinto at at least 50 miles an hour. Given the same circumstances, Neal stated, any car would have suffered the same consequences as the Ulrich's Pinto.[16] As reported in the *New York Times* and *Time*, the verdict brought a "loud cheer" from Ford's board of directors and undoubtedly at least a sigh of relief from other corporations around the nation.

Many thought this case was that of a David against a Goliath because of the small amount of money and volunteer legal help Prosecutor Cosentino had in contrast to the huge resources Ford poured into the trial. In addition, it should be pointed out that Cosentino's case suffered from a ruling by Judge Staffeldt that Ford's own test results on pre-1973 Pintos were inadmissible. These documents confirmed that Ford knew as early as 1971 that the gas tank of the Pinto ruptured at impacts of 20 mph and that the company was aware, because of tests with the Capri, that the over-the-axle position of the gas tank was much safer than mounting it behind the axle. Ford decided to mount it behind the axle in the Pinto to provide more trunk space and to save money. The restrictions of Cosentino's evidence to testimony relating specifically to the 1973 Pinto severely undercut the strength of the prosecutor's case.[17]

Whether this evidence would have changed the minds of the jury will never be known. Some, however, such as business ethicist Richard De George, feel that this evidence shows grounds for charges of recklessness against Ford. Although it is true that there were no federal safety standards in 1973 to which Ford legally had to conform and although Neal seems to have proved that all subcompacts were unsafe when hit at 50 mph by a 4,000-pound van, the fact that the NHTSA ordered a recall of the Pinto and not other subcompacts is, according to De George, "*prima facie* evidence that Ford's Pinto gas tank mounting was substandard."[18] De George argues that these grounds for recklessness are made even stronger by the fact that Ford did not give the consumer a choice to make the Pinto gas tank safer by installing a rubber bladder for a rather modest fee.[19] Giving the consumer such a choice, of course, would have made the Pinto gas tank problem known and therefore probably would have been bad for sales.

Richard A. Epstein, professor of law at the University of Chicago Law School, questions whether Ford should have been brought up on criminal charges of reckless homicide at all. He also points out an interesting historical fact. Before 1966 an injured party in Indiana could not even bring civil charges against an automobile manufacturer solely because of the alleged "uncrashworthiness" of a car; one would have to seek legal relief from the other party involved in the accident, not from the manufacturer. But after *Larson v. General Motors Corp.* in 1968, a new era of crashworthiness suits against automobile manufacturers began. "Reasonable" precautions must now be taken by manufacturers to minimize personal harm in crashes.[20] How to apply criteria of reasonableness in such cases marks the whole nebulous ethical and legal arena of product liability.

If such a civil suit had been brought against Ford, Epstein believes, the corporation might have argued, as it did to a large extent in the criminal suit, that the Pinto conformed to all current applicable safety standards and with common industry practice. (Epstein cites that well over 90 percent of United States standard production cars had their gas tanks in the same position as the Pinto.) But in a civil trial the adequacy of industry standards are ultimately up to the jury, and had civil charges been brought against Ford in this case the plaintiffs might have had a better chance of winning.[21] Epstein feels that a criminal suit, on the other hand, had no chance from the very outset, because the prosecutor would have had to establish criminal intent on the part of Ford. To use an analogy, if a hunter shoots at a deer and wounds an unseen person, he may be held civilly responsible but not criminally responsible because he did not intend to harm. And even though it may be more difficult to determine the mental state of a corporation (or its principal agents), it seems clear to Epstein that the facts of this case do not prove any such criminal intent even though Ford may have known that some burn deaths and injuries could have been avoided by a different placement of its Pinto gas tank and that Ford consciously decided not to spend more money to save lives.[22] Everyone recognizes that there are trade-offs between safety and costs. Ford could have built a "tank" instead of a Pinto, thereby considerably reducing risks, but it would have been relatively unaffordable for most and probably unattractive to all potential consumers.

To have established Ford's reckless homicide it would have been necessary to establish the same of Ford's agents, since a corporation can only act through its agents. Undoubtedly, continues Epstein, the reason why the prosecutor did not try to subject Ford's officers and engineers to fines and imprisonment for their design choices is "the good faith character of their judgment, which was necessarily decisive in Ford's behalf as well."[23] For example, Harold C. MacDonald, Ford's chief engineer on the Pinto, testified that he felt it was important to keep the gas tank as far from the passenger compartment as possible, as it was in the Pinto. And other Ford engineers testified that they used the car for their own families. This is relevant information in a criminal case which must be concerned about the intent of the agents.

Furthermore, even if civil charges had been made in this case, it seems unfair and irrelevant to Epstein to accuse Ford of trading cost for safety. Ford's use of cost-benefit formulas, which must assign monetary values to human life and suffering, is precisely what the law demands in assessing civil liability suits. The court may disagree with the decision, but to blame industry for using such a method would violate the very rules of civil liability. Federal automobile officials (NHTSA) had to make the same calculations in order to discharge their statutory duties. In allowing the Pinto design, are not they too (and in turn their employer, the United States) just as guilty as Ford's agents?[24]

IV

The case of the Ford Pinto raises many questions of ethical importance. Some people conclude that Ford was definitely wrong in designing and marketing the Pinto. The specific accident involving the Ulrich girls, because of the circumstances, was simply not the right one to have attacked Ford on. Other people believe that Ford was neither criminally nor civilly guilty of anything and acted completely responsibly in producing the Pinto. Many others, I suspect, find the case morally perplexing, too complex to make sweeping claims of guilt or innocence.

Was Ford irresponsible in rushing the production of the Pinto? Even though Ford violated no federal safety standards or laws, should it have made the Pinto safer in terms of rear-end collisions, especially regarding the placement of the gas tank? Should Ford have used cost-benefit analysis to make decisions relating to safety, specifically placing dollar values on human life and suffering? Knowing that the Pinto's gas tank could have been made safer by installing a protective bladder for a relatively small cost per consumer, perhaps Ford should have made that option available to the public. If Ford did use heavy lobbying efforts to delay and/or influence federal safety standards, was this ethically proper for a corporation to do? One might ask, if Ford was guilty, whether the engineers, the managers, or both are to blame. If Ford had been found guilty of criminal homicide, was the proposed penalty stiff enough ($10,000 maximum fine for each of the three counts equals $30,000 maximum), or should agents of the corporation such as MacDonald, Iacocca, and Henry Ford II be fined and possibly jailed?

A number of questions concerning safety standards are also relevant to the ethical issues at stake in the Ford trial. Is it just to blame a corporation for not abiding by "acceptable standards" when such standards are not yet determined by society? Should corporations like Ford play a role in setting such standards? Should individual juries be determining such standards state by state, incident by incident? If Ford should be setting safety standards, how does it decide how safe to make its product and still make it affordable and desirable to the public without using cost-benefit analysis? For that matter, how does anyone decide? Perhaps it is putting Ford, or any corporation, in a catch-22 position to ask it both to set safety standards and to make a competitive profit for its stockholders.

Regardless of how we answer these and other questions it is clear that the Pinto case raises fundamental issues concerning the responsibilities of corporations, how corporations should structure themselves in order to make ethical decisions, and how industry, government, and society in general ought to interrelate to form a framework within which such decisions can properly be made in the future.

NOTES

1. *The Indianapolis Star*, Sunday, Mar. 9, 1980, Section 3, p. 2.

2. Mark Dowie, "Pinto Madness," *Mother Jones*, September–October, 1977, pp. 18, 20. Subsequently Mike Wallace for "Sixty Minutes" and Sylvia Chase for "20-20" came out with similar exposés.

3. *Ibid.*, p. 30.

4. Ford news release (Sept. 9, 1977), pp. 1–3.

5. *Ibid.*, p. 5.

6. Dowie, p. 29.

7. *Ibid.*, pp. 22–23.

8. *Ibid.*, pp. 24, 28.

9. *Ibid.*, p. 28.

10. *Ibid.*, pp. 28–29.

11. *Ibid.*, p. 30.

12. *Ibid.*, p. 32. Dowie might have cited another example which emerged in the private correspondence which transpired almost a half-century ago between Lammot du Pont and Alfred P. Sloan, Jr., then president of GM. Du Pont was trying to convince Sloan to equip GM's lowest-priced cars, Chevrolets, with safety glass. Sloan replied by saying: "It is not my responsibility to sell safety glass. . . . You can say, perhaps, that I am selfish, but business is selfish. We are not a charitable institution—we are trying to make a profit for our stockholders. [Quoted in Morton Mintz and Jerry S. Cohen, *Power, Inc.* (New York: The Viking Press, 1976), p. 110.]

13. *Ibid.*, p. 31.

14. *Ibid.*, p. 32.

15. Transcript of report of proceedings in *State of Indiana v. Ford Motor Company*, Cause No. 11-431, Monday, Mar. 10, 1980, pp. 6202–6203. How Neal reconciled his "easiest way" point with his "making more profit for stockholders" point is not clear to this writer.

16. *Ibid.*, pp. 6207–6209.

17. *Chicago Tribune*, Oct. 13, 1979, p. 1, and Section 2, p. 12; *New York Times*, Oct. 14, 1979, p. 26; *The Atlanta Constitution*, Feb. 7, 1980.

18. Richard De George, "Ethical Responsibilities of Engineers in Large Organizations: The Pinto Case," *Business and Professional Ethics Journal*, vol. 1., No. 1 (Fall 1981), p. 4. *The New York Times*, Oct. 26, 1978, p. 103, also points out that during 1976 and 1977 there were thirteen fiery fatal rear-end collisions involving Pintos, more than double that of other United States comparable cars, with VW Rabbits and Toyota Corollas having none.

19. *Ibid.*, p. 5.

20. Richard A. Epstein, "Is Pinto a Criminal?", *Regulation*, March–April, 1980, pp. 16–17.

21. A California jury awarded damages of $127.8 million (reduced later to $6.3 million on appeal) in a Pinto crash in which a youth was burned over 95 percent of his body. See *New York Times*, Feb. 8, 1978, p. 8.

22. Epstein, p. 19.

23. *Ibid.*, pp. 20–21.

24. *Ibid.*, pp. 19–21.

HOOKER CHEMICAL AND THE LOVE CANAL

TIMOTHY S. MESCON* and GEORGE S. VOZIKIS†

Just prior to the turn of the century, Colonel William Love arrived in Niagara Falls, New York, with a dream. Love envisioned a canal that would connect the upper and lower Niagara Rivers across the peninsula, drop it over a 300-foot Niagara escarpment, and bring a new source of electrical power to the area. Love envisioned a model industrial city emerging in this beautiful upstate New York area. Initial support was slow in developing, so Love started digging the canal by himself until financial backers were identified. Unfortunately, the combination of an economic depression, which dried up Colonel Love's sources of funds, and the invention of alternating current (which meant that electricity could be transmitted over distances) brought an abrupt halt to Colonel Love's dream. The canal served as a swimming hole in the summer and as a skating rink in the winter for over 30 years until it was acquired by Hooker Electrochemical Company in 1942.

HOOKER CHEMICAL—A BRIEF HISTORY

Elon Huntington Hooker was the founder of the Development and Funding Company [1906], which was the predecessor of the Hooker Electrochemical Company, later renamed Hooker Chemical Company.

During both World Wars, Hooker Electrochemical Company was instrumental in America's effort to achieve independence in the field of industrial chemistry. The company built and ran five defense plants for the government, turning out scores of chemicals useful in products from synthetic rubber to waterproof tents. The company also participated in the Manhattan District Atomic Project. In the decade following World War II, the company's sales grew from $15 million to $54 million. The company was also producing more than 100 chemicals in three locations. In 1958, the company incorporated. Ten years later, Occidental Petroleum Corporation acquired the company through a stock exchange. One dollar invested in the Hooker Company in 1905 had grown to $3077. Today, Hooker is the tenth largest chemical company in the nation, with 1979 sales of $1.7 billion. Hooker Chemical Corporation has 30 plants in 11 countries, and employs more than 110,000 workers. Few Americans are ever out of reach of Hooker's products. The company's chemicals can be found in toothpaste, soap, gasolines, tires, inks, and diapers, to name just a few products.

Excerpted from "Hooker Chemical and the Love Canal," published in *Management Policy and Strategy*, 2d ed., edited by George A. Steiner et al. (New York: Macmillan Publishing Co., Inc., 1982). Reprinted by permission of Timothy S. Mescon.

*Department of General Business, Management, and Organization, University of Miami, Coral Gables, Fla.

†Professor of Management, University of Oklahoma, Norman, Okla.

THE LOVE CANAL

Between the years 1942–53 Hooker disposed its chemical wastes in the Love Canal. The Love Canal was considered an ideal landfill site for chemical residues and numerous other wastes for two basic reasons: (1) at the time, the canal area was sparsely populated, and (2) the soil was an impervious clay that was characteristic of the land in that part of New York state. Such impervious clay created a natural "vault" which would hold the chemical residues and other industrial wastes.

The sections of the canal used by Hooker were isolated as needed. The chemical wastes were transported to the site in drums and were then placed, either in the old canal bed or a new excavation, and covered with several feet of clay material.

By 1952, the Board of Education of the City of Niagara Falls wanted the Love Canal site for a school, and Hooker found itself facing the threat of seizure of the land by the law of eminent domain. Resulting from the persistence of the School Board in 1953 Hooker deeded the land to the city for $1. The deed contained the following admonition:

> Prior to the delivery of this instrument of conveyance, the grantee herein has been advised by the grantor that the premises above described have been filled, in whole or in part, to the present grade level thereof with waste products resulting from the manufacturing of chemicals by the grantor at its plant in the City of Niagara Falls, New York, and the grantee assumes all risk and liability incident to the use thereof. It is, therefore, understood and agreed that, as a part of the consideration for this conveyance and as a condition thereof, no claim, suit, action or demand of any nature whatsoever shall ever be made by the grantee, its successors or assigns, against the grantor, including death resulting therefrom, or loss of or damage to property caused by, in connection with or by reason of the presence of said industrial wastes. It is further agreed as a condition hereof that each subsequent conveyance of the aforesaid lands shall be made subject to the foregoing provisions and conditions.

After acquiring the land, the School Board subdivided it and built a school adjacent to the central portion of the canal. The northern part of the land was deeded to the city and the southern portion was eventually sold to a private developer. In time, despite the warning issued by Hooker, houses and shopping centers sprang up in the area (no homes, however, were built directly on the Love Canal property). The basements of many of these houses expanded into the impervious clay. When the construction crews removed the topsoil covering the surface of the Love Canal, rain and snow began to seep into the canal gradually forcing a chemical mixture, leachate, to flow out of sealed containers.

As early as 1958 some children playing above the Love Canal dump site had to be treated for chemical burns; this, however, was merely a minor indication of the problems to come. Throughout the 1970s heavy rains accelerated the erosion of the more than 199,900 tons of contaminated waste representing 150 chemical compounds in the area [EPA Hits Hooker, 1979]. As the waste oozed to the surface, some ominous statistics also began to emerge. An unusually high percentage of miscarriages, serious birth defects, liver abnormalities, chromosome breakdown, and cancer was detected in the area. Additionally, a strong smell emitted from the chemicals prompted one local resident to claim, "The whole area stinks" [Molotsky, 1979].

THE CONFLICT

On May 21, 1980, President Carter signed an emergency order under which the federal government and the state of New York will share the ($3–$5 million) cost of relocating 710 Love Canal area families to other housing. This move will be in addition to the 239 other families who were forced to abandon their homes in 1978 after toxic fumes were discovered in their basements and traces of trichlorophenal (which breaks down into dioxin and can cause cancer, nervous system depression, liver and kidney damage, and irritate skin and mucous membranes) were found in nearby drainage ditches. President Carter's action followed the release of a study conducted by the Environmental Protection Agency (EPA) that examined 36 residents in the area and concluded that 11 showed signs of chromosome breakdown.

In December 1979 the EPA filed a complaint against Hooker Chemical, the city of Niagara Falls and the Niagara Falls Board of Education. In part, the complaint stated,

> Hooker neither warned residents and developers in the vicinity that contact with materials at the canal could be injurious, nor did it take any action to prevent future injuries due to exposure of the wastes. [What Hooker Told Whom, When About Love Canal, 1980]

Only two of the nine school board members who accepted the deed to the land in 1953 can be found. Although the transference of the deed took place almost 30 years ago, Irma Runals, one of the school board members, who insists that Hooker warned no one of any dangers said, "By golly, you certainly would remember that" [Molotsky, 1979].

Minutes collected from the Board of Education meetings held in 1957 prior to the subdivision of the land, however, indicate that representatives from Hooker did indeed urge the Board not to approve construction on the land.

Arthur Chambers, appearing before the Board on November 7, 1957, as a representative of Hooker's Legal Department,

> reminded the board that . . . the land was not suitable for construction where underground facilities are necessary. It was their (Hooker's) intent that the property be used for a school and for parking. He referred to the moral obligation on the part of the Board of Education in the event the property is sold." [What Hooker Told Whom, When About Love Canal, 1980]

On November 22, Chambers reappeared before the Board and warned,

> there are dangerous chemicals buried there in drums, in loose form, in solids and liquids. It was understood the land would be used for a park or some surface activity if it was developed. [What Hooker Told Whom, When About Love Canal, 1980]

A 1979 study conducted by the American Institute of Chemical Engineers told a Senate environmental subcommittee that the original dump site was *well within federal guidelines* set in 1976 by the Resource Conservation and Recovery Act. According to the researchers, "the problem at Love Canal was a lack of remedial work" [Love Canal Lessons, 1980].

The Resource Conservation and Recovery Act was designed to control the treatment of hazardous wastes from their generation to their ultimate disposal. This 1976 law deals primarily with the regulation of *new* waste-disposal sites. To date, EPA officials have been somewhat reluctant to regulate dumps already in existence because the law requires that there be an "imminent hazard" to public health before the government can step in. (Hazardous wastes are defined by the EPA as those that are flammable, corrosive, or toxic to humans, or that react violently with chemicals. Some 36 million tons of hazardous wastes are manufactured each year.)

For its part, Hooker, which has not officially owned the land for 20 years, does not consider that it had any responsibility in the matter. The company did, however, volunteer to share the cost of the consulting engineers' study and to contribute one third of the original estimate for the cost of a remedial program.

The other two-thirds of the cost of recapping the southern portion of the canal was to be assumed by the school board and the city. However, because of the school board's inability to raise the necessary funds and the delay in rectifying the existing situation, a state of emergency was declared and the federal and state governments assumed the costs of the remedial program. According to sources at Hooker, the company is still willing to share the cost, as long as the school board and the local government also participate.

HOOKER'S PAST RECORD

Although Hooker does not claim responsibility for the Love Canal situation, it has admitted to falsifying records concerning releases of toxic waste in upstate New York and the pollution of wells on Long Island. An internal memo at Hooker's Durex division also disclosed that "Hooker had instructed supervisors on how to hide toxic waste and spills inside the plant from New York State Department of Environmental Control inspectors" [Galdston, 1979, p. 27].

Other dumping and storage acts on Hooker's part seem to solidify critics' concerns. Recent disclosures include the dumping of Kepone (a known carcinogen) into the James River in Virginia, runoff from improperly stored barrels of Mirex (a carcinogen) into Lake Ontario, which prompted health officials to bar all commercial and private fishing on the lake, and the release of Mirex being stored in rotting barrels into Lake Michigan.

A company report titled "Operation Bootstrap" indicates that Hooker employees frequently handled carcinogenic chemicals with little personal protection. "Operation Bootstrap" also revealed that a variety of dangerous gases (chlorine, phosphorous, chlorides, mercury, and so on) were being released into the air outside of the company's Niagara Falls facility. Moreover, in April 1979, Hooker employees showed a Buffalo, New York, newspaper reporter their "Hooker bumps," which were red bumps on their necks and faces caused by contact with trichlorophenal in the plant [Galdston, 1979, p. 27]. One outspoken critic has stated, "Of the 5500 chemical companies in the United States, Hooker Chemical Company has thus far been most frequently, almost consistently, associated with the worst instances of illegal and inadequate toxic waste dumping" [Galdston, 1979, p. 25].

AND NOW . . .

Currently, 44 states are pursuing plans for action in the waste disposal area. While Love Canal presents a serious problem, many experts are divided on whether the Love Canal is more the exception rather than the rule. Carl A. Goslini of the Chemical Manufacturers Association attempts to dispel the notion that chemical companies dump their wastes in clandestine manner by stating: "94 percent of all solid chemical (industrial) waste generated by the 54 largest chemical producers in the last 30 years repose in facilities owned by them. Of the remainder, 5 percent are in known other sites, only 1 percent in unknown facilities" [Evans, 1980].

Love Canal is only one of an estimated 100,000 industrial waste dumps in the United States. Additionally, there are some 18,500 municipal sites for the disposal of solid wastes and 23,000 sewage-sludge dumps; 1200 of these dumps have been classified as "dangerous" by the EPA [Hazardous Wastes–How Dangerous?, 1979]. The EPA estimates that the cost of cleaning up the most dangerous dumps could exceed $3 billion and that as much as $22 billion will be required to neutralize all *potentially* hazardous sites.

In the meantime Hooker is continuing with its clean-up program. The leachate that seeped out of the canal is being rechanneled into an underground tank from which it will be pumped through a charcoal filtering system to remove the toxic chemicals prior to being sent to the city waste-treatment plant. Finally a new clay cap is being placed over the entire site [McWilliams, 1979].

> One significant effect of the Love Canal situation has been the focusing of national attention on the whole subject of industrial waste disposal. In common with other corporations, Occidental had been concentrating on this problem, applying its research facilities and devoting money toward the development of a solution. But more is needed. It will take a strenuous effort by industry, government, and the academic community to solve the problem, but solve it we must so that we can continue to benefit from the contribution the chemical industry makes to our lives. And, equally important, so that there be no Love Canals tomorrow [McWilliams, 1979].

NOTES

"A Formula to Settle Toxic Dump Problems," *Business Week*, 14 January 1980, p. 34.

"An Alarming Silence on Chemical Wastes," *Business Week*, 7 May 1979, pp. 44–46.

"A Review of Hooker's Chemical Disposal Sites in the Niagara Frontier," *Hooker Chemical Company*, March 1979, pp. 3–4.

Beck, Melinda, "A Caustic Report on Chemical Dumps," *Newsweek*, October 22, 1979, p. 51.

Dionne, E. J. Jr. "New York Survey Lists Industrial Poisons," *New York Times*, 9 August 1978, p. 1:3.

"EPA Hits Hooker with Suits Asking $118MM for Clean Up of Hazardous Waste Dumps," *Chemical Marketing Reporter*, vol. 216, no. 26, December 24, 1979, p. 47.

Evans, M. Stenton. ". . . And Government Overreacts," *The Phoenix Gazette*, June 2, 1980, p. A-6.

Galdston, K. "Hooker Chemical's Nightmarish Pollution Record," *Business and Society Review*, Summer 1979, pp. 25–28.

Hammer, Stephen. "The Invisible Friend," *Oxy Today and Yesterday* #9, 1977, pp. 17–21.

Hazardous Wastes—How Dangerous?" *U.S. News & World Report*, November 5, 1979, p. 46.

"Hooker Beset by Disposal Problems, Sees Troubles Mount on Long Island," *Chemical Marketing Reporter*, 11 June 1979, pp. 3–24.

"Hooker and Velsicol Outline Cleanup Actions," *Chemical Week*, 4 April 1979.

"Hooker Tells Its Side of the Story," *Chemical Week*, 27 June 1979, p. 34.

"Love Canal Lessons," *The Wall Street Journal*, May 22, 1980, p. 24.

McNeil, Donald G., Jr. "Health Chief Calls Niagara Falls Waste Site A Peril," *New York Times*, 3 August 1978, p. 1–6.

McWilliams, Bruce. "Special Report: Love Canal," *Oxy Today* #13, 1979, p. 5.

Molosky, Irvin. "A Love Canal Warning No One Can Recall," *New York Times*, April 14, 1979, p. 22L.

"New Rule Asked For Controlling Unsafe Wastes." *New York Times*, 15 December 1978, p. 20.

Simon, Ellis. "Everyone Denies Liability in N.Y. Chemical Disaster." *Business Insurance*, 25 December 1978, p. 1.

Thomas, Robert E. *Salt and Water, Power and People.* New York, Hooker Electro Company, 1955.

"Upstate Waste Site May Endanger Lives." *New York Times*, 2 August 1978, p. 1.

"What Hooker Told Whom, When About Love Canal." *The Wall Street Journal*, June 19, 1980, p. 18.

THE MARKETING OF INFANT FORMULA
IN LESS DEVELOPED COUNTRIES

S. PRAKASH SETHI* and JAMES E. POST†

The activities of multinational corporations (MNCs) in less developed countries (LDCs) have been justified on many grounds. The foremost among the benefits accruing to the less developed countries are the transfer of superior technology and management skills; the creation of jobs and of a broader economic base, and so, an improved standard of living; and the provision of superior goods at reasonable prices. These benefits are possible because multinational companies operate from a large base of resources, thereby exploiting economies of scale; and because MNC research and development facilities ensure superior products through in-house testing and quality control. The last point is quite critical in the case of a variety of products and services. The consumers in LDCs usually do not have either the information or necessary skills to evaluate the multitude of new products that are introduced by the MNCs. These products are quite often outside their cultural frame of reference, and so evaluation through comparisons with local products is not possible.

The small size of total demand makes it unattractive for more than one or two companies to compete for the market. Thus the role of competition in disciplining the suppliers and providing the consumers with necessary comparative information is limited. The LDCs are generally deficient in institutional mechanisms for inspection and regulation that would ensure the production and sale of products in a manner that serves public interest while also ensuring reasonable profits to the MNCs.

DIMENSION OF THE PROBLEM

At the aggregate level, the assumption that MNCs serve public interest in host countries through their activities in the private sector is largely supportable. However, at the level of the single company or industry in the single country, this is not necessarily so. Therefore, while a MNC may not have deliberately violated any laws, its normal activities in pursuit of self-interest may have untoward social consequences. All marketing activities of individual firms have second order effects that extend far beyond the boundaries of the parties to the immediate exchange. Quite often, these effects are far more pervasive in their collectivity than visualized by individual firms when making simple transactions. While the users of the product or those indirectly affected by it are unable to seek adequate remedy and relief in the market place, the cumulative effect of their dissatisfactions results in transferring the issue from the private to public domain.

Condensed from "Public Consequences of Private Action: The Marketing of Infant Formula in Less Developed Countries," published in *California Management Review*, vol. XXI, no. 4 (Summer 1979), pp. 35–48. Copyright © 1979 by the Regents of the University of California. Reprinted by permission of the Regents and authors.

*School of Management and Administration, University of Texas, Dallas.

†School of Management, Boston University.

This article focuses on a study of the infant formula foods by large MNCs in less developed countries to demonstrate the nature of second order effects of primary activities, the promotion and sale of infant formula foods. The basic questions raised are:

- To what extent should a firm be responsible for the undirected use of its products? Ought not the demand for a product the marketing of which is legal be the ultimate count in the MNC's decision to undertake its manufacture and sale?

- Under what circumstances should a corporation exercise self-restraint in advertising? Does the corporation have an obligation to promote only those products which it knows will be used correctly? Should a competitor's successful manufacture and promotion of a product influence a company to enter the market and utilize similar tactics?

- The operation of the market economy assures that the second order effects of a firm's activities are in the public domain and so must be handled by government agencies, leaving individual firms to pursue their self-interest unfettered by external considerations. Is it feasible or desirable for a MNC to assume a posture that is primarily market-oriented? What role can the LDC government be expected to play in this area? Should there be a government-directed choice of products a private corporation could manufacture? Finally, once a private market-oriented issue gets into the public domain, what changes should MNCs make to assuage society's demands?

INFANT FORMULA FOODS: THE INDUSTRY[1]

Infant formula food was developed in the early 1920s as an alternative to breast-feeding. Sales rose sharply after World War II, and hit a peak in the late 1950s, following the 4.3 million births in 1957.[2] However, birth rates began declining in the 1960s, and by 1974 the annual number of births had declined to 3.1 million. The low birth rate caused a steep downturn in baby formula food sales.

The major U.S. and foreign companies engaged in the manufacture and marketing of infant formulas include Abbott Laboratories, which produces *Similac* and *Isomil* infant formulas through its Ross Laboratories division; American Home Products, which produces *SMA*, *S26*, and *Nursoy* infant formulas through its Wyeth Laboratories; Bristol-Myers, which produces *Enfamil*, *Olac*, and *Prosobee* through its Mead Johnson Division; Nestlé Alimentana, S.A., a Swiss multinational; and Unigate, a British firm. In their search for business, these companies began developing markets in third world countries, where population was still expanding, while baby food markets in developed countries were leveling off.

The international market for infant formula grew rapidly during the post-World War II era. Although a number of food companies had sold breast-milk substitutes in western Europe before that time, many of these products, made of evaporated milk or powdered milk, were not nutritionally equivalent to human milk, as are formulas. As prosperity returned to Europe and multinational firms expanded operations in Africa, South America and the Far East, infant formula became the "food of choice" for the children of expatriate Americans and western Europeans.

The large number of wealthy and middle-class persons able to afford infant formula in the U.S. and Europe made mass distribution and promotion of such products a widespread and acceptable phenomenon. In Africa, South America, and the Far East, however, the number of wealthy customers was fewer, and the size of the middle class was notably smaller. Local distributors were often used as a means of distributing the product. In an effort to expand sales, distributors, and sometimes the manufacturers themselves, began to promote the infant formula to broad segments of the population. This promotion reached the poor and those only marginally able to afford the product in less developed nations and produced the infant formula controversy.

Business Strategy

After intense competitive battles, Ross Laboratories and Mead Johnson emerged as the winners in the United States market. By the 1960s, the two firms commanded approximately 90 percent of the domestic infant formula business (Ross's *Similac* 55 percent, Mead Johnson's *Enfamil* about 35 percent). So entrenched were these sellers in the domestic market that Nestlé, the acknowledged worldwide industry leader with 50 percent of the market, never attempted to penetrate the U.S. market.

With the leveling off in the U.S. birth rate in the 1960s, both Ross and Mead Johnson began to look outside the U.S. for major growth opportunities. This effort led Ross to industrialized nations with higher disposable income and prospects for market penetration. Canada and Europe became major foreign markets for Ross's *Similac*. Mead Johnson looked primarily to the Caribbean where export was relatively easy. Puerto Rico, Jamaica, and the Bahamas became important Mead Johnson export markets.

Wyeth Laboratories, never a major seller of infant formula in the United States, began to sell internationally before World War II. Following the war, the company's presence as a pharmaceutical manufacturer was the base from which infant formula was marketed by affiliates in Latin America, Europe, and Southeast Asia. Today, Wyeth probably accounts for close to 15 percent of worldwide sales.

GROWTH IN INFANT FORMULA SALES IN LDCs

Studies point to an increasing trend toward bottle-feeding in LDCs. In developing nations, breast-feeding has declined substantially and the length of the nursing period has shrunk from over a year to a few months.

Three important environmental factors[3] account for the shift toward bottle-feeding in LDCs. These are the sociocultural changes in developing countries, the changing attitudes of health workers and health institutions, and the promotional activities of infant formula manufacturers.

The sociocultural factors influencing change in infant feeding can be understood primarily in terms of urbanization, which has caused the westernization of social mores and the need for mobility in employment. High income groups were the first to use infant formula, in imitation of western practices, and thus bottle-feeding came to represent a high-status modern practice. Low income groups tended to follow suit.

Too, the breast has come to be viewed as a sex symbol, which has led to embarrassment in using it for nursing, and fear that nursing will make the appearance of the breast less desirable. Finally, there is the convenience aspect: most places of employment do not provide facilities for a nursing woman, so bottle-feeding of the infant may become a necessity for a working woman.

Health professionals—doctors, nurses, and clinic workers—and the policies of the hospitals and clinics often, wittingly or unwittingly, endorse the use of infant formula. Although much of this activity originates in the promotional efforts by baby food formula manufacturers to the mother, the endorsement may appear to come from the health professionals themselves. Nurses and social workers who staff hospitals and clinics may encourage the use of bottle-feeding. In many hospitals newborn babies are routinely bottle-fed whether or not the mother plans to breast-feed later. Hospitals and clinics receive free samples of infant milk and special plastic milk bottles which nurses distribute to mothers. These nurses may also distribute "vaccination cards" which advertise infant formulas, and baby care booklets which recommend bottle-feeding.

INDUSTRY PROMOTION PRACTICES

Many observers claim that the infant formula industry's promotion is overly aggressive and has contributed to the decline of breast-feeding. The industry itself, however, feels that its promotion is generally responsible and performs a valuable function. Individual companies have concentrated on different promotional mixes, based on their orientation, i.e., pharmaceutical vs. processed foods; or depending on their market strategies, i.e., maintaining a dominant market position and protecting market share, or getting entry into new markets and increasing market share. Yet their impact from the public interest point of view is not very dissimilar. These practices can be summarized in the following categories.

Baby Food Booklets

One of the major forms of promotion used by baby food companies is the information booklet. Some typical titles are *The Ostermilk Mother and Baby Book: Caring for Your Baby*, published by Ross Laboratories, and *A Life Begins*, published by Nestlé. These booklets are distributed free in maternity wards of public hospitals, clinics, doctors' offices, and by nurses. They provide information on prenatal and postnatal care, with special emphasis given to how babies should be fed. Many of these books are directed to illiterate or semiliterate women, using pictures to show correct or incorrect feeding methods.

Some baby food booklets, usually pre-1975 versions, describe and illustrate bottle-feeding without mentioning breast-feeding. However, as public concern rose over the possible harmful effects of bottle-feeding, promotional booklets began to discuss breast-feeding and to recommend "mixed feeding," in which the bottle is used as a supplement to breast milk. Examples of this type include Nestlé's *Your Baby and You*, which suggests "an occasional bottle-feed . . . if you cannot breast-feed Baby entirely yourself."[4] A Mead Johnson pamphlet states "More babies have thrived on Mead Johnson formula products than on any other form of supplementary feeding." Cow & Gate recommends its milk to "be used as a substitute for breast-feeding or as a supplement."[5]

In discussing the use of supplements for feeding the baby, these booklets often emphasize reasons to discontinue or diminish breast-feeding. Nestlé, for example, in *A Life Begins*, asserts that bottle-feeding must be substituted for breast-feeding if the mother is ill, if her milk is insufficient for the baby or of "poor quality," or if the mother's nipples crack or become infected. These booklets also suggest that breast-feeding should be diminished to include solid food into the baby's diet. *The Ostermilk Mother and Baby Book* advises introducing solid foods for babies a few weeks old or even earlier, while Cow & Gate suggests feeding its brand of cereal to the baby from two to three months.[6]

Other Media Practices

Companies did promote their baby food products by advertising in magazines, newspapers, radio, television, and through loudspeaker vans. As with the baby care booklets, early advertisements usually did not mention breast-feeding: a magazine advertisement stated that Ostermilk and Farex products were "right from the start—the foods you can trust." Poster advertisements, often exhibited in hospitals and clinics, showed how to prepare baby formula, but gave only minimal attention to breast-feeding. Radio and television ads similarly emphasized bottle-feeding.

Free Samples and Gifts

One of the most widespread promotional techniques is the distribution of free samples, and the offer of free gifts to users or potential users of baby food formula. These usually take the form of samples of formula or free feeding bottles, and may be handed out by nurses and salesmen at hospitals, clinics, or in the home. A survey in Ibadan, Nigeria, found that 9 percent of the mothers surveyed had received samples. These had been given in equal proportion to more affluent mothers and to those who could not afford baby food formula. A spokesman from Nestlé admitted that sampling in the Philippines cost about 4–5 percent of turnover.[7] Free gifts are less often used as an inducement to buy.

Promotion Through the Medical Profession

Hospitals and physicians are a logical focus for promotion and sales-related advertising. The users of artificial feeding products are sensitive to the "scientific" quality of infant formula, and physicians were the appropriate counselors to give advice. Also, hospitals are becoming increasingly popular as the site for birth, and the newborns are typically fed at the hospital for the first few days of their lives. The decision a new mother makes before birth to feed her child "Brand X" formula could be changed by the hospital's decision to feed infants "Brand Y" or the physician's recommendation to feed "Brand Z." As a marketing matter, prebirth advertising can create consumer awareness of a product; it cannot create sales. Sales creation occurs in the physician's office or in the hospital. For these reasons, the medical community has become the focal point for infant formula promotion in industrialized and developing nations alike.

In general, all promotional methods such as booklets, free samples, posters, and the use of salespeople are employed in the hospitals and clinics. In addition, the use of "milk nurses" and "milk banks" functions to associate baby food formula with the medical profession. "Mother-craft" or milk nurses are fully or partially trained nurses hired by infant food formula companies, and instructed by them in "product knowledge." Most nurses are paid fixed salaries plus a travel allowance, but some may receive sales-related bonuses. A number of hospitals allow milk nurses to speak to mothers in maternity wards or clinics. Nurses visit mothers in their homes, and in some isolated areas, the milk nurses make formula deliveries. A 1974 study conducted by the Caribbean Food and Nutrition Institute found that Mead Johnson, subsidiaries of Nestlé, Glaxo, Ross Laboratories, and Cow & Gate all employed milk nurses in Jamaica. Mead Johnson employed twelve.[8]

Milk banks, usually set up in the hospitals and clinics that serve the poor, are sales outlets for commercial infant food formula. These banks sell formula at reduced prices to poor mothers. For example, at the milk bank at Robert Reid Cabral hospital in Santo Domingo, a pound tin of Nestlé's *Nido* is sold for 90¢, a 40 percent discount off the regular $1.50 price; Nestlé's *Nan* is sold for $1.35, a 33 percent discount off the regular price of $2.00.

CRITICISM OF INDUSTRY PROMOTION PRACTICES

All forms of promotion used by infant formula companies have been criticized by different observers. In general, critics claim that most forms of advertising are misleading or use "hard sell" techniques to turn mothers away from breast-feeding.

Baby Care Booklets

The main criticism of baby care booklets is that they ignore or de-emphasize breast-feeding. Critics feel that mothers reading these baby care booklets will be led to believe that bottle-feeding is as good as or better than breast-feeding. Even if the booklet directly states "Breast-feeding is best," critics assert that the overall impression is still misleading. The new trend in these books toward promoting "mixed feeding," or the early introduction of solid food is also questioned. The La Leche League International, an organization which promotes breast-feeding, observed that:

> . . . the supplementary formula is one of the greatest deterrents to establishing a good milk supply, and frequent nursing is one of the greatest helps. You see, the milk supply is regulated by what the baby takes. The more he nurses, the more milk there will be. If he's given a bottle as well, he'll gradually take less and less from the breast, and the supply will diminish.[9]

In addition, the use of a bottle and overdiluted formula, even as a supplement, can cause infection and malnutrition in the infant.

Promotion Through Media

The critics' objections to other media promotion is similar to their objections to the baby care booklets. They feel that even with the admission of the superiority of breast milk, media promotion remains essentially misleading in its encouragement of mothers to bottle-feed their children. A survey in infant feeding practices in Ibadan, Nigeria, revealed that of the 38 percent of 400 mothers who remembered having seen ads for formula, the majority recalled statements to the effect that the formula gives infants strength, energy, and power. None remembered having heard that breast milk is better for babies. In Nigeria, when ads for Ovaltine included the picture of a plump smiling baby, observers noted that there was a trend for mothers to feed their babies Ovaltine and water as a supplement. [10] This misinterpretation of ads is an obvious danger in a predominantly illiterate or semiliterate community.

Free Samples and Gifts

Free samples of baby food formula and feeding bottles, as well as gift gimmicks, are considered a direct inducement to bottle-feed infants. The widespread distribution of these items shows an unethical lack of concern for either informing mothers about the superiority of breast-feeding or for determining whether mothers have the economic ability to regularly buy infant formula after the first samples.

Promotion Through the Medical Profession

Critics find the promotion of infant formula through the distribution of free samples and literature or the display of advertising posters in hospitals and clinics especially dangerous. Dr. D. B. Jelliffe, head of the Division of Population, Family, and International Health at UCLA, called these promotional techniques "endorsement by association" and "manipulation by assistance." Jelliffe, along with many other critics, feels that companies providing hospitals and clinics with free samples and information on new developments in infant formula, as well as a barrage of advertisements, influence health care workers to favor and promote bottle-feeding to their patients. It is also argued that because mothers see posters and receive informational booklets and free samples at hospitals and clinics, they come to believe that the health profession endorses bottle-feeding. Thus, this type of promotion works two ways in influencing both the beliefs of professionals and the beliefs of mothers about the value of bottle-feeding.

The use of milk nurses also receives its share of criticism. Observers charge that the nurse uniform conceals the fact that the "nurses" are essentially salespeople who encourage mothers to bottle-feed. They assert that some nurses are paid on a sales-related basis, causing them to be even more eager to push for sales. In support of this belief, critics quote an industry man: "Some nurses will be paid a commission on sales results in their area. Sometimes they will also be given the added stick that if they don't meet those objectives, they will be fired."[11]

Milk Banks

Milk banks are used by companies to expand sales by encouraging bottle-feeding among the poor while still retaining the higher-income market. However, critics assert that the discount prices of the formula are still beyond the economic means of the people at whom the milk banks aim their services. For example, a milk bank in Guatemala

City sells Nestlé products for $1.00 per tin, a discount of 80¢ to $1.00 from the regular price. A tin lasts only a few days when properly prepared. However, since the women buying milk there generally have household incomes of between $15 and $45 per month, they commonly buy fewer tins and dilute them. This starts the baby on a cycle of malnutrition and disease.

THE INFANT FORMULA CONTROVERSY

The first criticism of the industry and its promotional activities is traceable to the late 1960s when Dr. Jelliffe, Director of the Caribbean Food and Nutrition Institute in Jamaica, conducted his research. His findings and criticism culminated in an international conference of experts held in Bogota, Colombia, in 1970, under the auspices of the U.N.'s Protein Calorie Advisory Group (PAG). Out of this meeting, and the 1972 follow-up session in Singapore, came increased professional concern about the effects of commercial activity related to infant feeding. The PAG issued an official statement (PAG, Statement #23) in 1973 recommending that breast-feeding be supported and promoted in LDCs, and that commercial promotion by industry or LDC governments be restrained.

The first public identification of the issue occurred in 1973 with the appearance of several articles about the problem in *The New Internationalist*.[12] This, in turn, spurred Mike Muller to undertake a series of interviews and observations which were eventually printed as *The Baby Killer*, a pamphlet published in 1974.[13] The popularization of the issue resulted in a German translation of Muller's work published in Switzerland under the title, *Nestle Tötet Kinder* (Nestlé Kills Babies); and in a lawsuit by Nestlé against the public action group that published the pamphlet. A period of intense advocacy issued from the trial in the Swiss courts. Thus, between 1974 and mid-1976 when the case was decided, considerable international media coverage was given the issue.

The pressure began in earnest in 1975 when shareholder resolutions were filed for consideration at the annual meetings of the American infant formula companies. This pressure has continued, and several institutional investors such as universities and the Rockefeller and Ford Foundations have taken public positions which sharply question the responsiveness of the firms to the controversy. Church groups have led the fight, and have developed their own institutional mechanism through the National Council of Churches, the Interfaith Council on Corporate Responsibility, to coordinate shareholders' campaigns. At the LDC level, the government of Papua New Guinea recently passed a law declaring that baby bottles, nipples and pacifiers are health hazards, and their sale has been restricted to prescription only. The objective was to discourage indiscriminate promotion, sale and consumption of infant food formulas.[14]

Recently, institutions have acted to broaden their popular base by launching a grass roots campaign to boycott Nestlé products in the United States. By linking public action groups throughout the U.S., the current campaign aspires to heighten First World pressure against the Third World's largest seller of infant formula foods.

Manufacturer Responses

The preproblem stage of the infant formula case existed prior to the 1970s. During this time, the adverse impacts on LDCs were not yet articulated. The MNC's response was of the social obligation type, answering only to prevailing law and market conditions. In effect, MNCs were free to conduct their business in ways most consistent with their own orientations and business strategies.

By the early 1970s the identification stage had been reached, as professional criticism grew and articles and stories began to appear in the mass media. The principal industry response to this professional concern was participation in the conference sponsored by PAG. Abbott (Ross), AHP (Wyeth), and Nestlé each sent representatives to these meetings as did a number of British, European, and Japanese companies. For most companies, this seemed to mark a decision point between what could be characterized as social obligation and social responsibility. Only a few firms, notably Abbott (Ross), took steps to mitigate their negative impact in the LDCs. AHP (Wyeth), Borden, Nestlé and others did not follow suit until 1974, when first plans for the formation of an international trade organization were laid.

The remedy and relief stage seems to have begun in 1975, with the Nestlé trial in Switzerland and the shareholder resolutions filed in the United States. In November 1975, representatives of nine MNC manufacturers met in Zurich and formed the International Council of Infant Food Industries (ICIFI). Nestlé, AHP (Wyeth), and Abbott (Ross) participated in these discussions along with several European and four Japanese companies. Others, such as Borden and Bristol-Myers, sent representatives to the sessions, but chose not to participate actively or to join the council. ICIFI's initial directive was to instruct members to adopt a code of marketing ethics which obliged them to recognize the primacy of breast-feeding in all product information and labelling; to include precise product-use information; and to eliminate in-hospital promotion and solicitation by personnel who were paid on a sales-commission basis. For those companies that joined, the council seemed to mark a passage into social responsibility as efforts were undertaken to mitigate negative social impacts.

There was criticism of the ICIFI code from the beginning, and Abbott (Ross) withdrew from the organization, arguing that the code was too weak. The company then adopted its own more restrictive code, which included a provision prohibiting consumer-oriented mass advertising. For ICIFI, the marketing code has been the most visible manifestation of concern for second-order impacts in LDCs. Additional criticism led to some incremental changes which strengthened the "professional" character of sales activity, but which have not yet proscribed all consumer-oriented mass advertising. Thus, ICIFI, the industry's mechanism for countering criticism and searching for means of addressing problems of product misuse in LDC environments, has been unable to reckon with any but the individual-level secondary impacts. Indeed, the critics continue to charge that the response at the user level has been insufficient.

Borden also moved from the social obligation to social responsibility stage. The company had shareholder resolutions filed with it in 1977. This filing perhaps facilitated a management review of promotional strategies in LDCs. In settling the resolution with the church groups before the meeting, Borden agreed to modify certain advertising and labelling of its powdered milk *Klim*; and to tightly oversee the marketing so as to minimize possible consumer misuse of the powdered milk product as an infant formula food. Separately, the company announced that it was withdrawing its infant formula *New Biolac* from two LDC markets in the Far East because it concluded it could not effectively market this product without extensive consumer advertising which was not permissible in the prevailing social-political environment.

As a public issue matures, companies may adopt actions which operate to prevent further growth in the legitimacy gap by minimizing or eliminating the underlying sources of criticism (a prevention stage). This has begun to occur in the infant formula controversy as both ICIFI and individual companies have taken action to prevent some of the secondary impacts discussed above. In 1977, Abbott (Ross) announced its intention to commit nearly $100,000 to a breast-feeding campaign in developing nations, and to budget $175,000 for a task force to conduct research on breast-feeding, infant formula, and LDCs. The company also announced a plan for a continuing cooperative effort with its critics in reviewing the situation. ICIFI has now also gone beyond its marketing code of ethics and has begun informally working with international health agencies to prepare educational materials, for use in LDCs, that would encourage breast-feeding and improve maternal and infant health care. The council is also involved in supporting scientific research of breast-feeding, infant formula products, and LDC environments.

Abbott (Ross) Laboratories' attempt to act in a way that will create positive impacts in LDCs signals a shift to a corporate social responsiveness. Granting that there is some danger of sending "double signals" to its sales force, the company seems to have adopted a posture that permits the sale of its products in appropriate circumstances, and assists the LDCs in encouraging breast-feeding where that is most appropriate.

CONCLUSION

The manner in which all organizations, particularly large corporations, respond to social change is a matter of great public concern. Their economic actions necessarily involve social changes and may have such an impact on established behavioral patterns and underlying cultural values and beliefs as to cause tremendous social stress. This is especially true in the case of LDCs. There is reason to believe that the effect of the modern corporation is even more profound in social and economic settings where there are fewer countervailing influences than exist in industrialized societies. These nations are in the process of becoming modernized and there is tension between the values of the old and the new, the technology of the past and the future, and the aspirations of the present with the traditions of the past. The modern corporation generally represents the new and the future. In such situations, it is not surprising that the impact of the corporation concerns those who care about the pace, the process, and the direction of development and change.

Infant nutrition is one area in which the complex interaction of changing social values, institutions, and technology has produced major changes in social habits. According to many public health and nutrition experts, there now exists a crisis of monumental proportions in LDCs as mothers abandon traditional breast-feeding practices in favor of bottle-feeding. In the view of some critics, the bottle has become a symbol of the most invidious intrusion of western technology into the lives and welfare of LDC populations. One might fairly conclude that the "great infant formula controversy" is one involving the politics of technology.

The objectives of MNCs and LDCs are not always congruent with each other. Nevertheless, there must be a common ground where the interaction between the two yields net benefits, both tangible and intangible, if any sustained cooperation is to take place. Conventional economic analysis shows direct costs and benefits of individual MNC-LDC cooperation, but usually overlooks social and political costs. These costs are difficult to calculate, as there is no common consensus of what they are or how they might be measured; and there is a fear that if these costs were specified, they could doom MNC projects. The cultural and sociopolitical costs are of critical importance. The long-range social acceptance on the part of the peoples in LDCs of MNC's investments depends on the decisions of MNC and LDC governments to taking these costs into account when developing economic projects.

NOTES

1. Much of this material comes from James E. Post, testimony in *Marketing and Promotion of Infant Formula in the Developing Nations*, Hearings before the Subcommittee on Health and Scientific Research of the Committee on Human Resources, 95th Congress, Second Session, 23 May 1978, pp. 116–125.

2. Robert J. Ledogar, *U.S. Food and Drug Multinationals in Latin America: Hungry for Profits* (New York: IDOC, North America, Inc., 1975), p. 128.

3. Johanna T. Dwyer, "The Demise of Breast Feeding: Sales, Sloth, or Society?" in *Priorities In Child Nutrition*, report prepared for the UNICEF Executive Board under the direction of Dr. Jean Mayer (E/ICEF/L. 1328, March 28, 1975), vol II, pp. 332–339.

4. Ledogar, op. cit., pp. 133–134.

5. Ibid.

6. Ibid., p. 142.

7. Frances M. Lappé and Eleanor McCallie, "Infant Formula Promotion and Use in the Philippines: An Informal, On-Site Report," Institute for Food and Development Policy (San Francisco, California, July 1977). Lappé is the author of the new book *Food First*.

8. V. G. James, "Household Expenditures on Food and Drink by Income Groups," paper presented at seminar on Natural Food and Nutrition Policy, Kingston, Jamaica, 1974.

9. *The Womanly Art of Breastfeeding*, 2nd ed. (Franklin Park, Ill.: La Leche League International, 1963). p. 54.

10. "Baby Food Tragedy," *New Internationalist*, p. 10; Mike Muller, *The Baby Killer: War on Want*, 2nd ed. (May 1975), p. 10.

11. Bristol-Myers Co., "The Infant Formula Marketing Practices," p. 13.

12. "The Baby Food Controversy," *The New Internationalist*, p. 10.

13. Muller, op. cit.

14. "Baby Bottles Banned in New Guinea," *The Dallas Morning News* (November 3, 1977), p. 8-C.

POLAROID IN SOUTH AFRICA

DHARMENDRA T. VERMA*

On Monday, November 21, 1977, Polaroid Corporation announced its decision to terminate its distributorship in South Africa thereby ending the "Experiment in South Africa" which it had begun six years earlier. In making this announcement, an official of Polaroid stated:

> We were presented on Wednesday, November 16, with information which suggested that Frank & Hirsch Pty. Ltd., the independent distributor of Polaroid products in South Africa, has been selling film to the government of South Africa in violation of a 1971 understanding. That understanding stipulated that the distributor refrain from selling any Polaroid products to the South African government.
>
> As a consequence of this new information, we initiated that same day an investigation from which we have now learned that Frank & Hirsch has not fully conformed to the understanding with regard to sales to the government.
>
> Accordingly, Polaroid is advising Frank & Hirsch that it is terminating its business relationship with that company.
>
> In 1971, when the question arose as to whether it was appropriate for Polaroid to continue to sell to a distributor in South Africa, we examined the issue carefully. We abhor the policy of apartheid and seriously considered breaking off all business with South Africa. We felt, however, that we should consider the recommendations of black Africans before making a decision. They urged us to maintain our business relationship and try to accomplish improvements in the economic and educational opportunities for black workers. We did succeed in persuading our distributor to give to black employees responsibilities much greater than they had had in the past and substantially to improve black salary rates. We also made contributions, which aggregate about one-half million dollars, to black African scholarship funds and other programs. In much of this activity our distributor cooperated effectively. We were therefore shocked to learn that the understanding not to sell to the government was not followed.
>
> With the termination of this distributorship in South Africa, we do not plan to establish another one.

THE SOUTH AFRICAN DISTRIBUTOR: REACTION

Polaroid Corporation's 1977 sales were over one billion dollars. The South African business was worth between three and four million dollars. This amounted to about half of the revenues of Frank & Hirsch (Pty.) Ltd., the South African distributorship. Helmut Hirsch, the owner of the distributorship is a "66-year-old German-Jewish emigree who escaped to South Africa from Nazi Germany. In the South African political scene he is considered a liberal. He is a member of the Progressive Party and a friend of Helen Suzman, a well-known critic of the Vorster regime. He has been the chairman of Dorkay House." (*The Boston Globe*, November 23, 1977.) The

Excerpted from "Polaroid in South Africa," published in *Proceedings of the Second National Conference on Business Ethics*, edited by W. Michael Hoffman (Washington, D.C.: University Press of America, 1979). Reprinted by permission of The Center for Business Ethics, Bentley College, and the author.

*Department of Management, Bentley College, Waltham, Mass.

company has distributed Polaroid products for the past 18 years and it also handled Japanese cameras, watches, and other imported equipment.

Following Polaroid's announcement, Helmut Hirsch issued a statement in Johannesburg on Tuesday, November 22, 1977, that said:

> On hearing allegations that Frank & Hirsch have supplied Polaroid products directly to departments of the South African government, we made an immediate investigation that revealed over the past several years a very small number of isolated cases where unbeknownst to us there were deliveries to the South African government. Frank & Hirsch regrets these isolated instances because they are not in keeping with the agreement between Frank & Hirsch and Polaroid. Immediate steps have been taken to avoid any recurrences.

The Boston Globe reported that in a telephone interview Hirsch confirmed that some sales of Polaroid products to the South African government violated the agreement with Polaroid. According to Hirsch, his investigation of the records showed three sales in 1975, two deliveries in 1976, and 12 transactions so far in 1977. The records do not go back further. However, he insisted that other sales to South African government agencies had not been restricted by the ban agreed upon in 1971. Hirsch claimed that "only some agencies were restricted—the Security Department, the Bantu (black) Reference Bureaus, and the military."

CIRCUMSTANCES LEADING TO THE POLAROID DECISION

Polaroid products were sold through the distributor to drugstores and photographic supply houses in South Africa. Polaroid management had known the South African government was using its film, but believed the purchases were made in the open market and not from its distributor. A 1971 agreement between Polaroid and its distributor had specified that no sales were to be made to the South African government.

Allegations of secret sales of Polaroid cameras and film to the South African military and Bantu (black) Reference Bureau that issue identification documents "passbooks" to blacks (an instrument of apartheid) were made by Indrus Naidoo, a former employee of Frank & Hirsch. Naidoo made a photostat of a delivery note covering one shipment of Polaroid film going to the Bantu Reference Bureau on September 22, 1975. This photostat copy was passed on to Paul Irish, an official of the American Committee on Africa (ACOA) in New York City. Irish released the copy to the press in mid-November 1977, only after Naidoo had left South Africa as an exile.

The Boston Globe (November 21, 1977) reported that Naidoo was interviewed by telephone while in Bonn, Germany, where he was on a speaking tour for the African Liberation Movement and he detailed the transactions between Frank & Hirsch and the South African government:

> Frank & Hirsch billed all the shipments to the South African government through Muller's Pharmacy, a drugstore in downtown Johannesburg. The films and cameras were placed in unmarked cartons and then transferred to unmarked transport vans for the drive to their destination . . . There were regular deliveries to the Voortrekker Hoogte military headquarters outside Pretoria, periodic deliveries to several local reference bureaus, and at least one large shipment of sunglasses to the Air Force . . . Since all billing was done through

Muller's Pharmacy, there would be no record of funds being received from the South African government.

Polaroid management was informed of the charges on Wednesday, November 16, and they dispatched Hans Jensen, the Export Sales Manager and a British auditor, to South Africa to investigate. Polaroid officials stated:

> Helmut Hirsch told us many times he was not selling to the South African government. As far as we were able to determine he had stuck to the agreement. However, we never took for granted they would follow our stipulation. That's why we have sent people there every year.

Mr. Jensen found several deliveries to the South African government in his examination of Frank & Hirsch records. In his telephone conversation with Polaroid officials, Jensen reported that Hirsch, the owner of Frank & Hirsch, was shocked: "He claimed he had no idea this was going on."

On Monday, November 21, 1977, in announcing Polaroid's decision to discontinue the distributorship, Robert Palmer, Director of Community Relations at Polaroid, described Polaroid officials as distressed.

> People are upset and disappointed . . . Over the past 6 years Polaroid influenced Frank & Hirsch to substantially raise its black employees' wages and we have contributed almost half a million dollars to several black groups in South Africa. Hirsch followed the program we outlined—equal pay for equal work, and black employees were moved into jobs the whites held. The distributor had only 200 black employees but I think our influence had a ripple effect on other U.S. Corporations . . . Now this "Experiment in South Africa" has come to an end.

POLAROID'S EXPERIMENT IN SOUTH AFRICA AND CONSEQUENCES: A PERSPECTIVE

In late 1970, internal (corporate) and external (community) questions were raised regarding Polaroid Corporation's involvement in South Africa.[1] Specifically, questions focused on the use of Polaroid's ID system by the government of South Africa in its passbook program. These passbooks had to be carried by all non-white South Africans and were seen as a means whereby the government enforced its apartheid system. In response, a Polaroid team was sent to South Africa to study the problem first hand. Based on its report, Polaroid management stated that they had reviewed their operations in South Africa and in January, 1971, announced an "Experiment in South Africa." The announcement included the following statements:

- We abhor Apartheid.

- We want to examine the question of whether or not we should continue to sell our products in South Africa.

- We do not want to impose a course of action on black people of another country merely because we might think it was correct.

A group of Polaroid employees, both black and white, then toured South Africa and returned with a unanimous recommendation to undertake an experimental program for one year with these goals:

- To continue our business relationship there except for any direct sales to the South African government.

- To improve dramatically the salaries and other benefits of the non-white employees of our distributor there.

- To initiate through our distributor well defined programs to train non-white employees for important jobs within that company.

- We would commit a portion of our profits earned there to encourage black education.

At the end of the year, in December, 1971, Polaroid management issued their report outlining the benefits of their year-long experiment. The report concluded:

> In a year's time the visible effects of the Polaroid experiment on other American companies had been limited, but the practical achievements in increased salaries, benefits, and education had shown what could be done. Therefore, the company decided to continue the program for the present.

In November, 1977, following a series of reviews and audits, Polaroid issued a report specifying some of the consequences of the six years following the initial decision to undertake the "Experiment" (see Exhibit 1). In conclusion, the report pointed out:

> We believe that it is still too soon to make a final judgment on our relationship to South Africa. We have found that the lack of knowledge concerning American business in South Africa has been as difficult to deal with as has the complexity of issues surrounding business practices in that country.
>
> We will continue to press, as constructively as possible, for change in South Africa. We will not, however, decide for black Africans what they need. The final determination will have to come from South Africans themselves. We intend to stay as long as black South Africans and moderate whites feel that progress is being made and that our presence there is helpful. We should acknowledge that our decision to continue is made easier by the fact that our South African distributor has been a willing participant in the changes affecting his work force.
>
> We agree with our thoughtful critics that the specific accomplishments of the Polaroid experiment affect relatively few black people. A growing number of people, however, are beginning to share our hope that the possibility of change in South Africa is real.

EXHIBIT 1 Polaroid in South Africa.

Polaroid's "Experiment" Update, November, 1977

- Our contributions are continuing to ASSECA (The Association for the Educational and Cultural Advancement of the African People of South Africa), though some concern has been expressed as to the slow pace of programs of this organization based mostly on the problem of a lack of full-time leadership. ASSECA has requested a full-time person from the United States.

- Our financial contributions have also continued to ASSET. In addition we made up for the loss suffered by the recent devaluation of the dollar. Several other companies have also made substantial contributions to ASSET (The American-South African Study and Educational Trust).

- We have also made additional contributions to the United States–South African Leader Exchange Program, the African-American Institute, and a contribution to AIESEC in South Africa—an organization of students in economics and business administration.

- With our encouragement and assistance, the Addison-Wesley Publishing Company of North Reading, Mass., donated over 22 thousand new text books for use in black South African schools.

- Training programs, medical benefits, legal aid, bursaries (scholarships) and loans have also been expanded at Frank & Hirsch.

There are some who sincerely believe that complete cessation of business with South Africa is the only solution to the existing problems. We respect that view though we continue to disagree with it. We believe that constructive engagement is the responsible course of action for an American company already there. Though Polaroid does not have plants, investments, subsidiaries or employees in South Africa, we have for a number of years sold our products through a local distributor, Frank & Hirsch (Pty.) Ltd. We feel for that reason alone we have a responsibility not to walk away from the problem.

We are pleased that some major U.S. (and other) employers in South Africa have initiated affirmative action programs. The Company's general feeling continues to be hopeful. We are aware of a number of companies with large investments there who have started serious new programs in the country. We will continue to review our efforts with our distributor and the programs to which we are making financial contributions on an annual basis. Visitors from South Africa and many other people with whom we have corresponded have encouraged us to continue. Press reports of the effects of our experiment have reinforced our decision to proceed.

U.S. CORPORATIONS AND SOUTH AFRICA: A DIFFERENT PERSPECTIVE

The non-profit Investor Responsibility Research Center (IRRC), Washington, D.C., released a study indicating that about 320 American companies have operations in South Africa. Some of the largest (with 1976 sales in South Africa) are Mobil Corporation (over $500 million); Caltex, a joint-venture of Standard Oil of California and Texaco ($500 million); Ford ($208 million); General Motors ($250 million); Chrysler (through a 24.9% interest in Sigma Motors, $190 million); IBM ($163 million or less). The U.S. Commerce Department estimates book value of U.S. investments in South Africa at $1.7 billion in 1976. For most American companies, South Africa represents 1% or less of their total sales. However, in the South African economy, some are significant. IRRC reported that American companies control 43% of the country's petroleum market, 23% of its auto sales and 70% of its computer business. (*The Wall Street Journal*, December 5, 1977)

The article further stated that some companies, such as General Motors, Ford and Control Data, have indicated they will limit further expansion there. Chrysler, International Telephone and Phelps Dodge have merged their subsidiaries into South African companies. Burlington Industries, Weyerhaeuser, Halliburton and Interpace have completely closed down their South African operations.

The call by a number of groups for complete withdrawal of U.S. investments in South Africa has been voiced on numerous occasions. Following the Polaroid announcement, a church group introduced a shareholder's resolution calling on the Eastman Kodak Company to ban all direct and indirect sales to the South African government. This was seen as a first step in a phased withdrawal of Kodak from South Africa. The resolution called on the corporation not to "make or renew any contracts or agreements to sell photographic equipment, including cameras, film, photographic paper and processing chemicals to the South African government."

Kodak and 53 other U.S. companies to date have signed a "Statement of Principles" regarding their operations in South Africa. These companies point to steps they have taken to improve the lot of their black employees and express confidence that in time the existing racial barriers can be pulled down. This "Statement of Principles" was drawn up by Reverend Leon Sullivan, a black minister from Philadelphia and a director of General Motors Corporation. *The Los Angeles Times* (December 29, 1977) reported:

> South Africa's Minister of Information, Connie Mulder, officially approved it (Statement of Principles). "In expressing a desire to contribute to the well-being of the black workers in South Africa, these American companies are to be commended," he said.

In a press release issued September 15, 1977, Dr. Leon Sullivan commented on the 54 corporate endorsements and the situation in South Africa:

> We are pleased with the response to date, but we will continue to invite other companies to participate . . . Some encouraging progress has been made during the last six months. I have been informed that racial signs are coming down; in some instances walls are being broken out to end segregation and new integrated facilities are being constructed; blacks are being selected and promoted to supervisory positions; and all companies are developing plans for aggressive future implementation of the six points. Within the next year we shall see if the effort is only a "ripple" or becomes a "tide for change."

At a business recognition dinner on October 5, 1977, attended by many senior corporate officials, Dr. Sullivan informed the executives that the Statement of Principles was being endorsed by non-U.S. groups such as the Federation of Swedish Industries and expressed the hope that "a world-wide effort against segregation and discriminating practices will be developed by businesses on a global scale." He pointed out that the European Economic Community recently announced its South African code of ethics which are very similar to the American Statement of Principles. (The EEC Code goes further in pushing companies to recognize black trade unions and to practice collective bargaining, as pointed out in *Business Week*, Ocotober 24, 1977.)

At the same dinner, U.S. Secretary of State Cyrus R. Vance said:

> . . . I think that all of you recognize by your presence here tonight the international business community operating in South Africa has an extremely important role to play. By adopting progressive employment practices for your South African Subsidiaries, you not only enhance the lives of those who work for you, you also demonstrate the promise of a society based on racial justice. . . . We believe that your efforts will set an example which will hasten the day when all the people of South Africa will realize their full human and spiritual potential. . . .

NOTES

1. For details describing the initial protest demonstrations and Polaroid's response, see the author's case, "Polaroid in South Africa (A)," ICH 9-372-624. The Polaroid "Experiment" along with local and worldwide reaction, are described in the sequel case "Polaroid in South Africa (B)," ICH 9-372-625. Both are distributed through the Intercollegiate Case Clearing House, Harvard University.

SUPPLEMENTARY READING FOR PART FOUR

Ball, George W., ed. *Global Companies: The Political Economy of World Business.* Englewood Cliffs, N.J.: Prentice-Hall, 1975.

Barbour, Ian G., ed. *Western Man and Environmental Ethics.* Reading, Mass.: Addison-Wesley, 1973.

Barnet, Richard J., and Ronald E. Muller. *Global Reach: The Power of the Multinational Corporation.* New York: Simon and Schuster, 1974.

Benningson, Lawrence A., and Arnold I. Benningson. "Product Liability: Manufacturers Beware!" *Harvard Business Review,* vol. 53, *3,* May–June 1974, pp. 122–132.

Blackstone, William T., ed. *Philosophy and the Environmental Crisis.* Athens, Ga.: University of Georgia Press, 1974.

Corporate Social Reporting in the United States. Report of the Task Force on Corporate Social Performance. Washington, D.C.: United States Department of Commerce, July 1979.

Galbraith, John Kenneth. "The Defense of the Multinational Company." *Harvard Business Review,* vol. 56, *2,* March–April 1978, pp. 83–93.

Goldman, Marshall I. *Ecology and Economics: Controlling Pollution in the 70's.* Englewood Cliffs, N.J.: Prentice-Hall, Inc., 1967.

Goodpaster, K. E., and K. M. Sayre. *Ethics and Problems of the 21st Century.* Notre Dame, Ind.: University of Notre Dame Press, 1979.

Howard, Niles, and Susan Antilla. "What Price Safety? The 'Zero-Risk' Debate." *Dun's Review,* September 1979, pp. 47–57.

Ledogar, Robert J. *Hungry for Profits.* New York: IDOC/North America, 1975.

Leiser, Burton, "Beyond Fraud and Deception: The Moral Uses of Advertising." *Ethical Issues in Business,* edited by Thomas Donaldson and Patricia H. Werhane. Englewood Cliffs, N.J.: Prentice-Hall, 1979.

Levitt, Theodore. "The Morality (?) of Advertising." *Harvard Business Review,* July–August 1970, pp. 84–92.

Lilly, William, III, and James C. Miller III. "The New Social Regulation." *Public Interest,* vol. 45, Spring 1977, pp. 5–51.

Linowes, David F. *The Corporate Conscience.* New York: Hawthorne Books, 1974.

Lowrance, William W. *Of Acceptable Risk.* Los Altos, Calif.: William Kaufman, Inc., 1976.

Mishan, E. J. *The Economic Growth Debate.* London: George Allen & Unwin, 1977.

Nelson, Phillip. "Advertising and Ethics." *Ethics, Free Enterprise and Public Policy,* edited by Richard T. De George and Joseph A. Pichler. New York: Oxford University Press, 1978.

Preston, Ivan L. *The Great American Blow-Up: Puffery in Advertising and Selling.* Madison, Wisc.: The University of Wisconsin Press, 1975.

Schultze, Charles L. *The Public Use of Private Interest.* Washington, D.C.: The Brookings Institution, 1977.

Stone, Christopher D. *Do Trees Have Standing?* Los Altos, Calif.: William Kaufman, Inc., 1972.

Turner, Louis. *Multinationals and the Third World.* New York: Hill and Wang, 1973.

von Hayek, F. A. "The Non Sequitur of the Dependence Effect." *Southern Economic Journal,* April 1961.

Weidenbaum, Murray L. *Business, Government and the Public,* 2d. ed. Englewood Cliffs, N.J.: Prentice-Hall, 1981.

Weinstein, Alvin S., et al. *Products Liability and the Reasonably Safe Product: A Guide for Management, Design and Marketing.* New York: John Wiley & Sons, 1978.

PART FIVE
QUESTIONABLE PRACTICES

In Part Five we examine three questionable business practices—bluffing, bribery, and price-fixing. All these forms of behavior are questionable because there are strong indications that their widespread practice would erode the foundations of business and undermine the very possibility of business activity. Like many other human pursuits, business has a set of rules by which it is conducted. Friedman (Chapter Four) has referred to these as the "rules of the game." Of our three questionable practices, two are expressly illegal, and therefore prohibited by game rules which require obedience to the law. A third—bluffing—is not illegal, but its ethical status has been questioned. Should any or all of these three practices be forbidden, or should they be regarded as acceptable moves in the business game? One of the purposes of this section of the text is to examine the rules of the game themselves, and their justification.

It may be helpful in reading this section to recall some of the elements of Kant's ethical theory, which was discussed in the general introduction to the text. Kant held that a practice is not moral unless it can be made into a universal law. Acts which we would not be willing to have everyone perform, or acts which, when universalized, are self-defeating, are considered by Kant to be immoral. Morality requires that you not make exceptions to the rules for yourself, that you do not permit yourself acts which you would not recommend to everyone. Those who do make exceptions of themselves are taking advantage of those who do obey the rules and using them as means to an end rather than treating them with the respect they deserve. According to Kant, it is only the prevalence of moral behavior which makes occasional immoral behavior profitable. If performed by everyone, immoral acts would no longer be advantageous.

Imagine a basketball game, for example, in which each player could change the rules at will. At one point carrying the ball is illegal; at another it is an accepted way of getting it from one part of the court to another. Now a basket is worth two points, now it is worth fourteen. Sometimes extensive physical contact with another player is penalized; at others the player with the ball is tackled by the opposing team, as in football. Under these circumstances, no "game" at all is possible.

The example illustrates that a game is made possible by its rules as much as it is by the players in it and the spirit of competition between them. Extending the game analogy to business, we might conclude that if business is to be carried on at all, there must be rules defining acceptable forms of behavior. Breaking these rules is wrong because they are a presupposition, a necessary condition, for business activity.

BLUFFING AND DECEPTION

It has generally been held that lying and deception are wrong, and the Kantian analysis described above supports this conclusion. If we admit that lying is morally permissible, then consistency demands that we allow everyone to do it. But if lying becomes universal, it is impossible to tell if someone is lying or telling the truth. Trust is eroded, and truth-telling becomes meaningless. Lying, which only makes sense against a background of truthfulness, ceases to be advantageous.

In our earlier discussion of business and consumer relations we concluded that lying and deception in business are wrong because they undermine the fair competition which is one of the presuppositions of business transactions. But is "bluffing" in business the same as lying? Does it really undermine the basis of business activity, or should it be permitted by the rules of the game as an acceptable game strategy?

Let us define a lie as a false statement made with the intent to deceive someone. If this definition is correct, then some forms of bluffing (for example, your claim that you would not accept less than $50,000 for your house when in fact you would) do seem to involve lying. Even if it is not an outright lie, a bluff involves deceiving another person or putting that person at a disadvantage, for if a bluff works, the person taken in by it will be paying a higher price or conceding more than he or she would otherwise have done.

Many thinkers argue that while lying and deception are wrong in other areas of human activity, in business they are sometimes permissible and even expected. Albert Z. Carr, for example, argues that business is a game with its own special rules, and that bluffing is an acceptable game strategy in business just as it is in poker. There *are* ethical rules for business, Carr believes: These might include upholding contracts, not defaming one's competitors, and in general obeying the law—but the prohibition against bluffing is not one of them. The goal of the business "game" is to maximize profit or to secure the best possible deal for ourselves or our firm. We are permitted to bluff whenever it helps to achieve this goal—and we can expect others to bluff us in return.

While they do not rule out all forms of bluffing, Richard E. Wokutch and Thomas L. Carson seem to argue that the practice requires a stronger defense than that offered by Carr. Because it involves lying and deception, which are prima facie wrong, the authors reason, bluffing demands special justification in order to establish that it is permissible. Wokutch and Carson agree with Carr that businesspeople seek to maximize profit and to obtain the best possible deal, but they do not believe that the fact that bluffing is advantageous for the person who does it is enough to justify the practice. We are not morally permitted to perform every action which advances our interests, especially actions which harm others or put them at a disadvantage.

Nor, they point out, is the argument that something is standard practice a justification. Slavery was standard practice in the South before the Emancipation Proclamation and torture was standard practice during the Spanish Inquisition, but that does not make slavery and torture morally acceptable. Wokutch and Carson suggest that the standard-practice argument is only convincing if it is supported by the premise that we have no duty to be truthful toward people we suspect of bluffing us.

Their conclusion bears some similarities to Carr's contention that bluffing is acceptable in business because it is expected behavior, and people are not deceived by it to the extent that they would have been if they had assumed that their fellow businesspeople were telling them the truth. When the acknowledged purpose of a negotiation is to gain as many concessions and to give as few as possible, bluffing becomes an acceptable negotiating tool. This kind of claim amounts to a suggestion that bluffing may be one form of deception which, even when widespread, does not undermine business activity as a whole. This does not mean, of course, that all forms of lying and deception are acceptable in business. Wokutch and Carson argue that business activity as a whole requires an atmosphere of trust.

BRIBERY

Much of the recent concern about bribery stems from the numerous disclosures of questionable foreign payments made in the middle 1970s. In an orgy of confession, more than 400 American corporations admitted to paying some $800 million in bribes, kickbacks, extortion fees, and "grease" payments to foreign political officials in order to secure or retain business. Among the offenders was Lockheed, which alone paid out $202 million in questionable payments to obtain sales for its faltering L-1011 aircraft. The 1977 Foreign Corrupt Practices Act, which declares such payments illegal, was passed in the shock which followed the disclosures. The scandal raises several important issues. What, if anything, is wrong with bribery? Is it morally permissible to bribe if bribery is a way of life in the culture in which you are doing business? Is the Foreign Corrupt Practices Act the best way of dealing with the problem of bribery in foreign countries?

Arguments against bribery generally turn on the importance of fair, open competition, which is essential to the workings of a free market system. In a free market system, companies compete to offer consumers the best possible product at the best possible price. Bribery takes advantage of competitors by shifting the terms of competition from quality and price to the size of the sum of money paid to a government official. Widespread bribery would make fair competition impossible. Bribery also injures the consumer, because the selection of an item on any basis other than quality and price could lead to the purchase of an inferior product.

Some claim that although the Foreign Corrupt Practices Act does forbid some immoral acts, the law itself has no moral justification. Mark Pastin and Michael Hooker take this position in their article attacking the act. Pastin and Hooker argue on utilitarian grounds that the act is wrong because it does not benefit the majority of the people it affects. In fact, they claim, the Foreign Corrupt Practices Act has serious and far-reaching negative consequences for American business, including loss of sales, loss of jobs, and a weakened ability to compete in foreign markets. Often, they suggest, the only way to secure a *superior* product for a client is to offer a larger bribe than a competing company which makes an inferior product. And a law forbidding American companies to offer bribes does not stop foreign officials from accepting bribes from non-American businesses.

Pastin and Hooker also offer a deontological argument against the act, suggesting that it places American business in a conflict of obligations. By cutting into corporate profits, the act forces organizations to break their promise (1) to shareholders to maximize return on investment and (2) to employees to provide job security.

But why are corporate promises to shareholders and employees more important than the obligation not to bribe? In his reply to Pastin and Hooker, Kenneth Alpern points out that the two authors provide no justification for this assumption. It is true that the rule against bribery is not absolute, Alpern agrees. But neither is the obligation to keep promises to shareholders and employees. Obligations to its constituencies do not entitle a corporation to perform immoral acts to further their interests.

Another important argument for not prohibiting bribery has been that it is common practice in many of the countries in which American firms do business. The claim that its payments were in accordance with "usual business practices" was one of the defenses offered by Lockheed, for example. Lockheed's reluctance to reveal the names of those who accepted the bribes, however, and the subsequent shame felt by their countries, suggest that although bribery may be prevalent in many places it is not morally acceptable in most. Even if it were, argues Alpern, this would not justify the practice, for as we have already noted in our consideration of bluffing, standard practices may be morally wrong. We ought to refrain from actions which we judge morally wrong, even if others do not agree with us. He concludes that American firms should be forbidden to offer bribes, even in countries in which bribery is standard practice.

PRICE-FIXING

Maintaining fair and open competition has traditionally been one of the major concerns of United States economic policy. As we have already mentioned above, competition is thought to maximize consumer freedom, provide the consumer with high-quality products at fair prices, and produce efficiency and rewards for creativity and initiative. The preservation of competition is the central goal of American antitrust regulation. Two major antitrust laws, the Sherman Act of 1890 and the Clayton Act of 1914, outlaw such anticompetitive practices as price-fixing, vertical and horizontal monopolies, and some types of interlocking directorates.

We focus here on price-fixing, or agreements among competing firms to cooperate in setting prices for their product rather than allowing them to be determined by the fluctuations of the market. Like bribery, price-fixing undermines competition; if widely practiced, it would make a free market system impossible. Price-fixing also deceives and takes advantage of consumers, for buyers are not really receiving what they believe they are receiving: the best possible deal as a result of competitive pricing.

Ironically, although price-fixing interferes with competition, it can also be seen as a natural outgrowth of market forces. Consider the following exchange between Senator Estes Kefauver of the Senate Subcommittee on Antitrust and Monopoly and Mark W. Cresap, Jr., president of Westinghouse, concerning the almost identical prices submitted by competitors on a 500,000-kilowatt turbine:

> *Kefauver:* . . . did you arrive at that price independently?
> *Cresap:* Yes, sir.
> *Kefauver:* You figured it yourself?

Cresap: We arrived at that particular one on the basis of the fact that General Electric Co. had lowered its costs for this type of machine, and we met it.

Kefauver: You mean you copied it from G.E.?

Cresap: No, we met the price.

Kefauver: Have you ever made one?

Cresap: Have we ever made . . . ?

Kefauver: A 500,000-kilowatt turbine?

Cresap: We had not at that time, no sir.

Kefauver: Have you made one yet?

Cresap: No.

Kefauver: Has G.E. ever made one?

Cresap: Yes, they are making one.

Kefauver: They have never made one, though?

Cresap: Well, this is the price that they established for this machine, and we met it.

Kefauver: You mean you copied it?

Cresap: We didn't copy the machine. We met the price because it was the lowest price in the marketplace.

Kefauver: In other words, you copied the figures exactly, $17,402,300, from General Electric?

Cresap: Senator, we had a higher price on the machine on our former book, and when they reduced, we reduced to meet them, to meet competition.

Kefauver: If you never made one, how would you know how much to lower or how much to raise?

Cresap: You would know by the basis of how much you needed the business, what the condition of your backlog was, what your plant load was, what your employment was, and what you thought you had to do in order to get the business.

Kefauver: In any event, you would not know whether you were making money or losing money on this bid, because you had never made one, and Mr. Eckert told us you had no figures on which to base this price. You just followed along with G.E. Is that the policy of your company?

Cresap: The policy of our company is to meet competitive prices, and this is the manner in which the book price on this particular machine was arrived at. . . .

Kefauver: Even if you lost money?

Cresap: Even if we lost money, if we needed the business to cover our overheads and to keep our people working. . . .

Kefauver: On something that you had never sold, that had never been made and that you have not made yet, and they have not made one yet, their price is $17,402,300, the same as yours.

Cresap: They would have to be, Mr. Chairman, if we are going to be competitive. We cannot have a higher price than our competition.

Kefauver: How about a lower price?

> *Cresap:*   If we had a lower price, I am sure they would meet it, if they wanted to get the business very badly.

The Westinghouse–General Electric conspiracy was part of the heavy electrical equipment antitrust case of 1961, which included some of the most significant violations of antitrust laws ever, and which were instrumental in focusing public attention on the problem of price-fixing. More recently, over 100 suits for antitrust violations have been filed against the paper industry. Litigation against the folding-carton industry alone comprises the largest price-fixing case since 1961. Jeffrey Sonnenfeld's and Paul R. Lawrence's detailed study of price-fixing in this industry explores some of the pressures which lead managers to engage in price conspiracy, and offers some suggestions for organizational change to help eliminate the practice.

In the case of the folding-carton industry, external factors leading to price-fixing include a crowded and intensely competitive market and the fact that folding cartons vary little between manufacturers, so that price becomes the primary basis for competition. When management fears that a business's survival is at stake, standards of conduct are likely to be sacrificed. Another important factor is the internal culture of the corporation. Sonnenfeld and Lawrence explain that many corporations inadvertently encourage price-fixing by personnel incentives, failure of legal staff to anticipate problems, and participation in trade associations. Their observations highlight the need for a change in the corporate ethos, something we examine in more detail in Part Six.

chapter fourteen
DECEPTION

IS BUSINESS BLUFFING ETHICAL?

ALBERT Z. CARR*

A respected businessman with whom I discussed the theme of this article remarked with some heat, "You mean to say you're going to encourage men to bluff? Why, bluffing is nothing more than a form of lying! You're advising them to lie!"

I agreed that the basis of private morality is a respect for truth and that the closer a businessman comes to the truth, the more he deserves respect. At the same time, I suggested that most bluffing in business might be regarded simply as game strategy—much like bluffing in poker, which does not reflect on the morality of the bluffer.

I quoted Henry Taylor, the British statesman who pointed out that "falsehood ceases to be falsehood when it is understood on all sides that the truth is not expected to be spoken"—an exact description of bluffing in poker, diplomacy, and business. I cited the analogy of the criminal court, where the criminal is not expected to tell the truth when he pleads "not guilty." Everyone from the judge down takes it for granted that the job of the defendant's attorney is to get his client off, not to reveal the truth; and this is considered ethical practice. I mentioned Representative Omar Burleson, the Democrat from Texas, who was quoted as saying, in regard to the ethics of Congress, "Ethics is a barrel of worms"[1]—a pungent summing up of the problem of deciding who is ethical in politics.

I reminded my friend that millions of businessmen feel constrained every day to say *yes* to their bosses when they secretly believe *no* and that this is generally accepted as permissible strategy when the alternative might be the loss of a job. The essential point, I said, is that the ethics of business are game ethics, different from the ethics of religion.

He remained unconvinced. Referring to the company of which he is president, he declared: "Maybe that's good enough for some businessmen, but I can tell you that we pride ourselves on our ethics. In 30 years not one customer has ever questioned my word or asked to check our figures. We're loyal to our customers and fair to our suppliers. I regard my handshake on a deal as a contract. I've never entered into price-fixing schemes with my competitors. I've never allowed my salesmen to spread injurious

*Served on the White House staff and as a special consultant to President Truman; free-lance writer (deceased).

rumors about other companies. Our union contract is the best in our industry. And, if I do say so myself, our ethical standards are of the highest!"

He really was saying, without realizing it, that he was living up to the ethical standards of the business game—which are a far cry from those of private life. Like a gentlemanly poker player, he did not play in cahoots with others at the table, try to smear their reputations, or hold back chips he owed them.

But this same fine man, at that very time, was allowing one of his products to be advertised in a way that made it sound a great deal better than it actually was. Another item in his product line was notorious among dealers for its "built-in obsolescence." He was holding back from the market a much-improved product because he did not want it to interfere with sales of the inferior item it would have replaced. He had joined with certain of his competitors in hiring a lobbyist to push a state legislature, by methods that he preferred not to know too much about, into amending a bill then being enacted.

In his view these things had nothing to do with ethics; they were merely normal business practice. He himself undoubtedly avoided outright falsehoods—never lied in so many words. But the entire organization that he ruled was deeply involved in numerous strategies of deception.

PRESSURE TO DECEIVE

Most executives from time to time are almost compelled, in the interests of their companies or themselves, to practice some form of deception when negotiating with customers, dealers, labor unions, government officials, or even other departments of their companies. By conscious misstatements, concealment of pertinent facts, or exaggeration—in short, by bluffing—they seek to persuade others to agree with them. I think it is fair to say that if the individual executive refuses to bluff from time to time— if he feels obligated to tell the truth, the whole truth, and nothing but the truth—he is ignoring opportunities permitted under the rules and is at a heavy disadvantage in his business dealings.

But here and there a businessman is unable to reconcile himself to the bluff in which he plays a part. His conscience, perhaps spurred by religious idealism, troubles him. He feels guilty; he may develop an ulcer or a nervous tic. Before any executive can make profitable use of the strategy of the bluff, he needs to make sure that in bluffing he will not lose self-respect or become emotionally disturbed. If he is to reconcile personal integrity and high standards of honesty with the practical requirements of business, he must feel that his bluffs are ethically justified. The justification rests on the fact that business, as practiced by individuals as well as by corporations, has the impersonal character of a game—a game that demands both special strategy and an understanding of its special ethics.

The game is played at all levels of corporate life, from the highest to the lowest. At the very instant that a man decides to enter business, he may be forced into a game situation, as is shown by the recent experience of a Cornell honor graduate who applied for a job with a large company:

This applicant was given a psychological test which included the statement, "Of the following magazines, check any that you have read either regularly or from time to time, and double-check those which interest you most. *Reader's Digest, Time, Fortune, Saturday Evening Post, The New Republic, Life, Look, Ramparts, Newsweek, Business Week, U.S. News & World Report, The Nation, Playboy, Esquire, Harper's, Sports Illustrated.*"

His tastes in reading were broad, and at one time or another he had read almost all of these magazines. He was a subscriber to *The New Republic,* an enthusiast for *Ramparts,* and an avid student of the pictures in *Playboy.* He was not sure whether his interest in *Playboy* would be held against him, but he had a shrewd suspicion that if he confessed to an interest in *Ramparts* and *The New Republic,* he would be thought a liberal, a radical, or at least an intellectual, and his chances of getting the job, which he needed, would greatly diminish. He therefore checked five of the more conservative magazines. Apparently it was a sound decision, for he got the job.

He had made a game player's decision, consistent with business ethics.

A similar case is that of a magazine space salesman who, owing to a merger, suddenly found himself out of a job:

> This man was 58, and, in spite of a good record, his chance of getting a job elsewhere in a business where youth is favored in hiring practice was not good. He was a vigorous, healthy man, and only a considerable amount of gray in his hair suggested his age. Before beginning his job search he touched up his hair with a black dye to confine the gray to his temples. He knew that the truth about his age might well come out in time, but he calculated that he could deal with that situation when it arose. He and his wife decided that he could easily pass for 45, and he so stated his age on his résumé.

This was a lie; yet within the accepted rules of the business game, no moral culpability attaches to it.

THE POKER ANALOGY

We can learn a good deal about the nature of business by comparing it with poker. While both have a large element of chance, in the long run the winner is the man who plays with steady skill. In both games ultimate victory requires intimate knowledge of the rules, insight into the psychology of the other players, a bold front, a considerable amount of self-discipline, and the ability to respond swiftly and effectively to opportunities provided by chance.

No one expects poker to be played on the ethical principles preached in churches. In poker it is right and proper to bluff a friend out of the rewards of being dealt a good hand. A player feels no more than a slight twinge of sympathy, if that, when—with nothing better than a single ace in his hand—he strips a heavy loser, who holds a pair, of the rest of his chips. It was up to the other fellow to protect himself. In the words of an excellent poker player, former President Harry Truman, "If you can't stand the heat, stay out of the kitchen." If one shows mercy to a loser in poker, it is a personal gesture, divorced from the rules of the game.

Poker has its special ethics, and here I am not referring to rules against cheating. The man who keeps an ace up his sleeve or who marks the cards is more than unethical; he is a crook, and can be punished as such—kicked out of the game or, in the Old West, shot.

In contrast to the cheat, the unethical poker player is one who, while abiding by the letter of the rules, finds ways to put the other players at an unfair disadvantage. Perhaps he unnerves them with loud talk. Or he tries to get them drunk. Or he plays in cahoots with someone else at the table. Ethical poker players frown on such tactics.

Poker's own brand of ethics is different from the ethical ideals of civilized human relationships. The game calls for distrust of the other fellow. It ignores the claim of friendship. Cunning deception and concealment of one's strength and intentions, not kindness and open-heartedness, are vital in poker. No one thinks any the worse of poker on that account. And no one should think any the worse of the game of business because its standards of right and wrong differ from the prevailing traditions of morality in our society.

"WE DON'T MAKE THE LAWS"

Wherever we turn in business, we can perceive the sharp distinction between its ethical standards and those of the churches. Newspapers abound with sensational stories growing out of this distinction:

> We read one day that Senator Philip A. Hart of Michigan has attacked food processors for deceptive packaging of numerous products.[2]

> The next day there is a Congressional to-do over Ralph Nader's book, *Unsafe At Any Speed*, which demonstrates that automobile companies for years have neglected the safety of car-owning families.[3]

> Then another Senator, Lee Metcalf of Montana, and journalist Vic Reinemer show in their book, *Overcharge*, the methods by which utility companies elude regulating government bodies to extract unduly large payments from users of electricity.[4]

These are merely dramatic instances of a prevailing condition; there is hardly a major industry at which a similar attack could not be aimed. Critics of business regard such behavior as unethical, but the companies concerned know that they are merely playing the business game.

Among the most respected of our business institutions are the insurance companies. A group of insurance executives meeting recently in New England was startled when their guest speaker, social critic Daniel Patrick Moynihan, roundly berated them for "unethical" practices. They had been guilty, Moynihan alleged, of using outdated actuarial tables to obtain unfairly high premiums. They habitually delayed the hearings of lawsuits against them in order to tire out the plaintiffs and win cheap settlements. In their employment policies they used ingenious devices to discriminate against certain minority groups.[5]

It was difficult for the audience to deny the validity of these charges. But these men were business game players. Their reaction to Moynihan's attack was much the same as that of the automobile manufacturers to Nader, of the utilities to Senator Metcalf, and of the food processors to Senator Hart. If the laws governing their businesses change, or if public opinion becomes clamorous, they will make the necessary adjustments. But morally they have in their view done nothing wrong. As long as they comply with the letter of the law, they are within their rights to operate their businesses as they see fit.

Violations of the ethical ideals of society are common in business, but they are not necessarily violations of business principles. Each year the Federal Trade Commission orders hundreds of companies, many of them of the first magnitude, to "cease and desist" from practices which, judged by ordinary standards, are of questionable morality but which are stoutly defended by the companies concerned.

In one case, a firm manufacturing a well-known mouthwash was accused of using a cheap form of alcohol possibly deleterious to health. The company's chief executive, after testifying in Washington, made this comment privately:

> We broke no law. We're in a highly competitive industry. If we're going to stay in business, we have to look for profit wherever the law permits. We don't make the laws. We obey them. Then why do we have to put up with this "holier than thou" talk about ethics? It's sheer hypocrisy. We're not in business to promote ethics. Look at the cigarette companies, for God's sake! If the ethics aren't embodied in the laws by the men who made them, you can't expect businessmen to fill the lack. Why, a sudden submission to Christian ethics by businessmen would bring about the greatest economic upheaval in history!

It may be noted that the government failed to prove its case against him.

The illusion that business can afford to be guided by ethics as conceived in private life is often fostered by speeches and articles containing such phrases as, "It pays to be ethical,"or, "Sound ethics is good business." Actually this is not an ethical position at all; it is a self-serving calculation in disguise. The speaker is really saying that in the long run a company can make more money if it does not antagonize competitors, suppliers, employees, and customers by squeezing them too hard. He is saying that oversharp policies reduce ultimate gains. That is true, but it has nothing to do with ethics. The underlying attitude is much like that in the familiar story of the shopkeeper who finds an extra $20 bill in the cash register, debates with himself the ethical problem—should he tell his partner?—and finally decides to share the money because the gesture will give him an edge over the s.o.b. the next time they quarrel.

I think it is fair to sum up the prevailing attitude of businessmen on ethics as follows:

We live in what is probably the most competitive of the world's civilized societies. Our customs encourage a high degree of aggression in the individual's striving for success. Business is our main area of competition, and it has been ritualized into a game of strategy. The basic rules of the game have been set by the government, which attempts to detect and punish business frauds. But as long as a company does not transgress the rules of the game set by law, it has the legal right to shape its strategy without reference to anything but its profits. If it takes a long-term view of its profits, it will preserve amicable relations, so far as possible, with those with whom it deals. A wise businessman will not seek advantage to the point where he generates dangerous hostility among employees, competitors, customers, government, or the public at large. But decisions in this area are, in the final test, decisions of strategy, not of ethics.

To be a winner, a man must play to win. This does not mean that he must be ruthless, cruel, harsh, or treacherous. On the contrary, the better his reputation for integrity, honesty, and decency, the better his chances of victory will be in the long run. But from time to time every businessman, like every poker player, is offered a choice between certain loss or bluffing within the legal rules of the game. If he is not resigned to losing, if he wants to rise in his company and industry, then in such a crisis he will bluff—and bluff hard.

Every now and then one meets a successful businessman who has conveniently forgotten the small or large deceptions that he practiced on his way to fortune. "God gave me my money," old John D. Rockefeller once piously told a Sunday school class. It would be a rare tycoon in our time who would risk the horse laugh with which such a remark would be greeted.

In the last third of the twentieth century even children are aware that if a man has become prosperous in business, he has sometimes departed from the strict truth in order to overcome obstacles or has practiced the more subtle deceptions of the half-truth or the misleading omission. Whatever the form of the bluff, it is an integral part of the game, and the executive who does not master its techniques is not likely to accumulate much money or power.

NOTES

1. *The New York Times*, March 9, 1967.
2. *The New York Times*, November 21, 1966.
3. New York, Grossman Publishers, Inc., 1965.
4. New York, David McKay Company, Inc., 1967.
5. *The New York Times*, January 17, 1967.

THE ETHICS AND PROFITABILITY OF BLUFFING IN BUSINESS

RICHARD E. WOKUTCH* and THOMAS L. CARSON†

Consider a standard case of bluffing in an economic transaction. I am selling a used car and say that $1,500 is my final offer, even though I know that I would accept considerably less. Or, suppose that I am a union representative in a labor negotiation. Though I have been instructed to accept $10 an hour if that is the highest offer I receive, I say that we will not accept a wage of $10 an hour under any circumstances. This sort of bluffing is widely practiced and almost universally condoned. It is thought to be morally acceptable. It is our contention, however, that bluffing raises serious ethical questions. For bluffing is clearly an act of deception; the bluffer's intent is to deceive the other parties about the nature of his bargaining position. Furthermore, bluffing often involves lying. The two examples of bluffing presented here both fit the standard definition of lying; they are deliberate false statements made with the intent of deceiving others.[1]

Common sense holds that lying and deception are matters of moral significance which are prima facie wrong. One could also put this by saying that there is a presumption against lying and deception; that they require some special justification in order to be considered permissible.[2] Almost no one would agree with Kant's view that it is wrong to lie even if doing so is necessary to protect the lives of innocent people. According to Kant it would be wrong to lie to a potential murderer concerning the whereabouts of his intended victim.[3]

Assuming the correctness of the view that there is a moral presumption against lying and deception, and assuming that we are correct in saying that bluffing involves lying, it follows that bluffing and other deceptive business practices require some sort of special justification in order to be considered permissible. Business people frequently defend bluffing and other deceptive practices on the grounds that they are profitable or economically necessary. Such acts are also defended on the grounds that they are standard practice in economic transactions. Are such grounds sufficient to justify lying and deception, given our present assumptions?

There are those who hold that lying and deception are never profitable or economically necessary. In their view, honesty is always the best policy. One incentive for telling the truth is the law, but here we are referring to lying or bluffing which is not illegal, or for which the penalty or risk of being caught is not great enough to discourage the action.

Those who hold that honesty is always in one's economic self-interest argue that economic transactions are built on trust and that a violation of that trust discourages an individual or organization from entering into further transactions with the lying

From *Westminster Institute Review*, vol. 1, no. 2, May 1981. Reprinted by permission of publisher and authors.

*Department of Business Administration, Virginia Polytechnic Institute.

†Department of Philosophy, Virginia Polytechnic Institute.

party for fear of being lied to again. Thus, some mutually beneficial transactions may be foregone for lack of trust. Moreover, word of deceitful practices spreads through the marketplace and others also avoid doing business with the liar. Thus, while some short run profit might accrue from lying, in the long run it is unprofitable. If this argument were sound, we would have a non-issue. Lying, like inefficiency, would be a question of bad management that would be in one's own best interest to eliminate.

Unfortunately, there are some anomalies in the marketplace which prevent the system from operating in a perfectly smooth manner. The very existence of bluffing and lying in the first place suggests that the economists' assumption of perfect (or near perfect) market information is not valid. Some transactions, such as buying or selling a house, are one-shot deals with little or no chance of repeat business. Thus, there is no experience on which to base an assessment of the seller's honesty, and no incentive to build trust for future transactions. Even when a business is involved in an ongoing operation, information flows are such that a large number of people can be duped before others hear about it (e.g., selling Florida swampland or Arizona desertland sight unseen). Other bluffs and lies are difficult or even impossible to prove. If a union negotiator wins a concession from management on the grounds that the union would not ratify the contract without it—even though he has reason to believe this is untrue—it would be extremely difficult for management to prove later that ratification could have been achieved without the provision. By the same token, some product claims, such as the salesman's contention that "this is the best X on the market," are inherently subjective. When the competing products are of similar quality, it is difficult to prove such statements untrue, even if the person making the statement believes them to be untrue. Another exception to the assumption of perfect information flows is the confusion brought on by the increasing technological complexity of goods and services. In fact, a product information industry in the form of publications like *Consumer Reports, Canadian Consumer, Consumer Union Reports, Money,* and *Changing Times* has arisen to provide, for a price, the kind of product information that economic theory assumes consumers have to begin with.

These arguments suggest not only that the commonly cited disincentives to bluffing and lying are often ineffective, but that there are some distinct financial incentives for these activities. If you can convince consumers that your product is better than it really is, you will have a better chance of selling them that product and you may be able to charge them a higher price than they would otherwise be willing to pay. It is also obvious that in a negotiating setting there are financial rewards for successful lies and bluffs. If you can conceal your actual minimal acceptable position, you may be able to achieve a more desirable settlement. By the same token, learning your negotiating opponent's true position will enable you to press towards his minimal acceptable position. This is, of course, why such intrigues as hiding microphones in the opposing negotiating team's private quarters or hiring informants are undertaken in negotiations—they produce valuable information.

An individual cannot, however, justify lying simply on the grounds that it is in his own self-interest to lie, for it is not always morally permissible to do what is in one's own self-interest. I would not be justified in killing you or falsely accusing you of a crime in order to get your job, even if doing so would be to my advantage.

Similarly, a businessman cannot justify lying or deception simply on the grounds that they are advantageous, i.e. profitable, to his company. This point can be strengthened if we remember that any advantages which one gains as a result of bluffing are usually counter-balanced by corresponding disadvantages on the part of others. If I succeed in getting a higher price by bluffing when I sell my house, there must be someone else who is paying more than he would have otherwise.

Economic necessity is a stronger justification for lying than mere profitability. Suppose that it is necessary for a businessman to engage in lying or deception in order to insure the survival of his firm. Many would not object to a person stealing food to prevent himself or his children from starving to death. Perhaps lying in an extreme situation to get money to buy food or to continue employing workers so that *they* can buy food would be equally justifiable. This case would best be described as a conflict of duties—a conflict between the duty to be honest and the duty to promote the welfare of those for/to whom one is responsible (one's children, one's employees, or the stockholders whose money one manages). However, it is extremely unlikely that bankruptcy would result in the death or starvation of anyone in a society which has unemployment compensation, welfare payments, food stamps, charitable organizations, and even opportunities for begging. The consequences of refraining from lying in transactions might still be very unfavorable indeed, involving, for example, the bankruptcy of a firm, loss of investment, unemployment, and the personal suffering associated with this. But a firm which needs to practice lying or deception in order to continue in existence is of doubtful value to society. Perhaps the labor, capital and raw materials which it uses could be put to better use elsewhere. At least in a free market situation, the interests of economic efficiency would be best served if such firms were to go out of business. An apparent exception to this argument about economic efficiency would be a situation in which a firm was pushed to the edge of bankruptcy by the lies of competitors or others.

It seems probable to us that the long term consequences of the bankruptcy of a firm which needs to lie in order to continue in existence would be better, or no worse, than those of its continuing to exist.

Suppose, however, that the immediate bad consequences of bankruptcy would not be offset by any long term benefits. In that case it is not clear that it would be wrong for a company to resort to lying and deception out of economic necessity. One can, after all, be justified in lying or deceiving to save individuals from harms far less serious than death. I can be justified in lying about the gender of my friend's roommate to a nosy relative or boss in order to protect him from embarrassment or from being fired. If the degree of harm prevented by lying or deception were the only relevant factor, and if bankruptcy would not have any significant long term benefits, then it would seem that a businessman could easily justify lying and deceiving in order to protect those associated with his business from the harm which would result from the bankruptcy of the firm. There is, however, another relevant factor which clouds the issue. In the case of lying about the private affairs of one's friends, one is lying to others about matters about which they have no right to know. Our present analogy warrants lying and deception for the sake of economic survival only in cases in which the persons being lied to or deceived have no right to the information in question.

Among other things, this rules out deceiving customers about dangerous defects in one's products because they have a right to this information; but it does not rule out lying to someone or deceiving them about one's minimal bargaining position.

We have argued that personal or corporate profit is no justification for lying in business transactions, and that lying out of economic necessity is also morally objectionable in many cases. But what about lying in order to benefit the party being lied to? There are certainly many self-serving claims to this effect. Some have argued that individuals derive greater satisfaction from a product or service if they can be convinced that it is better than is actually the case. On the other hand, an advertising executive made the argument in the recent Federal Trade Commission hearings on children's advertising that the disappointment children experience when a product fails to meet their commercial-inflated expectations is beneficial because it helps them develop a healthy skepticism. These arguments are not convincing. In fact, they appear to be smoke screens for actions taken out of self-interest. Deceptive advertising is almost always employed for reasons of self-interest, even though it is conceivable that consumers might benefit from it. For example, deceptive advertising claims may cause one to purchase a product which is of genuine benefit.

While lying and deception can sometimes be justified by reference to the interests of those being lied to or deceived, such cases are very atypical in business situations. As was argued earlier, successful bluffing almost always harms the other party in business negotiations. The net effect of a successful bluff is paying more or receiving less than would otherwise be the case.

But what of the justification that lying and deception are standard practice in economic transactions? Certainly, lying and deception are very common, if not generally accepted or condoned. Bluffing and other deceptive practices are especially common in economic negotiations, and bluffing, at least, is generally thought to be an acceptable practice. Does this fact in any way justify bluffing? We think not. The mere fact that something is standard practice or generally accepted is not enough to justify it. Standard practice and popular opinion can be in error. Such things as slavery were once standard practice and generally accepted. But they are and *were* morally wrong. However, the fact that bluffing is common can justify it indirectly. If one is involved in a negotiation, it is very probable that the other parties with whom one is dealing are themselves bluffing. It seems plausible to say that the presumption against lying and deception holds only when the other parties with whom one is dealing are not lying or attempting to deceive. Given this, there is no presumption against bluffing or deceiving someone who is attempting to bluff or deceive you. It should be stressed again that the prevalence of bluffing *per se* is no justification for bluffing. But, in fact, there is such a strong presumption for thinking that the other parties will bluff or lie in negotiating settings that one is justified in presuming that they are lying or bluffing in the absence of any special reasons to the contrary, e.g., dealing with an unusually naive or scrupulous person.

A further ground on which lying or deceiving in bargaining situations is sometimes held to be justifiable is the claim that the other parties do not have a right to know one's true bargaining position. It is true that the other parties do not have a right to know one's position, i.e., it would not be wrong to refuse to reveal it to them. But this is not to say that it is permissible to lie or deceive them. You have no right to know where I was born, but it would be prima facie wrong for me to lie to you about the place of my birth. So, lying and deception in bargaining situations cannot be justified simply on the grounds that the other parties have no right to know one's true position. This is not to deny that, other things being equal, it is much worse to lie or deceive about a matter concerning which the other parties have a right to know than one about which they have no right to know.

As we have argued, there appears to be a personal economic incentive in many cases for lying, cheating, and deception. We cannot, therefore, rely solely on the marketplace to eliminate these activities. Thus, we now consider what sorts of guidelines we can offer the individual buying or selling goods or services who is concerned about the morality of lying and bluffing but is also concerned about furthering his own economic welfare.

Bluffing is an attempt to distort one's true bargaining position. However, one could gain some negotiating advantage by simply concealing that position. Thus, if someone asks the minimum price you would accept for your house, you could say, "I want $50,000 for this house," without lying or deceiving anyone and without revealing the minimum offer you would accept. While this is clearly not as strong a position as "I won't accept a penny less than $50,000 for this house," if the prospective buyer felt that the house was worth $50,000 and that if he didn't offer that amount, someone else might buy it, he might be willing to pay that price. Whether or not this happens, of course, depends on the relative bargaining positions of the negotiators. In addition to this truthful negotiating approach, we make the following recommendations for personal and institutional responses to the problems involved in lying, bluffing, and deception in business:

1. Explicit consideration by negotiators and all persons engaged in economic transactions of the ethical issues involved in their activities. Even if there is no general consensus about the moral status of an action, a well thought out action would be preferable to one made without any attention to moral issues.

2. Focus on the morality of bluffing and lying as part of business ethics courses.

3. Strict legal definitions of deceptive practices in negotiations. If the market system can't provide adequate incentives for truth-telling, perhaps the legal system can.

4. Use of ethical advisors for opinions on the morality of certain economic transactions.[4] A resident philosopher would, of course, be practical only for large corporations and unions, but even individuals could seek counsel from trusted friends or clergy.

5. Further analysis of the moral status of lying and deception in economic transactions. The following questions seem particularly important: To what extent is the general presumption against lying and deception overridden when the other parties also are lying or deceiving, or when they have no right to the information in question? What is deception? What are the differences between lying and deception? Is it permissible to avoid lying by making true but deceptive statements?

6. The development of financial and other incentives for honesty in economic and political transactions and organizations.[5]

7. Public participation in deliberations on the issue of lying in business and business ethics in general. For example, public representatives on regulatory commissions considering these issues or on business panels seeking to develop codes of ethics would provide for the public scrutiny which is necessary for forthright consideration of ethical issues.[6]

While these steps would not eliminate the uncertainty about the morality of all the activities we have discussed, they would provide an improvement over decision making systems which ignore ethical issues.

NOTES

We are indebted to Thomas Beauchamp for comments on a previous version of this paper. Earlier versions of this paper were presented to a conference on Business and Professional Ethics at Kalamazoo College and Western Michigan University, November, 1979, and to the Philosophy Department at Denison University.

1. For a much more thorough defense of the claim that bluffing involves lying, with an appeal to a somewhat different definition of lying, see our paper, "The Moral Status of Bluffing and Deception in Business," in *Business and Professional Ethics*, ed. Wade L. Robison and Michael S. Pritchard (New York: Humana Press). Also see our paper "Bluffing in Labor Negotiations: Legal and Ethical Issues," with Kent F. Mursmann, *Journal of Business Ethics*, vol. 1, no. 1, January 1982.

2. The classic statement of this view is included in Chapter II of Sir David Ross' *The Right and the Good* (Oxford: Oxford University Press, 1930).

3. Immanuel Kant, "On the Supposed Right to Tell Lies from Benevolent Motives," (1797), In *Moral Rules and Particular Circumstances*, ed. Baruch Brody (Englewood Cliffs, New Jersey: Prentice-Hall, 1970), pp. 32 and 33.

4. John T. Steiner, "The Prospect of Ethical Advisors for Business Corporations," *Business and Society* (Spring, 1976): 5–10.

5. Jerry R. Green and Jean-Jacques Laffont, *Incentives in Public Decision Making* (Amsterdam: North-Holland Publishing Co., 1978); and William Vickery, "Counterspeculation, Auctions, and Cooperative Sealed Tenders," *Journal of Finance* (March, 1961): 8–37.

6. Points 6 and 7 are suggested by Sissela Bok, *Lying: Moral Choice in Public and Private Life* (New York: Pantheon Books, 1978).

chapter fifteen
BRIBERY

ETHICS AND THE FOREIGN CORRUPT PRACTICES ACT

MARK PASTIN* and MICHAEL HOOKER†

Not long ago it was feared that as a fallout of Watergate, government officials would be hamstrung by artificially inflated moral standards. Recent events, however, suggest that the scapegoat of post-Watergate morality may have become American business rather than government officials.

One aspect of the recent attention paid to corporate morality is the controversy surrounding payments made by American corporations to foreign officials for the purpose of securing business abroad. Like any law or system of laws, the Foreign Corrupt Practices Act (FCPA), designed to control or eliminate such payments, should be grounded in morality, and should therefore be judged from an ethical perspective. Unfortunately, neither the law nor the question of its repeal has been adequately addressed from that perspective.

HISTORY OF THE FCPA

On December 20, 1977 President Carter signed into law S.305, the Foreign Corrupt Practices Act (FCPA), which makes it a crime for American corporations to offer or provide payments to officials of foreign governments for the purpose of obtaining or retaining business. The FCPA also establishes record keeping requirements for publicly held corporations to make it difficult to conceal political payments proscribed by the Act. Violators of the FCPA, both corporations and managers, face severe penalties. A company may be fined up to $1 million, while its officers who directly participated in violations of the Act or had reason to know of such violations, face up to five years in prison and/or $10,000 in fines. The Act also prohibits corporations from indemnifying fines imposed on their directors, officers, employees, or agents. The Act does not prohibit "grease" payments to foreign government employees whose duties are primarily ministerial or clerical, since such payments are sometimes required to persuade the recipients to perform their normal duties.

From *Business Horizons*, December 1980. Copyright © 1980, by the Foundation for the School of Business at Indiana University. Reprinted by permission of the publisher and authors.

*Center for Private and Public Sector Ethics, Arizona State University.

†President, Bennington College.

At the time of this writing, the precise consequences of the FCPA for American business are unclear, mainly because of confusion surrounding the government's enforcement intentions. Vigorous objections have been raised against the Act by corporate attorneys and recently by a few government officials. Among the latter is Frank A. Weil, former Assistant Secretary of Commerce, who has stated, "The questionable payments problem may turn out to be one of the most serious impediments to doing business in the rest of the world."[1]

The potentially severe economic impact of the FCPA was highlighted by the fall 1978 report of the Export Disincentives Task Force, which was created by the White House to recommend ways of improving our balance of trade. The Task Force identified the FCPA as contributing significantly to economic and political losses in the United States. Economic losses come from constricting the ability of American corporations to do business abroad, and political losses come from the creation of a holier-than-thou image.

The Task Force made three recommendations in regard to the FCPA:

- The Justice Department should issue guidelines on its enforcement policies and establish procedures by which corporations could get advance government reaction to anticipated payments to foreign officials.

- The FCPA should be amended to remove enforcement from the SEC, which now shares enforcement responsibility with the Department of Justice.

- The administration should periodically report to Congress and the public on export losses caused by the FCPA.

In response to the Task Force's report, the Justice Department, over SEC objections, drew up guidelines to enable corporations to check any proposed action possibly in violation of the FCPA. In response to such an inquiry, the Justice Department would inform the corporation of its enforcement intentions. The purpose of such an arrangement is in part to circumvent the intent of the law. As of this writing, the SEC appears to have been successful in blocking publication of the guidelines, although Justice recently reaffirmed its intention to publish guidelines. Being more responsive to political winds, Justice may be less inclined than the SEC to rigidly enforce the Act.

Particular concern has been expressed about the way in which bookkeeping requirements of the Act will be enforced by the SEC. The Act requires that company records will "accurately and fairly reflect the transactions and dispositions of the assets of the issuer." What is at question is the interpretation the SEC will give to the requirement and the degree of accuracy and detail it will demand. The SEC's post-Watergate behavior suggests that it will be rigid in requiring the disclosure of all information that bears on financial relationships between the company and any foreign or domestic public official. This level of accountability in record keeping, to which auditors and corporate attorneys have strongly objected, goes far beyond previous SEC requirements that records display only facts material to the financial position of the company.

Since the potential consequences of the FCPA for American businesses and business managers are very serious, it is important that the Act have a rationale capable of bearing close scrutiny. In looking at the foundation of the FCPA, it should be noted that its passage followed in the wake of intense newspaper coverage of the financial dealings of corporations. Such media attention was engendered by the dramatic disclosure of corporate slush funds during the Watergate hearings and by a voluntary disclosure program established shortly thereafter by the SEC. As a result of the SEC program, more than 400 corporations, including 117 of the Fortune 500, admitted to making more than $300 million in foreign political payments in less than ten years.

Throughout the period of media coverage leading up to passage of the FCPA, and especially during the hearings on the Act, there was in all public discussions of the issue a tone of righteous moral indignation at the idea of American companies making foreign political payments. Such payments were ubiquitously termed "bribes," although many of these could more accurately be called extortions, while others were more akin to brokers' fees or sales commissions.

American business can be faulted for its reluctance during this period to bring to public attention the fact that in a very large number of countries, payments to foreign officials are virtually required for doing business. Part of that reluctance, no doubt, comes from the awkwardly difficult position of attempting to excuse bribery or something closely resembling it. There is a popular abhorrence in this country of bribery directed at domestic government officials, and that abhorrence transfers itself to payments directed toward foreign officials as well.

Since its passage, the FCPA has been subjected to considerable critical analysis, and many practical arguments have been advanced in favor of its repeal.[2] However, there is always lurking in back of such analyses the uneasy feeling that no matter how strongly considerations of practicality and economics may count against this law, the fact remains that the law protects morality in forbidding bribery. For example, Gerald McLaughlin, professor of law at Fordham, has shown persuasively that where the legal system of a foreign country affords inadequate protection against the arbitrary exercise of power to the disadvantage of American corporations, payments to foreign officials may be required to provide a compensating mechanism against the use of such arbitrary power. McLaughlin observes, however, that "this does not mean that taking advantage of the compensating mechanism would necessarily make the payment moral."[3]

The FCPA, and questions regarding its enforcement or repeal, will not be addressed adequately until an effort has been made to come to terms with the Act's foundation in morality. While it may be very difficult, or even impossible, to legislate morality (that is, to change the moral character and sentiments of people by passing laws that regulate their behavior), the existing laws undoubtedly still reflect the moral beliefs we hold. Passage of the FCPA in Congress was eased by the simple connection most Congressmen made between bribery, seen as morally repugnant, and the Act, which is designed to prevent bribery.

Given the importance of the FCPA to American business and labor, it is imperative that attention be given to the question of whether there is adequate moral justification for the law.

ETHICAL ANALYSIS OF THE FCPA

The question we will address is not whether each payment prohibited by the FCPA is moral or immoral, but rather whether the FCPA, given all its consequences and ramifications, is itself moral. It is well known that morally sound laws and institutions may tolerate some immoral acts. The First Amendment's guarantee of freedom of speech allows individuals to utter racial slurs. And immoral laws and institutions may have some beneficial consequences, for example, segregationist legislation bringing deep-seated racism into the national limelight. But our concern is with the overall morality of the FCPA.

The ethical tradition has two distinct ways of assessing social institutions, including laws: *End-Point Assessment* and *Rule Assessment*. Since there is no consensus as to which approach is correct, we will apply both types of assessment to the FCPA.

The End-Point approach assesses a law in terms of its contribution to general social well-being. The ethical theory underlying End-Point Assessment is utilitarianism. According to utilitarianism, a law is morally sound if and only if the law promotes the well-being of those affected by the law to the greatest extent practically achievable. To satisfy the utilitarian principle, a law must promote the well-being of those affected by it at least as well as any alternative law that we might propose, and better than no law at all. A conclusive End-Point Assessment of a law requires specification of what constitutes the welfare of those affected by the law, which the liberal tradition generally sidesteps by identifying an individual's welfare with what he takes to be in his interests.

Considerations raised earlier in the paper suggest that the FCPA does not pass the End-Point test. The argument is not the too facile one that we could propose a better law. (Amendments to the FCPA are now being considered.[4]) The argument is that it may be better to have *no* such law than to have the FCPA. The main domestic consequences of the FCPA seem to include an adverse effect on the balance of payments, a loss of business and jobs, and another opportunity for the SEC and the Justice Department to compete. These negative effects must be weighed against possible gains in the conduct of American business within the United States. From the perspective of foreign countries in which American firms do business, the main consequence of the FCPA seems to be that certain officials now accept bribes and influence from non-American businesses. It is hard to see that who pays the bribes makes much difference to these nations.

Rule Assessment of the morality of laws is often favored by those who find that End-Point Assessment is too lax in supporting their moral codes. According to the Rule Assessment approach: A law is morally sound if and only if the law accords with a code embodying correct ethical rules. This approach has no content until the rules are stated, and different rules will lead to different ethical assessments. Fortunately, what we have to say about Rule Assessment of the FCPA does not depend on the details of a particular ethical code.

Those who regard the FCPA as a worthwhile expression of morality, despite the adverse effects on American business and labor, clearly subscribe to a rule stating that it is unethical to bribe. Even if it is conceded that the payments proscribed by the FCPA warrant classifications as bribes, citing a rule prohibiting bribery does not suffice to justify the FCPA.

Most of the rules in an ethical code are not *categorical* rules; they are *prima facie* rules. A categorical rule does not allow exceptions, whereas a prima facie rule does. The ethical rule that a person ought to keep promises is an example of a prima facie rule. If I promise to loan you a book on nuclear energy and later find out that you are a terrorist building a private atomic bomb, I am ethically obligated not to keep my promise. The rule that one ought to keep promises is "overridden" by the rule that one ought to prevent harm to others.

A rule prohibiting bribery is a prima facie rule. There are cases in which morality requires that a bribe be paid. If the only way to get essential medical care for a dying child is to bribe a doctor, morality requires one to bribe the doctor. So adopting an ethical code which includes a rule prohibiting the payment of bribes does not guarantee that a Rule Assessment of the FCPA will be favorable to it.

The fact that the FCPA imposes a cost on American business and labor weighs against the prima facie obligation not to bribe. If we suppose that American corporations have obligations, tantamount to promises, to promote the job security of their employees and the investments of shareholders, these obligations will also weigh against the obligation not to bribe. Again, if government legislative and enforcement bodies have an obligation to secure the welfare of American business and workers, the FCPA may force them to violate their public obligations.

The FCPA's moral status appears even more dubious if we note that many of the payments prohibited by the Act are neither bribes nor share features that make bribes morally reprehensible. Bribes are generally held to be malefic if they persuade one to act against his good judgement, and consequently purchase an inferior product. But the payments at issue in the FCPA are usually extorted *from the seller*. Further it is arguable that not paying the bribe is more likely to lead to purchase of an inferior product than paying the bribe. Finally, bribes paid to foreign officials may not involve deception when they accord with recognized local practices.

In conclusion, neither End-Point nor Rule Assessment uncovers a sound moral basis for the FCPA. It is shocking to find that a law prohibiting bribery has no clear moral basis, and may even be an immoral law. However, this is precisely what examination of the FCPA from a moral perspective reveals. This is symptomatic of the fact that moral conceptions which were appropriate to a simpler world are not adequate to the complex world in which contemporary business functions. Failure to appreciate this point often leads to righteous condemnation of business, when it should lead to careful reflection on one's own moral preconceptions.

NOTES

1. *National Journal*, June 3, 1978: 880.

2. David C. Gustman, "The Foreign Corrupt Practices Act of 1977," *The Journal of International Law and Economics*, Vol. 13, 1979; 367–401, and Walter S. Surrey, "The Foreign Corrupt Practices Act: Let the Punishment Fit the Crime," *Harvard International Law Journal*, Spring 1979: 203–303.

3. Gerald T. McLaughlin, "The Criminalization of Questionable Foreign Payments by Corporations," *Fordham Law Review*, Vol. 46: 1095.

4. "Foreign Bribery Law Amendments Drafted," *American Bar Association Journal*, February 1980: 135.

MORAL DIMENSIONS OF THE FOREIGN CORRUPT PRACTICES ACT:
Comments on Pastin and Hooker

KENNETH D. ALPERN*

I

A number of considerations must be taken into account in order to determine whether a given law ought to be enacted or maintained. These considerations include the implications of the law for social welfare; its constitutionality; its efficacy, enforceability, and cost; its compatibility with personal rights; and the evenhandedness of the law compared with that of other laws governing similar activities. Usually no single factor is by itself dispositive. However, in the case of the Foreign Corrupt Practices Act (FCPA), one consideration, the morality of the law, has been crucial to its support. It is widely, if not universally, held that this law *is* supported by morality. In a recent paper,[1] Michael Hooker and Mark Pastin dispute this belief. They evaluate the FCPA from the perspectives of the two presently dominant theories of morality, end-point or utilitarian assessment and rule or deontological assessment, and conclude that neither theory provides a sound moral basis for this law.

This conclusion is mistaken. The FCPA is, in fact, supported by morality. I will show this by examining the deontological support for the act. I will not address utilitarian arguments directly, since an analysis of costs and benefits is likely to be inconclusive even if all the relevant empirical data could somehow be collected. Some of what I say, however, can be used to challenge, on conceptual grounds, much utilitarian criticism of the act.

II

Hooker and Pastin offer two argument sketches intended to show that the act does not receive support from deontological considerations. The key to the first argument is the claim that corporations have particularly weighty moral obligations to their investors and employees which override the moral obligation not to bribe. The key to the second argument is the claim that many of the activities made unlawful by the act are, in fact, of a type that is not morally objectionable. I will consider each argument in turn.

The first argument is roughly this:

1. The FCPA is essentially a prohibition of bribery. Hooker and Pastin allow this for the sake of argument. Actually, more than just bribery is unlawful under the act, and this fact is used in their second argument discussed in Section III below.

Presented at the Conference on Business and Professional Ethics at the University of Illinois at Chicago Circle, May 1981. Reprinted by permission of the author.

*Department of Philosophy, Virginia Polytechnic Institute.

2. Bribery is morally wrong—in the sense that there exists a prima facie moral obligation not to engage in bribery. This is to say that the prohibition of bribery is not absolute. It can be overridden by other considerations.

3. Corporations have moral obligations, again, merely prima facie, to protect the investments of their shareholders and the jobs of their employees. The federal government may also be under a prima facie moral obligation to secure the welfare of American business and workers.

In this paper, Hooker and Pastin leave the argument hanging at this point. But from these premises all that follows is that the moral rule against bribery is not the only deontological consideration that may be relevant. Something like the following must be added in order to complete their argument.

4. There are situations governed by the FCPA in which the prima facie moral obligations of corporations and government override the prima facie moral obligation not to bribe. That is, in some cases, considered individually and other things being equal, corporations *morally ought to bribe* and the government *morally ought not to punish* corporations for bribing. Thus, as the law now stands, some actions are required legally that are contrary to morality.

5. Cases in which the FCPA requires actions that are contrary to morality are numerous or are of great moral moment.

From this the conclusion is to be drawn that the FCPA does not have the support of morality from a deontological perspective on bribery and is therefore unacceptable.

There is much to agree with in this argument. Its pattern of reasoning is good; the premises do license the conclusion. It is certainly the case that any moral rule prohibiting bribery cannot be absolute. And it is surely true that corporations have some sort of obligation to pursue profit. I am even prepared to allow that there could conceivably be situations in which the prohibition of bribery is overridden by other obligations that corporations are under. Nonetheless, the conclusion is still false.

What gives the argument a large part of its appeal is its apparent discovery of a second moral principle, the principle that promises should be kept, which, in situations covered by the FCPA, weighs against the moral principle prohibiting bribery. If this second moral principle is recognized, the moral predicament of corporations would appear to involve being forced to choose between which of two conflicting moral principles to satisfy: keep promises or don't bribe.

But these principles appear to be of the same moral status: Both are basic principles of deontological moral theories. Given this equality of status, there would seem to be no a priori reason for favoring the principle prohibiting bribery over the principle requiring promise keeping. Hooker and Pastin do not go far enough into the argument to indicate what sorts of considerations are supposed to tip the scales in favor of promise keeping. Perhaps they have in mind some further deontological principles; or maybe at this point they would fall back on utilitarian considerations. In any case, they want us to believe that in situations governed by the act, the bribery rule conflicts with a rule for keeping promises, and that the promise-keeping rule is generally to be favored.

In order to show that this position is mistaken, I will argue that the supposed conflict is only apparent and that the introduction of the rule of promise keeping at this place in the argument is irrelevant and misleading. Furthermore, I will argue that the moral considerations which do properly stand in the place thought to be held by the obligation to keep promises can be demoted, on the basis of conceptual considerations, to where it will be clear that the prohibition of bribery generally takes precedence in a determination of the morally acceptable action. In order to make this case, we must look more closely at the way obligations to keep promises are supposed to enter the picture.

Hooker and Pastin mention three specific obligations deriving from the principle of promise keeping: (1) an obligation of corporations to promote the investments of their shareholders; (2) an obligation of corporations to protect the security of their employees' jobs; and (3) an obligation which the federal government may possibly be under to protect the welfare of American business and workers. I do not have enough space to examine all three of these obligations in detail, so I will concentrate on the one that I take to be most important, the obligation of corporations to their investors. At the end of this section I will offer a brief remark about each of the other two obligations.

How does the obligation of corporations to their investors come about? The essence seems to be this. Corporations are *agents* for their investors. In effect a corporation says: "If you allow us the use of your capital, we promise in return to work to increase the value of your investment."[2] Having made the promise to act as agents, corporations are morally obligated, by virtue of the moral rule that promises be kept, to promote the financial interests of their principals.

So corporations promise to promote their investors' financial interests and are morally obligated to them. What difference does this make to the morality of international corporate bribery? My answer is: None. The promise merely *transfers* the responsibility for looking after the investors' interests. It does nothing to affect the type or weight of the claim that can be made in behalf of those interests against other moral considerations. In the situations with which we are concerned, who the guardian is and how that guardianship comes about make no difference outside the relationship between the agent and the principal. If this were not the case, one could indefinitely increase the moral righteousness of one's causes merely by enlisting a series of agents, each promising the other to pursue one's ends. But this is ridiculous; moral weight does not accrue like the return due on a chain letter.[3]

Thus, any talk of the solemn promises or sacred trusts of corporations, while it may refer to actual obligations, is irrelevant to the issue at hand, which is the weight of investor interests against moral rules. There is no conflict here between a moral principle requiring that promises be kept and a moral principle prohibiting bribery. What stands in opposition to the moral rule prohibiting bribery is not a moral principle at all, but is, at best, merely the *self-interest* of the investors.

This, I think, considerably deflates the original argument against the FCPA. However, the attack could be relaunched with the observation that even unadorned self-interest has moral status and that even if this moral status is not, like the bribery rule, based on deontological considerations, it may nonetheless carry substantial moral weight. After all, the idea that satisfying interests is *morally* good is fundamental to all forms of utilitarianism and recognized as well in most other moral theories. Thus, the realigned attack would conclude, the interests of investors have moral weight in themselves and these interests may oppose and override the principle prohibiting bribery.

What is to be said of this argument? I think it must be admitted that investors' interests do have moral weight. However, I also think that it is quite unlikely that this weight will often be great enough to render international corporate bribery moral. First of all, what we have before us now is the opposition of *self-interest* and a moral rule. And within the deontological perspective, which we are being asked to take, moral rules are just the sort of things that override claims of self-interest. So, as long as we take the deontological perspective, there is strong a priori reason to hold that the rule prohibiting bribery controls.

A second line of defense against this argument can be developed out of the example Hooker and Pastin use to show that personal interests may sometimes override moral rules. It would in some circumstances be moral, they point out, to bribe a doctor—say if that were the only way in which to get essential medical treatment for a dying child. This example contains what I think are two characteristic, if not quite absolutely essential, features of such cases: (1) the personal interest at issue is not a mere desire, but a *dire need*, and (2) the rule is broken on a special occasion; it is not to be a continuing general policy to break the rule.[4] In contrast, when we are asked to reject the FCPA, we are asked to endorse a *policy* of bribery, and this for the promotion of interests that are not matters of life and death.

Yet it still might be objected that in cases of corporate investment the moral claim of the investors' interests is *considerable* and that it may well outweigh the bribery rule. There can be little justification for this objection. Indeed, the opposite is almost certainly true. The reason is that not all interests are of equal moral weight. Classical utilitarianism is mistaken in holding that equal additions to the sum total happiness or well-being are morally indifferent.

For example, an increase in happiness which satisfies a need is of greater moral moment than the same increment added to the total happiness by way of providing someone with adventitious pleasure. It is morally better to raise a person from poverty to security than to add an equal amount to the total happiness in contributing to a person's rise from ease to opulence. (Better a few more mouthfuls of rice for a starving Sudanese than a monthful of feasts for Bunky Hunt.) Thus, when it comes to comparing personal interests against moral rules, interests which rest in the satisfaction of mere desires which are not needs have little moral weight.

This point applies to the FCPA in two ways. First, although American investors include pension plans, philanthropic organizations, and people of modest income, the average American investor is still quite comfortable by world standards and return on investment is not a matter of survival. Second, even if return on investment were a matter of survival, the fact is that corporations can and do derive substantial profits from activities that do not call for bribery, and most American corporations have dealt successfully in international trade without having to resort to payments the FCPA makes unlawful.

One misunderstanding of the preceding argument must be forestalled. At issue is not a comparison of the degree of need of American investors and the degree of need of citizens of the country in which the bribery takes place. Rather, the point is that because American investors on the whole are not in dire need, the moral weight of their financial interests is small compared with the moral weight of moral principles.

It remains to say something, necessarily very brief, about the obligation of corporations to their employees and the obligation of the federal government to American business and workers. First, corporations are not morally obligated to secure profits by whatever means it takes in order to fulfill their responsibilities to their employees (cf note 3). There are restrictions, such as those imposed by law. If a corporation fails to meet its obligations because of the costs and effects of adhering to the law, then, other things being equal, the employees can have no *moral* complaint against the corporation.

In addition to the restrictions imposed on profit-seeking activities by the law, I submit that there are also moral restrictions. For example, corporations are not morally culpable for financial losses incurred by a failure to be ruthless, even when ruthlessness is within the limits set by the law. Employees (and other interested parties) cannot complain on *moral* grounds that they have suffered because the corporation failed to cheat, lie, deceive, bribe, or pay extortion.

Finally, consider the obligation of the federal government to promote and protect the welfare of American business and workers. Hooker and Pastin are not sure whether such an obligation actually exists, but assuming that it does, the argument against the FCPA would presumably go something like this:

1. Government is created to serve the citizens' interests.

2. Greater corporate profit is in the citizens' interest. (And therefore government should promote greater corporate profit.)

3. International corporate bribery secures greater corporate profit. Conclusion: Government should promote (or at least not prohibit) international corporate bribery, and so the FCPA should not be law.

This argument is open to criticism on a number of grounds, but I will comment only on the nature of the conclusion. The "should" in "Government should promote greater corporate profit" and in "Government should promote international corporate bribery" state *legal* or *political* obligations, but not always *moral* ones, for if what is in the citizens' interest or the means to satisfying it is *immoral*, the government cannot have a *moral* obligation to promote that interest by that means. That is, any *moral* obligation of the government's to promote a certain end or means extends only to those ends and means that can be determined antecedently to be moral. If acts of bribery are, all things considered, generally immoral—as I have been arguing—the government can have no *moral* obligation to condone activities calling for bribery. Thus, the question of whether or not the FCPA is moral is to be determined independently of any obligation of the government to protect business and worker welfare.

This concludes my comments on Hooker and Pastin's first argument. I now turn to their second argument.

III

In their second argument Hooker and Pastin marshal three distinct considerations behind the idea that "many of the payments prohibited by the Act are neither bribes nor share features that make bribes morally reprehensible." My general observation on this claim is that even if it is true, each of the three points falls before the fact that bribery is not the only morally objectionable form of behavior; an activity can be morally reprehensible even if it does not exhibit the morally reprehensible features peculiar to bribery. Let us take up each of the three considerations in turn.

1. Hooker and Pastin point out that quite often the payments in question are not bribes at all, but are *extorted* from corporations. Thus, the morally objectionable coercion of foreign officials characteristic of bribery is absent.[5]

   This may be true. Nonetheless, caving in to an extortion demand is morally objectionable in its own right. For one thing, to pay extortion is to participate in and foster the expansion of corruption in the country in which the payment is made. This naturally leads to the unjust concentration of power in the hands of the people who receive the payments and thereby contributes to the oppression of the people the recipients of the payments are supposed to serve. In addition, if the extortion payments are concealed, competition will be unfair and shareholders and the public at large will be deceived about the operations of a public corporation, while if the extortion is open and common knowledge, there will be an even more rapid disintegration of free bargaining and a return to the state of nature in which any form of influence and coercion is deemed acceptable.

   Some businesspeople may feel that the condition of international corporate competition is in fact that of the state of nature. However, this is hyperbole: Murder is still a fairly rare tactic in the competition for contracts; not everyone in the business community behaves like the Mafia. But even if this were not hyperbole, it still would not make such practices *moral*. It is also worth pointing out that the state of nature is not a condition we *want* to be in: Few of us *want* to deal with a government like that of Idi Amin's Uganda; still fewer of us would want to live in a world in which that was the norm.

2. Hooker and Pastin's second observation is that whereas bribery is objectionable, in part, because it tends to result in the purchase of inferior products for the parties represented by the recipients of a bribe, the fact is that in many cases *failure* to make a so-called bribe or extortion payment may be what leads to the purchase of inferior products.

   This, too, may be true, as, for example, where the corporation with the best product can secure a market only by making such a payment. However, this is not enough to justify the payment. To consider only the quality of the goods and services provided is to take too narrow a view. Rather, the *overall* result must be considered. This overall result will almost certainly include a more costly product, for the cost of the questionable payment must be made up somewhere, probably out of the foreign consumer's pocket, and perhaps the American's as well. But much more importantly, the effect of fostering corruption and injustice must also be included.

3. The final consideration raised by Hooker and Pastin is that the payments in question may be in accordance with local practice and thus may lack the morally objectionable feature of deceptiveness which is exhibited by bribery proper.

Once again, the observation may be true, but all it shows is that such payments need not exhibit every evil known to man. The other evils already mentioned still remain. That one's contribution to corruption, injustice, oppression, the disintegration of fair bargaining, and a return to the state of nature is acknowledged openly hardly does much to excuse it.

It might still be objected that if the society in which the business is being conducted engages in such practices, it would be wrong for us to try to impose our standards in dealings with them in their country.

This line of argument raises important conceptual issues about intercultural social, legal, and moral standards which are too complex to do justice to here. However, I can offer a few comments which I think considerably reduce the problems about how one ought to act. First, it is absolutely essential to distinguish between practices that are engaged in, recognized, and even tolerated and those that are condoned and held to be moral. To say simply that in many countries bribery is the norm disguises the fact that what is regularly done may not be what is held to be proper or moral even in the countries where that is the practice. A rough indicator of international moral judgment is the illegality of bribery in every part of the world.[6] Second, to require American corporations to adhere to "our" moral standards with respect to such activities as bribery and extortion is hardly to *impose* our standards on the rest of the world: For a Muslim to refrain from eating pork in England is not for him to impose Muslim standards on the British. Finally, there is some reason for us to refrain from a practice which *we* judge to be wrong and harmful to others even if we do not receive agreement: That settlers in the upper Amazon hunt native Indians for sport does not give us good reason to conform to that practice when in their company. Obviously, more needs to be said on these issues, but I hope that it has been made clear that a passing reference to moral relativism establishes nothing and that there are a number of lines of defense which can be taken against more serious relativistic criticisms.

My conclusion concerning Hooker and Pastin's second argument is that though all the practices prohibited by the act are not bribes and though some of the practices may not exhibit all the same morally objectionable features as bribery, these practices still exhibit morally objectionable features of their own, and so the law that prohibits them is on solid moral ground.

In closing, I want to add a few short remarks. First, in asserting that the FCPA is supported by morality, I am not claiming that the act prescribes the morally best behavior in every single case. All laws can be improved. Furthermore, I think that it is *conceptually* impossible for any general rule to classify all cases to which it may be applied properly and unambiguously. But admitting these problems, we should recognize that an imperfect law can still be moral and just.

Second, it should be noted that if Hooker and Pastin were correct, their arguments would go a long way toward justifying bribery and extortion *within* the United States by both foreign and domestic companies—unless we are to believe that a return to the state of nature is morally acceptable in one place—someone else's country—but not in another.

Finally, I think that I have shown that the FCPA is supported by considerations of morality. This should weigh heavily in favor of retaining the law. However, I do not claim to have necessarily provided *motivation* for supporting or adhering to the stipulations of this law. Morality may require sacrifice; in this case, at least, sacrifice of financial gain. For those who care more for financial gain and for the ruthlessness through which it can be obtained than for the moral values of justice and integrity, I cannot claim to have provided motivation.

NOTES

This paper is a slightly revised version of comments read at the Conference on Business and Professional Ethics at the University of Illinois at Chicago Circle, May 1981. A shortened version appears in *Ethical Issues in Business*, 2d. ed., edited by Thomas Donaldson and Patricia Werhane (Englewood Cliffs, N.J.: Prentice-Hall, 1983).

1. "Ethics and the Foreign Corrupt Practices Act," presented at the conference mentioned above and previously published in *Business Horizons* 23 (1980), pp. 43–47.

2. This promise must be understood as a promise to endeavor to a reasonable extent to increase investment value, not to maximize it at all costs.

3. The general moral principle here is, very roughly, that a promise to pursue the interests of another cannot increase the moral weight of those interests against moral considerations external to the relationship of promiser to promisee.

4. For continuing treatment of the child or when there is continuing and widespread corruption among doctors, it would be necessary to endorse bribery as a temporary policy. However, one's obligation in such a case would not be merely to engage in bribery, but rather to engage in bribery while doing what one can to rectify the situation. Regardless of the precise way this is to be worked out, a simple endorsement of bribery is not justified in such cases.

5. In practice it may be difficult to distinguish between bribery and extortion on the one hand, and goodwill gestures (such as gifts) and facilitating payments (so-called grease) on the other. However, the conceptual issue of the wrongness of extortion does not turn on how the practical problem is solved.

6. Judson J. Wambold, "Prohibiting Foreign Bribes: Criminal Sanctions for Corporate Payments Abroad" (*Cornell International Law Journal* 10 (1977), pp. 235–237). Wambold also found that though bribery generally is illegal, corporate contributions to political parties are acceptable in many countries. This complicates the moral evaluation of the FCPA. The next two points in my text suggest directions in which to go to defend the act in this connection.

chapter sixteen
ANTICOMPETITIVE BEHAVIOR

WHY DO COMPANIES SUCCUMB TO PRICE FIXING?

JEFFREY SONNENFELD* and PAUL R. LAWRENCE*

Down the centuries social analysts have frequently charged, "Laws are like spiderwebs, which may catch small flies but let wasps and hornets break through." As more and more corporations have been caught in the web of price-fixing laws, however, this charge has lost its punch. Senior business managers in industries that have never before known these problems, as well as previous offenders, are probably more concerned now about their corporate exposure to being indicted and convicted of price fixing than they were in any other recent period.

The reasons are not hard to find. As federal agencies, the courts, and Congress respond to the heightened post-Watergate expectations of the public, the law enforcement net has been substantially strengthened.[1] Instead of hearing protests over the legal immunity granted to the large and powerful, one now hears the anguish coming from the reverse direction. One can regularly read about prominent individuals and organizations that are overwhelmed by the stiff penalties they have incurred for behavior which may have been customary business practice in the past but which now violates social and legal standards.[2]

The costs of violating price-fixing laws are very high: lawyers' fees, government fines, poor morale, damaged public image, civil suits, and now prison terms. Justice Department statistics indicate that 60% of antitrust felons are sentenced to prison terms.[3] Thus, for very pragmatic reasons as well as for personal convictions, America's top executives are searching for fail-safe ways of meeting legal requirements. While top executives strongly complain about increasing government interference, they also acknowledge, "We operate through a license from society which can be revoked whenever we violate the terms of the license."

Executives in large decentralized organizations, however, find it increasingly difficult to carry through on their intentions. The considerable time and money corporations spend developing positive public images can be wasted by the careless actions of just one or two lower level employees. At the same time that organization

*Department of Organizational Behavior, Harvard Business School, Boston, Mass.

size and complexity increase, top executives find that the law imposes on them additional responsibility for the business practices of their subordinates.

Executives tremble over what may be going on in the field despite their internal directives and public declarations. One CEO well expressed the frustration common to executives in convicted companies:

> We've tried hard to stress that collusion is illegal. We point out that anticompetitive practices hurt the company's ethical standards, public image, internal morale, and earnings. Yet we wind up in trouble continually. When we try to find out why employees got involved, they have the gall to say that they "were only looking out for the best interests of the company." They seem to think that the company message is for everyone else but them. You begin to wonder about the intelligence of these people. Either they don't listen or they're just plain stupid.

Some executives we interviewed in researching this article believe with the CEO quoted that their employees who collude in price fixing are just not listening or are plain stupid. In our view it is less likely that the employees are deaf or stupid than that many well-meaning, ethical top managers simply are not getting their message down the line to loyal alert employees.

To better understand this lack of communication as well as other forces contributing to employees committing unlawful acts, we thought that it would be enlightening to look at the unfortunate experience of the forest products and paper industry in the midst of antitrust litigation. Looking just at antitrust cases in 1977, one can see that the paper industry was hit with separate prosecutions for price fixing in consumer paper, fine paper and stationery, multiwall bags, shopping bags, labels, corrugated containers, and folding cartons. In early 1978, over 100 suits have been filed against the industry.

In addition, a U.S. grand jury has been gathering information on competitive practices in the industry at large—which many suspect is part of a probe into industry collusion to restrain supply.[4] In fact, the *Wall Street Journal* recently stated that the paper industry is gaining the reputation as the "nation's biggest price fixer."[5]

The folding-box litigation has, by far, been the most damaging. The Justice Department has described this case as the largest price-fixing one since 1960. It is hard to understand how socially responsible companies could ever have found themselves in such a nightmarish situation. To find out, we discussed the various pressures and conditions in this industry with 40 senior, division, and middle level executives. Our investigation concentrated on the predicament of the large forest products companies that derive about 4% or 5% of their total company sales from folding-carton revenues.

The shock for those companies with strong, well-publicized ethical positions is perhaps most severe. In case the reader is skeptical, our interviews with the senior people in these companies left us without a shred of doubt about the sincerity and completeness of their personal commitment to legal compliance. In fact, the top people we spoke to in the major forest products companies desperately want to know how and why they got on the wrong side of the law so that they can be sure it never happens again.

HOW IT CAN HAPPEN

Before we discuss the factors that create a price-fixing prone industry and organization, we would like to point out that the various problematic situations that contributed to this unhappy end are certainly not unique to the paper industry. One can easily draw parallels between the paper industry's difficulties and the situations leading to price fixing in other very different industries. For such a comparison, we will at times glance at the 1960 electrical contractors' conspiracy. We hope too that no one will read this article without reflecting on his or her own company's situations.

Crowded and Mature Market

In the late 1950s and early 1960s, as the expansion of prepackaged and frozen foods kept the market growing at about 7% a year, the folding-carton business attracted new entrants. With low barriers to entry, competitors of all sizes saw this area as a great opportunity. Traditionally dominated by small family-run box-making shops, the industry became attractive to very large forest products companies, which integrated forward. These large companies first supplied the paperboard for box making, and then began to compete with their customers further down the line in making the actual boxes themselves.

The tendency toward overcapacity in paperboard production tempted these large paper companies to look on folding boxes as a way to unload excesses. Some blamed the softening of the box market on this attitude, claiming that "the big companies did not care about box prices because they were making their profit back at the paperboard mill."

Also harmful to the market in the intervening years was the halt of supermarket expansion as well as the growth of the use of substitute containers, such as plastics, which eroded the market share for paper containers. The industry is now very mature and has even suffered revenue as well as profit declines.

These declines place great pressure on middle level managers who are keenly aware that the constant use of existing capital equipment is the way to drive down unit costs.

When a manager feels his or her division's survival is in question, the corporation's standards of business conduct are apt to be sacrificed. In the 1960 electrical contractors' case the issue was also survival. A convicted General Electric division vice president explained:

> I think we understood it was against the law. . . . The moral issue didn't seem to be important at that time . . . it was a period of trying to obtain stability, to put an umbrella over the smaller manufacturers . . . I've seen the situation change, primarily due to over-capacity, to almost a situation where people thought it was a survival measure. . . . [6]

Job-Order Nature of Business

In the folding-box industry cost-cutting practices are also hampered by the nature of the production process. Boxes are generally manufactured for short job orders. One general manager said:

> Those guys up in headquarters think making boxes is like making paper, but papermaking is just following recipes. No two boxes are the same for us. Even with soap boxes, there are diverse product specifications.

Each of these jobs is costed and priced individually. Since each order is custom made, the pricing decisions are made frequently and at low levels of the organization. One salesman illustrated how a job-order business exposes a company to low-level price collusion:

> Every order is a negotiation, even when we've got a contract. Dialogue on prices is always on your mind. Any time I've met with a competitor, whether at a trade association meeting or in a customer's waiting room, one of us will eventually crack a smile and say, "You son of a bitch, you're cutting my prices again. . . ." Sometimes things go on from there and sometimes they don't. I think our company has been stupidly naive. It is impossible not to have talked price at some time.

Undifferentiated Products

Finally, while job specifications vary greatly between orders, the skills and equipment are fairly undifferentiated between companies. Several executives we interviewed concur with the following statement from one vice president:

> Part of the problem is that we're not competing with a unique article here. Our bags and boxes aren't really any better or worse than those of our competitors. You don't really go out and sell the product. Salespeople don't have any special product to sell. The only way to get a buyer is to sell at a lower price. Thus competitors may think that the only way to make it is to get together and fix prices.

Culture of the Business

In the electrical contractors' conspiracy, there were strong pressures to enforce the anticompetitive norms. A GE vice president describing the type of coercion placed on an executive who resisted the norms of collusion stated, "We worked him over pretty hard, and I did too; I admit it." One GE executive who was a target of this pressure from his colleagues committed suicide.[7] In one recent folding-box case, some executives threatened others with physical violence if they resisted raising prices.[8]

Another factor encouraging price fixing arises when a company with one culture acquires another with a quite different one. In several companies convicted of price fixing, senior executives acknowledge that rapid vertical integration brought their forest products companies into secondary converting businesses, which were little and poorly integrated.[9]

The parent companies often naively assumed that business practice and ethics in the two companies would automatically be congruent even if there were no common heritage. As an illustration of the sort of side practices that may come with a business acquisition, the management of one large forest products company learned to its shock that the box-making company it had just acquired had been running a house of prostitution as a customer service for years. One vice president stated:

The guys at the core of this conspiracy were acquired people from acquired companies and not part of our culture. That is just not the way we do business. Questions of ethics were never raised. We assumed that people do business ethically at our company. Apparently that was a simple-minded assumption.

Personnel Practices

On top of any other influences, the personnel practices used in many companies seemed actually to encourage people to engage in price fixing.[10] In a number of the companies convicted, management almost exclusively appraised individual performance on the basis of profits and volume. And not only advancement but also bonuses and commissions, which often exceeded 50% of base salary, were dependent on these measures. A division manager spelled out these practices:

> In the folding-carton division, our local salesmen have all been compensated with a base salary and a commission. Some bonus programs account for 60% of someone's compensation. People have been evaluated on the basis of profit and how forcefully they can execute a price increase. Thus, if he does this by price agreement with competitors, he'll build profit and price credits and get a reward.

So, instead of seeing the top people explicitly and officially acknowledge the difficult industry conditions, many of the lower officials see only strong pressures and inducements to "get the numbers no matter what." As one executive of a convicted company sadly acknowledged, "We've definitely run into some problems from jamming our corporate targets down everyone's throats."

Trade Associations

Over two centuries ago, Adam Smith, the dean of free market economics, warned:

> People of the same trade seldom meet together, even for merriment and diversion, but the conversation ends in a conspiracy against the public, or in some contrivance to raise prices.[11]

In keeping with this prediction, a sales manager of a convicted paper company complained that industry trade association activities can directly contribute to a company's involvement in conspiracy:

> You must limit the occasion of sin. You can't put yourself in a position of contact with competitors. I've dropped contact with personal friends in competing companies since this prosecution started, and I should have dropped such contacts sooner. I don't go to industry meetings at all. Now, finally, this whole company frowns on industry bullshit!

Virtually all the senior managers surveyed agree "that it's hard to talk about the costs of production without discussing prices." An executive at one of the relatively uninvolved companies proudly stated that his company has sharply curtailed the number of company employees participating in trade association meetings.

Corporate Legal Staff

Several corporate lawyers reluctantly acknowledge that their performance was related to their company's convictions. While in many companies antitrust memoranda and periodic legal lectures became more frequent after the landmark 1960 electrical contractors' conspiracy, legal departments in the paper companies still tended to react to problems rather than to anticipate them. The corporate counsel at one of the convicted paper companies explained:

> In the past, we practiced what we thought was our proper role, and that was to respond to legal questions. We sometimes did big group things like lectures, but we never sat down to talk the subject through with small groups of managers.

Similarly, another vice president of legal affairs conceded that, although his department is quite heavily involved in antitrust education now, "We've only really become anticipatory since the folding-carton case."

Thus the lawyers did not serve as a source for legal advice to avoid problems but allowed people to navigate to the brink of prosecution. A division manager in one of the convicted companies summed this up by giving his impression of the performance of the legal division:

> I can tell you that the lawyers here are a damned smart bunch of guys who can get you out of trouble once you've gotten into it. But we sure need more of an active force.

HOW TO AVOID IT

We have examined both the industry and the company factors that contributed to one industry's being so badly caught up in price fixing. It is time to take stock of the implications of our inquiry for managers who are resolved to avoid such traumatic experiences. How should managers respond to this predicament? The lessons are, in fact, fairly easy to perceive but at times very difficult to put into practice.

It is obvious but not trivial to say that managers in competing companies who would be fail-safe should move to the opposite poles from each and every one of the contributing factors we have identifed. But, of course, recognizing danger signs provides no more than a start toward solving the problem. Which factors are relatively controllable and which are not? What specific practices have we identified in our study that were helpful? What ideas and concepts can be useful in achieving compliance?

Managing the Market Conditions

Certainly very little in the market environment is under management's direct control. One may conclude that the conditions of the folding-carton industry are sufficiently hostile that a company would be justified in leaving the business entirely. Since four large companies have left the business over the past year, obviously some involved executives have reached that very conclusion. In our interviews, senior managers at one forest products company expressed sheer relief at being "liberated."

Those who have remained are striving for cost control and product differentiation to allow for longer runs and greater pricing freedom. Only a few have as yet succeeded in this effort. Many executives complain that their company could never remove itself from the brutal paper carton market unless top management made a really major commitment to a new strategy.

Managing the Company Culture

As we talked to executives in the forest products industry, we of course asked about their experience with management methods that could help control the price-fixing problem. One of the consistent and early points that came up was the example set for the company by the behavior of top management. We found one of the most frequent approaches senior management uses to encourage legal compliance is to cite its record in regard to social responsibility.

Psychological research on obedience,[12] business research on employee morality, and common sense all indicate that the behavior of those in authority serves as important role models to others.[13] Unless top management projects consistent and sincere company commitment, operating practices will not change.

This commitment, however, is a necessary but not a sufficient factor to ensure compliance. The major forest products companies where we interviewed have a long-standing reputation for the expression of public interest commitment by senior executives. Each company has its own internal maxim for, "We believe that ethics start at the front office." Unfortunately, these statements tend to stop here as well. A vice president of a convicted paper company explained:

> When we were small enough and in a stable environment, people all knew each other by first names. We could communicate informally, and we were successful in molding behavior through modeling. People could resolve gray areas of decision making by reflecting on how their superiors would handle such an issue. But, with our very explosive growth of the last decade and a half, this old approach has become problematic. Can we still communicate corporate standards to a lot of people in the same way we communicated to a few?

Price Decision Procedures. One of the factors contributing to price fixing was the practice in some of the companies studied of allowing specific price decisions to be influenced by salespeople and others below the general management level. In effect, because of bonus and commission arrangements, junior people were acting almost as profit center managers. Since these were the same people who might well see their competitors' sales representatives in the customers' waiting rooms, the scene for illegal action was set.

Some managers in the companies we studied have been reviewing their practices in this regard and making tighter definitions of who can legitimately take part in pricing decisions. It takes careful analysis of the multiple sources of relevant information concerning prices as well as an explicit commitment procedure to make such rules both workable and prudent.

Codes of Ethics. Attempts to move beyond top-level role modeling have led some executives to prepare codes of ethics on company business practices. In some companies, this document circulates only at top levels and, again, the word seems to have trouble getting down the line. An employee convicted of price fixing questioned the view that price fixers can be helped by ethical statements:

> A code of ethics doesn't do anything. I thought I had morals. I still think I do. I didn't understand the laws . . . not morals. What might to me be an ethical practice might have been interpreted differently by a legal scholar. The golden rule might be consistent with both views.

r̃or codes to really work, substantial specificity is important. One executive said his company's method was successful because the code was tied in with an employee's daily routine:

> There is a code of business conduct here. To really make it meaningful, you have to get past the stage of endorsing motherhood and deal with the specific problems of policy in the different functional areas. We wrote up 20 pages on just purchasing issues.

Individuals can be held responsible if they have been informed on how to act in certain gray areas. The company can show its commitment to the code by checking to see that it is respected and by then disciplining violators.

Several companies are developing ways to implement internal policing. Some executives think that audits could hold people responsible for unusual pricing successes as well as for failures.[14] Market conditions, product specifications, and factory scheduling could be coded, put on tables, and compared to prices. High variations could be investigated. One division vice president also plans to audit expense accounts to see that competitor contact is minimized.

Legal Training

As we noted earlier, executives in the convicted paper companies acknowledge that the lack of contact between them and company lawyers makes it hard to apply the law. Direct contact between operating managers and members of the legal staff seemed to be less frequent in the companies that were more heavily involved in the conspiracy.

Some companies have developed successful legal programs by fostering very close contact between the general managers and the legal division. In one such program there are two lawyers who specialize in traveling around and meeting the general managers.

Executives in a company which was not involved in the conspiracy agree with the need to tailor a program to the danger line of the organization. Outside counsel is extensively involved on two levels. First, attorneys meet with each saleman on a one-on-one basis. The lawyer digs up expense reports and other files and grills the salesman. This same procedure is then repeated at group and general manager meetings.

At the general manager and vice president levels, the legal staff puts on a simulated grand jury inquiry. In these dramatizations even the president sits on the witness stand to defend himself on the basis of documents prepared by his vice presidents. There is a great deal of tension surrounding these mock trials. The president of this company cited this trial as:

> . . . one of the most important ways we've sought to keep the organization sensitive to legal issues. We identify several hundred people with point-of-sales exposure and talk to a large percentage of that group. We're trying to get the lawyers to prepare a dossier and challenge each of these people. This confessional situation is a very intensive experience.

This procedure helps management spot problems so it can clear up misunderstandings before they become more serious. The possible interpretations of employee words and actions are made very clear. The president said that this sort of investigation on top of the usual lectures is needed to bring the message across:

> We've had attorneys giving their fire and brimstone talks to large groups for 10 to 15 years, and we have simply concluded that isn't strong enough medicine for this ailment. Our experiences in other parts of the company convinced us that this thoroughness is vital.

PROFESSIONAL PRIDE

Many industries share the exposures to price fixing we have highlighted. And the problems of ensuring compliance increase in complexity as the list of contributing factors grows. Our review of the specific compliance methods that are being used in the forest products companies with the better records provides a good start toward the development of a fail-safe approach. In our interviews we were also searching for a promising general approach—perhaps a philosophy of management—that could infuse a company and serve as an antibody to thoughts of price collusion.

We believe we did find such a condition in one company. The evidence we saw was largely indirect, but it can probably best be characterized as professional pride. This company is one of the handful that is largely successful in developing a differentiated set of products. It is no accident. Even in the face of all the industry difficulties we have cited there exists a very strong belief that "if we're not smart enough to make reasonable profits without resorting to any form of price fixing, we'll simply get out of the business."

This belief is translated at the individual level into "I'd rather quit than stoop to getting my results that way." In effect, this company's executives are making an old-fashioned distinction between clean, earned profits and rigged, dirty profits. It is literally unthinkable for them to want to make money the latter way. They have too much self-esteem.

Although executives and salespeople in this company widely share the strong code of behavior, it is not clear exactly how it has been disseminated throughout the organization. The best evidence is that when top managers emphasize professional pride and the distinction between clean and dirty profits, the commitment to achieve profits through legal means is clearly driven down the line. Such emphasis cuts out ambiguous signals that lead to junior people second-guessing top management's intentions.

NOTES

1. "Carter Trust Busters," *Newsweek*, September 26, 1977.
2. United States v. Park 421 U.S. Court 658 (1975); Tony McAdams and Robert C. Miljus, "Growing Criminal Liability of Executives." *HBR* March–April 1977, p. 36.

3. Timothy D. Schellhardt, "Price-Fixing Charges Rise in Industry Despite Convictions," *Wall Street Journal*, May 4, 1978, p. 31.

4. "13 Paper Concerns Face Price Fixing Charges," *New York Times*, December 23, 1977, p. D5; "Two Paper Firms are Convicted in Price-Fixing," *Wall Street Journal*, November 27, 1977, p. 3; "Indictment Cites 14 Paper Makers for Price-Fixing," *Wall Street Journal*, January 26, 1978, p. 3; Morris S. Thompson, "Aides of Box-Making Concerns Sentenced to Prison, Fined in Price-Fixing Case," *Wall Street Journal*, December 1, 1976, p. 4.

5. Schellhardt, "Price-Fixing Charges Rise," p. 1.

6. John Herling, *The Great Price Conspiracy* (Washington, D.C.: Luce, 1962), p. 241.

7. Herling, *The Great Price Conspiracy*, p. 249.

8. Schellhardt, "Price-Fixing Charges Rise," p. 1.

9. The recent acquisition spree may exacerbate this problem. See "The Great Takeover Binge," *Business Week*, November 14, 1977, p. 176.

10. Gilbert Geis, "White Collar Crime: The Heavy Electrical Equipment Antitrust Case in 1961," in *Criminal Behavior Systems: A Typology*, eds. Marshall B. Clinard and Richard Quinrey (New York: Holt, Rinehart and Winston, 1967), p. 150. Here it is explained that structural factors are major contributing elements to criminal behavior. Executives who were uncooperative with price-fixing training were transferred by the company. These issues are more fully discussed in: Laura Shill Schrager and James J. Short, Jr., "Toward a Sociology of Organizational Crime," presented at the American Sociological Association meeting, Chicago, August 1977.

11. Adam Smith, *The Wealth of Nations*.

12. Stanley Milgrim, *Obedience to Authority: An Experimental View* (New York: Harper and Row, 1974).

13. Raymond Baumhart, *An Honest Profit* (New York: Holt, Rinehart and Winston, 1968). This survey, based on 1,710 subscribers responding to an HBR poll, found most subordinates ultimately accept the values of chief executives. See also Archie B. Carroll, "Managerial Ethics: A Post Watergate View," *Business Horizons*, April 1975, p. 75.

14. William D. Hartley, "More Firms Now Stress In-House Auditing, But It's Old Hat at GE . . . Staff Doesn't Spare Top Brass Keeping Antitrust Vigil," *Wall Street Journal*, August 22, 1977, p. 75.

CASES FOR PART FIVE

LOCKHEED AIRCRAFT CORPORATION

DANIEL A. CZERNICKI*

Over a period of nine months after July 1975, 95 corporations with annual sales of $388 billion had voluntarily disclosed to the Securities and Exchange Commission (SEC) that they used bribes and kickbacks in the process of conducting business, both domestically and abroad.[1] That month the SEC suggested that companies in violation of disclosure laws might "lessen the need for SEC enforcement action" by cooperating with the SEC. Subsequent disclosures have shown corporate bribery to be much more prevalent in the United States than anyone had ever dreamed possible. Said one SEC official, "We now see corporate misdeeds being carried on in business to an extent that is sickening."[2]

For all the scandals surrounding those disclosures, none surpassed that of Lockheed Aircraft Corp. Lockheed has the unenviable distinction of having bribed more high-government officials with more money than any other known U.S. corporation. Their disclosures have had far-reaching repercussions, both for the company and the country.

This case examines Lockheed Aircraft Corp., the payoff scandal it is responsible for, and some of the resulting backlash the company faces as a result.

BACKGROUND

Lockheed Aircraft Corporation is engaged primarily in the design and manufacture of technologically advanced defense systems and equipment. It also builds commercial and military aircraft, ships, communication satellites, propulsion systems, undersea petroleum systems, rockets, air traffic control and radar systems, dams, and tunnels. Some of its better-known products include the L-1011 TriStar commercial airliner, C-130 cargo transport, S-3 and P-3 antisubmarine aircraft, Agena satellites, and Poseidon and Trident ballistic missiles.

To better understand Lockheed's problems, it is necessary to quickly examine some of the major aspects of the company's financial structure. In 1975, Lockheed had sales of $3,390,000,000 and a net income of about $45,000,000, which resulted

Excerpted from "Lockheed Aircraft Corporation," published in *Social Forces and the Manager*, edited by William R. Allen and Louis K. Bragaw. Copyright © 1982 by John Wiley and Sons, Inc., New York. Reprinted by permission of the publisher.

*Systems Engineer, Naval Underwater Systems Center, Newport, R.I.

in earnings per share of \$3.86.[3] No dividends were declared, nor have they been since 1969.

The company's capital structure is somewhat unusual in that it consisted of 97% debt and only 3% equity as of 12/31/74.[4] The primary reason for this imbalance is that after a period of rapid growth in the company's stock price in the early and mid-1960's, the bottom more or less fell out of the aerospace industry in 1969, and took Lockheed with it.[5] By 1971, the company faced bankruptcy. At that time Lockheed entered into a credit agreement with twenty-four banks providing for bank borrowings of \$400 million under revolving ninety-day notes and an additional \$250 million under revolving nine-month notes guaranteed by the U.S. Government. The terms of the agreement called for payment of the loans by December 31, 1975, and also precluded payment of cash dividends until the loans were paid. The credit agreement was conceived in part because the company anticipated increased earnings in future years through sales of its L-1011 TriStar airliner.

The government participated in the 1971 Credit Agreement for many reasons ranging from economic considerations (Lockheed is a major employer vital to the economies of California and Georgia) to national defense. To ensure the viability of its loan guarantees, the government created an Emergency Loan Guarantee Board (ELGB), with Treasury Secretary William E. Simon as chairman, tasked with acting as an independent board of directors to oversee Lockheed's operations. The board had the power to rescind the loan guarantees if necessary, an act that would probably force the company into bankruptcy. In conjunction with the ELGB, the government's General Accounting Office (GAO) audited the company, as part of the agreement.

In May 1975, the ELGB approved a two-year extension of the Credit Agreement. At that time the company owed \$195 million in guaranteed loans and \$400 million in nonguaranteed debt as part of the original agreement. The extension was requested by Lockheed's management because of problems encountered by the company in selling the L-1011 TriStar. At that time, only 158 of an anticipated 300 aircraft had been sold, no new orders had been taken in 1975, and tooling and start-up costs of \$515 million were yet to be recovered.

THE LOCKHEED PAYOFFS

The payoffs were accidentally forced out by the firm's auditors, Arthur Young and Co., as reported in *Aviation Week and Space Technology:*

> In early June, Arthur Young and Co., Lockheed's auditors, suggested that a statement saying the company had made no bribes abroad be included in the material for the annual meeting due to the recent disclosures about Northrop. Lockheed refused, and Young then declined to certify the financial statements unless the existence and extent of the bribes were acknowledged.
>
> "The loan board (ELGB) became aware of the extent but not the details of the bribes in mid-June," Simon said. "And the Lockheed board was told June 23."[6]

The company publicly acknowledged the bribes in early August in a press release the firm issued to announce its second-quarter earnings. *Newsweek* magazine carried the story:

The pattern was by now familiar, but the sheer size and scope of it were staggering. After months of repeated denials, Lockheed Aircraft Corp. a fortnight ago admitted that between 1970 and mid-1975 it laid out $202 million in payoffs to foreign politicians, political parties, agents and consultants in order to win overseas contracts. There was also one new twist. Lockheed's generosity may in a sense have been backed by taxpayer's money because of the $195 million in loan guarantees Congress granted the aerospace firm in 1971.

The story went on to say:

Lockheed wasn't apologetic. The payments, it said, "were made with the knowledge of management and management believes they were necessary. . . . The company also believes that such payments are consistent with practices engaged in by numerous other companies abroad, including many of its competitors." Moreover, the firm insisted that disclosure of any details concerning the payments might cost it hundreds of millions of dollars in foreign sales and "could result in a material adverse impact with respect to the company's future operations." Privately, Lockheed officials were even more blunt to both Sen. Frank Church's subcommittee on multinational corporations, which has been looking into foreign payoffs by U.S. companies, and to the Securities and Exchange Commission, which has been trying to negotiate a disclosure agreement with Lockheed. "They argue that full disclosure of these payments will destroy their company," an SEC official told Newsweek. "They claim they would be bankrupt, with tens of thousands out of work and the U.S. taxpayer loser of his $195 million."

As government investigators tell it, the vast program of payoffs centered around Lockheed's need to sell its L-1011 TriStar. Ever since the company got the government to guarantee some of its loans, it has consistently emphasized that its optimism about the future was based on the good prospect of recouping its massive investment in TriStar and turning a profit on the operation. . . . "You cannot avoid the conclusion," a government investigator said, "that the L-1011 sales effort is an absolutely frantic one greased by unbelievable sums."[7]

During the latter half of 1975 numerous hearings and meetings were conducted by the ELGB, the Senate Banking, Housing and Urban Affairs Committee, the Senate Foreign Relations subcommittee on multinational corporations, and the subcommittee on international economic policy of the House International Affairs Committee. Their primary purpose was to ascertain full details of the extent of Lockheed's bribes and how much, if any, information on details of the bribes should be made public. An attempt was to be made to strike a balance between the public's right to know and the purported adverse impact on the company's future foreign sales. In testimony before the Senate Banking Committee, Lockheed Chairman and Chief Executive Officer Daniel J. Haughton stated:

I believe that detailed disclosure now of our past sales activities, with the resultant public indictment of foreign officials, many of whom may be totally innocent, could result in severe and unjust consequences for them; could impose severe penalties on our company, our employees and our shareholders—impose them retroactively, even though those activities were not in violation of our law—without any offsetting public benefit.[8]

Apparently, the Senate Foreign Relations subcommittee on multinational corporations decided that full disclosure of evidence taken at its hearings *was* to the public's benefit—whatever the consequence to Lockheed.

The exact amount and all recipients will probably never be known because it is difficult to trace the portion of the $202 million that found its way into public officials' hands. Payments were usually made in cash (by the crate in the case of the Japanese bribes) and the only records kept, if at all, were scribbled notes for "peanuts, units, and pieces"—code words for bribery payments.[9] But the following payments disclosed by Lockheed in the hearings, are examples of payoffs that have been made.

Some $12.6 million in bribes was paid to Japanese officials, the largest in any single country. The bribes coincided with unexpected purchases of Lockheed F-104 Starfighters by the Japanese government in 1970 and the ordering of six L-1011 TriStars by All Nippon Airways in 1972. Of that amount, $7 million was paid to Yoshio Kodama, a founder of the ruling Liberal Democratic Party, and a well-known "fixer."[10]

Luigi Gui was Defense Minister of Italy in 1970, the year when the Italian government purchased fourteen C-130 transports from Lockheed for a total of $60 million, despite protests from other politicians that Italian-made planes were more cost-effective. Luigi lost his job as Minister of the Interior when Lockheed disclosed that it paid $2.2 million to Italian government officials in 1970, to ensure the sale of its planes.[11]

Prince Bernhard, husband of Queen Juliana of the Netherlands, reportedly accepted $1.1 million to help the company peddle its aircraft. The prince, a director of several major airlines and inspector general of the Dutch armed forces, denied the Lockheed allegations. However, the Dutch Cabinet quickly appointed a commission to investigate. It seems that his past is stained with shady dealings, including a bribe of $12 million in cash, $1 million in jewelry, and a private train that the prince negotiated for Juan Peron and his wife in order to perfect a $60 million sale of Dutch railroad equipment to the Peron government in 1951.[12]

WORLD REACTION

In the end, Lockheed's bribes backfired and demonstrated that in business policy planning it is the long haul that counts. Although the bribes secured significant foreign sales of its aircraft in the past, their disclosure was predicted to result in a far-reaching backlash that would trim Lockheed's foreign sales (originally forecast at almost $4 billion for the five years from 1975 through 1979) considerably in the future.[13]

Japan's first concrete reaction to the payoffs came in mid-February, when the Japanese government dropped plans to buy $650 million worth of Lockheed's long-range P-3C Orion planes.[14] And it was widely believed that the government would force privately owned All Nippon Airways to cancel options on three L-1011 TriStar jetliners. The Japanese Defense Agency began delaying decisions on almost all procurement programs, until the evidence could be weighed. And one Japanese government official said, "Lockheed will not be able to sell their aircraft in this country for some time in the future."[15]

Lockheed viewed these cancellations with horror, as they could well have a domino effect on the firm's foreign sales. The Canadian government delayed signing a $650 million order for Lockheed's P-3C aircraft because it had severe misgivings about the viability of Lockheed and the P-3C program in particular.[16]

In the Netherlands, news of the Prince's involvement was received with shock; never before had a member of the royal family been the target of such accusations.

Time suggested that confirmation of his misdeeds would force Queen Juliana (the Prince's wife) to abdicate her throne. [17] More important for the company, one of Lockheed's bankers stated that in Europe, "Politicians are going to think twice about buying Lockheed products if Prince Bernhard really did pocket $1 million."

LOCKHEED'S CONTINUING PROBLEMS

As a direct result of the widespread publicity given the Lockheed scandal around the world, pressure was mounting for Lockheed to do more about the scandal than simply announce a new policy banning payoffs. In addition to government officials, Lockheed's banks, and the general public, that sometimes forgotten group known as the stockholders was getting angry and contemplating action, as related in this *Business Week* article:

> *Business Week* has learned that a major public-interest law firm may bring a stockholder suit against Lockheed over its failure to disclose its foreign payoffs. One Lockheed watcher predicts that "if things get hot enough," Lockheed's board may be forced to hire an outsider to succeed Chairman Daniel J. Haughton, who is due to retire next fall at age 65. Kotchian, 61, who was promoted from president to vice-chairman and chief operating officer last October, has been expected to succeed Haughton. [18]

That prediction came true on February 20, 1976, when, under mounting pressure, Daniel J. Haughton and A. Carl Kotchian announced their resignations, effective March 1, 1976. *Fortune* carried the news in a story titled "The Unfolding of a Tortuous Affair":

> For the second straight month, scandal fouled the house of American business and ended the careers of executives whose hands were stained by bribery. Following hard on the revelations at Gulf, the Lockheed case raised broad questions about the need for new government controls, especially over the armaments industry, which has proved to be riddled with sleazy practices. Since 1970 Lockheed has paid $202 million in commissions and fees abroad to obtain $3.2 billion in foreign sales. Some $22 million eventually reached officials of foreign governments or airlines.
> When the famous names of some of those officials were bandied about last month, the resulting furor caused grave concern at the twenty-four banks whose support has kept Lockheed from collapsing. Chairman Daniel J. Haughton, 64, realizing that he had become, as he said, "the focal point of the crisis," called a special meeting of the board at which he and Vice Chairman A. Carl Kotchian, 61, submitted their resignations.
> A participant in the four-hour meeting says it was "a very tortuous affair. Haughton felt increasing pressures from the financial community. He was a bit of a sacrificial lamb." The board immediately installed Robert W. Haack, 59, an outside director, as temporary chairman. [19]

Aside from the moral implications of the payoffs on the integrity of Haughton and Kotchian, there was some question as to their management ability in the area of company strategy. Lockheed's problems began *before* revelations of the bribes became public knowledge, and were more deeply rooted than it seems. *Forbes* commented:

> Revelations about bribery in high places were the immediate cause of Haughton's and

Kotchian's dismissal. But in reality, it was a disastrous business decision a decade ago that brought the two men down and nearly toppled the company.

Oct. 1, 1967, *Forbes* did a cover story on Lockheed. In it we expressed the opinions that the company risked being overextended and that the decision to enter the commercial jet market with the L-1011 was quite clearly a gamble. The transcripts of our interviews with Haughton and Kotchian make fascinating reading today. They show how easy it is for dedicated, intelligent corporate bosses to make horrendously wrong decisions unless someone—bankers, stockholders or directors—stops them.

At the time we asked Kotchian why Lockheed—doing so well in defense business— was gambling on getting back into commercial aviation. . . . The commercial passenger jet business, Carl Kotchian said, "is a tremendous growth field." . . . So confident were Lockheed's brass they decided to build the L-1011 without a firm commitment from a single airline. Kotchian figured Lockheed could get 50% of the market, or 300 planes. Sold to date: 158.

It all sounded so good. But what if something should go wrong? What if airlines' passenger growth should slow down? What if inflation should get out of hand and escalate the plane's cost? Sound planning would have provided a cushion for such contingencies, but Lockheed, stretching itself thin, had little margin for error.

Once they had plunged in, the decision had its own momentum; a graceful pullback was out of the question. So Haughton and Kotchian plowed ahead. In the end Lockheed spent $1.2 billion on the L-1011. It will be lucky to break even. Without the continuing burden of L-1011 write-offs, the company would even now be hugely profitable—$9 a share after taxes, by some estimates.

The final irony from Haughton in 1967: "I don't want to be in the position where we rise or fall on one decision. I don't think the L-1011 is a do-or-die thing." To Haughton's discredit as manager—aside from the morality of Lockheed's alleged bribes—he did, in the end, let the decision become do-or-die and it nearly killed the company.[20]

NOTES

1. Michael Ruby, "Slow Motion," *Newsweek*, March 15, 1976, p. 77.

2. "The Corporate Rush to Confess All," *Business Week*, February 23, 1976, p. 22.

3. *Value Line Investment Survey*, Edition 1, April 9, 1976, p. 117.

4. Ibid., p. 117.

5. *Standard and Poor's Industry Surveys*, October 30, 1975 (Section 2), Aerospace, p. A 11.

6. William A. Shumann, "Lockheed Agrees to End Payouts Abroad," *Aviation Week and Space Technology*. September 1, 1975, p. 19.

7. Allan J. Mayer, "Show and Tell Time," *Newsweek*, August 18, 1975, p. 63.

8. "Lockheed Agrees to End Payouts Abroad," op. cit., p. 19.

9. "Japan—An Aftershock of the Lockheed Affair," *Business Week*, April 12, 1976, p. 43.

10. "The Big Payoff," *Time*, February 23, 1976, p. 28.

11. Ibid., p. 28.

12. Michael Ruby, "A Slap for the Prince," *Newsweek*, April 5, 1976, p. 68.

13. "GAO Ties Outlook for Lockheed to Loan Extension, L-1011 Sales," *Aviation Week and Space Technology*, February 16, 1976, p. 16.

14. "The Big Payoff," op cit., p. 29.

15. "Payoffs Cloud Export Prospects," *Aviation Week and Space Technology*, February 23, 1976, p. 14.

16. "The Unfolding of a Tortuous Affair," *Fortune*, March 1976, p. 27.

17. "Havoc in Holland," *Time*, February 23, 1976, p. 34.

18. "Lockheed's Bribes Backfire," *Business Week*, February 23, 1976, p. 24.

19. "The Unfolding of a Tortuous Affair," op. cit., p. 27.

20. "Anatomy of a Disaster," *Forbes*, March 15, 1976, p. 91.

SUPPLEMENTARY READING FOR PART FIVE

Armentano, Domenick T. *Antitrust and Monopoly.* New York: John Wiley & Sons, 1982.

Blodgett, Timothy. "Showdown on Business Bluffing." *Harvard Business Review,* May–June 1968, pp. 162–178.

Bok, Sissela. *Lying: Moral Choice in Public and Private Life.* New York: Pantheon Books, 1978.

Bork, Robert. *The Antitrust Paradox: A Policy at War with Itself.* New York: Basic Books, 1978.

Boulton, David. *The Grease Machine.* New York: Harper & Row, 1978.

Geis, Gilbert. "White Collar Crime: The Heavy Electrical Equipment Antitrust Cases of 1961." *Corporate and Governmental Deviance,* edited by M. David Ermann and Richard J. Lundman. New York: Oxford University Press, 1978.

Herling, John. *The Great Price Conspiracy.* Washington D.C.: Robert B. Luce, Inc., 1962.

Jacoby, Neil H., Peter Nehemkis, and Richard Eells. *Bribery and Extortion in World Business: A Study of Corporate Political Payments Abroad.* New York: Macmillan, 1977.

Richman, Barry. "Can We Prevent Questionable Foreign Payments?" *Business Horizons,* vol. 22, *3,* June 1979.

Shields, Geoffrey B. "The Cumshaw Pot." *Harvard Magazine,* June 1976, pp. 27–31.

PART SIX
THE FUTURE CORPORATE ETHOS

In Parts One and Five we explored some of the most important dilemmas faced by American business today. In this final part of the text we look toward the future of the American corporation. In particular, we wish to ask how the business organization of the future will meet the ethical challenges posed to it by society. Its ability to meet these challenges could prove to be crucial for business' very survival.

Observers of business sometimes speak as if business had no normative role to play in society, but this view is misleading. The legitimacy of business—the public's acceptance of its right to exist and its belief in the "rightness" of business as an institution—has always rested on business' connection with our highest social values and on its perceived contribution to what we view as the good life or the good society. While business has been essentially a profit-making institution, society has encouraged business to strive for profits in the belief that its doing so would promote the general welfare. Maximizing profits, then, has been the way in which business has discharged its social responsibilities. The "invisible hand" of the market system, it has been assumed, would function automatically to harmonize self-interest and bring about the good of society as a whole. And indeed business has made enormous contributions to American society. It has supported fundamental social values such as freedom of opportunity, productivity, growth, efficiency, and material well-being. It has encouraged enterprise and creativity. No society has a higher standard of living or such an abundance of goods and services.

The legitimacy of business still rests on public confidence in its contribution to a good society. In the past two decades, however, this confidence has eroded, and our conception of a good society has undergone some transformation. Observers of the American scene such as Gerald Cavanagh have concluded that business could be facing a genuine crisis in legitimacy.

Increasingly, Cavanagh explains, people are challenging the belief that economic well-being is identical with social well-being, or that the former leads automatically to the latter. On the contrary, many now feel that some of the same values which contributed to our economic success—growth, productivity, consumption, the profit motive—have led to unacceptably high social costs. Americans have lost confidence in the ability of the market system automatically to bring about the general welfare. Rather than encouraging business in the single-minded pursuit of profit and waiting for social well-being to follow, the public is demanding that business broaden the scope of its concerns and assume a more active role in solving social problems and in working for a good society. The social responsibility of business today, the American public seems to be saying, no longer ends with its economic responsibility.

Cavanagh maintains that the criteria for judging business performance must be broadened to include social measures such as justice, equality, and the fostering of a humane society, as well as economic measures. Although in the past we have looked to government to make changes in business' social role, Cavanagh calls for corporate executives to be sensitive to social demands without waiting for legislation. Only in this way, he argues, can business establish a new legitimacy for itself, based on broader standards of performance. Cavanagh suggests the inclusion of public interest directors on the board, the use of the corporate social audit, and the restructuring of internal corporate policies as ways of encouraging business sensitivity to social issues.

The view that business should assume social as well as economic responsibilities and take an active role in working toward social goals represents a challenge to the traditional understanding of the nature and functions of business. As we have worked through this text, we have seen the impact of this challenge in nearly every aspect of business activity. Traditionally, business organizations have been understood to be the private property of their shareholders. Managers were viewed as agents of the shareholders, bound by an agreement to serve their interests as the shareholders themselves would serve them—which, presumably, was to make a profit. As we have seen, however, the increasing separation of ownership and control and the decreasing confidence in the market system to contribute to public welfare have undermined the idea that management's sole responsibility is to shareholders. Business is now expected to exercise responsibility toward a range of "stakeholders," including consumers, employees, and the public at large.

Increasingly, society expects corporations not only to supply goods to consumers, but also to exercise care and foresight to make sure that the product is safe for consumer use. Manufacturers' liability for defective products has been extended to include even situations in which manufacturers could not have foreseen and prevented accidents. Some have suggested that corporations should refrain from encouraging indiscriminate consumption through advertising.

Society now demands that business avoid undue pollution and depletion of natural resources, and that it operate as much as possible in harmony with the natural environment. Business has been asked not simply to invest where it is most profitable, but to be sensitive to the social consequences of investment and to use its economic power to alleviate social injustice. It is expected not merely to provide jobs for members of the community, but also to offer a safe, healthy, and fulfilling work environment. Many thinkers have called for restrictions on the corporation's freedom to hire and fire and on the obedience and loyalty it demands from its employees. Increasingly, business organizations are being asked to adopt hiring policies which help solve problems of institutional racism. As the duties of business organizations are broadened to include social responsibilities, employees who resist or reveal illegal or unethical acts on the part of their employers may in fact be acting in the best interests of the corporation.

Many of the responsibilities corporations are being asked to assume are duties which, until now, have been associated with government. Traditionally, it has been government's job to promote social welfare; the job of business was to make money. Ironically, government has also traditionally been expected to keep its interference with business at a minimum, passing only those regulations necessary to preserve freedom of competition. As public dissatisfaction with business performance has increased, however, the relationship between business and government has shifted. Business is now subject to a multiplicity of "social regulations," many of which it feels are unfair and unnecessary. The restrictions placed on business by these regulations constitute a powerful argument for complying voluntarily with society's new demands.

How is business to respond effectively to public expectations, however, when all institutional attitudes and forces encourage corporate managers to place profits first? Today's manager is rewarded with success and esteem not for cutting down on the pollution of a local river or for improving employee satisfaction, but for maximizing profits. Indeed, as we have seen in many of the cases included in the text, pressures to sacrifice ethical concerns to profits are often severe. The corporation can create a closed context in which behavior that might be condemned elsewhere is found acceptable.

Christopher Stone argues that neither restrictions from outside nor internal structural reforms will succeed in getting the corporation to assume the new social responsibilities as long as the values, attitudes, and customs of the corporation remain unchanged. For this reason, Stone believes we must reform the "corporate culture"; we must attempt to change the things the corporation cares about.

Stone recognizes that a corporation cannot sustain a number of competing aims, and he believes that business must remain essentially a profit-oriented institution. While he accepts the corporate orientation toward profit, Stone does not believe that we should permit any and all acts—acts that harm others, for example—in the name of profit. He feels that business can be made to strive for profit within the limits required by ethics, and he lists a number of attitudes he would like to see adopted by corporations, not in place of, but in conjunction with, their profit orientation. Already, Stone notes, different corporations and industries possess recognizably different cultures. Precisely because a corporation is a culture of its own defined by norms, values, and mores which powerfully influence behavior, there is hope for change. Such change is necessary, both Stone and Cavanagh believe, if business is to ensure its legitimacy and integrity in the future.

chapter seventeen
DEVELOPING THE MORAL CORPORATION

THE CULTURE OF THE CORPORATION

CHRISTOPHER D. STONE*

Can we change those things that the corporation cares about? We can restructure the corporation's information processes so as to make it gather and channel vital data to those in a position to do something about it. But what is there to guarantee that the person in authority, supplied the information, will act upon it? What if he doesn't care that his company is running the risk of imposing long-range health hazards on the public? We can make companies install special officers in charge of particular problem areas. But what is there to guarantee that, the special executive having been instituted, the other officers will not undermine him in all the subtle ways available to them? We can provide arrangements to protect, and thus encourage, potential "whistle blowers" to come forward with information about the dangers and abuses that they see on their jobs. But what amount of protection will get the workers to come forward if they simply don't give a damn in the first place?

I do not want to leave the impression that "internal reform" measures cannot be rested upon anything firmer than the corporation's good intentions. On the contrary, there are any number of ways to link legal penalties (and rewards) to bona fide compliance, both of the company and of key individuals.

But we have to recognize too that, in the last analysis, the most these measures can do is *reduce* the resistance of the preexistent corporate cultures. So long as the underlying attitudes are left untouched, some measure of resistance—of circumvention, disregard, and foot dragging—is inevitable.

Should we hold out any hope of altering the very attitudes of corporate America? *Is there any chance at all?*

The answer, I am afraid, is that we are very limited in what we can do. It isn't just a matter of autonomy: No organization, of course, is going to hand control over gladly. There is, even beyond this, simply a limit to how many different, potentially competing aims and attitudes any institution can entertain. Universities aim to educate; armies, to fight; hospitals, to treat and cure. These shared, mutually understood goals provide a context against which commands are interpreted and actions synchronized.

*Department of Law, University of Southern California.

They provide a post against which the institution can measure its "success" and stabilize itself.

To be realistic, with the American business corporation the dominant orientation of the institution is going to remain toward profit, expansion, and prestige. Those who labor in it are going to remain concerned about providing for their wives and kids, about the approval of their peers, about "moving up" in the organization. What ideas can we gather up in our entire society that are powerful enough to set in competition with these, with "self-interest" as so many centuries of the culture have defined it?

To recognize these basic constraints is not to say we are powerless, however. We live with the fact that human beings are dominated by certain ego-centered goals/ drives (sexual gratification, power, self-preservation). But through various acculturating mechanisms we have been able, not to do away with these forces, but at least to put constraints on them. On a parity of reasoning, even if we accept profit *orientation* as a basic and inalterable fact of American corporate life, we don't have to accept, or expect, sheer corporate hedonism. What I am asking of our chemical companies, for example, is not that they abandon profits. Producing fertilizers and chemicals that will get the world fed would be, and should be, a profitable activity. But what we want, too, is that the companies will manifest enough concern about the effects their products are having on the health of the field workers who use them, that they will accept the internal structures we deem appropriate; that in cooperation with the imposed systems they will perform some amount of follow-up; that, if suspicious circumstances are apparent, they will undertake appropriate studies and notify health authorities; that they will make data available to interested parties—rather than cover up the apparent risks and deny their very possibility.

We could, in fact, attempt a listing of various attitudes desirable in connection with each of the various social roles that the corporation plays.

The corporation as citizen

- to be concerned with obeying the laws (even if it can get away with law breaking profitably)

- to aid in the making of laws, as by volunteering information within its control regarding additional measures that may need to be imposed on industry

- to heed the fundamental moral rules of the society

- not to engage in deception, corruption, and the like

- as a citizen abroad, to act decently to host country citizens, and not inimically to U.S. foreign policy

The corporation as producer

- to aim for safe and reliable products at a fair price

The corporation as employer

- to be concerned with the safety of the work environment

- to be concerned with the emotional well-being of its workers

- not to discriminate

The corporation as resource manager
- not to contribute unduly to the depletion of resources
- to manifest some concern for the aesthetics of land management

The corporation as an investment
- to safeguard the interests of investors
- to make full and fair disclosures of its economic condition

The corporation as neighbor
- to be concerned with pollution
- to conduct safe and quiet operations

The corporation as competitor
- not to engage in unfair competition, on the one hand, or cozy restrictions of competition, on the other

The corporation as social designer
- to be innovative and responsive in the introduction of new products and methods
- not to close its eyes to the fact that the movies it turns out, the shows it produces, the styles it sets, have an impact on the quality of our lives, and to concern itself with the impact responsibly

Some will say it is unlikely that corporations will ever do these sorts of things—that is, go much beyond whatever the law, and market competition, can absolutely force from them. How much do ordinary citizens meet some of these standards—report favorable errors on their tax returns, for example? Indeed, if Christianity "hasn't been tried yet" why should we suppose that it is corporations who are finally going to get it off the ground?

The possibility of something better is inherent, oddly enough, in the very development decried by Adolf Berle and Gardner Means in their famous *The Modern Corporation and Private Property* (1932). Berle and Means first called public attention to the fact that as the industrial sector was evolving from sole proprietorships to larger and larger corporations, the owners of the property in the traditional sense—the investors—were no longer the true managers of the companies. Formerly, the owner-investor had been his own manager, or had exercised tight control over the hired officers. But now the officers—the men who were calling the shots—were emerging with relative independence from the stockholders as the latter became increasingly passive and dispersed. The investors, moreover, were losing their link to the underlying corporate property; they sold their shares and bought stock in a new enterprise with perfect fluidity.

This situation, Berle and Means saw, contained the germs of a sort of "irresponsibility" that had not existed on such a scale before. But they were thinking of the relations between the managers and stockholders. This is the relationship that was of paramount concern to those analyzing the "corporation problem" in the thirties, when widespread tragedy to investors was very much a part of the intellectual and moral climate, rather than "consumerism," "environmentalism," and the like. And from this perspective, they were clearly right. But from the other perspective—that of the management's relations to interests "outside" the corporation—the same historical development provides at least a new wedge of hope for greater managerial accountability. For when the interests of management and ownership are one (as, most purely, in the case of a sole proprietorship) all the compromises management makes with profits come out of its own pockets. If the people who own the business decide to install an unrequired pollution filter, or establish day care for mother-workers, or go out of their way to investigate the health hazards of their products, *they* pay. But it is not so in the giant, broadly held companies. There, the "charitable" gestures of management do not come out of their own pockets. Thus, in theory—and I think in practice as well—the giant, broadly held company is more likely to be socially accountable, and less likely to engage in sharp, irresponsible conduct, than the small, closely held concern that served as Berle and Means's historical model.

WHY AREN'T CORPORATIONS MORE MORAL?

"Well, then," someone may ask, "why isn't the corporation more responsible than it is?" The answers are not all obvious; they are, moreover, important because any program to change corporate attitudes has to begin by identifying the particular asocial attitudes that we are up against.

The first point to remember is that while the corporation is *potentially* immune from a single-minded profit orientation, in any particular company that potentiality is able to become reality only after some satisfactory level of profits has been achieved. A corporation that is operating "on the margin" is going to cut as many corners as it can get away with on worker safety, product quality, and everything else.

Then, too, it would be a mistake to believe that the desire to turn profits is the only attitude that causes us problems. We know, for example, that many companies— especially the major dominant companies—go through periods in which they are well enough off that they could put a little something extra into, say, environmental protection, and not have to face (what is a real rarity) a shareholder coup d'état. The true range of attitudes we have to confront is much deeper and more complex than "profits"—but not necessarily any the less intractable.

One range of attitudes we might call "profit-connected." Even when the company is achieving enough profits that the managers can protect their own tenure, they may continue to pursue much the same course of conduct, but now as a reflection of other motives. Prestige in the business world comes of being connected with a firm listed on the New York Stock Exchange, one whose sales are rising, or which appears in the *Fortune* 500. The problem here is a lack of most other measures of success, other guarantors of prestige, than those which can be read off the company's ledgers.

Some other of the attitudes we are up against are even further removed from profits. Consider corporate insensitivity to their workers. The received wisdom on "blue-collar blues" is a purely economic one: that the worker is crushed in the corporation's never-ending push for profits. In part, this is true. But any bureaucracy, and not only the modern corporation, evolves toward depersonalized relationships. Its very "success" depends upon the mobilization of personalities into roles—the better for the synchronization of behavior. Thus, if corporations appear insensitive (to the world as well as to their workers) they may be insensitive for many of the same reasons that many nonprofit bureaucracies are insensitive (a hospital is the first example that comes to my mind). I am not saying that we therefore give up on attempts to sensitize them. I am just suggesting that if we are going to confront such problems, we have to be prepared to deal with subtler and more pervasive features than "capitalist greed."

In such actions as sabotage, we are involved, too, in very complex matters of group dynamics. In an institutional framework, men do things they ordinarily wouldn't. (The army is a dramatic example.) One reason for this is that the usual restraints on antisocial behavior operate through a self-image: "I can't see myself doing *that*." In an institutional setting, however, *that* isn't being done *by me*, but *through me* as an actor, a role player in an unreal "game" that everyone is "playing." The evidence in the electrical equipment industry's price-fixing case is shot through with this flavor of a huge game. So, too, is the entire Watergate affair. The Equity Funding scandal went so far as to involve role playing in the most literal sense—"forgery parties" at which people played the roles necessary to fake dossiers.

What I am getting at is that behavior that may seem on the surface to spring from profits or even venality may actually involve, and have to be dealt with as, something as far removed from venality as play. An ideal examination of "the culture of the corporation" (which I can present here only in outline) would try to identify a whole range of underlying institutional attitudes and forces, and proceed to identify the particular sorts of undesired corporate behavior that constitute their symptoms. These attitudes would include, for example: a desire for profits, expansion, power; desire for security (at corporate as well as individual levels); the fear of failure (particularly in connection with shortcomings in corporate innovativeness); group loyalty identification (particularly in connection with citizenship violations and the various failures to "come forward" with internal information); feelings of omniscience (in connection with inadequate testing); organizational diffusion of responsibility (in connection with the buffering of public criticism); corporate ethnocentrism (in connection with limits on concern for the public's wants and desires).

WHAT CAN BE DONE?

This definition of the corporate culture is barely even a first step. And we have to face the fact that we really know very little about how to change it. There are, it is true, plenty of people (industrial and management psychologists, for example) who study and attempt to alter attitudes within this matrix. Much thought has gone into motivating workers toward increased productivity. Sensitivity training has been invoked with executives to eliminate "interpersonal frictions" that threaten the corporation's "solidarity."

But how about calling to question the organization's own values? How about motivating workers to recognize and report clues that a substance they are working with may kill fish, or farm workers? Or to adopt a more positive attitude toward the law—even when the chances of the company's getting caught are slim? What I have discovered is that there is almost no literature available on these matters; when industrial psychologists have been called into a company, it is always by management with an eye toward getting some group to perform more "effectively" from the point of management's preestablished aims—not to challenge those aims, or to try to work into the organization "extraneous" values favored by the society at large.

Thus, to a large extent, the territory we are striking out into is unmarked. To map our way, we ought to begin by learning more about why different corporations—like different political administrations—seem to permeate themselves with their own characteristic attitudes toward law abidance and "good citizenship" generally. "Lawbreaking," some sociologists have observed, "can become a normative pattern within certain corporations, and violation norms may be shared between corporations and their executives." The atmosphere becomes one in which the participants (as at Equity Funding) "learn the necessary values, motives, rationalizations and techniques favorable to particular kinds of crime."

One would want to know, too, why different industries manage to evolve their own customs, habits, and attitudes. For example, the most recent and provocative survey I have seen involves a comparison of worker safety records in coal mines owned and operated by traditional coal mining companies with those owned and operated by steel firms.[1] The differences are striking. The ten major mining concerns experienced an average 0.78 deaths per million man-hours worked; but in the mines operated by the steel companies, there were on average only 0.36 fatalities per million man-hours. The injury statistics were more discrepant still. The ten major mining companies experienced, on average, 40.61 injuries per million man-hours; the steel-company-operated coal mines averaged 7.50. There are several possible explanations for these striking discrepancies. But one of the most common factors cited was simply an attitudinal one—that the steel companies have just not evolved what was called "a 'coal mentality' that accepts a great loss of life and limb as the price of digging coal."

> . . . Traditionally the steel companies' top corporate executives, being used to a relatively good safety record in their steel mills, have never been willing to tolerate poor safety performance in their mines. . . . "There's a paternalistic attitude [in the steel companies] that you don't find prevalent in [coal,]" admits the head of one large commercial coal operation.[2]

Why is it that different corporations, and different industries, exhibit these differences in attitude? Can we identify the variables that make some more responsible than others, and put this knowledge to work by directly manipulating those variables? We simply do not know the answer to these and many similar questions. But even in the absence of this knowledge we do have some good clues as to how attitudinal changes can be brought about—clues that suggest two broad approaches suited to two distinguishable situations.

The key characteristic of the first situation is that the attitudes we want to inculcate can be connected with, and find support in, norms and/or subgroups that preexist in the organization. An example of this is provided in the aftermath of the electrical equipment conspiracy cases.

Price-fixing in the industry—certainly in the heavy-equipment section of the industry—had become so widespread as to constitute something of a behavioral norm. To change this corporate culture that had grown up within it, Westinghouse appointed an outside advisory panel.

The advisory panel insisted not merely on the company's instructing its employees that price-fixing was illegal. Despite all the industry protests about the "vagueness" of the antitrust laws, none of those involved in the secret meetings had any doubts about the illegality of price-fixing. And that knowledge, of itself, obviously had not pulled enough freight. Instead, the panel decided to aim for an affirmative demonstration "that competition, properly pursued, can produce far more consistent profits than . . . conspiracy."[3]

In-house programs were established—management courses, workshops, conferences—all adopting the positive approach that the company's business success in the future, over the long haul, depended "to a considerable degree on the adoption . . . of policies of vigorous (and even aggressive) flexible, competitive initiative."[4]

The presentation, in other words, was not that the company had to "submit" to a stronger, outside force—that is, the government. Rather, the price-fixing was depicted as itself a foreign element, inimical to the more fundamental corporate ideal of increasing one's share of the market through better salesmanship, superior design, and the like—the norm of competition. In fact, I am authoritatively informed that at discussions among employees, a sentiment emerged that the price-fixing had been "the sales force's thing: a way to avoid the hard work of really going after sales." The same source reports that the design engineers actually resented what had been going on. Their self-esteem had been based on their ability to build better mousetraps; suddenly they discovered that their share of the market for heavy equipment had been fixed at a ratio that had no real bearing on their own contribution.

This brings me to the second point. Securing conformity to the compliance norm was not based solely on demonstrating its link to a preexistent, supposedly dominant, corporate *ideal*. In addition, there already existed within the organization certain *groups* potentially more supportive of the desired attitude than the corporation as a whole. Part of the trick of changing the attitude manifested by the corporation as a whole is to locate the critical support group and strengthen its hand. (The engineers have already been mentioned.) In the example at hand, lawyers were particularly crucial. Company lawyers "look bad," both among their peers and their co-workers, when something like widespread price-fixing is revealed to have been going on under their noses. What is more, along with their other functions, they, in particular, symbolize law abidance within the organization. In such a context, making the desired attitude more acceptable involves placing the symbolic custodian of the attitude more prominently in the corporate hierarchy. This was accomplished in the Westinghouse situation by requiring other employees to, for example, file reports with the lawyers whenever certain questionable activity was undertaken.

In a second class of situation, however, the problem of dealing with the corporate culture is stickier. I am thinking now of the cases where the attitudes the society wants to inculcate are at odds with all the dominant norms of the corporation and can find no alliance with any of the attitudinal groups I mentioned (the work group, industry, business community).

For example, where worker-safety problems are concerned, we can at least consider mobilizing some internal alliance with the unions; for product quality and safety, with the engineers; for resource conservation (as through recycling energy), with the investors. But consider, by contrast, the problem of getting "insiders" to give notice of the company's pollution; to halt industrial espionage and campaign law violations; to keep clear of political adventures in foreign countries; to exercise concern for land use aesthetics. In these cases, the attitudes desired by the "outside" world have barely a toehold on the "inside."

When we move into this area what we are faced with is nothing less than providing the organization with a new *internal rhetoric*—the special "vocabulary of motives" that every culture, and every cultural subgroup, provides its members with as its own "legitimate" reasons for doing things. These varying vocabularies involve more than just different ways of interpreting and explaining an act already completed. The range of available motives imposes boundaries on the alternatives a member of the group is prepared to consider. Today, a lower-level executive who recommended against a program on the grounds that "it will cause a lot of noise in the neighborhood" would be rather unlikely to get his recommendation advanced very far up the corporate hierarchy—unless he could convincingly append something about "we are likely to get fined (or zoned out)."

That is why any program to shift basic corporate attitudes has to involve, not replacing the profit motive ("will it sell?"), but at least providing respectable alternate vocabularies that can effectively be invoked, within some range of profit constraint, in special circumstances.

How can such a change be brought about?

A good deal depends upon the sort of gradual social evolution that is out of the control of any of us. As the general public becomes more and more informed and concerned about the environment, for example, some of that concern will gradually work its way through the corporation's walls, with the result that explanations today unacceptable—"out of place"—will become persuasive in time.

On the other hand, while much is in the hands of this sort of evolution, there are some deliberate measures that we can take. These possibilities include the following.

REWARDS FOR EXCELLENCE

At present, just about the only positive reward corporations achieve is in the form of profits (or sales, or other measures of financial growth). Essentially, all other social feedback is negative—public criticisms or legal punishments for doing things badly. This need not be the case. During World War II, for example, "E" awards were bestowed on defense companies that had exceeded their allotted production. The presentation of the "E" to a qualifying corporation was the occasion of a high ceremony, at which government representatives, executives, and workers joined. The company would get a flag, and each of the workers an "E" pin. Why should not the Environmental Protection Agency, for example, be authorized to give out its own Environmental Protection "E"s to companies that accelerate beyond their "cleanup" timetables, or come up with ingenious new environment-protecting methods?

THE SOCIAL AUDIT

A great deal has been written recently about devising a "social audit" for corporations to supplement their traditional financial audits. Their aim would be to represent on paper the total social costs and benefits of a corporation's activities, over and above those that are now reflected in its financial statements.

The problem with the traditional statements is that they developed to reflect the interests of the financial community. Investors—and potential investors—have no particular need for a breakdown of figures displaying, for example, how much the company has put into quality-control systems or how much it has done to increase minority worker mobility. A paper company's statement will reflect the cost of the lumber it consumes; but if it uses the local river as a sewer to carry away waste, and does not have to pay for the damages this causes downstream, those social costs will nowhere appear on the company's books. They don't affect earnings.

A reporting system that measured these hidden costs and benefits would be—if we had it—quite interesting. But at present, the details of how to implement it are wanting. Much of the value of a true audit, for example, is that it has a set, prescribed structure, designed to display the answers to a series of questions which are the same for all companies.[5] This the social auditors are nowhere near achieving. And it may well be beyond their grasp.

Against this background, I am inclined to agree with the suggestion of Bauer and Fenn that, at least while we are seeing what, if anything, corporate social audits may develop into, management ought to be encouraged to make them up for their own internal use only.[6] I myself have doubts as to how successfully and far the social audit can evolve even in such a private and nurtured atmosphere. But to my mind, the key point is that even if these experiments never do produce anything terribly useful informationally, along the lines of a true audit, there is still a chance of success from our present viewpoint: from the point of developing a new internal vocabulary of motive that might compete with "profitability" and the profit constellation (sales, costs, etc.). What new constellations of motive would evolve, one cannot say. I would rather suspect that, in contrast with the true audit, different companies would design incommensurable categories and structures, each appropriate to its own fields of operation, capital intensivity, and so forth. Then these categories, in turn, could be worked into the internal evaluation process, so that those divisions and persons who performed in the appropriate way would stand a chance of reward.

INTERCHANGES

There is no more primitive way to alter intergroup attitudes (hopefully, for the better) than to bring the groups together. On an intracorporate scale, there have been a number of experiments in "sensitivity" confrontations among executives and, to a lesser extent I believe, among management and workers.

But insofar as the boundary between the corporation and the outside world is concerned, the exchanges could barely be worse. The government, for its part, relies largely on lawsuits and the threat of suits—certainly a less than ideal way to communicate values. The public at large—or, at least, the activist groups that purport to speak for it—maintain a shrill criticism that is just overstated enough that managers (even otherwise sympathetic managers) can find grounds to dismiss it in their own minds. The corporate response to the public is either a cynical PR bluff, or a defensiveness no less shrill and hysterical than the criticisms it receives. In a recent interview,

Union Oil Company's president dismissed the environmental movement as "a question of people being irrational." Then, thinking a little further he added darkly, "It's more than that, actually. I don't know who's behind the Sierra Club, but it obviously isn't people of good will."[7]

What is called for, obviously, is some improved modes of communication and understanding—in both directions. Public criticism of corporate behavior certainly should be maintained. But it should be informed enough, and even sympathetic enough, that it does not induce so extreme and inflexible a defensiveness.

PUBLIC EDUCATION

Part of the problem corporate reformers face in changing the corporate culture has been mentioned: that the shriller their criticisms, the more the corporate community inclines to discount them as "one-sided" and ill-informed. The reform movement has some particularly sensitive problems, too, in taking its case to the public. How the issues are handled is important, not only because of the obvious implications for garnering legislative support, but because the reactions of the outside world are themselves one of the more significant determinants of the corporation's internal culture.

Altering corporate behavior may involve reexamining the views that prevail in the outside world. And in this regard, one has to be struck by the fact that while the public may be periodically exercised over corporations, corporate wrong-doing simply doesn't command the same dread and fascination as crimes committed by tangible human beings.

I strongly suspect—although I cannot prove—that where a corporation rather than an identifiable person is the wrongdoer, the hostility that is aroused is less even where the offense is more or less the same. For example, if we are subjected to the noise of a motorcyclist driving up and down our street at night, I think a deeper and more complex level of anger is tapped in us than if we are subjected to the same disturbance (decibelically measured) from an airline's operations overhead. It is not just that the one seems "uncalled for" while the other seems incidental to commerce and progress. It is also that where a tangible person is involved, we can picture him (even if that means only to fantasize him); whereas when the nuisances we are subjected to are corporate, there is no tangible target to fix our anger upon. And it all seems so hopeless anyway. The consequence, if I am right, is that while various small groups are turning increased publicity onto corporate wrongdoing, they are still a long way from bringing about effective changes in corporate laws and corporate performance. A reform movement, to be effective, needs both widespread indignation and widespread hope to sustain itself. Neither by itself will do. So long as the public continues to perceive the wrongs corporations do as impersonal, market-dictated, and somehow inevitable, the reformers will have as little success forcing a change in corporate consciousness as they will in marshaling a public opposition that can seriously challenge the corporation's legislative clout. In all events, those of us who aim to change things have a job to sort out and deal with the various reasons why corporate reform movements have not been more successful after so many decades of agitation. One principal reason, I am sure, is that the public little cares to be reminded, over and over, that it is being victimized by impersonal forces, without being told what it can do about it. I like to think that some of the ideas in this paper, expanded upon by others, will suggest the steps we might now begin to consider.

NOTES

1. "Coal-Mines Study Shows Record Can Be Improved When Firms Really Try," *Wall Street Journal*, January 18, 1973, p. 1, col. 6.

2. Ibid., p. 7.

3. Richard Austin Smith, *Corporations in Crisis* (New York: Doubleday, 1964), p. 165.

4. A Report from the Board of Advice to Westinghouse Electric Corporation (1962), p. 10.

5. "Enter the Social Auditors," *London Sunday Times*, June 21, 1973, p. 72, col. 5.

6. Raymond A. Bauer and Dan H. Fenn, "What Is a Corporate Social Audit?," *Harvard Business Review* 51 (January-February 1973): 43–44.

7. Digby Diehl, "Q & A: Fred L. Hartley," *West Magazine (Los Angeles Sunday Times)*, February 20, 1972, p. 30.

CORPORATE VALUES FOR THE FUTURE

GERALD F. CAVANAGH*

Because of competition and the nature of the free enterprise system, some now argue that business can do nothing substantial to solve society's ills.[1] According to this point of view, capitalism makes maximization of profit and growth inevitable. Government regulation is not successful in removing the undesirable by-products of the competitive corporation. If we acknowledge the many strengths and the now more obvious weaknesses of the American business system, this brings us to the core question: How does that system go about adapting to change? How are inefficiencies and inequities repaired? What means does the economic and business system have at its disposal that will enable it to meet the future with confidence?

Change is accomplished in the political process primarily through voting and the legislatures. There is no such instrument in the business sphere that can detect changing needs of *all* citizens, and thus help the system to adapt. On public interest issues Americans are generally committed to an open system and to consensus. This process often works slowly, but it does bring about changes in law and thus in life. On the other hand, when it comes to the inadequacies of the business system, we often need a good swat from a baseball bat to wake us up. It took the urban race riots to force us to realize the extent and injustice of job discrimination. Lake Erie died before we began to realize the dangers of pollution. In spite of predictions of serious long-term shortages, it took the energy crisis to awaken us to the dimensions of the problem, and many today still shrug off the possibility of any serious long-term energy shortage. Bank of America executives now acknowledge that it took the bombing and burning of a branch bank in Isle Vista, California, to force them to be more responsive to the needs of the larger society.[2]

A democratic people act when they personally feel a need. Hence a democracy works slowly, and generally requires a crisis to awaken its citizens to new public needs. Many of the needs now facing Americans are serious (dwindling resources, urban decay, nuclear disaster, pollution). If a crisis must affect each one of us before we understand the seriousness of each of these problems, there will be no time or flexibility left to find solutions.

A SUMMARY OF INADEQUACIES

American industrial society has managed prodigious feats of production and growth. In spite of this, it is also characterized by inadequacies in its values:

1. Acquisitive materialism is encouraged by a system that provides a rationalization for self-interest and selfishness.

Excerpted from *American Business Values in Transition* (Englewood Cliffs, N.J.: Prentice-Hall, Inc., 1976, pages 171–208.) Reprinted by permission of the publisher.
*College of Business and Administration, University of Detroit.

2. Freedom and productivity are dominant values, with less attention paid to how this freedom and productivity will be used.

3. Because of large organizations and the division of labor, individuals seldom feel a sense of human participation.

4. Traditional unbounded faith in scientific, technological, and industrial progress is increasingly questioned.

5. There is an inequality in the distribution of income and wealth, domestically and internationally.

6. Individual decisions based on self-interest increasingly fail to add up to acceptable and humane policy for society as a whole.

7. The cumbersome machinery of majority rule may not leave us sufficient time to solve the serious problems that face us.

BUSINESS: MOVER OR MOVED

Society's expectations with regard to business have expanded over the years. Recently the community has been asking that business look to employing minorities and women, try to keep the air and water clean, and contribute in other ways to the life of citizens. The question to be asked now is this: Although the changing expectations come from society as a whole, do actual changes in corporate policy come about because of government leadership and legislation, or because the firm itself sees these needs and responds to them on its own initiative?

Historically we have seen how most social innovations in business operations have come about through the prodding of the government and legislation (minimum wage, security and exchange regulations, environmental protection). The business sector seems to need a push. Furthermore, it also helps the formulation of new rules of the game, so that no one firm is at a disadvantage in introducing a socially desirable product or program at some cost in a highly competitive market.

Is the government therefore the sole agency for determining social priorities, and setting up programs and ground rules for acting? Government consultant and Harvard Business School professor George C. Lodge would answer yes: that is precisely the role of government.[3] Business can be effective in mobilizing its resources for whatever ends government decides, as it did in producing for World War II or the space program. In fact, Lodge maintains that business works best in a structured setting to meet objectives made explicit by outside elements. The more amorphous those needs and goals are, the less efficient and effective is business in addressing them.

In the late 1960s, after the civil disturbances, President Lyndon Johnson turned to business leaders and said: "Government has failed; now it is your turn to try to save the cities." Lodge finds both the request and the attempted response futile and unworkable. Business is not equipped to set social priorities or to solve social problems. Most members of the New Left agree and would not want business to set social priorities; they do not trust business to look to the best interests of society. Business by nature looks to its own advantage; it is expected to and structured to do so. It is therefore incapable of effectively determining needs and priorities for society as a whole.

Reacting to Johnson's statement, Lodge paraphrased the hoped-for response of the business person to a president, mayor, or cabinet officer who asks business to transform the cities:

> No, my friend. That is your job; we can only help you when you have decided what will be the direction, the speed, and the design—the ideological basis of the transformation. You are the politician; you are the elected ruler of the community; you are the sovereign state; you speak for the people. We serve you.[4]

It would therefore seem to him that business can respond to the prods and constraints of government direction and legislation, but is not able to initiate action on social problems. What is badly needed in any case, says Lodge, is a new ideology for business; the old pragmatic values are obsolete and no longer of any use.

There is a strong case here for separate, defined sectors and roles for business and government institutions. It is true that the business community has traditionally abhorred the interference of government in its affairs. Over the years, the Chamber of Commerce and business people themselves have taken the position that laws and regulations are intrusions that tend to hinder the free market, and so make the productive process less efficient. Moreover, it is true that every restriction and regulation tends to narrow the number of possible responses. Innovation will be hindered if all larger policy questions that stem from the expectations of society are turned over to government, with business given no choice but to follow along or object. Perhaps this is a solution, but it is one that will adversely affect flexibility and innovation within the firm, and as a result in society as well.

There is, however, another solution, and one that is probably more consonant with the latent desires of both business and government. Executives themselves are calling on their peers to be more sensitive to the expectations of society *without* waiting for legislation. It is true that, in highly competitive industries (autos, steel, rubber), a costly but socially desirable innovation (safety, pollution controls) will require legislation. The experience of Ford in trying to introduce the seat belt and General Motors' more recent attempt to sell the air bag as an option show that safety features, desirable as they may be, will often not be purchased. The firm that tries to absorb these costs is at a competitive disadvantage. Consumers want other motorists not to pollute, but would individually refuse to pay the costs of the necessary devices themselves. To bring about equal employment opportunity requires legislation, primarily to ensure something approaching fair and equal application of new policies and to avoid an individual firm's foot dragging.

On other issues, such as job enrichment, product quality, and even plant location and relation to the surrounding community, it is more difficult to formulate legislation. It is harder to specify policy and to apply measurements. Furthermore, legislation in these areas would severely constrain freedom of action and operation, and this in turn would undoubtedly affect efficiency and flexibility. In these areas, it is probably better if the firm takes the lead and does not wait for law. The government is therefore not the sole agency for determining social priorities, and hence policies and programs. Business firms and executives may appropriately take initiatives that will leave them more in charge of their own future direction. Executives are thus less constrained and regulated, but in turn take a broader view of the role of the firm and its purposes.

In this model, the government continues to oversee, regulate, and facilitate participation in the economic as well as the political sphere. But more grass roots initiative is expected from every segment of business, for the sake of the entire society. This grass roots participation is prodded, encouraged, and even policed by the various new activist groups—the consumer advocates, the equal rights proponents, and the shareholder activists. There is a danger that the stridency of their charges and the lack of real attention on both sides may cause lessened confidence in institutions and leaders. Nevertheless, their record of successes is quite remarkable, and they do represent a "third sector"[5] that has developed between public and private institutions to perform a watchdog function and help keep institutions and their leaders honest and sensitive to the needs of society.

ECONOMIC PLANNING

Economic planning is essential as industrial activities become more complex and interdependent. Because of the intricate demands of technology, capital, and markets, larger firms have long resorted to planning. The aggregate planning universally done by large firms in the private sector Galbraith calls "the planning system." The existence of a multiplicity of free, competitive, individualistic producers is a myth; a private planning system is the reality.[6] Moreover, such private-sector planning focuses on the growth and security of the individual firm, and is only secondarily concerned with the public welfare. It thus works to the best interests of the already powerful.

Economic planning for the public welfare is therefore even more essential. A major goal of public economic planning is to bring the goals and activities of private enterprise into better alignment with the overall goals of society. Adam Smith's "invisible hand" or the Physiocrats' "pre-established harmonies" no longer provide assurance that the pursuit of private gain will automatically work to the benefit of society.[7] Americans long ago decided that the free market was not a good indicator of what should be spent on such public goods as national security, fire protection, and parks. There are many other areas, such as the environment and the use of resources, in which the free market has not only not solved the problem, but has contributed to it.

The United States Congress, too, has recognized the necessity for economic planning and the anticipation of unforeseen and undesirable consequences of gross industrial growth. Beneath every tax, subsidy, and government regulation lie value judgments as to what sort of economic activities should be encouraged. Sometimes, unfortunately, these judgments are more influenced by special interest pressures than the public welfare. To look into these problems, Congress has recently established its own Office of Technology Assessment, through which it intends to review recent and proposed technological and industrial activities and innovations in order to examine all side effects—especially the otherwise unforeseen "downstream" effects.

But if we agree that free markets and competition generally do provide greater economic efficiency and also encourage self-reliance, a second question arises: Under what conditions and in what fashion can the strengths of free enterprise be retained? To put the matter differently, how can individual microdecisions be more effective in contributing to better macrodecisions with resulting benefit to society as a whole? It seems clear that long-term, global criteria such as job satisfaction, the use of finite resources, poverty, and hunger must increasingly become elements that enter into corporate decisions. These considerations can become part of corporate decision making either because of government-imposed constraints (tax incentives, regulations, subsidies) or because of the social responsiveness of the firms themselves. Incentives can be changed so that it will be to the best interest of the private firm to take into account public needs. Tax credits for recycling metals and for new, small enterprises, or additional taxes on excessive energy use would be examples.

Economic planning for the public welfare will therefore be carried out in two ways. First, those public goods that can best be provided by government directly (parks, police, urban public transportation) will continue to be so provided. Moreover, this segment of the economy may even grow. Second, on the basis of its long-term, global policies, government will encourage the private sector to also serve the public good through such incentives as new regulations and changes in tax laws. For these initiatives to be successful will require the wholesale reexamination and restatement of economic and public policy.

THE LACK OF CLEAR VALUES

The director of a research institute[8] reported a few years ago that young people were quite critical of the beliefs of their parents and adults in general. They were not critical of *what* they believed, but of what seemed to be a *lack* of beliefs and convictions. Their elders' values seemed to be largely inherited and absorbed passively from the surrounding culture; they had very little in the way of thought-out, internalized goals and values of their own.

Confusion and a lack of clear goals and values on the part of the young puts an even greater burden on their elders to reflect on their own values. If adults in a society, those who have traditionally been looked to as being experienced and wise, do not have some considered notion of their own life goals and aspirations, there would seem to be little hope for young people. It is especially important that individuals have fairly clearly articulated values in a time of rapid change. Otherwise, these persons are left with no rudder, pushed from one job or neighborhood to another by events. Without values and goals, they are not in control of their own careers, lives, or destinies. Opportunities, challenges, and crises now come rapidly, and individuals who have never reflected on what they do and why are unable to meet these events so that they, their families, and others may profit and grow. Rather, such people will be less fulfilled, their families confused and frustrated, and others hurt.

One of the functions of education is to enable and encourage students to reflect on their own values and make them explicit, so that they may then be able to grow and make clear life choices. Alvin Toffler, in analyzing precisely this problem, has harsh words for the schools:

. . . students are seldom encouraged to analyze their own values and those of their teachers and peers. Millions pass through the education system without once having been forced to search out the contradictions in their own value systems, to probe their own life goals deeply, or even to discuss these matters candidly with adults and peers . . . .

Nothing could be better calculated to produce people uncertain of their goals, people incapable of effective decision-making under conditions of overchoice.[9]

The need for individuals to search out and make explicit their own values and goals is underscored in a period of rapid change, and a primary vehicle for this sort of examination and evaluation is the school—yet the American school, from kindergarten to university, has failed in this respect. Educators maintain that education should be "objective," and that values are too controversial a field for a public institution.

When either an individual or an institution plans for the future, values and goals are essential for setting a direction, charting a course, and being in control of that future. Looking to the future is then not a frightening, debilitating experience, but one filled with opportunities for growth and satisfaction. Clearly stated goals and values are essential for another reason: From these building blocks come a value structure—an ideology. Out of living, planning, acting, plus reflection on those actions—out of a reciprocal relationship between action and reflection—come personal and institutional values and goals.

CLUES TO THE FUTURE

The problems and inadequacies of the American business system are no secret: many press on us from all sides; the more subtle ones are apparent to a discerning observer. These difficulties make the system unstable. It simply cannot continue as it is. Sharp shifts in attitudes have already taken place, and changes will continue, probably at an accelerating rate. The question then becomes, what is the direction and the substance of those changes? Future attitudes and policies will be affected by each of us, as citizens, consumers, and managers. It is imperative that we understand present needs and future trends, both for our own sakes and for that of the society in which we live.

In this final section, we will review the changes that are taking place. We will try to identify emerging values that will have a significant impact on the American business system of the future and on the ideology that supports it. We will try to avoid the charge of wishful thinking by adhering to what seem to be valid projections.

Central Role of the Person

A constant theme running through American life and thought is the importance of the individual person. Individualism, democracy, the free market, and the courts all have that principle as a foundation. As the average level of education rises and people's expectations also rise, they become less willing to suffer uninteresting work and being treated, along with capital, as merely one of the inputs into the production process. Business executives often proclaim "people are our most important asset."

In spite of rhetoric and research, however, many now feel that the central role of the individual person is but another of the unfulfilled promises of the American Dream. Ivan Illich goes further to maintain that our developed society and its institutions, especially the corporation, have made us more dependent and hence less free: "Our present institutions abridge basic human freedom for the sake of providing people with more institutional outputs."[10]

In a General Electric report distributed to its own management, *Our Future Business Environment: Developing Trends and Changing Institutions*, several of the main findings point to the growing importance of the individual person. The study predicts a rising tide of education: more persons completing more years of schooling. Such a person "will have more self-respect, will want to be treated more as an individual; will be far less tolerant of authoritarianism and organizational restraints; will have different and higher expectations of what he wants to put into a job and what he wants to get out of it."[11] Higher expectations will also bring an erosion of the traditional work ethic. The attitude that hard, unpleasant, and unrewarding work is to be tolerated because there is no way of avoiding it will be held by fewer and fewer persons. Where people have any choice at all, they will tend to search out work that is satisfying and rewarding. They will often be willing to work more hours and for less pay, if that work is fulfilling.

The business firm will find that, in order to compete, it must begin to see that the development of its people is as important an objective as providing goods and services. Without a work environment in which the individual is challenged, able to grow, and fulfilled, the firm will be at a severe disadvantage. This is, of course, especially true of the more talented and achievement-oriented white collar and blue collar workers. Although research indicates that there is a substantial minority of assembly-line workers who are happy with repetitive, undemanding work (for they can then escape into their personal daydreams), nevertheless the majority will want more challenging work.

One of the essential elements in the growth and development of the individual person is self-knowledge. Without self-knowledge in depth, we are unaware of our own needs and what moves us. We act without being aware of why we act. Without self-knowledge we find it more difficult to build on our strengths and to compensate for our weaknesses. Without self-knowledge we do not have adults, but only children grown old, armed with computers, television sets, and intercontinental ballistics missiles, none of which they really understand. A person obtains self-knowledge from reflection and feedback from others. Often enough, our business life leaves little room for either. What positive or negative feedback, what sense of accomplishment comes from repeatedly bolting a lug on a frame? When a job is repetitive and unchallenging and when a person's relation to his or her superior is impersonal and distant, there is no human relationship and little meaningful feedback. This is not the environment in which a person is able to grow.

A work environment that provides flexibility, that challenges the multitude of talents a person possesses, one in which co-workers and superiors relate and provide each other feedback on their efforts, is one in which an individual may grow as a person. On the other hand, persons fail to develop when they are so socialized by their schools, their firms, and their neighbors that they seek to be like other men and women—losing their individuality. Workers are increasingly asking for some sort of fulfillment from their jobs. Various attempts at job enlargement and organization development have been tried. Volvo assembles its automobiles in teams, rather than using the assembly line. General Motors and the other auto firms have experimented with other types of more challenging work arrangements. Some of these experiments have not been successful, but they do indicate the direction in which large firms realize they must go in order to provide a more humanly satisfying work environment.

Participation in Decision Making

In addition to job enlargement, many workers are also asking for a greater say in major decisions that are made in the plant. Various schemes have been worked out in the United States, Sweden, Yugoslavia, and in other countries to obtain worker input and even to share the responsibility for these decisions with workers. Decisions being made through consensus at the grass roots among workers (industrial democracy), as opposed to decisions being made exclusively at the top and handed down through the hierarchy, is a model now being used in many countries and in some plants in the United States.[12] It undoubtedly points in the direction industrial firms will move in coming decades.

Most job-enlargement attempts to make the work more attractive involve forming work teams. These teams work together, performing the job and distributing the work, taking breaks, and so on, in a fashion that is agreeable to the team. Where these work teams have been formed, job satisfaction generally increases, although efficiency and cost-per-unit sometimes suffer. The advantages and the problems in encouraging cooperation in the work place are fairly clear. The assembly line is the extreme of division of labor and mechanization: small, segmented jobs done by an individual in relative isolation. Although the efficiency of the assembly line cannot be denied, neither can its negative effects on job satisfaction. Much research and experimentation is being carried on by firms in an attempt to make that work more satisfying and rewarding to the individual.

The Corporation as a Servant of Society

The free market model of business and economics supports the view that the corporation is individual, isolated and competing with other firms to survive and grow. Success is measured in dollar terms. Those who hold this capitalist model would acknowledge that the purpose of the firm is to produce the goods and services society needs. Nevertheless, the firm is judged successful whether it makes short-lived, trivial, luxuries perhaps even at the cost of low-paid workers and pollution of a neighborhood, or whether it makes durable, high-quality, basic necessities. As long as a firm shows a profit and grows, Wall Street and *Barron's* will dub it a success. But it is becoming apparent that these criteria of success are much too narrow. The business firm, especially the corporation, is a servant of society. It is chartered by the state to provide for the needs of citizens. It is not an autonomous institution, intent exclusively on its *own* profit and growth.

In contrast to the "cowboy economy" out of which we have recently moved, in which production and consumption are the measures of success, the newer "spaceship economy" has as a measure of economic success "the nature, extent, quality, and complexity of the total capital stock, including in this the state of human bodies and minds included in the system."[13] This is a totally new concept for economists and business people who have been obsessed with production, consumption, profits, and growth. The notion of "more is better" is clearly myopic, and has very many undesirable consequences: pollution; intrusive advertising; long hours of debilitating work to produce unnecessary and fragile gadgets; disruption of urban and rural areas by ugly and unplanned asphalt, concrete, and factories; heart attacks and nervous strain stemming from obsessive competition and "keeping ahead of the Joneses"; and families uprooted because of job transfer. If human needs and desires could be met with less production and consumption, heretical as it sounds, the economy would actually be performing in a superior fashion. In short, additional production and consumption are not only not goals in themselves, but exclusive emphasis on them works to the detriment of people. This is a hard conclusion for economists and business people to accept. Their models and ideology work best for an economy of gross, indiscriminate production and consumption. There is a residual resistance to such a basic shift, since it would require rethinking goals and criteria of performance.

The decreasing relative importance of economic efficiency in production and distribution was also one of the conclusions of the General Electric report on the future business environment cited earlier. Efficiency is considered an organizational value, so that when the organization performs successfully, its importance will diminish. Then the more human values of "justice, equality, individual dignity" will become more important. In the final analysis, organizations exist to serve the needs of the citizens of the larger society, not vice versa.

New Measures of Success

The issues that have been discussed all point to one basic question: How do we measure the success of an economic system? These considerations indicate that priority is gradually shifting from efficiency and productivity to justice, equality, and providing the means for a humane life for all. Once a people attain a certain level of affluence, they find that their needs for material goods have been met. Hence, as "education induces a greater regard for self-development, materialism progressively loses much of its appeal as a prime motivating force."[14]

As more people find that the material goods they need are rather readily available, the *quality* of their lives becomes more important. However, agreeing on and measuring success with these more all-embracing criteria are still in infant stages. Not only do one person's notions of a better quality of life differ from another's but any sort of measurement of success in reaching those goals is also difficult. In contrast, the criteria of success in reaching the traditional business goals of greater efficiency and productivity are readily agreed upon. These criteria are constructed in such a way that they are also easily measurable and hence manageable. Determining quality of life goals, and also some criteria by which to measure success in achieving them, again underscores the point that ". . . the search for a new sense of meaning and purpose in life will become a matter of real importance."[15] We are again faced with basic questions: What sort of life do we want? What sort of society do we want for ourselves and for our children?

Recognition of the need for establishing some criteria of successful performance on larger quality of life issues has spurred a movement to develop some sort of "social indicators."[16] Both government and private agencies have attempted to outline social goals in the areas of health, learning and culture, income and poverty, justice, public order, housing, transportation, and the physical environment. In each of these areas, it is often difficult to agree on the purpose of the activity, to say nothing of arriving at a method of measuring progress toward the goal. Nevertheless, the growing social indicator movement shows that many are not only convinced of the need for a clearer statement of goals, but are already moving beyond that in an attempt to measure progress toward the attainment of those goals.

Parallel to the attempt to develop social indicators for society has been the search for a viable social audit for the corporation itself.[17] Several large companies, including Bank of America and American Telephone and Telegraph, have attempted various systems of measuring their performance in activities that affect the society around them. The more exact attempts, such as those of the management consultants of Abt Associates, try to measure the total dollar value of the firm's social contribution, and also the dollar costs to the larger society of the firm's operations, such as the pollution caused. It is exceedingly difficult to obtain accurate dollar figures on many of these less tangible items. Moreover, trying to obtain them might skew social efforts toward those that can be measured. Hence most firms are attempting a less accounting-like audit.

Another proposal for making the firm more sensitive to the needs of the larger society is through public representatives on the board of directors. Recognizing that even conscientious outside board members give only part of their time to the firm and are totally dependent for information on line management, both Arthur Goldberg and Robert Townsend have advocated a few public directors on every board who would be full-time and empowered to gather their own independent information.[18] The public interest could thus be represented by these relatively independent directors. If, for example, the corporation were planning on shutting down an inefficient inner-city plant in order to move the operation to a rural area, the public director could take it on him or herself to investigate the economic and social impact on the community. Thus the public director might argue for building a new plant within the same community. That director could argue the case directly at the board meeting, and if there were no response in cases that warrant it, he or she might even release the facts to the public at a press conference.

Arthur Goldberg, former associate justice of the Supreme Court and United States ambassador to the United Nations, while a director of Trans World Airlines (TWA), wanted independent outside directors. He proposed that the outside directors have a separate staff for information gathering and that they meet independently on issues. His request was turned down, and so he resigned from TWA's board. Goldberg's proposal was worthwhile, and TWA would have benefited in the long run if it had taken the leadership on this issue. Since his proposal, a number of firms have appointed representatives of the public and have also established public policy committees among their outside board members.

Business firms that are serious about their social responsiveness have begun to restructure their internal policies, procedures, and reward systems.[19] Fine-sounding speeches and policy announcements may be a good beginning, but unless they are implemented within the firm in some hardheaded fashion, they remain words. After the policy is clearly stated, generally a staff specialist is appointed to see that it is carried out. Clear goals are specified, and it is made clear to all management personnel that performance on social policy is one of the factors considered along with other more traditional criteria for salary increase and promotion. It is only when managers are rewarded on the basis of their social performance that they realize the policy is serious and not merely public relations.

Harmony with the Environment

In addition to meeting citizens' real needs, in the future the corporation will be constrained to operate in greater equilibrium with the natural environment. Scarcity of resources, pollution, and undesirable by-products all place limits on the direction and pace of economic and business growth. These physical constraints will become more obvious, and citizens' expectations of the firm living in harmony with them will become more pronounced.

When speaking of life as a whole, many opt for simplification. At present, for example, a great deal of time and energy is wasted in transportation. Much of the time that was saved in cutting down the hours of the work day is now absorbed in getting to and from work, stores, schools, and so on. This is not only a waste of human time and energy, but also a waste of petroleum and other natural resources. Similarly, time is wasted in filling out forms such as income tax returns, insurance applications, and questionnaires, and in listening to advertisements. In speaking to these same issues in the concluding paragraph of his book *Alienation and Economics*, Walter Weisskopf urges, "Wherever there is a choice between making more money and simplifying life, the latter road should be taken." He goes on to spell out the details:

> . . . abandonment of the purely activistic way of life, of getting and doing more and more for the sake of power over and control of the external world including our fellow beings; taking seriously the Kantian maxim that men should never be used as means but always as "ends"; putting more stress on being than on doing by cultivating receptivity to nature, to others, to art, to feelings; more listening rather than talking, also in relation to one's inner life; taking seriously intuition and insight by trying to resurrect what is valid in mysticism and religion; recovering the art of faith by breaking through the value-relativism of technical reason and cultivating the inner powers on which faith rests.[20]

Most of these new attitudes are already observable among many segments of our society, and they seem to be spreading.

Business management is now seen to be responsible not only for product, financing, and work force, but also for any pollution or undesirable side effects their operations bring about. As Peter Drucker puts it, "Managements of all institutions are responsible for their by-products, that is, the impacts of their legitimate activities on people and on the physical and social environment."[21] It is clear that the first responsibility lies with business managers themselves.

Necessity of a New Legitimacy for the Corporation

The legitimacy of any institution depends on the extent to which that institution can justify to its constituency and the larger society its right to exist. It is a political necessity that those who wield power in a society must establish their right to do so. In any society, whether democratic or not, a group or institution that seeks legitimacy must identify itself with some principle that is acceptable to the community as a whole. [22] If an institution does not possess the support and confidence of the majority of the people in a society, it will lose legitimacy, and its future is threatened. We already know that in recent years only about one-fourth of the American people have confidence in business and business leadership. It is but a short step from this lack of confidence to a questioning of the very role, purpose, and existence of the corporation.

Americans have always had ambivalent attitudes toward business and business people. In addition, citizens have recently come to expect the corporation to be more sensitive to the larger problems of society. If these expectations are not met, confidence and hence legitimacy will be further eroded. Peter Drucker entitles the last section of his recent book, *Management*, "The Need for Legitimacy."[23] In reacquiring legitimacy, Drucker rejects the enlightened self-interest model as automatically benefiting society: "This, by the way, is why the rhetoric of 'profit maximization' and 'profit motive' are not only antisocial. They are immoral." The strength of the model in the past has been the efficiency it encouraged; its weakness is its inadequacy in addressing vitally important social problems.

Interdependence of People, Institutions, Nations

In a world of more people, more elaborate tools and life styles, and quicker transportation and communication, peoples and institutions are becoming more interdependent. A military coup in Latin America or Asia is in our living room in a matter of hours via television. Malnutrition and starvation in Africa are brought home to us quickly, along with the fact that our use of lawn fertilizer, dog food, and even meat may play a role in depriving those Africans of life-giving grain.

The immense problems that face us face all nations: population, deteriorating environment, malnutrition, nuclear power and threat of nuclear warfare, balance of payments, dwindling resources, and inflation. No single nation, in spite of the threats and bravado of some who speak of "project independence," can face these problems alone. Some nations, such as Japan and England, are more dependent than others on outside sources of raw materials, but ultimately all peoples will depend more and more on each other. Looking on this extremely complicated interdependence tempts many social commentators to see the problems as immense and almost unsolvable. [24] Since peoples and nations seem unwilling to limit their own individuality, sovereignty, and greed, they are convinced that there is no hope for mankind.

In any case, the urgency and vital importance of the many problems that jointly face the nations of the world may force their leaders to work pragmatically to determine and carry out public policy together. The continued survival and well-being of all men and women may force nations to overcome nationalism, insularity, and greed in a way that ideals and altruism could not accomplish.

Religious Roots of a New Business Creed

Personal and societal goals for Americans have been heavily influenced by religion, especially Christianity and Judaism. The Protestant ethic stemmed from Christianity, and particularly Calvinist Christianity. Although it soon became very much a part of secular ideals and values, its religious roots are unmistakable—as indicated in its very name. Since religious values have had such a profound influence on business and economic life in the past, it is not inappropriate to ask whether religious ideals might have a significant impact in the future.

Along with a new concern for nature, sharing, feeling, and intuition is also "a greatly increased interest in, and tolerance for, the transcendental, religious, mystical and spiritual views."[25] Religion is thus a growing influence, especially insofar as it is built upon some personal experience. Institutional religions are wrestling with the questions of how to measure the validity of this experience, and how to provide an environment that will encourage it.

In any case, interest in the mystical and in deeper experiences, along with a concern for self-knowledge and sensitivity to self and the world around one, are all gaining ground. The person is thus seen as more than rational and organized; he or she is also deeply human and spiritual. This new recognition and emphasis is already having an effect on attitudes toward other persons, the environment, the city, and so on. From it will surely come attitudes that will also alter our business values.

One of the spreading new movements is one of liberation, whether it be women's liberation, liberation of minorities, or liberation of all men and women. The growth and success of the "theology of liberation" suggests that it may be an influence on men's and women's attitudes and ideals in the future. If so, this will mean a demand for self-determination, whether at work, at home, or in the city. Such self-determination is not the old-fashioned individualistic sort of demand, but one that is hammered out with others, in a community of men and women who look for their own and their society's fulfillment.

The alternatives presented by most of the social commentators who are looking at the future are stark: disruption, decay, and chaos, or developing new spiritual and human values and making them a habitual part of everyday personal life and institutional decision making. On this shrinking planet, economic and political planning must increasingly consider such larger issues. Paradoxically, it is "old fashioned" religion that has traditionally urged the viewpoint of concern for *others*, especially the poor, people in other nations, and future generations.

Concern for Others

Self-centeredness and insularity are the vices of the child. As a person, loved and cared for, matures, that same person tends to be less defensive and turned in on the self. He or she begins to move out toward others and to love. Love is a basic, human virtue. It is the act of a parent or a peer; it is an act of giving, often without hope of return. This sort of altruistic love is possible for any person, although it is more readily achieved by the person who has been loved. Self-giving love is essential for the growth of persons, families, and society, yet it is sometimes difficult. Speaking of this sort of love, economist Kenneth Boulding says:

> It always builds up, it never tears down, and it does not merely establish islands of order in a society at the cost of disorder elsewhere. It is hard for us, however, to learn to love, and the teaching of love is something at which we are still very inept.[26]

Much of the energy of the very poor is spent on obtaining the necessities of life. Once an individual's basic needs are reasonably satisified, that person more readily has the time and the inclination to be concerned with the needs of the larger society. Affluence can put a person in a position where he or she is no longer totally dependent, with all energies consumed in obtaining the next meal. Greater availability of food and shelter provides a physical and psychological security that can enable people to reach out beyond themselves and their own concerns. A certain amount of material security can be the foundation for loving and self-giving. The problems of human life, development of the person, and interdependence of persons and institutions can be far more readily approached. Western society is uniquely ready for greater love and concern for others, and the problems we face together could be better solved given such an attitude.

Vision and Hope

Some of the most widely read current social commentaries[27] find that the problems we face are so immense as to be almost unsolvable. These commentators, many of whom are veterans of research and policymaking themselves, find that our obsession with economic growth has blinded us to human needs. Although we profess democracy, people have control over their own lives and futures only very indirectly, if at all.

Nevertheless, the question becomes: Do we have the resources and the motivation to change the institutions that so much affect our lives and our values? Can we alter our institutions so that we are able to approach equal rights for all men and women? Can the values, structures, and institutions necessary for peace and justice throughout the world be built?

Vision and hope have always been characteristically American virtues. Ever since the days of the frontier, we have never had patience with defeatists or fatalists. It would be foolish to be naive about the enormity of the tasks before us, but it would also ensure failure if we were to give up before we have even tried to make our values, institutions, and society more human.

NOTES

1. Neil W. Chamberlain, *The Limits of Corporate Responsibility* (New York: Basic Books, 1974).

2. See Louis B. Lundborg, *Future Without Shock* (New York: Norton, 1974). Lundborg was chairman and is still a director of Bank of America.

3. George Cabot Lodge, "Top Priority: Renovating Our Ideology," *Harvard Business Review*, 48 (September–October 1970), 51.

4. *Ibid*.

5. Theodore Levitt, *The Third Sector* (New York: Amacom, 1973).

6. John Kenneth Galbraith, *Economics and the Public Purpose* (Boston: Houghton Mifflin, 1973), esp. pp. 55–175.

7. George F. Rohrlich, "The Challenge of Social Economics," in *Social Economics for the 1970's*, ed. George F. Rohrlich (New York: Dunellen, 1970), pp. 3–5.

8. Leo Cherne, "The Campus Viewpoint: An Analysis," *General Electric Forum,* 12 (Spring 1969), 5.

9. Alvin Toffler, *Future Shock* (New York: Random House, 1970), p. 370.

10. Ivan Illich, *Tools for Conviviality* (New York: Harper & Row, 1973), p. 12.

11. Ian Wilson, "Our Future Business Environment: Developing Trends and Changing Institutions," summary later published in *The Futurist* (February 1969), p. 17.

12. Ichak Adizes and Elisabeth M. Borgese, eds., *Self-Management: New Dimensions in Democracy* (Santa Barbara, Calif.: Clio, 1975).

13. Kenneth E. Boulding, "The Economics of the Coming Spaceship Earth," in *The Futurists,* ed. Alvin Toffler (New York: Random House, 1972), p. 237; see also Kenneth J. Arrow, "Social Responsibility and Economic Efficiency," *Public Policy,* 23 (Summer 1973), 303–17.

14. Ian Wilson, "How Our Values Are Changing," *The Futurist* (February 1970), p. 7.

15. *Ibid.* See also Herman Kahn and B. Bruce-Briggs, *Things to Come: Thinking About the Seventies and Eighties* (New York: Macmillan, 1972), esp. pp. 162–231.

16. See the more detailed discussion of social indicators and corporate appraisal criteria in another book in this series, Lee E. Preston and James E. Post, *Private Management and Public Policy* (Englewood Cliffs, N.J.: Prentice-Hall, 1974), pp. 130–41.

17. Raymond A. Bauer and Dan H. Fenn, Jr., *The Corporate Social Audit* (New York: Russell Sage Foundation, 1972); also by the same authors, "What Is a Corporate Social Audit?" *Harvard Business Review,* 51 (January–February 1973), 37–48.

18. Arthur J. Goldberg, "Debate on Outside Directors," *The New York Times,* October 29, 1972, Sec. F. p. 1; also Robert Townsend, "Let's Install Public Directors," and Donald E. Schwartz, "Reforming the Corporation from Within," *Business and Society Review,* 1 (Spring 1972), 63–70.

19. Robert W. Ackerman, "How Companies Respond to Social Demands," *Harvard Business Review,* 51 (July–August 1973), 91. Also, "Making Minority Policies Effective," in Theodore V. Purcell and Gerald F. Cavanagh, *Blacks in the Industrial World* (New York: Free Press, 1972), pp. 223–32.

20. Walter A. Weisskopf, *Alienation and Economics* (New York: Dutton, 1971), p. 192.

21. Peter Drucker confirms this in his *Management: Tasks, Responsibilities and Practices,* p. 312.

22. John G. Maurer, *Readings in Organization Theory* (New York: Random House, 1971), p. 361.

23. Drucker, *op. cit.,* p. 810.

24. See, for example, Robert Heilbroner, *The Human Prospect* (New York: Norton, 1974).

25. Willis W. Harman, "Humanistic Capitalism: Another Alternative," *Journal of Humanistic Psychology,* 14 (Winter 1974), 21.

26. Kenneth E. Boulding, *The Meaning of the Twentieth Century* (New York: Harper & Row, 1964), p. 146.

27. See for example, Donella Meadows et al., *The Limits to Growth* (New York: Signet Books, 1972): Heilbroner, *op. cit.;* and Richard C. Goodwin, *The American Condition* (Garden City, N.Y.: Doubleday, 1974).

SUPPLEMENTARY READING FOR PART SIX

Andrews, Kenneth R. "Can the Best Corporations Be Made Moral?" *Harvard Business Review,* May–June 1973, pp. 57–63.

Carr, Albert Z. "Can an Executive Afford a Conscience?" *Harvard Business Review,* July–August 1970, pp. 143–153.

Chamberlain, Neil. *The Place of Business in America's Future: A Study of Social Values.* New York: Basic Books, 1973.

Ouchi, William G. *Theory Z: How American Business Can Meet the Japanese Challenge.* Reading, Mass.: Addison-Wesley, 1981.

Schumacher, E. F. *Small Is Beautiful.* New York: Harper & Row, 1975.

Thurow, Lester C. *The Zero-Sum Society.* New York: Penguin Books, 1980.

FURTHER SUGGESTED READING ON BUSINESS ETHICS

The following list represents some of the leading anthologies, texts, case books, and monographs on business ethics which are relevant to a number of the specific issues explored in this text.

Allen, William R., and Louis K. Bragaw, Jr., eds. *Social Forces and the Manager.* New York: John Wiley & Sons, 1982.

Barry, Vincent, ed. *Moral Issues in Business.* Belmont, Calif.: Wadsworth Publishing Company, 1979.

Beauchamp, Tom, and Norman Bowie, eds. *Ethical Theory and Business.* Englewood Cliffs, N.J.: Prentice-Hall, 1979.

Bowie, Norman. *Business Ethics.* Englewood Cliffs, N.J.: Prentice-Hall, 1982.

Davis, Keith, William C. Frederick, and Robert L. Blomstrom, eds. *Business and Society: Concepts and Policy Issues.* New York: McGraw-Hill, 1980.

De George, Richard T. *Business Ethics.* New York: Macmillan, 1982.

De George, Richard T., and Joseph A. Pichler, eds. *Ethics, Free Enterprise and Public Policy.* New York: Oxford University Press, 1978.

Donaldson, Thomas. *Corporations and Morality.* Englewood Cliffs, N.J.: Prentice-Hall, 1982.

Donaldson, Thomas, and Patricia H. Werhane, eds. *Ethical Issues in Business: A Philosophical Approach.* Englewood Cliffs, N.J.: Prentice-Hall, 1979.

Garrett, Thomas, Raymond C. Baumhart, Theodore V. Purcell, and Perry Roets. *Cases in Business Ethics.* Englewood Cliffs, N.J.: Prentice-Hall, 1968.

Green, Mark, and Robert Massie, Jr., eds. *The Big Business Reader: Essays on Corporate America.* New York: The Pilgrim Press, 1980.

Ethics for Executives Series. Reprints from *Harvard Business Review.* Boston, Mass.: Harvard University Press.

Ethics for Executives: Part II. A *Harvard Business Review* reprint series. Boston, Mass.: Harvard University Press.

Heilbroner, Robert L., and Paul London, eds. *Corporate Social Policy.* Reading, Mass.: Addison-Wesley, 1975.

Hoffman, W. Michael, ed. *Proceedings of the First National Conference on Business Ethics: Business Values and Social Justice: Compatibility or Contradiction?* Waltham, Mass.: Center for Business Ethics at Bentley College, 1977.

————. *Proceedings of the Second National Conference on Business Ethics: Power and Responsibility in the American Business System.* Washington, D.C.: University Press of America, Inc., 1979.

Luthans, Fred, and Richard M. Hodgetts, eds. *Social Issues in Business,* 2d ed. New York: Macmillan, 1976.

Molander, Earl A., and David L. Arthur. *Responsive Capitalism: Case Studies in Corporate Social Conduct.* New York: McGraw-Hill, 1980.

Partridge, Scott H. *Cases in Business and Society.* Englewood Cliffs, N.J.: Prentice-Hall, 1982.

Sethi, S. Prakash. *Up Against the Corporate Wall,* 4th ed. Englewood Cliffs, N.J.: Prentice-Hall, 1982.

Steckmest, Francis. *Corporate Performance: The Key to Public Trust.* New York: McGraw-Hill, 1982.

Steiner, George A. *Business and Society,* 2d ed. New York: Random House, 1975.

————. *Issues in Business and Society.* New York: Random House, 1972.

Steiner, George, John B. Miner, and Edmund R. Gray. *Management Policy and Strategy,* 2d ed. New York: Macmillan, 1982.

Stevens, Edward. *Business Ethics.* New York: Paulist Press, 1979.

Stone, Christopher D. *Where the Law Ends.* New York: Harper & Row, 1975.

Sturdivant, Frederick D. *Business and Society: A Managerial Approach,* rev. ed. Homewood, Ill.: Richard D. Irwin, 1981.

Sturdivant, Frederick D., and Larry M. Robinson. *The Corporate Social Challenge: Cases and Commentaries,* rev. ed. Homewood, Ill.: Richard D. Irwin, 1981.

van Dam, Cees, and Luud Stallaert, eds. *Trends in Business Ethics,* vols. I–III. Leiden, Netherlands, and Boston, Mass.: Martinus Nijhoff, 1978.

Velasquez, Manuel G. *Business Ethics: Concepts and Cases.* Englewood Cliffs, N.J.: Prentice-Hall, 1982.

Walton, Clarence, ed. *The Ethics of Corporate Conduct.* Englewood Cliffs, N.J.: Prentice-Hall, 1974.

Williams, Oliver F., and John W. Houck, eds. *The Judeo-Christian Vision and the Modern Corporation.* Notre Dame, Ind.: University of Notre Dame Press, 1982.